DATE DUE			
May 14 '75			

SOCIAL LIFE IN BRITAIN
FROM THE CONQUEST
TO THE REFORMATION

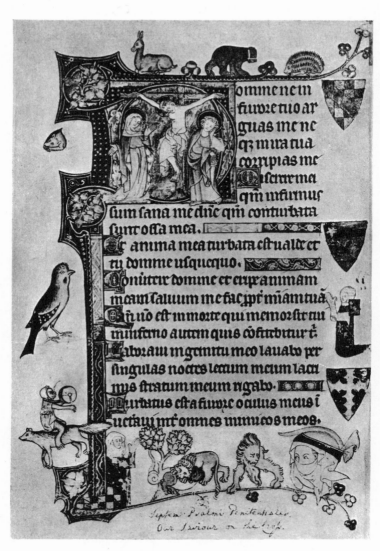

LEAF OF AN ENGLISH BOOK OF HOURS

SOCIAL LIFE IN BRITAIN
FROM THE CONQUEST TO
THE REFORMATION

COMPILED BY THE LATE

G. G. COULTON

BARNES & NOBLE, Inc.
NEW YORK
PUBLISHERS & BOOKSELLERS SINCE 1873

914.203
C83s
81650
Jan.1913

First published, 1918
Reprinted, 1968
by permission of the Cambridge University Press

L. C. Catalog Card Number: 68-23758

Printed in the United States of America

PREFACE

THOUGH this book is primarily intended to supply that background of social history which is necessary to a sympathetic comprehension of our own literature in the Middle Ages, it is hoped that it may appeal also to the general public; and that, in these extracts, our forefathers may be found speaking for themselves on all the main questions which interest intelligent people to-day.

A large proportion are translated (and many for the first time) from Latin or Old French. The rest are presented unmodernized (though sometimes, as the reader is warned, with some abridgment) in their medieval garb. To this end the compiler has made specially free use of such old translations as those of Trevisa, Lord Berners, and the *Alphabet of Tales*. Even where the episode was given more fully by a first-rate chronicler like Matthew Paris, it seemed preferable to reproduce it in Trevisa's naïve rendering of Higden's compilation; since here we have the actual English that Chaucer heard.

A very few of these illustrations have been chosen from other countries and from earlier or later dates. This, however, is only in cases where the thing described, though it happens to be recorded most clearly in such a foreign document, is also characteristic of medieval England, and could be inferred, though more laboriously, from genuine English sources. The story of Froissart's youth, for instance, may be applied without much modification to Chaucer and many others among our own youth at that day.

The compiler has attempted, so far as space would permit, to obtain a cumulative effect by multiplying testimonies on important points. For the sake of readers who may think such repetitions superfluous, and who may prefer to take a bird's-eye view of medieval history, the more important passages have been distinguished by an asterisk in the Table of Contents.

His hearty thanks are due to the following who have kindly permitted him to print copyright material: to the Committee of the Guildhall Library for the very numerous extracts from Riley's *Memorials of London*, to the Early English Text Society for a still more liberal use of their publications; to Messrs Constable and Co. for the extracts from *Arber's Reprints* (Section IV. No. 18 and V. 12), and from the *Paston Letters* (III. 22, XII. 4, 11), and to Dr R. L. Poole for an extract originally published in *The English Historical Review* (V. 9).

Finally, he is indebted for criticisms and suggestions to Sir A. T. Quiller-Couch, Prof. H. M. Chadwick, Dr H. F. Stewart, and above all to Mr A. R. Waller, whose help has been ungrudging and invaluable.

G. G. C.

GREAT SHELFORD,
Nov. 27, 1917.

FRONTISPIECE

The frontispiece is a photogravure of a leaf of a Book of Hours, preserved in the Fitzwilliam Museum, Cambridge. The following description of it is taken from *A Descriptive Catalogue of the Manuscripts in the Fitzwilliam Museum...* by Montague Rhodes James, Cambridge, 1895, pp. 398, 9.

191. FRAGMENTS (ENGLISH).

i. Two single leaves, 9½×6, 21 lines to a page. Cent. xiii (1280). English work. From the Lawrence sale; presented by S. Sandars, M.A., Trinity College, in 1892.

Verso. Bordered. A large initial, with punctured gold ground, of the Crucifixion; the Cross is green; there are three nails. On *L.* is the Virgin with hands outspread, on *R.* S. John with book, and hands to face. On the top of the border, a deer, a bear with muzzle, and a hedgehog. On *L.* a beast in a burrow, and a jay, and a monkey riding a fox, face to tail, and drumming.

At bottom is a lady praying, in a dress blazoned with her arms, then a lion fighting a dragon under a tree, a male head on two legs and a large female head, the mouth covered.

On *R.*, a shield, *gules* a cross engrailed *or*: a knight in mail and blazoned surcoat, praying: a second shield, of his arms, barry of six *argent* and *azure*, on a bend dexter *gules* bearing three mullets of five points *or*, for Grey: above this is a third shield, of the lady's, checky *or* and *azure*, a bend dexter *gules* with three lioncels *argent* (Clifford of Frampton). *Text. Domine ne in furore*, to ver. 7.

All this work is very fine....

The volume to which this belonged was sold at the Fountaine sale at Messrs Christie's in 1894, to Mr William Morris, and at his death passed into the possession of the Fitzwilliam Museum. It is of early date for a book of private devotion, not being a Psalter. Writing and decoration are of the best English sort.

TABLE OF CONTENTS

* (*For the signification of the asterisks, see Preface*)

SECTION I LAND AND FOLK

		PAGE
*1	Merry England	1
*2	Scotland	8
*3	Ireland	10
*4	Wales	17
5	Flanders	20
6	The Effects of the Conquest	20
7	Norman Manners	23
8	Stephen's Misrule	23
*9	The Law of Englishry	25
10	The Cornish Foreigner	26
11	The Wild West	27
*12	The English Tongue	28
13	English Tails	28
	*(a) 28 : *(b) 29	
14	English Drink	29
15	An Englishman's Privileges	30
	*(a) 31 : *(b) 32 : *(c) 32	
*16	As Others See Us	37
17	England in Civil War	42

SECTION II BIRTH AND NURTURE

*1	The Anatomy of Childhood	45
*2	The Father	47
3	Infant Damnation	47
*4	Baptismal Scenes	50
5	Proofs of Age	52
6	Decayed Schools	53
*7	An Old English School	54
*8	The Schoolmaster's Attributes	55
9	Co-Education	56
10	The Dangers of Grammar	56
	*(a), *(b), *(c) 57	
11	University Origins	58
	*(a), *(b)	

Table of Contents

		PAGE
12	The Model Student	59
*13	The Poor Scholar	61
	*(a) 61 : *(b) 62	
14	Hard Work	62
*15	Bible Education	62
16	Black Sheep	64
*17	University Discipline	64
18	Cambridge Riots	66
19	Forbidden University Sports	67
	(a) 67 : (b), (c) 68 : (d), (e), (f) 69	
*20	Life in a Royal College	69
21	A College Scrutiny	77
	(a) 77 : (b) 78 : (c) 79	
*22	A Day of Eton Life in 1530	81
23	University Reform	82
24	University Decay	83
*25	Froissart's Youth	84
*26	The Model Boy (Stans Puer ad Mensam) . .	90
27	School Verses	93
	*(a) 93 : *(b) 94	
*28	Wardship	94
29	University Expenses	95
30	Spoiled Children	95
*31	As Others See Us	96
32	Looking Back on the Middle Ages . . .	97
	*(a), *(b) 97 : *(c) 98	

SECTION III AUTHORS, SCRIBES AND READERS

1	Monastic Studies	100
	*(a) 100 : *(b) 101	
2	Writers' Pay	101
*3	A Writer's Bond	102
4	The Writer's Pains	103
	*(a), *(b)	
5	Hireling Writers	104
6	Chaucer's Copyist	105
7	A Scrivener's Gild	105
8	Literary Life in the Cloister	106
	(a) 106 : (b) 107 : (c) 109 : *(d), (e) 110	
*9	A Literary Archdeacon	111
10	A Great Chronicler	122
	*(a) 122 : (b), (c) 124 : (d) 125 : *(e) 126	
*11	Poet and Public	126

PAGE

*12 The Fight for Science 129
13 A Monastic Poet 136
14 Medieval Grub-Street 137
         *(a) 138 : **(b)*, **(c)* 141 : **(d)* 143 : **(e)* 144
*15 A Chronicler's Difficulties 146
16 Author and Patrons 148
*17 A Chronicler's Methods 149
*18 Poet and King 162
*19 Hoccleve's Autobiography 163
20 The Poet's Paradise 170
         *(a), **(b)*, **(c)* 170 : **(d)* 171
*21 Lydgate's Early Days 171
22 Our First Antiquary 176
23 Translators' Difficulties 179
         *(a) 179 : **(b)* 180
*24 The Love of Books 183

SECTION IV   CHURCH AND CHURCHMEN

1 A Dying World 187
         *(a) 187 : *(b)*, *(c)* 189 : *(d)* 190
2 Sacerdotal Authority 190
         *(a) 190 : *(b)*, *(c)* 191
3 Canon Law 192
         (a) 192 : **(b)* 194
4 Peter's Pence 195
5 Miracles 195
         *(a) 195 : **(b)* 196
6 I Stretch Lame Hands of Faith . . . 197
         *(a) 197 : *(b)* 198
7 Political Martyrs 200
         (a), **(b)* 201 : *(c)* 202 : *(d)* 203
8 Indulgences 203
         (a) 203 : **(b)* 204 : *(c)* 205 : **(d)* 206
*9 The Virtue of a Mass 207
10 Canterbury and York 209
11 An Archiepiscopal Visitation . . . 211
*12 A Model Parish Priest 213
13 Tithes 215
         *(a) 215 : *(b)*, *(c)*, **(d)* 216
*14 Parson and Parishioner 218
15 A Pious Family 221
16 A Wholesome Vision 227
17 Purgatory 227

PAGE

*18 A Vision of Heaven 229
 19 Foundation of a Religious Order 232
 20 Monastic Quarrels 236
 21 Abbot and Town 237
 22 St Dominic the Saviour 238
*23 Missionary Friars 239
*24 The English Mission 246
 25 Chaucer's Friar 249
       *(a), (b) 250
*26 A Pilgrimage Shrine 251
 27 The Flagellants 259
*28 Sidesmen's Reports 260
 29 Religious Education 263
       *(a) 263 : *(b) 264
 30 Church Music 265
       *(a) 265 : *(b) 266
*31 Excommunication 266
 32 A False Vow 267
 33 Degrees in Blasphemy 267
 34 Faith and Reason 268
       *(a), (b) 269
 35 Latimer's Conversion 271
*36 Utopian Monks and Clergy 271

SECTION V   KINGS, KNIGHTS AND WAR

 *1 The Conqueror's Character 274
  2 The Death of Rufus 275
  3 Henry II and His Sons 276
  4 The Daughters of Richard I 277
  5 John's Death 277
  6 Court and City 278
  7 Knightly Ideals and Realities 281
        *(a), *(b)
 *8 The Making of a Lord 282
  9 A Verray Parfit Gentil Knyght . . . 283
*10 The Squire in Hall and Bower . . . 286
*11 Crusaders' Redemptions 287
 12 Crusade Vows Broken 288
 13 Crusader and Wife 289
 14 A Crusader's Falsehood 290
*15 Speculation in Ransoms 291
*16 "They Blustreden Forth as Bestës, over Bankes
        and Hilles" 291
*17 The Fight of the Thirty 294

SECTION VI MANOR AND COTTAGE

PAGE

*1 A Model Manor 301
2 The Manorial Court 306
*3 The Peasant's Fare 308
4 Incidents of the Countryside 309
5 Essex Ploughboys 310
6 The Miller's Tricks 310
*7 Decay of Yeomanry 310
*8 Decay of Husbandry 312

SECTION VII TOWN LIFE

*1 London Folk-Mote 315
*2 An Unpardonable Word 317
3 Town and Fire 318
4 A London Garden 318
5 Old St Paul's 319
    (a), (b), (c)
6 Forbidden Sports 320
*7 The Town Peace 320
8 City Vagrants 321
9 Corrupt Wine 321
10 Fraudulent Traders 322
    *(a), *(b), *(c), *(d) 322: (e), (f) 323
11 Sea-Coal 324
12 The Liar's Reward 324
13 Child-Stealing 325
14 Chaucer's Lease 325
15 Cook-Shops 327
    *(a), *(b)
16 Trade Tricks 328
*17 The Plain-Spoken Butcher 329
*18 Town Sanitation 330
*19 Christmastide 332
20 Hock Days 332
*21 Profiteering 332
22 Town and Forest 333
23 Wild Birds at Charing Cross 333
*24 Through Italian Eyes 333

SECTION VIII RICH AND POOR

*1 The Orthodox Theory of Bondage 337
*2 The Unorthodox Theory 337
3 The Serf's Legal Status 338
*4 The Servant's Lot 339
5 Monastic Serfs 341

PAGE

6   The Serf at the Confessional   341
*7   Usurers in England.   .   .   .   .   :   .   342
8   An Archbishop Excommunicated   345
9   The Corrosion of Usury   346
10   A Mont De Piété   346
*11 Fines and Bribes   346
*12 Priests of Prey.   348
*13 The Poor Law Anticipated   350
14   The First Statutes of Labourers   350
         *(a) 350: *(b) 351
*15 The Rising Tide   353
16   Instigations to Revolt   354
17   A Premature Revolt   356
18   The Cry of Internationalism   359
         *(a) 359: *(b) 360
*19 Trade-Unions   362
20   The Bakers' Strike   363
21   Dives and Lazarus   364
22   The Knight Rebuked   365
*23 The Power of Money   367

    SECTION IX   HOUSE, DRESS AND MEALS

1   The Cat   371
2   The Dog   371
3   A Familiar Beast to Man   373
         *(a), *(b)
*4   Dinner and Supper   373
*5   Bread Rations   376
6   Beer and God's Law   378
7   A Friar's Praise of Wine   378
8   Extravagant Costume   379
         *(a), *(b) 379: *(c) 380
*9   Buying a New Suit   381
*10 Baronial Breakfasts   383
11   Extravagant Food   385
*12 By the Evening Fire   385
13   The Drudging Goblin   385
*14 Economy in Bedding   386

    SECTION X   SPORTS AND PASTIMES

*1   London Pastimes   387
2   Hawking   395
         *(a), *(b)
3   Sport and Church   396
         *(a), *(b) 396: *(c) 397

PAGE

4 The English Longbow 397
　　(a), *(b)* 397 : *(c)* 398 : *(d)* 399
5 Football 400
6 Forbidden Tourneys 400
　　(a) 400 : *(b)* 401
***7** The Actor's Status 403
8 King and Minstrel 404
9 A Minstrel's Trick 404
***10** God's Minstrels 405
11 A Minstrel's Whim 406
12 Miracle-Play and Miracles 407
13 Dance and Song for Bannockburn . . . 409
***14** The Demaundes Joyous 409
***15** Swimming 411

SECTION XI WAYFARING AND FOREIGN TRAVEL

1 The Greatest City in Europe 412
　　(a) 412 : *(b)* 414
***2** A Merchant Adventurer 415
3 A Journey to Avignon 420
4 Travel Prices 422
5 The Traveller's Gear 423
***6** Travellers' Tales 423
***7** The Wayfaring Friar 424
8 The Blind Man's Wayfaring 425
9 Forest Ways 425
10 A Trap for Travellers 426
***11** Pits in the High Road 426
12 A Stormy Crossing 427
***13** The Pilgrims' Sea Voyage 427
***14** A Travellers' Guide 430
***15** Becket on a Journey 431

SECTION XII WOMEN'S LIFE

***1** The Thirteenth Century Girl 433
2 Women's Education 434
3 Precocious Jealousy 434
***4** The Spinster's Lot 435
5 The Corrosive Dowry 436
6 The Law of Marriage 436
　　(a), *(b)*, *(c)* 437
7 A Marriage Arranged 438
8 Without the Parents' Consent 439
***9** Erasmus on Marriage 439

		PAGE
*10	Man and Wife .	441
*11	Wife to Husband	442
*12	The Model Housewife	444
13	Jealousy and Revenge	445
14	The Perfect Woman	446
*15	A Nunnery Visitation	451
16	Women's Labour	455
*17	Servants by Compulsion	455
*18	Women and General Councils	456
19	New Fashions .	457
20	The Order of the Garter	458
21	Women in Church	462
*22	A Protestant Woman	462

SECTION XIII   ARCHITECTURE AND THE ARTS

*1	The Artist's Inspiration	466
2	The Artist's Estimation	468
	*(a) 469: (b) 470	
3	The Architect's Reward	471
4	Lincoln Cathedral	472
5	The Perils of Originality	473
	*(a) 473: (b) 474	
*6	An Artist's Notebook	476
7	Angels in Art	479
8	The Octagon of Ely	480
9	Masonic Legend and Fact	481
*10	York Cathedral Masons	489
*11	Wyclif on Freemasonry	490
*12	Freemasons and Trade-Unionism	491
13	King's College Windows	492
14	The Beginnings of the Secular Stage	493
	*(a) 493: *(b) 494	

SECTION XIV   MEDICINE AND JUSTICE

*1	The Perfect Surgeon	496
2	An Anaesthetic	501
3	The Rashness of Inexperience	501
*4	" For Gold in Physik is a Cordial "	502
5	The Master-Surgeon's Oath	502
*6	A Medical Inquisition	503
*7	The Quack's Penance	503
8	Surgeon-Barbers	505
9	Medical Recipes	506

		PAGE
10	Toothache	507
	*(a), *(b), *(c)	
11	The Dangers of Water	508
12	Hospital Fare	508
*13	Every Man His Own Constable	509
*14	A Nation in Arms	510
*15	The Escape from Feudalism	513
*16	Piepowder Court	514
17	City Police	516
18	Lynch Law	516
19	Before the Wars of the Roses	517
*20	Torture by Law	517
*21	The Perils of the Law	519
22	Veterinary Medicine	520

SECTION XV SUPERSTITIONS AND MARVELS

*1	A Nest of Sorcery	521
*2	Roger Bacon's Forecasts	524
3	Charms in Medicine	526
4	A Charm to find Stolen Goods	527
5	Damages for Sorcery	527
6	The Witch's Fate	528
*7	Alchemist by Royal Appointment	529
8	Portents	530
9	Oliver the Flying Man	530
*10	Crocodile Tears	531
*11	The Remora	531
12	The Lamprey	532
*13	The Ghost of the Gog-Magog Hills	532
*14	The Enchanted Mere	534
*15	The Antipodes	535
*16	The Green Children	537
*17	Cloud-Ships	538

Plate I	Perpetual Motion	*Between pp.* 476–7
„ II	Laon Tower about 1250 A.D.	„ „
„ III	North-West Tower of Laon (present state)	„ „
„ IV	An Aisle-window from Reims	„ „

LIST OF ILLUSTRATIONS

Facing page

1. A DRINKING BOUT . ; 20
   From MS. Harl. 603, f. 51 vᵒ, reproduced in T. Wright, *Domestic Manners and Sentiments*, 1862, p. 29. This famous MS., which (like Eadwine's Psalter in the Library of Trin. Coll. Camb.) is copied from the Utrecht Psalter, may legitimately be exploited as approximately representing Anglo-Saxon dress and customs, since the representations are frequently such as might apply roughly to any date from the 9th to the 11th century.

2. ANGLO-SAXON DRESSES 21
   From J. Strutt, *Chronicles of England*, vol. II. (1779), p. 238, plate XI. "The general exterior habit of the men among the Anglo-Saxons, from the king to the husbandman, appears to have been nearly of the same form."

3. ANGLO-SAXON SCHOOL 24
   T. Wright, *l.c.* p. 117, from the Trin. Coll. Psalter.

4. A FIFTEENTH-CENTURY LECTURE-ROOM . . 25
   From the title-page of a volume of Albertus Magnus printed at Cologne in 1497.

5. BAPTISM 50
   Showing the medieval custom of immersion. From *The Life and Pageants of Richard Beauchamp, Earl of Warwick* (ed. Sir W. St John Hope and Viscount Dillon, 1914). The pictures were drawn about 1485 A.D.; they have sometimes been ascribed to the Earl's chaplain, John Rous, but are more probably by a professional artist. (Reproduced by kind permission of Viscount Dillon and Mr Emery Walker.)

6. PARENTS AND CHILDREN 51
   From 15th century manuscripts reproduced by T. Wright, *l.c.* pp. 370 and 402.

7. SWORD AND BUCKLER-PLAY 68
   From J. Strutt, *Sports and Pastimes*, plate XXVI. (MS. of 14th century).

8. MAYING IN THE FIELDS 69
   From a 14th century illumination figured by T. Wright, *l.c.* p. 289.

9. A ROSE-BATTLE 88
   From the Louterell Psalter (about 1320 A.D.) figured in *Vetusta Monumenta*, vol. VI., plate XX.

*Facing
page*

10. A PICNIC 89
From a 15th century MS. reproduced by T. Wright, *Womankind in
Western Europe*, 1869, p. 210.

11. A MONK WRITING 110
Eadwine, the Canterbury monk of the 12th century who copied the
Utrecht Psalter. As in other representations of the kind, he holds a
pen and a scraping-knife. The inscription round his portrait may be
Englished as follows :
The Writer [speaketh].
"Prince of writers am I; nor shall my praise and fame perish in days
to come; do thou, O my Letter, proclaim who I am."
The Letter [speaketh].
"Thine own writing, marked with this painted image, proclaimeth
thee to be Eadwine, whose fame shall live throughout the ages. The
glory of this book doth show forth thy skill; O God, do Thou vouch-
safe to receive this book and the writer's self as a gift acceptable unto
Thee." (By kind permission of the Council of Trinity College,
Cambridge.)

12. THE MINSTREL'S RECEPTION 111
From a MS. of the 15th century figured in T. Wright, *Domestic
Manners and Sentiments*, p. 366. (In this particular case, the minstrel
is a nobleman in disguise.)

13. THE WRITER'S SPECTACLES 170
From T. Wright, *l.c.* p. 439 (15th century).

14. LYDGATE AND HIS BOOK 171
H. Shaw, *Dresses and Decorations of the Middle Ages*, plate VI. From
a copy of the illumination representing the poet introducing his *Pilgrimage of the World*, in 1426, to Thomas, Earl of Salisbury, one of
the most distinguished captains of Henry VI's wars.

15. FLAGELLATION OF HENRY II 192
From J. Carter, *Ancient Painting and Sculpture*, 1838, plate XXXIX.
The original is a glass-painting, probably of the 14th century. "Four
monks, in the exact Benedictine habit and tonsure, with bundles of
twigs in their hands, stand two and two of a side, one of whom (probably the prior) addresses the king with great seriousness, while
another of them raises up his hand in astonishment and pity."

16. SAINT THOMAS OF LANCASTER 193
From the orphrey of an embroidered chasuble of the close of the 15th
century (*Journal of British Archaeological Association*, 1879, p. 385,
by kind permission of the President).

17. AN ABBOT'S FUNERAL 228
Abbot Islip of Westminster (d. 1532), from his Mortuary Roll, engraved in *Vetusta Monumenta*, vol. IV., plate XVIII. This illustrates
the enormous number of tapers which were kindled for the benefit of
rich men's souls at their obsequies.

Facing
page

18. SAINT GUTHLAC BUILDING A CHURCH . . . 229

From a 13th century MS. engraved in *Vetusta Monumenta*, vol. VI.,
plate XXIX. The Saint is shown tugging at a rope under direction of
the master mason.

19. THE SQUIRE AT TABLE 286

T. Wright, *l.c.* p. 152, from a 14th century MS.

20. A MEDIEVAL SHOP 287

J. H. Parker, *Domestic Architecture* (1859), part I., p. 37. This is a
15th century house in Double Butcher Row, Shrewsbury. The shop
occupied the ground-floor; the hall was on the next story; bed-
rooms above.

21. A RICH CITIZEN 322

Robert Attelathe, of King's Lynn (d. 1376), from J. S. Cotman,
Norfolk Brasses. Cf. Gough, *Sepulchral Monuments*, vol. I.,
p. 138.

22. A FORESTALLER IN THE PILLORY 323

From a MS. of about 1500, engraved in *Vetusta Monumenta*, vol. I.,
plate LXIX.

23. LADIES HUNTING 370

J. Strutt, *Sports and Pastimes*, plate II.

24. THE CAT 371

J. Jackson and W. A. Chatto, *Wood Engraving* (1861), p. 226. The
cut dates probably from about 1450.

25. A NORMAN FEAST 374

From the Bayeux Tapestry (*Vetusta Monumenta*, vol. VI., plate XI.).
The legend runs: " Here they made their dinner; and here the
Bishop is blessing the food and drink."

26. A FEAST WITH MUMMERS 375

About 1520 (T. Wright, *l.c.* p. 461).

27. ARCHERY PRACTICE 398

From the Louterell Psalter (*Vetusta Monumenta*, vol. VI., plate
XXIV.).

28. AN ENGLISH ARCHER 399

Costume du Moyen-Age (Brussels, 1847), vol. II., plate XXXIII. (15th
century).

29. A MEDIEVAL INN 424

Of the 15th century, at Norton St Philip's, Somerset (J. H. Parker,
Domestic Architecture (1859), part I., p. 47).

*Facing
page*

30. (*a*) THE BLIND WAYFARER 425
    T. Wright, *l.c.* p. 328 (MS. of 14th century).

    (*b*) CROWLAND BRIDGE
    A triple arch, spanning the junction of two streams. From J. Carter,
    Ancient Painting and Sculpture (ed. Meyrick, 1838), plate XLII.

31. A LADY ARTIST 436
    T. Wright, *l.c.* p. 428, from a 15th century MS.

32. WOMEN'S COSTUME 437
    Reproduced in J. Strutt, *Dresses and Habits* (ed. Planché, 1842),
    plate XXXVIII.; from MS. Cotton, Nero, c. IV.2. The illumination,
    of late 12th or early 13th century, shows a good lady modestly dressed,
    while the devil masquerades as an ultra-fashionable lady with long and
    elaborate sleeves.

33. WOMAN BREAKING CLODS 454
    From Louterell Psalter (*Vetusta Monumenta*, vol. VI., plate XXIII.).

34. SPINSTER AND CARDER 455
    Ibid.

35. AN ANCIENT CRUCIFIX 474
    Romsey Abbey. The date is disputed, but it is certainly earlier than
    the change alluded to in the text (p. 474, note 1). From a photograph
    kindly supplied by Dr F. J. Allen.

36. (*a*) A GLASS-PAINTER 475
    Proceedings of the Archaeological Institute, 1845 (Winchester), paper
    No. 4. From an early 15th century window in Winchester College
    Chapel. The legend runs: " Thomas, the worker of this glass."

    (*b*) CARPENTER, MASON, AND CLERK OF THE
    WORKS
    From the same window. Legend: " The Carpenter—William [Win-
    sore] the Mason—Sir Simon Membury."

37. AN OPERATOR IN THE FOURTEENTH CENTURY . 500
    From the frontispiece to John Arderne's treatise (E.E.T.S. No. 139,
    by kind permission of the Society). The illumination, of the 14th
    century, represents a Master in Medicine operating (Sloane MS. 2002,
    f. 24*b*).

38. LADY PHYSICIAN 501
    T. Wright, *Womankind in Western Europe*, p. 184.

39. A PORTENT IN THE SKY 530
    Bayeux Tapestry (*Vetusta Monumenta*, vol. VI., plate VII.). Legend:
    " These men marvel at the star "—a portentous comet which foretold
    Harold's fate.

40. A DEMON TOURNEY 531
    Louterell Psalter (*Vetusta Monumenta*, vol. VI., plate XX.).

SECTION I

LAND AND FOLK

1   MERRY ENGLAND

John of Trevisa, a Cornishman (1326-1402), was the most assiduous of medieval translators into English.   He was a Fellow first of Exeter College, Oxford, and then of Queen's, from which he was expelled in 1379 with the Provost and some others.   By 1387, at least, we find him as Vicar of Berkeley and chaplain to Lord de Berkeley, for whom his translations were done.   His translation of Higden's *Polychronicon* was thrice printed before 1527, and his *Bartholomew* twice; his "Descrypcion of Englonde," from Higden, went through five separate editions in thoᴗe early years.

Ralph Higden (1299?-1363?) was a monk of St Werburgh's, Chester. A doubtful story makes him the author of the Chester Miracle Plays. His *Polychronicon* is a world-history, with a geographical introduction, compiled with great diligence from the standard authors then accessible ; it was deservedly popular throughout the rest of the Middle Ages, since it exactly appealed to the average medieval mind.   The following extracts are very much abbreviated from Higden, and I have omitted the references to authorities (Bede, Giraldus, Solinus, etc.) from whom he draws.

Polychronicon Ranulphi Higden, vol. II.

(p. 3.)   After the ilondes of ocean now Bretayne schal be descreved.   By cause of Bretayne alle the travaile of this storie was bygonne.

(p. 13.)   As Fraunce passeth Bretayne so Bretayne passeth Irlond in faire weder and nobilte, but nought in helthe.   For this ilond is beest and bringeth forth trees and fruyt and [oxen] and other bestes, and wyn groweth there in som place.   The lond hath plente of foules and of bestes of dyvers manere kynde, the lond is plenteuous and the see also.   The lond is noble, copious, and riche of nobil welles and of nobil ryveres with plente of fische ; there is grete plente of small fische, of samon and of elys. So that cherles in som place fedith sowes with fische. There beeth ofte i-take dolphyns, and see calves, and baleynes, grete fisches as hit were of whales kynde, and dyvers manere schelfische. Among the schelfisch beeth muskles that haveth with ynne them margery perles of alle manere colour and hewe, of rody and rede, of purpur and of blew, and specialliche and moste of whyte. There is also plente of schellefische that men dyeth with reed fyn; the redenesse therof is wonder fyn and stable, and steyneth nevere with colde ne with hete, with wete ne with drie ; but evere the eldere the hewe is the fairer. There beeth also salt welles and hote welles; ther of renneth stremes of hote bathes i-deled in dyvers places, acordynge for man and womman, and for alle manere age, olde and yonge.

(p. 17.) There beeth schepe that bereth good wolle, there beeth meny hertes and wylde bestes and fewe wolves, therfore the schepe beeth the more sickerliche with oute kepynge i-lefte in the folde. In this ilond also beeth many citees and townes, faire and noble and riche; many grete ryveres and stremes with grete plente of fische; many faire wodes and grete with wel many bestes tame and wylde. The erthe of that lond is copious of metal ore and of salt welles ; of quarers of marbel of dyvers manere stones, of reed, of whyte ; of nesche[1], of hard; of chalk and of whyte lyme. There is also white cley and reed forto make of crokkes and stenes[2] and other vessel and brent tyle to cover with hous and cherches.

(p. 19.) Flaundres loveth the wolle of this lond, and Normandie the skynnes and the velles[3]; Gasquyn the iren and the leed; Irlond the ore and the salt ; al Europa loveth and desireth the white metal of this lond. Therfore a versifioure in his metre preyseth the lond in this manere[4]; Engelond

---

[1] soft.   [2] jars.   [3] fells.

[4] i.e. Henry of Huntingdon, *De Prerogativis Angliae*: " Anglia plena jocis, gens libera digna jocari "—the original of the phrase " merry England." Henry's words have been borrowed also by Bartholomaeus Anglicus in a well-known passage : see R. Steele, *Medieval Lore* (King's Classics), p. 87.

ful of pley, fremen well worthy to pleye; fre men, fre tonges,
hert fre; free heelth al the leden[1]; here[2] lond is more fre, more
better than here tonge.

> Straunge men that needeth,
> That lond wel ofte releveth.
> Whan hunger greveth,
> That lond alle suche men fedeth,
> (p. 21.) In londe, in stronde
> Wel wyde men speketh of Engelonde;
> Lond, hony, melk, chese,
> This ilond schal bere the prys.
> Of alle londes riches this lond hath nede to noon;
> Alle londes moot seche helpe nedes of this allone.

(p. 23.) In Bretayn, beeth many wondres; nevertheles
foure beeth most wonderful. The firste is at Pectoun [*the
Peak of Derbyshire*]; there bloweth so strong a wynde out of
chenes[3] of the earth, that it casteth up agen clothes that men
casteth yn. The secounde is at Ston-henge by sides Salisbury;
there beeth grete stones and wonder huge, and beeth arered
an high as hit were gates i-sette uppon other gates; notheles
hit is nought clereliche i-knowe nother perceyved how and
wherfore they beeth so arered and so wonderlicche i-honged.
The thridde is at Cherdhole [*Cheddar*]; there is grete holow-
nesse under erthe; of meny men haveth i-walked therynne
and i-seie ryveres and stremes; but nowher konneth they fynd
non ende. The ferthe is that reyn is y-seie arered uppon the
hilles and noon i-spronge aboute in the feeldes. Also there is
a grete ponde that conteyneth thre score ylondes covenable
for men to dwelle ynne; that pond is i-clipped aboute with
sixe roches; uppon everich roche is an egles nest. And thre
score ryveres renneth into that pond; and noon of them
alle renneth into the see, but oon. There is a pond i-closed
aboute with a wal of tyle and of stoon. In that pond men
wascheth and batheth wel ofte; and everiche man feleth the
water hoote or colde, right as he wolde hymself. There beeth
salt welles fer fram the see, and beeth salte alle the woke
longe, forto Saturday at none; and fresche from Saturday at

---

[1] folk.   [2] their.   [3] clefts.

none for to Monday. The water of these welles, whan hit is
i-sode, torneth in to smal salte, faire and white.

(p. 27.) In the contray aboute Wynchestre is a den; out
of that den alwey bloweth strong wynd, so that no man may
endure forto stonde to fore that den. Under the citee of
Chestre renneth that ryver Dee, that now to-deleth[1] Engelond
and Wales; that ryver everiche monethe chaungeth his
foordes, as men of the contrey telleth, and leveth ofte the
chanel; but where the water drawe more toward Engelond
other toward Wales, to what side that hit be, that yere men
of that side schal have the worse ende and be overcome, and
men of the other side schal have the better ende and be at
here above. Whan the water so chaungeth his cours, it
bodeth suche happes.

Take hede how greet light and brightnesse of Goddiss
myldenesse hath by-schyne Englischemen, seththe they torned
first to rightful byleve. So that of no men in oon province
beth i-founde so meny hool bodyes of men after thir deth in
likenese of evere lastynge life that schal be after the day
of dome, as it wel semeth in these holy seyntes Etheldred,
Edmond the kyng, Elphege, and Cuthbert. I trowe that it is
i-doo by special grace of God alle myghti, for the nacioun
that is i-sette, as it were, with oute the worlde, schulde take
hede to durynge of bodies with oute corrupcion and rotynge,
and be the more bolde and stedefast for to triste on the final
arisynge of deed bodies forto laste evermore after the day
of dome.

(p. 41.) In that arme of the see, that departeth this ilond
Mon and North Wales, is a swelowe that draweth to schippes
that seilleth, and sweloweth them yn, as dooth Scylla and
Charybdis, that beeth tweie perilous places in the see of
myddel erthe; therfore men may noght seile by this swolwe
but slily at the ful see.

Som tyme was stryf whether this ilond Man schulde ligge
to Britayne other to Irlond; and, for venemous wormes that
were i-brought thider leved there, hit was i-demed that the
ilond Man schulde longe to Bretayne. And in that ilond is

---

[1] divides.

sortilege and wicchecraft i-used. For wommen there sellith schipmen wynde, as it were i-closed under thre knottes of threde; so that the more wynd he wol have, he will unknette the mo knottes.

Thanatos, that is Tenet and is an ilond bysides Kent, and hath that name Tanatos of deth of serpentes, for there beeth none, and the erthe thereof sleeth serpentes i-bore in to other londes. There is nobil corn lond and fruytful; me troweth that that ilond was i-halowed and i-blessed of seynt Austyn, the first doctour of Englische men; for there he aryved first.

(p. 157.) As it is i-knowe how meny manere peple beeth in this ilond, there beeth also so many dyvers longages and tonges; notheles Walsche men and Scottes, that beeth nought i-medled with other naciouns, holdeth wel nyh thir firste longage and speche; but yif the Scottes, that were somtyme confederat and wonede with the Pictes, drawe somwhat after thir speche; but the Flemmynges that woneth in the weste side of Wales haveth i-left ther straunge speche and speketh Saxonliche i-now. Also Englische men, (they[1] thei hadde from the bygynnynge thre manere speche, northerne, sowtherne, and middel speche in the myddel of the lond, as they come of thre manere peple of Germania,) notheles by comyxtioun and mellynge firste with Danes and afterward with Normans, in many thynges the contray longage is apayred[2], and som useth straunge wlafferynge, chiterynge, harrynge, and garrynge grisbayting[3]. This apayrynge of the truthe of the tongue is bycause of tweie thinges, oon is for children in scole, agenst the usage and manere of alle othere naciouns, beeth compelled for to leve thire owne langage, and for to construe thir lessouns and there thynges in Frensche, and so they haveth seth the Normans come first in to Engelond. Also gentil men children beeth i-taught to speke Frensche from the tyme that they beeth i-rokked in their cradel and kunneth speke and playe with a childes broche; and uplondisshe men wil likne thym self to gentil men, and fondeth[4] with greet besynesse for to speke Frensce, for to be i-tolde of. This manere

---

[1] though.   [2] impaired.
[3] gabbling, chattering, snarling, croaking and hissing.   [4] strive.

was moche i-used to fore the firste moreyn[1] and is siththe
sumdel i-chaunged; for John Cornwaile, a maister of grammar,
chaunged the lore in gramer scole and construccioun of
Frensche into Englische; and Richard Pencriche lerned that
manere techynge of hym and othere men of Pencrich; so
that now, the yere of oure Lorde a thowsand thre hundred and
foure score and fyve, and of the secounde kyng Richard after
the conquest nyne, in alle the gramere scoles of Engelond,
children leveth Frensche and construeth and lerneth an
Englische, and haveth therby avauntage in oon side and disavauntage in another side ; here avauntage is, that they lerneth
ther gramer in lasse tyme than children were i-woned to doo;
disavauntage is that now children of gramer scole conneth na
more Frensche than can thir lift heele; and that is harme for
them and they schulle passe the see and travaille in straunge
landes and in many other places.   Also gentil men haveth now
moche i-left for to teche there children Frensche.   Hit semeth
a greet wonder how Englische, that is the burthe tonge of
Englisshemen and her owne langage and tonge, is so dyverse
of sown in this oon ilond, and the langage of Normandie is
comlynge of[2] another londe, and hath oon manere soun among
alle men that speketh hit aright in Engelond.   Nevertheles
there is as many dyvers maner Frensche in the reem of
Fraunce as i[s] dyvers manere Englische in the reem of
Engelond.   Also of the forsaide Saxon tonge that is i-deled
a-thre, and is abide scarsliche with fewe uplondisshe men, is
greet wonder; for men of the est with men of the west, as it
were undir the same partie of hevene, accordeth more in
sownynge of speche than men of the north with men of the
south; therfore it is that Mercii, that beeth men of myddel
Engelond, as it were parteners of the endes, understondeth
bettre the side langages, northerne and southerne, than northerne or southerne understondeth either other.   Al the longage
of the Northhumbres, and specialliche at York, is so scharp,
slitting, and frotynge[3] and vnschape, that we southerne men
may that longage unnethe understonde.   I trowe that that is

---

[1] plague.   [2] imported from.   [3] grating.

bycause that they beeth nyh to straunge men and naciouns
that speketh strongliche, and also bycause that the kynges of
Engelond woneth alwey fer from that cuntrey; for they beeth
more i-torned to the south contray, and yif they gooth to the
north contray they gooth with greet help and strengthe.

(p. 165.) Now of the maneres and of the doynges of the
medled peple of Engelond nedeth for to telle. But the
Flemynges that beeth in the westside of Wales beeth now by-
torned as though they were Englische bycause of companye
with Englische men, and they beeth stalworthe and stronge
to figte, and beeth the moste enemyes that Walsche men
hath, and useth marchaundyse and clothynge and beeth ful
redy to putte them self to aventures and to peril in the see
and in the lond bycause of greet wynnynge, and beeth redy
for to goo somtyme to the plowgh and somtyme to dedes of
armes whan tyme and place axeth.   Hit semeth of this men
a grete wonder that in a boon[1] of a wethres right schuldre,
whan the flesche is aweye i-sode and nought i-rosted, they
knoweth what hath be do, is i-doo, and schal be do, and as
hit were by a spirit of prophecie and a wonderful craft they
telleth what me[n] doth in fer contrayes, tokens of pees and
of werre, the staat of the reeme, sleynge of men, and spouse-
breche; soche they declareth certeynliche by schewynge of
tokenes and of sy[g]nes that beeth in suche a schulder boon....
But the Englische men that woneth in Engelond, that beeth
i-medled in the ilond, that beth fer i-spronge from the
places that they spronge of first, wel lightliche with oute
entisynge of eny other men, by there owne assent tornen to
contrary dedes.   And so unesy, also ful unpacient of pees,
enemy of besynesse, and wlatful[2] of sleuthe...that whan they
haveth destroyed there enemyes al to the grounde, thanne
they fighteth with themself, and sleeth everiche other, as a
voyd stomak and a clene worcheth in hit self....Notheles men
of the south beeth esier and more mylde; and men of the
north be more unstable, more cruel, and more unesy; the
myddel men beeth somedele partyners with bothe; also they

---

[1] bone.   [2] loathing.

woneth them to glotonye more than other men, and beeth
more costlewe in mete and in drynke and in clothynge. Men
troweth that they took that vyce of kyng Hardeknute that
was a Dane, for he sette twyes double messe at dyner and at
soper also. These men been speedful bothe on hors and on
foote, able and redy to alle manere dedes of armes, and
beeth i-woned to have the victorie and the maistrie in
everich fight wher no treson is walkynge; and beth curious,
and kunneth wel i-now telle dedes and wondres that thei
haveth i-seie. Also they gooth in dyveres londes; unnethe
beeth eny men richere in ther owne londe othere more gracious in fer and in 'straunge londe. They konneth betre
wynne and gete newe than kepe her owne heritage; therfore
it is that they beeth i-spred so wyde, and meneth that everich
other londe is thir owne heritage. The men beeth able to al
manere sleithe[1] and witte, but to fore the dede blondrynge
and hasty, and more wys after the dede, and leveth ofte
lightliche what they haveth bygonne....And as Hannibal
saide that the Romayns myghte nought be overcome but in
thir owne cuntray; so Englische men mowe not [be] overcome
in straunge londes, but in thir own cuntray thei beeth lightliche overcome....These men despiseth thir owne, and preiseth
other menis, and unnethe beeth apaide[2] with thir owne estate;
what byfalleth and semeth other men, they wolleth glad-
lyche take to them self; therfore hit is that a yeman arraieth
hym as a squyer, a squyer as a knyght, a knight as a duke
and a duke as a kyng.

2   SCOTLAND

Bartholomew the Englishman (Bartholomaeus Anglicus) has sometimes been confused with a quite different Bartholomew de Glanville of
a century later : both were Friars Minor.

Our Bartholomew studied in the Paris schools, joined the French
province of the Order, and taught with success at Paris. In 1231
he was sent to Saxony, where he taught theology in the Franciscan
convents. His great work, *De Proprietatibus Rerum*, was written probably between 1250 and 1260 ; it at once became a standard work, and
was one of the books hired at regulated prices by the scholars of Paris.

---

[1] sleight.   [2] pleased.

It was translated into French in 1372, into English by Trevisa in 1398, and into Spanish and Dutch a century later. Not only the Middle Ages but even later centuries were indebted to it for many of their notions about the universe ; it was republished in 1582, in a slightly modernized form, by Stephen Batman ; and it has been contended that Shakespeare knew the volume well. (See Mr C. L. Kingsford's article on Bartholomew in *Dict. Nat. Biog.* XXI. 409.) The first modern popularizer of Trevisa's *Bartholomew* was Mr Robert Steele (*Medieval Lore*, King's Classics, 1/6, an excellent volume to which readers should refer for much valuable matter for which there is no room here).

Lib. xv. cap. clii. *Of Scotia.*

The londe Scotia hathe the name of Scottes that [there] dwelle. The men are lyght of harte, fiers and couragious on theyr enmyes. They love nyghe as well death as thraldome, and they account it for slouth to dye in bed, and a great worshyppe and vertue to deye in a feldė fyghtynge agaynst enmyes. The men ben of scarse lyvynge, and many suffre hungre longe tyme and eate selde tofore the sonne goynge downe, and use fleshe, mylke meates, fyshe and fruites more than Brytons: and use to eate the lasse brede: and though the men bene semely ynough of fygure and of shape, and fayre of face generally by kind, yet theyr owne scottyshe clothynge dys-fygure them full moche. And scottes be sayd in theyr owne tonge of bodyes painted, as it were kytte[1] and slytte. For in olde tyme they were marked with divers fygures and shape on theyr fleshe and skyn, made with yren prickes, as Isidore saith, [in his] "de Vocabulis Gentium." And, bycause of medlyng with englishe men, many of them have changed the olde maners of scottes in to better maners for the more parte, but the wylde scottes and Iryshe acounte greate worshyppe to folowe theyr fore fathers in clothynge, in tonge, and in lyvynge, and in other maner doynge. And dispise some deale the usages of other men in comparison to theyr owne usage. And so eche laboreth to be above : they detract and blame all other and envye all other : they deride al other, and blame all other mens maners, they be not ashamed to lye: and they repute no man, of what nation, bloudde, or puissaunce so ever he be, to be hardy and valiant, but them

[1] cut.

selfe. They delyte in theyr owne : They love not peace. In that lond is plentuous ground, mery woodes, moyst ryvers and wells, many flockes of beastes. There ben erthe tyllers, for quantite of the place, inow.

3 IRELAND

Trevisa's *Higden*, I. 331 ff., abbreviated as before. Higden's chief authority here is Giraldus Cambrensis.

Irland is an iland grettest after Bretayne, and streccheth north from Brendans hilles anon to the ylond Columbyna, and conteyneth eighte dayes jorneis, evrich jorney of fourty mile.

(p. 333.) The lond is not playne ; but ful of mountaynes and of hilles, of wodes, of mareys, and of mores : the lond is nesche[1], reyny, and wyndy, and lowe by the see syde, and with ynne hilly and sondy. There is grete plente of noble pasture and of lese ; therfore bestes most ofte be dreve out of thir lese, leste they fede them self to ful and schende themself, and they moste ete at thir owne will. Men of that lond haveth here hele[2] alwey, and straunge men haveth ofte a perilous fluxe by cause of moysture of mete ; there cowes flesche is holsom and swynes flesch unholsom. Men of that lond haveth no fevere, but onliche the fevere agu, and that wel silde-whanne. Therfore the holsomnesse and helthe of that lond and the clennesse withoute venyme is worth all the boost and richesse of treen, of herbes, of spicerie of riche clothes, and precious stones of the est londes. Hit semeth that the helthe of that lond is bycause that there is noght gret passynge and exces in [cold] nother in hete....In this lond beeth mo kyn than oxen, more pasture than corne, more gras than seed. There is grete plente of samon, of lampreys, of eles, and of other see fisch ; of egles, of cranes, of pekokes, of corlewes, of sperhaukes, of goshaukes, and of gentil faucouns, and of wolfes, and of wel schrewed mys[3]. There beth attercoppes[4], bloodsoukers, and enettes[5] that dooth noon harm. There beeth veyres[6] litel of body and ful hardy

---

[1] soft.   [2] health.   [3] mice.   [4] spiders.   [5] newts.   [6] weasels.

and strong. There beeth bernakes[1], foules liche to wylde
gees; kynde bryngeth them forth wonderliche out of the
trees, as it were kynde worchynge agenst kynde. Men of religioun eteth bernakes in fasting dayes, for they cometh nought
of flesche nother beeth i-gete flescheliche bytwene fader and
moder: but they [*such monks*] beeth ful lewedliche i-meved,
for resoun is contrarie to that doynge. For yif a man hadde
i-ete of Adams thigh, he had i-ete flesch; and yit Adam com
nought of flesch, nother was i-gete flescheliche bytwene fader
and moder. But that flesch com wonderliche of the erthe,
so this flesche cometh wonderliche of the tree. In this lond
is plente of hony and of mylk and of wyn, and nought of
vyneyerdes. Solinus and Isidorus wryten that Irlond hath
no bees; netheles it wer better wryten that Irlond hath bees
and no vyneyerdes. Also Beda seith there is grete huntynge
of roobukkes, and it is i-knowe that roobukkes beeth noon
there. It is no wonder of Beda; for Beda knew nevere that
ilond with his eyghe; bot som tale tellere tolde hym suche
tales.

...Whete cornes beeth there ful smal, unnethe i-clansed[2]
with manis hond; out-take men, alle bestes beeth smallere
there than in other londes. There lacketh...venemous bestes;
therfore som men feyneth and favorabliche seith that Seynt
Patryk clensed that lond of wormes and of venemous bestes.
But it is more probable and more skilful[3], that this lond
was from the bygynnynge alwey with oute such wormes.
For venemous bestes and wormes dyeth there anon, and we
brynge then thider out of other londes; and also venym and
poysoun, i-brought thiderward out of other londes, leseth his
malys anon as he passeth the myddel of the see. Also powder
of erthe of that lond i-sowe in other londes useth awey
wormes so fer forth, that a torf of that lond i-doo aboute
a worme sleeth hym other maketh hym thrulle[4] thorugh the
erthe for to scape a way. In that lond cokkes croweth wel
litel to fore day; so that the firste cokkes crowe in that lond
and the thridde in other londes beeth i-liche fer to fore day.

---

[1] barnacle-geese.   [2] cleansed.   [3] reasonable.   [4] bore.

(p. 341.) Giraldus seith that Casera, Noes nece, dradde the flood and fligh with thre men and fifty wommen into that ilond, and wonede ther ynne first the laste yere to fore Noes flood....

(p. 351.) Solinus seith that men of this lond beeth straunge of nacioun, housles, and grete fighteres, and acounteth right and wrong one thyng, and beeth sengle of clothinge, scarse of mete, cruel of herte, and angry of speche, and drinketh firste blood of dede men that beeth i-slawe, and then wassheth there face therwith; and holdeth them apayde[1] with flesshe and fruit instede of mete, and with mylk instede of drynke, and useth moche playes and ydelnesse and huntynge, and travailleth ful litel. In thir child hode they beeth harde i-norisched and hard i-fed, and they beeth unsemeliche of maneres and of clothyng, and haveth breche and hosen al oon of wolle, and straight hodes that streccheth a cubite over the schuldres by hynde, and blak faldynges[2] instede of mantels and of clokes. Also sadeles, bootes, and spores they useth none, whan they rideth....They fighteth vnarmed, naked in body; nevertheles with tweie dartes and speres and with brode sparthes[3]. They fighteth with oon hond; and whan other wepene failleth, they haveth good puble-stones redy at hond. These men forsaketh tilienge of lond and kepeth pasture for beestes: they useth longe berdes and longe lokkes hongynge doun by hynde thir nolles[4]. They use no craft of flex and wolle, of metal, nother of marchaundise, but geveth them alle to idelnesse and to sleuthe, and counteth reste for likyng and fredom for richesse. And they[5] Scotlond the doughter of Irlond use harpe, tymbre, and tabour, and Wales useth harpe, and pipe, and tabour, nevertheles Irische men beeth connyng in tweie manere instrumentis of musyk, in harpe and tymbre that is i-armed with wire and with strenges of bras, In the whiche instrumentis, they thei pleye hastiliche and swiftliche, they maketh wel mery armonye and melody with wel thicke tunes, werbeles[6], and notes....

| [1] content. | [2] rough cloth. | [3] axes. |
| [4] heads. | [5] though. | [6] warblings. |

These men beeth of yvel maneres and of levynge ; they paieth none tethinges[1], thei weddeth lawefulliche none wyfes, they spareth not ther alies, bot the brother weddeth his brother wyf. They beeth besy forto betraye thire neighbores and othere. They beren sparthes in there hond instede of stanes, and fighteth therwith agenst them that tristeth to them beste ; the men beeth variable and unstedefast, trecherous and gileful. Who that deleth with them nedeth more to be war more of gile than of craft, of pees than of brennynge brondes, of hony than of galle, of malice than of knyghthode. They haveth suche maneres that thei beeth not stronge in werre and bataille, nother trewe in pees. They bycometh gossibs to them that they wolleth falseliche betraye in gosibrede and holy kynrede ; everiche drinketh otheres blood, whan it is i-sched. He loveth somdel ther norice and there pleieng feres[2] whiche that souketh the same melk that they souketh, while they beeth children. And they purseweth there bretheren, ther cosyns, and there other kyn ; and despiseth thir kyn, while they beeth on lyve, and awreketh ther deeth, and they beeth i-slawe.

(p. 359.) In this lond and in Wales olde wyfes and wymmen were i-woned, and beeth yit (as me pleyneth) ofte forto schape them self in liknes of hares for to melke there neighebores keen, and so stele thire melk, and ofte grehoundes renneth after them and purseweth them, and weneth that they be hares. Also som by craft of nygramauncie maketh fat swyne that beeth reed of colour and noon other, and selleth them in chepinge and in feires ; but anon as these swyne passeth ony water they torneth agen in to thir owne kynde, where it be straw, hey, gras, other torves. But these swyn mowe not be i-kept by no manere craft forto dure in liknesse of swyn over thre dayes. Among these wondres and othere take hede that in the uttermeste endes of the world falleth ofte newe mervailles and wondres, as thei[3] kynde pleyde with larger leve priveliche and fer in the endes than openliche and nygh in the myddel. Therfore in this ilond beeth meny grisliche mervayles and wondres.

---

[1] tithes.   [2] playfellows, here = foster-brethren.   [3] though.

Meny men telleth that in the northe side of Irlond is the ilond of lyf; in that ilond is no man that may deie; but whan they beeth i-holde with hard siknesse they beeth i-bore out to the next ilond, and deie there.

There is also Patrick his purgatorie, that was i-schewed at his prayere to conferme his prechynge and his lore, whan he preched to mysbileved men of sorwe and peyne that evel men schal thole[1] for thire wicked wordes, and of joye and of blisse that gode men schal fonge[2] for there holy dedes. He telleth that who that suffreth the peynes of that purgatorie, yif it be enjoyned hym for penaunce, he schal nevere suffre the peynes of helle, but he dye fynalliche with oute repentaunce of synne, as the ensample is i-sette more ful at this chapitres ende. Thei this sawe myght be sooth, it is but a jape. For no man that dooth dedely synne schal be i-saved, but he be verrey repentaunt, what sommever penaunce he doo; and every man that is verray repentaunt at his lifes ende of al his mysdedes, he schal be sikerliche i-saved and have the blisse of hevene, though he nevere [hear] speke of Patrik his purgatorie.

(p. 371.) Touchynge Patrik his purgatorie take hede that the secounde Seynt Patryk, that was abbot and nought bisshop, whyle he preched in Irlond studied wel faste besily for to torne thilke wicked men, that levede as bestes, out of there yvel lyf for drede of the peynes of helle, and for to conferme them in good lyf by hope of the grete blisse of hevene; and they seide that they wolde nought torne, but [if] some of them myghte knowe somwhat of the grete peynes and the blisse, that he spak of, whyle they were here on lyve. Thanne Seynt Patrik preied to God alle myghty therfore; and oure Lord Jesus Crist apperede to Patrik, and took hym a staf, and the text of the gospel that beeth in the contray in the erchebisshops ward. Thanne oure Lorde ladde Patrik into a wilde place, and schewed hym there a round pitte that was derke with ynne, and seide: Yif a man were verray repentaunt and stable of byleve, and went in to this pitte, and waked there

---

[1] endure.   [2] take.

inne a day and a nyght, he schuld see the sorwes and the
peynes of evel men and the joye and the blisse of goode men;
than Crist vanysched out of Patrik his sight, and Patrik rered
there a chirche and dede there chanouns reguler, and closed
the pitte aboute with a wal; and is now in the chirche yerde
right at the est ende of the chirche, and is fast i-loke with
a strong gate. For no man schulde niseliche[1] wende yn with
oute leve of the bisshop and of the priour of the place. Meny
men went yn there and come out agen in Patrik his tyme,
and tolde of peynes and joye that they hadde i-seie; and
mervayles that they sey beeth yit there i-wrete. And by
cause therof meny men torned and were converted to right
byleve. Also meny men wente yn and come never agen. In
kyng Stevene his tyme, king of Engelond, a knyght that
heet Owen went into Patryk his purgatorie, and come agen,
and dwelled al his lyf tyme afterward in the nedes[2] of the
abbay of Louth that is of the ordre of Cisterciens, and tolde
meny men of wondres that he hadde i-seie in Patrykes purgatorie.

No man is enjoyned forto wende in to that purgatorie, bote
i-counseilled wel faste that they schulde not come there; but
yif he wil nedes entre, he schal first be i-sent to the bisshop of
the place, and he schalle counsaile hym for to leve; and yif the
man is stable, and wil nede take the wey, the bisshop schal
sende hym with lettres to the priour of the place; and the
priour schal counseille hym to leve. And[3] he wil take that wey,
he schal be i-brought into the chirche, and there he schal be
in prayers and in fastynge fiftene dayes. And after fiftene
dayes he schal be housled[4] and i-lad to the dore of purgatorie with processioun and letanye; and there he schal be
counseilled to leve that weye. Than yf he is stedfast and
stable, the dore schal be i-opened, and he schal be i-blessed,
and he schal blesse hymself also, and goo yn a Goddes half[5],
and holde forth his wey. Than the dore schal be faste i-loke
forto another day. Whan the day is come, the priour cometh
to the dore erliche and by tyme, and openeth the dore; and

[1] foolishly.　[2] business.　[3] if.　[4] take the Eucharist.　[5] in God's name.

yif the man is i-come, he ledeth hym in to the chirche with processioun; and there he schal be fiftene dayes in prayers and fastinge[1].

Here Girald maketh mencioun, that as men of this nacioun beeth more angry than other men and more hasty for to take wreche, while they beeth on lyve; so seyntes and halowes of this lond beeth more wrecheful than seyntes of other londes. Clerkes of this lond beeth chast, and biddeth meny bedes, and dooth greet abstinence a day, and drynketh al nyght; so that it is acounted for a myracle that leccherie reigneth nought there, as wyn reigneth. And, as moche schrewes among them beeth of alle schrewes worste, so good men among them (theis there beeth but fewe,) beeth goode at the best. Prelates of that contray beeth wel slowe in correccioun of trespas, and besy in contemplacioun, and nowt of prechynge of Goddes word. Therfore it is that alle the seyntes of that lond beeth confessoures, and non martir among them; and no wonder, for wel nyh alle the prelates of that contrey beeth i-chose out of abbayes in to the clergie, and dooth as monkes schulde.

(p. 381.) In this lond, in Wales, and in Scotland, bee belles and staves with croked hedes, and othere such thinges for relikes, in grete reverence and worschippe; so that men of this lond dredeth more forto swere uppon eny of thilke belles and gold battes than uppen the gospel. The chief of alle suche relikes is i-holde Jesus his staf that is at Develynge[2]; with the whiche staf they seith that the first Patrik droaf the wormes out of Irlond.

Yf me axeth, how it may be that dyverse manere bestes and of dyverse kynde, that beeth kyndeliche i-gete bytwene male and female, come and beeth in ilonds after Noes flood, me troweth that suche bestes swam in to ilondes aboute, and firste to the nexte, and so forth in to othere; othere men seillinge into othere londes broughte with them suche bestes for love of huntinge; other aungelles at God Almyghties

---

[1] For Froissart's reference to St Patrick's Purgatory see below, Section III., piece 17 *ad fin.*
[2] Dublin.

heste broughte suche bestes in to ilondes aboute; other the
erthe brought them forth ferst and fulfilled thoo Goddes heste,
that heet the erthe brynge forth gras and quyk bestes.

4   WALES

From the medieval translation of Higden printed in the Rolls Series
under that of Trevisa, from MS. Harl. 2261 ; abbreviated as before ; I. 395.

That londe whiche is callede now Wallia, other Wales in
Englische, was callede somme tyme Cambria, of Camber the
son of Brute, whiche was lorde of hyt.   That londe is plentuous
in frutes, flesche, fische, horses, oxen, and schepe bothe wylde
and tame.   That londe is apte also to alle seedes, gresse,
cornes, medoes, feldes, and woodes, with herbes and floures,
floodes and welles, vales and hilles.   The vales in hit brynge
furthe foode, and the hilles metalles.   And the matere and
substaunce amonge theyme is hony, mylke, and whitemeite[1].
Methe and bragotte[2] be there, as ale habundantely in that
cuntre; which londe bryngethe furthe plentuousely what so
ever thynge that is necessary to the lyf.

(p. 401.)   The use of that cuntre differrethe from the rite
of Englonde in clothenge, in fyndenge[3], and in mony other
thynges.   A mantelle and a schurte be the nowble thynges
of vesture amonge theyme, whiche use to bere fewe clothes
in wynter thaughe winde blawe ryghte coldely; whiche
sytte, stonde, and slepe despisenge schetes ; with owte hud-
des, cootes, or tabardes, bare on the legges; whiche use
unnethe to go eny other way, thaughe thei scholde mete a
kynge; fightenge with short speres in conflictes, amonge whom
the men in foote be more stronge then the horse men.
Woodes be to theym as for towres, and marras[4] for places of
defence ; whiche take fleenge as fighte, whan they thenke
tyme and opportunite.

(p. 405.)   The peple of that cuntre wille suffre hungre
longe, luffenge the commune foode, inquirenge not the arti-
ficialle operacion of cookes at the dyners of theyme, eitenge
brede made of otes and of barly, brode, rownde, and thynne, as

---

[1] milk foods.   [2] spiced ale.   [3] food.   [4] marshes.

C.

2

hit besemethe suche bloode. That peple dothe eite selde whete that is baken in an ove[n]; the meites of whom be buttyr, mylke, and chese; whiche provoke a man to drynke methe and ale, whiche thei do use daily. Thei accompte that wyne most principalle whiche is moste redde, whiche peple usenge to drynke seasethe not from communicacion and talkenge of ydelele thynges. Salt and lekes be to theyme solace at meyte, and after; acomptenge that a grete solace to yiffe a caldron with potages to men syttenge abowte and to divide to every man his porcion, kepenge to hym the remanente. But the infortuny of flesche nyouthe[1] theim moche, eitenge salmon hoote, ageyne the precepte of phisike. Whiche inhabite howses, whom thei make of litelle roddes; not nye to gedre, as thei use to make edificacions in cites. This peple useth to devoure the goodes of other men after that thei have devourede theire owne goodes, eitenge that thei fynde, returnenge after that to theire owne places, spendenge theire life in ydelnesse and in slauthe. The consuetude is of Walche men to giffe water to theire gestes to drynke. And if thei wasche theire feete, thei thenke that thei be wellecommen.

Men of that cuntre vse in theire festes a crowde[2], an harpe and trumpes. But at the deth of a man thei crye lyke to wylde bestes in exaltenge the bloode of Troy, of whom they toke begynnenge. That peple thenkethe men nye to theyme by bloode whome a C. degrees do separate. Neverthelesse thei be obediente to pristes, worschippenge theyme as the angelles of God. The prophecy of Merlyne and wycche crafte was wonte to begile theyme and to move theim to batelles. But nowe thei chaunge theire maneres gretely in to better exercise thro the communicacion of Saxones. Thei tylle feldes and gardynes, and applye theim to inhabite townes, usenge haburgeones and goenge with schoes, refreschenge theim in meites after curtesy, slepenge in beddes after the consuetude of Englische rather then after the maner of theim usede afore tyme. And if the cause be inquirede why thei lyve so now rather then in tymes afore, hyt may be ansuerede and seide that rychesse be the cause ther of, but

---

[1] hurts.　　　　[2] small fiddle.

now the drede of theire goode withdrawethe them from the exercise of conflictes.

(p. 412.) *Of the mervayles of Wales.* At Brehenoc[1] is a water habundante in fisches of diverse coloures, where a man may see in clere tymes mervellous edifienges, where a mervellous noyce and sownde be herde. And if the prince of that londe come, the bryddes synge and make grete melody to him, schewenge not pleasure and comforte to eny other man.

(p. 417.) Also there is a region at Penbroke whiche is vexed moche by the illusion of develles, whiche can not be made clene thro eny crafte other preiers, whiche, movenge that londe, doth prenosticate a grete fall of the peple of that cuntre.

(p. 423.) There be hilles in Snawdonia of a grete altitude, in so moche that a man may unnethe goe from the foote of hit to the highte of hit in a day. Whiche hilles men of that cuntrie calle Eriri, that sowndethe in Englishe the hilles of snawe, whiche be sufficiaunte in pastures to alle the bestes in Wales; in the altitude of whom be ii. waters, oon of whom concludethe an yle movede to and fro with the wynde, in so moche that drovers of bestes mervaile theyme to be caryede from oon place to an other sodenly.

(p. 427.) Also there is an other yle contiguate to that place, conteynenge heremites; and if there be discorde amonge theyme, myce gedre anoon and devoure the meites of theyme, whiche grevaunce dothe not cease tille that peace be reconsilede among theim. Also that peple of that cuntre be replete with the melancholy lyke to the peple of Yrlonde, so seyntes of that cuntre be prompte un to vengeance; where belles and croked staves be hade in grete veneration, as men use in Yrlonde and in Scottelande whiche peple drede more to swere by theym then on a masse booke. Also at Basyngwerc spryngethe an holy welle, whiche is of so grete fervence that hit castethe owte thynges caste in to hit, whiche bredethe so grete a water that myghte suffice to alle Wales; whiche water giffethe grete helpe to seke peple; where thou schalle fynde stones havenge in theym as dropes of

[1] Brecon.

blood, in the signe of the holy bloode whiche floede owte from the throte of Seynte Wenefride. For whiche offence the doers of hit and alle theire childer and successores berke in the maner of dogges, un til thei aske the suffrage and helpe of Seynte Wenefride at that welle, other elles at the cite of Schrewisbury where sche restethe now, hade there in grete veneracion.

5 FLANDERS

This brief description of our present allies seems worth including as typical of the medieval point of view, and as containing an interesting reference to our own land. Trevisa's *Higden*, I. 289.

And theygh Flaundres be a litel lond, it is ful plenteuous of meny profitable thinges, and of richesse of pasture, of bestes, of marchaundise, of ryveres, of havenes of the see, and of good townes. The men of Flaundres beeth faire, stronge, and riche; and bringeth forth meny children, and beeth pecible to thir neighebores, trewe to straungeres, noble craftes-men and greet makeres of cloth that they sendeth aboute wel nygh al Europa. The lond is pleyne and skarse of wode; therfore in stede of wode they brenneth torfes, that smelleth wors than wode, and maketh fouler as[h]es. Braban is by south est Flaundres, and is plenteuous of marchaundise and of makynge of clooth. For of wolle, that they haveth out of Engelond, they maketh clooth of dyvers coloures and sendeth in to othere provinces and londes, as Flaundres dooth. For, they Engelonde have wolle at the beste, he hath nought so grete plente of good water for dyvers coloures and hewes as Flaundres hath and Braban. Nevertheles at Londoun is oon welle that helpeth wel to make good scarlet, and so is at Lyncolne in certeyne place in the brook that passeth by the toun.

6 THE EFFECTS OF THE CONQUEST

William of Malmesbury, *De Gestis Regum*, Lib. III. tr. J. A. Giles (Bohn, 1847, pp. 278-280).

This [Battle of Hastings] was a fatal day to England, a melancholy havoc of our dear country, through its change of

A Drinking Bout

ANGLO-SAXON DRESS

masters. For it had long since adopted the manners of the Angles, which had been very various according to the times : for in the first years of their arrival, they were barbarians in their look and manners, warlike in their usages, heathens in their rites; but, after embracing the faith of Christ, by degrees, and in process of time, from the peace they enjoyed, regarding arms only in a secondary light, they gave their whole attention to religion....Nevertheless, in process of time, the desire after literature and religion had decayed, for several years before the arrival of the Normans. The clergy, contented with a very slight degree of learning, could scarcely stammer out the words of the sacraments; and a person who understood grammar, was an object of wonder and astonishment. The monks mocked the rule of their order by fine vestments, and the use of every kind of food. The nobility, given up to luxury and wantonness, went not to church in the morning after the manner of Christians, but merely, in a careless manner, heard matins and masses from a hurrying priest in their chambers, amid the blandishments of their wives. The commonalty, left unprotected, became a prey to the most powerful, who amassed fortunes, by either seizing on their property, or by selling their persons into foreign countries; although it be an innate quality of this people, to be more inclined to revelling, than to the accumulation of wealth. There was one custom, repugnant to nature, which they adopted ; namely, to sell their female servants, when pregnant by them and after they had satisfied their lust, either to public prostitution, or foreign slavery. Drinking in parties was a universal practice, in which occupation they passed entire nights as well as days. They consumed their whole substance in mean and despicable houses; unlike the Normans and French, who, in noble and splendid mansions, lived with frugality. The vices attendant on drunkenness, which enervate the human mind, followed ; hence it arose that engaging William, more with rashness, and precipitate fury, than military skill, they doomed themselves and their country to slavery, by one, and that an easy, victory. "For nothing is less effective than rashness ; and what begins with violence, quickly ceases, or is repelled." In fine, the English at that time wore short garments reaching to the mid-knee; they had their hair cropped; their beards shaven; their arms laden with golden bracelets; their skin adorned with punctured designs. They were accustomed to eat till they became surfeited, and to drink till they were sick. These latter qualities they imparted to their conquerors; as to the rest, they adopted their manners. I would not, however, have these bad propensities ascribed to the English universally. I know that many of the clergy, at that day, trod the path of sanctity, by a blameless life; I know that many of the laity, of all ranks and conditions, in this nation, were well-pleasing to God. Be injustice far from this account; the accusation does not involve the whole indiscriminately.

Moreover, the Normans, that I may speak of them also, were at that time, and are even now, proudly apparelled, delicate in their food, but not excessive. They are a race inured to war, and can hardly live without it; fierce in rushing against the enemy; and where strength fails of success, ready to use stratagem, or to corrupt by bribery. As I have related, they live in large edifices with economy; envy their equals; wish to excel their superiors; and plunder their subjects, though they defend them from others; they are faithful to their lords, though a slight offence renders them perfidious. They weigh treachery by its chance of success, and change their sentiments with money. They are, however, the kindest of nations, and they esteem strangers worthy of equal honour with themselves. They also intermarry with their vassals. They revived, by their arrival, the observances of religion, which were everywhere grown lifeless in England. You might see churches rise in every village, and monasteries in the towns and cities, built after a style unknown before; you might behold the country flourishing with renovated rites; so that each wealthy man accounted that day lost to him, which he had neglected to signalize by some magnificent action.

7   NORMAN MANNERS

Henry of Huntingdon, *Hist. Anglorum*, Lib. VI. *ad fin.*, speaking of the reign of William I.

For it is the nature [of the Normans] that, when they have so cast down their enemies as to add no more to their burdens, then they proceed to oppress each other, reducing their own folk with their lands to poverty and devastation. This appeareth more and more plainly in Normandy, England, Apulia, Calabria, Sicily and Antioch, lands of great fertility which God hath subjected to the Normans. In England, therefore, unjust taxes abounded in those days, and abominable customs. All the great folk were so blinded with greed for gold and silver, that the poet's word was true of them: "All must needs get and get, while none asks how his gains are gotten." The more talk there was of right, the more acts of unrighteousness; those who were called Justiciaries were the fountainhead of all injustice. Sheriffs and reeves, whose duty was to dispense law and justice, were more savage than the thieves and robbers, and more barbarous than the most barbarous of all. The king himself had farmed out his lands as dearly as he could; he would transfer them to another who offered more, and again to another, ever making light of his own covenant, and greedy of greater gain. So in this year 1087 God sent plagues of sickness and famine upon England; so that he who escaped the fever died of hunger. He sent also tempests and thunder, whereby many men were slain; nor did He spare either oxen or sheep.

8   STEPHEN'S MISRULE

From the *Anglo-Saxon Chronicle*, R. S., vol. II. p. 230.

When king Stephen came to England (a. 1139), he held an assembly at Oxford, and there he took the bishop Roger of Salisbury, and Alexander bishop of Lincoln, and the chancellor Roger, his nephew, and put them all into prison, till they gave up their castles. When the traitors perceived that he was a mild man, and soft, and good, and did no justice, then did they all wonder. They had done homage to

him, and sworn oaths, but had held no faith; they were all
forsworn, and forfeited their troth; for every powerful man
made his castles, and held them against him; and they filled
the land full of castles. They cruelly oppressed the wretched
men of the land with castle-works. When the castles were
made, they filled them with devils and evil men. Then took
they those men that they imagined had any property, both
by night and by day, peasant men and women, and put them
in prison for their gold and silver, and tortured them with
unutterable torture; for never were martyrs so tortured as
they were. They hanged them up by the feet, and smoked
them with foul smoke; they hanged them up by the thumbs,
or by the head, and hung fires on their feet: they put knotted
strings about their heads, and writhed them so that it went to
the brain. They put them in dungeons, in which were adders,
and snakes, and toads, and killed them so. Some they put
in a "crucet hûs," that is, in a chest that was short, and narrow,
and shallow, and put sharp stones therein, and pressed the
man therein, so that they brake all his limbs.

(p. 231.) In many of the castles were [instruments called]
a "lâð and grim," these were neck-bonds, of which two or
three men had enough to bear one. It was so made, that
[it was] fastened to a beam; and they put a sharp iron
about the man's throat and his neck, so that he could not in
any direction sit, or lie, or sleep, but must bear all that iron.
Many thousands they killed with hunger; I neither can nor
may tell all the wounds or all the tortures which they inflicted on wretched men in this land; and that lasted the
nineteen winters while Stephen was king; and ever it was
worse and worse. They laid imposts on the towns continually, and called it "censerie." When the wretched men
had no more to give, they robbed and burned all the towns,
so that thou mightest well go all a day's journey and thou
shouldst never find a man sitting in a town, or the land tilled.
Then was corn dear, and flesh, and cheese, and butter; for
there was none in the land. Wretched men died of hunger;
some went seeking alms who at one while were rich men;
some fled out of the land. Never yet had more wretchedness

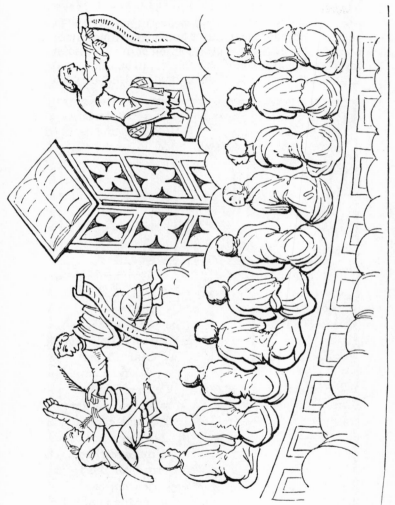

ANGLO-SAXON SCHOOL

Ad laudem ac honorez indiuidue trinitatis pa-

tris .filij. et spūssancti .gloriosissimeʒ virginis Marie In
cipiunt ꝑmentaria questiones et dubia pulcerrima ꝑtinen
tia.cum textu Arestotelis in octo libros de physico auditu
iuxta doctrinam exquisitissimā venerabilis dñi Alberti. in
Bursa Lauretiana floretissimi agripinēsis gymnasij edita

Albertus magnus
cum discipulis suis

A FIFTEENTH-CENTURY LECTURE-ROOM

been in the land, nor did heathen men ever do worse than they did; for everywhere at times they forbore neither church nor churchyard, but took all the property that was therein, and then burned the church and all together. Nor forbore they a bishop's land, nor an abbot's, nor a priest's, but robbed monks and clerks, and every man another who anywhere could. If two or three men came riding to a town, all the township fled before them, imagining them to be robbers. The bishops and clergy constantly cursed them; but nothing came of it; for they were all accursed, and forsworn, and lost. However a man tilled, the earth bare no corn; for the land was all fordone by such deeds: and they said openly that Christ and his saints slept. Such and more than we can say, we endured nineteen winters for our sins.

9   THE LAW OF ENGLISHRY

From the *Dialogue of the Exchequer*, composed by Richard, Bishop of London and Treasurer, who died in 1198. The present translation is from the text in W. Stubbs, *Selected Charters*, 1890, p. 201 (Bk I. ch. x.). Although the distinction between Norman and English was so nearly obliterated among freemen before 1200, the law here referred to was not finally repealed until 1339.

THE MASTER. *Murdrum* is, properly, the secret death of a man whose slayer is unknown; for the word *murdrum* signifieth *secret* or *hidden*. Now, in the earlier state of this realm after the Conquest, those English who were left were wont to lie in wait for the dreaded and hated Normans, and secretly to slay them here and there in woods or secluded places, as opportunity might offer. The kings and their ministers, therefore, did for some years inflict the most exquisite forms of torture upon the English, yet without full effect; until at length they imagined this following device. Wheresoever a Norman was found thus slain, if the slayer did not show himself or even betray himself by flight, then the whole of that district called the Hundred was fined on behalf of the royal treasury, some in thirty-six pounds sterling and some in forty-four, according to the diversity of districts and the frequency of murders; which (as we hear) was decreed in order that this general penalty might secure the safety of way-farers, and that all men might be spurred on either to punish the crime or to hand over to justice that man who had brought so enormous a loss upon the whole neighbourhood. Thou must know, as aforesaid, that they who sit at the Exchequer are free from the payment of these fines.

THE DISCIPLE. Should not the secret death of an English-man, as of a Norman, be imputed as *murdrum*?

THE MASTER. Not at the first institution of this law, as thou hast heard; but now that English and Normans have lived so long together, and have intermarried, the nations have become so intermingled (I speak of freemen only) that we can scarce distinguish in these days betwixt Englishman and Norman; excepting of course those serfs bound to the land whom we call *villeins,* and who cannot leave their con-dition without leave of their masters. Wherefore, in these days, almost every secret manslaughter is punished as *murdrum,* except those of whom (as I have said) it is certain that they are of servile condition.

10   THE CORNISH FOREIGNER

Adam de Marisco, or Adam Marsh, was third successor to Grosseteste as Lecturer in the Franciscan School at Oxford about 1247. His Italian contemporary Salimbene characterized him as "one of the greatest scholars in the world"; and Roger Bacon repeatedly couples him with Grosse-teste as "perfect in all wisdom." His letters are printed in the 1st vol. of *Monumenta Franciscana,* R. S., 1858: the following translation is from p. 134, addressed to Grosseteste.

I have not yet fully conferred with Master Robert Marsh [my brother], concerning persons apt for the prebend for which you have asked me to recommend. But, as I now see the matter, there occurs to me Master Solomon of Dover ...Master Peter of Aldham,...and Master Richard of Corn-wall, who, reverend Father, is not altogether unknown unto you ; a man lacking in command of the English tongue, yet of most honest conversation and unblemished reputation, learned in human and divine literature.

11   THE WILD WEST

John de Grandisson, Bishop of Exeter 1327–1369, was cousin to the Sir Otho de Granson from whom Chaucer translated his *Compleynt of Venus*. The following description of his diocese is translated from two letters written, soon after his enthronement, (i) to his patron, Pope John XXII., and (ii) to several friendly cardinals at the Court of Avignon (*Register of John de Grandisson*, ed. Hingeston-Randolph, vol. I. pp. 95, 97). I have taken the liberty of compressing the two descriptions, which complement each other, into one.

Purposing to survey the possessions and buildings appertaining to my see, I travelled to the border parts of Cornwall. That land adjoineth England only with its eastern boundary ; the rest is everywhere surrounded by the ocean, far beyond which, to the North, lie Wales and Ireland. Southwards, it looks straight over to Gascony and Brittany ; and the men of Cornwall speak the Breton tongue. To the West of St Michael's Mount, the immensity of ocean stretches without bound or limit. My see possesseth also certain sea-girt islands [i.e. Scilly], whereunto no bishop ever goeth, but they have been wont to send a few friars, as I have not [yet] done.

Here I am not only at the end of the world but even (if I may so say) at the ends of the very end. For this diocese, which includes Devon and Cornwall, is divided from the rest of England, and girt on all sides but one by an ocean which is rarely navigable, and frequented only by the natives of the land. It aboundeth sufficiently in home-fed flesh of beasts and at times in Gascony wine; but it is less fertile in corn and other things necessary to man. My episcopal manors I found terribly destroyed and despoiled, in hatred of my predecessor who was so inhumanly murdered[1], my lands waste and untilled, and an utter default of cattle and seed corn.

[1] Grandisson succeeded (after a very brief episcopate of John de Berkeley) to that Bishop Stapeldon whose murder is recounted in the *French Chronicle of London* (Camden Soc. 1844), p. 52.

12   THE ENGLISH TONGUE

The Brut, E.E.T.S., 1908, p. 315.

And in the xxxviii yere of his regne [1363], hit was
ordeyned in the parlement, that men of lawe, bothe of the
temporall and of holy chirche lawe, fro that tyme forth shold
plede in her moder tunge.

13   ENGLISH TAILS

For a learned disquisition on this strange legend see G. Neilson,
Caudatus Anglicus, 1896. The two following extracts show how widely
it was believed. Already about 1155, Robert Wace described the incident
which Robert Manning paraphrased into English in his *Chronicle* (about
1300). The second extract is from Fazio degli Uberti, a Florentine who
compiled, about 1370, a popular encyclopedia in verse. When Fazio
writes "I saw," he speaks only metaphorically; the scheme of his poem
is that Solinus the ancient geographer leads him everywhere and shows
him everything, as Virgil and Beatrice led Dante. References in foreign
medieval satire to the tailed Englishman are innumerable: as Mannyng
puts it "ffor tailles al Englische kynde ys blamed."

(*a*)   Mannyng's *Chronicle*, R. S., p. 527. St Augustine, the Apostle of
the English, is preaching in Kent.

> Toward Rouchestre he tok his weye,
> Godes worde for to seye.
> Byside Rouchestre y the londe,
> South est thethen[1], a folk he fond
> That to Godes werk gaf no tent,
> Ne no grace in them non hent[2];
> But there he stod them to preche,
> And ther savacion for to teche,
> Byhynd him on his clothes they henge,
> Righe[3] tailles on a strenge.
> When they had done that vyleny,
> They drof hym thenne wyth maistri;
> ffer weys they gan hym chace,
> Tailles they casten in hys face.
> Thys holy man God bisought,
> ffor they hym that vileny wrought,
> That on them and on al ther kynde,
> Tailled, alle men schulde hem fynde.

[1] thence.   [2] got.   [3] =the fish ray or skate.

And God graunted al that he bad,
ffor alle that kynde tailles had,—
Tailles hadde, and tailles have;
ffro that vengaunce non may them save.—
ffor they wyth tailles the godeman schamed,
ffor tailles al Englische kynde ys blamed;
In manie sere[1] londes seyd,
Of tho tailles we have umbreyde[2].

(*b*)   Fazio's *Dittamondo*, Lib. IV. c. 23 (ed. 1826, p. 350).

The people of this land are white and fair to see, even as
in Ethiopia they are black and hideous.   Many clear foun-
tains and cold baths we found there, and great plains, and
divers beasts in thick woods.   Divers also are the fruits,
and broad the pastures; fair towns and noble cities adorned
with palaces and lofty walls; great and noble rivers without
fords, and abundance of flesh, corn and fish.   Justice is strong
in those lands.   One thing I saw not—but it was a strange
thing to hear, and all bear it out as true, wherefore it behoveth
me to set it down even as I heard it—that among these islands
is one islet where folk are born with tails, but short, such as
the tail of a stag or some like beast.   It is true that, when
each [child] is loosed from his swaddling-clothes, the mothers
flee into other parts, to avoid this mischief[3].   It is noised
among these people, but I give it no faith, that there are such
wondrous trees as to beget birds for fruit[4].

14   ENGLISH DRINK

From the Chronicle of the Italian friar Salimbene, who wrote about
1285 (*Monumenta Germaniae, Scriptores*, XXXII. p. 219).

So the French delight in good wine, nor need we wonder,
for wine " cheereth God and men," as it is written in the ninth
chapter of Judges....It may be said literally that French and
English make it their business to drink full goblets.   Wherefore

---

[1] several.   [2] upbraiding.
[3] The legend was often localized, as we have seen, at Rochester; and it was
said that mothers went over the bridge to Stroud for their confinement, so as to
avoid the curse.
[4] i.e. the barnacle-goose: see above No. 3.

the French have blood-shot eyes; for from their ever-free potations of wine their eyes become red-rimmed, and bleared and bloodshot. And in the early morning, after they have slept off their wine, they go with such eyes to the priest who has celebrated Mass, and pray him to drop into their eyes the water wherein he has washed his hands. But Brother Bartolommeo Guiscola of Parma was wont to say at Provins (as I have often heard with mine own ears) "ale, ke malonta ve don Dé; metti de l'aighe in le vins, non in lis ocli"; which is to say, "Go; God give you evil speed! Put the water in your wine when ye drink it, and not in your eyes!" The English indeed delight in drink, and make it their business to drain full goblets; for an Englishman will take a cup of wine and drain it, saying, "Ge bi: a vu," which is to say "It behoveth you to drink as much as I shall drink," and therein he thinketh to say and do great courtesy, and he taketh it exceeding ill if any do otherwise than he himself hath taught in word and shown by example. And yet he doth against the scripture, which saith, "...Wine also in abundance and of the best was presented, as was worthy of a king's magnificence. Neither was there any one to compel them to drink that were not willing" (Esther, i. 7). Yet we must forgive the English if they are glad to drink good wine when they can, for they have but little wine in their own country. In the French it is less excusable, for they have greater plenty; unless, indeed, we plead that it is hard to leave our daily wont. Note that it is thus written in verse, "Normandy for sea-fish, England for corn, Scotland [or Ireland ?] for milk, France for wine."

15   AN ENGLISHMAN'S PRIVILEGES

Sir John Fortescue was born about 1394 and died about 1476: he became Chief Justice of the King's Bench in 1442. He adhered to the Lancastrian party, and accompanied queen Margaret into exile in 1463 At the end of this exile, about 1470, he wrote for Prince Edward his celebrated treatise *De Laudibus Legum Angliae*. The translation here used is that of Robert Mulcaster the educational reformer, first printed in 1573. Fortescue's slightly later work, *On the Governance of the Kingdom of England*, is no less important than the *De Laudibus* for English constitutional history. For Fortescue's influence on political thought in the

17th and 18th centuries, see Dr C. J. A. Skeel's article in *Transactions of the Royal Hist. Soc.*, third series, vol. x. (1916). The special value of his work is the contrast it marks between political and social life in England and France—a contrast true on the whole, though Fortescue very naturally exaggerates a good deal. I print from the edition of 1616.

(*a*) (Ch. 9, p. 25b.) For the king of England cannot alter nor change the lawes of his Realme at his pleasure. For why, hee governeth his people by power, not only royall, but also politique[1]. If his power over them were roial only, then he might change the lawes of his realme, and charge his subjects with Tallage and other burdens without their consent, and such is the dominion that the civill Law[s] purporte, when they say, The Prince his pleasure hath the force of a Law. But from this, much differeth the power of a King whose government over his people is politique, For he can neither change Lawes without the consent of his subjects, nor yet charge them with strange impositions against their wils. Wherfore his people do franckly and freely enjoy and occupie their own goods, being ruled by such lawes as they themselves desire, Neither are they pilled either of their owne king or of any other. Like pleasure also and freedome have the subjects of a king ruling only by power royal, so long as hee falleth not into tyrannye. Of such a King speaketh Aristotle in the third Booke of his Civill Philosophie, saying, that it is better for a Citie to bee governed by a good King, then by a good Lawe. But forasmuch as a King is not ever such a man, therefore Saint Thomas in the Booke, which hee wrote to the King of Cyprus, Of the governance of Princes, wisheth the state of a Realme to bee such, that it may not bee in the kings power to oppresse his people with tyrannie, Which thing is performed onely, while the power Royall is restrained by power politique. Rejoice therefore, O soveraigne Prince, and bee glad, that the Lawe of your Realme, wherein you shall succeed, is such, for it shall exhibite and minister to you and your people no small securitie and comfort. With such Lawes (as saith the same St. Thomas) shoulde al man kinde have beene governed, if in Paradise they had not transgressed Gods commandement,

---

[1] i.e. by constitutional government.

with such Lawes also was the Sinagogue ruled, while it served under God only as King, who adopted the same to him for a peculiar kingdome. But at the last, when at their request they had a man king set over them, they were then under royall Lawes onely brought very lowe. And yet under the same Lawes, while good Kings were their Rulers, they lived wealthily; and when wilfull and tyrannous Kings had the government of them, then they continued in great discomfort and misery, as the booke of Kings doth more plainly declare.

(*b*) (Ch. 18, p. 39 b.) Now whether the statutes of England be good or not, that onely remaineth to bee discussed. For they proceed not only from the Princes pleasure, as doe the lawes of those kingdomes that are ruled onely by regall governement, where sometimes the statutes doe so procure the singular commodity of the maker, that they redound to the hinderance and dammage of his subjects. Sometimes also by the negligence and oversight of such princes, and their sleight regard, respecting onely their owne commodities, they are so unadvisedly made, that they are more worthy to have the name of disorders, then of well ordered Lawes. But statutes can not thus passe in England, for so much as they are made not only by the Princes pleasure, but also by the assent of the whole Realme: so that of necessitie they must procure the wealth of the people, and in no wise tende to their hinderance. And it cannot otherwise be thought but that they are replenished with much wit and wisdome, seeing they are ordained not by the devise of one man alone or of a hundred wise Councellers onely, but of moe then three hundred chosen men, much agreeing with the number of the ancient Senatours of Rome: as they that know the fashion of the Parliament of England, and the order and manner of calling the same together, are able more distinctly to declare. And if it fortune these Statutes, beeing devised with such great solemnity and witte, not to fall out so effectually as the intent of the makers did wish, they may bee quickely reformed, but not without the assent of the commons, and states of the Realme, by whose authority they were first devised.

(*c*) (Ch. 35, p. 78.) Call to remembrance, most worthy

Prince, after what sort you sawe the wealthy Villages and
Townes (as touching store of Corne) in the Realme of Fraunce,
while you were there a sojourner, pestered with the Kings
men at armes and their horses, so that skant in any of the
great townes there you could get any lodging. Where, of the
inhabiters you learned, that those men, though they continue
in one village a moneth or two, doe not, nor will paye any
thing at all, either for their owne charges, or for the charges of
their horses; but, which is worse, they compelled the inhaby-
tants of the Villages and towne dwellers, when ther they came,
to provide of their owne proper costes, out of the villages
adjoyning, wine and flesh for them, and other thinges that
they needed, at dearer prices, then they might have bought
the same at home. And if any refused thus to doe, they were
anonne by plaine Stafford Law[1] forced to do it : And when
they had spent all the victuals, fewell[2], and horsemeat, in one
towne, then those men went to an other towne, wasting the
same in like manner, not paying one penie for any necessaries,
either for themselves or else for their concubines and harlots,
whereof they ever carried about with them great abundaunce,
nor for hosen or shooes, and other like, even to the lest point
or lace ; but they compelled the townsmen where they tarried
to beare al their expenses. And thus were al the villages and
unwalled townes of the land used, so that there is not the least
village there, free from this miserable calamity, but that it is
once or twise every yere beggered by this kinde of pilling.
Furthermore the King suffreth no man to eate salt within his
kingdome, except hee buy it of the king at such price as
pleaseth him to assesse. And if any poore man had rather
eat his meat fresh then to buy salt so excessively deare, he is
immediatly compelled to buy so much of the kings salt at
the kings price, as shall suffice so many persons as he keepeth
in his house. Moreover, al the inhabiters of the realme give
yerely to the king the iiij. part of all the wines that their
grounds beareth : and every Vintener the fourth peny of the
price of the wine that he selleth. And besides all this, every

---

[1] A punning proverbial phrase, "under threat of beating."
[2] fuel.

village and borough paieth yerely to the king great summes
of mony assessed upon them for the wages of men at armes,
so that the charges of the kings army, which is ever very great,
is maintained by the poore people of the villages, boroughes,
and townes of the realme.　And yet moreover, every village
findeth continually ij. Crossebowes at the least, and some
moe, with al furniture and habiliments, requisit for the kings
service in his wars, as oft as it pleaseth him to muster them,
which he doth very oft.　And, these things not considered,
other exceeding great tallages are yerely assessed upon every
village of the same realme to the kings use, wherof they are
no yere relesed.　The people, being with these and divers other
calamities plaged and oppressed, doe live in great misery,
drinking water daily, neither do the inferior sort tast any
other licor, saving only at solemne feasts.　Their shamewes[1] are
made of hemp, much like to sackcloth.　Wollen cloth they
weare none except it be very course, and that only in their
coates under their said upper garments; neither use they any
hosen, but from the kne upward : the residue of their legs go
naked.　Their women go barefoot saving on holidaies ; neither
men nor women eate any flesh there, but only larde of bacon,
with a smal quantity wherof they fatten their pottage and
broths.　As for rosted or sodden meat of flesh they taste none,
except it be of the inwards sometimes and heades of beastes,
that be killed for gentlemen and marchants.

But the men at armes, they devoure and consume all their
pulleine, so that they have scant the egges left to eat for
special dainties.　And if they fortune at any time to grow
some what welthy in substance, so that any of them bee
counted rich, hee is by and by charged to the Kings Subsidie
more deepely then any of his neighbors, so that within short
time he is made equall in poverty with the rest of his beggerly
neighbours.　And this, as I suppose, is the state of the comon
and rascall people of that nation.　But Gentlemen and Nobles
are not so oppressed, and overcharged with exactions.　But
if any of them chaunce to be accused of any crime, though it
be by his enemies, he is not ever wont to be cited or called

[1] short gowns.

before an ordinarie Judge: but many times it hath beene seene, that he hath in that behalfe beene talked with in the Kinges Chamber, or elsewhere in some private place, and sometimes onely by a Pursevant or Messenger: and immediately as soone as the Princes conscience hath, through the report of others, judged him guiltie, hee is without any fashion of judgement put in a Sacke, and in the night season by the Marshalls servants hurled into a River, and so drowned. After which sort you have heard of many moe put to death, then that have beene by ordinarie processe of the Lawe condemned. Howbeit the Princes pleasure, as say the Civill lawes, hath the force of a Lawe. Also, while you were abyding in Fraunce, and nigh to the same Kingdome, you hearde of other great enormyties like unto these, and some much worse then these detestable and damnable, done no otherwise but under the colour of that Lawe, which heere to rehearse would continue our talke too long a time. Now therefore, let us see, what the effecte of the Law politique and Regal, which some of your progenitors would have charged into this civill, hath wrought in the Realme of Englande; that you, being instructed with the experience of both Lawes, may the better by their effectes judge whether of them ye ought rather to choose, seeing the Philosopher, as afore is rehersed, doth say, that contraries laid together do more perfectly appeare.

Within the Realme of England, no man sojorneth in an other mans house, without the love and the leave of the good man of the same house: saving in common Innes, where, before his departure thence, he shall fully satisfie and pay for all his charges there. Neither shal he escape unpunished, whosoever he be, that taketh another mans goods without the good will of the owner thereof. Neither is it unlawfull for any man in that Royalme to provide and store himself of salt, and other merchandises, or wares, at his owne will and pleasure, of any man that selleth the same. Howbeit, the King, though the owners would say nay, may by his Officers take necessaries for his house, at a reasonable price, to bee assessed by the discretions of the Constables of the towns: Neverthelesse, he is bound by the Lawes to pay there-

3—2

fore, either presently in hand, or else at a day to bee limited and set by the higher Officers of his house: for by his Lawes hee may take away none of his Subjectes goods, without due satisfaction for the same. Neither doth the King there, either by himselfe or by his Servants and Officers, levie uppon his subjectes Tallages, Subsidies, or any other burdens, or alter their laws, or make newe Lawes, without the expresse consent and agreement of his whole Realme in his Parliament. Wherefore every inhabiter of that Realme useth and enjoyeth, at his pleasure, all the fruites that his lande or cattel beareth, with al the profits and commodities which, by his owne travell, or by the labour of others, hee gaineth by lande or by water: not hindered by the injurie or wrong detainement of any manne, but that hee shall bee allowed a reasonable recompence. And heereby it commeth to passe, that the men of that Land are rich, having aboundaunce of Gold and Silver, and other things necessarie for the mainetenance of mans life. They drinke no water, unlesse it bee so that some, for devotion and upon a zeale of pennance, doe abstaine from other drinke. They eate plentifully of all kindes of flesh and fishe. They weare fine wollen cloth in all their apparel. They have also aboundance of bedde coverings in their Houses, and of all other wollen stuffe. They have great store of all hustlements[1] and implementes of householde. They are plentifully furnished with al instruments of husbandrie, and all other things that are requisite to the accomplishment of a quiet and wealthie life, according to their estates and degrees. Neither are they sued in the Law, but only before ordinarie Judges, where by the Lawes of the Land they are justly intreated. Neither are they arrested or impleaded for their moveables or possessions, or araigned of any offence criminall, bee it never so great and outragious, but after the Lawes of the Lande, and before the Judges aforesaid. And these are the fruits, which, governement politique and regall conjoyned, doth beare and bring foorth : whereof now appeare evidently unto you the experiences of the effects of the Law, which some of your progenitors travelled to abolish. Before, also, you saw

[1] furniture.

plainly the effectes of the other Lawe, which they with such
earnest endevour laboured to advance and place in steade of
this Lawe; so that, by the fruites of them both, you may know
what they are: and did not ambition, riot, and wanton lust,
which your said progenitors esteemed above the wealth of the
Realme, moove them to this alteration.

16   AS OTHERS SEE US

The *Italian Relation of England* (Camden Soc., 1847) is a private
report drawn up by the Venetian envoy for the information of his government, about 1500 A.D.   I extract from it such portions as seem best
calculated to correct or complement Fortescue's too rosy descriptions.
The translation is that of the Camden Society Editor, with few alterations.
The narrator, however, falls into demonstrable exaggerations on his side.

(p. 20 ff.)   The English are, for the most part, both men
and women of all ages, handsome and well-proportioned;
though not quite so much so, in my opinion, as it had been
asserted to me, before your Magnificence went to that kingdom; and I have understood from persons acquainted with
these countries, that the Scotch are much handsomer; and
that the English are great lovers of themselves, and of everything belonging to them; they think that there are no other
men than themselves, and no other world but England; and
whenever they see a handsome foreigner, they say that "he
looks like an Englishman," and that "it is a great pity that
he should not be an Englishman"; and when they partake of
any delicacy with a foreigner, they ask him, "whether such
a thing is made in *his* country?"   They take great pleasure
in having a quantity of excellent victuals, and also in remaining a long time at table, being very sparing of wine when
they drink it at their own expense.   And this, it is said, they
do in order to induce their other English guests to drink wine
in moderation also; not considering it any inconvenience for
three or four persons to drink out of the same cup.   Few
people keep wine in their own houses, but buy it, for the most
part, at a tavern; and when they mean to drink a great deal,
they go to the tavern, and this is done not only by the men,
but by ladies of distinction.   The deficiency of wine, however,
is amply supplied by the abundance of ale and beer, to the

use of which these people are become so habituated, that, at an entertainment where there is plenty of wine, they will drink them in preference to it, and in great quantities. Like discreet people, however, they do not offer them to Italians, unless they should ask for them; and they think that no greater honour can be conferred, or received, than to invite others to eat with them, or to be invited themselves; and they would sooner give five or six ducats to provide an entertainment for a person, than a groat to assist him in any distress.

They all from time immemorial wear very fine clothes, and are extremely polite in their language; which (although it is, as well as the Flemish, derived from the German) has lost its natural harshness, and is pleasing enough as they pronounce it. In addition to their civil speeches, they have the incredible courtesy of remaining with their heads uncovered, with an admirable grace, whilst they talk to each other. They are gifted with good understandings, and are very quick at every thing they apply their minds to; few, however, excepting the clergy, are addicted to the study of letters; and this is the reason why any one who has learning, though he may be a layman, is called by them *a Clerk*. And yet they have great advantages for study, there being two general Universities in the kingdom, Oxford, and Cambridge; in which are many colleges founded for the maintenance of poor scholars. And your Magnificence lodged at one named Magdalen, in the University of Oxford; of which, the founders having been prelates, so the scholars are also ecclesiastics.

The common people apply themselves to trade, or to fishing, or else they practise navigation; and they are so diligent in mercantile pursuits, that they do not fear to make contracts on usury.

Although they all attend Mass every day, and say many Paternosters in public, (the women carrying long rosaries in their hands, and any who can read taking the office of our Lady with them, and with some companion reciting it in the church verse by verse, in a low voice, after the manner of churchmen,) they always hear mass on Sunday in their parish church, and give liberal alms, because they may not offer less than a piece of money, of which fourteen are equivalent to a golden ducat [i.e. a groat]; nor do they omit any form incumbent upon good Christians; there are, however, many who have various opinions concerning religion.

(p. 28.) The riches of England are greater than those of any other country in Europe, as I have been told by the oldest and most experienced merchants, and also as I myself can vouch, from what I have seen. (p. 29.) But above all are their riches displayed in the church treasures; for there is not a parish church in the kingdom so mean as not to possess crucifixes, candlesticks, censers, patens, and cups of silver; nor is there a convent of mendicant friars so poor, as not to have all these same articles in silver, besides many other ornaments worthy of a cathedral church in the same metal. Your Magnificence may therefore imagine what the decorations of those enormously rich Benedictine, Carthusian, and Cistercian monasteries must be.

(p. 30.) I saw, one day (being with your Magnificence at Westminster, a place out of London) the tomb of the Saint King Edward the Confessor, in the church of the aforesaid place Westminster; and indeed, neither St Martin of Tours, a church in France, which I have heard is one of the richest in existence, nor any thing else that I have ever seen, can be put into any sort of comparison with it. But the magnificence of the tomb of St Thomas the Martyr, Archbishop of Canterbury, is that which surpasses all belief. This, notwithstanding its great size, is entirely covered over with plates of pure gold; but the gold is scarcely visible from the variety of precious stones with which it is studded, such as sapphires, diamonds, rubies, balas-rubies[1], and emeralds; and on every side that the eye turns, something more beautiful than the other appears. And these beauties of nature are enhanced by human skill, for the gold is carved and engraved in beautiful designs, both large and small, and agates, jaspers and cornelians set in relievo, some of the cameos being of such a size, that I do not dare to mention it: but everything is left far behind by a ruby, not larger than a man's thumb-nail, which

[1] a delicate rose-red variety of ruby.

is set to the right of the altar. The church is rather dark, and particularly so where the shrine is placed, and when we went to see it the sun was nearly gone down, and the weather was cloudy; yet I saw that ruby as well as if I had it in my hand; they say that it was the gift of a king of France.

The population of this island does not appear to me to bear any proportion to her fertility and riches. (p. 32.) They generally hate their present, and extol their dead sovereigns. Nevertheless they reject the Roman code of laws, and adopt those given to them by their own kings. Nor are proceedings carried on in this country by the deposition of any one, or by writing, but by the opinion of men, both in criminal and civil causes. And if any one should claim a certain sum from another, and the debtor denies it, the civil judge would order that each of them should make choice of six arbitrators, and when the twelve are elected, the case they are to judge is propounded to them: after they have heard both parties, they are shut up in a room, without food or fire, or means of sitting down, and there they remain till the greater number have agreed upon their common verdict. But, before it is pronounced, each of them endeavours to defend the cause of him who named him, whether just or unjust; and those who cannot bear the discomfort yield to the more determined for the sake of getting out sooner. And therefore the Italian merchants are gainers by this bad custom every time that they have a dispute with the English; for, although the native arbitrators chosen by the English are very anxious to support the cause of their principal, before they are shut up, yet they cannot stand out as the Italians can, who are accustomed to fasting and privations, so that the final judgment is generally given in favour of the latter. This practice extends also to criminal causes, and any one may be accused of great and glaring crimes, and be put to the torture, though he may openly deny the truth of the accusation. But when the chief magistrate of the place has received notice of any such malefactor, he causes him immediately to be thrown into prison, and then twelve men of that place are elected, who must decide according to their consciences, whether the prisoner has or has not committed the crime of which he is accused, and if the greater number vote that he has, he is considered to be guilty. He is not, however, punished at that time; but it is necessary that twelve other men should be chosen, who must hear the cause over again; and if their verdict should agree with the former one, the days of the delinquent are brought to a close. It is the easiest thing in the world to get a person thrown into prison in this country; for every officer of justice, both civil and criminal, has the power of arresting anyone, at the request of a private individual, and the accused person cannot be liberated without giving security, unless he be acquitted by the judgment of the twelve men above named; nor is there any punishment awarded for making a slanderous accusation. Such severe measures against criminals ought to keep the English in check; but, for all this, there is no country in the world where there are so many thieves and robbers as in England; insomuch, that few venture to go alone in the country, excepting in the middle of the day, and fewer still in the towns at night, and least of all in London. Such is the bad effect that has arisen from an excellent cause.

There are three estates in England, the popular, the military, and the ecclesiastical. The people are held in little more esteem than if they were slaves.

(p. 35.) In another way, also, the priests are the occasion of crimes; in that they have usurped a privilege that no thief nor murderer who can read, should perish by the hands of justice; and, when anyone is condemned to death by the sentence of the twelve men of the robe, if the criminal can read, he asks to defend himself by the book; when, a psalter, or missal, or some other ecclesiastical book, being brought to him, if he can read it he is liberated from the power of the law, and given as a clerk into the hands of the bishop. But, notwithstanding all these evasions, people are taken up every day by dozens, like birds in a covey, and especially in London; yet, for all this, they never cease to rob and murder in the streets. (p. 37.) And if the King should propose to

[1] See Fortescue's own testimony (Section XIV., no. 12) and Sir Thomas More's (Section VI., no. 8).

change any old established rule, it would seem to every Englishman as if his life were taken from him; but I think that the present King Henry will do away with a great many, should he live ten years longer.

I dare say that your Magnificence will have been surprised, when I stated that there was only one Chief Justice in the whole kingdom ; and will, perhaps, have imagined that I meant to imply that the Dukes of Lancaster, York, Suffolk, and many others dispensed justice in their own countries; but these English noblemen are nothing more than rich gentlemen in possession of a great quantity of land belonging to the crown; and any King who had several sons, or kinsmen, and persons of merit, not only gave them great estates to enjoy, but also conferred upon them the titles of duke, marquess, or earl, assigning to each of them some small influence over the revenue of the place from which their title is derived ; as, for instance, 200 crowns per annum (40 *l.* sterling) are paid to the Duke of York, from the royal dues of the city of York; and the jurisdiction, both civil and criminal, and the fortresses remain in the hands of the Crown. It is, however, true that the Church of [Durham], which is on the borders of Scotland, has several castles in her own power, and exercises temporal jurisdiction, and coins some small pieces of money.

17 ENGLAND IN CIVIL WAR

Philippe de Commines is already of the Renascence ; he is a philosophic historian ; but unfortunately his remarks about England are too fragmentary for quotation with the following exception. (Book v. *ad fin.* Trans. M. Danett. 1596, p. 201.)

(p. 201.) Thinke you that an unwise Prince, being accompanied with fooles, can smell a far off how great a mischiefe division among his subjects is ? or beleeve that it can hurt him ? or proceedeth of God ? He eateth and sleepeth no whit the woorse for it ; he hath neither fewer horses in his stable, nor fewer robes in his wardrobe, but many mo companions. For he allureth men unto him by promises, and by parting among them the spoiles and offices of those whom he hath banished ; he giveth also of his owne to win thereby fame and renowme; but, when he shall least thinke of it, God will raise up an enimie against him whom peradventure he never mistrusted. Then will he waxe pensive, and suspect those whom he hath injuried, yea he will feare such as indeede owe him no evill will : yet notwithstanding he will not have his refuge to God in this extremitie, but seeke to redresse this inconvenience by force. Have we not seene in our daies examples heerof even among our next neighbors? Have we not seene the late King of England Edward the fourth of that name, heire of the house of Yorke, utterly destroy the house of Lancaster, under the which both his father and he had lived many yeeres? Further, the said King Edward having done homage to King Henry the 6. being of the house of Lancaster, did he not afterward hold him prisoner many yeeres in the tower of London, the chiefe citie of the realme, where in the end he was put to death?

Commines goes on to tell the well-known story of the Wars of the Roses, with all the conspiracies and executions which attended them : after which he proceeds :

In like maner we have seene of late the crowne of Spaine altered after the death of Dom Henry that last died. For the said Dom Henry had to wife the King of Portugales sister last deceased, by whom he had issue a goodly daughter, which notwithstanding succeeded not hir father, but was put from the crowne under colour of adulterie committed by hir mother. But the matter ended not without great contention and war : for the King of Portugale tooke part with his neece, and divers great Lords of Castile joined with him : yet notwithstanding the said Dom Henries sister, wife to the son of Dom John King of Arragon, obtained the crowne and possesseth it yet at this day : and thus this partage was made in heaven, as divers others are. Further, you have seene of late daies the King of Scotland and his sonne, being thirteene yeeres of age, in battell the one against the other : the sonne and his faction prevailed, and the King was slaine upon the place. This King murthered his owne brother, and was charged with divers other crimes, namely the death of his sister and such like. You see alsc the Duchy of Gueldres out of the right line, and have heard what impietie the Duke last deceased used against his father. Divers other examples I could rehearse which should manifestly appeere to be punishments and scourges of God, which scourges are the principall cause of wars, whereof insue mortality and famine, all the which evils proceede of lacke of faith. Wherefore I conclude, (considering the wickednes of men, especially of great men, who know not themselves, neither beleeve that there is a God,) that it is necessarie for every Prince and governor to have an adversary to keepe him in feare and humilitie, otherwise no man should be able to live under them or neere them.

SECTION II

BIRTH AND NURTURE

1 THE ANATOMY OF CHILDHOOD

Bartholomaeus Anglicus, tr. Trevisa, Bk VI. c. 5, 6 (ed. 1536, f. 72 a).

Of the little chylde.

The chyldes fleshe that is newe borne is tendre, nesshe[1], quavy[2] and unsadde[3]. Therfore dyvers remedies and fode ben necessary to the chylde, as saith Constantine li 3. capit. 32. And he saythe, that chyldren that be newe borne shulde be swathed in roses grouned with salte, that theyr membres may be comforted, and delyvered, and clensed of cleymye[4] moysture. Thanne the roofe of the mouthe and gommes sholde be froted[5] with ones finger wette in hony, to clense and comforte the inner partye of the mouthe, and also to excyte and to kyndle the chyldes appetyte with swetnesse of the hony. And he sholde be ofte bathed and anointed with [oil of myrtle or of roses], and al the limes shuld be anointid and rubbed with this oile, and namely the lymmes of males, the whiche bicause of traveyle ought to be more harde and sadde than the lymmes of females. And also it is nedefulle that they shulde be brought a-slepe in derke places, tyl theyr sighte be gadred[6] and joyned: For a place that is to bryghte, departeth and devydeth the syghte, and hurteth the small eyen, that be yet full tendre, and ofte maketh children to loke a squinte. And therfore they shold not be brought nor layde in to bright aier, leest the spirite of sight be dyvyded and departed. And of all thyng it nedeth to be ware of evill milke and of corrupted norysshinge and feding, that

---

[1] soft.   [2] flaccid.   [3] unsteadfast.
[4] clammy.   [5] rubbed.   [6] gathered.

the chyldren be not fed therwith. For by unclennes of nourices, and suckinge of clammy milke lyke glewe, comen full many soores and greves, As whelkes, blaynes, pimples in the mouth, spewing, fevers, crampe, the flyxe[1], and suche other. And if the chylde be syke, medicines shall be gyven to the nouryce, and not to the chylde. And she shall be ruled according to good diet, so that the virtue of the nouryce be in stede, supplye, and fulfyll the defaute of the chylde, as saith Constantine there. For of good disposicion of the milke cometh good disposicion of the chylde. And contrayre wyse. For of corrupte mylke of the nourice comen unkindly soores and greves in the chyldes littell body. And that is by reason of the tendernes of the chyldes kynde, and also for the easy changing of mylk fode. And for tendernes the lim[m]es of the chylde may easely and sone bowe and bende and take dyvers shapes. And therfore chyldrens membres and lymmes ben bounde with lystes[2] and other covenable bondes, that they ben not croked nother evyll shapen....

Children ben nesshe of flesshe, lethye[3], and pliant of body, able and lyghte to moevynge, wytty to lerne. And lede theyr lyves without thoughte and care. And sette theyr courages onely of mirth and lykynge, and drede no perylles more than betynge with a rodde : and they love an apple more than gold....Whan they bene praysed, or shamed, or blamed they sette littell therby. Through stiring and movynge of the heate of the flesshe and of humours, they ben lightly and soone wrothe, and soone pleased, and lightly they forgyve. And for tendernesse of bodye they ben soone hurte and greved. And maye not wel endure hard traveille. For moving of hote humours, whiche have the maystry in them, they moeve lightely and ben unstedfaste and unstable. Through great and strong heate they desyre moche meate. And so, by reason of superfluite of meate and of drynke, they falle ofte and manye tymes in to divers syknesses and evylles.

[1] flux.   [2] bandages.   [3] lithe.

2　THE FATHER

Trevisa's *Bartholomew*, Bk VI. cap. 15.

The fader is dyligent and besy, and lo[v]yth kindely his chylde, in so moche that he sparyth his owne mete to fede his chyldren.　And that is generally forthe in all kynde of beastes, out-take fewe, in whome kynde gothe out of kynde, and therfore they ben not busy and carefulle aboute theyr yonge, but they do beate theym awaye, as Aristotle libro 6. sayeth of the egle, that with his bylle and wynges beate and dryve away theyr yonge.　A man loveth his chylde and fedeth and nouryssheth it, and setteth it at his owne borde whan it is wayned.　And teacheth hym in his yougthe with speche and wordes, and chasteth hym with betinge, and setteth hym and putteth him to lerne under ward and kepynge of wardens and tutours.　And the father sheweth hym no gladde chere, leste he waxe prowde; and he loveth mooste the sonne that is like to hym, and loketh ofte on hym.　And gyveth to his chyldren clothynge, meate, and drynke, as theyr age requyreth, and purchaseth londes and herytage for his chyldren, and cesseth not to make it more and more....The more the father loveth his chylde, the more busyly he teacheth and chastyseth hym and holdethe hym the more streyte under chastisynge and loore, and whan the chylde is mooste loved of the father it semeth that he loveth hym not: for he betyth and greveth hym ofte, lest he drawe to evyll maners and tatches[1], and the more the child is like to the fader, the better the father loveth hym.　The fader is ashamed, if he here any foule thing tolde by his chyldren.　The fathers herte is sore greved, if his chyldren rebel ayenst him.

3　INFANT DAMNATION

R. of Brunne, *Handlyng Synne*, E.E.T.S., 1901, p. 298, abbreviated. The theory of the damnation of unbaptized infants was not invented by Calvin, but was taught by St Augustine, and whole-heartedly accepted by all orthodox theologians throughout the Middle Ages.

Ofte we here the lewed men seye
That erre ful moche oute of the weye

[1] faults.

That of the Jewës seye sum oun,
"They ne wote whether they be saved or noun";
But of sum prestes ys gretter tene[1],
That so of the Jewës also wene;
Certes, they are alle yn were[2],
And yn the feyth they are not clere,
For, shal never Jewe that deyeth Jewe,
Of hevene blys have part ne prewe[3],
But he be crystened yn the holy gaste[4],
And yn the sacrament be ful stedfast.

Lo, here a wurde to leve[5] youre drede!
Yn the Gospel that we rede,
That god Jhesu us allë techeth
Thurgh seynt Mark, that hyt precheth,
"He that beleveth and ys baptysed,
He shal be saved, so ys dyvvysed;
And he that beleveth nat, forsothe and ywys,
Bothe body and soulë, lore he ys."
Loke howe ye mow be a-bawed[6],
That seye that the Jewe ys saved!
Gyf a chylde be dedë bore—
Thogh hyt were quyk yn wombe byfore—
And, receyve nat the bapteme,
Of hevene may hyt never cleme[7];
With-outë doute, beleve ye thys,
That hyt shal never come to blys;
Ne peyne of hetë, ne of colde,
Hyt shal non fele, no ryght hyt wolde;
Hyt noght mysdyd, ne served wo,
Ne to nonë shal hyt go;
Thys ys peyne with-outen ende,
Hyt shal never to Joyë wende,
Gretë grace ys to them lent,
That here receyve thys sacrament[8].

---

[1] misfortune.   [2] error.   [3] proof.   [4] ghost.
[5] relieve.   [6] abashed.   [7] claim.
[8] Though medieval theologians often explain, as here, that the lost infants will suffer no actual bodily torment, yet most thinking men, even then, must have

Y shal yow telle of a mydwyfe,
That loste a chylde, bothe soule and lyfe.
This mydwyfe whan the childe was bore,
She helde hyt on here lappe before;
And whan she sawe that hyt shulde deye,
She bygan loude for to crye,
And seyd "God and Seynt Jone
Crysten the chylde, bothe flyssche and ‚bone."
Thys mydwyffe noghte elles seyde,
And yn the cherche-yerde they wulde hyt have leyde
As another chylde shulde he be
That hade receyvede the solempte,
The prest askede the mydwyffe,
Gyfe hyt were cristenede whan hyt hade lyffe,
And who hyt cristened, and on what manere
And what was seyde, that any myghte here?
The mydwyffe seyde unto the prest,
"Thys herde they that stood me nest[1],
'That God almyghty and seynt Joun
Gyve the chylde cristendom yn flesshe and boun.'"
Than seyd the preste, "God and seynt Jame
Gyve the bothe sorow and shame,
And Crystys malysun have thou for-thy,
And alle the outher that were the by!
Yn evyl tymë were thou bore,
For yn thy defaute, a soule ys lore,"
She was commaunded she shuld no more
Come eftesones there chyldryn were bore.

echoed the words which Bishop Fisher quoted approvingly from Chrysostom :
"if one would think the grief of 10,000 hells, all that yet is nothing like to be
excluded from that blessed countenance and to be hated of Christ" (*Fisher's
English Works*, E.E.T.S., Extra Series, 1876, p. 287: cf. 374 and 426, in both of
which latter places the last six words are omitted, showing that Fisher thought
them unessential).
[1] next.

4   BAPTISMAL SCENES

When a man of any property died, it was very important for the heir to prove that he was of full age, and therefore immune from the heavy burdens of wardship, &c. These *proofs of age* were made by the concurrent testimony of a number of neighbours and friends. In later times this evidence partook very much of the nature of "common form"; see a very interesting article in *The English Historical Review*, vol. XXII. (1907), pp. 101, 526.

But at the time to which the following extracts refer the evidence may be taken as genuine, or, at the very least, as probable, and therefore as almost equally significant for the social historian. They are from the 2nd and 7th volumes of the *Calendar of Inquisitiones Post Mortem*.

Vol. II. p. 500 (19 Edw. I.).

Philip Paynel.

John de C. says that the said Philip was born at Pyriton on the day of the Assumption about the first hour, 53 Hen. III., and was baptised in the baptistry of St Mary's Church, Pyriton, by Richard then Vicar, on the morrow at the morning hour. Philip Basset, uncle of the said Philip's mother, who was then at his manor of La Fasterne, being asked to be godfather, sent his friends Hugh de Courteney and John de Pyriton to lift him from the font and give him the name of the said Philip Basset, and Agnes then the wife of Roger de W. held him and was his godmother. He is certain of the time, for one John de Frie of Pyriton married one Emma at Hockday before the said Philip's birth, and the witness met him leading his wife with a great company and struck one William Champeneys, who was very abusive, heavily on the head with a staff, for which he was sore amerced in the hundred [Court] of Worth, and made great pecuniary amends.

Vol. II. p. 505 (20 Edw. I.).

Roger Alayn, alias Aleyn of Purscadel.

Henry le Chamberlang and others say the same, for at that time one Roger Cosyn, uncle of the said Roger, was rector of the church, and immediately after his birth wrote the date in the missal of the church, which they have often seen, and they say that on Monday after the Conception, 20 Edw. I., the said Roger was 22.

BAPTISM

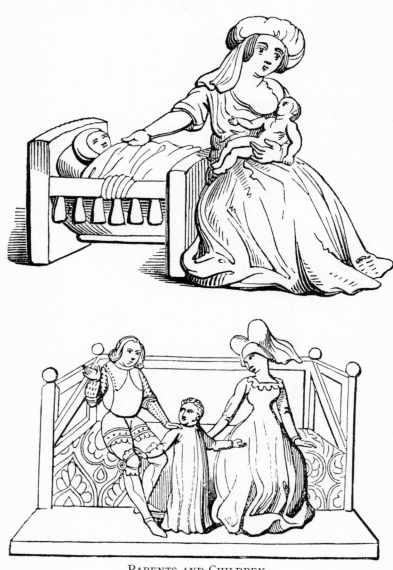

PARENTS AND CHILDREN

Vol. VII. p. 138 (2 Edw. III.).
Robert de La Legh.

Walter de Ludeworth, aged 33 years, says as the said John ; and this he knows because a certain Walter Man had a daughter born, name Alice, and took the said Walter [de Ludeworth] with him to the aforesaid church of Wermuth, and caused him, then aged nine years, to lift the said daughter from the sacred font, on the same 2nd November, and then and there he saw the aforesaid Robert baptised before the said Alice, whereby a long delay occurred, for which cause she wept, and he knows by the age of the said Alice, who survives, that the aforesaid Robert has completed the age of 24 years, as they have often computed among themselves.

John de Hewith, aged 50 years, says the like, and knows it because on the same 2nd of November his sister Iseult died, whose death is inserted in the calendar of the church of Suthwermuth, and because on the 2nd of November 24 years will have elapsed. He then saw the said Robert baptised with great solemnity, the priest sprinkling the holy water excessively in his face and in his eyes from the sacred font, wherefore he was angry for a long time with the aforesaid priest ; and therefore he well knows that the said Robert has completed the age of 24 years.

Vol. VII. p. 194 (3 Edw. III.).
Beatrice de Longevill née de Hastang.

John Lamb, aged 48 years, agrees, and knows it because he was present in the said church when John de Dalderbi, then bishop of Lincoln came there within a month after the said Beatrice was born, to confirm certain children, and there he saw her in the hands of the rector of the said church to be confirmed by the said bishop[1].

Vol. VII. p. 379 (7 Edw. III.).
Richard Darches.

Richard of A., aged 43 years, says the same, and knows it because on the day of his (the said Richard's) birth he

---

[1] Confirmation was administered at any age by the medieval bishops ; and (as orthodox contemporaries frequently tell us) very irregularly.

brought the news to Margaret de la Rokaylle his aunt, and had for it a silk purse with half a mark.

Vol. VII. p. 385 (7 Edw. III.).

Roger Dole, aged 50 years, says the like, and recollects it because his son Robert was buried at Reston, and there stood Thomas Hildeyerd, to whom it was then announced that Emma his wife had brought forth the said Elizabeth, and for the news he promised him [Roger] the robe in which he was clothed.

5   PROOFS OF AGE

It is of great social interest to see how these proofs were made ; a typical series of testimonies is therefore appended here, from *Calendar of Inquisitiones Post Mortem*, vol. VII. p. 457.

William, son of William le Marchal of Kyngestanleye, Gloucester. Proof of age, 22 May, 8 Edward III.

He is 21 years and 6 weeks of age and more, and was born in the town of Kyngestanleye, and baptised in the church there, on Thursday in the feast of Rogations (*sic*), 2 Edward II.

John Potelyn says he knows this, because on that Thursday, Alice, his daughter, died at Gloucester, and was buried at the church of St Oswald.

John Clavyle says that, on the previous Wednesday, William de Tyderynton espoused Margery de Heygrave, his kinswoman, at Staverton by Gloucester.

Gilbert le Carpenter says that on Saturday next after that Thursday, the bishop of Landaff came to Kyngestanleye, and consecrated a certain altar of St Katherine in the church there.

William Despenser says that, on that Thursday, John de Feckenham, chaplain, was instituted in the church of Bradele.

Thomas de Bacar says that on the Friday next following Agnes his wife was going to Gloucester, and in going by the way she fell, and broke her right leg.

Hugh de Dodebrugg says that on the Monday next before that Thursday, Adam his son became a friar at the house of St Augustine of Oxoneford.

Richard Thursteyn says that on that Thursday he and

several of his neighbours were robbed in the forest of Dene, between Gloucester and the abbey of Tynterne.

Walter le Deyer says that on that Thursday John le Taverner, of Circestre, came towards his house by the way near the wood of Wetyndon, and met robbers, who killed the said John there, and robbed him of 10*l.*

John le Gurnay says that on the previous Wednesday Sir Richard, vicar of Ledeneye, his brother, was buried.

John le Weler says that on the Friday following Elizabeth, his sister, fell into a certain marlpit, within her close near Leyecroft, and broke her neck.

Richard Pynnock says that on that Thursday he lifted from the font in the church of Kyngestanleye John, son of William Despenser, who was baptised in the same water in which the said William was baptised.

6 DECAYED SCHOOLS

Macaulay, arguing in 1847 before the House of Commons in favour of compulsory state education, had to meet the plea that voluntarism "will do all that is necessary, if we will only wait with patience." He retorted "wait with patience! Why, we have been waiting ever since the Heptarchy." His allusion was probably to the decree of the council of Cloveshoe in 747 which has sometimes been interpreted as implying a national system of education, though, in fact, it was only an attempt to combat the ignorance prevailing in the majority of monasteries. Though medieval grammar-schools were far more numerous than was supposed before A. F. Leach began his researches, they were always irregularly spaced and their existence was precarious. The best illustration of this may be found in the petition of William Byngham, a London priest, to Henry VI. in 1439. Byngham begged leave to found at Cambridge a college called "God's House," on the following plea: the whole document is printed in A. F. Leach, *Educational Charters and Documents*, 1911, p. 402.

"The Clergie of this youre Reaume...is like to be empeired and febled by the defaute and lak of Scolemaistres of Gramer, in so moche that [the founder, William Bingham] hath founde in [your] Lande, ouer the est partie of the wey ledyng from [South]hampton to Coventre, and so forth no ferther north than Rypon, LXX Scoles voide or mo, that weren occupied all at ones within L yeres passed, whereof as now ben almost none, nor none mowen be hade in your Universitees over those that nedes most ben occupied still there."

7 AN OLD ENGLISH SCHOOL

Aelfric was Abbot of Evesham, and wrote his *Dialogue* about the year 1,000 ; see A. F. Leach, *Educational Charters and Documents*, 1911, pp. xvi, 36. It is possible that the *personnel* of our early schools was not always so miscellaneous as Aelfric here represents ; his object was to bring into his Dialogue as many useful words and phrases as possible ; but there is a general verisimilitude in his descriptions. The text may be found in full in Wright and Wülcker's *A.-S. Vocabularies*, 1884, 1. 88 : long extracts are translated by Leach, *l.c.* 36.

Disciple. We boys beseech thee, O master, teach us to speak Latin rightly ; for we are unlearned, and speak corruptly. *Master.* What will ye speak ? *D.* What care we, so that we only speak rightly, not basely or in old wives' fashion ? *M.* Will ye be flogged in your learning ? *D.* We love rather to be beaten for learning's sake than to be ignorant ; but we know that thou art a kindly man, who will not beat us unless we compel thee. *M.* I ask *thee*, then ; what sayest thou ? what is thy daily work ? *D.* *I* am a professional monk, and I shall sing daily my seven services with the brethren, and am busy with reading and psalmody ; yet in the mean time I would fain learn to speak in the Latin tongue. *M.* And these thy fellows, what know they ? *D.* Some are ploughers, others shepherds, some are cowherds and some also are hunters, fishers, fowlers ; some are merchants or cobblers or salters or bakers in this place.

[Each then describes his own daily occupation, the monk last of all, adding : "and now we stand here before thee, ready to hear what thou wilt say to us."]

M. When will ye sing vespers or compline ? *D.* When the time is come. *M.* Hast thou been beaten [in the monastery] to-day ? *D.* No, for I kept myself cautiously. *M.* And thy fellows ? *D.* Why dost thou question me of this matter ? I dare not reveal our secrets unto thee ; each knoweth in his own heart whether he have been beaten or not... *M.* Where sleepest thou ? *D.* In the dormitory, with the brethren. *M.* Who waketh thee for the night-services ? *D.* Sometimes I hear the bell and arise ; but sometimes my master arouseth me harshly with a rod.

8 THE SCHOOLMASTER'S ATTRIBUTES

Matthew Stokys or Stokes, born at Eton and afterwards fellow of King's, became Esquire Bedell and Registrary. The University Register from 1531 onwards is in his writing, and perhaps from as early as 1523. He compiled an invaluable memorandum-book of University customs, extracts from which are printed in Dean Peacock's *Observations on the Statutes of the University of Cambridge*, 1841. In medieval, as in Roman, law, an office was always conferred symbolically by the handing over of some visible sign ; e.g. the pallium, ring and crosier which figure so largely in the Investiture controversy. The Master of Arts received his cap on this occasion, the Master of Grammar, as will be seen, his "palmer" (for application to the erring boy's hand) and his birch.

THE ENTERYING OF A MASTER IN GRAMER.

The Bedyll shall sett the Masters of Gramer to the Fathers place at vij of the Clocke, or betwene vii or eyght, Than the Father shal be brought to Saynt Mary Chyrch to the Masse begynyng at viij[th] of the Clocke: he shall cume behynde, and hys eldyst sonne nexte hym on hys ryght honde, lyke as is sayde afore of the Inceptours in Arte. When masse is done, fyrst shall begynne the acte in Gramer. The Father shall have hys Sete made before the Stage for Physyke, and shall sytt alofte under the Stage for Physyke[1]. The Proctour shall say, *Incipiatis*. Whan the Father hath arguyde as shall plese the Proctour, the Bedyll in Arte shall bring the Master of Gramer to the Vicechauncelar, delyvering hym a Palmer wyth a Rodde, whych the Vycechauncelar shall gyve to the seyde Master in Gramer, and so create hym Master[2]. Than shall the Bedell purvay for every master in Gramer a shrewde Boy, whom the master in Gramer shall bete openlye in the Scolys, and the

[1] "St Mary's Church, and, during the time of its rebuilding from 1478 to 1519, the churches of the Austin and Grey Friars, were fitted up, during the celebration of these solemnities, with stages, like a theatre, for the chancellor, noblemen and heads [of houses], for the doctors of the different faculties, for the regent and non-regent masters, for the different religious orders, with places for the proctors, father, prævaricator, philosopher, and other actors in the proceedings of the day. This practice continued, with a gradual diminution of splendour and interest, until about the year 1740."

[2] "This mode of creating masters in grammar, *ferulâ et virgis*, was followed in the University of Oxford. (Wood's *Hist. Univ. Oxon.* Lib. II. p. 4.) The statutes of the faculty of grammar in that university were the same as those of Cambridge, and were probably derived from some common source."

master in Gramer shall give the Boye a Grote for hys Labour, and another Grote to hym that provydeth the Rode and the Palmer; etc. *de singulis.* And thus endythe the Acte in that Facultye.

Nota, That the Bell Ryngar shall provyde a Rodde and a Palmer for the Masters in Gramer, and he shall have of every master in Gramer for hys Labour iiij[d].

Nota, That the Inceptour in Gramer shall gyve to the Vice-chauncelar a Bonett, and to the Father and to eche off the Proctours a Bonett; and iff there be but on Inceptour, he shall do thys; and iff there be moo then on, then to pay thys emong them.

9　CO-EDUCATION

Trevisa's *Higden,* vol. VII. p. 183.

...In these dayes [about 1050 A.D.] a famous clerk, Barbosus, was at Irland, and a man of wonderful religioun, so moche that he helde a greet scole of clerkes and lewed men and maydons; but, for he schare[1] the maydens in manere of his scolers, he was put out of Irlond.

10　THE DANGERS OF GRAMMAR

Walsingham, *Historia Brevis,* R.S., vol. II. p. 9 (A.D. 1381), speaking of Wat Tyler and his fellow-rebels.

We must judge them by their works; for they slew the father of the whole clergy, the head of the English Church, the Archbishop of Canterbury. See too what they did against the faith; how they compelled masters of grammar schools to swear that they would never again teach grammar to children! And what more? they strove to burn all ancient muniments, and slew all such as could be found capable of commemorating to posterity either ancient records or modern events; it was perilous to be recognized as a clerk, and far more perilous if any were caught bearing an inkhorn at his side.

This attitude of the rebellious commons towards learning may be illustrated by that of the extremists among the governing classes, as recorded in the parliamentary proceedings of subsequent years.

[1] i.e. made them adopt the clerical tonsure.

(*a*) A.D. 1388 (Knighton, R.S. 1895, vol. II. p. 298).

[At this parliament of Cambridge,] new statutes were published for the profit of the common people, and many which had been published in the reign of Edward III. were renewed, concerning labourers, artificers, servants....For in those days there grew up among the common people such pride in divers fashions of dress and ornament that scarce one of the people was distinguished from another by splendour of dress or adornment. The poor differed not from the mighty, the needy from the rich, the serf from his lord nor the priest from his flock; but each imitated another and strove to bring in some newer guise and to surpass his betters in pride of dress or ornament....

These Statutes (i) reinforced the Statutes of Labourers, and (ii) added (p. 302):

Item, it is ordained and agreed that all such as have been wont to labour at plough or cart, or other work or service of husbandry, up to the age of 12 years, that such do abide henceforward in the aforesaid labour, without being put to any trade or craft; and if any covenant of apprenticeship be made in contravention of this, let it be null and void.

(*b*) A.D. 1391 (*Rotuli Parliamentorum*, vol. III. p. 294).

§ 39. *Item*, the Commons pray the King that it may please him to ordain...that no serf or villein henceforward put his children to school, in order to procure their advancement by clergy; and this we beseech in maintenance and salvation of the honour of all free men in the kingdom.

Responsio. Le Roi s'avisera[1].

(*c*) *Statutes of the Realm*, 7 Henry IV.

Let no man or woman, whatsoever be their estate or condition, set their son or daughter, of whatever age, to serve as apprentice to any trade or work within the Cities or Boroughs of this realm, unless he have land or rent to the value of twenty shillings a year at least; but let the children be set to serve at the same labour as their parents have used, or to other labours as their estates require, under pain of a year's imprisonment,

---

[1] i.e. the petition is rejected or shelved.

and fine or ransom at the King's will. Provided however that every man or woman, of whatsoever estate, be free to set their son or daughter to learn letters at any school which may please them within this realm.

11 UNIVERSITY ORIGINS

(*a*) *Oxford* (if we are to accept Dr Rashdall's extremely probable hypothesis) developed from a local school to a real University in consequence of the following royal edict of about 1165 recalling all English clerks (which would include scholars) from abroad. The text is in *Materials for the History of Abp Thomas Becket*, R. S., vol. I. p. 54.

Let all clerks who have revenues in England be warned to come back to England, as they love their revenues, there to enjoy the same; and, if they return not within this term, let their said revenues be confiscated to the royal treasury. Let this be done throughout all the counties of our realm.

(*b*) *Cambridge*, Roger of Wendover, R. S., vol. II. p. 51.

About this same time [A.D. 1209] a certain clerk who was studying in Arts at Oxford slew by chance a certain woman, and, finding that she was dead, sought safety in flight. But the mayor and many others, coming to the place and finding the dead woman, began to seek the slayer in his hostel which he had hired with three other clerks his fellows; and, not finding the guilty man, they took his three fellow-clerks aforesaid, who knew nothing whatsoever of the homicide, and cast them into prison; and, after a few days, at the king's bidding but in contempt of all ecclesiastical liberties, these clerks were led out from the city and hanged. Whereupon some three thousand clerks, both masters and scholars, departed from Oxford, so that not one of the whole University was left; of which scholars some pursued their study of the liberal Arts at Cambridge, and others at Reading, leaving Oxford utterly empty.

12 THE MODEL STUDENT

The ideal student is described in a 14th cent. statute of University College, Oxford, quoted by Mr Hulton on p. 29 of his *Rixae Oxonienses*, 1892. It was hoped that this College would prove itself "a society of clerks living honourably in a manner befitting saints, not fighting or using scurrilous or low words, not reciting, singing, or willingly hearing songs or tales of an amatory or indecent nature, not taunting or provoking one another to anger, and not shouting so as to disturb the studies and repose of the industrious." The actual Oxford and Cambridge student is portrayed in lifelike detail by Dr Rashdall in the second volume of his *Universities of Europe*, and by Prof. R. S. Rait in his little monograph *Life in the Medieval University*. Here, so far as our space permits, we have collected instances of the two extremes of student life at Oxford and Cambridge, where contrasts were perhaps more strongly marked between rich and poor, and between the boy of 13 or 14 and the well-to-do rector or canon of mature age, than even in other departments of medieval life.

Of St Edmund Rich (Archbishop of Canterbury and patron saint of St Edmund's Hall, Oxford, and of many modern Roman Catholic schools and colleges), there is an excellent description in Green's *Short History*. Dr Rashdall has claimed, with much reason, that no equal to St Edmund, intellectually and morally, sat upon the throne of Canterbury until the appointment of Abp Temple. The following extract is from Trevisa's *Higden* VIII. 217, considerably abbreviated.

From his firste childhod this used his wittes to the studie of godnes by occupacioun of gostliche lyvynge. In token therof he made his avow to Oure Lady; by his moder counsaille he used the [shirt of] heyre, and faste every Friday to brede and to water, and used every Sonday and holy day to seie al the Sawter[1] or he wolde dyne. In his childhood he lernede his gramere and was so disesed with the heedache that he hadde non hope to spede afterward in lore. His moder spak to hym and seide, "Sone, I trowe that the lewednesse and unsemeliche tonsure that thou usest is cause of thy woo"; thanne afterward he usede tonsure as a clerk, and was hool of al that woo. In a tyme he walked by hym self in a mede bysides Oxenforde, and a faire child appered to hym and seide, "Heyl my luf, I wondre that thou knowest me nought, and nameliche while I am alwey by thy side in scole and in other places; therfore what thou seest in my forheede i-wrete, prynte it everiche

---

[1] Psalter.

nyght in thyn owne forheed." The writynge was "Iesus
Nazarenus rex Judeorum," that is "Jesus of Nazareth kyng
of Jewes:" therafter he lerned to have oure Lordes passioun
alwey in his mynde. Ones, for besynesse of a lessoun that he
moste rede, he forgat it; than whan the day gan to spring the
olde enemy bonde faste his hondes for he schulde nought
blesse hym self, and he prayde in his herte, and the enemy
fil[1] doun from hym bytwene the bed and the wal. They[2] he
were nought infra sacros[3] he was a maister of aart, and usede
to here a masse and seie his houres everiche day or he wolde
rede, and was profitable to his scolers, for he taughte them to
here masse also. Whan he feng[4] money of his scolers he leyde
it in a wyndowe, and seide "Pouder to pouder and askes[5] to
askes;" but the money was ofte i-take awey with his felawes
in game, other elles priveliche with theofes. Whanne he redde
arithmetic his moder that was deed appered to hym in his
sleep and axede hym and seide, "What figures beeth thees
that thou studiest ynne?" and he answerde, "Such and suche,"
and than sche peynted thre cercles in her right hond, as they
sche wolde men[e] the Fadir and Sone and Holy Goost, and
seide, "Sone, studie thou in these figures after this tyme."
Seelde he sat in chirche, but he badde his bedis stondynge
other knelynge; ffor he was a nobil prechour, a scharp arguer,
and a mylde lyst[en]er. For greet knelynge his kneen were
harde as the sooles of his feet. Everiche day he seide thre
payre of matyns and of houres of the day, of oure Lady, of
the Holy Gost, with Placebo and Dirige. A-nyght after his
firste sleep he wolde ary̆se and seie certeyn psalmes and prayers.
Yif eny envious word come in place, he wolde chaunge the
theme, and passe to the betir matire; he wolde have no benefice with cure, but oon. The tyme of etynge and slepynge
and rydynge, whanne he myghte noughte studie, he tolde hit
al y-lost. As ofte as he openede his bibel he wolde worschippe hit with a cros. And in the heyres that he werede
unnethe[6] myghte eny worme be y-founde. Hym schamed
nought to drawe of his owne hosen and schoon. Everiche
man that he mette in the way that wolde be schryve[n] to

[1] fell. [2] though. [3] in Holy Orders. [4] took. [5] ashes. [6] scarcely.

hym, he wolde light doun of his hors and hire his schrifte, and spare for no lette of comynge to his in, neyther for wynde ne for rayn ne for other wedir. He ferde as the olyve tree that holdeth to itself the bitternesse in the rynde, and heldeth[1] out to the other the swetnes of the oyle, so he was hard to hym-self and esiliche and goodliche to other men. He beet his brest ofte with his hond, and his knees agenst the grounde so that clerkes that leye in selers under hym myghte unnethe sleepe. For worschippe of oure Lady he worschipped alle wommen, but therby was he nevere i-wemmed[2].

13   THE POOR SCHOLAR

(*a*) St Richard of Chichester was born at Wych in Worcestershire, the son of well-to-do parents. He was studious from his childhood; in youth, he preferred his studies to an advantageous marriage which had been arranged for him. The rest here following is translated from John Cap-grave's life of the Saint in *Acta Sanctorum Bolland.*, Ap. 3 (Ed. 1675, I. p. 279).

Richard therefore hastily left both [his father's] lands and the lady, and all his friends, and betook himself to the University of Oxford and then to that of Paris, where he learned logic. Such was his love of learning, that he cared little or nothing for food or raiment. For, as he was wont to relate, he and two companions who lodged in the same chamber had only their tunics, and one gown[3] between them, and each of them a miserable pallet. When one, therefore, went out with the gown to hear a lecture, the others sat in their room, and so they went forth alternately; and bread with a little wine and pottage sufficed for their food. For their poverty never suffered them to eat flesh or fish, save on the Sunday or on some solemn holy day or in presence of companions or friends; yet he hath oftentimes told me how, in all his days, he had never after led so pleasant and delect-able a life.

---

[1] poureth.   [2] corrupted.

[3] *Cappa*, a long garment fastened down the front, statutory for all clergy and therefore for university students. The university gown on the one hand, and the priestly cassock on the other, are lineally descended from the medieval *cappa*. See Rashdall, *l.c.* II. 636 ff., where, however, "boots" (*caligae*) should be "hosen."

(*b*)   *Statutes of the Realm*, 22 Hen. VIII. c. 12 § 4.

And be yt enacted by the aucthoryte aforsayde that
Scolers of the Universities of Oxford and Cambrydge that
goo about beggyng, not beyng aucthorysed under the Seale
of the sayde Universities, by the Commyssary Chauncelloure
or Vichancelloure of the same, and all and syngular Shyp-
men pretendyng losses of theyre shyppes and goodes of the
see goyng aboute the countrey beggyng wythout suffycyent
aucthoryte wytnessyng the same, shall be punysshed and
ordered in maner and fourme as ys above rehersed of stronge
beggers [i.e. § 3, "to be tyed to the end of a Carte naked and
be beten wyth Whyppes thoroughe oute the same market
towne or other place tyll his Body be blody by reason of
suche whyppyng; and after suche punysshement and whyppyng had, the person...shalbe enyoyned upon his othe to
retourne forthewyth wythout delaye in the nexte and
streyght waye to the place where he was borne, or where
he last dwelled before the same punysshement"].

14   HARD WORK

Adam Marsh is pleading that a meritorious young brother-friar, Walter
of Maddeley, may be better furnished by the authorities with means for
continuing his studies.   An incident of this same Walter's life will be
found below, Section XI., no. 7.

By reason of which [neglect] he is compelled not only to
exhaust his vital spirits by the vehemence of his studies, but
also to wear out his bodily strength, day by day, by writing
with his own hand ; though (as saith the prophet Job) his
strength is not the strength of stones, nor is his flesh of brass.

15   BIBLE EDUCATION

Roger Bacon, *Opus Tertium*, ed. Brewer, R. S., 1859, p. 54.   Dr Rashdall has given prominence to the startling fact "that the 'religious
education' of a 'bygone Oxford,' in so far as it ever had any existence,
was an inheritance not from the Middle Ages but from the Reformation.
In Catholic Europe it was the product of the Counter-Reformation."
Universities of Europe, II. 701.

Therefore [moral philosophy] should first be learnt, that
men might know to what end and for what reasons they

work; in order that such philosophy might become the rule of all human work, and that man might do naught but by this science. Wherefore all, from their youth up, are instructed by the Church in those things which pertain to faith. And we ought to be far better instructed in the knowledge of Christ than we now are, from our youth up. For God's Law should be read to children, that they might ever grow accustomed to the truth of the faith, and especially the simplest and most moral books of the Old and New Testament, even as some are now taught from Bibles in verse; but it would be better that they should hear and construe the Gospels in prose, and the Epistles, and the Books of Solomon; since that versified Bible mutilates everything, and is worthless.

For man should first be taught in those things which pertain to the salvation of his soul, that he may grow accustomed always to go on from good to better; wherefore the Jews, in their youth, learn first of all the Law of God. Boethius also, in his *De Disciplina Scolarium*, teacheth that boys should first be instructed in Seneca's works; which he therefore saith (as Bede expoundeth) because those are moral books, and boys should first learn from such as Seneca. Not thus are they now taught, but in the fables and insanities of Ovid[1] and other poets, wherein all possible errors in faith and morals are set forth....Wherefore our youth conceive evil manners from their early days; and, when they have made experience of these things, they increase more and more therein. ...Wherefore, seeing that the multitude knoweth nothing of this science [of morals] from their youth up, therefore men have minds darkened and blinded which can never grow except in vanities and falsehood, and in evil quibblings and a most plentiful lack of wisdom. Hence it is that the multitude of students neglect all that is fair and profitable in philosophical science, and philosophy is perishing among us. Nay, the very books of this science, by Aristotle and Avicenna, Seneca and Cicero and other writers, cannot be obtained without great expense, partly because their best books have

---

[1] Ovid is perhaps the classic most frequently cited by medieval writers.

not been translated into Latin, and partly because no copy of their others can be found, even at great universities.

16   BLACK SHEEP

Anstey, *Munimenta Academica*, R. S., vol. I. p. 320. This Oxford Statute of 1432 may be compared with the almost contemporary petition of the Commons against student-bandits, translated on p. 597 of my *Medieval Garner*. Dr Rashdall remarks that "there are historic battle-fields on which less [blood] has been spilt" than on Oxford High Street (*l.c.* II. 403).

Item—seeing that the peace of this kindly [*almae*] University is seen to be frequently broken by divers persons who, under pretence of being scholars, wait and lurk within the University and its precincts, but outside the Halls and under tutelage of no Principal—men known by the abominable name of "Chamberdeacons," who sleep all day and by night haunt the taverns and brothels for occasions of robbery and manslaughter—therefore it is decreed by the said University that all and every scholar do dwell in that Hall or College wherein his common contributions are registered, or in Halls thereunto annexed, which share with the aforesaid in commons or battels, under pain of imprisonment for the first offence. If, moreover, having been once admonished by the Chancellor or his Commissary, or by the Proctors, they neglect to transfer themselves to those abodes aforesaid, then let them be banished and cut off from the University, as rotten members thereof, within eight days.

17   UNIVERSITY DISCIPLINE

Anstey, *Munimenta Academica*, R. S., vol. I. p. 304 (A.D. 1432).

Item, seeing that the unbridled continuance here of exe-crable discussions, while multiplying vices and idleness, hath wellnigh blackened the fair manners, the famous learning and the sweet fragrant report of this University of Oxford ; seeing also that, in these days of ours, a money-fine is more feared than any other penalty, and the imposition of such a fine upon the offenders is accounted the readiest means of ending such troubles, therefore the Masters of this University in congregation have unanimously ordered and decreed that every man lawfully convicted of breaking the peace be mulcted of a sum of money, according to the quantity and quality of his offence, over and beyond all other accustomed penalties : *viz.*

For threats of personal assault, 12^d ; for bearing arms contrary to the statutes, 2^s; for drawing of weapons for violence or for thrusting with shoulder or striking with fist, 4^s; for striking with stone or staff, 6^s 8^d; for striking with knife, dagger, baselard or sword, with axe or any such weapon of war, 10^s; for bearing a bow and shooting therewith with intent to harm, 20^s; for assembling of armed or other persons, and conspiring or confederating against the execution of justice or to inflict bodily harm upon any man, 30^s; for resisting the execution of justice, or night-walking, 40^s; in addition to satisfaction for the party aggrieved. And we ordain that if any Master or Scholar, or any other person, do favour any other man's cause for that he is his fellow-country-man, or do withstand him for that he is of a different country[1], or do give any manifest occasion whereby any quarrel between country and country may be like to arise ; or, again, if any be lawfully convicted of aiding and abetting the arousing or fomenting of such quarrel, he shall pay, over and above the wonted penalties for disturbers of the peace....

Here follows a long list of penalties graduated according to the offender's pecuniary circumstances, which shows that the authorities expect to find Masters and well-beneficed clergy among these lawbreakers. The records of actual trials, published by J. E. T. Rogers in *Oxford City Documents* (1891) and by Anstey in *Munimenta Academica*, show a startlingly large proportion of offenders among the senior members of the University.

[1] This refers to the standing feud between North and South, the Trent being the rough boundary. An extremely interesting account of one of these fights in 1383, which lasted three days and cost much bloodshed, is related by the chronicler Adam of Usk (ed. Maunde Thompson, 1904, p. 7) and Knighton (R. S. II. 309). As Dr Rashdall says, the settlement of the dispute between the Northern and Irish scholars in Oxford in 1252 "reads like a treaty of peace between hostile nations rather than an act of university legislation"; and the existing records of coroners' inquests show that, in practice, "nothing worse happened to [the majority of these Oxford homicides] than being compelled to go to Cambridge" (*Univ. of Europe*, II. 363, 683).

18 CAMBRIDGE RIOTS

C. H. Cooper, *Annals of Cambridge*, vol. I. The curious reader may refer also to the town and gown fight of 1261 A.D. (*ibid.* p. 48), the Peasants' Revolt at Cambridge (p. 120), the attack upon King's College in 1454 with "guns and habiliments of war" (p. 205), and the fight between the Prior of Barnwell and the Mayor (p. 277).

p. 160 f.   1418 A.D.

Complaints of the Mayor, Bailiffs, and Commonalty
[of Cambridge, to the King's Council].

II. That on the vigil of St. James the Apostle, many scholars, with the assent and at the excitation and abetting of the before mentioned persons, armed in a warlike manner, caused great terror to the mayor, by laying in wait to kill him and his officers, if they on that night had issued out of their houses ; and that when they perceived they could not effect their malicious purpose, they affixed on the mayor's gate a certain schedule, to his great scandal, and so that the mayor and burgesses dared not to preserve the peace.

This schedule was in these terms :—

BILLA POSITA SUPER HOSTIUM MAJORIS.   CITATIO
PEREMPTORIA.

Looke out here Maire with thie pilled[1] pate,
　And see wich a scrowe[2] is set on thie gate ;
Warning thee of hard happes,
　For and it lukke thou shalt have swappes[3] :
Therefor I rede keepe the at home ;
　For thou shalt abey[4] for that is done ;
Or els kest[5] on a coate of mayle ;
　Truste well thereto withouten faile.
And great Golias, Joh. Essex,
　Shalt have a clowte with my karille axe[6],
　Wherever I may him have.
And the hosteler Bambour, with his goat's beard,
　Once and it hap shal be made afeard,
　So God mote me save !

---

[1] bald.　　[2] scroll.　　[3] blows.　　[4] abide the penalty.　　[5] cast.
[6] curtal-axe, cutlass.

And yit with thie catchepoles hope I to meete,
  With a fellowe or twayne, in the playne streete,
  And her gownes brake;
And that harlot[1] Hierman, with his calves snowte,
  Of buffets full sekerly shall bern a rowte[2],
  For his werkes sake.
And yet shall Hankyn Attilbrigge
  Full yerne for swappes his tayle wrigge,
  And it hap arith[3].
And other knaves, all on heape,
  Shall take knockes full good cheape,
  Come once winter nith.
But nowe I praye to God Almyth,
  That whatsoever yowe spare,
That metche sorowe to him bedith,
  And evill mote he fare!

Amen, quoth he, that beshrewed the Mair's very visage.

19   FORBIDDEN UNIVERSITY SPORTS

Tennis and all other ball-games were forbidden in the streets and within the college precincts; cf. the Statutes of King's College which will be found just below. The current legend as to the prohibition of marbles on the Senate House steps at Cambridge is doubtless a traditional distortion of this early legislation.

(*a*)   Anstey, *Munimenta Academica*, R. S., vol. I. p. 18 (1250? A.D.).

It is decreed and ordained that no feast of any nation[4] be henceforth celebrated in any church solemnly and with the accustomed assembly of Masters and Scholars or other acquaintance (except so far as any man desireth to celebrate devoutly the feast of some saint of his own diocese in the church of his own parish, but without inviting the Masters or Scholars or any other of his acquaintance from another parish, even as none such are invited on the feasts of St Catherine, St Nicholas, and so forth). We command also the observance of this [following] decree, with the authority of the Chancellor, under pain of the greater excommunication: that no [master

---

[1] rascal.   [2] bear a quantity.   [3] aright.
[4] i.e. North or South, Irish, Welsh, etc.

or scholar] dance with masks, or with any noise whatsoever, in the churches or the streets, nor go about garlanded or crowned with a crown woven of leaves or the like, under pain of excommunication which we hereby pronounce, and of long imprisonment[1].

(*b*)   *ibid.* I. 24 [1252?].

At least once in every year, let a general inquisition be made, by authority of the Chancellor, among the Principals and Manciples [of Halls] specially sworn for this occasion, concerning peacebreakers and public taverners and such as practise the game of buckler-play.

(*c*)   *ibid.* II. 526, A.D. 1442.

The deposition of John ffelerd, servitor to Oliver Hore, sworn and examined concerning a breach of the peace between himself and William Bishop of St John's Hall....

He saith that he and his friend were communing together concerning the game vulgarly called *swerd and bokelere*, or *pykyd staff*, saying that such games come from merriment of heart; and, among other things, the said William said to this aforenamed John, *sofft and ffayre!* whereunto John made answer *sofft and ffayre ynogh!*   Then William departed and brought back with him two scholars whose names are unknown, and the aforesaid William said unto the same John, "where is he who would fain play at this game aforesaid," adding, "where are the weapons?"   "Here am I," replied John; "and here are the weapons"; and the said William with his fellows laid hold on the staff at one end, and the said John would have drawn it away by the other end.   Then said the same William and his fellows, "Leave us the staff!" and he would not, but tore it with great force from them, and so he smote the said William even unto the shedding of blood[2]; but before he smote him, a

---

[1] Cf. the Statute of 1432 (p. 312) imposing a fine of 6*d.* on all Regent masters who wander about irreverently during mass or funeral services at the University Church.

[2] And was therefore *ipso facto* excommunicate: see the decree of Innocent II. in Gratian's *Decretum*, Pars II. Causa xvii. q. 4, c. 29: "If any man, instigated by the devil, commit such a sacrilege as to lay violent hands upon a clerk or monk, let him be anathema, nor let any bishop presume to absolve him (except on his

SWORD AND BUCKLER PLAY

Maying in the Fields

certain scholar coming with the said William drew out a knife called *hangere*, wherewith he would have smitten John ffelerd; which John aforesaid was convicted of this [assault] before me Master John Kexby, chancellor of Oxford University.

(*d*) *ibid.* II. 602.

A.D. 1450, August 22, Thomas Blake, currier, William Whyte, barber, John Karyn, glover, "husbundemen[1]," appeared before us, Master J. Beek, D.D. and Master Gilbert Kymer, Chancellor of this kindly [*almae*] University of Oxford and Commissary General [of the Bishop of Lincoln], and with their hands on the holy Gospels abjured the game of tennis within the city of Oxford and its precincts.

(*e*) *ibid.* 666.

July 3, 1456, [——] Medeley, for shooting by night at the proctor of the northern nation and his attendants, was convicted and imprisoned; he gave up his bow and paid twenty shillings.

(*f*) *ibid.* 668.

Aug. 7, 1457. Oweyn the Clerk, vicar of St Giles's Church, swore on the Gospels to keep the peace, gave up his club, and paid two shillings[2].

Three other accounts of celebrated Oxford brawls are translated in my *Medieval Garner*, pp. 286, 449, 450; and many more in Mr Hulton's *Rixae Oxonienses*, 1893, the best book on this subject.

20 LIFE IN A ROYAL COLLEGE

The Statutes of Eton and King's College, Cambridge, give perhaps the best idea of later medieval school and college life, because they repeat and summarize all that had been most approved in previous legislation on the subject. The earliest complete English statutes (those of Merton, Oxford) exercised to the last a great influence upon all others, and

---

deathbed) until he appear before the Pope and receive his mandate." The official commentator is careful to explain that the application of violent feet comes under the same category as violent hands. The law was so interpreted, however, as to permit the layman to use violence in self-defence; this explains the drift of John's evidence.

[1] Householders.

[2] If we are to believe an emendation in the MS. the culprit here was not Vicar, but Parish Clerk of St Giles's.

came to Cambridge through its first college, Peterhouse. (Rashdall, *l.c.* II. 484, 492, 560–1.) Wykeham's statutes for New College mark another definite step forward; and King's was modelled on New College, as Eton was on Winchester. The following excerpts are translated from *King's College and Eton College Statutes*, ed. J. Heywood and T. Wright, 1850.

(p. 21.) We ordain that all and several who are to be elected for the years of probation in our Royal College of Cambridge be poor and needy scholars and clerks, who have received the first clerical tonsure, adorned with good manners and conditions, and sufficiently taught in grammar[1].

(p. 67.) We ordain that, in fruitful years and times of abundance, when there is plenty of victuals in store, there shall be faithfully paid through the Bursars, for each scholar admitted to the three years of probation, and each perpetual fellow, and each chaplain ministering in the said chapel and residing personally in the same college on full commons, sixteen pence per week for commons....And in years of greater dearth, when such shall befall, let these commons be proportionally and equally augmented, from the common store aforesaid, even to the sum of seventeen or eighteen pence, according to the quality and exigencies of the season, and the increased price of corn for the time being....To every clerk or other servant and valet of the said King's College, personally residing therein, the bursar shall pay ten pence; to every chorister and other groom or page of the said college, eight pence each for their weekly commons.

(p. 71.) *Item*, that all and several fellows, scholars, chaplains and clerks of our King's College aforesaid, sitting daily at table in their Hall, have the Bible publicly read in their presence [during the meal], or other writings of the holy Fathers and Doctors of the Church....To which reading let all fellows, scholars, chaplains and clerks listen diligently, feasting in silence; nor let them in anywise impede such reading by verbosities, babblings, cries, laughter, murmurs, or other inordinate tumult. Moreover, when they happen to

---

[1] Rashdall and A. F. Leach have shown conclusively that these words must not be taken too literally; that our colleges were not founded for the very poor; and that from the first the scholars were mainly of the middle classes, and often of good family.

speak one with another, whether in hall and at table or in
their chambers, or chapel, or elsewhere within the said King's
College, or the precincts or garden thereof, let them speak
in modest and courteous wise; and, if they be fellows or
scholars, let them employ the Latin speech, unless they be
constrained to some other idiom by the presence of strangers
or layfolk, or by any other reasonable cause. Neither shall
any one of them in any wise impede any other studying or
wishing to study in the said King's College, nor keep him at
sleep-time from sleep or rest, by games or tumults or noises,
or by any other practices.

(p. 72.) Moreover—seeing that, after bodily refection
through food and drink, men are commonly rendered the
more ready for buffooneries and indecorous speech, and (what
is yet worse) for detractions and quarrels, and for the per-
petration of many other perilous misdeeds, paying then less
heed to such-like excesses than when they are on a fasting
stomach, whereby they oftentimes move the minds of other
simple folk to quarrels, revilings, and excesses—therefore we
decree, ordain, and will that every day after dinner (and likewise after supper on supper-days)[1], after grace duly said for
that which hath been received...then, without further delay,
when the loving-cup hath been administered to all who wish
to drink, and after the potations in Hall at the hour of curfew,
let all the seniors, of whatsoever condition or degree, betake
themselves to their studies[2] or to other places, nor let them
suffer the juniors to tarry longer in Hall, save only on the
principal holy-days, or when College Councils are to be held
in Hall after the meal, or other arduous business touching
the said Royal College; or again when, in honour of God
or of His Mother or of some other saint, the fellows are in-
dulged with a fire in Hall at wintertide. Then it shall be
lawful for the scholars and fellows, after dinner or supper, to
make a decent tarrying in Hall for recreation's sake, with

---

[1] There was no supper on ecclesiastical fast-days.

[2] By this time the word *studium*, among other senses, was sometimes used for
the small wooden closets, like modern cubicles, which afforded fellows and scholars
extra privacy within the larger chambers : see the 5th extract here below.

songs and other honest pastimes; and to treat, in no spirit of
levity, of poems, chronicles of realms, the wonders of this world,
and other things which are consistent with clerical propriety[1].

(p. 80.) We ordain that [our students] go not about
alone[2], without a fellow or scholar of the said King's College,
or one of the common servants thereof, or some other companion of mature age and good character; and let them walk
modestly and without confusion—save only to processions,
sermons, churches, or the Schools, for which purposes we
permit them to go alone if they cannot well find such a companion. Further, we prohibit all and singular the fellows
and scholars aforesaid from wearing red or green hosen,
piked shoes[3], or striped hoods, on any pretext, within or
without the University: nor shall they wear swords or long
knives or other offensive or even defensive arms, nor belts or
girdles adorned with gold or silver, within the College or
the University or the town of Cambridge, either publicly or
privately, except for some necessary cause to be approved
by the Provost, or by the Vice-Provost, Deans, and Bursars[4].
Furthermore we ordain that no scholar or fellow let his hair
or beard grow; but that all wear the crown and tonsure
accordant to their order, degree, and condition, honestly and
duly and decently[5].

(p. 83.) Since it befitteth not poor men, and specially
such as live by charity, to give the children's bread unto dogs,

---

[1] This clause is repeated almost verbatim in the Statutes of Eton College, and
is, in fact, borrowed from Wykeham's ordinations for Winchester and New College,
Oxford. Of the *mirabilia mundi* here alluded to, a few specimens will be found
in the last Section of this book; the chronicles would mostly be popular compilations of the Higden type.

[2] This rule of walking two and two is one of the many monastic customs
introduced into college life.

[3] Red and green cloths were the most expensive, and therefore most worldly;
the long pointed toes of fashionable shoes were a commonplace of later medieval
satire. Heywood and Wright's text here has *sæcularibus*, by an obvious error for
sotularibus.

[4] It was permitted, for example, to travel armed to and from the University,
for fear of robbers.

[5] By the *corona* the hair was cropped close to the ears and the nape of the
neck; by the *tonsura* a small bald patch was made at the top; but *tonsura* is
often used for both operations.

and we find it written elsewhere *Vae sit eis in peccatum, qui in avibus coeli ludunt*[1], therefore we command, ordain and will that no scholar, fellow, chaplain, clerk, or servant whatsoever to the said King's·College, do keep or possess dogs, hunting or fishing nets, ferrets, falcons, or hawks ; nor shall they practise hunting or fishing. Nor shall they in any wise have or hold within our Royal College, singly or in common, any ape, bear, fox, stag, hind, fawn, or badger, or any other such ravening or unaccustomed or strange beast, which are neither profitable nor unprofitable. Furthermore, we forbid and expressly interdict the games of dice, hazard, ball and all noxious inordinate unlawful and unhonest sports, and especially all games which afford a cause or occasion for loss of coin, money, goods or chattels of any kind whatsoever, whether within King's College or elsewhere within the University....And it is Our will firmly and expressly to prohibit all of the aforesaid fellows &c. from shooting arrows, or casting or hurling stones, javelins, wood, clods or anything whatsoever, and from making or practising, singly or in common, in person or by deputy, any games or castings whatsoever, within the aforesaid King's College or its enclosed precincts or gardens, whereby, directly or indirectly, the Chapel or Hall or other buildings or edifices of our said College may suffer any sort of harm or loss in the glass windows, walls, roofs, coverings, or any other part thereof, within or without. (p. 149.) *Item*, whereas through incautious and inordinate games in the Chapel or Hall of our said King's College, which might perchance be practised therein by the wantonness of some students, the said Chapel and Hall might be harmed and even deformed in its walls, stalls, paintings and glass windows ; we therefore, desiring to provide against such harm, do strictly command that no casting of stones or balls or of anything else soever be made in the aforesaid collegiate Chapel Cloister, Stalls, or Hall; and we forbid that dancing[2] or wrestling, or other incautious and inordinate sports whatsoever, be practised at any time within the Chapel, Cloister or Hall aforesaid[3].

---

[1] Baruch iii. 17.   [2] Chaucer, *C. T.*, A 3328.
[3] Official Visitors in the Middle Ages not infrequently report that the glass of

(p. 118.) *Item*, seeing that holiness befitteth the Church of God...we ordain that all fellows and scholars aforesaid enter into and issue from the said Chapel humbly, modestly and devoutly ; and, within the Chapel itself, let their conversation be quiet and pleasing to God.... Nor let them in any wise make murmurs, babblings, scoffing, laughter, confabulations or indiscreet noises ; lest, through their inordinate tumult and the various sounds of voices and their other talk among themselves the devotion or exercise of those singing psalms in the choir be in any wise impeded. Nor let any business be done in Chapel which regardeth not the worship of God's name ; seeing that the Chapel is for the business of divine praise.

(p. 131.) Seeing that the miserable burden of distracting want doth oftentimes turn scholars aside from that tillage of God's field whereunto they are otherwise able, and maketh them to desert their studies, we therefore have thought fit to bestow £200 sterling for the special use of the said Provost, fellows and scholars...so that the said Provost may borrow £5, and any fellows or scholars (in the order in which they shall expose their indigence to the guardians of this Chest), up to the number of thirty-five, may borrow £2 each ; the rest may borrow £1. 13s. 4d. and no more.... Let the wardens be sworn that they will deliver no sum to any man, whether by way of loan or otherwise, without some real and sufficient pledge or caution of the true value of more than half the money borrowed ; and that such pledge or caution, unless within a year of the loan it be released, redeemed and acquitted, be sold forthwith within a month of this lapsed year, unless it chance to fall in time of vacation.

(p. 133.) We ordain that, in each of the upper chambers of the said King's colleges, two fellows at least shall keep together, so far as the number of fellows shall suffice and extend. In the lower chambers, which have space for three

church or cloister has been broken by tennis-balls: the citizens of Exeter regularly played tennis in the Cathedral cloister. (Cf. Shillingford's Letters, Camden Soc., 1871, p. 101: "In especiall in tyme of dyvyne service, ungoodly-ruled peple (most custumably yong peple of the said Comminalte) within the said Cloistre have exercised unlawfull games...and most atte tenys, by the which the walles of the saide Cloistre have be defowled and the glas wyndowes all to-brost.")

studies each, let three scholars or fellows always keep; among all which scholars and fellows let each have his separate bed wherein he may lie alone[1]; and that in each lower chamber aforesaid there shall be one fellow superior to the rest in maturity, discretion and learning, who shall supervise the other students in the chamber, and shall veraciously certify and inform (under bond of an oath which he shall make to the College, the Provost, Vice-Provost and Deans, from time to time, according as there shall be need or occasion) concerning their manners and conversation and studies…. Moreover we strictly and expressly ordain that no dweller in the aforesaid upper rooms…whether in washing his head or hands or feet or any other thing, or in any other manner whatsoever, do spill water, wine, beer, or any other liquor whereby those in the lower rooms may be grieved in their persons, goods or chattels, or in any way molested.

(p. 96.) *Item*, seeing that detractors, conspirators, maintainers[2] and whisperers—arousing or maintaining discord, envy, wrath, strife, quarrels, or matter of dissension among the scholars or fellows—do damnably cause frequent harm, scandal and schism, provoking hatred and altogether expelling charity, we do therefore command, ordain and will, and firmly prescribe to the said Provost and all fellows and scholars of our Royal College, both present and future; yea, more, in the bowels of Jesus Christ we do pray and beseech them, in regard of their happiness in this life and in the life everlasting, and under threat of God's judgment, that in all things and above all things they shall always have, faithfully keep, and observe both unity and mutual charity among themselves, with peace and concord and brotherly love, seeing that there is by nature a certain brotherhood among the fellows of one College; and

---

[1] It is characteristic of this royal and rich foundation, and of Wykeham's sumptuous college at Winchester, that this provision was made for comfort. At Eton, the juniors had to sleep two in a bed (cap. XXXVI. p. 576); at Wells choir school, three in a bed. The *Northumberland Household Book* shows how even an Earl's chaplains had sometimes to put up with similar discomforts: see Section IX., no. 13.

[2] A *maintainer* was one who, often for money, took up a quarrel that was not his own; the word has this sense in the Statute of Maintenance.

let them, so far as in them lieth, yearn and be zealous for the fostering of these virtues. Let all scurrilities of whatsoever kind, and all words of envy, contumely, conspiracy, contention, quarrel or harm, all whisperings and strife and evil speech and derision, all words whatsoever that bring harm or weariness or scandal or insult, all comparisons between race and race[1], family and family, noble and commoner, excellent or special prerogatives, for the sake of malicious provocation, be utterly and expressly restrained from the mouths of all persons whatsoever, both within and without the College, whether in public or in private....(p. 171.) Also that each scholar, in his admission to this our Royal College, after his year of probation, shall swear that he will not favour the opinions, condemned errors, or heresies of John Wycliffe, Reginald Pecock, or any other heretic whatsoever, so long as he shall live in this world, under pain of perjury and expulsion *ipso facto*.

(p. 143.) Moreover,...we ordain that in future, at the mandate of the Provost for the time being, at least thrice a year, all and singular the fellows, scholars, chaplains, clerks, and choristers, shall be summoned and assemble in the College chapel, on some convenient day with least impediment to their studies or other scholastic acts, after previous notice of at least three days....Then let the Provost, fellows and scholars cause these our Statutes to be publicly and distinctly read and rehearsed in the common Hall or in some other convenient place....Then let a scrutiny and examination be made by the Provost and one of the senior fellows...concerning the life and conversation, manners, conditions, profit in scholastic studies and keeping of our Statutes and Ordinances; and also let cautious and diligent enquiry be made of all things needing correction and reform in King's College or in the persons that dwell therein; in which scrutiny faults shall be corrected according as they are discovered by this inquisition....Furthermore we ordain that no fellow or scholar of our College, who may be accused or reported of crimes, excesses, or faults, shall demand that a copy of the things

---

[1] e.g. the feud between North and South, English, Welsh and Irish, etc.

brought forward and discovered against him be communicated, published, given or delivered to him; nor that the names of his accusers and denouncers be revealed to him.

21 A COLLEGE SCRUTINY

College statutes provided for periodical *scrutinies*, corresponding to the daily Chapters and the periodical visitations of monasteries, in which the Fellows and Scholars were bound by custom (and often, as at King's and Pembroke, Cambridge, by a statutory oath) to inform against each other. Three such scrutinies at Merton, Oxford, have survived by a fortunate chance, and are printed by J. E. T. Rogers (*Hist. Ag. and Prices*, II. 1866, pp. 670 ff.). The following translation is abbreviated by the omission of merely corroborative evidence. At the first scrutiny 19 Fellows testified (but there is a lacuna in the MS.); at the second 28, and at the third 22, some more than once.

(*a*) July 20, 1338.

WESTCOMBE speaketh of silence broken at meals; *item*, of discord betwixt Wyly and Fynemer. HUMBERSTON, that two Fellows are delinquent, as unwilling to bear the College burdens whereunto they are bound; *item*, that the College is overburdened with horses. FYNEMAR, that Elyndon, when he speaketh with the Fellows, will not let them speak. *Item*, that Wantyng, Wyly and Elyndon are most rebellious. *Item*, that Wantyng and Elyndon, in treating of College business, will not give their advice like the other Fellows. *Item*, that Elyndon and Wyly have undue private means [*habent uberius*], GOTHAM, nothing. BERNARD, that mutual charity is not kept between the Warden and the other Fellows. *Item*, that there is a default of auditors, five should be assigned, we have but three. SUTTON, the default is this: that those assigned will not audit the accounts without Wyly and Wantyng. MIDLOND, that we have too few Fellows. ELYNDON, that the Warden should amend his ways, oftentimes saying that those of Founder's kin [*de sanguine*] are ill dealt with in the matter of vesture and learning. That the Warden hath frequently been absent without reasonable cause. *Item*, there hath been much talk in this matter, yet none hath noted how Fynemer maltreats him, and that none complain of this matter save his [Fynemer's] abettors; and that the Warden is too grievous to him, dealing unjustly with him in that he maintaineth Fynemer against him; and that Fynemer hath uttered mortal threats against Wyly, and that in private converse he speaketh ill to others of this deponent, Elyndon.

(*b*) Dec. 1338.

HANDELE, that there should be an election [of further Fellows]. WESTCOMBE; let it be ordained that the Fellows may have access to the library. Of the money bequeathed by the schoolmasters [*scolasticos*]. HUMBERSTON, that the College is overburdened with horses. REGHAM, of mutual charity between the Warden, Elyndon, and Wantyng. That the Chaplain be corrected in the matter of hosen[1] and vesture. WYLIOT, that there is no progress in the faculty of Arts as was wont, neither within the College nor without. DOYLY, that John the Chaplain keepeth a servitor and daily contendeth with him, accusing him of theft. WANTINGE, of silence at table, of the hosen of William the Chaplain, that John should behave himself more decently in chapel, and that the chaplains should sing mass daily. WYLY, that John Chaplain should be corrected in the matter of the servitor whom he keepeth in his room, and for his negligence in chapel; that the Dean should enforce silence at table; that the Fellows revile each other; that the rest change not their new garments yearly, whereas they were wont to transfer their old garments then [at new year] without rebuke. *Item*, that injury hath been done him by one of the Fellows, whereof he hath oftentimes made complaint, and no fine hath yet been imposed upon the offender; that the Statutes bind the Warden to be present when the Statutes are read; that those things said at the last scrutiny concerning the Warden's person have not yet been all amended, therefore let the Warden now be corrected in person for those things whereof he hath not corrected himself.

---

[1] *Caligas.* Even Dr Rashdall has fallen into the same snare as some other editors of visitations and translated this *boots.* From at least the end of the 12th century the word loses its classical sense and is used for *hosen*: e.g. all the entries of *caligae* in Rogers's *Hist. Ag. and Prices* show that they were made of cloth. These Fellows were clerics; and, as we not infrequently find with monks and other clerics, they are complained of for wearing the tight-fitting hosen which Chaucer's Parson, and all other disciplinarians of the age, condemned as indecent even for the laity.

BOCKYNGHAM, that the Fellows should [not] use indecorous [*inhonestis*] hosen, according to the ancient custom which was wont to be kept.

(*c*)   March 1339.

MIDLETON, that William the Chaplain hath oftentimes transgressed against the Fellows. HANDELE. It is expedient that the seniors should be called upon to make peace between Wyly and Fynemer[1]. WESTCOMBE, of the tumult of the Fellows in their chambers. HUMBRESTON, of the discord betwixt Wyly and Fynemer ; *item*, that the Fellows keep dogs and that the progress of studies is hindered by idleness. *Item*, that the Rule is not kept, in that we have no manciples. *Item*, it would be expedient to farm out the land in Little Wolford. FYNEMER, that Wyly, assigned before this in statutory form to audit the accounts, refused ; after which, having been thrice warned and called upon by the Fellows, he refused again, like a rebel, and therefore falleth under the statutory case [of rebellion]. *Item*, that he receiveth commons unjustly, taking beyond his due share ; wherefore those who should proceed against him are too remiss. WANTYNG, that the Warden should not do such injustice to the seniors as he hath begun to do. WYLY, that we should send to Stratton to inquire concerning the lands and other possessions of the College. SUTTON, that they ought to have a keeper of pledges, and have not ; for lack of which, as it is said, certain books are sold, and neither the College nor the Fellows profit thereby. *Item*, that the Warden doth not make execution against the College debtors, and specially the bailiff of Elham ; and that Wanting oweth the bailiff of Elham £7. 1*s*. 4*d*. of College property. *Item*, that he should not interfere in the scrutinies, seeing that he hath excused himself from other College business. *Item*, that Waneting hath borrowed College money and not paid, but excuseth himself because the Warden regardeth him not as competent to labour. CLEANGRE, that a new fashion hath been introduced, for there are so many writers at the scrutiny. HANDELE would have a set of Decretals and Decrees put in the library. *Item*, that there should be a division of the

---

[1] In 12 cases the evidence of discord among the fellows is repeated.

College books. BOKYNGHAM, that Wanting sold College horses at Elham and keepeth the moneys in his hands; neither hath he paid, nor the bailiff. *Item*, that Elyndon provoketh the Fellows to wrath. MONBY, that there were too many writers at the scrutiny. *Item*, that Wantyng absented himself without cause from the election of Fellows. *Item*, that he and Elyndon, in business matters, made no answer except under protest. *Item*, that Wyly broke out against Fynemer publicly, in the presence of all the Fellows. FYNEMER, that Wyly reviled him because the bailiff of Elham gave Wantyng £7. 1s. 4d. of College money for College use, but he hath given credit, and the payment of this money is not in Wantyng's hands. *Item*, that Elyndon transgressed in words against Fynemer without cause. LEVERYNTON, of the discord among the Fellows. *Item*, that the seneschal is not present in chapel on holidays, but absent for the greater part. WYLY demandeth amendment for the things said by Elyndon and Wantyng, and warneth the warning of charity; that the Warden should correct these things, and those which before were said unto the Warden at the scrutiny, and specially how Elyndon hath said that the reputations of certain Fellows are tarnished etc. [*sic*]. *Item*, that Duraunt accused Wyly that he and other seniors intended to impede the election; and this he had from those who were of late in London. *Item*, of the injustice done unto him elsewhere by Fynemer etc. [*sic*]. MIDELTON, that Elham is guilty of breaking the Hall door. HANDELE would wish that peace should be made at the earliest opportunity. *Item*, that the juniors should show reverence to the seniors, and that all and singular should be publicly admonished to keep mutual charity, and that each should do this in so far as in him lieth. HUMBRESTON that, according to the Statutes, it is the Warden's duty to take some impartial Fellows as assessors and to put an end to this quarrel between Wyly and Fynemer. *Item*, that Wantyng hath borne himself irreverently towards the Warden, calling him *Robert* before all men[1]. *Item* that, according to the form of the Statutes, we should have stewards in the manors to visit them, for the sparing of expense.

[1] The warden was Robert Treng, who died of the plague in 1350.

22 A DAY OF ETON LIFE IN 1530

The Grammar School of Saffron Walden was founded in 1525 expressly on the model of Winchester and Eton ; the headmasters of those famous schools were therefore asked to supply information as to their current practice. The following is the Eton Headmaster's account of his own arrangements, printed first by T. Wright and again with corrections by A. F. Leach, *Educational Charters and Documents*, p. 450. Compare the letters from an Eton schoolboy in *Paston Letters*, 1900, vol. III. p. 240, reprinted in my *Medieval Garner*, p. 638.

This ys the order of the same schole [Eton] usyd by me Richard cox, scholemaster.

They come to schole at vj of the Clok in ye mornyng; they say Deus misereatur with a Colecte ; at ix they say de profundis and go to brekefaste. With in a quarter of an howre cum ageyne and tary [till] xi and then to dyner, at v to soper, afore an Antheme and De profundis.

Two prepositors in every forme, whiche doth give in a schrowe[1] the absents Namys at any lecture and shewith when and at what tyme, both in the fore none for the tyme paste, and at v.

Also ij prepositors in the body of the Chirche, ij in the qwere, ffor spekyng of Laten in the thred forme and all other, every one a custos and in every howse a monytor.

Whan they go home ij. and ij. in order, a monitor to se that they do soe tyll they come at there hostise[2] dore.

Also prevy-monytors how many the Mr wylle.

Prepositors in the feld whan they play, for fyghtyng, rent clothes, blew eyes[3], or siche like.

Prepositors for yll-kept hedys, unwasshid facys, fowle clothis and sich other.

Yff there be iiij or v in a howse, monytors for chydyng and for latyn spekyng.

When any dothe come newe, the master doth inquire fro whens he comyth, what frendys he hathe, whether there be any plage. No man gothe owte off the schole, nother home to his frends, with owt ye masters lycence. Yff there be any

---

[1] scroll.   [2] host's (*or* hostess's).   [3] black eyes.

dullard the Mr gyvith his frends warnyng and puttyth hym away, that he sclander not the schole[1].

23   UNIVERSITY REFORM

Sir Edmund Dudley, the able but unscrupulous minister of Henry VII., was committed to the Tower by Henry VIII. immediately after his accession.   He wrote in prison his *Tree of the Commonwealth* (1509), a remarkable and illuminating treatise on the political and social conditions of his age, which was only printed in 1859.   The following is from p. 31.

But for a suretie, the [oftener] that a Prince pareth[2] his fruite, and then the paringe by discrecion be disposed, the better will his fruite be, and the more will it have the s[c]ent of his materiall propertie.   What is the paringe of the fruite of good example to the Clergie, but the encrease of vertue and coninge?   Of itself, it is right laudable, and the paringe right proper for good example.   What shall yow of the clergie doe with this paringe?   Is there any folk have need thereof?   I trowe never more neede, and soe greate nede that if you decide not your paringe right hastelie, I feare me the encrease comeinge will fall in this realme.   Looke well upon your twoe universities, how famous they have ben, and in what condicion they be nowe.   Where be your famous men that were wonte to reade Divinitie in every Cathedrall Church, and in other great Monasteries?   Where be the good and substanciall scollers of grammar that have ben kepte in this realme before this tyme, not onlie in every good toune and cittie, and in other places, but also in Abbies and Priories, in prelates houses, and oftentymes in the houses of men of honour of the temporalitie?   Wherefore the greate prelates with the help of other of the clergie, pare of theis paringe of thencrease of vertue and connynge, and throwe them into

---

[1] By the original Ordinances of Harrow School (1590) it was one of the Headmaster's duties to "have regard to the manners of his Scholars, and see that they come not uncombed, unwashed, ragged or slovenly." There were three monitors, two to keep ordinary school discipline (including, at Winchester and Eton, the substitution of Latin for English speech) and another privately appointed to note the faults and omissions of the other two. (*Harrow*, by J. F. Williams, 1901, pp. 24, 28.)
[2] prune.

your universities in plenteous mauner, soe that every one of
you in your diocese do this, as well in your Cathedrall church
as in Abbies and Priories, and in all other places convenient.

24   UNIVERSITY DECAY

Thomas Lever, a Lancashire man, took his B.A. at Cambridge in
1542 and became Master of St John's in 1553. The following extract is
from a sermon preached at St Paul's Cross in 1550, before the citizens of
London. Though the final effect of the Reformation was to give Oxford
and Cambridge, under Elizabeth and the Stuarts, a greater share in the
national life than ever before or since, yet the first effects of the change of
religion were highly prejudicial to the Universities. The 3rd chapter of
vol. III. of *The Cambridge History of English Literature*, while laying
great stress upon the temporary damage done, is strangely silent as to
the final result. Lever's Sermons, ed. Arber, 1870, p. 120.

If ye hadde anye eyes ye shoulde se and be ashamed that
in the great abounaance of landes and goods taken from
Abbeis, Colleges and Chauntryes for to serve the kynge in all
necessaryes, and charges (especially in provision of relyefe for
the pore, and for mayntenaunce of learnynge), the kynge is so
dysapoynted that bothe the pore be spoyled, all mayntenance
of learnyng decayed, and you only enryched. But, for because
ye have no eyes to se wyth, I wyll declare that you may heare
wyth youre eares, and so perceyve and knowe, that w[h]ere
as God and the kynge hathe bene moste liberall to gyve and
bestowe, there you have been moste unfayethfull to dyspose
and delyver. For accordying unto gods word and the k[y]nges
pleasure, the universities, which be the scholes of all godlynes
and vertue, should have bene nothyng decayed, but much
increased and amended by thys [the] reformacion of religion.…

For before that you did beginne to be the disposers of the
kinges liberalitye towardes learnyng and poverty, there was in
houses belongynge unto the unyversyte of Cambryge, two
hundred studentes of dyvynytye, manye verye learned, whyche
bee nowe all clene gone, house and manne, young towarde
scholers, and old fatherlye Doctors, not one of them lefte : one
hundred also of an other sorte, that havyng rych frendes or
beyng benefyced men dyd lyve of theym selves in Ostles and
Innes, be eyther gon awaye or elles fayne to crepe into

Colleges and put poore men from bare lyvynges. Those
bothe be all gone, and a small number of poore godly
dylygent studentes now remaynynge only in Colleges be not
able to tary and contynue theyr studye in the universitye, for
lacke of exibicion and healpe. There be dyvers ther whych
ryse dayly betwixte foure and fyve of the clocke in the
mornynge ; and, from fyve untyll syxe of the clocke, use
common prayer wyth an exhortacion of gods worde in a
commune chappell ; and from sixe unto ten of the clocke use
ever eyther pryvate study or commune lectures. At ten of
the clocke they go to dynner, whereas they be contente wyth
a penye pyece of byefe[1] amongest iiij, havyng a fewe porage
made of the brothe of the same byefe wyth salte and otemell,
and nothynge els. After thys slender dinner they be either
teachynge or learnynge untyll v. of the clocke in the evenyng,
when as they have a supper not much better then theyr dyner.
Immedyatelye after the whyche, they go eyther to reasonyng
in problemes or unto some other studye, untyll it be nyne or
tenne of the clocke ; and there, beyng wythout fyre, are fayne
to walk or runne up and downe halfe an houre to gette a heate
on their feete whan they go to bed.

25   FROISSART'S YOUTH

Translated, with many omissions of irrelevant passages, from the
chronicler's autobiographical poem *Espinette Amoureuse* (ed. Buchon,
vol. III. pp. 479 ff.). We need not here enquire how far the author has
always confined himself to literal fact ; he has certainly set himself to
portray a poet's childhood and youth, and that is enough for the purpose
of this present book.

In my youth, such was my temper that I loved pastime
passing well ; and, as I was then, such am I still, though
yesterday be not to-day. While I was yet but twelve years
old, I hungered and thirsted to see dances and caroles[2], to
hear minstrels and words of solace ; so it was my nature to
love hotly all such as love hawks and hounds. When there-

[1] beef.
[2] A round dance in which the performers sang also ; see Manning of Brunne,
Handlyng Synne, ll. 8987 ff.

fore I was put to school, wherein the ignorant are taught, I found there the little girls whose tender youth was even as mine own; and I, who was a little boy, would serve them with gifts of pins or apples or pears, or with a ring of glass; and, for to say sooth, methought it was great prowess to win their grace—as in truth it is; for I say none otherwise to-day. And then I was wont to think in my heart "When will my day come, that I shall be able to love in very sooth?" for thereunto was my nature inclined, and everywhere men proclaim that all joy and all honour cometh from arms and from love.... But what age, to say truth, think ye that I had when Love, by his wounds, taught me his precious balms? Very young was I in years: never yet had I tired of children's games as they are played before the age of twelve. When I was grown a little wiser, then I must needs be more fully subject to my masters; for they taught me the Latin tongue, and, if I varied in repeating my lessons, I was beaten.... I could not rest; for I fought with other children, beat and was beaten; so distraught was I that I oftentimes went home with torn raiment; there again I was reproached full oft or beaten. But be assured that my parents lost their labour; for this never turned me aside, but, as soon as I saw my fellows pass by on their way, full soon I found some excuse to escape and join their play.

But, so help me God! so happily did I pass those days that all things turned unto me for delight, whether speech or silence, whether movement or rest; for I had time at my choice. In those days I took more account of a chaplet of violets to give to those little girls, than I take now for twenty silver marks from the hand of a count.... Though my body was yet weak and tender, yet my heart would fain be everywhere, and specially wheresoever there was plenty of violets and roses and peonies, wherein (God help me!) I took more delight than in aught else. And when the season changed and winter came, with his rain and foul weather, then I delighted to take my pastime in reading romances, and specially such as treated of love.

I remember how an adventure befel me while my young

years ran on their course; never thereafter did it depart from my heart; wherefore it shall be set down here.

'Twas in the jolly month of May: no doubt or fear had I when I entered into a fair garden. The hour was yet early, little after the break of dawn; there lay no heaviness upon my mind, but all things brought me pure delight, in that fair weather that reigned and that promised to reign. The small fowls, for their part, vied with each other in melody, all in glad harmony without note of discord; for never saw I dayspring or morn so fair as this. The firmament was still spangled with stars on high; but the daystar had already set out on his chase to drive black night before him.... I stayed my steps a moment to muse on these fowls and their song, and to contemplate the young trees that stood so thick around; above me rose a bush of that flower that men call white-thorn, whose blossom is so fair that we care little for the thorn...

[Here Venus appears to the poet, and promises him success in love if he do but persevere in her worship.]

After this adventure of mine, even as young men stray afield from place to place, for company or for pastime, so I fell upon a place where I came to terms with the God of Love, even as it is here told. Right at the hour of prime a maiden sat in that place reading a romance; I moved to greet her, and named her by name, and said, " Fair sweet lady, how call you this romance?" She forthwith, closing her mouth[1], laid her hand upon the book and made courteous answer, saying, " Cleomades is his name; well is the book made, and well doth it treat of love; you shall hear it, and shall tell me how it pleaseth you." Then I beheld her sweet face, her fresh colour and her grey eyes. No fairer could have been desired; with her long lintwhite locks and her hands so fine that the freshest lady in the world could show no fairer; God of truth! how fair and dainty she was, how gay her bearing and how

---

[1] It is only with the advent of the printed book that reading has become a silent occupation. Philip heard the eunuch reading to himself, yet aloud; St Augustine discusses at great length the probable reasons why St Ambrose was so eccentric as to read silently. (*Confess.* Bk VI. c. 3.)

slender her body! Then spake I, "Lady, I am at one with
that which I hear you read; for I love those things better than
melody of harp or any other music." Then the damsel read
on, in a place which provoked to mirth; no words of mine can
tell how sweetly her lips moved; they scarce seemed to touch
the words, so low and so soft she laughed—yea, and not too
long, but even to the point, as the best-born and most prudent
lady in the world. Then, when she had read a space, she
prayed me of her grace that I would read a little in turn; and
I, who had neither desire nor courage to refuse her, read two
or three pages more. She listened well (God regard her!)
while I read; then we left that book and entered upon other
talk; but it was ever of single words, as is the wont of young
folk in their play, when they talk at leisure for solace and for
pastime. But full well I know that the God of Love fell upon
me at that hour, and smote me with the most amorous of his
arrows.

(483. 6.) Once I sat beside my fair, jesting of I know
not what; then she, of her courtesy, said, "Young man,
prithee lend me a romance to read, for to read for pure joy is
a pleasant craft." "Certes, fair lady, I will do your behest,
and will furnish you with a book wherein you will find great
solace"; for then it came into my mind that I had the book
called *Bailiff of Love*. And within myself I said, "Thou seest
well, thou darest not speak of love to this lady so debonnair;
therefore will I write all mine intent in a letter, and enclose it
in the book." Fair and well was my ballade written, in a
little scroll; then I slipped it into the romance and put it
into her hands. With much joy she took it; to the end, or
near to the end, she read the book, and many thanks she gave
me in rendering it again. Full fain was I of her good will,
and hastily did I open the book to see whether the ballade
lay therein; but alas! there it lay, neither more nor less, but
even as I had placed it when the book came into her hands.
"Ha!" said I, "here is a strange matter! for the fair lady
hath left my ballade even in the same place where I laid it; at
least she might have looked a little thereon!"

(485 a.) It befell one day that I went out after dinner to

play in a garden where were many delights of roses, of lilies and other flowers, and of much other solace. There, under a fair green rose-tree, I plucked a crimson rose and went softly, gladly, to my lady's hostel. Such was my fortune that I found her there; then besought I that she would accept this rose *par amours*. Forthwith she answered, as one unwilling to receive it, yet in soft and kindly words, " Leave it where it is; for it is in good hands." Then said I, " Nay, lady, but take it, for thus shall it come into better hands, by my soul ! " Softly then she took it, and smiled a little as she spoke; and I betook me again to that spot whence I had plucked it, seeing that I knew none fairer for solace of sweet garden-ground.

Again it befell within a brief while after, in an hostel that stood hard by the home of my lady so sweet and fair, we sat five or six of a like age, merry of heart and eating of fresh fruit in solace and in great revel. My lady was with us, and sweet was her mien; yet I dared make no semblant that would betray us to the rest; forth I went at last, still hoping for her mercy.

Thus passed my days of youth betwixt Reason and Love. Reason would that I should suffer; and Love, that I should offer my heart and show that fair lady how I lived for her, how I did nought but for her love. " It is good now," said I, " that I should speak and pray her fair for mercy; willingly (said I) will I speak so soon as I shall find occasion." Thereunto then bent I my mind. One day we set ourselves to dance; others were there beside us two; and I held her by the finger, for she was leading me forward. I, then, that followed, holding her finger, fairly and softly I pressed it in mine; such joy and delight drew I thence as no tongue may tell ! Whensoever her turn came to sing, I was full blithe and ready to sing again; ah me ! how merry then was I ! At last we set ourselves down upon a bench; and then I caught fairly at my chance of speech, and spake out with my tongue: " Certes, fair lady, your sweet semblaunt, your gentle bearing and your lightness of limb are cause of all my joy; no longer can I dissemble. If I had leisure now to speak, and that we two were here

A Rose Battle

A Picnic

alone, I would swear it to you by my solemn faith." Then
she eyed me for a while, yet so as no man might observe, and
answered with these brief words, "Would you indeed do as you
say, and is it with good sense that you would have my love?"
and thereupon she arose and said, "Let us dance on; in this
pastime of dancing I find no heaviness."

(486 *a*.) Even thus the time went by; one day I came in
time to see her; another day, not. Then fell I into melancholy
to think that she was as friendly with other folk as with me.
I therefore, who loved her from the bottom of my heart, would
sigh full oftentimes, "Ah me! she hath made now a new
friend! she plays and laughs with every man; her looks are
common to all!"

The tale goes on with medieval minuteness of detail. A confidante
secretly conveyed a "ballade" of Froissart to the lady, who, however,
rippled with laughter over it (487 *a*). She then announced that the lady
was on the point of marriage ; and our hero, after his first idea of slaying
the rival, fell into a deadly fever (479 *b*, 480). He was partly consoled,
on recovery, by the confidante, who procured him the mirror in which the
lady's face had so often been reflected (490 *a*). In imagination he saw
there the long lintwhite locks and his mistress "tressing" them with her
ivory comb (491 *b*). He travelled long in foreign lands, and returned
to find the lady married, but apparently more favourable. His change
of colour touched her; she gave him three violets (495 *a*). Soon after,
with a friend, he went to a feast where he knew his lady would be :

(496 *b*.) In the first days of jolly May...God! how fair was
the season! The air was clear and windless and serene, and
the nightingales sang aloud, rejoicing us with their melody.
Clear and fresh was the morn, and we came to a thorn-bush
all white with blossom; lance-high it stood, with fair green
shade beneath. Then said one, "Lo! a place made for our
pleasant repose; here let us break our fast!" Then with one
accord we brought forth the meats; pasties, hams, wines and
bakemeats, and venison packed in heath. There was my lady
ruler of the feast; and then it pleased her to say, for comfort
of my martyrdom, that she retained me for her own; whereat
my heart opened a fathom wide.

But *Male-bouche*, the envious backbiter of all medieval romance, came
now in between them (497 *a*). His next interview, therefore, was less happy:

(497 *b*.) One evening it befell that I stood all peaceably

hard by my lady's house; and, by my soul! it befell also that she came thither per adventure. I, who endured so many evils for her sake, was bold to whisper to her as she passed, "Come hither by my side, *douce amie*." But she, as one in wrath, made reply, "No friend here for you!" and went and sat her down elsewhere. When, therefore, I could see all this, I remained quietly in mine own place. What did she then? Ye shall know. Again she passed by me; and, in passing, she caught me by my long hair; believe me, more than three hairs stayed in her hand when she had passed. Then thought I, "Here is great hardship! I set my fortune at small price, for I love and am not beloved."

This, then is the end; yet Froissart is as unrepentant as the Wife of Bath:

(498 *b*.) Yet should I have been of little worth if I had lacked such salvation as this: it is a great advancement for a young man, and a fair and good and most profitable beginning of life. Thereby is he made courteous and able, and his vices are changed to virtues; never was such time lost; for by such means many men have been advanced, more than I could tell or number.

26   THE MODEL BOY (*Stans Puer ad Mensam*)

By John Lydgate (1370?-1451?) from *The Babees Book*, E.E.T.S., p. 32, with a few alterations for the sake of clearness.

My dere childe, first thiself enable
With all thin herte to vertuous disciplyne
Afor thi soverayne standing at the table,
Dispose thi youth aftir my doctryne
To all norture thi corage[1] to enclyne.
First when thu spekist be not rekles,
Kepe feete and fingeris and handes still in pese.

Be symple of chiere, cast nat thyn eye aside,
Agenst the post lete nat thy bak abyde;
Gaase nat aboute, tournyng overalle;
Make nat thy myrrour also of the walle,
Pyke nat thy nose, and in especialle

¹ heart.

Be right wele ware, and sette hieron thi thought,
By-fore thy soverayne cracche[1] ne rubbe nought.

Who spekithe to the in any maner place,
Rudely cast nat thyn eye adowne,
But with a sadde[2] chiere loke hym in the face;
Walke demurely by strete in the towne,
Advertise thee withe Wisdom and Reasoune.
Withe dissolute laughters do thow non offence
To-fore thy soverayn, whiles he is in presence.

Pare clene thy nailes, thyn handes wasshe also
To-fore mete, and whan thow dooest arise;
Sitte in that place thow art assigned to;
Prease[3] nat to hye in no maner wise;
And til thow se afore thee thy service,
Be nat to hasty on brede for to byte,
Of gredynesse lest men wolde the endwyte.

Grennyng and mowes[4] at the table eschowe;
Cry nat to lowde; kepe honestly silence;
To enboce[5] thy jowis[6] withe mete is nat diewe;
Withe ful mowthe speke nat, lest thow do offence;
Drynke nat bretheles for hast ne necligence;
Kepe clene thy lippes from fat of flesshe or fisshe;
Wype clene thi spone, leve it nat in thy disshe.

Of brede I-byten no soppis that thow make;
In ale nor wyne withe hande leve no fattenes;
Withe mowthe enbrewed[7] thy cuppe thow nat take;
Enbrewe no napery for no rekelesnes;
For to souppe loude is agenst gentiles;
Never at mete begynne thow nat stryf;
Thi tethe also thow pike nat withe no knyf.

Of honest myrthe late[8] be thy daliaunce[9];
Swere none othes, speke no ribawdrye;
The best morsel, have in remembraunce,
Hole to thyself alwey do nat applie;

---

[1] scratch.   [2] steadfast.   [3] press.   [4] grimaces.   [5] bulge out.
[6] jaws.   [7] wet.   [8] let.   [9] sport.

Part[1] withe thy felaw, for that is curtesie:
Laade nat thy trenchour withe many remyssailes[2];
And from blaknes alwey kepe thy nayles.

Of curtesye also agenst the lawe,
Withe sowne[3] dishonest for to do offence;
Of old surfaytes[4] abrayde[5] nat thy felawe;
Toward thy soverayne alwey thyn advertence;
Play withe no knyf, take heede to my sentence;
At mete and soupper kepe thee stille and soft;
Eke to and fro meve[6] nat thy foote to oft.

Droppe nat thi brest withe sawce ne withe potage;
Brynge no knyves unskoured to the table;
Fil nat thy spone, lest in the cariage
It went beside, whiche were nat comendable;
Be quyke and redy, meke and servisable,
Wele awaityng to fulfille anone
What that thy soverayne comaundithe the to be done.

And whereso ever that thow dyne or soupe,
Of gentilesse take salt withe thy knyf;
And be wele ware thow blow nat in the cuppe.
Reverence thy felawe, gynne withe hym no stryf;
By thy powere kepe pees al thy lyf.
Interrupt nat, where so thow wende,
None other mans tale, til he have made an ende;

Withe thy fyngres make thow nat thy tale;
Be wele avised, namly[7] in tendre age,
To drynk by mesure[8] bothe wyne and ale;
Be nat copious also of langage;
As tyme requyrithe, shewe [not] thy visage,
To gladde ne to sory, but kepe atwene tweyne,
For losse or lucre or any case sodayne.

Be meke in mesure, nat hasti, but tretable[9];
Over moche is nat worthe in no maner thyng;

---

[1] share.   [2] remnants.   [3] sound.   [4] excesses.   [5] upbraid.
    [6] move.   [7] especially.   [8] moderately.   [9] tractable.

To children it longithe nat to be vengeable,
Sone meeved and sone forgyvyng;
And as it is remembrid bi writyng,
Wrathe of children is sone overgone,
With an apple the parties be made atone.

In children werre[1] now myrthe and now debate,
In theyr quarel no grete violence;
Now pley, now wepyng, [selde] in one estate;
To theyr playntes gyve no credence;
A rodde refourmythe al theyr insolence;
In theyr corage no rancour dothe abyde;
Who sparithe the yerd[2], al vertu set aside.

Go, litel bille, bareyn of eloquence,
Pray yonge children that the shal see or reede,
Thoughe thow be compendious of sentence,
Of thi clauses for to taken heede,
Whiche to al vertu shal theyr yowthe leede.
Of the writyng, thoughe ther be no date,
If ought be [a]mysse—worde, sillable, or dede,—
Put al the defaute upon Johne Lydegate.

27   SCHOOL VERSES

(a) *Rel. Ant.* vol. I. p. 116. "The Song of the Schoolboy at Christmas" from MS. Sloane, No. 1584, of the beginning of the 16th century, or latter part of the 15th, fol. 33, 2°, written in Lincolnshire or Nottinghamshire; perhaps, to judge by the mention of persons and places, in the neighbourhood of Grantham or Newark.

Ante finem termini baculus[3] portamus,
Capud hustiarii[4] frangere debemus;
Si preceptor nos petit quo debemus ire,
Breviter respondemus, non est tibi scire.
O pro nobilis docter[5], now we youe pray,
Ut velitis concedere to gyff hus leff to play.
Nunc proponimus ire, withowt any ney,
Scolam dissolvere, I tell itt youe in fey.

---

[1] strive.   [2] rod.   [3] *sic*: read *baculos.*   [4] *hostiarius* = usher.
[5] *sic*: read *prenobilis doctor.*

Sicut istud festum merth is for to make,
Accipimus nostram diem owr leve for to take.
Post natale festum, full sor shall we qwake,
Quum nos revenimus latens for to make[1].
Ergo nos rogamus, hartly and holle[2],
Ut isto die possimus to brek upe the scole.

(*b*) *Rel. Ant.* vol. I. pp. 289–90. [From MS. Lansd. fol. 99 r°, of the time of Henry VII.]

Nulla gratia[3] perit nisi gratia gramaticorum.
Est et semper erit litil thanke in fine laborum.

Si meus iste liber tingatur sorde, magister
Infringet natibus verbera dira meis.

28 WARDSHIP

Wardship was a frankly profitable job in medieval society; wards were openly bought and sold ; see, for instance, the case of Stephen Scrope in *Paston Letters*, ed. 1900, Introd. p. clxxv. and vol. I. pp. 91 ff. " He bought me and sold me as a beast " wrote Scrope of Sir John Fastolf. Three accounts of such wardships, from the purely business side, are given in Riley's *Memorials of London*, pp. 379, 446, 448. The second of these is here printed, because it is rarer to find such full accounts of girls' wardships than of boys'.

ACCOUNT of John Bryan, citizen and fishmonger, delivered on the first day of December, in the 4th year etc., in the Chamber of the Guildhall of London, before the auditors by William Walworthe, the then Mayor, assigned ; for the time that he was guardian of the body and chattels of Alice, daughter of John Reigner, blader[4], an orphan of the said city ; at the instance of Richard Fraunceys, fishmonger, her husband, then present.—

He charges himself with 100 marks received to the use of the said Alice; and with profit thereupon for five years, at 4 shillings in the pound yearly, according to the custom of the said city, amounting to 100 marks.—Sum total, 200 marks.

He claims allowance of one half of such increase, namely 2 shillings in the pound yearly for five years, for his trouble as to the same, according to the custom of the City, making

---

[1] to do Latin exercises. [2] wholly. [3] *sic*: for *gratia nulla*. [4] Or corndealer.

50 marks. For the board of the said Alice, at 8 pence per week, making 34*s*. 8*d*. yearly, in the whole, 8*l*. 13*s*. 4*d*. For her clothes, linen and woollen, and bed, 13*s*. 4*d*. yearly, making in the whole, 3*l*. 6*s*. 8*d*. For dressing and doctoring[1] the head of the same Alice, and for her teaching, shoes, and other small necessaries, 13*s*. 4*d*. yearly, making in the whole, 3*l*. 6*s*. 8*d*. For his expenses upon a plea in the Courts of the Bishop of London and of the Archbishop, for the marriage contract of the said Alice, 4*l*. 13*s*. 4*d*.—Sum total, 53*l*. 6*s*. 8*d*.

29   UNIVERSITY EXPENSES

Riley's *Memorials of London*, p. 379 : a guardian accounts for his ward's property in 1374.

Also,—for the board of the said Thomas, during the said 13 years ; 2 shillings per week being paid by the same Robert while he was at the Schools at Oxford, for his board there, and the same throughout the said time, making 104 shillings yearly, and in the whole—67*l*. 12*s*.

Also,—for the clothes, linen and woollen, and shoes, of the same Thomas for the said 13 years, at 40 shillings yearly, expended by the said Robert—26*l*.

Also,—for the teaching of the same Thomas for ten years out of the said thirteen, at 2 marks yearly, by the same Robert paid, making 20 marks.

Also,—for sundry expenses, namely, his riding at Oxford and elsewhere, and for moneys laid out upon a master for the said Thomas, at the rate of 20 shillings yearly, making in the whole 13*l*.

30   SPOILED CHILDREN

Sir E. Dudley, *Tree of the Commonwealth*, 1859, p. 35.

And ye honeste merchantes and other welthie commoners, be not ashamed to give to your children [due care]. Let not the femynine pittie of your wives destroy your children ; pompe them not at home in furred coates, and their shirtes to be warmed against their uprising, and suffer them not to

---

[1] *ornatu et medicamine.*

lie in their beddes till tenne of the clocke, and then a warme breakfaste ere his handes be washed : his nature is soe tender, he may neither learne ne labour. " Mr John," he must be called ! and his fathers servauntes set their bodies to some busynes, and that betymes. Remember yourselves howe ye wonne your thriftes. Dandell them not to derelie[1], lest follie fasten on them ; for oftentimes all that you leave, though ye were longe in gettinge thereof, with much penurie and paine, shortlie they spende it with unthriftie manner.

31   AS OTHERS SEE US

Italian Relation of England, A.D. 1500 (Camden Soc. 1847), p. 24.

The want of affection in the English is strongly manifested towards their children; for after having kept them at home till they arrive at the age of 7 or 9 years at the utmost, they put them out, both males and females, to hard service in the houses of other people, binding them generally for another 7 or 9 years. And these are called apprentices, and during that time they perform all the most menial offices; and few are born who are exempted from this fate, for every one, however rich he may be, sends away his children into the houses of others, whilst he, in return, receives those of strangers into his own. And on inquiring their reason for this severity, they answered that they did it in order that their children might learn better manners. But I, for my part, believe that they do it because they like to enjoy all their comforts themselves, and that they are better served by strangers than they would be by their own children. Besides which the English being great epicures, and very avaricious by nature, indulge in the most delicate fare themselves and give their household the coarsest bread, and beer, and cold meat baked on Sunday for the week, which, however, they allow them in great abundance. That if they had their own children at home, they would be obliged to give them the same food they made use of for themselves. That if the English sent their children away from home to learn virtue and good manners, and took them back again when their apprenticeship was over,

---

[1] too dearly.

they might, perhaps, be excused; but they never return, for the girls are settled by their patrons, and the boys make the best marriages they can, and, assisted by their patrons, not by their fathers, they also open a house and strive diligently by this means to make some fortune for themselves; whence it proceeds that, having no hope of their paternal inheritance, they all become so greedy of gain that they feel no shame in asking, almost "for the love of God," for the smallest sums of money; and to this it may be attributed, that there is no injury that can be committed against the lower orders of the English, that may not be atoned for by money.

32   LOOKING BACK ON THE MIDDLE AGES

Sir Thomas Elyot (1499?–1546) published in 1530–1 his *Booke of the Governour*, in which he precedes Ascham as an educational reformer. Like his elder contemporary Erasmus, he looked upon the education of his time with a horror which—making due allowance for the exaggerations natural to enthusiastic admirers of the classics—had only too much foundation in justice. The quotations are from the first edition (Berthelet, 1531) with references also to H. H. S. Croft's edition, 1880.

(*a*)   Fol. 28 *a* : Croft, vol. I. p. 50 (Bk I. chap. ix.).

By a cruell and irous maister the wittes of children be dulled; and that thinge for the whiche children be often tymes beaten is to them ever after fastidious; whereof we nede no better autor for witnes than daily experience.

(*b*)   Fol. 45 *b* : Croft, vol. I. p. 113 (ch. xiii.).

The seconde occasion wherfore gentylmens children seldome have sufficient lernynge is avarice: for where theyr parentes wyll nat adventure to sende them farre out of theyr propre countrayes, partly for feare of dethe, whiche perchance dare nat approche them at home with theyre father; partly for expence of money, whiche they suppose wolde be lesse in theyr owne houses, or in a village with some of theyr tenantes or frendes; havyng seldome any regarde to the teacher, whether he be well lerned or ignorant. For if they hiare a schole maister to teche in theyr house, they chiefely enquire with howe small a salary he will be contented, and never do inserche howe moche good lernynge he hath, and howe amonge

well lerned men he is therin estemed, usinge therin lasse
diligence than in takynge servantes, whose service is of
moche lasse importance, and to a good schole maister is nat
in profite to be compared. A gentil man er he take a cooke
in to his service, he wyll firste diligently examine hym, howe
many sortes of meates, potages, and sauces, he can perfectly
make, and howe well he can season them, that they may
be bothe pleasant and nourishynge; yea and if it be but a
fauconer, he wyll scrupulously enquire what skyll he hath in
feedyng, called diete, and kepyng of his hauke from all
sickenes, also how he can reclaime her and prepare her to
flyght. And to suche a cooke or fauconer, whom he findeth
expert, he spareth nat to gyve moche wages with other
bounteous rewardes. But of a schole maister, to whom he
will committe his childe, to be fedde with lernynge and instructed in vertue, whose lyfe shall be the principall monument
of his name and honour, he never maketh further enquirie
but where he may have a schole maister, and with howe litel
charge; and if one be perchance founden, well lerned, but he
will nat take paynes to teache without he may have a great
salary, he than speketh nothing more, or els saith, What? shall
so moche wages be gyven to a schole maister whiche wolde
kepe me two servantes? To whom maye be saide these wordes,
that by his sonne being wel lerned he shall recieve more
commoditie and also worship than by the service of a hundred
cokes and fauconers[1].

(c) Fol. 59*b*: Croft, vol. I. p. 163 (Bk I. chap. xv.).

Lorde God! howe many good and clene wittes of children
be nowe a dayes perisshed by ignorant scholemaisters! Howe
litle substancial doctrine is apprehended, by the fewenesse
of good gramariens!...I call nat them gramariens, whiche

[1] This is borne out by the *Northumberland Houshold Book* (ed. Bp Percy, 1770,
pp. 46–49). The "scolemaister techynge Gramer" was to have £5 a year—plus
board and lodging, as in the case of the other servants. Higher or equal wages
were given to the Chamberlain, Steward, Treasurer, Controller and Supervisor
and Herald, and two senior Gentlemen of the Chapel (from £6. 13*s*. 4*d*. to £10 or
more); the Secretary, the Senior Priest of the Chapel, and "every one of my
Lord's counsel" received £5. The Clerk of the Kitchen received £3. 6*s*. 8*d*.; the
yeoman-falconer £2 and the groom-falconer £1.

onely can teache or make rules, wherby a childe shall onely lerne to speake congrue latine, or to make sixe versis standyng in one fote, wherin perchance shal be neither sentence nor eloquence.... Undoubtedly ther be in this realme many well lerned, whiche (if the name of a schole maister were nat so moche had in contempte, and also if theyr labours with abundant salaries mought be requited,) were righte suffycient and able to induce their herers to excellent lernynge, so they be nat plucked away grene, and er they be in doctrine sufficiently rooted. But nowe a dayes, if to a bachelar or maister of arte studie of philosophie waxeth tediouse, if he have a spone full of latine, he wyll shewe forth a hoggesheed without any lernyng, and offre to teache grammer and expoune noble writers, and to be in the roome of a maister : he wyll, for a small salarie, sette a false colour of lernyng on propre wittes, whiche wyll be wasshed away with one shoure of raine. For if the children be absent from schole by the space of one moneth, the best lerned of them will uneth[1] tell wheder *Fato*, wherby Eneas was brought in to Itali, were other[2] a man, a horse, a shyppe, or a wylde goose. Al though their maister wyll perchance avaunte hym selfe to be a good philosopher.

[1] scarcely.   [2] either.

SECTION III

AUTHORS, SCRIBES AND READERS

1   MONASTIC STUDIES

(*a*) *Rule of S. Benedict* (c. 48).

Of Daily Handiwork. Idleness is the enemy of the soul ; therefore the brethren should be occupied at certain times in working with their hands, and at certain other hours in godly reading. Wherefore we think fit thus to dispose both these times. From Easter to the first of October let them go forth early and labour at necessary work from Prime until almost the fourth hour; and from the fourth until about the sixth let them busy themselves with reading.... From the first of October until the beginning of Lent, let them read a full hour until the second hour ; then let them say Tierce, and let all work until None at the work enjoined them.... After refection let them busy themselves with their reading, or with the Psalms. Again, in Lententide, let them read from early morn to full Tierce, and then busy themselves until the full tenth hour with whatsoever work has been enjoined upon them. And in these days of Lent let each take one volume for himself from the library, and let him read that book fully, from beginning to end, [during the year]. These volumes must be given out on the first day of Lent. But, above all, let one or two seniors be deputed to go round the monastery at those hours which are assigned for reading, lest perchance some slothful brother be found who spends his time in idleness or in talk, and who is not intent upon his reading, thus wasting not only his own time but that of others also. If such a one be found (though God forbid that there should be such !) let him be admonished once and twice ; and, if he amend not then, let him be subjected to regular discipline [i.e. to corporal punishment], that the rest may fear to follow in his steps. On Sundays let them spend their time in reading, except those who are deputed for the various services. But if any monk be so negligent and idle that he will not or cannot meditate or read, let some work be enjoined upon him, that he be not wholly unoccupied.

(*b*) Lanfranc's Canterbury Constitutions (*Opera*, ed. J. A. Giles, vol. I.).

On the second day in Lent, before the brethren enter the Chapter House, the keeper of the books should have the volumes collected in the said Chapter House and spread out upon a carpet, save only such as shall have been given out for reading during the past year, which must be brought in by the brethren, each bearing his own volume in his own hands, according to the warning which the aforesaid keeper shall have given in the Chapter of the day before. Then let the sentence of St Benedict's Rule be read concerning the observance of Lent, and let a sermon be made upon this theme; after which the keeper shall read his list of the books borrowed by the brethren for the year past. Each monk, hearing his name pronounced, shall render back the book which had been committed to him for reading during the year ; and, if he be conscious of not having read it to the end, he shall fall down and confess his fault and beseech indulgence. Then shall the said keeper give unto each of the brethren some other book to read, distributing them in order and writing down on the spot both the titles of the books and the names of the readers.

2   WRITERS' PAY

J. E. T. Rogers, *History of Agriculture and Prices*, vol. II. (1866).

(p. 579.) *Farley* (A.D. 1320). Fee paid to a certain clerk of Oxenford, for translating Hebrew into Latin, two pence.

(p. 579.) *Carleon* (A.D. 1320). To labourers making lime, at 2^d per diem ; carrying stone, at 2^d per diem.

(p. 579.) *Usk* (A.D. 1320). To threshers, per diem 2^d.

(p. 612.)   *Clare* (A.D. 1324).   The countess keeps a scriptor at Clare [castle] for 16 weeks engaged in writing a book called *Vitae Patrum,* and pays him 8 shillings[1].

(p. 583.)   *Oxford* (A.D. 1374).   Writing the third part of a Bible of the edition of Nicholas de Lyra, and parchment, 29 shillings.

3   A WRITER'S BOND

Codex Dunensis, ed. Kervyn de Lettenhove (Brussels, 1875) (pp. 216, 217). This MS., belonging to the Cistercian Abbey of Dunes, near Dunkirk, contains no document later than 1325; its contents date mostly from the late 13th century.

To all who shall inspect these present letters, the Archdeacon of Orleans wisheth health in the Lord.

Know ye that, in our presence, Robert of Normandy, an English writer, hath promised by his faith to write, continue and finish according to his ability, for Master W. de Lion, clerk[2], the commentary of Innocent [IV.] on the Decretals, even as he hath begun to write in the second book, and in letters as good as those wherewith he hath begun, for the sum of four pounds of Paris money to be paid by the said Master to the said Robert, even as he shall gain by writing in piecework[3]. Moreover the said writer hath promised by his faith that he will accept no other work until the book aforesaid shall have been wholly completed. The same Robert hath promised by his faith that, if he should desist from writing, continuing and finishing the work aforesaid, he shall be kept in prison and in iron bonds within the house of the said Master, never to go forth until the said work shall have been altogether completed; and, if he fail in this his promise, he hath coven-

---

[1] *Vitae Patrum* contains about 317,000 words : he therefore wrote at the rate of about 3,300 words a day on an average, even including the frequent holy days. His pay comes to 6*d.* a week *plus* board and lodging ; an ordinary artisan's pay. Very elaborate writing was of course far more expensive than this : a legendary for Winchester College in 1396 cost about 4*s.* 6*d.* per 1,000 words. The poet Hoccleve earned £4 a year as a scribe in a public office. (*Works*, Early English Text Society, vol. III. p. 30.)

[2] The editor notes that one Jean de Lion was a monk at Dunes in 1268—probably a brother of W. de Lion.

[3] Professional scribes reckoned their work by divisions of a standard length, called *peciae*. The *livre parisis* was equal to about 6*s.* 8*d.* sterling.

anted that our provost or our servant may seize him wheresoever he be found, and bring him to the house of the Master aforesaid to keep his prison there, as hath been already rehearsed, promising by his faith that he will in no wise contravene the aforesaid covenant or any part thereof. And, for the keeping of these aforesaid articles, the same Robert hath pledged, by his faith, to the aforesaid Master W., his own person and his heirs, and all his goods, whether movable or immovable, present or future, renouncing by his faith, in this matter, all help of canon or civil law, all privilege of crusade granted or to be granted, all hurt, deception, circumvention, exception of fraud, and all other exceptions which might be objected or laid against these letters present, submitting himself in this matter, by his faith, to the jurisdiction of the Court [Christian] of Orléans.

P. 217 contains a similar bond by the same scribe, to copy out a commentary on Justinian's Code for £10 *parisis*, and to undertake no other work in the meantime. On this occasion the penalty for breach of contract is not prison, but two other scribes solemnly pledge themselves to complete the work in case of Robert's failure.

4   THE WRITER'S PAINS

(*a*) Wattenbach, *Schriftwesen des Mittelalters*, 1896 (I. 287), from a MS. written by the monk Ludwig of Wessobrunn.

The book which you now see was written in the outer seats [of the cloister]; while I wrote I froze; and, what I could not write by the beams of day, I finished by candlelight[1].

(*b*) *Reliquiae Antiquae* (I. 287). From a MS. of the time of Henry VII.: compare Hoccleve's complaint in No. 19.

Three fingers write, yet the whole body is in travail : they who know not how to write deem it no labour !

[1] Adam Marsh's letters show us that it was looked upon as a most unusual thing to write by night—as indeed the rudimentary lighting arrangements of the Middle Ages must have made it a severe trial to the eyes. (*Monumenta Franciscana*, Rolls Series, vol. I. pp. 141, 345.)

5   HIRELING WRITERS

At an early date (as we see in No. 3) the hired *scriptor* began to take the place of the purely monastic copyist. The Westminster Consuetudinary of 1266 makes provision for the professional as well as for the monastic scribe ; and at St Albans, the most remarkable of all English abbeys for its literary activities, this process had begun still earlier. The best copying (and the best art generally) of the later Middle Ages was done not by monks but by laymen or lower clerics.

Gesta Abbatum Monasterii S^{ti} Albani, R.S. (p. 57).

In the days of Abbot Paul [1077–1093], among other things, a certain warlike Norman noble, at the abbot's persuasion, bestowed upon us two-thirds of the tithes of his domain in Hatfield, which he had received at the distribution [of the spoils] ; and, at the wish of the Abbot Paul, who loved books, he assigned these tithes for the making of books for the Abbey; for the knight himself was a literate man, a diligent hearer and lover of the Scriptures. To this office were added certain tithes in Redbourne ; and the Abbot decreed that certain daily allowances should be given to the scribes from the charities of the brethren and of the cellarer, since such gifts were ready to eat, in order that the scribes might not be hindered in their work[1] ; on account of which allowances he gave better endowments by way of reparation to the almoner, that his conscience might not be hurt. There, then, the Abbot caused such noble volumes as were necessary for the Church [*or* Abbey] to be written by choice scribes whom he sought from afar ; and of pure courtesy (for he was a most courteous man), he bestowed upon the aforesaid Sir Robert, for the use of the chapel in his manor of Hatfield, two sets of vestments, a silver chalice, a missal and other necessary books. Moreover, each forbade that, by reason of the aforesaid gifts of tithes to the scriptorium, or of the Abbot's gift, anything else should be written or given henceforward for this knight. So, after that Paul had thus liberally bestowed upon the said knight his first set of books, he forthwith ordained the writing of choice books in this scriptorium

---

[1] i.e. they were to receive dishes straight from the convent kitchen, instead of allowances of uncooked food which they would have to prepare in their own quarters.

which he had made; and [Abp] Lanfranc lent him archetypes
to copy from.

6 CHAUCER'S COPYIST

Chaucers wordes unto Adam, his owne Scriveyn.

Adam scryveyne, if ever it thee byfalle
Boece or Troylus for to wryten nuwe,
Under thy long lokkes thowe most have the scalle[1]
But after my makyng thowe wryt more truwe.
So offt a daye I mot[2] thy werk renuwe,
It to corett and eke to rubbe and scrape;
And al is through thy neglygence and rape[3].

7 A SCRIVENER'S GILD

From the *York Memorandum Book* (Surtees Soc. 1912, vol. I. (p. 56),
of the late 14th century). Compare the similar evidence in H. T. Riley,
Memorials of London, 1868, p. 557.

Scriveners of Text.

These are the ordinances made among the scriveners of
the city of York by their common assent.

First. If any stranger scrivener come to the city to dwell
therein, if he be able and sufficient for the place of a master, he
shall forthwith be made free of the city; and if he be unable
to practise as master in the said craft, he shall put himself to
apprenticeship with some master, to learn his art, until he be
well taught and able to copy as a master in the same craft.

Item, that no master scrivener take an apprentice for a
less term than five years; and that the said apprentice be of
the age of 16 years at least; and that the master take none
other to teach but such as are his apprentices.

And those who have not the freedom of York, and are
taught and informed to write, shall dwell with masters of the
said craft in that city aforesaid, to take a proper wage according
to their ability to work in the said craft.

And that no man of this craft act against this ordinance
in any of the above-said points, under fine of twenty shillings

---

[1] scab. [2] must. [3] haste.

sterling; viz. ten to the Council Chamber and ten to the profit of their pageant and of the light[1] which appertaineth to the said craft.

8 LITERARY LIFE IN THE CLOISTER

Ordericus Vitalis (1075–1143?) was son of a French priest, Odeler, who came to England as confessor to Roger, earl of Shrewsbury. Odeler not only persuaded the earl, after many years, to build a monastery at Shrewsbury, but entered it himself with half of his property. Though Orderic was sent in early life to the abbey of Ouche or St-Evroul in Normandy, he never lost his affection for England, and frequently styles himself *Angligena*. He and his somewhat discursive *Historia Ecclesiastica* are admirably characterized by Dean Church in his *St Anselm*, 1870, pp. 101 ff. The following translations are partly taken (with slight changes) from Church : the page-references are to the originals in Migne, *Patrologia Latina*, vol. 188.

(a) *Hist. Eccl.* Lib. v. (c. 17, col. 425).

The aforesaid Odeler, my father [when the monastery at Shrewsbury had been finished], fulfilled to the letter all that he had promised ; for he gave two hundred pounds of silver, and his son Benedict to be a monk ; and after earl Roger's death, he himself took the cowl there. In that house he served God seven years according to the Rule of St Benedict; and on Friday in Whitsun week, after very many labours borne for God's sake, he covered his sins by uncovering them with confession and bitter tears, and died anointed and fortified with the holy Eucharist....

Lo! here is a digression, be it of what account it may, about the building of the monastery on my father's land, which is now inhabited by the family of Christ, and where my father himself, as I remember, an old man of sixty, willingly bore to the end the yoke of Christ. Forgive me, good reader, and let it not be an offence to thee, I pray thee, if I commit to record something about my father, whom I have never seen since the time when, as if I had been a hated step-child, he sent me forth for the love of his Maker into exile. It is now forty-two years ago ; and in those years many changes have been, far and wide, in the world. While I often think of these things, and commit some of them to my paper, carefully

---

[1] The light maintained in the Gild Chapel.

resisting idleness, I thus exercise myself in inditing them. Now I return to my work, and speak to those younger than myself—a stranger, to those of the country—about their own affairs, things that they know not; and in this way, by God's help, I do them useful service.

(*b*) *Ibid.* Lib. XIII. (c. 22, col. 981).

Behold, worn out with age and infirmity, I desire to end my work, and for many reasons prudence requires it. For I am now [1141] passing the sixty-seventh year of my age in the worship of my Lord Jesus Christ, and while I see the foremost men of this world crushed by heavy disasters of the most opposite sort, I dance for joy, in the safe estate of obedience and poverty.   There is Stephen, king of the English, sighing in prison ; and Lewis, king of the French, leading an expedition against the Goths and Gascons, is vexed with many and frequent cares.   There is the church of Lisieux, whose bishop is dead, and which is without a pastor; moreover, when it will have one, and of what sort, I know not. What shall I say more ? Amid these things, I turn my speech to thee, O Almighty God, and with double force beseech thy goodness that thou wouldest have mercy on me.   I give thee thanks, O King most high, who didst freely make me, and hast ordered my years according to thy good pleasure.   For thou art my King and my God, and I am thy servant and the son of thine handmaid, who, from the first days of my life, according to my power, have served thee. For on Easter eve I was baptised at Attingesham [Atcham], which village is in England on the Severn, that great river of Severn.   There, by the ministry of Ordric the priest, thou didst regenerate me by water and the Holy Ghost, and didst put upon me the name of that same priest, my god-father. Then, when I was five years old, I was delivered over to school in the city of Shrewsbury, and there I offered to thee the first services of clerkship in the church of the holy apostles, St Peter and St Paul.   There Sigward, the famous priest, taught me for five years the letters of Carmenta Nicostrata[1], and broke me

[1] Carmentis (otherwise Nicostrata) was \ables to have introduced the alphabet into Italy.   See frontispiece to R. S. Rait, *Life in the Medieval University*, 1912.

in to psalms and hymns and other necessary instructions; meanwhile, thou didst exalt the aforesaid church, built on the river Mole, which belonged to my father, and by the pious devotion of Count Roger didst build there a venerable monastery. It did not seem fit to thee that I should longer be thy soldier there, lest with my relations, who often to thy servants are a burden and hindrance, I should suffer some disquiet, or run into some loss in the fulfilment of thy law through the carnal affection of my relations. Therefore, O glorious God, who didst command Abraham to go forth from his country and his father's house and kindred, thou didst put into the heart of Odeler my father to give up all his claim in me, and to put me absolutely under thy yoke. So he delivered me to Rainald the monk, a weeping father his weeping child, and for the love of thee appointed me to banishment : and he never saw me afterwards. Young boy as I was, I took not on me to dispute my father's wishes, but in everything I willingly assented, for he had promised on his part that, if I would become a monk, I should after my death possess Paradise with the innocent. Gladly was this engagement made between me and thee, my father being its minister ; and I left behind my native country and my parents and all my kin, and my acquaintance and friends; and they, weeping and bidding me farewell, with loving prayers, commended me to thee, O most high Lord God. Hear their supplications, I beseech thee, and graciously grant what they desired, O merciful King of Sabaoth.

So being ten years old I crossed the British Sea, and came an exile to Normandy, where, unknown to all, I knew no man. Like Joseph in Egypt, I heard a strange language. Yet by the help of thy favour, among these strangers I found all gentleness and friendliness. In the eleventh year of my age, I was received to the monastic life by the venerable Abbot Mainer, in the monastery of Ouche, and on Sunday, the 21st of September [1085], I was tonsured after the manner of clerks, and for my English name, which sounded harsh to Normans, the name of Vitalis was given me, borrowed from one of the companions of St Maurice the martyr, whose martyrdom was at that time celebrated [Sept. 22]. In this house for fifty-six years, by thy favour, have I had my conversation, and by all the brethren and dwellers in it I have been loved and honoured much more than I deserved. Heat and cold and the burden of the day have I endured, labouring among thine own in the "vineyard of Sorech"; and the "penny" which thou hast promised I have confidently waited for, for thou art faithful. Six abbots have I reverenced as my fathers and masters, because they were in thy place: Mainer and Serlo, Roger and Garin, Richard and Ranulf. They were the lawful heads of the convent of Ouche; for me and for others they kept watch, as those who must give account; within and abroad they used good husbandry, and, with thee for their companion and helper, provided all things necessary for us.

On March 15 [1091], when I was sixteen years old, at the bidding of Serlo, our abbot-elect, Gilbert, Bishop of Lisieux, ordained me sub-deacon. Then after two years, on the 26th of March [1093], Serlo, Bishop of Séez, laid on me the office of deacon, in which grade I gladly ministered to thee fifteen years. Lastly, in the thirty-third year of my age, William, Archbishop of Rouen, on the 21st of December [1107] laid on me the burden of the priesthood. On the same day, he ordained 244 deacons and 120 priests, with whom, in the Holy Ghost, I devoutly approached thy holy altar, and have now for thirty-four years faithfully performed thy service unto thee with a willing mind.

(*c*) *Ibid.* Lib. v. prologue (addressed to his abbot, Garin) (col. 374).

First, therefore, I chose to obey your commands and those of our venerable abbot Roger, by beginning a short history of our monastery of St Evroul; a work which our predecessors have exhorted each other to perform, but which none was willing to begin; for all preferred silence to speech, and untroubled repose to the care of searching out past events. They would gladly, indeed, have read the acts of their abbots and brethren, and the story how those small possessions were got together, and increased by needy yet devout founders and by the immense solicitude of our forefathers; but they would not bend their minds to the slow labour of composition or writing. At length I myself, borne hither as a ten-year-

old English boy from the most distant confines of Mercia
and thrown as a barbarous and unknown stranger among the
more expert inhabitants of this house, have attempted, by
God's inspiration, to publish among Normans the story of
Norman deeds and Norman affairs.

(*d*) *Ibid.* Lib. IV. (c. 25, col. 372).

Many other misfortunes [beyond those which I have just
related] are impending over the world; so many that, if all
were recorded, they would fill more than one vast volume.
But now I am benumbed with the winter frosts and must
turn to other duties; wherefore I am resolved here to lay
down my weary pen and to end this fourth book. When the
soft air of sweet spring shall return, then I will turn again to
those matters which I have omitted or have treated too
briefly; and, with God's help, I will clearly and truly set
forth the events of our countrymen in war and peace.

(*e*) *Ibid.* Lib. V. prologue (col. 449).

All men, so long as they live, ought to learn day by day,
and to profit from the comprehension of the manly examples
of bygone heroes. Many things which seem almost unheard-
of come oftentimes to the ears of inexperienced folk; and we
moderns are often struck by the sudden emergence of unex-
pected chances and changes; whereby the mental vision of
the unlearned is dimmed, unless they are able to read of past
events. It is for this that studious folk search into hidden
things, and, in charity to their fellow-men, seize exultingly
upon whatsoever seems likely to profit all well-meaning minds.
Benevolence prompts their labour; and they ungrudgingly
display the past to the eyes of posterity; yet the idle sometimes tear, as with dogs' teeth, whatsoever these men's skill
hath produced. Wherefore certain envied folk, when wounded
by the teeth of these envious, oftentimes lose their spirit and
cease from the work which they have begun, and which perchance will fall thenceforth into eternal silence. Thus, for
the slightest occasion, the world sometimes suffers lamentable
loss....We read such complaints oftentimes in the writings of
our forefathers; and we mourn with famous teachers who be-

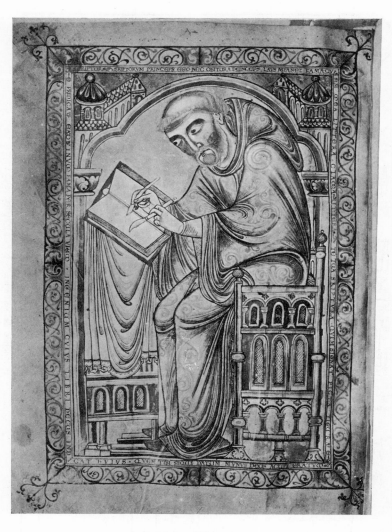

A Monk Writing

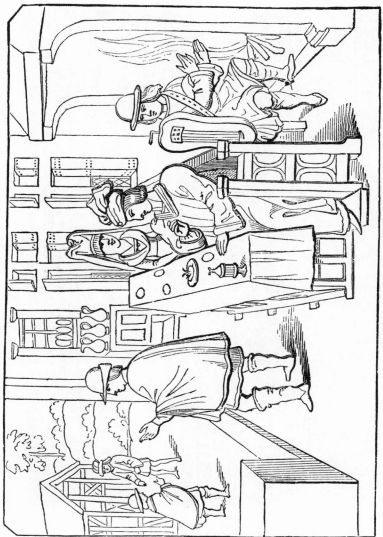

THE MINSTREL'S RECEPTION

moan the insults of their rivals....Therefore I beseech those men to hold their peace and to cease from troubling, who neither write on their own behalf nor look kindly upon the writings of others, nor even correct peaceably the things which they find amiss. Let them learn that which they know not ; or, if they cannot learn, let them at least suffer their fellows to publish what they hold to be true[1] !

9　A LITERARY ARCHDEACON

Giraldus Cambrensis (1147–1222 ?), of mingled Norman and Welsh blood, spent most of his life in an attempt to revive in his own person the supposed metropolitan rights of the see of St Davids.　He was a prolific author—his books on Ireland and Wales are among the best of their kind in the Middle Ages, and his *Gemma Ecclesiastica* and *Speculum Ecclesiae* treat very frankly of Church reform.　But all through his writings run two subjects—the Bishopric of St Davids and himself.　Though undisguisedly vain, Giraldus was neither meanly selfish nor treacherous. " His whole life had been one rebellion against the see of Canterbury ; but it was on behalf of the more ancient see of St Davids.　He utterly refused to revive the controversy when King John wanted to make Giraldus and his cause a tool in his warfare against Stephen Langton and the Canterbury monks."　The following extracts are translated, with the omission of many superfluities, from *De rebus a se gestis* (R. S., vol. I.) in which the author tells his own life in the third person.　For further information the reader should refer to H. Owen's *Gerald the Welshman*.

(p. 45 ff.)　Gerald was born in South Wales, on the coast of Demetia, not far from the chief town of Pembroke, namely, at the castle of Manorbier, where his parents were of noble rank. For his mother was Angarath, daughter of Nesta, the noble daughter of Rhys, Prince of South Wales, and his father was the noble William de Barri.　Gerald, therefore, being the youngest of four blood-brethren, when his elder brothers in their boyish games were wont, in the sand or the dust, to build castles and cities and palaces, as a prelude to their later life, this Gerald, I say, as a like prelude, ever bent his whole mind to the building of monasteries and churches in play.　His father, oftentimes noting and marvelling at this his custom, took it for a prognostic of the future, and determined with wise

---

[1] Similar complaints on the part of monastic writers are extraordinarily frequent ; e.g. Aimoin of Fleury, Ekkehard IV and Ekkehard V, Ralph Glaber, Guibert of Nogent and Caesarius of Heisterbach.

forethought to set him to letters and liberal studies : moreover with playful praise he was wont to call the boy his "little bishop."

It came to pass one night that the land was troubled by an invasion of enemies, and all the able men of the town rushed in haste to arms. Which, when the boy saw, and when he heard the tumult, he wailed aloud and besought a safe asylum, asking that he might be carried to the church; wherein, with a marvellous spirit of prophecy, he presaged that the peace of the Church and the immunities of God's House should be most firm and sure. When all men heard these words of his, the tumult ceased, for they pondered this boy's speech in their hearts, and, discussing among themselves, they recalled with amazement that his words promised them greater safety in this remote church, exposed to the blasts of heaven and to the hazards of chance, than in any city crammed with men and arms and well fortified with towers and walls.... In these first days, therefore, the boy was no little hindered by the companionship of his brethren, who played with him on holidays and extolled with all their might the business of their knightly profession, for a boy's manners are formed by those who dwell with him. Wherefore he was slow indeed to profit by the teaching that they set before him. At length, however, he was much moved by the rebuke and instant correction of the then Bishop of St Davids (who was his own uncle), David, of pious memory ; and also by two clerks of the same bishop, one of whom rebuked him by declining the adjective "durus, durior, durissimus," and the other "stultus, stultior, stultissimus," which insult stirred him deeply, so that he began to profit more through shame than the rod, finding in this disgrace his most efficient preceptor. Afterwards, therefore, he was so wrapped in the vehemence of his studies that within a short time he far surpassed all his schoolfellows of the same age in his native land. In process of time he thrice crossed the sea to France for the sake of further study and profit, and studied in three stages of seven years in liberal learning at Paris, until at length, rivalling the most excellent preceptors, he taught there the Trivium with great success, and won distinguished praise in the art of rhetoric. Wherein he was so entirely given up to study, so utterly devoid of frivolity or buffoonery in his acts or mind that, whensoever the Masters in Arts would give an example of good scholars, they were wont to cite Gerald first of all....

He came home from Paris in 1172, was at once promoted to important offices in the Church, and fought boldly in his native Wales, though not with entire success, against customs which defrauded the clergy of part of their tithes, and against the concubinary priesthood. The many controversies of his later life may be partly explained at least by his own public criticism: " Even as the laymen of Wales are thieves and reivers of other men's goods, so are the Welsh bishops robbers of churches." This, he tells us complacently, raised a laugh at the King's court, but can scarcely have smoothed his way as a reformer at home.

(p. 45 ff.) (A.D. 1177.) After these achievements, Gerald, who thought that nothing had been done so long as anything remained to be done, and who never looked backwards but always pressed forward and mounted unrestingly from step to step,—Gerald, I say, for the sake of greater and riper wisdom, heaped together a treasure of books and set himself again to cross into France and to apply himself afresh with all his heart to the humaner studies, that he might raise high upon his foundation of arts and literature the walls of Civil and Canon Law, and cover all in at last with the sacred roof of Holy Scriptures, so that the building, bound together by this triple structure, might be formed with all strength of joint. In that city, for many years he had applied his studious mind first to the laws of the Empire, then to those of the Pope, and at last to the sacred Scriptures; and at length he obtained such grace in causes of Canon Law, (which were wont to be discussed on Sundays,) that, on such days, as the news of his coming lecture was bruited about at Paris, so great was the concourse to his pleasant voice, of almost all the doctors with their scholars, that even the greatest house could scarce contain his auditors. For with such rhetorical persuasion did he support the living reasons of Civil and Canon Law, and so did he adorn the causes with schemes and colours of words and with the marrow of wise sentences, and with such marvellous artifice did he fit the sayings of philosophers and authors into their proper places, that, the more wise and learned his hearers were, the more greedily and attentively did they apply their hearts and their minds to listen and fix it all in their memory. For they had been enticed and soothed by such sweetness of his words that, hanging on his lips as he spoke, they listened without weariness or satiety, even though his speech were long and prolix and such as in most cases begetteth tediousness. Wherefore also the scholars everywhere vied with each other in writing out his cases word for word, as they came from his own lips, and embraced them with great desire. For one day, when a great concourse had come from all parts to hear him— after he had ended speaking and while the murmur of the multitude expressed the favour and praise of all his auditors— a certain eminent doctor, who also had lectured in arts at Paris, and had long studied at Bologna in law—his name was Master Roger the Norman, who afterwards was made Dean of the cathedral church of Rouen—this Roger, I say, broke out into the following words: " Certainly there is no science under the sun which, if it be brought by chance to Paris, doth not thrive there far and incomparably better than anywhere else."

I have thought it therefore not beside the purpose to insert here the beginning of that case which I then read and this in guise of proemium :

The subjoined specimen of rhetoric is more to the taste of the 12th century than of our own, but the reader may be interested to hear Gerald's further account of its effect.

A certain noble man, a Canon of the cathedral of Paris, and son of the Castellan of Montmorency, who shortly afterwards became Dean of Notre-Dame, being a studious person and greedy of learning and literature ; this man, I say, as he departed from the audience, whereat he had been present with many others, accosted Gerald secretly, and asked him how many years he had spent upon Civil and Canon Law at Bologna. Hearing then that Gerald had never been at Bologna, he asked again where he had studied in law, and, hearing again that Gerald had passed only three years in this study at Paris, he withdrew in amazement. Moreover Gerald's own preceptor in the laws, whom he visited after dinner, applauding and rejoicing in this great glory of his own pupil, spoke in Gerald's hearing, "Of a truth I would not for a plea of a hundred shillings" (which was a form of expression of Bologna) "that you should have failed to speak so admirably to-day in so great a consistory, and before so vast an audience of scholars. For, as Jerome saith, 'The profit and growth of scholars is the praise and glory of their preceptors.'"......

(p. 49.) But to return to the point and to the course of our matter. After Gerald had spent a long time in study, he thought to return home, but was compelled vainly to await his messengers long beyond the time that had been fixed for their returning and bringing his money. But since his creditors, to whom he was much in debt, lay hard upon him from day to day in importunate impatience, therefore, sad and anxious at heart, and almost driven to desperation, he repaired to the chapel of St Thomas of Canterbury in the church of St Germain l'Auxerrois, which had been built and dedicated in his honour by the Archbishop of Reims, brother to King Louis [VII.], in the very first days of his martyrdom. To this, as to his last refuge, he came with his companions to pray devoutly for the martyr's help; for he knew, as wise Master Philo saith, that where human aid fails, we must then have recourse to divine. Therefore, having heard a solemn mass of the martyr, and made his oblation, he received forthwith without delay the reward of his devotion. For in that same hour his messengers arrived prosperously, to his great rejoicing, by the marvellous disposition of God, who chooseth for His saints from among worldly things which happen in their own course, and whose pleasure it is that things which are certainly given of His pure grace should be obtained as it were by prayers and merits.

(p. 50.) Gerald therefore on his way to England came to Arras in Whitsun week, and abode at a hostelry hard by the market-place, during which days there was a great stir in the city. For the great Philip, Count of Flanders, was then dwelling in this his town and had caused a quintain to be set up in the market-place, which covered a great square space in the midst of the city; which quintain was in the form of a strong shield, firmly hung to a post whereupon the aspirants to knighthood and the lusty youth might practise themselves in warlike sports at full gallop, and make trial of their strength either by breaking their lances or by piercing through the shield. Gerald therefore, who beheld all this from the upper chamber of his hostelry (and would that I could add, strong enough in mind to despise it all as a vain show), saw the Count himself and a great host of nobles with him, both knights and barons clad in silk; he saw such a host of goodly chargers rushing past at the gallop, such a forest of lances broken, that, beholding all these things with great attention, he was scarce able to contain himself with wonder. Yet when this had endured but for the space of a single hour, and the whole square had been crowded all that while with that great press of noblemen, suddenly Count Philip departed and the rest slipped away behind him; so that, where all had lately been so full of vain show, now neither man nor beast could be seen, nor anything but the bare and desert market-place. Wherefore, concerning this and like pomps, Gerald is always wont to show how great a proof and demonstration they give us that all things under the sun are subject to vanity, even as phantoms which swiftly pass away; and how all things in this world endure but for a moment.

(p. 51 ff.) Proceeding therefore on his journey and crossing the sea of Flanders he came to Canterbury, and ate on the day of the Holy Trinity with the monks of that monastery in their refectory at the Prior's bidding. Sitting then in that hall with the Prior and the greater monks at the high table he noted there, as he was wont to relate, two things; that is to say, the excessive superfluity of signs, and the multitude of the dishes. For the Prior sent so many gifts of meat to the monks who served him, and they on their part to the lower tables, and the recipients gave so many thanks and were so profuse in their gesticulations of fingers and hands and arms and in the whisperings whereby they avoided open speech, (wherein all showed a most unedifying levity and licence,) that Gerald felt as if he were sitting at a stage play or among a company of actors and buffoons; for it would be more appropriate to their Order and to their honourable estate to speak modestly in plain human speech than to use such a dumb garrulity of frivolous signs and hissings. Of the dishes themselves and their multitude what can I say but this, that I have oft-times heard him relate how six courses or more were laid in order (or shall I not say in disorder?) upon the table; and these of the most sumptuous kind. At the very last, in the guise of principal course, masses of herbs were brought to all the tables, but they were scarcely touched, in face of so many kinds of fishes, roast and boiled, stuffed and fried—so many dishes tricked out by the cook's art with eggs and pepper—so many savouries and sauces composed by that same art to stimulate gluttony, and to excite the appetite. Add to this, that there was such abundance of wine and strong drink—of piment and claree[1], of new wine and mead and mulberry wine, and all intoxicating liquors in so much abundance—that even beer, which the English brew excellently (especially in Kent), found no place; but rather beer stood as low in this matter as the pot-herbs among other dishes. I say, ye might see so excessive and sumptuous a superfluity here in meats and dishes as might weary not only the guest who partook thereof, but even the beholder. What then would Paul the Hermit have said to this? or Anthony? or Benedict, father and founder of monastic life? Nay, to seek examples far nearer to our own times, what would our noble Jerome have said, who, in his *Lives of the Fathers*, extols with such praise the parsimony and

---

[1] For *piment and claree* see Chaucer, *C.T.*, A 1471 and 3378. They are thus described by Bartholomaeus Anglicus, lib. xix. c. 58–9, tr. Trevisa. "*Claret* is made of wyne and of honye and swete spicery: for good spicery is grownde to smalle powder, and put in a lynnen bag that is fayre and clene, with hony or with sugre; and the best wyne is put upon the spicery....And the wyne shal be ofte put theron, unto the vertu of the spicery be in corporat into the wyne, and be claryfyed. And so claret draweth of the wyne myghte and sharpnes, and holdeth of the spicery good smell and odour, and borroweth of the hony swetnes and savour. *Pigmentum*...is [spice] beten in a morter, of the which spiciry, by Pigmentary crafte, is made liking drynke and Electuaries." Peter the Venerable forbade piment to the monks of Cluny, for reasons of expense and temptation to drunkenness. *Statuta*, c. 11: Migne, *P. L.* 189, c. 1029: his contemporary, St Bernard, was of the same mind.

abstinence and moderation of the early Church, saying among other things that the Church, in proportion as she hath grown in wealth, hath much decreased in the virtues? Moreover, Gerald would sometimes say (as is not beside the mark to relate here) how the monks of St Swithun at Winchester, with their Prior at their head, grovelled in the dust before Henry II., King of England, and complained to him with tears and wailing that their bishop, Richard, who was in place of an abbot to them, had taken away three of their daily dishes. Whereupon the King asked how many dishes remained, and they answered, "Ten, for it is an ancient custom with us to have thirteen." "How!" said the King, "I and my court am content with three dishes. Perish therefore your bishop unless he reduce your dishes in the monastery to as few as my dishes at court!" To what purpose is this waste? especially among men vowed to Religion and wearing the religious habit, for these superfluities might have been sold and given to the poor. Now this is the reason which they give and whereby they colour their proceedings, that this excessive multitude of dishes hath been invented and suffered in their Order for the sake of increasing and multiplying their alms. Yet they would be better counselled, and scandal would better be avoided, and it would more profit their honour and modesty, if they were content with fewer dishes and would feed the poor of Christ with those superfluities; whereby they might temper their appetite and cut off occasion of scandal and bring far greater and more wholesome increase unto their alms.

Gerald therefore, proceeding on his way to London, found Richard, Archbishop of Canterbury, in a certain manor of his not far from that city; by whom he was kept that night and received with honourable hospitality as one who had been his beloved and familiar friend. [He proceeded to Southwark and visited the Bishop of Winchester.] And the Bishop, to whom he had been well known, seeing him come in with his companions, and the tokens of St Thomas of Canterbury hanging round their necks, and marvelling at the sudden coming of this Gerald, whom he knew to have been so long in France, and whom he believed still to be there—the Bishop, I say, embraced him with a kiss and set him down by his side, and bade his servants entertain Gerald's companions.

(p. 57.) Moreover Gerald's fame increased and spread from day to day, and when King Henry II. was busy among the Marches of Wales, in pacifying that country, Gerald was called to court by the council of the King's great men. Then—at the instant prayers of the King himself, with promises and commands to boot—though most unwilling and reluctant, because, even as the scholar's life is esteemed above all others, so the life of the courtier is most detested—he at last joined the King's train and became his clerk[1]. When therefore he had followed the court for many years in faithful service, and with much profit for the pacifying of Wales and the keeping of peace, yet, on account of his kinship to Rhys ap Griffith and other princes of Wales, he received nothing but empty promises from that King who enriched and promoted so many unworthy persons. Yet in secret council the King would commend him highly to his lords, approving his manners and moderation and modesty and his tried fidelity; and saying again and again that, had he not been born in Wales and so near of kin to the princes of that country, and especially to Rhys, he would copiously reward him with ecclesiastical dignities and rents and make him a great man in his kingdom.

(p. 65.) Now it befel in mid-Lent, at the Sunday "Laetare Jerusalem," that John, Archbishop of Dublin, called together his suffragan bishops and held a council in the cathedral of the Holy Trinity, and on the first day himself preached concerning the sacraments of the Church. On the second day, Albin, Abbot of Bolkinglas, who was afterwards Bishop of Ferns, preached at great length concerning clerical continence—in which sermon he cast all the blame upon the clergy who had come from Wales to England and to Ireland, teaching that the Irish clergy had been of great purity until they had been infected by the con-

---

[1] For a description of the discomforts endured by scholars at court, see the extract in my *Medieval Garner* (pp. 128 ff.) from Gerald's brother-archdeacon, Peter of Blois. Walter Map is equally uncomplimentary in his *De Nugis Curialium* (Camden Soc. 1850, chap. 1, entitled "Comparison between the King's Court and Hell").

tagion of these foreigners, since evil communications corrupt
good manners, and he who toucheth pitch shall be defiled
thereby. And, to crown all this confusion, at the end of his
sermon, our[1] clergy of the parts around Wexford accused each
other incessantly before the Archbishop and the whole council
concerning concubines who had been publicly taken and
brought home, and with whom marriages had been publicly
solemnized. And this being proved by the immediate production of witnesses (for Gerald moved the Archbishop to
this in order that public justice might at once be done), they
convicted each other amid great derision and mockery from
the Irish clergy. The Archbishop, however, in order that he
might repress the mockery of the Irish and show how such
uncleanness and enormities displeased him, gave summary
sentence against those convicted, and suspended them both
from their offices and from their benefices. So on the third
day the Archbishop entrusted to Gerald the duty of preaching; and he, taking his text from the pastoral office, began by
confessing what could be said truly to the praise of the Irish
clergy. He then proceeded to speak of their faults and
excesses, and especially the vice of drunkenness, first blaming
all in common and then turning to their prelates, whom he
irrefragably convicted of carelessness and pastoral negligence.
Wherefore I have thought it not irrelevant to insert here that
part of his sermon which may be found in the last chapter of
his *Topographia Hibernica*.......

When our Gerald had thus gained a great name and
wide renown in this island, between Easter and Pentecost he
crossed over to Wales, where he applied his whole mind with
all diligence to the consummation of his *Topographia*, which he
had already begun. In process of time, when the work had
been completed and corrected, willing to place his lighted
candle not under a bushel but on a candlestick, that it might
show its full light, he purposed to go to Oxford, where the
English clergy were most flourishing and most excellent in
learning, and there to read his book before this eminent
audience. And, since the work was divided into three parts,

[1] i.e. Welsh and English.

by reading one daily, he spread it over three days. On the first he received and entertained in his hostel all the poor of the whole city whom he had called together for this purpose ; next day he entertained all the doctors of the different faculties, and their pupils of greatest fame and renown; and on the third day the rest of the scholars with the knights, the citizens, and others of the borough. This was indeed a sumptuous and noble undertaking, whereby he renewed in some fashion the glorious ancient times of the poets; nor can either the present age nor any past age in England show such a day.

(p. 80.) Archbishop Baldwin of Canterbury asked Gerald whether he had taken from any of our hagiographers or expositors those truths concerning the allegorical exposition of the natures of birds which he had given in the first book of his *Topographia*. When therefore Gerald had answered that all was his own, the Archbishop replied that these were written in the same spirit wherein the great Fathers wrote, and added this also, that Gerald should not permit the grace of this excellent style which God had given him to lie idle, but should always use it and continually write, that his time might not be lost in idleness, but that by continual study and praiseworthy labour he should extend the memory of his name to future ages and thus earn perpetual grace and favour, not only from future generations, but from all save the envious of our own age. For he said and repeated that Gerald should prize God's gift of so gracious a style far more than earthly riches that must soon perish, or worldly dignities that must swiftly pass away. "And," said he, "thou shouldst indeed be grateful, since thy works can neither pass away nor perish, but the more ancient they shall become in process of time, the dearer and more precious they will be to all men for all eternity."

(From Gerald's *Letters*, p. 417.) Therefore let those know who envy me, that I have hitherto led no idle nor easy life, nor with God's grace will I ever lead such a life while strength remains to me. Wherefore let the envious call me at their pleasure a foolish and mad old man; let them gnaw and rend and cease not to bark at me ; for I, according to the warnings and salutary precepts of the holy man whom I have often cited, will not relinquish that grace of style which God hath given me from on high. Truly it is my desire unweariedly to exercise my studious mind in the study of literature theology philosophy and history, even as it hath always been my past custom, and not only to linger over these things in zealous charity for the erudition of posterity, but even so to die, and thus to breathe out my vital breath when my hour shall come. Yet to write books, and especially to strike out new thoughts, is a perilous thing to-day as in the past; and it exposeth us on all sides to the calumnious detraction of the envious.

(p. 419.) Here therefore, in my studies and in my books, elaborated with much toil for the profit of posterity, is matter to burst the sides of our envious rivals, matter for the present time to tear to pieces in wrath, and for posterity to praise. Let the present rend them, and posterity read them. Let the present loathe them, and posterity love them. Let the present reprove, let posterity approve.

10   A GREAT CHRONICLER

Matthew Paris is certainly the greatest of British chroniclers, and has possibly no superiors until the Renascence. He took the cowl at St Albans in 1217, was appointed historiographer to the Abbey on the death of Roger of Wendover (1235), and brought his chronicle down to the year of his own death (1259). The following passages are translated from Luard's edition in the Rolls Series.

(*a*) *Chronica Majora*, IV. 643, A.D. 1247. Henry III., having received some drops of Christ's blood from the Holy Land, caused this precious relic to be solemnly translated to the splendid abbey church he was then building at Westminster :

But when [these relics] were being examined, and some, slow of belief, were yet hesitating, then the lord Theodoric, Prior of the Hospitallers, said to the Bishops and others that sat around..." Why then should all these men of so great reputation have given their testimony to this assertion, appending thereunto their signs manual as manifest pledges of their good faith ? " And his words, though he was an unlearned man, were approved by all, both Bishops and others, that heard them. But now to our purpose again. When the said Bishop [of

Norwich] had finished his eloquent sermon, he announced to the exultant crowd that whosoever should assemble to venerate the most holy blood here kept should freely earn, by the gratuitous grant of all prelates who had come hither, an indulgence of one year and 116 days of penance enjoined upon them. And, seeing that some of those present yet hesitated and grunted [*obgrunnirent*]—disputing how our Lord, who on the third day after His passion rose in all fulness and integrity, could have left blood upon this earth—this question was then exactly determined by the Bishop of Lincoln [Grosseteste], as is written below in my Book of Additions, even as I, who write this page, heard it myself and recorded most plainly word for word, and have marked with this sign[1]. And, while this great and magnificent solemnity proceeded in the Abbey Church, the Lord King sat gloriously on his royal throne, clad in a golden garment of the most precious brocade of Bagdad, and with a slight crown of gold (such as we call *garlanda*) on his head. Then he let summon his own half-brother, with many of his fellows that there bare him company, waiting to be knighted with all due pomp and ceremony; which brother, with others of his fellows, the Lord King girt with his knightly belt amid great rejoicing. And while the King sat on his royal throne aforesaid, seeing me who write this, he called me and bade me sit down on the step which rose between the floor and his throne, saying "Hast thou seen all these things, and hast thou firmly impressed them in thy heart?" Whereunto I made answer "Yea, my lord; for it is worthy to be remembered, since this is truly a glorious day here spent." Then the King added this also "In truth I am assured this day that the Lord hath deigned to work a most glorious miracle, as a foretaste of His more plenteous lovingkindness and of the wonders that will be wrought in future by His grace. This befel at early dawn, and therein do I rejoice. I beseech thee therefore—and, in beseeching thee, I command to boot—to show forth all these things fully and expressly in a clear hand,

---

[1] Drawing of chalice covered with corporal; the document comes on p. 138 of the *Additamenta*, but will scarcely add to Grosseteste's reputation as a philosopher.

that they may be indelibly recorded in thy book, and that the memory thereof may never be lost to posterity, even to the remotest ages." Moreover he invited me, after these words, to dine, and three of my companions with me. And that same day he commanded that all monks who had come to the ceremony should be feasted at his own expense, in the refectory with the monks of Westminster; and other guests also were there entertained, and most splendidly and ceremoniously were they feasted.

(*b*) *Ibid.* (pp. 617–18).

This same year [1258] the Lord King came to St Albans... and he tarried there a whole week. And, seeing that I who write this was continually with the King, at table, in his court, and in his bedchamber, he directed my pen with great diligence and friendship.... At the same time, on the 9th day of March, there came to St Albans certain masters of Oxenford, about nine Masters of Arts, who complained bitterly before the King, in St Oswin's chapel, against the Bishop of Lincoln, who was attempting to restrict the liberties of the scholars in violation of the ancient and approved statutes of the University. And a day was appointed for answering them, at the coming Great Parliament, in order that the pleas might be heard on either side and that peace might be made. So, that day, the Brother who writeth these words spake thus unto the Lord King: "My Lord, for God's sake have a care of the Church, which is now tottering to her fall. For the University of Paris, nurse and mistress of so many holy prelates, is now sore troubled; and if like troubles fall at the same time upon the University of Oxford, which is the second school of the Church, then there will be great cause to fear the total ruin of the Church." "Nay, God forbid!" said the King, "and specially in mine own time."

(*c*) *Ibid.* (p. 44). Letter of Innocent IV. to the Abbot of St Albans.

Since it hath been represented to us by our beloved son the abbot of St Benet of Holm, in the diocese of Trondhjem, that the said abbey hath been deformed by the negligence of his predecessors in those things that pertain to the monastic

Order, and that none can be found in those parts who is well
acquainted with the statutes and observances of that Order,
we therefore, at the instance of the said Abbot, earnestly
beseech and exhort your Discretion, and command you by
these our Apostolic letters, to send our beloved son Brother
Matthew [Paris], your monk, who is reported to be of approved life and experienced in Religion, to that abbey aforesaid, in order that he may inform and instruct the said Abbot
and his monks in the regular discipline and statutes which
appertain unto the said Order.   And let this be done with all
convenient haste, for the reverence of God and of our Apostolic
See and of our own person.   Given at Lyons [A. D. 1248].

(*d*) *Ibid.* (p. 35).

This year [1248]..., in Norway, the devastating flames
raged so horribly in the three chief cities as to strike wonder and
amazement into all men's hearts.   One of these cities, Bergen,
was reduced to ashes, save only four monasteries, and the
King's palace, chapel and chambers.   For in that city eleven
parish churches were consumed, with certain episcopal mansions ; and this flame of vengeance for men's sins flew even
unto the King's castle in that city, trailing after it a sheet of
flame like a devouring dragon of the length of five bowshots.
Wherefore the citizens were most certainly assured that this
betokened the severity of God's vengeance ; for the greater part
of the castle, which was built of huge flinty stones, was reduced
to ashes.   Moreover, on the morrow, God sent His fearful and
horrible thunderbolts down upon the site of that city ; so that
a sudden bolt struck a certain great vessel from England which
had come to her moorings that night, blasting one man of her
crew and either wounding or bruising horribly all the rest ; her
mast was shattered into the smallest splinters and cast into the
sea ; and all the ships in that haven, two hundred or more, were
shaken.   I who write this had come in that stricken ship ; but
at that very hour I was singing mass in a church by the shore,
intoning, as it were, my song of sea-triumph, as one who would
render thanks to God after the perils of the deep.   When the
Lord King [of Norway] had heard this, for my sake who had

been in that ship he bade that a better and greater mast should be given to that ship.

(*e*) Thos. Walsingham, *Gesta Abbatum*, R.S. I. 395.

In his time [Abbot John II., 1235–60] flourished and died Dom Matthew Paris, monk of St Albans, a man of eloquence and renown, fulfilled of innumerable virtues, a magnificent historiographer and chronographer, a most excellent composer in the Latin tongue, and one who kept that saying in his heart: "idleness is the enemy of the soul." This man's fame was so spread abroad that it had recommended him even to men of remote parts who had never seen his face. He collected from ancient times even unto the end of his own life, and wrote down fully in his books, the deeds of great men in Church and State, with sundry and marvellous chances and events, whereby he bequeathed to posterity a marvellous knowledge of the past. Moreover he was so subtle a workman in gold and silver and other metals, in carving and in painting, that he is believed to have left no equal in this world of the West. Let us therefore take him for our pattern, and labour without ceasing at wholesome works, that we may share with him in the rewards of heaven.

11   POET AND PUBLIC

Rutebeuf was born, probably at Paris, in the first half of the 13th century: his earliest contemporary allusion refers to about the year 1255, and his latest to 1285. I have here strung together a series of his autobiographical allusions, from poems which will be found in vol. I. of Jubinal's edition (1839).

To avoid interruption, the passages are here presented continuously. And if, in this case, we are travelling beyond Great Britain, it is because a minstrel's life was essentially the same in all countries, and Rutebeuf has told fairly succinctly the very same story which we can infer from dozens of scattered notices in our own literature. Rutebeuf's confessions should be compared with those of François Villon, as collected (e.g.) in R. L. Stevenson's essay on that poet.

(p. 291.) *Lay of Charlot the Jew.* It is a common story everywhere (as all men and women know) that, when a man makes a marriage or a feast, whereunto well-nurtured folk come, the minstrels soon get wind of this ; for they ask for nothing better. Then they flock to his house, up hill and down dale, some on foot and others on horseback. Cousin William[1] made some such marriage feast for the common behoof, whereat were many fair folk, which seemed both fair and noble. Well they ate and well they drank; how many we were, I myself cannot tell, though I was among them. Right joyous was the cheer they made; it is long since I saw such noble fare or such delights; so help me God! all the fair folk are departing; good gentility is gone, and all men think only of their own. So to this spousal came the minstrels in full riding-boots; none was slow of speech: "give us" (quoth they) "either patronage or money, as is right and reason, that each may go content to his home."

(pp. 1–3.) *Lay of the Poverty of Rutebeuf.* I know not where to begin, so copious is my matter, in speaking of my poverty : for God's sake I pray you, frank king of France [Louis IX.], give me some goods! Great king, I lack food and have lacked it long; no man offers, no man gives to me. I cough with cold, I gape with hunger, whereby I am consumed and mal-treated; mattress I lack, bed I lack; from Paris to Senlis there is none so poor as I. Sire, I know not whither to turn; my ribs know well the taste of horse-litter; straw-bed is no bed, and on mine lieth naught but straw.

(pp. 25–27.) *The Lay of Winter Misery.* Poor sense hath God the king of glory given me, and poor memory, and poverty of this world's goods. Chill are my loins when the east-wind blows; it comes and blows me through and through. God so tempers His seasons to me that black flies bite me in summer, and white flies in winter. I am like the wild osier, or like the bird on the bough; in summer I sing, and in winter I weep and make lament; like the tender bough I cast my leaves at the first touch of frost. The dice that we buy at the dicemaker's have spoiled me of all my garments; dice are my death; they watch and spy on me, they assail and defeat me; that is my bane.

(pp. 6–17.) *The Marriage of Rutebeuf* and *The Complaint*

---

[1] This William, whom Rutebeuf calls satirically cousin, was pantler (pane-tarius) to the Count of Poitiers, brother of St Louis; we may remember that Chaucer's wife was probably *panetaria* to the Duchess of Lancaster.

of Rutebeuf. For myself, what boots it to disquiet myself? Men say "the fool that fooleth not loseth his seasonable time"; was it without reason that I took a wife? Now have I neither cot nor house; and, worst of all, to the greater comfort of all who hate me to the death, I have taken to me such a wife as no man else can love or prize; she was poor and marred when I took her; and now am I the married man no less poor and marred than she. Gentle she is not, nor fair; she hath fifty years in her dish; lank and lean, I fear no rival in her love; since the day when God was born of Mary in the manger, never was such a wedding as this of mine! By the Lord who hath all things, little had I when I took my wife, and she still less. I can do no handiwork; no man will ever know mine abode, so poor it is; never shall my door stand open, for my house is too bare and poverty-stricken and foul; often I have neither bread in the hutch nor paste in the kneading-trough. Blame me not, therefore, if I have no haste to go home, for there I find no good cheer; no creature holds my coming dear if I bring naught with me; that is the chief of all my woes, that I dare not to knock empty-handed at mine own door! Know ye how I bear myself? My feast is in the hope of what the morrow may bring.

The foster-mother cries on me daily for money; she distrains and pinches me for the child's food, else will she send him home to bray on his own hearth; may the Lord God who brought him into the world give him nourishment and send his sustenance, and may He grant me also some relief, that my poverty may press me less, and that I may help my child better and assure him better sustenance than now! All hath been pledged that pledge I could, and all is taken from my house; for I have lain three months without sight of a friend. Evil cometh never alone; all that was to befal me hath now befallen. Where are now those friends whom I had held so dear and loved so well? Methinks they are too few and far between; ill were they sown from the first, and they have come to nought.

12   THE FIGHT FOR SCIENCE

By far the best brief biographical sketch of Roger Bacon is Prof. A. G. Little's in *Roger Bacon* (commemoration volume, Oxford, 1914). He was born about 1214, and was already a famous lecturer at Oxford and Paris before he joined the Franciscans. The story of his earlier imprisonment rests upon an error; from about 1256–66 he was incapacitated not by prison, but by a breakdown of health. On June 22, 1266, Pope Clement IV., who as a cardinal had already become interested in Bacon's writings, sent him a command for a copy of these, "written in a fair hand [*de bona littera*], with all possible expedition...and as secretly as possible...notwithstanding any contrary command of your Superior or any constitution of your Order[1]." Bacon found none of his past works worthy of sending to the Pope, but set to work at once upon a series of new works which should embody his philosophical views. "His first project," writes Prof. Little, "was an elaborate one, including a systematic and scientific treatment of the various branches of knowledge; he worked at this, writing parts of the Communia Naturalium and Communia Mathematicae, for some months ('till after Epiphany,' i.e. January 6, 1267), but found it impossible. He then started again on a more modest scale and wrote in the next twelve months the preliminary treatise known as the Opus Majus, which was supplemented by the Opus Minus, and, subsequently, by the Opus Tertium. The Opus Minus and the Opus Tertium were both of them introductions to and summaries of the Opus Majus with some additions (chiefly on the dangerous subjects of alchemy and astrology) and further elucidation of special points."

In 1277 the Bishop of Paris issued, at the bidding of Gregory X., a decree condemning 219 current "errors," some of which had been held even by St Thomas Aquinas; on the whole, the decree was an attack upon the liberal thought of the time. In that same year the heads of the Franciscans and Dominicans concerted measures of censorship to allay certain wordy disputes between the members of the two Orders. We know that Bacon's works would have come naturally under both these bans; it is therefore natural that he should have been struck. The Minister General committed him to prison—which would include deprivation of books and writing materials—and his doctrines were condemned. A new Minister was elected in 1289; it is possible that Bacon was released in 1290; but it is only too probable that he remained there till 1292, when he worked at his unfinished *Compendium Studii Theologiae*. He probably died in this year. My extracts are translated from

---

[1] Constitutions of Franciscan Chapter General, 1260, drawn up under the presidency of St Bonaventura : "*item*, we decree that henceforth no new writing be published outside the Order, unless it have first been diligently examined by the General or Provincial Minister and the Delegates in General Chapter; and whosoever shall do contrary to this decree, let him fast three days on nothing but bread and water, and let that writing be taken from him."

Opera Inedita, ed. Brewer, R. S. 1859. Other passages emphasizing the difficulties of a scholar in the thirteenth century are translated in my *Medieval Garner*, pp. 338 ff.

(p. 3.) To the most holy father and lord Pope Clement, supreme Pontiff by the grace of God, your servant writeth as follows, kissing in spirit the blessed feet of your Holiness.

(p. 7.) I recall how for ten years I have now been an exile from that fame which I formerly won in the schools; and I recognize mine own littleness, my manifold ignorance, my stammering speech and scratching pen. With all this I wonder at your Wisdom, which now deigneth to demand works of philosophy from me who am now unheard of all men, even as a man already buried and eaten up by oblivion.... The head of the Church hath made request of the unworthy sole of the Church's foot; the Vicar of Christ and governor of the whole world deigneth to solicit me, who am scarce to be reckoned among the atoms of the universe!... My gratitude is not small; nay, it behoves me to be the most grateful of all men, since your Holiness hath requested of me that very thing which I have yearned for with burning desire, which I have toiled for with bitter sweat, which I have pushed forward at great expense of money. Nevertheless the foundations are not yet laid—the very stones and timber—until I shall have diligently investigated the mastery of sciences and languages, and other things requisite for building the edifice of wisdom[1]. For the marvels of arts and sciences are subject to so many difficulties (and especially in these times of ours, when we are waiting for the days of Antichrist and his followers, on whose behalf the Devil is full of fury, that he may in divers manners confound the study of wisdom, as I shall make plain in later pages of my book) that remedy will never be applied unless through the prudence of the Pope. But, where so great an authority as his stands over us, there can be no difficulty; for his power penetrates the heavens, looses the bonds of purgatory, treads hell under foot, and holds the whole world in subjection.

(p. 13 ff.) But this delay was necessary, and against mine

[1] It seems necessary here to read *donec* for Brewer's *hoc est*, which leaves the sentence ungrammatical.

own will, who grieved then and grieve still thereat. For, when you last wrote, the things which you believed me to have written had not yet been composed. In truth, before I became a friar, I composed no philosophical book; nor, since I came into this Order, have I ever been asked to do so by those who are set in authority over me. Nay, a grievous Constitution hath even been made to the contrary, under pain of loss of our book and of several days' fasting on bread and water, if any writing done in a friary be communicated to others. But I could not get it copied in a fair hand [*littera bona*] save by scribes who are not friars; and such scribes would then make copies for themselves or for other folk, whether I would or not, even as things are so frequently published at Paris through the copyists' frauds. Certainly, if I had been able to communicate my writings freely, I would have composed many books for my brother who is a student, and for others of my friends. But when I saw no hope of publication I neglected to write. Wherefore, when I offered myself to your Highness as ready, you must know that this meant for future writing of books not yet written; therefore Raymond de Laon, your clerk, was altogether deceived when he recommended me to you. For although I had sometimes hurriedly written a few chapters on divers matters, at the instance of my friends, here is no notable writing worthy to be offered to your Wisdom; for they are things of which even I take no account, wherein is nothing continuous or complete. Nevertheless the greatness and authority of your Reverence kept me long idle, since I knew not at first what I could offer worthy of your attention. Then, considering that nothing should be presented to your Highness but such as was magnificent, to your Blessedness nothing but what was excellent, to your Wisdom nothing save of the fairest, it is no wonder that I delayed in setting to work....For the treatise on Optics alone, which I here send you, could not be written by any other in less than a year..., nay, nor in ten. For, howsoever well he knew the matter, he would need to make many experiments of these things, and to practise an almost infinite number of described figures, which demand much time, and to write it all out five or six times until he had one tried and trustworthy book. I say nothing here of other and greater subjects, until a more convenient time.

To this add other and far more grievous causes of delay, which oftentimes drove me almost to despair. Truly, an hundred times I thought of breaking off my work; and, had it not been for the reverence due to the Vicar of Christ, and the profit of mankind which could be procured through him alone, I would not have gone through with these impediments in this business—nay, not for all the churchmen in the world, howsoever they might have besought me and insisted.

The first impediment came through those who are set over me. Since you wrote nothing to them in my excuse, and since I could not nor should not reveal unto them your secret, they lay hard upon me, with unspeakable violence, that I, like the rest, should obey their will; which I could not do, bound as I was by your command to proceed with your work, notwithstanding any contrary command of my prelates. Know therefore that, not being excused by you, I was involved in more and more grievous hindrances than I can tell; yet perchance I may explain in another place certain particulars of these hindrances, writing with mine own hand for the weightiness of the secret which I have to tell.

Another kind of hindrance, which alone was enough to ruin the whole project, was my lack of money. For I had to spend more than sixty pounds *parisis* in this matter; whereof I will give full and sufficient account in its own place[1]. I marvel not that you had no thought of these expenses, seeing that you, sitting aloft over the whole world, must needs think of so many weighty affairs that no man can measure the cogitations of your heart. But the mediators who bore the letters were careless, in that they said naught of the expenses; and they themselves would not lay out a single penny, albeit I said to them that I would keep an exact account, and that each should have his own restored unto him. I myself, as you know, neither have money nor can have money; nor, by consequence, can I borrow, since I have no means of repaying.

---

[1] i.e. £20 sterling : the equivalent of £300 to £400 in our own day.

I sent therefore to my rich brother in our own country; but he, having taken the king's part [in the Barons' wars], was driven from his home together with my mother and brethren and the whole family; nay, he was oftentimes taken by the enemy and put to ransom. Wherefore he was too impoverished and ruined to succour me, nor have I had any answer from him even unto this present day.

Considering therefore your Reverence's command, I solicited many great folk—some of whom you know well by face, but not their inward mind—saying that I had to transact a certain business for you in France (which business I unfolded not) which could not be performed without great expense. But no tongue can tell how many of these men called me shameless, how many repelled me, how many lured me with false hopes, and what confusion I suffered in mine own person. Nay, not even my friends would believe me, seeing that I was unable to unfold this business to them; wherefore this way was debarred unto me. At last, therefore, in greater anguish than I can express, I compelled succour, as it were, from poor men who were my familiar friends, constraining them to spend all their substance, and to sell much and set the rest to pledge, even oftentimes at usury; and I promised them that I would render you a full and faithful account of the expense, and pledged my faith to procure full payment on your part. Yet these folk were so poor that I oftentimes broke off this work, and despaired, and ceased to labour further; wherefore, had I not known that you had forgotten to take these expenses into account, for all the world I would never have proceeded; rather would I have given mine own body to prison. For all these causes therefore hath this delay come to pass, for which I am vehemently grieved; for not only is your Clemency now sick with hope deferred, but I also have sustained grievous loss, as you may well think from what I have already said, and as shall be more certainly and clearly set forth below.

(p. 58.) My fourth reason [for thus insisting] is on my own account; for I have laboured in many ways at science from my youth up, and at languages, and at all the aforesaid branches of learning; whereby I have collected much profitable learning and have also ordered other folk in that way. For I have sought the friendship of all wise men in this western world, and have caused young men to be instructed in tongues and figures and numbers and tables and instruments and many necessary things. And I have examined all things that are requisite hereunto, and know now how we must proceed, and by what means, and in the face of what hindrances; but how to proceed I know not, for lack of the aforesaid moneys.

Yet, if any man would expend as much as I myself have already expended in my life, certainly a great part of the work might be completed. For during those twenty years wherein I laboured especially in the study of wisdom, neglecting the opinions of the common sort, I expended more than £2000 sterling[1] on these things—on secret books, and various experiments, and languages and instruments and tables and such like matters; and also in seeking the friendship of wise men and in teaching others who should help me in languages, in figures, in numbers, in tables, in instruments, and in many other things. Nor is it my intention to bestir your Clemency that the multitude or their leaders may be corrected by violence, nor that I should contend with them; but I only insist upon these things by reason of the aforesaid four causes. And, if it pleased your Wisdom that [my writings] should be published, copies would be given first of all to such as are wise, and then little by little to all who wish, that no man may be coerced. And yet I know that all would wish for copies; but all are not worthy of all sciences.

(p. 60.) Nevertheless, since your Wisdom hath so long been busied in Church affairs and in various cares for the State, and since no man on the throne of the Apostles can find much time for studies, and these things whereof I write are of great difficulty and foreign to the sense of many men—therefore I was more solicitous to find a fit mediator for presentation to your Reverence, than for the words of my own writings....Wherefore I set my thoughts on a certain poor youth whom, some five or six years ago, I caused to be instructed in languages

---

[1] i.e. from £30,000 to £40,000 in modern money.

and mathematics and optics, wherein is the whole difficulty of the things which I now send. Moreover, I taught him freely by word of mouth, after receiving your command, since I felt that I could find none other at present who knew my mind so well. Wherefore I thought to send him to you, as a ready mediator if your Wisdom should deign to make use of him; and, if not, he could none the less bear my writings to your Majesty....He came to me in poverty, and a mere boy; I caused him to be nourished and taught for the love of God, especially since I had found no other youth so able both for study and for [practical] life. And he hath profited so far that he might earn all that he needs in great abundance, and better than any other scholar of Paris, although his age be only twenty years or twenty-one at most.

(p. 63.) Nor is it only for that cause that I send this messenger; but also that you may see how nothing is difficult to a man of diligence and confidence, though a negligent or craven-spirited scholar shutteth himself from all that is good. For this youth came to me at the age of fifteen, and in poverty, having neither livelihood nor sufficient masters nor patron to take pity on his destitution; nor did he learn for as long as a single year, since he must needs work as servant to those who gave him the necessities of life; nor in his studies did he find for two whole years any man who would teach him a single word; notwithstanding all which impediment, he now knoweth many great matters by reason of his own confidence and diligence....Wherefore I am fully persuaded that there is no difficulty of youth or of learning which may not be surmounted, if men have the will to learn, and confidence, and diligence. Nor is there any such difficulty in languages or sciences, but only in the teachers themselves, who will not or cannot teach. For, from our youth up, we find no profitable teachers; and therefore we languish our whole lives long, and know very little in the end. But, if we had capable teachers, I doubt not that we should learn more in one year than we now learn in twenty—all which I am ready to prove in practice; and I will stake my head on its success.

I have laboured much in sciences and languages. For forty years have I now laboured since first I learned the alphabet; and I was always studious; and for all but two years of those forty I have been always at the university [*in studio*]; and I have spent much money, as others commonly spend much. Yet I am assured that within a quarter of a year, or half a year at most, I would teach with mine own mouth all that I know to a resolved and confident man; provided only that I had first written a compendious manual thereof. Yet it is well known that no man hath laboured in so many languages and sciences as I, nor hath laboured so hard therein; for, before I became a friar, men marvelled that I could live through such excessive labour; yet afterwards I have been as studious as before; not indeed that I have laboured so hard, for it was no longer necessary, by reason of mine exercise in wisdom.

13   A MONASTIC POET

Robert Mannyng of Brunne (i.e. Bourne) took the cowl at the monastery of Sempringham in 1288, and wrote his *Handlyng Synne* in 1303. The following autobiographical passage illustrates also the author's limitations as a French scholar, in his translation of a simple abstract word like *manuel*. His *Handlyng Synne* is, however, an extremely interesting translation from the almost contemporary *Manuel des Pechiez* of William of Wadington : my references here and elsewhere are to Furnivall's edition, E.E.T.S., 1901–3.   P. 2, l. 43.

For lewdë men y undyrtoke
On englyssh tunge to make thys boke.
For many ben of swyche manere,
That talys and rymys wyl blethly here ;
Yn gamys, and fests, and at the ale,
Love men to lestene trotëvale[1] :
That may falle ofte to vylanye,
To dedly synne, or other folye ;
For swyche men have y made this ryme
That they may weyl dyspende here tyme,
And there-yn sumwhat for to here,
To leve al swychë foul manere.

---
[1] nonsense.

To alle crystyn men undir sunne,
And to godë men of Brunne,
And speciäli, alle be name,
The felaushepe of Symprynghame,
Roberd of Brunnë greteth yow
In all godenesse that may to prow.

Of Brunnëwake yn Kestevene,
Syxe myle be-syde Symprynghame evene,
Y dwelled yn the pryorye
Fyftenë yere yn cumpanye,
In the tyme of gode dane[1] Ione
Of Camelton, that now ys gone:
In hys tyme was y there ten yeres,
And knewe and herd of hys maneres;
Sythyn with dane Ione of Clyntone,
Fyve winter wyth hym gan y wone;
Dane Felyp was maystér that tyme
That y began thys englyssh ryme.
The yeres of grace fyl than to be
A thousynd and three hundred and thre.
In that tymë turnede y thys
On englyssh tunge out of frankys,
Of a boke as y fonde ynne;
Men clepyn the bokë "handlyng synne."

In frenshë ther a clerk hyt sees,
He clepyth hyt "manuel de pecches."
"Manuell" ys "handlying with honde";
"Pecches" ys "synne," y undyrstonde.
These twey wurdys that beyn otwynne[2],
Do hem togedyr, ys "handlyng synne."

14   MEDIEVAL GRUB-STREET

The theory of the multiple authorship of *Piers Plowman*, propounded by Prof. Manly in the second volume of the *Cambridge History of English Literature*, has not yet been supported by the exact kind of proofs there promised; and the majority of scholars probably follow M. Jusserand in maintaining, until further evidence, the single authorship.

---

[1] *dominus*, the courtesy-title of a monk.   [2] apart.

For the purpose of this present book, the question is comparatively irrelevant. As illustrations from the life of writers who lived from hand to mouth in Chaucer's London, the following extracts are almost equally enlightening whether the lifelike touches be strictly autobiographical or colourable fictions; and, again, they tell the same social tale whether they refer to one man or to a group of like-minded writers. The references are to Skeat's edition, Oxford 1886.

(*a*) **The School of Life** (C, VI. I, p. 118).

Thus ich a-waked, God wot, whanne ich wonede[1] on Corne-
hulle,
Kytte and ich in a cote, clothed as a lollere,
And lytel y-lete by[2], leyve[3] me for sothe,
Among lollares of London and lewede[4] heremytes;
For ich made of[5] tho men as reson me tauhte.
For as ich cam by Conscience, with Reson ich mette
In an hote hervest, whenne ich hadde myn hele[6],
And lymes to labore with, and lovede wel fare,
And no dede to do bote drynke and to slepe.
In hele and in unite on me aposede[7];
Romynge in remembraunce thus Reson me aratede[8].
"Canstow serven," he seide, "other[9] syngen in a churche,
Other coke[10] for my cokers, other[9] to the cart picche,
Mowe other mowen[11], other make bond to sheves,
Repe other be a repereyve[12] and a-ryse erliche,
Other have an horne and be haywarde[13] and liggen oute
a-nyghtes,
And kepe my corn in my croft fro pykers and theeves?
Other shappe[14] shon other clothes, other shep other kyn kepe,
Heggen[15] other harwen[16], other swyn other gees dryve,
Other eny other kyns[17] craft that to the comune nedeth,
Hem that bedreden be by-lyve to fynde[18]?"
"Certes," ich seyde, "and so me God helpe,
Ich am to waik to worche[19] with sykel other with sythe,

---

[1] lived.   [2] esteemed.   [3] believe.   [4] ignorant.
[5] composed verses on (*or* thought of).   [6] health.
[7] Being in health of body and in unity of mind, a man began to discuss with me.
[8] reproved.   [9] or.   [10] make haycocks.   [11] stack hay.   [12] foreman reaper.
[13] guardian of hayfield.   [14] shape.   [15] hedge.   [16] harvest.   [17] kind of.
[18] In order to find a livelihood for the bedridden.   [19] work.

And to long, leyf me, lowe for to stoupe,
To worchen as a workeman eny whyle to dure."
"Thenne havest thow to lyve by," quath Reson, "other
    lynage[1] riche
That fynden the thy fode[2]? for an ydel man thow semest,
A spendour that spende mot[3], other a spille-tyme,
Other beggest thy by-lyve aboute at menne hacches[4],
Other faitest[5] up-on Frydays other feste-dayes in churches,
The whiche is lollarene lyf that lytel ys preysed,
Ther ryghtfulnesse rewardeth ryght as men deserveth.
Other thow art broke, so may be, in body other in membre,
Other ymaymed throw som myshap wherby thow myght be
    excused?"
"Whanne ich yong was," quath ich, "meny yer hennes[6],
My fader and my frendes founden me to scole,
Tyl ich wiste wyterliche[7] what holy wryt menede[8],
And what is best for the body, as the Bok telleth,
And sykerest[9] for the soule; by so[10] ich wolle continue.
And yut fond ich nevere, in faith, sytthen my frendes
    deyden[11],
Lyf that me lyked, bote in thes longe clothes.
Yf ich by laboure sholde lyve and lyflode[12] deserven,
That labour that ich lerned best, ther-with lyve ich sholde.
And ich lyve in Londone and on Londone bothe,
The lomes[13] that ich laboure with and lyflode deserve
Ys *pater-noster* and my prymer[14], *placebo* and *dirige*,
And my sauter som tyme and my sevene psalmes[15].
Thus ich synge for hure[16] soules of such as me helpen,
And tho that fynden me my fode vouchen saf, ich trowe,
To be welcome whanne ich come other-whyle in a monthe,
Now with hym and now with hure[17]; and thus-gate[18] ich begge
With-oute bagge other botel bote my wombe one[19].

---

[1] lineage.   [2] food.   [3] must.   [4] gates.   [5] idlest.   [6] years hence.
[7] certainly.   [8] meant.   [9] safest.   [10] provided that.
[11] died.   [12] livelihood.   [13] tools.   [14] book of religious instruction.
[15] i.e. he earned his living by singing memorial services for the dead, which, as
a clerk in minor orders, he was competent to do. *Dirige* is the origin of our
dirge.
[16] their.   [17] her.   [18] in this way.   [19] but my belly alone.

And al-so more-over me thynketh, syre Reson,
Men sholde constreyne no clerke to knavene[1] werkes ;...
For-thy[2] rebuke me ryght nouht, Reson, ich yow praye ;
For in my conscience ich knowe that Crist wolde that ich
   wrouhte.
Preyers of a parfyt man, and penaunce discret,
Ys the leveste labour that oure Lord pleseth."...
Quath Conscience, "by Crist! ich can nat see this lyeth[3] ;
Ac[4] it semeth nouht parfytnesse in cytees for to begge,
Bote[5] he be obediencer[6] to pryour other to mynstre."
"That ys soth," ich seide ; "and so ich by-knowe[7],
That ich have tynt[8] tyme, and tyme mysspended ;
And yut, ich hope, as he that ofte haveth chaffared[9],
That ay hath lost and lost, and atte laste hym happed[10]
He bouhte suche a bargayn he was the bet[11] evere,
And sette hus lost at a lef[12] at the laste ende,
Suche a wynnynge hym warth[13] thorw wordes of hus grace ;
   Simile est regnum celorum thesauro abscondito in agro,
                                                  et cetera:
   Mulier que invenerit dragmam unam, et cetera;[14]
So hope ich to have of hym that is al-myghty
A gobet[15] of hus grace, and bygynne a tyme,
That alle tymes of my tyme to profit shal turne."
"Ich rede the," quath Reson tho, "rape[16] the to by-gynne
The lyf that ys lowable[17] and leel[18] to the soule"—
"Ye[19]! and continue" ; quath Conscience ; and to the kirke
   ich wente.
And to the kirke gan ich go, God to honourie,
By-for the crois on my knees knocked ich my brest,
Sykynge[20] for my synnes, seggynge[21] my *pater-noster,*
Wepyng and wailinge, tyl ich was a slepe.

[1] servile.   [2] therefore.
[3] Skeat would translate "I cannot see that this is to the point"; but it
seems simpler to understand "that this is false."
[4] but.   [5] unless.   [6] officer in a monastery.   [7] confess.   [8] lost.
[9] chaffered.   [10] it befel him that.   [11] better.   [12] cared not a leaf for his loss.
[13] such a gain he got.
[14] Parables of the Hid Treasure and the Lost Piece of Silver.
[15] fragment.   [16] haste.
[17] praiseworthy.   [18] leal.   [19] yea.   [20] sighing.   [21] saying.

(b) "**Who ne'er his bread with tears hath ate**"
(B, X. 147, p. 296).

"For thi mekenesse, man," quod she, "and for thi mylde
  speche,
I shal kenne[1] the to my cosyn that Clergye is hoten[2].
He hath wedded a wyf with-inne this syx monethes,
Is sybbe[3] to the sevene artz[4], Scripture is hir name.
Thei two, as I hope after my techyng,
Shullen wissen[5] the to Do-Wel[6], I dar it undertake."

Thanne was I also fayne as foule of faire morwe[7],
And gladder than the gleman that golde hath to yifte[8],
And axed hir the heighe weye where that Clergye dwelte;
"And telle me some token," quod I, "for tyme is that I
  wende."

"Axe the heighe waye," quod she, "hennes to Suffre-
Bothe-Wel-and-Wo, yif that thow wolt lerne,
And ryde forth by Ricchesse, ac[9] rest thow naught therinne;
For, if thow couplest[10] the ther-with, to Clergye comestow
  nevere.
And also the likerouse launde that Lecchery hatte[11],
Leve hym on thi lefte halve a large myle or more,
Tyl thow come to a courte, Kepe-wel-thi-Tonge-
Fro-Lesynges[12]-and-lither[13]-Speche-and-likerouse-Drynkes.

Thanne shaltow se Sobrete and Symplete-of-Speche,
That eche wighte be in wille his witte the to shewe,
And thus shaltow come to Clergye, that can many thinges."

(c) **The School of Nature** (B, XI. 312, p. 358).

And slepynge I seigh[14] al this; and sithen[15] cam Kynde,
And nempned[16] me by my name, and bade me nymen[17] hede,
And thorw the wondres of this worlde wytte for to take.

---

[1] introduce. [2] called. [3] kin.
[4] The Seven Arts of the University Curriculum : Grammar, Logic, Rhetoric,
Music, Arithmetic, Geometry and Astronomy.
[5] show. [6] Do-Well; the personification of Good Works.
[7] as glad as a bird is of a fair morn. [8] gift. [9] but.
[10] dost associate. [11] hight. [12] lying. [13] evil.
[14] saw. [15] then. [16] named. [17] take.

And on a mountaigne that Mydelerd[1] hyghte, as me tho[2]
    thoughte,
I was fette[3] forth, by ensaumples to knowe
Thorugh eche a creature and kynde my Creatoure to lovye.
I seigh the sonne and the see, and the sonde after,
And where that bryddes and bestes by here makes[4] thei
    yeden[5],
Wylde wormes in wodes, and wonderful foules
With flekked fetheres and of fele[6] coloures.
Man and his make I myghte bothe byholde;
Poverte and plenty, bothe pees and werre,
Blisse and bale bothe I seigh at ones,
And how men token mede[7], and mercy refused....
Briddes I bihelde that in buskes made nestes;
Hadde nevere wye[8] witte to worche the leest.
I hadde wonder at whom and where the pye lerned
To legge the stykkes in whiche she leyeth and bredeth;
There nys wrighte[9], as I wene, shulde worche hir neste to
    paye;
If any masoun made a molde[10] ther-to, moche wonder it were.
And yet me merveilled more how many other briddes
Hudden and hileden[11] her egges ful derne[12]
In marcys and mores, for men sholde hem nought fynde,
And hudden here egges whan thei there-fro wente,
For fere of other foules and for wylde bestis....
Moche merveilled me what maister thei hadde,
And who taughte hem on trees to tymbre so heighe,
There noither buirn[13] ne beste may her briddes rechen.
    And sythen I loked upon the see, and so forth upon the
    sterres,
Many selcouthes[14] I seygh ben nought to seye nouthe.
I seigh floures in the fritthe[15] and her faire coloures,

---

  [1] The habitable earth, the *Middangeard* of Norse mythology and cosmography,
which postulated a fairly compact mass of habitable land surrounded on all sides
by sea: cf. Section XV., no. 18.
    [2] then.   [3] fetched.   [4] mates.   [5] went.   [6] many.
    [7] lucre.   [8] wight.   [9] carpenter.
  [10] The pattern from which the mason traces his work upon the stone.
  [11] covered.   [12] secretly.   [13] man.   [14] marvels.   [15] forest.

And how amonge the grene grasse grewe so many hewes,
And somme soure and some swete; selcouthe me thoughte;
Of her kynde and her coloure to carpe¹ it were to longe.

Ac that moste moeved me and my mode chaunged,
[Was,] that Resoun rewarded and reuled alle bestes,
Save man and his make; many tyme and ofte
No resoun hem folwed; and thanne I rebuked
Resoun, and righte til hym-selven I seyde,
"I have wonder of the," quod I, "that witty art holden,
Why thow ne suwest² man and his make that no mysfait
    hem folwe?"

And Resoun arated me and seyde, "recche the³ nevere,
Whi I suffre or nought suffre; thi-self hast nought to done;
Amende thow it, if thou myghte; for my own tyme is to
    abyde.
Suffraunce is a sovereygne vertue and a swift veniaunce⁴.
Who suffreth more than God?" quod he; "no gome⁵, as
    I leve!
He mighte amende in a minute-while al that mys-standeth
Ac he suffreth for somme mannes good, and so is owre
    bettre...."

Tho caughte I coloure anon, and comsed to ben aschamed,
And awaked ther-with; wo was me thanne
That I in meteles⁶ ne myghte more have yknowen.
And thanne seyde I to my-self and chidde that tyme;
"Now I wote what Do-Wel is," quod I, "by dere God, as
    me thinketh!"
And as I caste up myn eyghen, One loked on me, and axed
Of me, what thinge it were? "Ywisse, sire," I seide,
"To se moche and suffre more, certes," (quod I,) "is
    Do-Wel!"

(d) Crabbed Age (B, xx. 182, p. 588).

And Elde anone [came] after me, and over myne heed yede.
And made me balled bifore, and bare on the croune,
So harde he yede over myn hed, it wil be seen evre.

---

¹ talk.   ² followest.   ³ reck thou.   ⁴ vengeance.
⁵ person.   ⁶ dreams.

"Sire evel-ytaughte Elde," quod I, "unhende[1] go with the!
Sith whanne was the way over mennes hedes?
Haddestow be hende," quod I, "thou woldest have asked
    leve!"
"Ye! leve lordeyne!" quod he, and leyde on me with age,
And hitte me under the ere, unethe[2] may ich here;
He buffeted me aboute the mouthe and bette out my tethe,
And gyved me in goutes, I may noughte go at large.
And of the wo that I was in my wyf had reuthe,
And wisshed ful witterly[3] that I were in heuene....

    And, as I seet in this sorwe, I say how Kynde passed,
And Deth drowgh niegh me; for drede gan I quake,
And cried to Kynde out of care me brynge.
"Loo! Elde the hoore hath me biseye[4],
Awreke me, if yowre wille be, for I wolde ben hennes."
"Yif thow wilt ben ywroken, wende in-to Unite[5],
And holde the there evre tyl I sende for the,
And loke thow conne some crafte ar thow come thennes."
"Conseille me, Kynde," quod I, "what crafte is best to
    lerne?"
"Lerne to love," quod Kynde, "and leve of alle othre."
"How shal I come to catel[6], so to clothe me and to fede?"
"And thow love lelly," quod he, "lakke shal the nevere
Mete ne worldly wede whil thi lyf lasteth."
And there, by conseille of Kynde, I comsed[7] to rowme
Thorw Contricioun and Confessioun, tyl I cam to Unite.

(e) **Wander-Years** (B, VII. 138, p. 246).

The prest and Perkyn [in my dream] apposeden either
    other,
And I thorw here wordes a-woke, and waited aboute,
And seigh the sonne in the south sitte that tyme,
Metelees and monelees on Malverne hulles.

(B, VIII. I, p. 252.)

Thus y-robed in russet I romed aboute,
Al a somer sesoun, for to seke Do-Wel.

---

[1] evil.   [2] scarcely.   [3] certainly.   [4] visited.   [5] i.e. Holy Church.
[6] chattels.   [7] commenced.

(B, xv. 1, p. 436.)

Ac after my wakyng it was wonder longe,
Ar I couth kyndely[1] knowe what was Do-Wel.
And so my witte wex and wanyed, til I a fole were,
And somme lakked[2] my lyf, allowed[3] it fewe,
And leten[4] me for a lorel[5], and loth to reverencen
Lordes or ladyes or any lyf elles,
As persones in pellure[6] with pendauntes of sylver;
To serjeauntz ne to suche seyde [I] noughte ones,
"God loke yow, lordes!" ne louted faire;
That folke helden me for a fole; and in that folye I raved
Tyl Resoun hadde reuthe on me and rokked me aslepe.

(B, xviii. 1, p. 520.)

Wolleward and wete-shoed[7] went I forth after,
As a reccheles renke[8] that of no wo reccheth,
And yede forth like a lorel al my lyf-tyme,
Till I wex wery of the worlde, and wylned eft[9] to slepe,
And lened[10] me to a Lenten [tide], and longe tyme I slepte;
And of Crystes passioun and penaunce the people that of-
    raughte,
Reste me there, and rutte faste[11], tyl *Ramis-Palmarum*[12];
Of gerlis[13] and of *Gloria Laus* gretly me dremed,
And how *Osanna* by orgonye old folke songen....

(B, xviii. 424, p. 548.)

Tyl the daye dawed [in my dream] these damaiseles
    daunced,

---

[1] intimately.   [2] blamed.   [3] approved.   [4] considered.   [5] wastrel.
[6] furs.

[7] i.e. shirtless and barefooted, like a religious penitent; cf. W. Map, *De Nugis Curialium*, ed. Wright, p. 65.

[8] fellow.   [9] again.

[10] "And idled about till Lent-time" (Skeat); but it seems simpler to understand "and rested one Lenten-tide."

[11] "And rested there, and dreamt (*lit.* snored) hard of Christ's passion and penance, that reached to the people."

[12] Palm Sunday, in the service for which came the words "all glory, laud, and honour," and "hosannah!"

[13] children.

C.

That men rangen to the resurexioun ; and right with that
I waked,
And called Kitte my wyf and Kalote my doughter—
"Ariseth and reverenceth Goddes resurrexioun,
And crepeth to the crosse on knees[1], and kisseth it for a
juwel !
For Goddes blissed body it bar for owre bote,
And it afereth the fende ; for such is the myghte,
May no grysly gost glyde there it shadweth ! "

Thus I awaked & wrote what I had dremed,
And dighte me dereley and dede me to cherche,
To here holy the masse, and to be houseled after.
In myddes of the masse, tho men yede to offrynge,
I fel eftsones a-slepe.

15   A CHRONICLER'S DIFFICULTIES

Thomas Burton was nineteenth abbot of the Cistercian monastery of
Meaux in Yorkshire.   He resigned in 1399, and spent his retirement,
until overtaken by blindness, in compiling a history of the monastery
down to the year 1404.   His preface, which might be paralleled by many
similar documents from other houses, shows the difficulties which often
beset a medieval chronicler even in a rich abbey, through the carelessness
of his predecessors and contemporaries.   Burton's words go far to explain
the complaint of the Oxford Chancellor Thomas Gascoigne about 50 years
later : " In old days the kings had, in the monasteries they had founded,
excellent writers of the books of great doctors and of chronicles ; but now,
alas ! in our monasteries more books are spoiled and fail and perish
than those which are written afresh " (*Lib. Verit.*, ed. Rogers, p. 73 ; cf.
pp. 106, 112, 145).   It will be noted that Burton, like Ordericus Vitalis and
many other medieval monastic writers, arms himself beforehand against
the envy of his domestic critics.

Chronicon de Melsa, R.S., vol. I. p. 71.

When I see how the memory of the famous men who
have been abbots of this house of Meaux hath almost utterly
perished through the sloth of negligent men, I am grieved to
the heart and must grievously groan and sigh ; not only
because so many and excellent lights of the church (that

---

[1] For the ceremony of creeping to the cross, see D. Rock, *Church of our
Fathers*, ed. Hart and Frere, 1905, vol. IV. pp. 279, 287.

is, so many glorious deeds of our noble ancestors) are hidden and set under a bushel, but also because so many wise and learned men our predecessors, while they feared not to heap up the treasures of their own wisdom, took no heed to commit to public writing the praiseworthy acts of their fore-fathers. I therefore, desiring to put an end to this great negligence so far as in me lay (though I knew well mine own utter unworthiness for the task), have at length, after tedious scrutiny, collected together certain ancient scrolls and neglected parchments, some of which I found exposed to the rain [that dripped through the roof], and others set aside to be burned. In these documents I have abridged whatsoever was too lengthy, and explained more clearly whatsoever was obscure; I have perused the registers, and filled in their omissions from other registers or trustworthy documents; and these collections I have at last compiled into the following work. Therefore, if any reader find herein matters whereof he knew nothing, let him not suppose that I have composed them out of mine own head; let him rather be assured that there is nothing in this book but such as I have either found written in other men's books[1], or from divers written records, or from frequent and trustworthy hearsay, or from that which I myself have seen. Accordingly I beseech all who shall read this chronicle, such as it is, either to blush that they themselves do nothing to correct ancient neglect, or at least to be ashamed of carping at me who am attempting to amend [this neglect]. Moreover, if any be offended at my brevity of narration or at the rudeness of my style, there will be nothing to hinder any other from writing another such book after his own fashion; nay, he may do so the more easily, in proportion as the truth is more clearly narrated in this work.

[1] Most of his narratives of public events are in fact, after the usual fashion of monastic chroniclers, taken from other well-known writers.

16   AUTHOR AND PATRONS

The following, put into continuous form, is a cento of autobiographical fragments collected from Froissart's *Buisson de Jonece*, written in 1366 (Buchon, vol. III. pp. 500–1).

[My first patron was] the good lady who now rots in earth, but who was once queen of England ; Philippa was the noble lady called ; God have mercy upon her soul ! Truly am I bound to pray for her and to proclaim her largesse ; for it was she who made and created me. So also her daughter [in law], duchess of Lancaster, who died fair and young, at about the age of 22 years ; gay and glad she was, fresh and sportive ; sweet, simple and of humble semblance, the fair lady whom men called Blanche. The queen's daughter Isabel also, lady of Coucy, fervently must I pray for her soul, for I found her of great courtesy. From the earl of Hereford, again, I once had great comfort, and my lord of Mauny, and his son of Pembroke. "And the great lord Despenser, who spends so freely in largesse, what hath he done for thee ? " What ? much indeed ! for never was he weary of giving to me, wherever he might be ; no stones or staves, but horses and florins beyond number ; he is one among my masters whom I count for lord. Another who is much familiar with me is the good lord of Coucy, who hath oftentimes filled my hand with good florins of red gold. Beraut also, the count Dauphin of Auvergne, and his son the Duke of Bourbon. Charles, king of France, did me much good in my youth. To the duke and duchess of Brabant owe I great thanks ; for they have always been such to me that I have found them and their friends and their household liberal and courteous to me. The duke Albert hath always received me gladly, and also the lords of Blois, Louis and John and Guy, and the good lord of Beaumont and the lord of Moriaumé. There are others too who will come and become my masters, for they are young and the future is theirs ; of such may I make record when I write another book ; but these whom I now rehearse to you are those who have already given and done liberally to me.

I know not if I have named Amedeus count of Savoy :

but at Milan, in Lombardy, the good count gave me a cote-hardie worth twenty golden florins[1]. Reason have I to tell the praises of the noble king of Cyprus, at whose bidding Sir Tiercelet de la Barre gave me at Ferrara forty ducats, one after another. Alas! what, am I about to forget the king of Scotland? or the good earl of Douglas, with whom I have had great pastime? Warmly was I welcomed in the lands of the earls of Moray and the Marches, of Sutherland and of Fife; if I went back to those parts, welcome should I be again; but by that time I should be bald, feeble, impotent, downcast and melancholy; for my life passeth as a shadow.

17   A CHRONICLER'S METHODS

(Autobiographical fragments from Lord Berners's translation, Pynson's ed., 1523, 1525; reprint of 1812, vol. II. p. 43.) I have silently corrected a good many small errors, especially in proper names, for many of which the early printer was very likely responsible. This cento begins at p. 309 of the Globe Edition of Froissart. The earlier part of this autobiography has already been given in Section II. of the present book.

(A.D. 1388.)   And therfore I John Froyssart, who have taken on me to cronycle this present hystorie, at the request of the highe renomed prince sir Guy of Chatillon, erle of Blois, lorde of Avesnes, Beaumoot, Schoonhove, and of la Goude, my soverayne mayster and good lorde, consydring in myselfe howe there was no great dedes of armes likely towarde in the parties of Picardy or Flaunders, seyng the peace was made bytwene the duke and them of Gaunt, and it greatly anoyed me to be ydell, for I knewe well that after my deth this noble and highe hystorie shulde have his course, wherin dyvers noble men shulde have great pleasure and delyte; and as yet I thanke god I have understandyng and remembraunce of all thynges passed, and my wyt quicke and sharpe ynough to conceyve all thinges shewed unto me, touchyng my princypall mater, and my body as yet able to endure and to suffre payne: all thynges consydred, I thought I wolde nat lette to pursue my

---

[1] i.e. at the wedding of Lionel Duke of Clarence, at which Froissart (and possibly Chaucer) was present. A cote-hardie was a close jacket.

sayde first purpose; and to thentent to knowe the trouthe of
dedes done in farre countries, I founde occasion to go to the
highe and mighty prince Gaston, erle of Foix and of Bearn;
for I knewe well, that if I might have that grace to come into
his house, and to be there at leysar, I coude nat be so well
enformed to my purpose in none other place of the worlde;
for thyder resorted all maner of knightes and strange squyers,
for the great noblenes of the sayd erle.   And as I ymagined,
so I dyd, and shewed to my redoubted lorde the Erle of
Bloyes myne entent; and he gave me letters of recommenda-
cions to therle of Foiz.

   (p. 50 f.)   In the season that I enterprised to go se the erle
of Foiz, and to se the dyversities of the countreys, where as
I had never ben before, whan I departed fro Carcassone, I
lefte the waye to Tolouse.....................and than I came
to the good cytie of Pamyers, parteyning to the erle of
Foiz, and there I taryed, abydinge for some company goyng
into the countre of Bearne, where the erle was; and whan
I had taryed there a thre dayes in great pleasure, for the
cytie was delectable, standyng among the fayre vynes, and
envyroned with a fayre ryver large and clere, called Ariege,
and on a day it so fortuned, that thyder came a knyght of the
erle of Foiz, fro Avignon warde, called sir Espaenge de Lion,
a valyant and an experte man of armes, about the age of
l. yeres: and so I gate me into his company, and he was
greatly desyrous to here of the maters of Fraunce; and so we
were a six dayes in our journey, or we came to Orthez: and
this knyght every day, after he had sayd his prayers, moost parte
all the day after he toke his pastyme with me, in demaundyng
of tidynges; and also whan I demaunded any thyng of hym,
he wolde answere me to my purpose; and whan we departed
fro Pamyers, we past by the mount of Cosse, whiche was an
evell passage, and so we came to the towne and castell of
Artigat, whiche was frenche, but we passed by it, and so came
to dyner to a castell of therle of Foiz, halfe a leage thens,
called Carlat, standynge highe on a mountayne; and after
dyner the knight sayd to me, sir, let vs ryde toguyder fayre
and easely, we have but two leages to ryde to our lodgyng:

and so I was content to do; than the knight said, we have this day passed by the castell of Artigat, which dothe moche domage in this countre, Peter Danchyn kepeth it, and hath taken and stollen out of the realme of France more than threscore thousande frankes. Than I demaunded how that might be: I shall shewe you, quod the knight....

(p. 53.) Than I said, ah, saint Mary, was this Mongat suche an expert man of armes? ye truely, sir, quoth he, and in war he dyed, in a place wher as we shall passe within this thre dayes, in a countre called the Layre, in Bigore, by a towne called La Cieutat. Well sir, quod I, and I shall remembre you therof, whan we come ther.

Than the next day the knight had counsayle to passe the ryver by botes by the towne of Casseres : so we rode thider, and dyd so moche that we past the ryver of Garonne with great payne and parell, for the bote that we were in was nat very great; it coude nat take at one tyme but two horses and their kepars, and they that ruled the bote ; and so whan we were over we rode to Casseres, and abode there all that daye, and in the meane tyme that our supper was a dressyng, this knight said to me, sir Johan, let us go and se the towne ; and so we passed along through the towne, and came to the gate towarde Palaminiche, and went out therat and came to the dykes; than the knyght shewed me a pane of the wall, and said, sir, se you yonder parte of the wall whiche is newer than all the remnant. Yea sir, quod I. Well, quod he, I shall shewe you why it is so ; it is a ten yere past sithe it fortuned....

(p. 54 f.) And than we wente to our supper. And the nexte day we rode alonge by the ryver of Garon, and passed by Palaminiche, and than we entred into the lande of the erle of Commynges and Armagnake, and on the other syde was the ryver of Garon, and the lande of therle of Foiz ; and as we rode, this knight shewed me a stronge towne, called Martres-le-Toussac, parteyninge to therle of Comynges, and on the other syde of the ryver on the mountayne he shewed me two castelles parteyninge to the erle of Foiz, the one called Mountmirall, and the other Mountclare : and as we rode bytwene these townes and castelles alonge by the ryver of

Garon, in a fayre medowe, this knight sayd to me, sir Johan, I have sene here many fayre scrimysshes and encountrynges bytwene the Foizois and Armynakes, for as than there was no towne nor castell but that was well furnysshed with men of warre, and so they warred eche vpon other.

So in suche devyses we rode all that day alonge by the ryver of Garon, and what on the one syde and on the other, we sawe many fayre castelles and fortresses ; all that were on our lyfte hande parteyned to therle of Foiz, and the other syde parteyned to therle of Armynake. And so thus we passed by Montpesac, a fayre castell and a stronge, standyng on an highe rocke, and underneth was the towne and the highe way, and without the towne a lytell, there was a place called la Garde, and a towre bitwene the rocke and the ryver, whiche towre had a gate and a portcolyse of yron ; sixe men might well kepe this passage agaynst all the worlde, for there coulde no man passe but two on a front, what for the towre on the one syde, and the ryver on the other syde. Than I sayd to the knyght, sir, here is a stronge passage, and a myghtie countre. It is true, quod the knight, and though thentre be stronge, yet the erle of Foiz dyde conquere it ones, and he and all his passed the same waye, with the helpe of the archers of Englande, that he had as than in his company, and the great desyre that they had to passe into the countre. Come ryde nere me sir, quod he, and I shall shewe you howe it was....

(p. 60 f.) And so with these wordes we came to the towne of Tourney, where as we shulde rest all night. So than the knight seased of his talkyng, and I remembred well where we lefte agaynst the next day, and we were lodged at the signe of the Starre, and toke our ease ; and at supper tyme, the capitayne of Malvoysin, called sir Raymonde of Lane, came to se us, and supped with us, and brought with hym four flaggons of the best wyne that I dranke of in all my journey: those two knightes talked long togider, and whan it was late the knight departed and retourned to the castell of Malvoysin: and the next mornyng we mounted on our horses, and departed fro Tourney and passed by a [ford] the ryver of

Lesse, and rode towarde the cytie of Tarbe, and entred into Bigore ; and we lefte the waye to Lourde, to Bagneres, and to the castell of Mountgaylliard on the lyfte hande ; and we rode towarde a vyllage called La Cieutat, and dyd coost it, and came to a wode in the lande of the lorde of Barbasan, and we came nere to a castell called Mascaras, at the entre of the countre of Layre. Than the knight said to me, Sir Johan, beholde here the place of Layre, and beholde it well and advyse the countre, which semed to me right strange : I thought myselfe but as lost ther, if I had nat ben in the company with that knight : than I remembred the wordes that this knight had shewed me ii. or thre dayes before of that countre of Layre and of the Mongat of Lourde : than I sayd to hym, Sir, ye shewed me the last daye, that whan we shulde be in the countre of Layre, that ye wolde shewe me the maner of the Mongat of Lourde, and howe he dyed. It is true, sir, quoth the knyght ; come on and ryde by me, and I shall shewe you....They fought this day hande to hande ; Ernalton Bysset with the Mongat of saynt Basyll ; they dyde many a feate of armes bytwene them, and they fought so long till they were so wery that they coude ayde themselfe no lengar : and ther was slayne on the place two capitayns, the Mongat of Lourde, and on the other parte Ernalton Bysset. Than ceased the batayle by agrement of bothe parties, for they were so wery that they coude scante holde their axes in their handes. Some unarmed them, to refresshe themselfe, and lefte their armure in the place. They of Lourde bare awaye with them the Mongat slayne, and the frenchemen bare Ernalton Bysset to Tarbe : and to thentent that this batayle shulde be had in remembraunce, wher as the two squyers fought, there was set a crosse of stone ; beholde yonder is the crosse ; and with those wordes we came to the crosse, and there we sayd for their soules a Pater noster and an Ave maria....By my faythe, sir, than quod I, ye have well declared the mater ; I never herde it before, and nowe that I knowe it, I shall putte it in perpetuall memorie, if god gyve me grace to retourne into my countrey ; but, sir, if I durste, I wolde fayne demaunde of you one thynge ; by what insydent

the erle of Foiz sonne dyed? thanne the knyght studyed a
lytell and sayd, Sir, the maner of his dethe is right pytuous,
I wyll nat speke therof; whan ye come to Ortaise[1], ye shall
fynde them that wyll shewe you if ye demaunde it. And than
I helde my peace, and we rode tyll we came to Morlaas.

The next day we departed and roode to dyner to Bougarber, and so to Arthez, and there we dranke, and by sonne
setting we came to Ortaise; the knight alighted at his owne
lodgynge, and I alyghted at the [sign of the] Mone, wher
dwelte a squier of the erles Ernalton de Pyne, who well receyved
me, bycause I was of Fraunce: Sir Spayne of Leon wente to the
castell to therle, and founde hym in his galarye, for he had but
dyned a lytell before, for the erles usage was alwayes, that it was
hyghe noone or he arose out of his bedde, and supped ever at
mydnight; the knight shewed hym howe I was come thider,
and incontynent I was sente for to my lodgynge, for he was
the lorde of all the worlde that moost desyred to speke with
straungers, to here tidynges. Whan the erle sawe me, he
made me good chere, and reteyned me as of his house, wher
I was more than xii. wekes, and my horse well entreated;
the acquayntaunce of hym and of me was, bycause I had
brought with me a boke, whiche I made at the [request] of
Wenceslas of Boesme, duke of Luzenbourge and of Brabant,
whiche boke was called the Melyador, conteyninge all the
songes, baladdes, rundeaux, and vyrelayes, whiche the gentyll
duke had made in his tyme, whiche by imagynacyon I had
gadered toguyder, whiche boke the erle of Foiz was gladde to
se; and every night after supper I reed theron to hym, and
whyle I reed there was none durst speke any worde, bycause
he wolde I shulde be well understande, wherin he tooke great
solace; and whan it came to any mater of questyon, than he
wolde speke to me, nat in Gascoyne, but in good and fayre
frenche.

(p. 79 f.) And on a day I sawe a squyer of Gascone,
called the Bascot[2] of Maulyon, a man of a fyftie yere of age,
an expert man of armes and a hardy, be semynge: he alighted

---

[1] This is Berners's usual form for *Orthez.*
[2] *Bascot* and *Bourg* (see next page) are variants of *bastard.*

at my lodgynge in Ortaise, at the signe of the Moone, at
Ernalton du Puy's: he brought with hym his somers and
caryages, as thoughe he had ben a great barone, and was
served bothe he and his servauntes in sylver vessell: and whan
I herde his name, and sawe therle of Foiz and every man do
hym so moche honour, than I demaunded of sir Espaygne de
Lion, and sayd, Sir, is nat this the squyer that departed fro
the castell of Trygalet, whan the duke of Anjou laye at siege
before Malvoysin? Yes, truely, quod he, it is the same, and
he is a good man of armes and a good capitayne: and so
than I fell in aquayntaunce with hym, for he was lodged there
as I was: and a cosyn of his, called Ernalton, capitayn of
Carlate in Auvergne, with whome I was well acquaynted,
helped me to be aquainted with him, and in lykewise so dyd
the Bourg of Compare: and at a tyme, as we were talkyng
and devysinge of armes, sytting by the fyre abyding for
mydnight, that therle shulde go to supper, than this squiers
cosyn began to reken up his life, and of the dedes of armes
that he had ben at, sayeng howe he had endured as moche
losse as profite. Than he demaunded of me, and sayd, sir
John, have ye in your hystorie any thyng of this maters that
I speke of? and I answered and said, I coude nat tell tyll I
here them: shewe forthe your mater, and I wyll gladly here
you; for paradventure I have herde somwhat, but nat all.
That is true, quod the squyer; than he began to saye thus:...
Than the Bascot sayd to me, sir Johan, are ye well enformed
of my lyfe? yet I have had other adventures, whiche I have
nat shewed, nor wyll nat speke of all. Sir, quod I, I have
well herde you.

(p. 109 f.) Saynt Mary, quod I to the squyer that shewed
me this tale, Howe is it that therle of Foiz coude knowe on
one day what was done within a day or two before, beynge so
farre of? By my faythe, sir, quod he, as it appered well, he
knewe it. Than he is a devyner, quod I, or els he hathe
messangers that flyeth with the wynde, or he muste nedes
have some crafte. The squyer began to laughe, and sayd,
Surely he muste knowe it by some arte of Nigromansye, or
otherwyse. To saye the trouthe, we can nat tell howe it is, but

by oure ymaginacions. Sir, quod I, suche ymaginacion as ye have therin, if it please you to shewe me, I wolde be gladde therof; and if it be suche a thynge as ought to be secrete, I shall nat publysshe it, nor as long as I am in this countre I shall never speke worde therof. I praye you therof, quod the squyer, for I wolde nat it shulde be knowen that I shulde speke therof; but I shall shewe you as dyvers men speketh secretelye, whan they be togyder as frendes. Than he drewe me aparte into a corner of the chapell at Ortayse, and than began his tale and sayd :...(p. 113) Lo, sir, quod the squyer, thus I have shewed you the lyfe of Orthone, and howe a season he served the lorde of Corasse with newe tidynges. It is true, sir, quod I; but nowe as to your firste purpose: Is the erle of Foiz served with suche a messangere? Surely, quod the squier, it is the ymaginacion of many that he hath suche messangers ; for ther is nothynge done in any place, but and he sette his mynde therto, he wyll knowe it, and whan men thynke leest therof : and so dyde he whan the good knightes and squyers of this countrey were slayne in Portugale, at Juberothe. Some saythe, the knowledge of suche thynges hath done hym moche profyte; for and there be but the value of a spone loste in his house, anone he wyll knowe wher it is. So thus than I toke leave of the squyer and went to other company, but I bare well awaye his tale.

(p. 609 ff. A.D. 1394.) Trewe it was, that I sir Johan Froissart, (as at that tyme treasourer and chanon of Chymay, in the erldome of Heynaulte, in the diocese of Liege), had great affectyon to go and se the realme of Englande, whan I had ben in Abbevyle, and sawe that trewce was taken bytwene the realmes of Englande and Fraunce, and other countreis to them conjoyned, and there adherentes, to endure four yeres by see and by lande. Many reasons moved me to make that voyage; one was, bycause in my youthe I hadde been brought up in the court of the noble kynge Edwarde the thyrde, and of quene Philyppe his wyfe, and amonge their chyldren, and other barones of Englande, that as than were alyve, in whome I founde all noblenesse, honour, largesse, and courtesy; there-fore I desyred to se the countre thynkynge therby I shulde lyve moche the lengar, for I hadde nat been there xxvii. yere before, and I thought, though I sawe natte those lordes that I lefte alyve there, yet at the leest I shulde se their heyres, the whiche shulde do me moche good to se, and also to justifye the hystories and maters that I hadde written of them : and or I toke my journey, I spake with duke Aubert of Bavyere, Erle of Heynaulte, Hollande, Zelande, and lorde of Freese, and with my lorde Wyllyam erle of Ostrevaunt, and with my right honourable lady Jahane duchesse of Brabant and of Lusenbourge, and with the lorde Engerant, lorde Coucy, and with the gentyll knyght the lorde of Gomegynes, who in his youthe and myne had been toguyder in Englande in the kynges courte; in lykewise so had I sene there the lorde of Coucy, and dyvers other nobles of Fraunce, holden great housholdes in London, whan they laye there in hostage for the redempcion of kynge Johan, as than Frenche kynge, as it hath been shewed here before in this hystorie.

These sayd lordes, and the Duchesse of Brabant, coun-sayled me to take this journey, and gave me letters of recommendacyon to the kynge of Englande and to his uncles, savynge the lorde Coucy : he wolde nat write to the kynge bycause he was a Frencheman, therfore he durste nat, but to his doughter, who as than was called duchesse of Irelande ; and I had engrosed in a fayre boke well enlumyned, all the matters of amours and moralytees, that in four and twentie yeres before I hadde made and compyled, whiche greatly quickened my desyre to go into Englande to se kyng Rycharde, who was sonne to the noble prince of Wales and of Acquitayne, (for I hadde nat sene this kynge Richarde sythe he was christened in the Cathedrall churche of Burdeaux, at whiche tyme I was there, and thought to have goone with the prince the journey into Galycia in Spaygne ; and whanne we were in the cytie of Aste, the prince sente me backe into Englande to the Quene his mother).

For these causes and other I hadde great desyre to go into Englande to se the kynge and his uncles. Also I hadde this said fayre boke well covered with velvet, garnysshed with clapses of sylver and gylte, therof to make a present to the

kynge at my fyrst commynge to his presence; I hadde suche
desyre to goo this voyage, that the payne and traveyle greved
me nothyng.   Thus provyded of horses and other necessaries,
I passed the see at Calais, and came to Dover, the xii. daye of
the moneth of July; whanne I came there I founde no man
of my knowledge, it was so longe sythe I had been in
Englande, and the houses were all newly chaunged, and yonge
children were become men, and the women knewe me natte,
nor I theym; so I abode halfe a daye and all a nyght at
Dover; it was on a Tuesdaye, and the nexte daye by nyne of
the clocke I came to Canterbury, to saynt Thomas shrine,
and to the tombe of the noble prince of Wales, who is there
entered right richely; there I herde masse, and made myne
offrynge to the holy saynt, and thanne dyned at my lodgynge;
and there I was enformed howe kyng Richarde shulde be
there the nexte daye on pylgrimage, whiche was after his
retourne out of Irelande, where he had ben the space of nyne
monethes or there about: the kyng hadde a devocyon to
visyte saynt Thomas shrine, and also bycause the prince his
father was there buryed.   Than I thought to abyde the kynge
there, and so I dyde; and the next daye the kynge came
thyder with a noble company of lordes, ladyes, and damoselles:
and whan I was among them they semed to me all newe
folkes, I knewe no persone; the tyme was sore chaunged in
xxviii. yere[1], and with the kynge as than was none of his
uncles; the duke of Lancastre was in Acquitayne, and the
dukes of Yorke and Glocestre were in other busynesses, so
that I was at the firste all abasshed, for if I had sene any
auncyent knyght that had ben with kyng Edwarde, or with
the prince, I had ben well reconforted and wolde have gone to
hym, but I coulde see none suche.   Thanne I demaunded for
a knyght called sir Rycharde Stury, whyder he were alyve or
nat? and it was shewed me yes, but he was at London.   Than
I thought to go to the lorde Thomas Percy, great seneschall of
Englande, who was there with the kyng: so I acquaynted me
with hym, and I founde hym right honorable and gracyous,

---

[1] Froissart speaks loosely: a page before he has specified this period as " vingt
sept ans tous accomplis."

and he offred to present me and my letters to the kynge, wherof I was right joyfull, for it behoved me to have some meanes to bringe me to the presence of suche a prince as the kynge of Englande was; he wente to the kynges chambre, at whiche tyme the kynge was gone to slepe, and so he shewed me, and badde me retourne to my lodgynge and come agayne. And so I dyde; and whan I came to the bysshoppes palays, I founde the lorde Thomas Percy redy to ryde to Ospring, and he counsayled me to make as than no knowledge of my beynge there, but to folowe the court: and sayd he wolde cause me ever to be well lodged tyl the kyng shulde be at the fayre castell of Ledes, in Kent. I ordered me after his counsayle and rode before to Ospring; and by adventure I was lodged in an house where was lodged a gentyll knyght of Englande, called sir Wyllyam Lysle; he was taryed there behynde the kynge, bycause he had payne in his heed all the nyght before: he was one of the kynges prevy chambre; and whan he sawe that I was a straunger, and as he thought, of the marchesse of Fraunce, bycause of my langage, we fyll in acquayntaunce toguyder: for gentylmen of Englande are curtesse, treatable, and gladde of acquayntaunce; than he demaunded what I was, and what busynesse I had to do in those parties; I shewed hym a great parte of my commynge thyder, and all that the lorde Thomas Percy hadde sayd to me, and ordred me to do. He than answered and sayde, howe I coulde nat have a better meane, and that on the Friday the kyng shulde be at the castell of Ledes; and he shewed me that whan I came there, I shuld fynde there the duke of Yorke the kynges uncle, wherof I was ryght gladde, bycause I had letters dyrected to hym, and also that in his youthe he hadde sene me, in the courte of the noble kyng Edwarde his father, and with the quene his mother. Than on the Friday in the mornyng sir Wylliam Lysle and I rode toguyder, and on the waye I demaunded of hym if he had been with the kynge in the voyage into Irelande. He answered me yes. Than I demaunded of hym the maner of the hole that is in Irelande, called saynt Patrykes purgatorie, if it were trewe that was sayde of it or nat. Than he sayde,

that of a suretie suche a hole there was, and that he hymselfe
and another knyght of Englande hadde ben there whyle the
kynge laye at Duvelyn, and sayd howe they entred into the
hoole and were closed in at the sonne goynge downe, and
abode there all nyght, and the nexte mornyng issued out
agayne at the son risyng. Than I demaunded if he had any
suche strange sightes or vysions as were spoken of. Than he
sayd, howe that whan he and his felowe were entred and past
the gate that was called the purgatorie of saynt Patryke, and
that they were discended and gone downe thre or four paces,
discendyng downe as into a cellar, a certayne hoote vapure
rose agaynst them, and strake so into their heedes, that they
were fayne to syt downe on the steeres, whiche are of stone;
and after they had sytte there a season, they had great desyre
to slepe, and so fell aslepe and slepte there all nyght. Than
I demaunded that if in their slepe they knewe where they
were, or what visyons they had. He answered me, that in
slepyng they entred into great ymaginacyons and in marvey-
lous dremes, otherwyse than they were wont to have in their
chambres: and in the mornynge they issued out, and within
a shorte season clene forgate their dremes and visyons, wherfore he sayde he thought all that mater was but a fantasy.
Than I lefte spekyng any further of that matter, bycause I
wolde fayne have knowen of hym what was done in the
voyage in Irelande: and I thought as than to have demaunded
what the kyng had done in that journey; but than company
of other knyghtes came and fell in communycacion with hym,
so that I lefte my purpose for that tyme. Thus we rode to
Ledes, and thyder came the kyng and all his company, and
there I founde the lorde Edmonde duke of Yorke. Than
I went to hym and delyvered my letters fro the erle of
Heynaulte his cosyn, and fro the erle of Ostrevaunt. The
duke knewe me well, and made me good chere, and sayde:
Sir Johan, holde you alwayes nere to us, and we shall shewe
you love and courtesy: we are bounde therto for the love of
tyme past, and for love of my lady the olde Quene my mother,
in whose courte ye were, we have good remembraunce therof.
Than I thanked hym as reason requyred. So I was advaunsed

by reason of hym and sir Thomas Percy, and sir William
Lysle; by their meanes I was brought into the kynges
chambre, and into his presence by meanes of his uncle the
duke of Yorke.   Than I delyvered my letters to the kyng,
and he toke and reed them at good leysar.   Than he sayd to
me that I was welcome, as he that hadde ben and is of the
Englysshe courte.   As on that daye I shewed nat the kynge
the boke that I hadde brought for hym, he was so sore
occupyed with great affayres, that I had as than no leysar to
present my boke.   The kyng was sore busyed there in counsayle for two great and mightye maters:

(p. 612.)   And whan they had taryed at Ledes a four
dayes, the kyng retourned to Rochester and so to Elthame,
and so I rode forthe in the kynges company.

(p. 618.)   I have delyght to write this mater at length,
bycause to enfourme you of the trouthe: for I that am auctour
of this hystory was presente in all these maters, and this
valyaunt knyght syr Rycharde Sturye shewed me every
thynge; and so it was, that on the sonday folowynge all
suche as had ben there were departed, and all their coun-
saylours, except the duke of Yorke, who abode styll about the
kynge; and the lorde Thomas Percy and syr Rycharde Stury
shewed my busynesse to the kynge.   Than the kynge desyred
to se my booke that I had brought for hym: so he sawe it in
his chambre, for I had layde it there redy on his bedde.
Whanne the kynge opened it, it pleased hym well, for it was
fayre enlumyned and written, and covered with crymson
velvet, with ten botons of sylver and gylte, and roses of golde
in the myddes, wyth two great clapses gylte, rychely wrought.
Than the kyng demaunded me wherof it treated, and I
shewed hym how it treated maters of love; wherof the kynge
was gladde and loked in it, and reed it in many places, for
he coulde speke and rede French very well; and he tooke it
to a knyght of hys chambre, named syr Rycharde Creadon, to
beare it into hys secrete chambre: and the same sonday I
fell in acquayntaunce with a Squyer of Englande, called
Henry Castyde, an honest man and a wyse, and coud well
speke Frenche: he companyed wyth me, bycause he saw the

kyng and other lordes made me good chere, and also he had
sene the boke that I gave to the kyng: also syr Rycharde
Stury had shewed hym howe I was a maker of hystories.
Than he sayd to me as herafter foloweth....

(p. 763.) This kyng Richarde reigned kynge of Englande
xxii. yere in great prosperite, holdyng great estate and sig-
norie: there was never before any kyng of Englande that
spente so moche in his house as he dyd, by a C. M. [100,000]
florens every yere: for I sir John Froissart, chanon and
treasourer of Chimay, knewe it well, for I was in his court
more than a quarter of a yere togider, and he made me good
chere, bycause that in my youthe I was clerke and servaunt to
the noble kynge Edwarde the thirde his grauntfather, and
with my lady Philyp of Heynault, quene of Englande, his
grandame; and whan I departed fro hym it was at Wynsore,
and at my departynge the kyng sent me by a knight of his,
called sir John Golofer, a goblet of sylver and gylte, weyeng
two marke of silver, and within it a C. nobles, by the which I
am as yet the better, and shal be as long as I lyve; wherfore
I am bounde to praye to God for his soule, and with moche
sorowe I write of his dethe.

18   POET AND KING

John Gower was of a good Kentish family. He was possibly a merchant;
certainly he did part of his literary work in a house within the precincts of
the priory of St Mary Overey, Southwark; within this priory he was
married in 1397, and he probably lived there until his death. The following lines are from the first redaction of his *Confessio Amantis*, ed.
Macaulay, p. 2; they describe the occasion which led him to compose
this book.

> Bot for men sein, and soth it is,
> That who that al of wisdom writ
> It dulleth ofte a mannes wit
> To him that schal it aldai rede[1],
> For thilke cause, if that ye rede,
> I wolde go the middel weie
> And wryte a bok betwen the tweie,

[1] advise.

Somwhat of lust, somewhat of lore,
That of the lasse or of the more
Som man mai lyke of that I wryte:
And, for that fewe man endite
In oure englissh, I thenke make
A bok for king Richardes sake,
To whom belongeth my ligeance
With al myn hertes obeissance
In al that evere a liege man
Unto his king may doon or can...
As it bifel upon a tyde,...
In Temse whan it was flowende,
As I be bote cam rowende,
So as fortune hir tyme sette,
My liege lord par chaunce I mette;
And so befel, as I cam nyh,
Out of my bot, whan he me syh,
He bad me come in to his barge.
And whan I was with him at large,
Amonges othre thinges seid
He hath this charge upon me leid,
And bad me doo my besynesse
That to his hihe worthinesse
Som newe thing I scholde boke[1],
That he himself it mihte loke
After the forme of my writynge.
And thus upon his comandynge
Myn herte is wel the more glad
To write so as he me bad.

19　　HOCCLEVE'S AUTOBIOGRAPHY

We know a little of Thomas Hoccleve's life from scattered entries in the Privy Council Proceedings and the Patent and Pells-Issue Rolls; but for most we are indebted to autobiographical passages in his own poems. These have been admirably pieced together by Furnivall, in his preface to the first volume of the poet's works (E.E.T.S., Extra Series, LXI. 1892). The following sequence is almost entirely in Furnivall's or in Hoccleve's

[1] write in a book.

own words: but the present compiler has silently made several emenda-
tions which seem required by the sense, and made other slight alterations
to avoid a multiplicity of notes.

In his *Dialog*, finished in 1422, he says "of age I am fifty winter and
thre." He must therefore have been born in 1368–9. The date of his
englishing of *De Regimine Principum* is 1411–12; and in that poem he
says that he had been then 24 years, come Easter, in the Privy-Seal
Office.

> "In the office of the prive-seel I wone;
> To write there is my custume and wone
>   Unto the seel; and have twenty yere
>   And foure, come Estren, and that is nere."
>   —Ed. Wright, p. 29.

He must therefore have gone into that office in 1387–8, when he was
19 or 20 years of age.

Of his wild youth in the office of the Privy Seal he gives an account
in his *Male Regle* (pp. 28 ff.).

> My freendes seiden un-to me ful ofte,
> My mis-reule me cause wolde a fit;
> And redden[1] me, in esy wyse and softe,
> A lyte and lyte to withdrawen it;
> But that nat mighte synke in-to my wit,
> So was the lust y-rootid in myn herte.
> And now I am so rype un-to my pit[2],
> That scarsely I may it nat asterte[3]....
>
> Reson me bad and redde as for the beste,
> To ete and drynke in tyme attemprely;
> But wilful youthe nat obeie leste[4]
> Un-to that reed, ne sette nat ther-by.
> I taken have of bothe outrageously,
> And out of tyme nat two yeer or three,
> But xx[ti] wyntir past, continuelly,
> Excesse at borde hath leyd his knyf[5] with me....
>
> The outward signe of Bachus and his lure,
> That at his dore hangith day by day,
> Excitith [us] to taaste of his moisture
> So often, that man can nat wel seyn "nay."

---

[1] advised.   [2] grave.   [3] escape.   [4] cared not to obey.
        [5] taken his place as a fellow guest.

For me, I seye I was enclyned ay
With-outen daunger thithir for to hye me,
But if swich charge up on my backe lay
That I moot it forbere, as for a tyme

Or but I were nakidly bystad¹
By force of the penyless maladie,
For thanne in herte kowde I nat be glad,
Ne lust had noon to Bachus, hows to hie.
Fy! Lak of coyne departith compaignie,
And hevy purs, with herte liberal,
Qwenchith the thirsty hete of hertes drie,
Wher chynchy² herte hath ther-of but smal.

I dar nat telle how that the fresshe repeir
Of Venus femel lusty children deere,
That so goodly, so shaply were, and feir,
And so plesant of port and of maneere,
And feede cowden al a world with cheere,
And of atyr passyngly wel byseye³,
At Poules Heed⁴ me maden ofte appeere
To talke of mirthe & to disport & pleye.

Ther was sweet wyn ynow thurgh-out the hous,
And wafres⁵ thikke; for this conpaignie
That I spake of been sumwhat likerous,
Where as they mowe a draght of wyn espie—
Sweete, and in wirkynge hoot for the maistrie⁶
To warme a stomak with—thereof they dranke.
To suffre them paie had been no courtesie:
That charge I tooke, to wynne love and thanke....

¹ bare of coin (nakedly bested).   ² niggardly.   ³ arrayed.
⁴ The "Paul's Head" was one of those city taverns of which a contemporary writes so feelingly in a corner of a Trin. Coll. Cambs. MS. (599, fol. 208, printed by Dr M. R. James in his Catalogue).

> He that wyll in Es[t]chepe ete a goose so fat
> With harpe pype and song
> He must slepe in Newgate on a mat
> Be the nyght never so long.
>   [As Aristotle saith]

⁵ sweet cakes.   ⁶ strength.

Of him that hauntith taverne of custume,
At shorte wordes, the profyt is this :
In double wyse his bagge it shal consume,
And make his tonge speke of folk amis ;
For in the cuppe seelden founden is,
That any wight his neigheburgh commendith.
Beholde & see what avantage is his,
That god, his freend, and eek himself, offendith

But oon avauntage in this case I have :
I was so ferd with any man to fighte,
Cloos kepte I me; no man durste I deprave[1]
But rownyngly[2] I spak, nothyng on highte.
And yit my wil was good, if that I mighte
For lettynge of my manly cowardyse,
That ay of strookes impressid the wighte[3],
So that I durste medlen in no wyse.

Wher was a gretter maister eek than y,
Or bet aqweyntid at Westmynstre yate,
Among the taverneres namely,
And cookes, whan I cam eerly or late ?
I pynchid nat at[4] them in myn acate[5],
But paied them all that they axe wolde ;
Wherfore I was the welcomere algate,
And for a ' verray gentil man' y-holde.

And if it happid on the Someres day
That I thus at the taverne hadde be,
Whan I departe sholde & go my way
Hoom to the privee seel, so wowed[6] me
Heete & unlust and superfluitee
To walke un-to the brigge & take a boot
That nat durste I contrarie them all three,
But did as that they stirred me, god woot.

And in the wyntir, for the way was deep,
Un-to the brigge I dressid me also,

---

[1] abuse.   [2] in a whisper.   [3] weight.
[4] chaffered not with.   [5] bargain.   [6] wooed.

And ther the bootmen took up-on me keep,
For they my riot knewen fern ago:
With them was I y-tugged to and fro,
So wel was him that I with wolde fare;
For riot paieth largely everemo;
He styntith nevere til his purs be bare.

Othir than 'maistir' callid was I nevere,
Among this meynee, in myn audience.
Me thoghte I was y-maad a man for evere:
So tikelid me that nyce reverence,
That it me made larger of despense
Than that I thoght han been. O flaterie!
The guyse of thy traiterous diligence
Is, folk to mescheef hasten & to hie....

No force of al this! go we now to watche
By nightirtale out of al mesure;
For, as in that, fynde kowde I no matche
In al the Privee Seel with me to endure;
And to the cuppe ay took I heede & cure,
For that the drynke apalle¹ sholde noght.
But whan the pot emptid was of moisture,
To wake aftirward came nat in my thoght.

But whan the cuppe had thus my neede sped,
(And sumdel more than necessitee,)
With repleet spirit wente I to my bed,
And bathid there in superfluitee.
But on the morn was wight of no degree
So looth as I to twynne fro my cowche.

Hoccleve meant at first to be a priest:—"I whilom thought Have
ben a preest; now past is the raas," *De Reg.*, p. 52, ll. 1147–8. He
probably entered the Privy-Seal Office till he could get a benefice promised him, and then meant to be ordained and take the endowment.
But no benefice came.   Instead, after twelve years' office-work, Hoccleve
got from Henry IV., on Nov. 12, 1399 (six weeks after his accession), the
grant of £10 a year for life, until the King should promote him to an
ecclesiastical benefice, without cure of souls, with £20 a year, in other

---

¹ slacken.

words, quarter him on a convent. Then, as no benefice or corrody[1] was given him, he tired of waiting for it, and drifted into marriage :

Harl. 4866, lf 26, bk, ed. Wright, p. 53, st. 208, l. 1456.

I gasyd longë firste, & waytid faste
After some benefice, and whan non cam,
By proces[2] I me weddid attë laste.
And, God it wot, it sore me aghaste
To byndë me where I was at my large;
But done it was: I toke on me that charge.

(HOCCLEVE.)

He married for love, not money (*Reg.* 56/1559–61), and after his "skittish youth" (as the old Beggar terms his own gay time, *Reg.* 22/590), settled down into poverty and sad old age.

Over his writing or copying work, Hoccleve groans to his old Beggar, *De Reg.*, pp. 36–7.

Harl. 4866, lf 18, bk, st. 142.

Many men, fadir, wenen that writynge
No travaile is; thei hold it but a game :—
Art hath no foe, but swich folk unkonynge :—
But who-so list disport hym in that same,
Let hym continue, and he shal fynd it grame[3]·
It is wel gretter labour than it seemeth;
The blyndë man of coloures al wrong deemeth.

A writer mot thre thynges to hym knytte,
And in those may be no disseverance ;
Mynde, ee and hand, non may fro othir flitte,
But in them mot be joint contynuance.
The mynd, al hoole with-outen variance,
On the ee and hand awaytë mot alway,
And thei two eek on hym; it is no nay.

Who-so schal wrytë, may nat holde a tale
With hym and hym, ne synge this ne that;
But alle his wittës grete and smale
Ther must appere, and halden them ther-at,

---

[1] *corrody*, originally a month's allowance, is most often used in the sense of a pension from a monastery, in kind or in money. Such corrodies were generally bought, or exchanged for some *quid pro quo*; but kings frequently claimed and exercised the privilege of compelling monasteries of royal foundation to grant corrodies to royal clerks, etc.

[2] in process of time.   [3] grief.

And syn he spekë may, ne syngë nat,
  But bothë two he needës moot forbere:
  His labour to hym is the alengere[1].

Thise artificers, se I day be day,
  In the hotteste of al her bysnysse,
Talken and synge, and makë game and play,
  And forth thir labour passith with gladnesse;
  But we laboure in traveillous stilnesse;
    We stowpe and stare upon the shepës skyn,
    And keepë muste our song and wordës in.

Wrytyng also doth grete annoyës thre.
  Of which ful fewë folkës taken heede
Sauf we oure self; and thisë, lo, thei be:
  Stomak is one, whom stowpyng out of dreede
  Annoyeth soore; and to our bakkes neede
    Mot it be grevous; and the thrid, our eyen,
    Up-on the-whytë mochel for to pryen.

What man that thre and twenti yere and more
  In wryting hath continued, as have I,
I dar wel sayn it smerteth hym ful sore
  In every veyne and place of his body;
  And eyen most it greeveth trewely
    Of any crafte that man can ymagyne:
    Fadir, in feith, it spilt[2] hath wel-ny myne.

Yet he is too vain to wear spectacles, he tells us (st. 7).

Thow foul book, un-to my lord seye also,
That pryde ys un-to me so greet a fo,
That the spectacle forbedith he me,
And hath y-doon of tyme yore ago;
And, for my sighte blyve hastith me fro,

And lakkith that that sholde his confort be,
No wonder thogh thow have no beautee.
Out up-on pryde, causer of my wo!
My sighte is hurt thurgh hir adversitee.

                                   (HOCCLEVE.)

[1] more grievous (ailing).   [2] spoiled.

20   THE POET'S PARADISE

(*a*)   *Piers Plowman*, B, x. 300–5, p. 308.

"For if hevene be on this erthe, and ese to any soule,
It is in cloistere or in scole, be many skilles I fynde;
For in cloistre cometh no man to chied ne to fighte,
But alle is buxumnesse[1] there and bokes, to rede and to
    lerne."

This is not an original sentiment. St Jerome writes (*Super Matthiam*,
c. 18) "I confess the truth; if there be a paradise on this earth, it is
either in a monastery or in the wilderness." Peter of Blois (Ep. xii.)
writes "for, according to the feeling of my heart, if there be a paradise
in this present life, it is either in cloister or in the schools."

Monasteries not infrequently took in boarders; and we have several
instances of this in literary history. John Gower spent his last days in
the monastery of St Mary Overey, as Chaucer at Westminster; but both
these poets had their own private houses within the precincts. Robert
Henryson, in his *Abbay Walk*, may intend to represent himself under
the same conditions :—

Allone as I went up & down
    In ane Abbay was fair to se,
Thinkand quhat consolatioun
    Was best in-to adversitie....

John Awdelay, however, the Shropshire poet, seems to have been an
ordinary pensioner or corrodian in the abbey of Haughmond. The first
of the three following autobiographical extracts is translated from the
Latin : the other two are in his own words. He wrote a series of
religious poems which have no special literary merit. (*Poems of John
Audelay*, Percy Soc., 1844, pp. vi and x: see also *Mod. Lang. Review*,
vol. v. pp. 473 ff.) *Capellanus*, in medieval Latin, is frequently used in
the sense of hired priest, like the modern *curate*.

(*b*)   This book was composed by John Awdelay, *Capellanus*
(who was blind and deaf), during this his visitation [from God],
to the honour of God and the example of other men, in the
monastery of Haughmond, A.D. 1426 : may God have mercy
on his soul.

(*c*)   As I lay seke in my langure,
    In an abbay here be west,
This boke I made with grete dolour,
    When I myght not slepe ne have no rest;

[1] obedience.

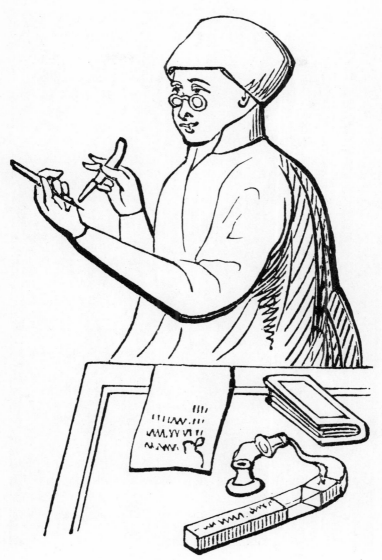

THE WRITER'S SPECTACLES

LYDGATE AND HIS BOOK

Offt with my prayers I me blest,
  And sayd hilé to heven kyng,
I knowlache, Lord, hit is the best.
  Mekelé to take thi vesetyng,
Ellis wot I wil that I were lorne.
  Of al lordis be he blest!
Fore al that ye done is fore the best,
Fore in thi defawte was never mon lost,
  That is here of womon borne.

(*d*) The MS. concludes with the following lines, which inform the reader that he may have a copy on condition that he will pray for the author's soul.

Cujus finis bonus ipsum totum bonum,
  Finito libro, sit laus et gloria Christo!
No mon this book he take away,
  Ny kutt owte noo leef, y say for why;
For hyt ys sacrelege, sirus, y yow say,
  [He] beth acursed in the dede truly;
Yef ye wil have any copi,
  Askus leeve and ye shul have,
To pray for hym specialy,
  That hyt made your soules to save,
Jon the blynde Awdelay;
  The furst prest to the Lord Strange he was,
  Of thys chauntré here in this place,
  That make thys bok by Goddus grace,
Deeff, sick, blynd, as he lay,
Cujus anime propicietur Deus.

21   LYDGATE'S EARLY DAYS

John Lydgate was born about 1372, and therefore was a contemporary of Hoccleve. Like Hoccleve, he was a devoted pupil of Chaucer; but he wrote not only far more but also far better poetry than his contemporary. Without laying too much stress on the following confession of his youthful indiscipline, we may infer from his poems in general that he had no deep vocation for the monastic life.

Minor Poems of Lydgate, E.E.T.S., Extra Series, 1910, pp. 351 ff., with a few alterations for the sake of clearness

Duryng the tyme of this sesoun ver,
  (I mene, the sesoun of my yeres grene,)
Gynnyng fro chyldhode strecched up so fer
  To the yeres accounted ffull fyftene,
  B' experyence, as it was weel sene,
The geryssh[1] sesoun, straunge of condiciouns,
Disposed me to unbrydeled passiouns.

Voyd of resoon, given to wilfulnesse,
  Froward to vertu, of thryfte take litel hede,
Loth to lerne, I loved no besynesse,
  Save pley or merth; was straunge to spelle or rede,
  Folowyng alle appetytes longyng to childhede,
Lyghtly turnyng, wylde and selden sad,
Wepyng for nowght, and anone after glad.

For litel wroth to stryve with my felawe,
  As my passiouns did my brydell lede,
Of the yerd[2] sumtyme I stood in awe,
  To be skowr[g]ed, that was al my drede;
  Loth toward skole, I lost my tyme in dede,
Lyke a yong colt that ran without brydell,
Made I my frendes ther good to spend in ydell.

I had in custome to come to skole late,
  Nat for to lerne, but for a contenaunce[3],
With my felawes was redy to debate,
  To Jangle or Jape was sett all my pleasaunce;
  Wherof rebuked, this was my chevesaunce[4],
To forge a lesyng, and therupon to muse,
Whanne I trespaced, my-selven to excuse.

To my better I did no reverence,
  Of my sovereynes gaf no force[5] at all,
Wex obstinat by Inobedience
  Ran in-to gardeynes, apples ther I stall;
  To gadre frutes spared nedir hegge nor wall,
To plukke grapes in other mennes vynes
Was I more redy, than for to sey matynes.

---

[1] garish.   [2] stick.   [3] appearance.   [4] trick.   [5] heed.

My lust was all to skorne folke and jape,
  Shrewed turnes ever among them to use;
To skoffe and mowen like a wantoun ape;
  Whan I dyd evele, other I koude accuse;
  My wyttes fyve in waste I did all use,
Redier cheri-stones for to telle
Than gon to chirche, or here the sacryng belle.

Loth to ryse, lother to bedde at eve,
  With unwasshe hondes redy to dyner,
My pater noster, my crede, or my beleve,
  Cast attë cok[1], lo, this was my maner!
  Waved with eche wynd, as doth a reedspere,
Snybbed of my frendes, sucche teeches[2] t' amende,
Made a deef ere, list not to them attende.

A chyld resemblyng which was not lyke to thryve,
  Froward to God, rekles in his servyce,
Loth to correccioun, slow my-selve to shryve,
  All good themes redy to despise,
  Chief bel-wether of [feynyd] truandice,
This is to mene, myself I coude feyne,
Sicke like a truant, and felt no maner peyne.

My port, my pas, my foot allwey unstable,
  My loke, myn eyen, unsure and vagabound,
In alle my werkes sodeynly chaungeable,
  To all good themes contrarye I was founde,
  Now oversadd, now mornyng, now jocunde,
Wilfull, rekles, made stertyng as a hare,
To folowe my lust for no man wold I spare.

Entryng this tyme into relygioun,
  Onto the plowe I put forth myne hond,
A yere complete made my professioun,
  Consideryng litel charge of thilke bond;

---

[1] Compare the moral saw scratched on a pillar of Barrington church (Cambs.) in a 15th century hand :

> Lo fol how the day goth,
> Cast foly now to the Cok ;
> Ryth sone tydyth the Wroth,
> It ys almast xij of the clok.

[2] faults.

Of perfeccioun ful gode exaumple I fond,
Ther techyng good, in me was [all] the lacke,
With Lothes wyf I loked often abak.

Taught of my maystres by vertuous disciplyne
  My lookes restreyne, and kepe clos my syght,
Of blyssed Benet to folowe the doctryne,
  And bere me lowly to every maner wyght,
  By the advertence of myn inward syght,
Cast to godward of hole affeccioun,
To folowe thempryses of my professioun.

His holy rewle was onto me rad,
  And expouned in ful notable wyse,
By vertuous men, religious and sad,
  Ful weel experte, discrete, prudent, and wys
  Of observaunces of many a gostly empryse;
I herd all weel; but, touchyng to the dede,
Of theis when taught I toke litel hede!

Of religioun I wered a blak habite,
  Only outward as by apparence,
To folowe that charge I savoured but ful lyte,
  Save by a maner connterfete pretence;
  But in effecte ther was none existence[1],
Like the image of Pygmalyon,
Shewed I lyfly, and was made but of ston.

Upon the ladder, with staves thryes thre
  The ix. degrees of vertuous mekenesse
Called in the Reule 'grees[2] of humylite,'
  Wheron t' ascende my feet me lyst not dresse,
  But by a maner feyned fals humblenesse,
So covertly, when folkes were present,
One to shewe outward, another in myn entent.

First, where as I forsook myne owne wylle—
  Shette with a lock of obedience,
T' obeye my sovereynes, as it was ryght and skylle,
  To folowe the skole of perfygt pacience,

---

[1] reality.   [2] steps.

To myn eymes doon worshep and reverence—
Folowyng the revers, I toke all another weye,
What I was boden, I koude weel disobeye.

With tonge at large and brotel[1] conscyence,
  Ful of wordes, dis-ordinat of language,
Rekeles to kepe my lyppes in silence,
    Mouth, eyen, and eres token ther avauntage,
    To have ther cours onbrydeled by outrage,
Out of the reynes of attemperaunce,
To sensualyte gaf I the governaunce.

Watche out of tyme, ryot and dronkenesse,
  Unfructuous talkyng, intemperat diete,
To veyn fables I dyd myn eres dresse,
    Fals detraccioun [also] was to me swete,
    To talke of vertu me thought it was not mete
To my corage nor my compleccioun,
Nor naught that sowned toward perfeccioun.

One with the firste to take my disporte,
  Last that arose to come to the quere,
On contemplacioun I fond but small comforte,
    Holy histories did to me no chier,
    I savoured more in good wyne that was clere,
And every houre my passage for to dresse,
As I seyd erst, to ryot or excesse.

I kowde grucche, and fond no cause why,
  Causeless ofte compleynyng on my fare,
Geynst my correcciouns answered frowardly,
    Withoute reverence, list no man to spare,
    Of all vertu and pacience I was bare,
Of rekles youthe I list non hede to take,
What Cryst Iesu suffred for my sake.

Which now remembrying in my later age,
  Tyme of my childhode, as I reherse shall,
Wythinne xv [yeres], holdyng my passage
    Myd of a cloyster, depicte vpon a wall,

[1] evil.

I saugh a crucifyx, whos woundes were not smalle,
With this [word] " vide," wreten there besyde,
" Behold my mekenesse, O child, and leve thy pryde."

The which word, whan I dyd vndirstond,
     In my last age takyng the sentence,
Theron remembryng, my penne I toke in honde,
     And gan to wryte with humble reverence,
     On this word, " vide " with humble diligence,
In remembraunce of Crystes passioun,
This litel dite, this compilacioun....

22   OUR FIRST ANTIQUARY

William of Worcester or William Botoner (1415–82 ?) is probably
the earliest of known English antiquaries.   The son of well-to-do Bristol
citizens, he drifted into the service of Sir John Fastolf ; and the dispute
over that knight's rich inheritance led to a quarrel between Worcester and
Sir John Paston which seems less discreditable to the former than to the
latter.   To form an adequate notion of his career, the reader should refer
to Prof. Tait's article in the *Dict. Nat. Biog.* LXII. 441, and compare it
with the biography of John Leland (*ibid.* XXIII. 13).   The following
extracts from the *Paston Letters* (1900) illustrate his trials as a servant in
Fastolf's household and as a litigant for some provision after Fastolf's
death.   He seems to have got a reasonable reward for his services in the
end, according to the notions of that time ; III. 73.

Letter to John Paston, I. 300, A.D. [1454].

Aftyr dewe recomendacion wyth my simple service pre-
cedyng, please your maistershyp to wete, that as to such
remembraunce that ye desyre me to contynew forth to the
uttermost, I shall wyth gode wille, so as my maister wille
licence me, as oft as I can, th' officer to hafe leysure to be
wyth me, for ye know well I can not do it alone, etc.

And where as ye of your pleasure wryte me or calle me
Maister Worcestr, I pray and requyre yow foryete that name
of maistershyp, for I am not amended by my maister[1] of
a ferthyng yn certeynte, but of wages of housold in comune
entaunt come nows plaira[2].   By Worcestr or Botoner I hafe
[vs.] yerly, all costs born, to help pay for bonetts that I lose.

---

[1] I am no better for being master.

[2] "As much as we please."   Botoner fed with the servants, where there was
rough plenty.

I told so my maister thys weke, and he seyd me yerstenday he wyshed me to hafe be a preest, so I had be disposed, to hafe gofe me a lyvyng by reson of a benefice, that anothyr most gefe it, as the Byshop, but he wold ; and so I endure *inter egenos ut servus ad aratrum*[1].

Forgefe me, I wryte to make yow laugh ; and our Lord bryng my maister yn a better mode for othyrs as for me.

At Caister, ijd day of September.

I pray yow displeser not your servaunt be so long, for my maister lettet hym.

Your,
W. Wyrcestyr.

I. 369, A.D. 1456. To John Paston.

My maister demaundyth me sondry tymes when ye shall be here. I coude not sey till thys day be passed. William Geney shall be here to morn, so wold Jesus ye were her then. I asked licence to ryde yn to my contree, and my maistr dyd not graunt it ; he seyd hys wille was for to make, etc. Y ansuerd, it fyt not me to know it. God gefe hym grace of holsom councell, and of a gode disposicion ; *non est opus unius diei, nec unius septimanæ*[2].

Wryt hastly, vj. day Januar.
W. Botoner.

I. 403, A.D. [1456]. To John Paston.

Please you to wete that I hafe remembred of the langage that I hafe late lerned W. Barker had to yow and othyrs of his accomptes apposyng[3], and of that they be not hole bethyn[4] us, but yn division, etc. Sir, as I may sey yow, hyt was nevere othyrwyse, ne nevere ys lyke to be ; for now they hafe do with Lowys, he that ys next shall be yn the same as was yn gelosye ; for when my maister comaundyth such as

---

[1] "Among the destitute, as a serf at the plough."

[2] "It will take more than one day—or one week for the matter of that—[to amend Fastolf's temper]."

[3] The apposing of accounts was the calling of the responsible person to reckoning.

[4] between.

C.

of force (by reson of her [*their*] occupacion) most be nere hym, to do a message to hys felow, or question of hym, hyt shall be ymagyned amonges our felyshyp that he doth make maters to my maister.   And so it ys ymagyned of me when I wryte lettres to London, to Bokkyng or Barker, that yn such maters as please hem not, then it ys my doing ; yff it take well to theyr entent, then it ys her [*their*] doyng.   And yn gode feyth, so it was ymagyned of me and othyrs that wrote, by my maister comaundment, to Castre, to the parson of Blofeld, Geffrey Spyrlyng, and othyrs, that of such maters as was lykyng to hem and coude be sped by help of my maister frendes as by theyr solicytyng, then it was seyd that it was theyr avice, labour, and doyng And yff the maters went not to my maister entent, ne that they coude not bryng aboute the mater, then it was imagyned and jangled that it was my wrytyng and doyng.   I bare nevere my maister purs, ne condyt nevere chargeable mater alone of hys yn lawe, for my discrecion ne connyng know not whate such maters menyth....
I am eased of my spyrytes now that I hafe expressed my leude[1] menyng, because of my felow Barker, as of such othyr berkers ayenst the mone[2], to make wysemen laugh at her folye.   Our Lord kepe yow.

Wryt at Castre the xij day of October.

Your

W. Botoner....

Foryefe me of my leude lettre wrytyng, and I pray yow laugh at it.

I. 509.   To an anonymous friend, complaining of John Paston's un-friendliness in the matter of Fastolf's inheritance.

My maister also (God yelded is[3] sowle) graunted to me a liffelode accordyng to my degre, that I, my wiffe, and my childre, schulde have cause to prey for hym.   My wiffes uncle was present in his chapell at Castre as wele as my wiffe, and comaunded her oncle to chese[4] the londe.   This is trowthe be the blissed Sacrament that I receyved at Pasch.   And because I demaunded my right and duute of my Maister

---

[1] uneducated.   [2] against the moon.   [3] repay it to his.   [4] choose.

Paston, he is not plesed. I have lost more thanne x. mark
worthe londe in my maister servyce, by God, and not I
be[1] releved, alle the worlde schal knowe it elles that I have
to gret wrong. Wolde God I kowde plese bothe Maister
Paston and my oncle in reson, who preserve you.

Wrete hastely the vij. day of Feveryere.

         Your,

            W. Botoner, *dit* Wurcester.

23   TRANSLATORS' DIFFICULTIES

The plea that the pre-Reformation Church upheld the principle of
"the open Bible" rests mainly on extreme ignorance of medieval conditions, but sometimes on demonstrable perversions of well-known facts,
which are alluded to as notorious not only by Wycliffites, but even by
orthodox writers; see the evidence collected by Miss A. C. Paues in
her introduction to *A XIV. Century English Biblical Version*, 1904,
pp. xxviii–xxxi.

(*a*) How much prejudice existed in the clerical mind against the
vulgarization of all Latin works (even when, as in the case of Higden's
chronicle, the book treats only incidentally of religious subjects) may be
gathered from Trevisa's *Dialogue between a Lord and a Clerk*[2], which is
here given from the edition of Trevisa's *Higden* printed by Peter Treveris
in 1527 (fol. 2*a*). It will be noted that Trevisa, like some monastic authors,
anticipates considerable difficulty from "bakbyters."

The Clerke. A grete dele of these bokes stondeth moche
by holy wryte, by holy doctours and by phylosophye; thenne
these bokes sholde not be translated into Englysshe.

The Lorde. It is wonder that thou makest so febel argu-
mentes, and haste goon so longe to scole. Arystoteles bookes
and other bookes also of logyke and of phylosophye were translated out of greke in to latyn. Also, at prayenge of kyng
Charles, Johan Scot translated Denys bokes out of greke in
to latyn, and then out of latyn in to frensshe; then what hath
Englysshe trespaced, that it might not be translated into
Englysshe? Also Kynge Alurede that founded the unyversyte of Oxenford translated the beste lawes in to Englysshe

---

[1] unless I be.

[2] This, with other valuable prefaces of the same kind, may be found in
modernized spelling, but complete, in Dr A. W. Pollard's *XV. Century Prose and
Verse*, 1903, pp. 193 ff.

tongue, and a grete dele of the Psalter out of latyn in to Englysshe, and caused Wyrefryth bysshop of wyrcette to translate saynt Gregoryes bokes the Dyalogues out of latyn in to Saxons. Also Cedmon of whytby was enspyred of the holy goost and made wonder Poysyes in Englysshe nigh of all the storyes of holy wryte. Also the holy man Beda translated saynt Johans gospell out of latyn in to englysshe. Also thou wotest [where] the Apocalypsys is wryten in the walles and roof of chappell bothe in latyn and in frensshe[1]. Also the gospell and prophecye and the ryght fayth of holy chyrche muste be taught and preched to Englysshe men that can noo latyn ; thenne the gospell and prophecye and the right fayth of holy chyrche muste be tolde them in englysshe, and that is not done but by Englysshe translacyon; for suche Englysshe prechyng is very translacyon; and suche Englysshe prechynge is goode and nedefull; thenne Englysshe translacyon is good and nedefull.

The Clerke. Yf a translacyon were made that myght be amended in ony poynt, some men it wolde blame.

The Lord. Yf men blame that is not worthy to be blamed, thenne they by to blame.

The Clerk is presently overpersuaded and decides to make the venture of faith ; "thenne god graunte us grace redely to gynne, wytte and wysdome wysely to worche." And then, on fol. 2 *b*, comes the prologue to his translation, in which something of his original fears may still be traced :

For blame of bakbyters wyll I not blynne, for envye of enemyes, for evyll spytyng and speche of evyl spekers wyl I not leve to do this dede; for travayll wyll I not spare. Comforte I have in nedefull makynge and plesynge to god and in knowynge that I wote that it is your wyll for to make this translacyon clere and playne to be knowen and understonden.

(*b*) The following extract from Caxton, on the other hand, shows what difficulties the conscientious translator encountered even when there was no question of his incurring religious censure by setting before an unlearned public things which the Church insisted on locking up in

---

[1] i.e. in the chapel of Berkeley Castle.

the Latin tongue. It is from the Prologue to his *Eneydos* (1490), E.E.T.S.,
Extra Series, 1890, p. 1.

After dyverse werkes made, translated and achieved,
havyng noo werke in hande, I, sittyng in my studye where
as laye many dyverse paunflettis and bookys, happened that
to my hande came a lytyl booke in frenshe, whiche late was
translated oute of latyn by some noble clerke of fraunce,
whiche booke is named Eneydos, made in latyn by that noble
poete and grete clerke vyrgyle.......And whan I had advysed
me in this sayd boke, I delybered and concluded to translate
it in-to englysshe and forthwyth toke a penne and ynke and
wrote a leef or tweyne whyche I oversawe agayn to corecte
it. And whan I sawe the fayr and straunge termes therin,
I doubted that it sholde not please some gentylmen whiche
late blamed me, sayeing that in my translacyons I had over
curyous termes whiche coude not be understande of comyn
peple and desired me to use olde and homely termes in my
translacyons. And fayn wolde I satysfye every man; and, so
to doo, toke an olde boke and redde therin, and certaynly the
englysshe was so rude and brood that I coude not wele
understande it. And also my lorde abbot of westmynster
ded do shewe to me late, certayn evydences wryton in olde
englysshe, for to reduce it in-to our englysshe now usid. And
certaynly it was wreton in suche wyse that it was more lyke
to dutche than englysshe; I coulde not reduce ne brynge it
to be understonden. And certaynly our langage now used
varyeth ferre from that whiche was used and spoken whan I
was borne. For we englysshe men been borne under the
domynacyon of the mone, whiche is never stedfaste but ever
waverynge wexynge one season and waneth and dyscreaseth
another season[1]. And that comyn englysshe that is spoken
in one shyre varyeth from a nother. In so moche that in my
dayes happened that certayn merchauntes were in a shippe
in tamyse, for to have sayled over the see into zelande; and,
for lacke of wynde, thei taryed atte forland, and wente to

---

[1] Medieval English writers frequently criticize their nation for instability; the
impression was probably derived in part from the political revolutions under
Henry III., Edward II., Richard II. and the Wars of the Roses.

lande for to refreshe them. And one of theym named sheffelde,
a mercer, cam in-to an hous and axed for mete ; and specyally he axyd after eggys ; And the goode wyf answerde, that
she coulde speke no frenshe. And the marchaunt was angry,
for he also coude speke no frenshe, but wolde have hadde
egges and she understode hym not. And thenne at laste a
nother sayd that he wold haven eyren ; then the good wyf
sayd that she understod hym wel. Loo! what sholde a man
in thyse dayes now wryte, egges or eyren? certaynly it is
harde to playse every man by cause of dyversite and chaunge
of langage. For in these dayes every man that is in ony
reputacyon in his countre, wyll utter his commynycacyon
and maters in suche maners and termes that fewe men shall
understonde theym. And som honest and grete clerkes have
ben wyth me, and desired me to wryte the moste curyous
termes that I coude fynde. And thus bytwene playn rude and
curyous I stande abasshed, but in my judgemente the comyn
termes that be dayli used ben lyghter to be understonde
than the olde and auncyent englysshe. And for as moche
as this present booke is not for a rude uplondyssh man to
labour therin, ne rede it, but onely for a clerke and a noble
gentylman that feleth and understondeth in faytes of armes,
in love, and in noble chyvalrye. Therfor in a meane bytwene
bothe, I have reduced and translated this sayd booke in to
our englysshe, not over rude ne curyous, but in such termes
as shall be understanden, by goddys grace, accordynge to my
copye. And yf ony man wyll enter-mete in[1] redyng of hit,
and fyndeth suche termes that he can not understande, late
hym goo rede and lerne vyrgyll, or the pystles of ovyde, and
ther he shall see and understonde lyghtly all, yf he have a
good redar and enformer. For this booke is not for every
rude and unconnynge man to see, but to clerkys and very
gentylmen that understande gentylnes and scyence. Thenne
I praye alle theym that shall rede in this lytyl treatys, to
holde me for excused for the translatynge of hit. For I
knowleche myselfe ignorant of connynge to empryse on me
so hie and noble a werke. But I praye mayster John Skelton,

[1] undertake to.

late created poete laureate in the unyversite of oxenforde, to oversee and correcte this sayd booke, And taddresse and expowne where as shalle be founde faulte to theym that shall requyre it. For hym, I knowe for suffycyent to expowne and englysshe every dyffyculte that is therin. For he hath late translated the epystyls of Tulle and the boke of dyodorus syculus, and diverse other werkes oute of latyn in-to englysshe, not in rude and olde langage, but in polysshed and ornate termes craftely, as he that hath redde vyrgyle, ovyde, tullye, and all the other noble poetes and oratours to me unknowen.

24   THE LOVE OF BOOKS

Richard de Bury, a cleric of good birth, became tutor to Edward III.; then royal clerk and ambassador, papal chaplain, and bishop-expectant with an income *pro tempore* equivalent to not less than £30,000 or £40,000 in modern money. In 1333 he became bishop of Durham. He was a great book-collector, and his *Philobiblon* is the most remarkable of medieval treatises on books ; but a distinguished contemporary accuses him of having paraded borrowed learning, and ascribes the real authorship of the book to the Dominican Robert Holcot; and a few known facts lend some colour to this accusation. Whether Holcot or Bury, however, the actual writer was evidently a sincere book-lover ; and he has found a model editor in Mr E. C. Thomas (1888). Mr Thomas's translation has been republished in *The King's Classics* : the extracts here given are by the present compiler.

Cap. 1. That desirable treasure of wisdom and knowledge, which all men covet by natural instinct, doth infinitely tran-scend all earthly riches.... Where dost thou most gladly hide, O chosen treasure? and where shall our thirsty souls find thee? Surely it is in books that thou hast pitched thy tent ; for there hast thou been set by the most Highest, the Light of Lights, the Book of Life ! There do all receive who ask, and all find who seek, and to all who unweariedly knock it is opened without delay. Here the Cherubim stretch out their wings, that the learner's understanding may be raised on high, and may survey from pole to pole, from the rising of the sun to the going down thereof, from the north and from the south.... Lastly, we must weigh what comfortable teaching there is in books, how easy and how secret. How safely do we lay bare before a book, without false shame, the poverty of our human ignorance! Books are masters who teach us without rod or ferule, without reviling or wrath, without [gifts of] garments[1] or money. If thou comest to visit them, they sleep not ; if thou wilt question them, they hide nothing ; they murmur not at thine errors, they have no laugh of scorn at thine ignorance.

Cap. 3. From the aforesaid we draw a corollary pleasing to ourselves but acceptable, we fear, to few : to wit, that no man should be withheld from buying books, at however great a price, if only his means will permit—unless, indeed, he must needs resist the malice of the vendor, or await a more opportune season for buying. For, if it be wisdom alone which giveth a book its price, and if wisdom be a treasure which no man can number, so that (as these premisses suppose) the price of books is more than tongue can tell, how then can that be a dear bargain wherein an infinite good is bought? Wherefore Solomon, that sun among men, exhorteth us to buy books gladly and sell them unwillingly, saying in the 23rd chapter of Proverbs, "Buy the truth, and sell not wisdom."

Cap. 4. [The author makes Books complain of neglect at the hands of the beneficed clergy.]

But enough of this ; for it irks us to remember what gifts we have conferred on this degenerate race of clerks, since all gifts to the ungrateful seem rather wasted than conferred. Let us dwell now for awhile upon the injuries wherewith they repay us, their insults and injuries, wherein we cannot recite one of each kind ; nay, scarce can we come near to naming the kinds themselves. First, we are expelled by main force from those houses of the clergy which are our own by hereditary right :—we, who had once our cells of quiet in the inner chamber, but who in these abominable days, sad to relate! are utterly cast forth and bear reproach without the gates; for our places are now taken either by dogs or birds, or by that two-footed beast whose cohabitation with the

---

[1] Cf. the Bedell's instructions in Section II., no. 8 : "The Inceptour in Gramer shall gyve to the Vice-chauncelar a Bonett," etc. At other universities the expense was sometimes greater, and the candidate for a degree was obliged to give gowns.

clergy hath been forbidden from ancient times—that beast whom we have ever taught our scholars to flee as they would flee the asp or the basilisk. Hence it is that she, who hath ever implacably envied our studies, spying us at length in our corner, with no defence but the webs woven around us by spiders now defunct, seizes us with frowning brow and bitter words; and, laughing us to scorn, proves us to be superfluous and unwelcome guests among all the household furniture. She complains that we are unprofitable for all domestic services, and counsels that we should be exchanged for precious head-gear, fine linen and silk and double-dyed scarlet; for garments furred with vair; for linen and for wool. Nor doth she err here, if she could see our inmost hearts, if she had read Theophrastus or Valerius[1], or at least had heard, marked, and inwardly digested the twenty-fifth chapter of Ecclesiasticus.

Cap. 17. You will see perchance some headstrong youth, sitting slothfully at his studies...his finger-nails are filthy, black as jet, and with them he marks the place where the matter takes his fancy. He distributes innumerable straws, laying them conspicuously in divers places of the book, that the wheatstalk may recall whatsoever his memory may let slip. These straws, which are never withdrawn, remain undigested in the book's belly, first distending it to the bursting of its wonted clasps, and then rotting in the neglect and oblivion to which they have been left. He shrinketh not from eating fruit or cheese over his open book, nor from moving his cup carelessly over it; and, having no bag at hand, he leaves in his book the fragments that remain.... Then he leans his elbows on the book and takes a long sleep in exchange for his brief study, and bends back the margins of the leaves to smooth out the wrinkles, to the no small detriment of the volume. Now the rain is over and gone, and the flowers appear on our earth; and this scholar whom we

---

[1] *Wife of Bath's Prologue*, 669:

> He hadde a book that gladly, nyght and day,
> For his desport he woldë rede alway.
> He clepëd it 'Valerie' and 'Theofraste,'
> At whichë book he lough alwey ful faste.

describe, this neglector rather than inspector of books, will stuff his volume with violets, primroses, roses and four-leaved clover.   Then he will paw it over with hands wet with water or sweat; then with dusty gloves he will fumble over the white parchment, and hunt for his page, line by line, with a forefinger clad in this ancient leather.   Then, at the prick of some biting flea, the sacred volume is cast aside, scarce to be closed again for another month, when it is so clogged and swollen with dust that it resists all efforts to close it.

But we must specially keep from all touch of our books those shameless youths who, when they have learned to shape the letters of the alphabet, straightway become incongruous annotators of all the fairest volumes that come in their way, and either deck with their monstrous alphabets all broader margins that they can find around the text, or rashly presume to write with unchastened pen whatsoever frivolous stuff may happen to run at that moment in their heads.... There are thieves also, who shamefully mutilate our books, cutting down the lateral margins, to the very quick of the written text, as material for their own epistolary correspondence, or stealing for various evil uses the blank pages which guard the book's ends; a sort of sacrilege which doth merit to be prohibited under strictest threat of excommunication.

Moreover, scholastic decency imperatively demands that, whensoever we return to study from our meals, we should wash our hands before reading; no finger dipped in grease should either turn the leaves or even open the clasps, before such ablution.   Let no whimpering child be suffered to admire the pictured capital letters, lest his slimy hand defile the parchment; for whatsoever the child seeth, that must he also touch.   The unlearned also, for whom a book is the same whether it be held open upright or topsy-turvy, are utterly unworthy of any communion with books.   Let the clerk see to it also, that the sooty scullion reeking straight from the fleshpots lay no unwashen finger on the lily-white page; let him who ministereth to your precious volumes be one who walketh without blemish.   A decent cleanliness of hand would be most profitable both to books and to scholars, if scabs and pustules were not marks of the clerical character.

SECTION IV

CHURCH AND CHURCHMEN

In this section there is no attempt to exploit fully such sources as Matthew Paris or Jocelin of Brakelond. The latter is, in fact, altogether avoided; his chronicle is so brief, so accessible in *The King's Classics*, and casts so many different sidelights on Church life under the Angevins, that it should be read in its entirety.

1   A DYING WORLD

The whole Middle Ages may be looked upon as a long process of suffering and convalescence from the barbarian invasions, which influenced European thought down to and beyond the Reformation. Men's minds were constantly haunted by the Apocalypse and the more dismal chapters of the Prophets; much of the unprogressiveness of the Middle Ages in certain directions may be traced to this numbing belief in the imminence of the Last Judgment. The following four extracts will suffice, out of very many which might be chosen; one of the passages in which Roger Bacon records his despair of the present world may be found in *A Medieval Garner*, p. 342.

(*a*)   St Gregory the Great, *Hom. in Ezech.* c. II. Hom. vi. § 21 (Migne, *P.L.* vol. 76. 1009).

I ask, what is there now in this world to please us? Everywhere we see sights of mourning and hear the groans of men. Cities are ruined, towns are desolate, fields lie waste; the land hath become a wilderness. No husbandman is left in the fields; scarce a citizen remains in the cities; and even these scant remnants of humanity live under daily and unceasing plagues—plagues of divine justice which have no end, because the guilty actions themselves are not yet amended thereby. Some we see led into captivity, others maimed, others slain; what therefore, my brethren, do we see of pleasure in this life? Nay, if we yet love such a world as this, it is not joys but wounds that we love.

We see what is now left of Rome, once the mistress of the world. We see the manifold oppression of immeasurable pains, the desolation of her citizens, the enemies that press daily upon her, the ruins that grow from day to day, so that in her we may see that fulfilled whereof Ezekiel speaketh [c. xxiv. *v.* 3, 5, 10, 11], "set a pot, set it on, and also pour water into it.... Take the choice of the flock, and burn also the bones under it, and make it boil well, and let them seethe bones of it therein.... Heap on wood, kindle the fire, consume the flesh, and spice it well, and let the bones be burned. Then set it empty upon the coals thereof, that the brass of it may be hot, and may burn, and that the filthiness of it may be molten in it, that the scum of it may be consumed."...... But now, behold! all the mighty men of this world are taken away from Rome; therefore *the bones are sodden away.* Lo! the commons fail and fall; *the flesh of it is consumed.* Therefore let the word go forth : *Heap on wood, kindle the fire, consume the flesh, and spice it well, and let the bones be burned.* For where is the Senate now, and where the People? The bones are crumbled away, the flesh is consumed, all pomp of worldly dignities is extinguished in the city; the whole substance thereof hath been sodden away ; and we, who yet remain, are we not daily given over to the sword, and to innumerable tribulations? But why do I thus speak of men, when we see the destruction so increasing that the very buildings crumble to ruin? Wherefore the prophet aptly addeth this word concerning our city, now so empty, *that the brass of it may be hot, and may burn.* For now the very pot itself is consumed, wherein aforetime the flesh and bones had melted away; which is to say that, after the inhabitants have failed, the very walls now fall. But where now are those who were wont to rejoice in her glory? where is their pomp and pride, their often and immoderate mirth?...

And this which we have said of the breaking in pieces of the city of Rome, we know to have come to pass also in all the cities of the world. Some parts have been wasted with slaughter, others devoured with the edge of the sword, others tormented with famine, others swallowed up with earthquakes. Let us therefore with all our soul scorn this present world, as already brought to nought ; let us close our yearnings for this world now at least, at the very end of this world's existence ; let us do what we can, and imitate the deeds of good men.

(*b*) Adam de Marisco, or Marsh, was an intimate friend of Grosseteste and Simon de Montfort, and one of the earliest and most distinguished of medieval teachers at Oxford. The following extract is from his letter to Pope Innocent IV. about 1250 A.D. (*Monumenta Franciscana*, R.S., vol. I. 1858, p. 420). Almost equally strong expressions may be found elsewhere : e.g. to Grosseteste, p. 147, and Simon de Montfort, p. 266.

Since it seems that the world is now in its old age, and we are come to the end of all things, and the Saviour's prophecy is fulfilled, who saith that iniquity shall abound and the love of many shall wax cold, so that it is already as if Satan were loosed, and those horrors were abroad which St Paul fore-telleth [2 Tim. iii. 1] :...therefore, I say, more horribly than in any past times we now see, throughout all regions of the habitable globe, how wickedness runs riot : the Gospel is dis-obeyed, laws are gainsaid, churches are laid waste, kingdoms made desert, the priesthood shaken to its foundations, princes cast down, clergy trodden under foot, knighthood scattered abroad, religion profaned, and the commonalty ruined. We see bitter malice, ferocious murders, filthy defilements, violence in prelacies, wicked perfidies, vehement seditions, knavish discords, jarring schisms and deliberate treachery ; so that, in all these things, the direst havoc of infernal torments seems to be falling upon mankind.

Almost equally interesting is the long Welsh prophecy of Antichrist and the Day of Judgment printed with a translation in *Transactions of the Society of Cymmrodorion*, vol. IV. (1881), pp. 106 ff. Antichrist, the author thinks, will appear in the year 1403 A.D. ; and "the Masters of the Arts, did they rightly know how, conjecture that the world will end at the end of the seventh thousand years from the beginning of the world," since "the Creator at the beginning formed several things in sevens." But it is best to take our last examples from the beginning of the Reformation period.

(*c*) Bishop Fisher (*English Works*, E.E.T.S., Extra Series, 1876, p. 337).

Before the coming of Antichrist there shall be a notable

discession and departing from the faith of the Church. And it is not unlike to be at this same time, by the occasion of this most perilous heretic [Luther].

(*d*) Sir T. More, *The Third Booke of Comfort against Tribulacion* (*Workes*, ed. 1557, p. 1213*b*. The book is in the form of a dialogue between two Hungarian nobles, Anthony and his nephew Vincent: More wrote it in his prison at the Tower in 1534).

Anthony. Verely, if we people of the christen nacions were such as woulde god we were, I would litle feare all the preparacions that the gret Turk could make.   No! nor yet, beyng as badde as we be, I nothing doubt at all, but that in conclusion, howe base so ever chrystendome be broughte, it shall springe up agayne, tyll the tyme be come verye nere to the daye of dome; whereof somme tokens as me thinketh are not comen yet....For, as appereth in thapocalips and other places of scrypture, the faith shal be at that tyme so far faded, that he shall for the love of hys electes, lest thei should fall and perish, abbredge those daies and accelerate his coming.   But, as I saye, me thynketh I misse yet in my minde some of those tokens that shall by the scripture come a good while beefore that.

2   SACERDOTAL AUTHORITY

To realize the reaction against sacerdotal pretensions which forms an important factor in later medieval life and literature, we must understand clearly what those claims were.

(*a*) From the bull of Boniface VIII., *Unam Sanctam*, published in 1302. This bull is incorporated in Canon Law (*Extrav. Com.*, l. I. tit. viii. c. I).

That there is one holy Catholic and Apostolic Church we are compelled by faith to hold and maintain....As the truth testifieth, it is the part of the spiritual power to teach and judge the earthly power....Moreover, we declare that all human beings are subject to the Pontiff of Rome; and we assert, define and pronounce this tenet to be essential and necessary to salvation.   Given at our palace of the Lateran, in the 8th year of our pontificate.

(*b*) The bull *Clericis Laicos*, published by Boniface VIII. in 1296, asserted the complete immunity of the clergy from taxation by the state. Though both England and France openly resisted it in practice, it laid down a theory which was never formally retracted by the Church. The translation is from D. Wilkins, *Concilia, etc.*, vol. II. (1737), p. 222.

That the laity are bitterly hostile to the clergy is a matter of ancient tradition which is plainly confirmed by the experience of modern times also; for the laity, not content with their own limits, press with unbridled presumption to things unlawful; to wit, lacking the prudence to observe that they have no lawful power over the persons or goods of clerks or ecclesiastics, they impose grievous burdens and taxes upon prelates, churches and regular or secular clerics...without licence from the Apostolic See....We therefore, willing to put an end to such acts of injustice, with the advice of our brethren, do decree by our Apostolic authority that [all clergy who pay such taxes without Papal permission], and all Emperors, Kings, Dukes, Earls,...and all persons of whatsoever rank or condition, who impose, exact or receive such taxes...or all who knowingly aid and abet the same, whether openly or secretly, shall *ipso facto* incur the sentence of excommunication....From which sentence of excommunication and interdict no man may be absolved, unless on his deathbed, without the special authority and licence of the Apostolic See; since we do hereby intend utterly to repudiate this so horrible abuse of the secular power.

(*c*) Bishop Quivil (or, more probably, Quenel) of Exeter was one of the many solid and careful prelates who did honour to the medieval English church. He held a Synod in 1287, the constitutions of which are among our most important documents for the relations between clergy and people (D. Wilkins, *l.c.*, p. 152, § XLII.).

Certain layfolk, especially bailiffs and nobles...as we learn from frequent complaints, have in these modern times (*modernis temporibus*) fallen into such audacious madness that, the more they inflict outrage, loss and insult upon the clergy and their goods, the more they rejoice and boast themselves therein. Alas! unhappy wretches, walking in darkness! Is not God our Father who created us? and is not the Church our Mother in whom we were born again

by baptism? and is it not written in Canon Law[1]: "He
that stealeth anything from his father or his mother and
saith: This is no sin, is the partner of a murderer"? Is it
not plain and strange madness that the son should attempt
to lord it over his father, the disciple over his master? and
that a man should strive to subject by unjust obligations
those whom he believes to have the power of binding and
loosing him not only on earth but in heaven also?

3   CANON LAW

Canon Law, which lies at the foundation of so many medieval theories,
grew up very gradually from different attempts to codify the decisions
(1) of Popes, (2) of Church Councils, (3) of Church Fathers of acknowledged authority, and (4) of Emperors dealing with Church affairs. It is
a characteristically medieval production; no scholar now denies that a
large proportion of it is either altogether spurious or wrongly attributed,
while there is great conflict of opinion even within the Roman Catholic
Church as to its authority or its binding force. Great portions of it have
admittedly full papal authority; concerning other considerable portions,
neither Popes nor orthodox commentators have yet ventured to pronounce
any definite decision. The two following extracts illustrate the two opposite
poles of medieval opinion; the enormous majority, however, would have
disagreed with Bacon. One of the very few medieval writers who went
even further than Bacon, condemning some of the most important parts
of Canon Law as spurious, was Bishop Pecock, of Chichester, whose
criticisms may be found in his *Repressor*, R. S. 1860, vol. II. pp. 323-53.

(*a*)   R. Bacon, *Opp. Ined.*, R. S., p. 84.

What I would fain say is this: that, as among the Hebrews
of old the State was governed by God's law [in the Old Testa-
ment], so now among Christians should it be ruled by God's
law [in both Testaments]. For if all wisdom be mainly contained in the Bible, as its principal source, then at least we
may say that the State should be mainly ruled thereby. But
now it is not so; for in God's church a civil lawyer is more
renowned and is more quickly promoted to dignities—even
though he know naught but civil law, and be ignorant of
canon law and theology—than a master in theology. And it is
strange that, whereas canon law is drawn from Holy Scripture

---

[1] Gratian's *Decretum*, Pars II. Causa xii. q. ii. c. 6; a decree of Pope Anacletus,
based on Prov. xxviii. 24 and developing the argument here adopted by Bishop
Quivil.

FLAGELLATION OF HENRY II

SAINT THOMAS OF LANCASTER

and from the expositions of the saints as from its fountain-head, yet it doth not turn mainly to those sources, either in study or in ecclesiastical practice. For this canon law should in justice be expounded, and harmonized, and corroborated, and confirmed from the Holy Scriptures, since to them it owes its origin. But now it is mainly expounded and harmonized and discussed through civil law, whereunto it is altogether attracted both in study and in practice, which is altogether unjust; although indeed civil law may rightly be used in subservience to canon law, as a servant to a mistress.

O therefore that the cavils and frauds of lawyers might be put down, and that causes might be settled without din of litigation, as was men's wont forty years ago! O that I might live to see this with mine own eyes! For if we removed the din of litigation and the cavils and abuses of lawyers, then clergy and laity alike would enjoy justice and peace. For, if once canon law were purged from this superfluity of civil law, and were ruled by divinity, then would the Church be gloriously ruled, according to her proper dignity. For there are and would be many who, if this were so, would never cease from the study of wisdom until they had fulfilled their aim, if they had their livelihood meanwhile; and some would complete theology, some philosophy, and others would rectify canon law and reduce it to its proper state....

But, most blessed Pope and most wise Lord, may your Majesty deign to consider this; for you alone can apply the remedy, since there never was a Pope so truly learned in the law as you, nor (as I believe) shall be; and, though there be some who know law well, yet there is no hope that such men will be elected to the papacy. But it hath been prophesied some forty years since, and to many men hath it been revealed in visions, that in our days there shall be a Pope who shall purge canon law and God's Church from the cavils and frauds of lawyers, and that justice shall be done everywhere without din of litigation; and it shall come to pass, through the goodness and truth and justice of this Pope, that the Greeks shall come back to the obedience of the Roman Church, and most of the Tartars shall be converted to the Faith, and the Sara-

cens shall be destroyed, and there shall be one fold and one
shepherd, as this word sounded in the prophet's ears.   And
one man, who saw this by revelation, said and still saith that
he himself shall see these wonderful works done in his own
time; and certainly all could be done within a year, or less, if
it pleased God and the Supreme Pontiff; wherefore it follows
that all might be done within your reign ; God preserve your
life that you may perform this!...I have made a sign here in
the margin, that your Holiness in your wisdom may take
good note of this; more especially, because you have the
Church of God in your power, and the whole world under
your direction.

(*b*)   Constitution of Abp Arundel in 1409, with notes by Bp Lyndwood,
the recognized official commentator (Lyndwood's *Provinciale*, Oxon. 1679,
pp. 297 ff.).

Moreover, let no man presume to dispute, whether publicly
or secretly, concerning the Articles determined by the Church,
as contained in the Decrees, Decretals and our Provincial
Constitutions, or in local synodal decrees, unless such dispute
be directed solely to the understanding of the true sense
thereof; nor again shall any man call in doubt the authority
of the said Decrees, Decretals or Provincial Constitutions, or
the power of whosoever may have composed the same; nor
shall any teach contrary to that which is therein determined....
He therefore who shall assert, teach, or preach the contrary,
or who shall pertinaciously imply the same (unless indeed he
repent under the form and manner elsewhere prescribed by
Us, and abjure his error as there prescribed), shall incur the
pains of Heresy, and possibly of a relapsed heretic; and he
shall be condemned as such for all effect of law.

Lyndwood's notes (A.D. 1430).

Articles.   He addeth not, *of Faith,* but (as may be seen)
determined by the Church, intending thereby that heresy is
incurred not only by opposition to the Articles of Faith but
also by opposition to what hath been determined by the
Church even though this concern not the articles of faith ;
and this is in accord with that which is written in the Gre-

gorian Decretals, Lib. v. tit. 7, cap. 9 and in the Clementines, Lib. v. tit. 3, cap. 3.

By the Church: that is, by the prelates of the Church.

Whosoever may have composed; whether such author be the Pope as universal ordinary, or the Archbishop in his own province or the Bishop in his diocese.

Imply. From this it is plain that a man may offend not only in words, but also in signs or gestures; and this is true, so far as such may display his inward mind or intention.

Possibly; that is if, after abjuring, he fall again into his former errors.

4   PETER'S PENCE

The Brut, E.E.T.S., 1908, p. 316.

And in the same yer [1365] hit was ordeyned that seynt Petris pens, fro that tyme forth shold not be payd, the whiche Kyng Ina, sumtyme King of Englond, of the cuntre of West-Saxons, that bygan to regne in the yer of our Lord DClxxxix, ferst graunted to Rome, for the scole of Engelond ther to be continued.

5   MIRACLES

It is not generally recognized how many thinking men in the Middle Ages did all they could to clear their faith from reliance on the merely miraculous. St Augustine and St Gregory the Great, in words which were often echoed in later generations, take up a standpoint which, logically, approaches nearly to "modernism"; though, of course, neither writer pushed his thought to its logical conclusion. In this connection, and as a corrective to the crude materialism of the masses which is typified in the third extract, it is worth while to insert two passages from the *Magna Vita S. Hugonis* (R.S., 1864). It must be added that, though the biographer portrays Hugh as no admirer of the miraculous *per se*, he believes his hero to have worked many miracles himself.

(a)   *The Saint's View.*

p. 97. [St Hugh] had so deeply and perfectly drunk in, to the bottom of his soul, that gravity and humility laid down by the writers of the holy Carthusian Order, that he seemed to admire or strive after nothing less than the prodigies of miracles; nevertheless, when he read or heard of such miracles wrought by holy men, he gladly related them and held them in high veneration. He related them (I say) to the commendation of those who had shown forth such wonders, and for the discipline of such as marvelled thereat; but for himself the mere sanctity of a saint was his real miracle, and that alone sufficed him for an example. And to him the one universal miracle was that hearty and intimate remembrance of his Creator which was never absent from his mind; and the stupendous and inexplicable multitude of God's mighty works.

p. 245. A certain cleric, though in mortal sin, yet presumed to officiate at Mass, saying meanwhile in his own heart "thinkest thou that Christ's body and blood is truly made, touched, and taken by me, a foul sinner?" In answer to his doubts, the host turned to actual flesh, which, when broken, gave forth blood.

Many faithful flocked together from the neighbourhood, on every side, to see with their own eyes these mighty works of God; and they with the utmost reverence magnified the Lord who alone doeth wondrous things....They who brought this news from the priest to the Bishop looked that he would go forthwith to see the miracle, with eager devotion of heart. But he had no sooner heard their tale than he made reply, saying "Good! in God's name let them keep to themselves the signs of their own unfaith! What is this to us? Do we marvel at particular images of this divine gift—we who daily behold, with the most faithful eyes of the spirit, the whole unbroken image of this heavenly sacrifice? Let that man go and gaze with bodily eyes upon those tiny crumbs [of God's body], who seeth not the whole with the inward eye of faith...." Thus he held back his own household from their purpose of curious sightseeing.

(*b*) *Popular Preaching.*

An Alphabet of Tales (E.E.T.S., 1904). A 15th century translation, through the French, of Latin anecdotes for preachers; most of the stories are very popular, occurring in all kinds of similar compilations. p. 71: Latin title "A Bird's Prayer is sometimes heard."

Cesarius [of Heisterbach] tellis how som tyme ther was a burd that was lernyd to speke. So on a tyme sho flow away in the feldis, and the Goshalk [pur]sewid after hur and wold hafe kyllid hur. And whan sho saw hym com, as sho was lernyd

at home, sho began to cry, and sayd; "Sancte Thoma! adiuva
me! A! Saynt Thomas, helpe me!" And onone[1] this goshalk
fell down dead, and this burd esskapid and had none harm.
Lo, surs, what vertue it is to call on Saynt Thomas, martir of
Cantyrbery, in any tribulacion!

6   I STRETCH LAME HANDS OF FAITH...

The uniformity of medieval faith has often been much exaggerated by
modern writers : thoughtful and plain-spoken writers of the time often
show indications of embarrassment.   It would be difficult to choose better
illustrative passages here than the following two from *Piers Plowman*
(abbreviated).

(*a*)   B, X. 414 ff. and 452 ff., pp. 320, 322.

On Gode Fridaye I fynde a feloun was ysaved,
That had lyved al his lyf with lesynges[2] and with thefte ;
And, for he biknewe[3] on the crosse and to Cryste schrof[4] hym,
He was sonnere[5] saved than seynt Johan the baptiste,
And or Adam or Ysaye or eny of the prophetes,
That hadde yleine[6] with Lucyfer many longe yeres.
A robbere was yraunceouned[7] rather than thei alle,
With-outen any penaunce of purgatorie to perpetuel blisse.
    Thanne Marye Magdaleyne; what womman dede worse?
Or who worse than David that Uries deth conspired?
Or Poule the apostle, that no pitee hadde
Moche crystene kynde to kylle to deth?
And now ben thise as sovereynes wyth seyntes in hevene,
Tho that wroughte wikkedlokest, in worlde tho[8] thei were.
And tho that wisely wordeden, and wryten many bokes
Of witte and of wisdome, with dampned soules wonye[9].
    The doughtiest doctour and devynoure of the trinitee,
Was Augustyn the olde and heighest of the foure[10],
Sayde thus in a sarmoun (I seigh it writen ones),
    *Ecce ipsi idioti rapiunt celum, ubi nos sapientes in
    inferno mergimur :*

---

[1] anon.   [2] lies.   [3] confessed.   [4] shrove.   [5] sooner.
[6] lain.   [7] ransomed.   [8] when.   [9] dwell.
[10] The four styled *Doctor* in Canon Law are Ambrose, Augustine, Jerome and
Gregory.   The passage here quoted is really from St Augustine's *Confessions*,
l. VIII. c. 8.

And is to mene to Englisshe men more ne lasse,
" Aren none rather yravysshed fro the righte byleve
Than ar this cunnynge clerkes that conne many bokes ;
Ne none sonner saved ne sadder[1] of bileve,
Than plowmen and pastoures and pore comune laboreres."
Souteres[2] and shepherdes, suche lewed jottes[3],
Percen[4] with a *pater-noster* the paleys of hevene,
And passen purgatorie penaunceles at her hennes-partynge[5],
In-to the blisse of paradys for her pure byleve,
That inparfitly here knewe and eke lyved.

Yee ! men knowe clerkes that han cursed the tyme,
That evere thei couth or knewe more than *credo in deum patrem;*
And pryncipaly her *pater-noster* many a persone hath wisshed.

I se ensamples my-self, and so may many an other,
That servauntes that serven lordes selden falle in arrerage,
But tho that kepen the lordes catel[6], clerkes and reves.
Right so lewed men and of litel knowynge,
Selden falle thei so foule and so fer in synne,
As clerkes of holikirke that kepen Crystes tresore,
The which is mannes soule to save, as god seith in the gospel.

(*b*) B, x. 28, p. 286.

Thilke that god moste gyveth, leste good thei deleth,
And moste unkynde to the comune that moste catel weldeth[7].
Harlotes[8] for her harlotrye may have of her godis,
And Japeres[9] and Jogeloures[10] and Jangelers of gestes.

Ac[11] he that hath holy writte ay in his mouth,
And can telle of Tobye and of the twelve apostles,
Or prechen of the penaunce that Pilat wrought
To Jesu the gentil that Jewes to-drowe[12] :—
Litel is he loved that suche a lessoun scheweth.

But tho that feynen hem folis[13], and with faityng libbeth[14],
Agein the lawe of owre lorde, and lyen on hem-selve,

---

[1] more steadfast.   [2] cobblers.   [3] unlearned fellows.   [4] pierce.
[5] hence-parting.   [6] chattels.   [7] dispose of.   [8] rascals.   [9] jesters.
[10] buffoons.   [11] but.   [12] tortured.   [13] fools.   [14] live as idle beggars.

Spitten and spewen and speke foule wordes,
Drynken and dryvelen and do[1] men for to gape,
Lickne[2] men and lye on hem that leneth[3] hem no giftes,
Thei conne namore mynstralcye ne musyke, men to glade,
Than Munde the mylnere[4] of *multa fecit deus!*[5]
Ne were here vyle harlotrye[6], (have god my treuthe,)
Shulde nevere kyng ne knight ne chanoun of seynt Poules
Gyve hem to her yeresgive[7] the gifte of a grote!
    Ac if thei carpen[8] of Cryst, this clerkis and this lewed,
Atte mete in her murthes whan mynstralles ben stille,
Thanne telleth thei of the trinite a tale other tweyne,
And bringen forth a balled[9] resoun, and taken Bernard to
    witnesse,
And putten forth a presumpsioun to preve[10] the sothe.
Thus thei dryvele at her deyse[11] the deite to knowe,
And gnawen god with the gorge whan her gutte is fulle.
    Ac the careful may crye and carpen atte gate.
Bothe afyngred[12] and a-thurst and for chele[13] quake;
Is none to nymen hym nere[14], his noye[15] to amende,
But hoen[16] on hym as an hounde and hoten[17] hym go
    thennes.

Freres and faitoures han founde suche questiouns
To plese with[18] proude men sithen the pestilence tyme,
And prechen at seint Poules for pure envye of clerkis,
That[19] folke is noughte fermed in the feith, ne fre of her
    goodes,
Ne sori for her synnes; so is pryde waxen
In religioun and in alle the rewme amonges riche and pore,
That preyeres have no power the pestilence to lette.
[For god is def now a dayes and deyneth nouht ous to
    huyre[20],
And good men for oure gultes he al to-grynt[21] to dethe;][22]

---

[1] cause.   [2] mimic.   [3] give.   [4] miller.
[5] God's wonderful works (Ps. xxxix. 6).   [6] nor, but for their vile ribaldry.
[7] year's-gift, Christmas box.   [8] talk.   [9] bald.   [10] prove.
[11] their dais.   [12] hungry.   [13] chill.   [14] bring him near.   [15] suffering.
[16] hoot.   [17] bid.   [18] wherewith to please.   [19] so that.   [20] to hear us.
[21] ground.   [22] These two lines are inserted from C-text.

Elyng[1] is the halle uche[2] daye in the wyke,
There the lorde ne the lady liketh noughte to sytte.
Now hath uche riche a reule to eten bi hym-selve
In a pryve parloure, for pore mennes sake,
Or in a chambre with a chymneye[3], and leve the chief halle,
That was made for meles, men to eten inne.
I have yherde hiegh men etyng atte table,
Carpen, as thei clerkes were, of Cryste and of his mightes
And leyden fautes uppon the fader that fourmed us alle,
And carpen ageine clerkes crabbed wordes ;—
"Whi wolde owre saveoure suffre such a worme in his blisse,
That bigyled the womman and the man after,
Thorw whiche wyles and wordes thei wenten to helle,
And al her sede for here synne the same deth suffred ?
Here lyeth yowre lore" thise lordes gynneth dispute,
"Of that ye clerkes us kenneth of Cryst by the gospel ;
    Filius non portabit iniquitatem patris, &c.[4]
Whi shulde we, that now ben, for the werkes of Adam
Roten and to-rende[5] ? resoun wolde it nevere ;
    Unusquisque portabit onus suum, &c."[6]
Suche motyves thei moeve[7], this maistres in her glorie,
And maken men in mysbileve that muse moche on her
    wordes.

7 POLITICAL MARTYRS

A medieval commonalty had always one not ineffective way of political protest ; any statesman who had suffered in a popular cause, without respect to his personal character, was canonized by the popular voice ; prayers were addressed to him, and miracles were worked not only at his tomb but elsewhere by his intercession with God. Becket, Simon de Montfort, Edward II. and Henry VI. are well-known examples ; but perhaps the most curious case in English history is that of the selfish and inglorious Thomas Earl of Lancaster, who lost his head in 1322 and was sainted as a protest against the government of Edward II. Here will be found three out of many documents referring to his cult, and one to that of Edward II. It may be noted in this context that the body of Abp Boniface

---

[1] ailing.   [2] each.   [3] fireplace.
[4] The son shall not bear the iniquity of the father (Ezech. xviii. 20).
[5] be destroyed.   [6] Each shall bear his own burden (Gal. vi. 5).
[7] move.

of Canterbury, whose high-handed proceedings may be found described below (No. 11), worked miracles after his death (L. Wadding, *Annales Minorum* IV. 241 : " He was buried at Hautecombe in 1270, and having worked many miracles, is venerated as a saint by all the people of Savoy "). There was naturally some difference of opinion as to such miracles—as, indeed, there sometimes was in the case of the greatest saints—and there can be little doubt that Higden's comments in extract (c) represent the point of view of most thinking men in his age.

(a)   *The Brut* (E.E.T.S. 1906) I. 228 ff.

And sone after the Gode Erl Thomas of Lancastre was martrede, a preste, that longe tyme hade ben blynde, dremede in his slepyng that he shulde gone unto the hull[1] there that the gode Erl Thomas of Lancastre was don unto deth, and he shulde have his sight agein....And when this miracle was knowen amonges men, the peple come thither on every side, and knelede, and made here praiers at his tombe that is in the Priori of Pountfrette, and praied that holy martre of socour and of helpe, and God herd here prayere.   Also there was a yonge childe drenchede in a welle in the toune of Pountfrette, and was dede iij daies and iij nyghtes ; and men come and laide the dede childe oppon seint Thomas tombe, the holy martre ; and the childe aros there fram the deth unto lif, as meny a man hit saw....Also ther was a riche man in Coundone [Condom] in Gascoigne ; and soche a maladie he had, that al his right side rotede, and felle awaie from him ; and men might se his lyvere and also his hert.   [*His friends prayed to St Thomas, who came in a vision and healed him.*]   And this gode man come into Engelande, and toke with him iiij felawes, and come to Pountfrette, and come to that holy martre, and dede here pilgrimage ; but the gode man that was sik come thither al naked saf his breche ; and when thai hade done, thai turnede home ageyne into here contre, and told of the miracle wher-so that thai come.   And also ij men have bene helede there of the morimal[2], through helpe of that holy martre, though that evel be holde incurable.

(b)   From the *French Chronicle of London*, tr. Riley in *Chronicles of Old London*, 1863, p. 257.

At this time [1322] God wrought many miracles in the

---

[1] hill.   [2] putrid sore (Chaucer, *C. T. Prologue*, l. 386).

Church of Saint Paul, at the tablet there which the said Thomas of Lancaster made ; in remembrance that the king had granted and confirmed the Ordinances which were made by Saint Robert de Winchelse, Archbishop of Canterbury, and by all the great and wise men of England, to the great profit of all the realm. In which place, the crooked were made straight, the blind received their sight, and the deaf their hearing, and other beneficial works of grace were there openly shown.... And after this, at the Translation of Saint Thomas [7 July], by the King's writ, issued from Chancery, the tablet in the Church of Saint Paul, as also the wax taper that was there offered in devotion to the martyr, was with great rigour taken away and removed ; but still, for all that, the devotion of the people was not wholly put an end to, oblations being still made at the pillar from which the tablet had been hung.

(c) Trevisa's *Higden*, VIII. 313.

Of this erle and of his dedes is ofte greet stryf among comoun peple, whether he schulde be acounted for seyntes other none. Some seyn yis, for he dede many almes dedes, and worschipped men of religioun, and mayntened a trewe querel, as it semed, to his lyves ende ; also his enemyes durede afterward but a while, and deyde in schentful[1] deeth. Other seien the contrarie, and telleth that he was an housbonde man, and rought[2] nought of his wyf, and defouled a greet multitude of gentilwommen and of gentil wenches[3]; yif eny man offended hym a lite, he lete slee hym anon. And postataes[4] and evel doers he favored strongliche, for he schulde nought be i-punsched by the lawe. Also he wolde commytte all his doynges to oon of his secretaries to doo with as he wolde. Also, that he folowe[d][5] schamefulliche in tyme of fyghtinge for the right anon to the deth; and suche on[e] schulde nought be acounted a saynt, nameliche whan he was i-take and i-slawe mauger his teeth[6]. But offrynges and liknes[7] of myracles that

---

[1] shameful.   [2] though he was a married man, he recked.

[3] Higden "hominem videlicet conjugatum neglecta uxore sua generosa innumerosas mulierculas polluere."

[4] apostate : the technical term for a "religious" who had deserted his monastery.

[5] vacillated.   [6] slain against his will.   [7] appearance.

now beeth i-doo[1] in the place there he was byheded, what issue they schulde take it schal be knowe after this tyme. [Cf. *ibid.* 325.]

(*d*) F. Devon, *Issues of the Exchequer*, 1837, p. 259 (18th year of Richard II. Ap. 24).

To Peter Merk and James Monald. In money paid to them by the hands of the same Peter, in discharge of 6*l.* 19*s.* which the Lord the King commanded to be paid them for so much money by them paid for costs incurred about the carriage and portage of a gold cup and a gold ring set with a ruby; also *a Book of the Miracles of Edward, late king of England, whose body was buried at the town of Gloucester*—to wit, from London to the City of Florence, to make a present of the same to our most holy Father Pope Urban, on behalf of the Lord the King.

8 INDULGENCES

(*a*) The strictly orthodox official view, from Bp Lyndwood's *Provinciale*, ed. 1679, pp. 336–7.

The Mystic Treasury is that of the merits of the whole Church, and of those made perfect in the Church, and also of Christ Himself. For this Treasure is collected from the abundance of superfluous merits which many saints have paid and weighed out beyond the measure of what they owed[2], and from the tribulations by them endured, whereof the merit is so great as to exceed all the penalty [of sin] owed by any living man; and especially the passion and merits of Christ, the least drop of whose blood or sweat would suffice for the expiation of all the sins that ever were; for all they are as nothing in respect of this...; and the other good works done by true believers, all which are laid up in the Casket and Treasure-house of the Church, the dispensation whereof is granted to all who have the care of Christ's Mystical Body, and the key of the whole Church militant; that is, generally, to the Supreme Pontiff, but locally also to the other Bishops

[1] are wrought.
[2] ex abundantia meritorum quae multi sancti ultra mensuram debitorum supererogaverunt et impenderunt.

in their dioceses and Archbishops in their provinces, provided only that they do not exceed the quantity limited by [Canon] law.

Lyndwood, however, and all medieval theologians, either assume or explain that the indulgence cannot take effect unless the receiver have confessed to a priest and be truly penitent.

(*b*) From Lyndwood's younger and equally orthodox contemporary Thomas Gascoigne, Chancellor of Oxford University, who wrote about 1450 and was more concerned than Lyndwood with the practical results of the system (*Loci e Libro Veritatum*, ed. Rogers, 1881, *passim*). All these are foreshadowed in the Bull of Boniface IX. (1390), printed by M. J. J. Jusserand in his *Wayfaring Life*, appendix 26.

(p. 86.) The sixth river of Babylonian confusion and destruction [of the Church] is the false faith which some men have in indulgences granted by the Pope, or by man; which [faith] is not of God, for such men have not what is required for such a pardon in God's sight [*here follow five pages setting forth the orthodox theory of indulgences after St Thomas Aquinas and other similar authorities ; then he proceeds*, p. 91] : O ! how often have I heard worldly men of carnal life say proudly, " I care not how often I implead men, or gain great wealth for my own enjoyment, or impoverish the widows and the destitute by cunning sleights and crafty tricks ; for, however ill I may live, by visiting such-and-such a church and by offering money there I can get a plenary remission of guilt and penalty for my sins ! " O how blind of soul are those who say such falsehoods ! How is that man loosed from bonds, who is yet held in bonds ? How is he loosed from sin, while he leaveth not his iniquity, nor doeth either in will or in deed the good works which he oweth to God ?... The men of our time [*homines moderni*] say " We reck not of any sin ; but we do whatsoever pleaseth us as though it were lawful ; we have sinned, and no vengeance hath overtaken us ; and, if we sin again, we need have no fear, for the Kingdom of God is nigh unto us, and Rome is even at our doors ; for we can easily and quickly get us pardon for our guilt, and remission of all the penalty thereof, if we give money for a papal indulgence."... A certain doctor at Bâle wrote there a great discourse of papal indulgences, wherein he affirmeth that he hath found

no indulgences granted and sealed, after the fashion that is
used in these days of ours, within the first thousand years
after Christ; nor hath he found described, in the writings of
any saint, any indulgences after the fashion now used....
Sinners say nowadays, "I care not how many or what evils
I do in God's sight; for I can easily and quickly get plenary
remission of all guilt and penalty by an absolution and
indulgence granted me by the Pope, whose written grant
I have bought for 4*d.* or for 6*d.*, or have won as a stake for a
game of tennis [with the pardoner]." For these indulgence-
mongers wander over the country and give a letter of pardon
sometimes for 2*d.*, sometimes for a good draught of wine or
beer, sometimes as a stake for a game of tennis, or even for
the hire of a harlot or for carnal love. For Pietro da Monte
who, about the year 1440, collected immense sums for indulgences granted by Pope Eugenius, when he went on ship-
board to leave England, said to Doctor Vincent Clement:
"By God!" (quoth he) "Pope Eugenius shall never have
one penny from these full money-bags, unless I first get
his promissory letters granting me the Archbishopric of
Milan[1]!"

(*c*) The view of the ideal Parish Priest (Myrc's *Festial*, E.E.T.S.,
Extra Series, 1905, p. 74). John Myrc or Mirk was prior of Lilleshall in
Shropshire and flourished about 1400 A.D. He wrote books for the help
of parish priests in their ministrations: a rhyming book of "Instructions,"
printed by the E.E.T.S. in 1868, and *Liber Festialis*, a book of sermons
for Sundays and festivals, interspersed with anecdotes, which was printed
with some alterations by Caxton. He wrote also a Latin book of Instructions, which is still in MS.

And yet, yn more confort of all Godys pepull, yche fyfte
yere, the pope of Rome grauntythe a full remyssion of all
synnys to yche man and weman that comyth to Rome that
yer. But, for all men may not come thedyr and have thys

---

[1] Compare this with the statement of Cardinal Gasquet (*The Eve of the
Reformation*, 1900, p. 437): "In the literature of the period, it must be remembered, there is nothing to show that the true nature of a 'pardon' or indulgence
was not fully and commonly understood. There is no evidence that it was in any
way interpreted as a remission of sin, still less that any one was foolish enough
to regard it as a permission to commit this or that offence against God."

pardon, therfor the Pope of Heven, Ihesu Cryst, of his specyall grace grauntythe all men and woymen full pardon of hor synnys yn hor deth-day, so that thay woll kepe by hor lyve thre thyngys that ben nedefull to hom. The wheche ben these : full contricion wyth schryft, full charite wythout feynyng, and stabull fayth wythout flateryng. And, sothly, wythout thes thre, ther may no man have pardon at Rome ne elleswher. Wherfor he that wyll be asoylet of the Pope of Heven, and have playne remyssyon of hys synnys, he most be full contryte, that ys, ynwardly sory for hys synnys and his gyltes; and so schryve hym clene, and be yn full purpos never forto synne more. Whoso dothe thus, leve[1] he wele, God forgevyth hym his trespas, and full perdon therof.

(*d*) The "Broad-Church" view in the later fourteenth century. (Exactly the same sentiment is expressed in the less orthodox version of *The Lay Folk's Catechism*, E.E.T.S., 1901, lines 877 ff.) *Piers Plowman*, B, VII. 173, p. 248.

Now hath the pope powere pardoun to graunte the peple
With-outen eny penaunce to passen in-to hevene;
This is owre bileve as lettered men us techeth,

> *Quodcumque ligaveris super terram, erit ligatum et in celis, &c.*[2]

And so I leve lelly (lordes forbode ellis!)[3]
That pardoun and penaunce and preyeres don save
Soules that have synned sevene sithes[4] dedly.
Ac[5] to trust to thise triennales[6], trewly me thinketh,
Is nought so syker for the soule, certis, as is Dowel.

For-thi[7] I rede[8] yow, renkes[9] that riche ben on this erthe,
Uppon trust of yowre tresoure triennales to have,
Be ye nevere the balder[10] to breke the ten hestes[11];
And namelich[12], ye maistres mayres and jugges,
That han the welthe of this worlde, and for wyse men ben
holden
To purchace yow pardoun and the popis bulles.

[1] believe.   [2] Matt. xvi. 19.
[3] I believe loyally (God forbid it should be otherwise!).   [4] times.
[5] but.   [6] a soul-mass said daily for three years.
[7] therefore.   [8] counsel.   [9] men.
[10] bolder.   [11] commandments.   [12] specially.

At the dredeful dome, whan dede shullen rise,
And comen alle bifore Cryst acountis to yelde,
How thow laddest thi lyf here and his lawes keptest,
And how thow dedst day bi day the dome wil reherce;
A poke-ful of pardoun there, ne provinciales lettres[1],
Theigh ye be founde in the fraternete of alle the foure ordres,
And have indulgences double-folde, but if Dowel yow help,
I sette yowre patentes and yowre pardounz at one pies
hele[2]!

9 THE VIRTUE OF A MASS

R. of Brunne, *Handlyng Synne*, E.E.T.S., 1901, p. 324. This anecdote
is the more valuable for being given on Manning's own authority.

A man yn Southfolke onës deyde
Besydë Sudbyry, men seyde.
For that man, swych[3] grace was dyght,
That hym was graunted to come a nyght
For to spekë wyth hys wyfe
To amende the defaute of hys lyfe:
"Gyf a messe were for me doun
With gode mannes devocyoun,
Y hope," he seyd, "to blys go,
And be delyverd of alle my wo;
Y prey the, pur charyte[4],
To travayle so moche for me."
She graunted hym that ychë bone[5],
And ros up on the mornë sone,
And un-to the frerës gede,
For there hoped she best to spede.
She cam, and spak with a frere,
And preyd she myght hys messë here,
And for here housbunde soule to synge,
And she wulde gyvë hym offrynge.

---

[1] Letters from the Minister Provincial of one of the four Orders of Friars,
setting forth that the recipient was of their Fraternity—i.e. had conferred benefits
on them for which they made him or her partakers in their merits and prayers. Cf.
Jocelin of Brakelonde, tr. Clarke, 1907, p. 3.

[2] heel of a magpie (*or*, last remnant of pie-crust).

[3] such.   [4] pour charité.   [5] particular boon.

The frere ded here a messe
Yn comune, as the servyse ys ;
Whan thys messë sungë was
She went home a godë pas.
The nyght aftyr, than come he,
"Slepest thou ? " he sayd ; "Nay," seyd she,
"Be ye yyt," she sayd, "yn blys ?
The messë for yow sungen ys.'
    "The messe," he seyde, "thou dedyst be do¹,
A party² hyt halpë ther-un-to ;
My parte y had, of that messe,
As of thyng that comune ys ;
Gyf one for me were specyale seyde,
That outher for me blys had nede,—
Gyf the prest were of lyfe so gode
That God hys preyer undyrstode—
Y hopë than, grace to have,
That hys messë myght me save."
Ofte he seyd[ë] to hys wyfe
"A prest ! A prest ! of clenë lyfe."
On the mornë, sone she yede
To the frerës eft god spede,
And shewed hyt to the pryour,
And prey[ed] hym of socour,
"Gyf he had any brother,
That he hoped, were better than other,
That wyl syngë me a messe
For a man that dedë ys ;
And at myn esë he shal have,
To a pytaunce³, that he wyl crave."
    The pryor spake un-to a frere,
And prey[ed] hym on alle manere
That he wulde a messë synge
For that soule that she made preyng.
    The frerë was an holy man ;
And ar⁴ that he hys messe bygan,

---

¹ didst cause to be sung.   ² partly.
³ extra allowance in a monastery, generally of food or drink.   ⁴ ere

He preyde to God hys orysoun
Yn ful grete afflyccyoun,
That hyt myght be hym to pay[1],
The messe that he shulde synge that day.

Whan the messe was do to ende,
He bad the womman home to wende,
"And, whan thou more eftë[2] heres,
Cum and sey to ourë freres."

The nyght aftyr, lesteneth now,
He come, and seyd, "Slepest thou?"
"Nay," she seyd; "how farë ye?"
"Weyl," he seyd, "and so wurth the[3]."
"Were ye pay[ed][4] of that messe,
That, for yow, sungyn ys?"
"Ye," he seyd, "graunte mercy,
Thys messe to me ys more wurthy
Than alle the worlde, an hunder sythe[5],
Ne myght have made me halfe so blythe;
Hys preyer was to God so dere,
That he besoghte, that wlde[6] he here,
Gyf he had preyd for an hundred mo,
Fro pyne to blys, he had broght tho;
For what thyng he hade asked bone[7],
God had graunted hyt hym as sone;
And have gode day, for now y wende
To the joye with-outyn ende."

10   CANTERBURY AND YORK

The quarrel for precedence between the two archbishops was at least
as old as the Conquest; the acutest moment was in 1176, an incident
which I have translated at length on p. 127 of my *Medieval Garner*,
and may give here in Thomas Fuller's summary. (*Ch. Hist.* bk III.
sect. iii. § 3.)

A synod was called at Westminster, the pope's legate being
present thereat; on whose right hand sat Richard, archbishop
of Canterbury, as in his proper place; when in springs Roger

---

[1] please.   [2] again.   [3] may it be to thee.   [4] pleased.
[5] times.   [6] would.   [7] as a boon.

of York, and finding Canterbury so seated, fairly sits him down on Canterbury's lap; (a baby too big to be danced thereon!) yea, Canterbury's servants dandled this lap-child with a witness, who plucked him thence, and buffeted him to pur- pose....Here the pope interposed, and, to end old divisions, made a new distinction,—"primate of all England," and "primate of England"; giving the former to Canterbury, the latter to York. Thus when two children cry for the same apple, the indulgent father divides it betwixt them; yet so that he giveth the bigger and better part to the child that is his darling.

The "last flash" of the controversy, as Fuller puts it, may be found in the following complaint of the Archbishop of York to Pope Nicholas III. in 1280 (*Letters from the Northern Registers*, R. S., p. 60).

Lo, most reverend Father, on my return to England [from your court]....I set up my cross in the midst of the English seas as a token of my primacy, as is always wont to be done, and was quietly bearing it through the diocese of Canterbury, when Master Adam of Hales, official to the Archbishop of Canterbury, together with certain accomplices and adherents of his own and the Devil's, rushed violently upon me and my train like a brazen-faced madman, and wickedly dashed my cross to pieces; yet blessed be the Lord! I soon procured another and caused it to be carried erect before me....Nor was he con- tent with these revilings and assaults; for, when I entered the city of London, on the morrow he hastened to make a fierce assault upon me and mine with an immense multitude of armed men bearing staves, axes, swords and divers other weapons, to the huge scandal of us all....Moreover, most exalted Father, my Lord of Canterbury, through his official and his servants, wheresoever I passed through his province in wonted fashion for the business of mine own church, did most cruelly prohibit and interdict to me and mine all lodgings, places of resort, and victuals, as though we had been heretics or folk cut off from the faithful by the actual sentence of excommunication; and, wheresoever I go or stay, he layeth the whole neighbourhood under ecclesiastical interdict.

11 AN ARCHIEPISCOPAL VISITATION

Matthew Paris, *Hist. Major*, R. S., vol. v. p. 121. It must be noted (1) that the Archbishop was in the right in insisting on his legal power of visitation, and the Canons wrong in resisting; (2) that, in his later *Hist. Minor*, Matthew Paris makes the Archbishop behave more mildly, though still very differently from modern standards; and (3) that his appointment had been a matter of political favouritism; he was son to the Count of Savoy, and uncle to Henry III.'s queen.

On May 12, 1250, the Canons of St Paul had refused to admit the Visitation and had been excommunicated:

On the morrow, therefore, still swelling and inflamed with the wrath of yesterday, and wearing a coat of mail under his vestments (as witnesses relate), he came to visit the Canons of St Bartholomew's Priory, [Smithfield]. When he arrived and entered the church, he was met by the Subprior (for the Prior was away) followed by his convent in solemn and reverent procession, with much light of waxen tapers and loud peals from the church-bells, and clad in very precious choir-copes, whereof the most precious was worn by their leader, the Subprior. The Archbishop, paying little heed to the honour thus shown unto him, said that he was come to visit the Canons. Now they were all in the midst of the church, i.e. in the choir—the Canons, the Archbishop, and the Archbishop's train in a disorderly throng. Then answered one Canon for the rest, that they had a Bishop of experience and diligence, whose office it was to visit them when it was needful, and that they neither would nor should be visited by any other man, lest it should seem to be in contempt of the Bishop. The Archbishop, at these words, was moved to most inopportune and indecent wrath. He fell upon the Subprior, and, forgetting his own rank and the sanctity of his predecessors, he impiously smote that holy man—a Priest, a Religious, in the midst of the church—he smote him (I say) with impious fist, again and again, first on his aged breast, then on his venerable face, and lastly on his hoary head, crying loudly all the while "thus, thus should these English traitors be handled!"; and at length, raving with horrible oaths which may not be repeated here, he bade them forthwith bring his sword. Then, when the tumult waxed fiercer, and the Canons strove to free their Subprior from the hands of this violent oppressor, the Archbishop tore with his own hands that precious cope wherein the Subprior was clad, and tore away the clasp (which men call *morse* in the vulgar tongue), which was trodden under foot and lost in that tumultuous crowd, though it was precious with silver and gems: nay, and the cope itself, of most costly workmanship, was trodden and torn, to its irremediable damage. Yet even thus the Archbishop's fury was not turned away; for, thrusting the holy man violently from him, and driving him backwards, he so furiously crushed the Subprior's aged body against the arm-rest that divided two stalls, as to shake his bones to the very marrow, and to bruise his heart within him. The rest, seeing such immoderate wrath in the Archbishop, hardly tore their half-dead Subprior from the brink of destruction, driving his oppressor back. Then, as the Archbishop fell backwards, his vestments fell apart and his coat of mail was clearly seen by many men, who shuddered to see an Archbishop in armour; whereupon many augured that he was come not to visit and to correct faults, but rather to stir up bloody strife. Meanwhile the Archbishop's unruly Provençal attendants fell truculently upon the rest of the Canons, unwarlike, unarmed and unprepared as they were; and not only the Archbishop himself, but also some of these attendants at his bidding, maltreated many of the holy men, smiting them, tearing their vestments, overthrowing them and treading them down. The Canons therefore, foul with bruises and blood; maltreated, dishevelled and torn, came to the Bishop of London, with grievous complaints and tears at this detestable deed.

The Bishop advised them to complain to the King, who, however, sided with the Archbishop, though the Londoners nearly broke into open riot against the Archbishop.

12   A MODEL PARISH PRIEST

John Capgrave (1393–1464) was born at Lynn, where he became head of the Austin Friary, and finally Provincial of his Order in England. He was a voluminous writer, mostly in Latin ; his chief patron was Humphrey, Duke of Gloucester. His *Life of St Gilbert* is founded on the official Latin life of the saint. It was dedicated to the then Master of the Order of Sempringham and especially intended (as the author tells us in his own preface) "for the solitary women of your religion which unnethe can understand Latin, that they may at vacant times read in this book the great virtues of their master." The following extract is from E. E. T. S., vol. 140 (1910), pp. 62–5.

This man Gilbert was bore in that same place cleped Sempingham.   His fader was bore in Normandye, his modyr lady of this place be-for seide.   His fader as thei say was a knyte of Normandye whech cam in-to this lond with Kyng William at the Conquest and weddyd the lady of this place.... Than was this man medeled[1] with too blodis, Norman of the fader side, Englisch of the moderis side....So semeth it that this man was not bore of no wrecchid nacion, ne of no servage, but of puple[2] gentil and fremanly and large[3], both on the fadir side and the modir.   He was in his yong age and in his simplinesse ful gracious, lich on-to Jacob, whom for his clennesse and innocens the modir Rebecca, thorw inspiracion of God, preferred to be lord of all his bretherin, lich as this man is preferred to be maystir of al this religion....He was at that age set to skole and lerned groundly in thoo scienses whech thei clepe liberal, as gramer, retorik, logik and swech[4] othir. But his corage[5] at that tyme was mor enclyned to lerne good maneris than sotil conclusiones, eke be-cause aftirward that he was ordeyned to be a techer of vertuous lyvyng, it was convenient that he schuld first be a disciple in that, in schole of honestie.   In al his yong age was he clene fro swech vices as childyrn use, as lying, wauntown ragyn[g], and othir stynkyng condiciones.   Evene thann be-gan he to be lich a religious man, to whech lyf he was applied be[6] God.

In that same seculer lyf and in that tendyr age, he folowyd

---

[1] mingled.   [2] people.   [3] generous.   [4] such.   [5] heart.   [6] by.

as he coude and myth[1], the reules of religious lyf, and to them all of whech[2] he had ony power he ful benyngly gaf exaumple the same reules to folow. For first was he a maystir of lernyng to the smale petites, swech as lerne to rede, spelle and synge. Tho childyrn that were undyr his disceplyne he taute not only ther lessones on the book, but be-side this, he tawt for to play in dew tyme, and here playes taute he that thei schuld be honest and mery with-outen clamour or grete noyse. For thoug he had not at that tyme experiens of the good customes whech be used a-mongis religious men in monasteriis, yet had our Lord God at that age put in his brest these holy exercises, for he taute thoo disciples that he had to kepe silens in the cherch ; all an on our[3] to go to bedde and eke to ryse to her lessones ; all went thei to-gidyr to their pley or ony othir thing. His moost labour and grettest desir was to wynne soules to God with word and eke ensaumple, for the best sacrifise on-to God is the gelous love of soules.... Whan he was promoted to the ordre of presthod, and had soules in governauns, and eke had receyved power to make ministracion of the goostly giftis whech be vertue of oure Lordes blod ar left in the cherch, than, as a trewe steward of his Lordes tresour,...the word of good exhortacion was not hid in him, but he delt it oute frely to them that wold lerne. For his auditorye was so endewyd with lernyng that it sempt[4] in all her[5] governauns the[y] had be norchid[6] in monasterye amongis the servauntis of God. Thei used non insolent drynkyngis, ne no longe sitting there, ne used not to renne to wrastillingis, ber-baytingis and swech othir onthrifty occupaciones, whech summe men now on dayes preferr be-for dyvyne servyse ; this used thei nout, but thei used to pray devoutly in the cherch, to pay treuly ther tythes, to walk aboute and visite pore men, to spend ther good in swech weye as is plesauns of God and coumfort to pore. Who-so had seyn them with-inne the cherch, he myth[7] sone discerne whethir thei wer Gilberd parischones or nowt, he had tawt them so wel to bowe ther bakkes and ther knes to God and so devoutly to bid ther bedes.

---

[1] might. [2] over whom. [3] at one hour. [4] seemed. [5] their. [6] nourished.
[7] might.

13   TITHES

(*a*)   From Quivil's *Exeter Constitutions*, § LIII. (D. Wilkins, *Concilia, etc.*, vol. II. 1737, p. 158).   Tithes, mortuaries, and customary offerings at Easter etc. were a cause of constant friction between parson and people.

O marvellous and ineffable loving-kindness of our God, who, although He hath commanded that tithes and firstfruits be yielded to Himself, as to Him who hath the whole earth and the fulness thereof, not for His own profit but for that of His priests...yet doth also, as giver of all good things, reward fourfold with the abundance of His benefits all who fully pay that tithe which He deigneth to receive—to wit, with abundance of harvest, with health of body, with indulgence of their sins, and with the gracious prize of His heavenly kingdom! Let none therefore, through avarice, lose so great benefits as this....

Seeing that contention ariseth oftentimes between rectors of churches and their parishioners—since it is sometimes doubtful what and how much should be given for tithes when there are so few cows or sheep that no cheese can be made from their milk, or when in like manner there are too few calves, lambs, kids, chickens, piglings, geese, or fleeces, to be divided by ten, since there are not ten in all—therefore it is our will to hand down a certain rule in these matters; for in leaving them to local custom we should rather increase than remove the matter for quarrels, since the customs themselves are disputed and denied.   We therefore decree that one farthing should be given as tithe for each lamb, kid or pigling below the number of seven[1].   If there are seven, let one be given for tithe; and next year whatsoever is lacking from the number ten shall be allowed for in tithing....For the milk of

---

[1] These rates are certainly moderate; between 1285 and 1290 we find piglings [*porcelli*] ranging from 2½*d*. to 3*d*. (or exceptionally even 1*s*. 7*d*.); lambs from 4*d*. to 8¾*d*. (exceptionally, 1*s*. 3*d*.); calves from 2*s*. 1¼*d*. to 2*s*. 9*d*.; so that Quivil's tithe-rate seems to represent really only about one-twentieth of the selling price of the animal.   (J. E. T. Rogers, *History of Agriculture and Prices*, vol. II. pp. 194 ff.)

each cow, if no cheese be made, let a penny be given; for that of each milch-ewe a farthing and for each she-goat a half-penny....Again, seeing that certain persons, for their tithe of milk (which hath hitherto been given in cheese, according to the custom hitherto approved in our diocese), maliciously bring the milk itself to church, and—what is more wicked still—finding there no man to receive it, pour it out before the altar in contumely to God and His Church; and others [*a long list of similar frauds and subterfuges*].—We therefore, by the authority of God the Father Almighty, and of St Peter Prince of the Apostles, our patron saint, and with the approbation of the present holy synod, excommunicate all such evildoers with their aiders and abettors, until they shall have made competent satisfaction for their misdeeds.

(*b*) Myrc, *Instructions for Parish Priests*, E. E. T. S., 1868, p. 21. Myrc was probably Chaucer's younger contemporary.

> The gret sentence I write here,
> That twies or thries in the yere
> Thou shalt pronounce, without lette,
> Whan thi parisse is togidir mette
> Thou shall pronounce this idous[1] thing,
> With crosse and candell and bell knylling;
> Speke oute redely, fir noght thou wond[2],
> That all mowe[3] the understonde.

By auttorite of god almighte ffader and son and holy gost, and of al the Seyntes of heven. ffirst we accursen al them that broken the pece of holy chirch of sturben hit;...also all thilk[4] that, for wrath or for hate of eny person or vicary, propor tithinges with-holden, or destroyen with hem self or with her bestes, or beren awey, and all that consenten thereto.

(*c*) Chaucer, *C. T. Prologue*, l. 477.

> A good man was there of religioun,
> And was a Poore Persoun of a Toun....
> Ful looth were hym to cursen for his tithes.

(*d*) *An Alphabet of Tales* (E.E.T.S., 1904) is an English 15th century translation from a Latin-French collection of anecdotes for the use of

---

[1] hideous.   [2] for thou shalt not fear.   [3] may.   [4] those.

preachers, like *Gesta Romanorum*.   Most of them are from 13th century collections such as Caesarius of Heisterbach or Étienne de Bourbon; but the translation shows clearly also what was to the taste of English congregations.   The following is from p. 385 (Tale DLXXVII.).

Jacobus de Vetriaco tellis how som tyme ther was a hus-band-man that was ane yll payer of his tenndis[1], and he wold seldom offer bod[2] if it were on solempne dayis, and than he wold offr a fals peny or ane yll[3].   So on a passch-day[4] hym happend emang other to com unto the howselburde[5], and the preste, that knew that he usid evur to offer a fals peny, when he had gyffen other men ther howsell, he gaf this husband, in-stead of his howsell, the same yll peny that he offerd. And he chewid and feld [th]at it was hard, and grapid[6] in his mouthe what it was, and he fand it was the same fals peny that he had offerd; and when he saw it he had grete mervell therof, and made mekull sorow.   So when mes was done, he come unto the preste wepand and sayd; "A! sur, my syn is so grete that it happend me this day [th]at the sacrament [th]att ye gaff me is turnyd in-to a fals peny."   And the preste ansswerd hym agayn and said; "This thyng happynd not unto the with-oute som cawce[7], and therfor thou haste done som horrible syn.   Tell me what it is!"   And with grete shame he tolde hym in confession, and said; "I shryfe me[8] that I was so attemptid with covatice[9], that evur when other folk offerd gude sylver I offerd alway ane ill penye."   And than the preste said unto hym; "This was the jugement [th]at thou tolde me off; and herefor in-stede of the sacrament thou fand in thi mouthe ane ill peny.   And therfor thou moste make restitucion."   And so he did, and promysid that evur after fro thens furth he sulde trewlie pay his tend and offer gude sylver. And so the preste asoylid[10] hym and gaff hym his howsell, and evur after he was a gude man.

---

[1] tithes.   [2] but.   [3] bad one.   [4] Easter.   [5] communion table.
[6] felt about.   [7] cause.   [8] confess.   [9] covetousness.   [10] absolved.

14   PARSON AND PARISHIONER

From MS. Lambeth 51, fol. 5 *b*. The present compiler owes the communication of this passage, and the description of the MS., to the courtesy of the Provost of King's College, Cambridge. It is "an immense compilation, apparently only extant in this copy, of revelations of the other world, extracted from the lives of saints and the *Vitae Patrum*, by Peter, Prior of Holy Trinity, Aldgate, London (1197–1221). His other principal works were the *Pantheologus* and *De Adventu Messiae*, the latter a series of dialogues with a Jew." Cf. Wharton, *Anglia Sacra*, I. 113.

Like St Gregory the Great and other similar compilers of medieval visions, Peter explains in his Prologue that such collections are necessary to counteract the faithlessness of his contemporaries (f. 2). Although (he says) nearly all nations of mankind have now cast away their idols and believe in One God, yet there are still some who believe that there is no God ; and that the world is ruled by chance ; and there are many who "consider only what they see, believing neither in good nor in evil angels, nor in life after death, nor in any other spiritual and invisible things. Therefore, I, Peter, minister of the Church of the Holy Trinity in London, have collected, out of the lives and acts of the saints, the revelations and visions vouchsafed to them into this book, which I call *Liber Revelationum*....I have confined myself to those which have occurred since Christ's passion, excluding from my view the Old and New Testaments, which are accessible to all who care to look at them."

Some of the anecdotes are taken from Peter's own experience ; and the following passage has been selected because it would be difficult to find any in medieval literature which casts a more quiet and natural light upon everyday relations between a parish priest and his well-to-do parishioners (f. 5 *b*).

Moreover, not only that man's soul exists, but also that it has in it by nature something of the divine and a knowledge of future things, may be proved not only by those things which prophets and other saints are wont to foretell, but also by those things which men often see in sleep, and which afterwards come to pass even as they saw them.

There was a certain faithful man of good deed and good repute named John, in that village of England which is called Orpington, who was wont to tell the following tale to me, Peter, who write these things. "One night" (he said) "as I slept in my own bed at home, it seemed that I rose from my couch early one Saturday and ordered my horse to be saddled. Then (as it seemed) I mounted him and rode to my own church of Cray to hear Mass. When I had come thither I left my servant-lad outside with my horse, and came into church even as they were singing the *Alleluia Veni Sancte Spiritus*; for the parish priest, Gilbert by name, had already begun his Mass of the Holy Ghost and the clerks were singing *Alleluia* even as I came in. Then I heard the Gospel and remained in church until the whole Mass was sung through. After which I went out to my horse. When I had come to him, it seemed to me that at that moment the servant-lad of the aforesaid priest came with his master's horse ready to fetch him. Whereupon I asked the priest's groom whither his master meant to go, and the lad answered, To the Chapter of Eynsford. I waited therefore awhile by the side of my horse until the priest left the church and came to me. And when, in answer to my question, he answered that he was indeed going to the Chapter of Eynsford, then I made reply " I too am going to my sister's house, which is on the way. If thou therefore wilt go thither, let us ride together." With this the priest accorded ; and we rode on until we came to a certain field wherein (as it seemed to me) I saw a white sow, fat and well-liking, but marked in many places with black spots ; behind her (as it seemed) followed many well-liking sucking-pigs marked in like manner with their mother. Then said the priest to me, for he rode by my side, "Sir John, dost thou see these sucking-pigs following their mother ? Mark now my words. Although there are ten of them, yet their master will not give me a single one for tithe, albeit he be mine own parishioner." At this speech of the priest I, John, stood and reined in my horse for awhile, and it seemed to me that in counting the pigs I found only nine ; wherefore I turned round to the priest and said, "All ye priests are too greedy, looking ever to your own advantage rather with eyes of ambition than with sober judgment. For, if it so please thee, Sir Priest, number now these sucking-pigs, and thou shalt not find them enough for the law to grant thee a tithe thereof, seeing that they are but nine." The priest, marvelling at this word, and numbering those pigs once more, remained still of the same mind, and said, " I have counted ten of them"; which when I had denied, these diverse beliefs bred between us a certain pleasant and friendly contention. In short, as it seemed in my dream, we each promised solemnly to the other that whosoever could be convicted of having counted wrong, should be condemned to pay four gallons of wine to the other. Then we set about to number the pigs with great diligence, and I won my wager; and lo! even as I exulted in this my victory, I wakened from my sleep.

In process of time, although this dream had slipped from my memory and from my mind and although I thought thereon no longer, yet on the morrow there came to pass all that I had seen in my dream, even to the very last jot and tittle, and whatsoever I had already seen in my sleep I now saw with my waking eyes. For, to sum up briefly what I have already told at length, on the Saturday morning I rode to the aforesaid church; heard the same *Alleluia* and Gospel and Mass of the Holy Ghost; and, going forth, heard from the priest's groom that his master purposed to go to the aforesaid Chapter. I waited there for the priest to come out; and, as we rode together by common consent, we came to the aforesaid field, wherein I saw a sow with her sucklings like at every point to those which I had seen in my dream. Then at last I recalled what I had seen in my sleep; for I swear to you with a solemn oath that I knew that sow and her piglings by sight better than any of my own pigs at home. At this sight, then, I recalled my dream; and, marvelling at this strange thing, I reined in my horse for a moment and laughed. The priest, wondering that I halted with so sudden a change of countenance, asked me wherefore I laughed; and I was fain to elude his question with such perfunctory and obscure answers as I could find. Then the priest looked at the piglings and said all even as I had heard in my dream; and when I, for my part, answered concerning the cupidity of priests and the number of the pigs, with no less exact repetition of my vision, then we pledged ourselves that the victor should receive from the conquered four gallons of wine. After which we diligently counted the pigs, and I was victor.

" Which " (said John) " delighted me more with what I learned thereby than for my earthly gain ; for I was thus taught by mine own experience how the soul hath in it somewhat of divine, and thenceforward I was most firmly convinced that the soul liveth evermore."

15   A PIOUS FAMILY

From MS. Lamb. 51, fol. 23 *a*.

In the days of Henry the First, king of England, there befel a vision of marvellous import to a certain good and holy man, grandfather to me, Peter, fourth Prior of Holy Trinity, London, who here describe this man's vision, in so far as I can remember it after the lapse of so many years that have gone by since my father Jordan was wont to relate it to me in my boyhood. This same vision was told in past years by my grandfather aforesaid, Ailsi by name, to his son Jordan, who was then a youth ; which same Jordan retold it, in so far as the lapse of years had yet left it in his memory, to his said son Peter, then but a child but now verging on his sixtieth year....

There lived in Cornwall a man named Ailsi, simple and upright and godfearing, who kept himself from evil ; inasmuch as he strove, his whole life long, to please God and St Stephen by good works. With such loving devotion did he cling to St Stephen, and to the canons of St Stephen in Cornwall[1], from whom he himself held his land, that he might be thought by a special prerogative of affection to have deserved this vision which God vouchsafed to show him. For St Stephen familiarly revealed to him many hidden matters and prophecies, and graciously cherished him in all his anxious cares, and oftentimes healed his infirmities, in order that by such frequent consolations he might give him to understand how pleasing was his life and his conversation to God. For St Stephen oftentimes appeared unto him in the likeness of a man of venerable aspect, as to his faithful and prudent servant whom the canons had chosen for their

---

[1] i.e. of Launceston = Llanstephan.

treasurer for the building of the tower of his church, committing to his care and governance not only the work itself, but also the workmen and servants thereof. The saint, therefore, would come to him in a vision and show him how he wished all things to be done, diligently teaching him which of the workmen were faithful and should be kept, which were faithless and should be sent away.

Here follow three miracles, showing St Stephen's help and satisfaction in the work.

(f. 24 *a*.) Moreover this Ailsi was once sick of a grievous infirmity in one of his eyes, so that all his neighbours believed that this eye must irrevocably perish, since no physician could bring any effectual remedy to his sickness. In which infirmity he suffered such grievous pain that at last he broke into impatience; and, departing from St Stephen's work, he took his way homeward, thus meanwhile addressing to the saint (to whom he had so often spoken as friend with friend): "O blessed Stephen, Stephen!" said he, "long time have I laboured in thy service; yet now, methinks, in vain. For if I had served the Earl of Moreton, who is now Lord of Cornwall, so faithfully as I have long served thee, he would have enriched me with many gifts; but thou, to whom I have committed myself and my whole soul and all that I possess, givest me over now to torture." And thus, with frequent repetition of these and suchlike reproaches, wrathfully inveighing the while against St Stephen, and much anxious communing within his own mind, he came to his own house[1]. But that night the blessed Stephen visited him, rebuking him mildly and gently for his evil words, and bringing him

---

[1] For this medieval habit of making the Saint responsible for prayers unfulfilled, see *A Medieval Garner*, p. 5. Perhaps the most interesting examples of all are in the *Miracles de St Benoît*, ed. Certain, 1858, pp. 59, 149, 184, 185, 283, 327, 353. A peasant-woman at Harnicourt, for instance, failing to get justice by humble prayers, tucked up St Benedict's altar-cloth, beat the altar soundly and cried, "Effete old Benedict, idle and slothful, what doest thou? why sleepest thou?" After this, her prayers were heard. Cf. also Gervase of Canterbury's account of the conflagration at his Cathedral in 1174 (R. S., vol. I. p. 5). The crowd, furious and indignant at the disaster, "hurled grisly curses [*enormia quaedam maledicta*] against God and His Saints, the patrons of that edifice."

solace with full health of body; for he touched his eye and blessed it....

(f. 25 *a*.) This man of God then, this Ailsi, was so familiar with St Stephen (with whom in truth he oftentimes spake face to face as a man speaketh with his friend), that the saint's person became well known to him through these frequent and familiar sights and colloquies, and Ailsi was wont to describe him to his acquaintance. Wherefore it came to pass that, even as he himself was a good and holy man, and was styled "the holy" by reason of his frequent visions of St Stephen, so also he begat and fostered and brought up his children in the fear of the Lord; who themselves also were justified in their kinship to him; so that all who knew the father were wont to call his sons "the half-saints." For this godly man Ailsi had (over and beyond the daughters whom he begat, and who also strove their best to follow in the footsteps of their father's sanctity) four sons, each of whom in like manner did in some degree follow after his father's holiness; and all clave to St Stephen, after their father's example, with special and singular affection....His eldest, Bernard, and Nicholas his second, so grew up in all goodness that through their learning and their virtues they earned the close familiarity and affection of king Henry of England, and were esteemed first among the foremost at his court. One became a royal chaplain; another was a canon of Merton.

These two brethren, Bernard and Nicholas, gave to the church of St Stephen, together with many other gifts, a dark blue banner embroidered with gold; in the midst whereof is woven the Agnus Dei; and beneath, the stoning of St Stephen; and at the four corners the symbols of the four evangelists; which banner is still held there in great veneration. Moreover these same brethren gave also to that church a carpet, and an ivory casket full of relics, adorned with silver clasps and studs; which casket was once their writing-case, and still contains their great silver inkstand.

The third of these brethren was called Jordan of Trecarl, who was a layman like his father; a man just in his generation, after that he was grown to man's estate; most humble

and quiet and mild of heart ; a lover of peace, affable to all
men, and of marvellous kindness to his enemies; to his
servants and serfs he was almost a companion. He was
learned in the secular law and customs beyond all his
brethren, and famous among all men ; and, by reason of his
greater learning in these matters, he was frequented by all
who were in necessity; yet he would maintain no cause for
gain unless he knew it to be just; wherefore he was
wondrously loved and venerated by all. He, though younger
than these two others, received the paternal inheritance because he was a layman. He loved St Stephen with all his
strength and with all his heart....

(f. 26 a.) The fourth son of the aforesaid man of God,
Ailsi, was named Paganus, for that he was long time a
pagan ; that is, he lived twelve years before he was baptized[1].
In a brief space after his baptism, God took him to Himself,
lest his mind should be changed by the malice of the world.
After the death of this child, the holy man began to ponder
within himself concerning the future state of the blest ; but,
seeing that neither he, as a layman, knew aught thereof, nor
could any other man give him any sure tidings, he remained
in great anxiety of mind ; and, the less he knew of the pains
of the damned or the rewards of the blest, the more solicitous
he was to learn these things. But God would not that His
beloved servant should long waver among such doubts and
ignorances ; therefore He sent unto Ailsi, in a vision of the
night, his son Paganus aforesaid, to inform him of all these
things and to lead him down to the place of hell-pains, and
up to the mansions of the blest.

He dreamed that he was going on a pilgrimage, with
a company of other pilgrims, to Jerusalem, and that he had
already performed a great space of his journey. On their
way, therefore (so it seemed), they all descended in a troop
from a certain mountain into a dale, wherein so thick a cloud
stretched from side to side that each was parted from his

---

[1] Though there were not infrequent complaints that, through negligence or bad
management, large numbers of children died unbaptized, I know of no other case
like this, where pious parents deliberately deferred baptism.

fellow, nor could Ailsi find any man to teach him whither he went. So this man of God, finding himself left thus desolate, began to cry and shout for his fellows; but no man answered him. Pushing forward therefore, and praying as he went, and calling on God and St Stephen for help, never despairing of their succour but always pressing on, he came to the bottom of that vale, where he saw a great river, whereof his eye could measure neither length nor breadth, both for its own immensity and for the darkness of that cloud. In great doubt of mind, he set himself now to go hither and thither on the bank of that stream, both up and down, if by any chance he might find a bridge and pass over to the other bank. But, finding none, nor any trodden way, he stood there weary and downcast and almost despairing, as knowing neither what to do nor whither to turn. As he thus looked this way and that, praying in bitter trouble for the help of God and St Stephen, then the fullness of his devotion earned him an answer to his prayer. For, among his direst doubts, behold! his own son Paganus stood by his side, and greeted him; and, being greeted in return, asked him what he would have and whither he went. The father, amazed and afraid at the sight of this his son whom he knew to be dead, cried aloud, "Art thou then my Paganus, and art thou not dead?" To whom the other made answer, "I am indeed thy dead son Paganus; but by God's will I am come hither for thy succour."

[Paganus carries his father on his back across the stream, and shows him first the torments of the damned, and then the delights of the blessed; these do not differ sufficiently from the conventional medieval descriptions to warrant their insertion here. The closing sentences, however, are interesting in their resemblance to the last stanzas of *Pearl*, except the obvious deviation from the Apocalypse in the matter of the temple.]

In the midst of that vast plain [of Paradise] was a temple so great and fair that it was a marvel to see; whereunto the blessed souls would enter and tarry awhile to praise God; and then after a while they would go forth again; but ever they praised the Lord and rendered Him infinite thanks for His lovingkindnesses bestowed upon them. This temple was all glittering with gold, within and without, and adorned with an infinite variety of colours and pictures, and spangled everywhere with precious gems that cast their light all around. What more shall I say? All the souls there were making merry with hand-clapping and singing, and prayer and praise and blessing of God. When therefore Ailsi had noted all this, and while he stood rapt in excess of joy at this great tranquillity of the souls, and this delightful plain of Paradise, and the beauty of this temple, then said the son unto him: "Beloved father, here dwell I now with these holy souls; and here I enjoy the utmost tranquillity and delight, waiting ever patiently for the time of my assumption to heaven, where the angels and the spirits of those made perfect see the Lord of lords in Sion. To this place of joy and quiet thou thyself also, dearest father, shalt be brought after thy death, when thou hast first suffered punishments for the evils which thou hast done in the flesh. Now, therefore, must thou return unto the world, and to thine own household; and then, when thou hast lived but a brief while longer, thou shalt be laid with thy fathers, ending thy life in a good old age. But now, having seen, both by the pains of some souls and by the glory and quiet of others, what are the things which should be avoided and what should be embraced, thou knowest enough to safeguard thyself and to forewarn others." Then the father, being thus certified of his son's death and of his own return to the world, was grieved beyond all that tongue can tell, standing in doubt and in amazement; until at length he said, "Be sure, my son, that I will never leave thee, nor ever tear myself away from this joy!" "Nay," said the boy; "for no man may come to dwell in this place but if he die first." Nevertheless the father would have used force with his son, that he might stay in that place; and there arose a long dispute between those twain, the one refusing by all means to depart, and the other showing how he must first taste of death; until at last both child and vision melted away together, and the father awoke to find himself in his own house, much troubled by reason of this dream.

16   A WHOLESOME VISION

Myrc's *Festial*, E.E.T.S., 1901, p. 5. It must be remembered that, as the Church was the poor man's Bible, so the most conspicuous paintings in the churches often represented, with the crudest realism, the Last Doom and the pains of hell.

Seynt Bede telleth that ther was a husbond-man yn Englond that fell seke, and lay as for ded from the eventyde tyll the morow. Then aros he, and departed his godys[1] yn thre partyes, and his partye he gaf to pore men, and yede[2] and was made a monke yn an abbay that stod by a watyr syde. Ynto the whech watyr ych[3] nyght he yede yn, wer hyt never soo coold froste, and stod ther long tyme of the nyght. And when he was asket, why he put hymselfe ynto so moche penaunce, he unswered: "Forto eschoyn[4] the more payne that I have seyn," and ete barly-bred, and dranke watyr all his lyfe aftyr. And he wold tell to relygyous men the payne that he segh, that was soo gret, that he cowthe not tel hit openly. He sayde that an angyll lad hym ynto a place that on the toon[5] syde was suche a colde, that no tong myght tell the payne therof; and on that other syde was suche a hete, that no man myght tell the payne therof...and sowles wern cast out of that won into the tother. And so that angyll schewet hym the fyre that come out at the mowthe, that was the fyre of hell; that was so hote, that als ferre as he myght seen hit, hym thoght he brennet for hete. And yn the lees therof he segh sowles bulmyng[6] up and don, cryyng horrybuly, and a noyse of fendes cryyng; "Sle[7], sle, sle, sle, sle, sle, opon the broche[8], rost hote, cast ynto the cawdren[9], setthe[10] fast yn pyche, and cood[11], and brymston, and hot leed!"

17   PURGATORY

Ibid., p. 269.

In Die Animarum Sermo Brevis ad Parochianos.

Good men and woymen, as ye kneweth wel, the morow aftyr All-halow-day ys evermor Sowlemasse-day, that ben yn purgatory yn Goddys pryson and have gret nede to be

---

[1] goods.   [2] went.   [3] each.   [4] avoid.   [5] one.   [6] swirling.
[7] slay.   [8] spit.   [9] cauldron.   [10] seethe.   [11] tar.

holpon. Wherfor, as holy chyrche thys day worschepyth all the seyntes of Heven generaly yfere[1], hopyng to be holpen by thom, ryght soo, on Sowlesmasse-day, holy chyrch makyth mynd, and syngyth and redythe generaly for all the sowles that ben yn purgatory, havyng full beleve forto relesch[2] thom of thor payne, othyr[3] yn parte, othyr yn all. Wherfor ych[4] crysten man and woman schall, as thys day, helpe the sowles that ben yn payne, for soo thay mown[5] and they woll; for the lest prayer that ys made for thom dothe thom ese, so thagh[6] a man say but thus: "God have mercy on all crysten sowles!" so that he that sayth thus, be yn charyte and out of dedly synne. Then schull ye know wele that thre thynges helpen soules most out of penance, that ys: devot prayng, almes-gevyng, and masse-syngyng.

Devot prayer helpyth moch a man sowle; for, as a lord that hath a man yn dystres, at the prayer of his godde servand, other he relesches all, other som[e], soo God, at the prayer of his trew servand, releschuth a sowle that he prayth for, othyr yn party, other yn all.

(p. 270.) Also almes-gevyng helpyth moch thom; for as watyr quenchethe fure yn our syght, ryght soo almes-dede qwenchethe the fure that brenneth thom yn thor payne....

The thrydde helpe that the sowle hathe ys massys syngyng; for when any soule apereth to any man, evermore he wylneth[7] and prayth forto have massys songen for hym. For ryght as mete and drynke conforteth a man when he ys febull, ryght soo the sacurment comfortethe and strenktheth the sowles that hyt byn don fore....

(p. 271.) In the [Golden Legend] we fynden how that fyschers of Seynt Tybaude yn the hot hervest token yn thor nettes a gret clot of yse[8], and beron hyt to hym, for he was pottagur[9]; and wyth that yse thay refreschet the grete hete of his fete, as oft as hit was layde to. Then herd he a voyce that spake to hym out of the yse and sayde: "I am a sowle that dray my penons[10] her; and woldyst thou syng thrytty masses contynuantly I schuld be delyverd of my penance."

---

[1] together.   [2] release.   [3] either.   [4] each.   [5] are able.   [6] though.
[7] desireth.   [8] ice.   [9] gouty.   [10] dree my penance.

AN ABBOT'S FUNERAL

SAINT GUTHLAC BUILDING A CHURCH

Then thys good man sayde he wold. And soo, when he had sayde a quantyte of thes massys, be steryng[1] of the fende on[e] come to hym, and told hym how all the towne was at debate, and yche was redy to sle[2] other, and he most nedes come forto ses[3] thom, and soo he dyd. Eftsones he began ageyne, and when he had seyd halfe the masses, then come ther another and told hym how enmyes wer comen, and bysegyd the towne, and he most nedys go and ordeyne therfor ; and so he laft hys masse. Eftsones and yet he beganne ageyne. And when he had songen all the masses but the last, then come ther a worde that all hys place and moche of the towne was on fure, and he most helpe hymselfe, lest he wer brent. Then sayde he "thagh all bren and I bothe, with the helpe of God I wyll syngne this masse." And when the masse was sayde, hit was fonde[4] all fantesy of the fend and noght els ; and then was the yse molten away, and so the soule holpen.

And pray we so to Jhesu that he wol help all the sowles that we ben bonden her forto pray for. Amen.

18 A VISION OF HEAVEN

This Revelation was really made to a monk of Eynsham, near Oxford, in 1196. It was recorded in Latin by his brother Adam, the biographer of St Hugh of Lincoln, who was afterwards Prior of Eynsham. The present English version was printed about 1480 with the misreading *Evesham*, and reprinted by Arber in 1869. See H. E. Salter, *Cartulary of the Abbey of Eynsham*, vol. II. 1908, p. 257.

Revelation to the Monk of Evesham (Arber), p. 107.

...what brightnes and clerenes of light was there within-forthe al aboutys, no man aske ne seche of me; for y can not only [not] telle hit by worde but also y can not remembre hit in mynde. That gloryous schyning light was brighte and smothe, and so raveshte a man that behylde hit that hit bare a man above hym selfe by the grete brightnes of lyghte; yn so mekyl that what-sumever y sawe before hit was as no thing, me thought, in comparyson of hit. That bryghtnesse, thawghe hyt were inestymable, neverthelesse hyt dullyd not a mannys syghte : hyt rathyr scharpyd hyt. Sothly hyt schynyd ful mervelusly ; but more ynestymably hyt delytyd a man that

[1] by instigation.　　[2] slay.　　[3] put an end to.　　[4] found.

behylde hyt, and wondirfully cowpulde[1] a mannys syghte to se hit. And wythynforthe no thyng y myght see, but lighte and the walle of crystalle throw the whyche we came yn. And also fro the gronde vppe to toppe of that walle were grycis[2] ordende and dysposyd feyre and mervelusly, by the whyche the joyful company that was cum yn at the forseyde gate gladly ascendyd uppe. Ther was no labur, ther was no difficulte, ther was no taryng yn her ascendyng; and the hier they wente the gladder they were. And, yn thys vision that y saw, so mekylle y concevyd yn my sowle of joy and gladnes that, wat-sumever may be seyde of hyt by mannys mowthe, ful lytyl hyt ys and onsufficient to expresse the joy of myne herte, that y had there.

Therfore when y had seyn al these syghtys above seyde, and many othyr innumerable, my lorde sent Nycholas that hylde me by the hande seyde schortly thys to me. Loo sonne (he seyde) now a party[3] aftyr they peticion and grete desir thow haste seyne and beholde the state of the worlde yat ys to cumme, as hyt myghte be to possible. Also the perels of hem that offendyn and erryn, the peynys of synners; the reste also of hem yat have done her purgacion, the desyrys of hem that be goyng to hevynward, and the joys of hem that now byn cumme to the courte of hevyn and also the joy of crystis reynynge. And now thow muste go ageyne to they selfe and to thyne, and to the worldys feyghtyng. Treuly thow schalt have and perceve the joys that thow haste seyne, and mekyl more, yeffe thow contynew and persever in the drede of god. And when he had seyde thys to me he browghte me forthe throwe the same gate that we came yn; wherfor ful hevy and sory was y and more than a man may suppose; for wele y knew that y must turne ageyne fro that hevynly blysse to thys worldys wrechidnes. And gretely he exhortyd me, how y schulde dyspose me to abyde the day of my callyng oute of my body yn clennes of herte and of body, and mekenes of spirite wyth dylygent kepyng of my religyon. Dylygently

---

[1] accorded with. The Latin here has *coaptabat*, which the translator has rendered literally by *coupled*.

[2] steps.　　[3] partly.

(he seyde to me,) kepe the commaundementys of god, and dyspose they levyng aftyr the example of ryghtwes men. And truely so hyt schal be, that aftyr the terme of they bodely levyng thow schal be admyttyd blessydly to her feleschippe everlastyngly.

And whyle the holy confessour sent nycholas thys wyse spake yet with me, sodenly y harde ther a solenne pele and a rynggyng of a mervelus swetenes, and as al the bellys yn the worlde or what-sumever ys of sownyng[1] had be rongyn to gedyr at onys. Trewly yn thys pele and rynging brake owte also a mervelus swetenes, and a variant medelyng[2] of melody sownyd wyth alle. And y wote not whether the gretnes of melody, or the swetnes of sownnyng of bellys was more to be wondirde. And to so grete a noyse y toke good hede, and ful gretly my mynde was suspendyd to here hyt. Sothly anone as that gret and mervelus sownnyng and noyse was cessyd, sodenly y saw my selfe departyd fro the swete feleschippe of my duke and leder sent Nicholas. Than was y returnyd to my selfe ageyne. and anone y hard the voycis of my brethyrne that stode abowte our bedde; also my bodely strenthe cam ageyn to me a lytyl and a litil, and myn yes opinde to the use of seying, as ye sawe ryghte wele.

Ful delectable hyt was to hym, as he seyde, fro that tyme forthe, as ofte as he harde any solenne pele of ryngyng of bellys; by cause hyt wolde then cum to hys mynde ageyne, the ful swete pele and melody the whyche he herde when he was amonge the blessyd sowlys yn paradyse. Sothely, aftyr that he was cum to hym selfe and hys brethirne had tolde hym that now ys the holy tyme of yestyr[3], than fyrste he beleved, when he harde hem rynge solenly to complen. For then he knew certenly that the pele and melodye, that he herde yn paradyse wyth so grete joy and gladnes, betokynde the same solennyte of yestir yn the whyche owre blessyd lorde and savyur jhesus criste rose uppe visibly and bodely fro dethe on to lyfe, to [w]home wyth the fadyr and the holy gooste be now and evermore everlastyng joye and blysse Amen.

---

[1] sounding.   [2] mingling.   [3] Easter.

19 FOUNDATION OF A RELIGIOUS ORDER

St Gilbert was born in or before 1089 at Sempringham in Lincolnshire, then on the edge of the fens. His father was a wealthy Norman knight named Jocelin; his mother, a Saxon lady. In 1131 he founded a small community which soon grew into the only purely English Monastic Order of the Middle Ages. He died in 1189 "at the age of more than 100 years," says his contemporary biographer, and was canonized by Innocent III. in 1202. There is an excellent study of his life and work by Rose Graham (1901), though her chapter on the Dissolution must be read with some caution. St Gilbert's life was first written in Latin by Roger, his successor in the Mastership of the Order, and translated into English by the Lynn friar John Capgrave in 1451. The following extract comes from pp. 81–90 of that life (E.E.T.S., vol. 140, 1910).

In that same time (that is to say in the reign of King Harry the Second) were in the town of Sempringham certeyn maydenes seculer, whos soules the seed of Goddis word, sowyn be this same Gilbert, had so touchid that thei were rype on-to religion lich as corn is white to hervest. These same maydenes, desyring to be victouris of her kynde[1] and eke of the world, every day entendyd to no othir thing but to plese and to be kynt[2] to that spouse whech is in hevene. This [being] aspied be Seynt Gilbert (specialy whan he had in his avow mad a promisse that his possession of Sempyngham and of Tyrington schuld be gove[3] to God, ferthermor that he wold geve this to [the] pore, and eke he fonde no men at that tyme wold lyve so streytly as these women were disposed for this cause), he determyned to gyve these goodes to swech pore whech were por in spirit and myth[4] chalange the kyngdam of Hevene for them and for othir. This man Gilbert mad him frendes with swech rychesse as he had, whech frendis schuld receyve him in-to everlasting tabernacles. The first frendes that he made wer not of men but of wommen....Oure Gilbert be-gan his perfeccion at the febiller kende, for to the febiller kynde nature techeth that we schuld do our benefetes....And be-cause that no man whech servyth God may serve wel God and be occupied with temporal besinesse, eke be-cause virginite is a tendir thing and may sone be tempted of the sotil deceytes of the serpent, the Devele, whech is ful eld of tyme and ful sotil of

---

[1] over their nature. [2] kind. [3] given. [4] might.

kynde and sone deceyveth virginite, namely whann it is sette
so open that it is schewid to the world,—for tresour openly
bore is put in gret perel,—for this cause he sperd[1] these
virgines fro the noyse of the world, fro the sith[2] of men, that
thei whech schuld entyr in-to the privy chaumbyr of the spouse
thei schuld only entende on-to[3] the swete halsyng[4] of the same
spouse....And though thei lyved in flesch and not aftyr the
flesch, yet wost he wel as longe as thei were in flesch, be-side[5]
swech neccessaries as [be]longe to the flesch, thei myth not
lyve, therfor al thing that is nedful to our fleschly febilnesse,
as mete, or drynk, or clothing, or houses, all these ordeyned
he to these maydenes and ther servauntis in best maner, in
mesur and discrecion. That is to seyn, swech houses as long to
religion, with a cloystir, or a clauser, wallid abowte, and in thoo
houses he sperd the handmaydenes of our Lord, evyn for to
dwelle ther in solitarie lyf; and this werk was undyr the wal
of the cherch of Seynt Andrew, in the strete or town of
Sempyngham, on the north side, first axid and had the counsel
and the help of Alexaunder, than bischop of Lincoln. Dore
was there non mad in the wal but on[e], and that was not open
but swech tyme as schal be touchid afterward ; there mad he
a wyndown thorw whech thei myth receyve swech neccessaries
as longe to her lif. For, though thei wer in the world he wold
put them oute of the world, fro ther lond, fro ther kynrod,
from ther fadir hous....Thus bonde he ther bodies with-inne
thoo walles at that same place Sempingham.

But he wold not, though he prisoned ther bodyes, bynde
ther soules fro God, but this was his entent to close them,
be-cause that conversacion in the world is wone to departe
many men fro that familiarite whech thei schuld have with
God. Eke be-cause that thei myth no-where go oute, therfor
he ordeyned on-to ther servyse certeyn maydenes not lerned,
in a pore seculer habite, whech schuld brynge on-to that
wyndowne mad in the wal all thing that was necessary for
them, and receyve of them at that same hole swech thingis
as was convenient to bere out. That same hole left he ope,
but not evyr ope, for it was opened but at certeyn tymes

[1] he (Gilbert) shut out.   [2] sight.   [3] listen unto.   [4] greeting.   [5] without.

whech wer assigned, for he wold a sperd[1] it for evyr if it had
be so that men or wommen myth a leved with-oute mete or
drynk or other necessaries. For a dore was mad beside, but
nevyr open with-oute his special comaundment, not for the
maydenes to go owt, but for him to entyr on-to them for
goostly coumfort, or techyng of religion, or visiting of the
seke, or swech othir neccessarie causes ; eke of that dore was
he gayler[2] him-self; no man bare that keye but he. Whidir
that he went, wher-evyr he dwelt, the keye of that dore was
with hym, so was he gelous lover of there clennesse. Aftir
this he stodyed sor that there schuld no thing owtward breke
that pes whech these solitarye folk had in ther clauser. He
lerned eke of religious men and wise men that it was not
convenient, ne sykir[3], that seculer maydenes rennyng a-boute
the world schuld serve swech solitarye persones; for evel
speche often tyme appeyreth[4] ful good maneres, and eke thei
that runne so a-boute schuld bryng clatering tydingis, whech
myth apeyre[5] the soules of the nunnes. For this cause thoo
same seculer maydenes, with the good counsel of ther fader
Gilbert and part[l]y with ther owne devocion, desired to have
a religious habite and so dwelle with the nunnes ; and as thei
desired so had thei. For ther, whan thei wer clad in a ful
pore lyf, thei served the nunnes and lyved in ful honest conversacion....

Than say our fader in his inwardly consideracion that,
with-outen mennys solace and purvyaunce, womennes besinesse profitith but lytyl ; therfor chase he certeyn men whech
schuld ovyr-se ther possessiones and have governauns of all
tho grete materes whech longed on-to them. Summe of these
chase he of his plowmen and of his servauntes, summe of pore
mennes childyrn and beggeres whech he had norched fro ther
childhod. He was lich the servaunt of whech the gospel
spekith, that at the comaundment of our Lord went in-to the
lanes and stretes of the cite, and swech as he fonde pore or
febil, brou[gh]t and compelled them to enter, that his lordis
hous schuld be ful....Thus be processe of tyme, be the wil of
our Lord God,...many rich men, noblemen of Ynglond, that is

---

[1] would have shut.   [2] jailor.   [3] safe.   [4] corrupteth.   [5] impair.

to seye, Erles, Barones, and othir,...offered many possessiones to our fader Gilbert; and monasteries, in many provynces, undyr his reule and governauns, thei be-gunne to edifie; of whech helpes Alisaundr biscop of Lincoln was first, and Kyng Herry the secunde, he confermed all. Our fadir Gilbert receyved these possessiones with ful gret dred; and summe was he in maner coact[1] to receyve; summe refused he and wold not have them, because his desir was fro the begynnyng of his ordre that his progenie schuld lyve in honest poverte. Honest poverte clepe we, that a man is not in myschef for his dayly nede, ne he hath neythir no gret superfluite of good. This was the cause that he wold not have ovyr mech whan it was gove him, for often-tyme it is seyn that a-mong gret multitude of puple and gret plente of richesse rise ful gret spottis of pride, as it is said be the wise man: In the multitude of the puple joye of the kyng [Prov. xiv. 28]. For his first purpos at his beginnyng was for to a kept no moo but thoo [first] sevene whech he had sperd up, that as long as thei lyved there schuld be no moo. But he sey[2] be the wil of our Lord that rich men had multiplied many monasteries to encres[3] of this ordre; he wold not be contrarie to Goddis wil, ne lette the devocion of the geveres, ne be rekles of the sustentacion to the servauntis of God, knowing wel that this was Goddis vertu, and not his; wherfor, he comitted al this disposicion to the profund councell of our Lord whech use[th] the servyce both of good and evel after his plesauns.

Whan our maystir Gilbert say[4] thus the childyrn of God grow soo undir his tuycion and say them profiten day be day in the weye of God on-to the tyme in whech thei were gretly magnified, he demed of him-self (as it longith to good soules to have them-self in litil reputacion), so demeth he him-self on-worthi for to be in swech heith[5] that he schuld have governauns ovyr so many parfit persones.

He therefore attended a General Chapter of the Cistercians, at which Pope Eugenius III. was present, and besought them to assume the government of this new Order.

His answer had he of the Pope and of the abbotis whech

---

[1] forced.   [2] saw.   [3] increase.   [4] saw.   [5] such height.

were present : thei saide it was not convenient that prelatis of
ther order schuld be preferred to the governauns of an-othir
ordre, specialy wher wommen were.   Thus frustrat of his purpos, he took his leve, and, be the comaundment of the Pope and
counsel of the prelates there present, he was mad maystir and
principall ovyr that congregacion whech he had begunne.

20   MONASTIC QUARRELS

Medieval disciplinarians constantly refer to the temptations to bad
blood among these cloistered communities, both male and female; cf.
Piers Plowman, c. VII. 128 ff., though the author is there more tender to
the male religious than many official disciplinarians are.   Fights and
bloodshed are not infrequently recorded, but seldom anything so grave as
the following incident, which was aggravated by the folly of a Norman
abbot who wished to impose new-fangled methods of psalmody upon
his Saxon subjects.   One account may be found in *The Anglo-Saxon
Chronicle*, R. S., vol. II. p. 184; that here printed is from Trevisa's *Higden*,
vol. VII. p. 299.   A milder affair is recorded in W. H. Bliss's *Calendar of
Papal Letters*, II. p. 213 (1321 A.D.).

This yere [1081] was a corsed stryf bytwene the monkes
of Glastyngbury and the unthryvynge[1] abbot Thurstan, that
kyng William hadde i-brought thider out of the abbay of
Cadoni [Caen], and made hym abbot of Glastingbury, that
cowthe non manere witte of redynes[2].   Among his other lewed-
nes and folie he despised Gregori his song and offys[3], and bigan
to compelle the monkes for to use the song of oon[4] William
monk of [Fescamp].... He wasted and spend the cherche
good and catel[5] in leccherie, and chalengede cruelliche the
ordre and service of the monkes, and with drough[6] therwith
there mete and drynke; thereof come chidynge and strif of
wordes and discord of wittes and of thowghtes, ffor Lucanus
seith, "Fastynge folk conneth[7] nought drede."   Thanne after
chidynge and stryf men took wepone.   And the abbot, with his
men of armes, fel i-armed on the monkes, slowgh tweyne at
the highe awter[8] and woundede eyghtene, and schot arewes to
ymages and schrynes of the cherche.   The monkes, as they
were i-dreve[9] to by nede, defended. them self as wel as they

---

[1] ignominious.   [2] knew no kind of prudence.   [3] service.   [4] one.
[5] chattels.   [6] withdrew.   [7] know.   [8] altar.   [9] impelled.

myghte yn everiche side with foormes and stooles and candle-
stikkes, and woundede som of the knyghtes.   This cause was
i-meoved[1] to-fore the kyng, and the abbot was i-chaunged and
i-torned to his owne abbay in Normandie.

21   ABBOT AND TOWN

This story is told from a very different point of view by Bartholomew
de Cotton, himself a monk of Norwich at the time (*Hist. Anglicana*,
R. S., pp. 147 ff.). The king certainly took the monks' side ; and it is
probable that the citizens on the whole were the worst offenders in this
affray.

Chronicles of Old London (H. T. Riley, 1863, p. 150).

This year [1271], in the month of August, there befell at
Norwich a certain most unhappy calamity, and one hitherto
unheard of by the world, as among Christians ; for the
Cathedral Church in honour of the Holy Trinity, which had
been founded there from of old, was burnt by fire, purposely
applied, together with all the houses of the monks built within
the cloisters of the said church.   And this took place through
the pride of the person who at that time was Prior of this
Convent ; as from the following facts may be ascertained.
For by assent and consent of this same Prior, the grooms
and servants of the monks very frequently went into the City,
beating and wounding men and women, both within their
houses and without, and doing much mischief.   This Prior also
used to endeavour to draw away men of the franchise from
the commons of the City, in order that they might be under
his own jurisdiction, and severed from the commons.   Also,
whereas the monks have a fair by ancient custom each year,
it happened this year, about the Feast of Holy Trinity, that
after the citizens had come with their merchandize there, and
the greater part of them, at the end of the fair, had returned
home, the servants of the monks, wickedly assaulting those
who remained, beat and wounded them, and slew some ; and
for this they never cared to make any amends; but, always
persevering in their malice and wickedness towards the
citizens, perpetrated all manner of mischief.   The citizens

[1] brought.

however, no longer able to endure so many evils, and such
violence as this, assembled together and had recourse to arms,
in order that they might repel force by force ; which this most
wicked Prior understanding, brought over a great multitude
of malevolent persons from Yarmouth, who had been robbers, plunderers, and malefactors, during the disturbances
in the realm.　All these persons, coming by water to the
Convent, ascended to the belfry where the bells were hung,
fortified it with arms, just as if it were a castle, and took aim
with their bows and arbalests therefrom, so that no-one could
pass along the streets or lanes near the Convent, without
being wounded.　The citizens, seeing these acts of violence,
were of opinion that these misdoers were acting manifestly
against the peace of his lordship the King, in thus setting up
a spurious castle in his city.　Accordingly, meeting together,
and coming to a determination to seize these persons and to
bring them to judgment in the King's name, they provided themselves with arms; and, approaching the closed gate of the court-
yard, on being unable to enter it by reason of the armed men
by whom it was defended, set fire to it, and ruthlessly burnt
the gate.　The fire spreading, however, the belfry was burnt,
and all the dwellings of the monks, as well as, according to
what some say, the Cathedral Church, alas ! together with all
the relics of the saints, books, and ornaments, of the church ;
so that whatever could be burnt was reduced to ashes, a
certain chapel only excepted, which remained unburnt.　The
monks however, and all who were able, took to flight and
made their escape ; though still, some persons on either side
were slain.

22　ST DOMINIC THE SAVIOUR

Myrc, *Liber Festialis*, p. 73 (E.E.T.S., Extra Series, 1905).

Thus, good men, ye most[1] understond how gret vengeans
God toke on the world for wykednesse of synne; and now,
more harme ys, the pepull ar as full of synne as thay wer
that tyme ; and therfor God will take vengeans, [n]er[2] the
prayers of holy sayntys and specyaly of our lady.

---

[1] must.　　　　[2] but for.

For this I rede yn the lyfe of Seynt Domink. When he was on a nyght yn his devocyons he segh our Lord Jhesu holdyng thre speres yn his hond, redy forto schote to the world for vengeans. Then come our lady anon, and kneled before hym, and sayde: "My dere sonne and swet, what wyll ye do?" Then sayde he: "Dere modyr, the world ys full of pride, and of covetyse and of lechery; wherfor, wyth these thre swerdys, I woll schote at hom[1]." Then sayde our lady: "My swete sonne, have mercy, and yet abyde a whyle; I have on[e] trew servand, the wheche schall goo, and preche, and turne the world to the." And so scho send forth Saynt Domink, and bade hym go, and preche Godys worde, and turne the pepull; and so he dude.

Thus, good men, ye have herde how by prayer [of] our lady and by prechyng of thys good man, God spared to do vengeans that tyme. But nowe, more harme ys, the pepull ys combyrt[2] wyth the same synne, and ys full like to be smytten wyth the same vengeans other[3] with wors; for now the pepull settythe but lytyll by God: for, thagh thay heren prechyng and techyng, they wyll not amende hom, ny[4] leve her synne. Wherfor God smytythe yn parte now, and woll [smyte] hereaftyr well hardye and sarre[5]. Wherfor ye schull pray to God to hold up his hond of vengeans that hyt fall not yn our dayes; but that we may come to amendement and have the blysse that he bo[u]gt us to. To the wheche blysse God brynge you and me, yf hit be hys wyll. Amen.

23 MISSIONARY FRIARS

The most vivid account of Franciscan missionary journeys is that of Jordan of Giano, an Italian friar who took a prominent part in the German mission. The best edition of his memoirs is that of Böhmer (Paris, Fischbacher, 1908). Jordan dictated these to a younger brother-friar at Halberstadt, probably within a few months of his own death, in the year 1262. Taking our ideas of the early fervour of the Order from Jordan and from Thomas of Eccleston, we shall be able to mark how far it had decayed in the days of Chaucer and *Piers Plowman*.

(c. 3.) In the year of our Lord 1219, and the 13th year of his conversion, Brother Francis held a general Chapter

[1] them.   [2] cumbered.   [3] or.   [4] nor.   [5] sorer.

at Sta Maria della Porziuncola, and sent brethren to France, Germany, Hungary, Spain and those provinces of Italy which the brethren had not yet reached. The brethren on the French mission, when asked whether they were Albigenses, answered *Yes*, not knowing the Albigenses, or that such heretics existed; wherefore they themselves were taken for heretics. But at length the bishops and masters, reading their Rule and seeing that it was evangelic and catholic, consulted pope Honorius on that matter; who sent letters testifying to the authentic approval of the Holy See for their Rule, and declaring the brethren to be true catholics and special sons of the Roman Church. The German mission was led by brother John of Parma with some 60 or more brethren. When they were come into Germany, not knowing the language, and when men asked whether they desired lodging or meat or any such thing, they answered *Ja*, and thus received kindly welcome from some folk. Seeing therefore that this word procured them humane treatment, they resolved to answer *Ja* to all questions whatsoever. Wherefore, being once asked whether they were heretics, come now to infect Germany after the same fashion wherewith they had already perverted Lombardy, they answered *Ja*; so that some were cast into prison, and others were stripped of their raiment and led to the common dancing-place, where they were held up for a laughing-stock to the inhabitants. The brethren therefore, seeing that they could make no fruit in Germany, came home again; and this deed gave the brethren so cruel a report of Germany, that none dared return thither but such as aspired to martyrdom. The Hungarian mission was brought by sea to that country by a certain bishop of Hungary; and when they began to scatter and go through the land, the shepherds set their dogs upon them and, speaking no word, beat them incessantly with the butts of their spears. When, therefore, the brethren disputed among themselves why they should be thus treated, one said: "Perchance they would have our frocks"; which, therefore, they gave up; yet even so the shepherds ceased not to smite them. So he said, "Perchance they will have our breeches also"; which again they gave;

whereupon the shepherds ceased to beat them and suffered them to depart unclad. And one of these same brethren told me that he had thus suffered fifteen times....So, after these and like sufferings, they came back to Italy. Of the brethren sent to Spain, five were crowned with martyrdom....But when the martyrdom and life and legend[1] of these brethren had been brought to St Francis, finding himself commended in that writing, and seeing that the brethren boasted of the passion of these five—being himself a great despiser of his own person, and holding all praise and glory in the utmost contempt—he repudiated the legend and forbade that it should be read, saying: "Let every man glory in his own sufferings, and not in other men's." So all that first mission was brought to nought. Perchance the time was not yet come, since the wise man saith that to every thing there is a season under heaven.

(c. 16.) So in the year 1221...St Francis celebrated a General Chapter at Sta Maria della Porziuncola,...and the brethren there assembled were reckoned at three thousand.... What tongue could tell the charity, patience, humility, obedience and brotherly cheerfulness which reigned at that time among the brethren? And, albeit the multitude of brethren was so great, yet the people ministered unto us so cheerfully that, after seven days, the brethren were constrained to close their gates against further gifts, and to tarry yet two days in order to consume these offerings. Now, at the end of this Chapter, St Francis bethought him that the Order had not yet been built up in Germany; and, because he was then infirm, brother Elias spake for him whensoever he would have spoken to the people. So St Francis, sitting at the feet of brother Elias, twitched him by the frock; and he, bending down to learn the Saint's will, rose again and said: "Brethren, thus saith the Brother" (that is to say, St Francis, whom the brethren called *The Brother* by excellence). "There is" (he said) "a certain land called Germany, wherein dwell Christian and devout folk who, as ye know, often traverse our land with

---

[1] The *legenda* of a medieval saint was a brief account of his life, divided into chapters for liturgical recitation.

long staves and wide boots[1], singing praises to God and His saints, visiting the Holy Places in the heat of the sun and the sweat of their brow. And, seeing that the brethren once sent thither were evil intreated and came home again, therefore the Brother would constrain no man to go thither; but if any man, inspired with zeal for God and men's souls, will now go thither, the Brother will give him the same commission—nay, an ampler commission still—than to those who go beyond the sea. Wherefore, if there be any willing to go, let them now arise and stand apart." Then some ninety brethren, inflamed with love, offered themselves for death; and, departing from the rest according to the Saint's bidding, they waited until it should be ordered who and how many and how and when they were to go.

Now there was a certain brother present at that Chapter who was accustomed in his prayers to beseech the Lord that his faith might not be corrupted by the Lombard heretics or shaken by the ferocity of the Germans ; but rather that God of His mercy would deign to deliver him from both. He, seeing many brethren arise and show their readiness for the German mission, and thinking that they would soon be martyred there, and grieving that he knew not the names of those brethren who had been martyred on the Spanish mission, was resolved to order things better in this case. Arising, therefore, from the throng, he went to these ninety, and asked of them one by one : " Who and whence art thou ? " for he thought it would redound much to his glory if they chanced to be martyred, and he could say : " I knew that man, and I knew that other." But among this company was a certain brother named Palmerio, a deacon, who was afterwards warden of the friary at Magdeburg ; a jocund and sportive man, from Monte Gargano in Apulia. So when that curious brother had come to Palmerio asking : " Who art thou, and what is thy name ? " then he answered " My name is Palmerio" ; and, laying hands on him, he added : " Thou too art of us and shalt go in our company," wishing to take this brother with him among those very Germans of whom he had oftentimes

---

[1] *ocreis*, boots or gaiters: medieval writers use the word in both senses.

besought the Lord that He might send him whithersoever
He would, so that it were not to Germany. Now therefore,
shuddering at that name *Germans,* he made answer : " I
am not of your company ; but I came hither desiring to
know your names, not to go with you." But the other, over-
mastering him in his jocund way, clave fast unto him and
drew him to the ground, for all his resistance in word and in
deed, and constrained him to sit down among the rest ; and
meanwhile, while this curious brother was thus held captive
there, he was assigned to another province and proclamation
was made : " Let such a brother go to such and such a province." But while these ninety were awaiting their answer,
brother Caesarius the German, of Speyer, was chosen Minister
Provincial of Germany, with power to choose whom he would
from that company. He, finding this curious brother among
the rest, was counselled by them to take him. And, seeing
that he desired not to go thither, and ceased not to protest,
saying : " I am not of your company, for I arose not with the
purpose of going with you," he was led to brother Elias.
And the brethren of the province whereunto he had been
assigned, seeing that he was a weakly man and that the land
of Germany is cold, strove to retain him ; whereas brother
Caesarius sought by all means to take him. At last brother
Elias cut short this strife, saying : " I command thee, brother,
by holy obedience, to resolve once for all whether thou wilt
go or leave it." He therefore, thus constrained by obedience,
and still doubting what to do, feared to choose for conscience
sake, lest in so choosing he should seem self-willed ; for he
feared the journey on account of the cruelty of the Germans,
lest his patience should fail him for suffering and his soul be
in mortal peril. Halting thus between two opinions, and
finding no counsel in his own heart, he went to that sorely
tried brother who (as we have said) had suffered fifteen
times in Hungary, and besought his advice, saying : " Dearest
brother, thus and thus hath it been commanded to me, and I
fear to choose and know not what to do." To whom the other
made answer : " Go then to brother Elias and say : ' Brother,
I am unwilling either to go or to stay ; but I will do whatsoever

thou shalt bid me ' : truly thus shalt thou be freed from thy
perplexity." Thus then he did, and brother Elias commanded
him by holy obedience to go with brother Caesarius to Germany. And he is that brother Jordan of Giano who writeth
these present words ; thus it was that he went to Germany ;
but he escaped from that fury of the Germans which he
had feared, and was among the first to plant the Order of
Friars Minor in that land, with brother Caesarius and other
brethren.

(c. 21.) So brother Caesarius, calling together his brethren
at Trent, and admonishing them to keep all humility and
patience, sent them before him to Bozen by twos and threes,
setting one over temporal things and another over the
spiritual. Then the lord Bishop of Trent entertained the
brethren for a few days as they came in succession, and
licensed them to preach in his diocese. Then they passed
from Bozen to Brixen, where they were kindly received by
the bishop. From Brixen they entered upon the mountain
ways, and came after men's dinner-time to Sterzing. Seeing,
therefore, that the men had no bread at hand, and the
brethren knew not how to beg [in German], hoping still that
by eventide they would come to some place where men would
have pity and refresh them, they came to Mittenwald[1].
Here, in great want, they assuaged, or rather provoked, their
gnawing hunger and their thirst with two mouthfuls of bread
and seven turnips, yet with a joyful heart; and, having taken
counsel among themselves how they should so fill their empty
bellies as to sleep after this day's journey of seven [German]
miles, they resolved to drink of the pure brook that ran
beside the road, lest their empty belly should murmur. At
dawn they arose again in hunger and emptiness and went on
their way : but they had scarce gone half a mile when their
eyes began to grow dim and their legs to fail, and their knees
were loosened and their whole body languished with fasting ;
wherefore, in the anguish of their hunger, they picked berries
and fruit from the thorns and the divers trees or bushes

---

[1] Jordan's memory has betrayed him here: Mittenwald comes at a slightly
different point of the pass.

which they found by the way. Moreover, seeing that it was a Friday, they feared to break their fast; yet it seemed somewhat to comfort them that they bore these fruits and berries, whereof they might have eaten in extremest need. Thus, therefore, now resting by the road, and now creeping painfully forward, they came to Matrey; and lo! God, to whom the poor is abandoned, was solicitous to provide for the needs of His poor servants; for, as we entered into that town, we met two hospitable men who bought us two penny-worth of bread; but what was this among so many? And, for it was the season of turnips, we begged turnips and supplied what was lacking in bread. After which dinner, rather filled than fed, we went on our way; and thus, passing by villages and towns and monasteries, we came at last to Augsburg.

There can be little doubt that Jordan, though he does not name himself, was again the hero of this next episode. The friars were tramping from Salzburg to attend a Provincial Chapter at Worms.

(c. 27.) On their way, they entered into a certain village to find food, wherein they begged by two and two from house to house; but men answered them in the German tongue: "God berad!" which is being interpreted "May God provide for you[1]!" One of the brethren, seeing that with these words nothing was given to them, thought within himself, "This *God berad* will slay us to-day!" Wherefore he ran before the brother who was wont to beg daily, and began to beg in the Latin tongue. Then answered the Germans, "We understand no Latin; speak to us in German." So that brother, speaking corruptly, said, "Nich tiudisch" (which is to say, "No German," the words *I know* being understood). And he added in German: "Bread, for God!" Then said they, "Ha! thou sayest in German that thou knowest no German," and they added, "God berad!" So that brother, exulting in spirit and smiling and making as though he knew not what

[1] Böhmer notes that the Bavarian peasants still say *Helf Gott!* as a pious formula of refusal. Compare *Reliquiae Antiquae*, vol. II. p. 74 (*The Demaundes Joyous*, printed by Wynkyn de Worde) "Q. What people be they that love not in no wise to be prayed for?—A. They be beggars and poor people, when men say *God help them*, when they ask alms"; and *P. Plowman*, c. XII. 44.

they said, sate him down upon the bench; whereupon the man and his wife, looking at each other and smiling at his importunity, gave him bread, eggs and milk. He, therefore, seeing that by such profitable dissimulation he might relieve not only his own necessities but those of the brethren also, went to twelve houses and begged in like fashion; whereby he gained enough to feed his seven brethren.

We may end with a final specimen of the good friar's pious importunity. He had been sent on a deputation to the Pope to protest against brother Elias's tyranny and violations of the Franciscan Rule.

(c. 63.) In the year 1238 the brethren of the province of Saxony...were compelled to appeal to the Pope. So brother Jordan, when he came into the Pope's presence and had saluted him, and had received the command to withdraw, would by no means go forth from the chamber, but rather hastened with jocund face to his Holiness's bed[1], and drew forth his naked foot and kissed it, saying, "Lo! we have no such relics as this in Saxony!" And, when the lord Pope would still have sent them forth, brother Jordan said: "Nay, my lord, we have no petition for ourselves, for we live in all abundance and glory; but you are the father and protector and corrector of our Order, therefore are we come to see you." So at last the Pope was merry, and sat up in his bed and asked wherefore they were come.

He now went carefully into the question; and Jordan's deputation finally retired, having succeeded in its main object.

24   THE ENGLISH MISSION

Though Thomas of Eccleston lacked himself the extraordinarily engaging personality of Jordan, his chronicle is longer and far more detailed. The reader must use some caution, however, in accepting commentaries on Thomas such as those of Dr Brewer in his introduction to *Monumenta Franciscana*, R. S., 1858, Dr Jessopp in his *Coming of the Friars*, and Father Cuthbert in his translation of the Chronicle. Eccleston tells us plainly himself that he looks back on a past heroic age: yet he wrote about 1258. By far the best edition is that of Prof. A. G. Little (1909): but I give here the pagination of the Rolls edition, as the most accessible: my translation is abridged here and there.

[1] It was common for kings, nobles and dignitaries to receive audiences either in or on their beds.

(p. 5.) In the year 1224 the Friars Minor first landed in England at Dover; four clerics and five lay-brethren. [Of the four clerics, only two were in Holy Orders.] (p. 71.) These nine were charitably conveyed over to England by the monks of Fécamp, and hospitably provided with all necessaries. At Canterbury, they abode two days at the Cathedral Priory; then four went forthwith to London, and the other five repaired to the Priests' Spital, where they abode until they had found an habitation. Soon afterwards a little room was granted unto them within the school-house. Here, from day to day, they sat almost continually enclosed; but at eventide, when the scholars were gone home, the friars came into their chamber and lit their fire and sat by the hearth. Here, when the time of Collation[1] came, they sometimes set on the fire a pot full of beer-dregs, wherein they dipped a bowl and drank all round, each saying some word of edification. And (as one hath borne witness who was of this same pure simplicity, and who was found worthy to share and partake in holy poverty) their drink was at times so thick that, when the bowl had to be warmed, they poured water in, and thus drank cheerfully. The like frequently befel them at Sarum, where the brethren so jocundly and joyfully drank their dregs round the kitchen fire at Collation, that each thought himself happy to snatch them in friendly fashion from the other. (p. 8.) It befel also that two brethren came in great distress to one friary, when there was no beer in the house. Then the Warden, taking counsel with the elder brethren, let them borrow a gallon of beer; yet on such terms that the friars of the house, who were entertaining the guests, should make but a false show of drinking thereof, for charity's sake. (p. 9.) Even in the London friary, I myself have seen the brethren drink beer so sour, that some preferred water; and I have seen them eat the bread called *tourte* in vulgar parlance[2]. Moreover, when there was no bread, I have for some

[1] Collation was a sup of drink and a mouthful of bread before retiring to bed; from monastic use it passed to the medieval colleges: see H. Rashdall, *Universities etc.* II. 655, and Section II., no. 20 of this present book: "the potations in Hall at the hour of curfew."

[2] A rough whole-meal bread, the roughest kind ordinarily baked; then came

time eaten [porridge of] spelt there, in the presence of the Provincial Minister and the guests.

But the four brethren aforesaid, proceeding to London, abode with the Friars Preachers, who received them kindly, and with whom they dwelt fifteen days, eating and drinking of what was set before them as most familiar guests. Then they hired for themselves a house in Cornhill, wherein they built cells, stuffing the partitions with grass. Here they dwelt in their first simplicity until the next summer, without any chapel, for as yet they had no privilege of setting up an altar and celebrating divine service. Here did the sweet Lord Jesus sow that grain of mustard-seed which afterwards became greater than all herbs. (p. 10.) It is worthy of note that, in the thirty-second year from the advent of the Friars Minor to England, the brethren living in the English province were numbered at 1,242, in forty-nine friaries.

The first to be received was a youth of great promise, pre-eminent in bodily beauty, brother Solomon. He was wont to tell me that, while he was yet a novice, the care of the temporal things was committed unto him, and he went to beg alms at his sister's house. She, bringing him a loaf, turned away her face, and said "Cursed be the hour that I ever set eyes on thee!" but he took the bread cheerfully and went his way. He kept so strictly to the prescribed form of extreme poverty, that he sometimes suffered so from cold as to seem on the point of death; and the brethren, having no other means of warming him, were inspired by holy charity to excogitate a pious subtlety; for they all gathered together and warmed him by pressing him to their bosom, as her litter lieth about a sow. [One day] the brethren ate at the table of the Archbishop and came home barefoot to the Canterbury friary, through snow so deep that all who saw it shuddered to see them go. After this [brother Solomon] was taken with an infirmity of one foot, whereof he lay sick in London for two years, so that he could scarce move from place to place but if another would bear him. In this infirmity he

bis, then *white*, and then fancy breads such as simnel, manchet, etc. See Riley, *Memorials of London*, p. 644.

was honoured with a visit from brother Jordan of holy
memory, Master of the whole Order of Friars Preachers, who
said unto him : " Brother, be not ashamed if the Father of
our Lord Jesus Christ draw thee to Himself by one foot."
When therefore he had thus lain a long while in the cellar,
where he had not been able to hear mass (for the brethren
sang no mass in the friary, but went to hear divine service
and to sing their masses in the parish church), then his infirmity became so desperate that, as the surgeons judged, his
foot must needs be cut off. But, when the axe was brought,
and the foot had been bared, a little blood and matter came
forth, which promised some hope; wherefore that hard judgment was deferred for a while. Meanwhile he conceived a
certain hope that, if he were led to some saint, he might
recover his foot and his health. Wherefore, when brother
Agnello [the Provincial minister] came, he bade that brother
Solomon should be taken to some shrine beyond the sea without delay, and as conveniently as might be. It came to pass,
then, that his faith belied him not; nay rather, he waxed
so strong as to walk without crutch, and to celebrate mass.
(p. 17.) At Cambridge the Brethren were received first by
the burghers of the town, who granted unto them the Old
Synagogue, hard by the Castle. But, seeing that the neighbourhood of the prison was intolerable to them (for the
gaolers and the brethren had but one door of entrance) the
king gave them ten marks wherewith to buy a rent which
should satisfy his exchequer for the rent of their site; and
thus the brethren built a chapel so miserably poor, that a
single carpenter in one day made and set up 14 pairs of
rafters.

25 CHAUCER'S FRIAR

There is overwhelming evidence to show that all thoughtful people,
orthodox or unorthodox, recognized clearly the decadence of the mendicant orders before the end of the fourteenth century. The following two
extracts from *Piers Plowman* do but put into picturesque language an
indictment which can be substantiated from the most unimpeachable
business records. A third long passage at the very end of the book is
still more unfavourable (B, xx. 211 ff.).

(*a*) B, III. 35, p. 64.

Thanne come there a confessoure coped as a frere,
To Mede[1] the mayde he mellud[2] this wordes,
And seide ful softly, in shrifte as it were,
"Theigh[3] lewed[4] men and lered[5] men had leyne by the[6] bothe,
And falsenesse haved yfolwed the al this fyfty wyntre,
I shal assoille[7] the my-selve for a seme[8] of whete,
And also be thi bedeman[9] and bere wel thi message
Amonges knightes and clerkis, conscience to torne."

Thanne Mede for here mysdedes to that man kneled,
And shrove hire of hire shrewednesse[10], shamelees, I trowe,
Tolde hym a tale and toke hym a noble[11],
Forto ben hire bedeman and hire brokour als[o].

Thanne he assoilled hir sone[12], and sithen[13] he seyde,
"We han a wyndowe a wirchyng wil sitten us ful heigh[14]:
Woldestow glase that gable and grave there-inne thi name,
Siker[15] sholde thi soule be hevene to have."

(*b*) B, XV. 148 ff.

" I have lyved in londe[16]," quod I, " my name is Longe Wille,
And fonde I nevere ful charite bifore ne bihynde!"...
"Charite," quod he, " ne chaffareth noughte, ne chalengeth, ne craveth.
As proude of a peny as of a pounde of golde,
And is as gladde of a goune of a graye russet
As of a tunicle of Tarse[17] or of trye[18] scarlet.
He is gladde with alle gladde, and good tyl[19] alle wykked,
And leveth[20] and loveth alle that owre lorde made.
Curseth he no creature, ne he can bere no wratthe,
Ne no lykynge hath to lye ne laughe men to scorne.
Al that men seith, he let it soth[21] and in solace taketh,
And alle manere meschiefs in myldenesse he suffreth ;
Coveiteth he none erthly good but hevene-riche blisse[22]."

[1] The personification of Ill-gotten Gain. [2] spoke. [3] though.
[4] ignorant. [5] learned. [6] thee. [7] absolve. [8] horseload.
[9] one who prays for hire. [10] wickedness. [11] 6*s*. 8*d*. [12] soon. [13] then.
[14] a window is being made in our church that will cost us a very high price.
[15] certain. [16] land. [17] China silk. [18] choice. [19] to. [20] believeth.
[21] he allows the truth of all that men say. [22] the bliss of heaven.

"Hath he any rentes or ricchesse or any riche frendes?"
"Of rentes ne of ricchesse ne reccheth he nevere."...
For he ne is noughte in lolleres ne in lande-leperes[1] her-
    mytes,...
For charyte is goddis champioun, and as a good chylde
    hende[2],
And the meryest of mouth at mete where he sitteth.
The love that lith in his herte maketh hym lyghte of
    speche,
And [he] is companable and confortatyf, as Cryst bit[3] hym-
    selve,
      Nolite fieri sicut ypocrite, tristes, &c. (Matt. vi. 16),
For I have seyn hym in sylke, and somme tyme in russet,
Bothe in grey and in grys[4] and in gulte herneys[5],
And as gladlich he it gaf to gomes[6] that it neded....
I have seyne Charite also syngen and reden,
Ryden and rennen[7] in ragged wedes,
Ac biddyng[8] as beggeres bihelde I hym nevere....
And in a freres frokke he was yfounde ones,
Ac it is ferre agoo, in seynt Fraunceys tyme;
In that secte sitthe to selde[n] hath he be[n] knowen.

26   A PILGRIMAGE SHRINE

St Mary of Walsingham, in Norfolk, was one of the most popular of
medieval pilgrimage-places for English folk. Erasmus, in the form of a
dialogue between Ogygius (himself) and Menedemus, describes his own
visit to the place some time before the summer of 1514, when he left
England. Erasmus's friend Aldridge, who accompanied him to Walsingham, was then a Cambridge student, and soon afterwards became Master
of Eton College. The *Colloquies*, from which this description is taken,
were begun in 1518. The translation therefrom is that of N. Bailey, 1733.
(Ed. 1877, pp. 241 ff.: Colloquy no. 37.)

Me. But what wind carried you to England? *Og.* A
very favourable wind, and I had made half a promise to the
beyond-sea she-saint [our Lady of Walsingham] to pay her
another visit within two or three years. *Me.* What did you

---

[1] vagabond.   [2] courteous.   [3] bade.   [4] grey squirrel-fur.
[5] gilded armour.   [6] men.   [7] run.   [8] but begging.

go to ask for of her? *Og.* Nothing new but those common matters, the health of my family, the increase of my fortune, a long and a happy life in this world, and eternal happiness in the next. *Me.* But could not our Virgin Mary have done as much for you here? She has at Antwerp a temple much more magnificent than that beyond sea. *Og.* I will not deny that she is able, but one thing is bestowed in one place and another thing in another; whether this be her pleasure merely, or whether she, being of a kind disposition, accommodates herself in this to our affections. *Me.* I have often heard of James, but, prithee, give me some account of that beyond-sea lady. *Og.* I will do it as briefly as I can. Her name is very famous all over England, and you shall scarce find anybody in that island who thinks his affairs can be prosperous unless he every year makes some present to that lady, greater or smaller, according as his circumstances are in the world. *Me.* Whereabouts does she dwell? *Og.* Near the coast, upon the furthest part between the west and the north, about three miles from the sea; it is a town that depends chiefly upon the resort of strangers. There is a college of Canons Regular there,...This college has little else to maintain it but the liberality of the Virgin, for all presents of value are laid up; but as for anything of money or lesser value, that goes to the support of the flock and the head of it, which they call the prior. *Me.* Are they men of good lives? *Og.* Not much amiss. They are richer in piety than in revenue. There is a clever neat church, but the Virgin does not dwell in it herself, but upon point of honour has given it to her Son. Her church is on the right hand of her Son's....And she does not dwell there neither, for the building is not finished; the doors and windows are all open, and the wind blows through it; and not far off is a place where Oceanus the father of the winds resides. *Me.* That is a hard case; where does she dwell then? *Og.* In that unfinished church that I spoke of, there is a little boarded chapel with a little door on each side to receive visitors. There is but little light to it but what comes from the tapers; but the scent is very grateful. *Me.* All these things conduce to religion. *Og.* Nay, Menedemus, if you saw the inside of it you would say it was the seat of the saints, it is all so glittering with jewels, gold, and silver....

At the north side there is a certain gate, not of a church, don't mistake me, but of the wall that encloses the church-yard, that has a very little wicket, as in the great gates of noblemen, that he that has a mind to get in must first venture the breaking of his shins and afterwards stoop his head too. *Me.* In truth, it would not be safe for a man to enter in at such a little door. *Og.* You are in the right of it. But yet the verger told me that some time since a knight on horseback, having escaped out of the hands of his enemy, who followed him at the heels, got in through this wicket. The poor man at the last pinch, by a sudden turn of thought, recommended himself to the holy Virgin that was the nearest to him, for he resolved to take sanctuary at her altar, if the gate had been open. When, behold, which is such a thing as was never heard of, both man and horse were on a sudden taken into the churchyard and his enemy left on the outside of it stark mad at his disappointment.

Me. And did he give you reason to believe so wonderful a relation? *Og.* Without doubt. *Me.* That was no easy matter to a man of your philosophy. *Og.* He shewed me a plate of copper nailed on the door, that had the very image of this knight that was thus saved, and in the very habit which was then in fashion among the English, which is the same we see in old pictures, which, if they are drawn truly, the barbers and dyers and weavers in those days had but a bad time of it. *Me.* Why so? *Og.* Why, he had a beard like a goat, and there was not a wrinkle in any of his clothes—they were made so strait to his body that the very straitness of them made his body the more slender. There was also another plate that was an exact description of the chapel and the size of it. *Me.* Then there was no doubt to be made of it. *Og.* Under the little wicket there was an iron gate, no bigger than what a man on foot could just get in at; for it was not fit that any horse afterwards should tread upon that place which the former knight had consecrated to the Virgin. *Me.* And very good reason.

Og. From hence towards the east, there is another chapel full of wonders; thither I went. Another verger received me. There we prayed a little; and there was shewn us the middle joint of a man's finger. I kissed it, and asked whose relic it was? He told me it was St Peter's. What, said I, the Apostle? He said it was. I then took notice of the bigness of the joint, which was large enough to be taken for that of a giant. Upon which, said I, Peter must needs have been a very lusty man. At this, one of the company fell a laughing. I was very much vexed at it, for if he had held his tongue the verger would have shewn us all the relics. However we pacified him pretty well, by giving him a few groats.

Before this little chapel stood a house, which he told us, in the winter time, when all things were buried in snow, was brought there on a sudden from some place a great way off. Under this house there were two pits brimful, that were fed by a fountain consecrated to the holy Virgin. The water was wonderful cold, and of great virtue in curing pains in the head and stomach. *Me.* If cold water will cure pains in the head and stomach, in time oil will quench fire. *Og.* But, my good friend, you are hearing that which is miraculous; for what miracle is there in cold water quenching thirst? *Me.* That shift goes a great way in this story. *Og.* It was positively affirmed that this spring burst out of the ground at the command of the holy Virgin.

I, observing everything very diligently, asked him how many years it was since that little house was brought thither? He said it had been there for some ages. But, said I, methinks the walls don't seem to carry any marks of antiquity in them. He did not much deny it. Nor the pillars, said I. He did not deny but those had been set up lately; and the thing shewed itself plainly. Then, said I, that straw and reeds, the whole thatch of it seems not to have been so long laid. He allowed it. Nor do these cross beams and rafters that bear up the roof seem to have been laid many years ago. He confessed they were not. And there being no part of that cottage remaining, said I to him, How then does it appear that this is the very cottage that was brought so far through the air? *Me.* Prithee, how did the sexton extricate himself out of this difficulty? *Og.* He presently shewed us an old bear's skin tacked there to a piece of timber, and almost laughed at us to our very faces for not having eyes to perceive a thing that was so plain. Therefore, seeming to be satisfied, and excusing our dulness of apprehension, we turned ourselves to the heavenly milk of the blessed Virgin....

That milk is kept upon the high altar in which Christ is in the middle, and his mother, for respect sake, at his right hand; for the milk represents the mother. *Me.* Why, is it plain to be seen then? *Og.* It is preserved in a crystal glass. *Me.* Is it liquid then? *Og.* What do you talk of being liquid, when it has been put in above 1500 years ago? It is so concreted, you would take it for beaten chalk tempered with the white of an egg. *Me.* But why don't they shew it open? *Og.* Lest the milk of the Virgin should be defiled by the kisses of men. *Me.* You say very well, for I believe there are some who put lips to it, that are neither pure nor virgin ones. *Og.* As soon as the officer sees us, he runs presently and puts on a surplice and a stole about his neck, and falls down very devoutly and worships, and by and by gives us the holy milk to kiss....After this, by our interpreter, (if I remember right,) one Robert Aldridge, a well-spoken young man, and a great master of the English tongue, I inquired as civilly as I could, what assurance he had that this was really the Virgin's milk. And truly I desired to be satisfied of this with a pious intention, that I might stop the mouths of some impious persons who are used to scoff at all these things. The officer first contracted his brow without speaking a word ; thereupon I pressed the interpreter to put the same question to him again, but in the fairest manner that could be, and he did it in so obliging a manner that if he had addressed himself to the mother herself in these terms, when she had but newly lain in, she would not have taken it amiss. But the officer, as if he had been inspired with some enthusiasm, looking upon us with astonished eyes, and with a sort of horror, cursing our blasphemous expression, said, What need is there for your putting this question, when you have an authentic record? and had turned us out of doors for heretics, had not a few pence pacified his rage.

Me. But how did you behave yourselves in the interim?

Og. Just as if we had been stunned with a cudgel, or struck with thunder; we sneaked away, humbly begging his pardon for our boldness; for so a man ought to do in holy matters. Thence we went to the little chapel, the dwelling of the Virgin Saint. In our way thither an expounder of sacred things, one of the minors, offers himself; he stares upon us as if he had a mind to draw our pictures; and having gone a little farther, another meets us, staring upon us after the same manner; and after him a third....We were just upon the point of going away, but walking about and looking round us to see if there was anything worth taking notice of, the chapel officers come to us again, leering at us. Pointing at us with their fingers, they advance to us, retreat, run backward and forward, nod as if they would fain have said something to us, if they had had courage enough to have done it. *Me.* And was not you afraid then? *Og.* No, not at all; but I looked them full in the face very cheerfully, as who should say speak and welcome. At length one of them comes up to me and asked my name. I told it him. He asked me if I was the person that a matter of two years ago set up a votive table in Hebrew letters? I told him I was. *Me.* Can you write Hebrew then? *Og.* No; but they call everything Hebrew that they cannot understand. But by and by, upon calling, as I suppose, came the...sub-prior. He saluted me very courteously. He told me what great pains had been taken to read those verses; what wiping of spectacles there had been to no purpose; how often one grave doctor of divinity, and another of law, had been brought thither to expound the table. One said the letters were Arabic, another said they were fictitious ones; but at last they found one that made a shift to read the title. It was written in Latin words and Latin capitals. The verses were Greek in Greek capitals, which at first sight looked like Roman capitals. Being requested, I turned the verses into Latin, word for word. They would have given me a reward for this small service, but I positively refused it, affirming that there was nothing so difficult that I would not, with all the readiness in the world, undertake for the sake of the holy Virgin.

How little Erasmus has here abused the satirist's licence of exaggeration, may appear from the official visitation of Walsingham Priory by Nicke, Bishop of Norwich, a "hammer of heretics," in 1514, probably a few months after Erasmus's visit. (*Vis. of Dioc. Norwich*, Camden Soc., 1888, p. 113.) The following extracts are compressed, by the omission of repetitions and minor complaints, from the evidence of the first few monks called upon in order of seniority to testify as to the state of the priory: their full evidence may be found translated in the eleventh of my *Medieval Studies*. They should be compared with Mr Hamilton Thompson's exhaustive translations of Lincoln visitations which are in course of publication by the Lincoln Record Society, and the Canterbury and York Society.

Dom Edmund Warham, Sub-prior, being questioned and examined, saith that the Prior hath never paid any moneys into the common chest within his term of office. He saith also that the Brethren are disobedient, incorrigible, quarrelsome and indisciplined.

Dom Thomas Bynham, examined, saith that...if any of the Brethren please John Smyth and his wife, he pleaseth the Prior also; and whosoever displeaseth them displeaseth the Prior. And that Smyth's wife hath access alone to the priory, and (as is believed) to the Prior's bedchamber. He saith that the Prior warned all the Canons together before the Visitation, that they should deliberate among themselves what they should depose or say at the Visitation, saying [to them] as followeth: "Take heed and beware; for the Lord Bishop will have jurisdiction for the time of the visitation; but when he is departed I shall reign again, in spite of him, and I shall look upon you according to the ill ye have deserved of me[1]." He saith that he believeth the Prior to possess 2,000 marks in coined money. He saith that the priory tenements in the town of Walsingham are going to ruin [*patiuntur ruinam*]. *Item*, the sick are almost perishing [*quasi pereunt*] through neglect; for they have no provision beyond that which is provided for the healthy....*Item*, that the Prior oftentimes goeth alone in the dusk to the Chapel of our Lady; and, without the knowledge of any of the Brethren, he dealeth at his will with the money and jewels there received....

Dom John Walsingham, third Prior, saith that the Prior said publicly in chapter-house among the Brethren, "Doo the best that ye can and complayn what yee woll, it shall be never the better."

---

[1] *Juxta demerita.* Visitors and Synods legislated vainly against these temptations to conspiracy or intimidation: see *English Historical Review*, January, 1914, pp. 37–8.

And another time he said, "And I wist that my lorde shulde be against me I shulde so provide that my Lorde [i.e. the Bishop] shulde doo me litle hurt." And another time he said, "When my lorde is goon I shall rule and aske him noon leave."...Robert Angos of the Black Lion knoweth whereof to depose concerning the Prior's conversation; so also knoweth Peter Burgate....

Dom Robert Parker...saith that, every day, the Prior sendeth to Smyth's wife a dish of the best meats brought up to his table. Also he goeth to the Chapel by night and taketh what he will, at his own pleasure. He saith that the Prior hath an old fool; and that he compelled this fool to put on a surplice and to walk publicly in a procession....The Prior smote a husbandman, from which blow the man died within a month....

Dom William Rase, examined, saith that Doms William Bettes, Thomas Wells, and John Clenchwarton go forth from the priory by night, and sit eating and drinking in John Smyth's house until eleven of the clock....

Dom John Lowe agreeth with Dom William Rase concerning the Prior's threatening words. *Item*, he saith that the Prior is lavish in giving monastery goods without the Chapter's consent....*Item*, John Smyth's wife buyeth fish in the market for the convent, to the scandal of the priory. *Item*, she hath kept the keys of the malt and corn-chambers, and taketh what she will. *Item*, she is called the Prior's lady, and hath of the best food and wine. *Item*, Doms Richard Docking, William Bettes, John Clenchwarton, Thomas Wells and David Norwich are of the Prior's part, and fawn and flatter him; moreover they sit up eating and drinking even unto mattins in John Smyth's house; and when they are come to mattins they sleep all the while. *Item*, Dom William Hutton cometh not to choir, but sitteth all day in the house commonly called "the halibred hous," eating and drinking daily therein....

Dom John Ailesham, examined, agreeth with respect to the Prior's threatening words in chapter....*Item*, this deponent, at the Prior's bidding, gave the Sacrament of the Eucharist to the Prior's fool, who was not wont to communicate....John the son of Gresham of Walsingham, rebuked one of the Brethren for sitting in the town at an undue hour; to whom that Brother thus made answer: "As long as I do noo wors then our fader prior doithe he can not rebuke me." The Prior loveth not the students, saying that they are minded to overturn religion....Smyth's wife rode to Canterbury on the Prior's horse. He agreeth with the rest concerning the dishes sent daily to Smyth's wife from the Prior's table.

27 THE FLAGELLANTS

Confraternities of flagellants grew up at different periods of excite-
ment or distress in the Middle Ages ; in all cases they seem to have
finally drifted or been driven into unorthodoxy : see Fleury, *Hist.
Ecclésiastique*, an. 1260, 1349, 1414 ; and Baluze, *Vitae Paparum
Avenionensium*, 1693, vol. I. col. 483 (dancing mania). Like other
similar extremes, they were comparatively infrequent in England.

Robert of Avesbury, *Historia Edwardi Tertii*, ed. Hearne, 1720,
p. 179.

Of the Public Penitents. In this same year [of the Plague]
1349, about Michaelmas, more than six score men came
through Flanders to London, mostly from Zealand and
Holland. These scourged themselves twice a day in the
sight of the people, some in St Paul's cathedral and others
in other parts of the city ; and this was the manner of their
penance. From the waist to the heels they were wrapped
in linen cloth, leaving all the rest of their body naked ; each
wore on his head a cap marked before and behind with a
red cross ; each in his right hand bare a scourge with three
lashes, and in each lash one knot, from the midst whereof
stood out hither and thither sharp points like needles. Thus
then, in the midst of the procession, these penitents followed
one after the other, barefooted, lashing their bare and bleeding
bodies with these scourges aforesaid, while four of them sang
a chant in their own tongue, to which four others answered
at the end, after the fashion of a Christian Litany. Then, in
this procession, all together fell thrice to the ground, where
they lay with hands outstretched in the form of a cross,
chanting all the while as before ; and at last each of these
prostrate penitents, stepping over his fellow, smote him with
the scourge there as he lay ; and thus from one to the other,
from the first even unto the last ; after which each clad
himself in his daily garb, and, with their caps still on their
heads, they returned to their lodgings. And this same
penance, it is said, they repeated every night also.

28 SIDESMEN'S REPORTS

At episcopal, archidiaconal (and possibly ruridecanal) visitations it was required that "sidesmen" (*synods-men*) should appear from each parish to testify. Very few of such testimonies have been preserved ; the following, which go into more intimate detail than any others, are translated from the register of Bp Stapeldon of Exeter, in the order in which they are entered by the editor (F. C. Hingeston-Randolph, 1892). The visitation took place in 1301.

(p. 107.) *Clyst Honiton.* They say that their parish priest is of honest life and good conversation, and hath been there 22 years, honestly fulfilling his priestly office in all that pertaineth to a parish priest ; but he is now broken with age and insufficient for the cure of the parish.

(p. 111.) *Colyton.* They say that sir Robert [Blond], their Vicar, is an honest man and preacheth to them as best he can [*quatenus novit*], but not sufficiently, as they think[1]. They say also that his predecessors were wont to call in the Friars to instruct them for the salvation of their souls ; but this Vicar careth not for them, and, if by chance they come, he receiveth them not and giveth them no help on their way ; wherefore they beseech that he may be reprimanded.

(p. 130.) *Culmstock.* They say that William their Vicar is a man of good life and honest conversation, as also is his Clerk ; and he teacheth his parishioners well in the visitation of the sick and the baptism of infants, and in all those things pertaining to his office, except that, as it seems to them, he tarrieth too long between Matins and Mass on feast-days ; they know naught else to reprehend in him.

(p. 133.) *Dawlish.* They say that the Vicar, whom they hold for a good man, resideth not personally, but hath in his place sir Adam, a Chaplain, who beareth himself well and honestly and teacheth them excellently in spiritual things.

---

[1] The ignorance of the parish clergy was often astounding ; a good many records of their examinations are translated in *A Medieval Garner*, pp. 270–9. Roger Bacon puts it only a little more brutally than his contemporaries Thomas Aquinas and Bonaventura when he writes "just as boys gabble through the psalter which they have learnt ; and as clerks and country priests recite the church services (of which they understand little or nothing) like brute beasts " (*Opp. Ined.*, R. S., p. 413).

But Randolph the Chaplain hath kept his concubine for ten years or more; and, though often rebuked, he persisteth incorrigibly. The parish clerk is continent and honest.

(p. 170.) *Ashburton.* They say that the Vicar beareth himself well and honestly in spiritual matters, and they know naught of mortal and hidden sin[1].

(p. 194.) *Branscombe.* They say that Thomas, their Vicar, beareth himself well in all things and preacheth willingly, and visiteth the sick, and doth diligently all that pertaineth to his priestly office. Of the clerk and the other parishioners they know naught but what is good and honest.

(p. 296.) *Chapel of Norton, in Newton St Cyres.* The jurors say that, in the time of Master William de Staneweye, who formerly held this chapelry to farm[2], the Rector of Newton was wont to find a Chaplain who, every Sunday, was accustomed to read the Gospel to the parishioners of the chapelry of Norton, to sprinkle holy water, and to distribute holy bread[3], to sing Mass each Wednesday and Friday, and to celebrate a full service for them at Christmas and Easter; and to hear their confessions in Lent and likewise baptize their children; but in the last days of the aforesaid William all these things aforesaid were withdrawn, until the time of the present farmer, who hath restored all except that the Gospel is not read to them, nor have they holy bread or water as of old; in which matter they beg for succour.

(p. 337.) *St Mary Church.* The parishioners say that, until the days of the present Vicar, they were wont to maintain the Chancel in all things and to be immune from paying tithe for the restoration of the church; but the present Vicar, though he maintaineth not the Chancel, yet receiveth the tithe and compelleth them to pay. *Item,* they say that Agnes

---

[1] The sidesmen were bound to testify as to the morals not only of the clergy but also of the parishioners.

[2] A church or chapelry might not be farmed out to a layman, but they were frequently farmed out to clerics: e.g. the monks of Norwich Cathedral thus let out their appropriated churches in the city.

[3] *Panem benedictum,* the *Eulogia* of the Greek Church and the *Pain Bénit* of the modern French church: see D. Rock, *Church of our Fathers,* 1905, vol. I. p. 110 and vol. IV. p. 214.

Bonatrix left five shillings in pollard coin[1] for the upkeep of
St Mary's church, which the Vicar hath received and detains.
Item, Master Roger le Rous left a certain sum of money to
the same end, which the said Vicar is said to have received
in part. *Item*, they say that the Vicar feedeth his beasts of
all kinds in the churchyard, by whom it is evilly trodden
down and vilely defouled. *Item*, the said Vicar taketh to
the use of his own buildings the trees blown down in the
churchyard. *Item*, he causeth his malt to be malted in the
church, wherein he storeth his wheat and other goods; whereby
his servants go in and out and leave the door open, and the
wind blowing into the church at time of tempests is wont to un-
cover the roof. They say moreover that he preacheth well and
exerciseth his office laudably in all things, when he is present.
But oftentimes he departeth to abide at Moreton-Hampstead,
now for a fortnight and now for a week, so that they have
then no Chaplain, except when sir Walter, the Archdeacon's
Chaplain, is present, or some other casual Chaplain is procured. [It is also presented that the church is in bad repair,
one of the 3 dependent chapels is in ruins, and the other 2
are dilapidated.]

(p. 345.) *Salcombe-Regis*. The parishioners say that Robert,
the Vicar, doeth competently all things that concern divine
service. On the other points they make no deposition, because, as they say, they know nothing.

(p. 368.) *Sidbury*. They say that Walter the Vicar
beareth himself excellently in all things, preaching well and
laudably exercising his priestly office. The Clerks also bear
themselves honestly. Of mortal sin they know nothing.

(p. 378.) *Staverton*. They say that sir Walter, the Vicar,
beareth himself well and honestly, and teacheth them excellently in spiritual things; nor is there, as they assert, any
defect in him. Of hidden mortal sin they know naught.
And his Vicarage, as they assert, is worth ten marks.

---

[1] So it seems necessary to interpret the *vs ballardorum* of the text. In 1300
the *pollard* was to pass for half its face value (Riley, *Memorials of London*, p. 42);
and Walsingham under the year 1301 records the difficulties arising from the
circulation of this coin. Cf. also Rogers, *Hist. Agric. and Prices*, I. 178.

(p. 380.)   *Stoke-Canon.*   The parishioners say that William, Chaplain of this place, beareth himself honestly, and all is well in spiritual things, as their understanding goeth (*ut intelligunt*).

(p. 388.)   *Thorverton* ⎫
(p. 397.)   *Upottery* ⎬   [No report on spiritual matters; considerable dilapidations in
(p. 409.)   *Winkleigh* ⎭   Churches, etc.]

29   RELIGIOUS EDUCATION

(*a*)   " All is well in spiritual things, as their understanding goeth " is a lifelike phrase which admits of further comment. The following passage from the autobiography of a most orthodox and hard-working visitor in N. Germany, which is perhaps unique of its kind, throws a vivid light on the patriarchal relations between clergy and people in a good parish. It is translated from Johann Busch, *Liber Reformationis Monasteriorum*, ed. Grube, p. 441. Busch found himself saddled with the archidiaconate of Halle ; at his first synod he found startling ignorances among the clergy, but he inserts this episode as a counterpoise.

I asked one sidesman, a peasant-farmer, " Have all your fellow-parishioners kept the commands of God and Holy Church ? " He answered, " I know not to the contrary." "And are all in your village faithful and good Christians, keeping holy-days, not witches or suchlike folk ? " He answered, " Yes." Then said I, " If thou be a good Christian, then say the Lord's Prayer and Ave Maria in German." Whereupon, in the hearing of all, he repeated them in good German. Then said I, " Now repeat the Creed "; and he repeated it fully and quite clearly in good German. So I said to him, "You believe that God will judge the quick and the dead. At that last judgment will all be dead, or all alive ? " " I know not," said he ; " but this I know, that God will then judge the quick and the dead."...Then I continued, " You have said that you believe the resurrection of the flesh. You seem to be forty or fifty years old. Your father, grandfather, and great grandfather are dead, and so are all that have gone before them....If their graves were opened, nothing would be found but perhaps a bit of a rib or of a skull or of some other bone ; for all the rest is fallen to dust. Do you believe that all these dead folk...will get again the same

bodies and limbs which they had while living on this earth...
down to the very skin and hair?" He answered, "I believe
that God is almighty; if He wishes it, He will certainly do
it; and I believe He does wish it." Lastly I said, "How
long is eternal life? is it as long as a hundred years?" To
which he replied, "What sayest thou? It is longer than a
good hundred thousand years." Then said I, "Thou hast
spoken very well; I give thee leave to depart." The Bürger-
meister of Halle, and many others who stood by, said then,
"If Father Busch had questioned us so closely, we could not
have answered him so exactly" (*tam formaliter*). I asked at
dinner-time (for all we priests dined together with the priest
of St Mary's at Halle), "How did that farmer know how
to answer so exactly?" And they told me that the priest
of that parish forbade their suffering any man to dine or
make merry with them at the tavern, until he had first said
his Pater, Ave, and Creed; "wherefore," said they, "they
speak to each other of these things, and have got so perfect
a memory and understanding thereof."

(*b*) The other side of this subject is shown by a series of synodal
decrees of the Church, in all countries. That of Abp Peckham, in 1281,
formed a model for other English archbishops and bishops, who repeat
his pleas, sometimes almost textually, all down the Middle Ages. It has
been argued by some modern apologists that these decrees constitute
a proof of pastoral care on the part of the medieval Church; but these
writers omit the two tell-tale opening sentences.

D. Wilkins, *Concilia*, vol. II. (1737), p. 54, "Of the Instruction of the
Simple."

The ignorance of priests casteth the people into the ditch
of error; and the folly or unlearnedness of the clergy, who
are bidden to teach the faithful concerning the Catholic
Faith, doth sometimes tend rather to error than to sound
doctrine. For some blind clergy do not always visit those
places which are known to need most the light of truth,
as saith the Prophet: "The little ones have asked for bread,
and there was none to break it unto them"; and as another
Prophet crieth: "The needy and the poor seek for waters,
and there are none; their tongue hath been dry with thirst"
(Lam. iv. 4; Is. xli. 17). Wherefore, in remedy of these

dangers, We decree that every priest having charge of a flock do, four times in each year, that is, once in each quarter, on one or more solemn days, either personally or by deputy, expound to the people in the vulgar tongue, without any fantastic texture of subtlety, the fourteen articles of the Faith, the Ten Commandments, the two Evangelical Precepts of charity; the Seven Works of mercy; the Seven Deadly Sins, with their progeny[1]; the Seven Chief Virtues; and the Seven Sacraments of Grace. And, lest any should excuse himself from these duties on the plea of ignorance (albeit all ministers of the Church are bound to know these things), we expound them here in a brief summary.

Here follows the summary, occupying two folio pages: the similar summary published by Bp Quivil for Exeter diocese runs to eight pages. Compare Latimer's words at the end of his *Sermon at Stamford* (Parker Soc., 1844, p. 307):

"Marvel not that I use at the sermon's end to make prayer, for I do it not of singularity; but when I am at home, and in the country where I go, sometime poor people come and ask at me, I appose them myself, or cause my servant to appose, of the Lord's prayer; and they answer, some, 'I can say my Latin *Paternoster*'; some, 'I can say the old *Pater noster*, but not the new.' Therefore [that] all that cannot say it may learn, I use before the sermon and after to say it. Wherefore now I beseech you, let us say it together:

Our Father, which art," etc.

30   CHURCH MUSIC

(*a*) From Bp Percy's notes to the *Northumberland Houshold Book*, 1770, p. 445.

There is a passage in an old Play, entitled "𝕿𝖍𝖊 𝕴𝖓𝖙𝖊𝖗𝖑𝖚𝖉𝖊 𝖔𝖋 𝖙𝖍𝖊 𝖋𝖔𝖚𝖗 𝕰𝖑𝖊𝖒𝖊𝖓𝖙𝖘," written about the beginning of Henry the VIIIth's reign, which shews what high regard was anciently paid to Church Music.

HUMANITY says,

" 𝕻𝖗𝖞𝖐-𝖘𝖔𝖓𝖌 𝖒𝖆𝖞 𝖓𝖔𝖙 𝖇𝖊 𝖉𝖎𝖘𝖕𝖞𝖘𝖊𝖉,
𝕱𝖔𝖗 𝖙𝖍𝖊𝖗𝖊𝖜𝖎𝖙𝖍 𝕲𝖔𝖉 𝖎𝖘 𝖜𝖊𝖑𝖑 𝖕𝖑𝖊𝖘𝖞𝖉,

[1] Chaucer's *Parson's Tale* is a free translation from one of these manuals on the Seven Deadly Sins.

𝔥onodtreꝺ, praꝑsꝑꝺ, anꝺ serbꝑꝺ
𝔦n the 𝔠hurch oft tꝑmes among."

YGNORAUNCE answers,

"𝔦s 𝔊oꝺ dtell pleasꝑꝺ, trodtost thou, therbꝑ?
𝔫aꝑ, naꝑ, for there is no reason dthꝑ:
𝔣or is it not as gooꝺ to saꝑ plaꝑnlꝑ
       Gyf me a spade?
𝔞s *Gyf me a spa, ve, va, ve, va, vade?*
𝔟ut ꝑf thou dtꝑlt habe a song that is goꝺe,
𝔦 habe one of 𝔯obin 𝔥oꝺe
𝔱he best that eber dtas maꝺe."

(b) *An Alphabet of Tales*, E.E.T.S., 1904, p. 85 (Tale cxx.).

Jacobus de Vetriaco tellis how that ther was a preste that trowid he was a passand gude synger, not-with-stondyng he was not so. So on a day ther was a gentyl-womman that satt behynd hym and hard hym syng, and sho began to wepe ; and he, trowyng that sho wepid for swettnes of his voyse, began to syng lowder than he did tofor; and ay the hyer sho h[e]ard hym syng, the faster wepud sho. Than this preste askid hur whi sho wepud so as sho did, and sho answerd hym agayn and sayd ; "Sur, I am a pure gentill-womman, and the laste day I had no calfe bod[1] one ; and the wulfe come and had it away fro me; and evur when that I here you syng, onone[2] I remembre me how that my calfe and ye cried [a]like." And when the preste hard this, onone he thoght shame, and remembred hym that that thing [th]at he thoght was grete lovyng unto God, was unto Him grete shame and velany ; and fro thens furth he sang nevur so lowde.

31   EXCOMMUNICATION

Ibid. p. 215 (Tale cccxii.).

Jacobus de Vetriaco tellis how som tyme in the bisshopprik of Lincoln ther was a smyth, and he dispysyd the sentens of the kurk ; and thai cursid hym. So on a day he satt at meatt with other folk, and ther come in-to the howse unto thaim a

---

[1] but.   [2] anon.

swyne of Saynt Antons[1]. And he tuke bread and keste unto it, and said; "Now sall itt appere whether this Anton swyne will eatt of my bread that am cursyd, or nay." And the swyne smellid the bread and wolde not eate it. And than he bad one of his felous take the same bread and giff it; and so he did, and yitt it wold not tuche it. And the toder[2] that satt aboute gaff it of ther bread, and onone the swyne eate itt.

32   A FALSE VOW

Ibid. 1905, p. 521 (Tale DCCLXXXII.).

We rede in "Libro de Dono Timoris" how som tyme ther was a man that had bothe a cow and a calfe unto the mownte of Saynte Michaell, betwix the bowndis of Bretayn and Normondie, [th]at he mot esskape the flowyng of the see that umwhile[3] occupied that way. And the flude come on hym and he cried of Saynt Michall and sayd; "O thou blissid Michaell, delyver me and I sall gyff the this calve." And when he was delyverid he sayd; "Saynt Michell was bod[4] a fule that trowed at I wolde hafe gyffyn hym my calfe." So afterward hym happend to be taken with the same flude. And than he cryd of Saynt Michaell and prayed hym delyver hym and he sulde gyff hym bothe the cow and the calfe. So he was delyverd and sayd as he did befor. So the iij time he went thedur [to] feche home this cow and this calfe, and sodanlie as he come hamwerd, the se-flude umlappid bothe hym and the cow and the calfe, and drownyd thaim all thre, and that onone[5].

33   DEGREES IN BLASPHEMY

Ibid. p. 83 (Tale CXVIII.).

Cesarius tellis how on a tyme ij men played at the dyce, and when the tane[6] of thaim began to lose, he began to wax wrathe with the toder and speke grete wurdis, and ravie and flite[7] with God for that he wan nott. And the toder, when he

---

[1] The hospital of St-Antoine in Dauphiné had branches all over Europe. The swine belonging to these hospitals were privileged; distinguished by bells round their necks, they roamed the streets when other swine were forbidden: cf. H. T. Riley, *Memorials of London*, 1868, p. 83.

[2] other.   [3] sometimes.   [4] but.   [5] anon.   [6] one.   [7] quarrel.

hard hym flite with God and speke grete wurdis, flate with hym
agayn and bad hym hold his tong ; and he wold not, bod evur
when he loste, blasfemyd owder[1] God or our Ladie.   So, as thai
satt threpand[2] thus, thaim thoght thai hard a voyce above thaim
that sayd ; " I hafe suffred hedur-toward[3] injurie and wrong to
be done unto my selfe, bod I will nor may not suffre no langer
the injurie and wrong done unto my moder."   And onone[4] this
[blasphemer], as he lenyd opon the tabels, was sodanlie strekyn
with a wown[5] that all men myght se, and bafid[6] att his mouthe
and swelte[7].

34   FAITH AND REASON

We have seen that Fellows and Scholars of King's College, Cambridge,
were kept in orthodoxy by a statutory oath to abjure the errors not
only of Wyclif, but also of Bp Reginald Pecock, who claimed stoutly
to be a true Catholic.   Pecock was born in Wales, became fellow of
Oriel in 1417, attracted the notice of Humphrey, Duke of Gloucester,
became Bp of St Asaph in 1444 and of Chichester in 1450.   About 1449
he had published his *Repressor*, an elaborate criticism of the Lollards'
position in the light of reason and history, as Pecock understood them.
In this book he made concessions to reason which stirred the wrath of
the orthodox clergy.   While the storm gathered, he was writing his still
more liberal *Treatise on Faith*.   He was publicly accused in the Council
of Westminster towards the end of 1457, subjected to frequent examinations by a commission of enquiry, and finally bidden to choose between
recantation and the stake.   "Pecock" (writes Babington in his Preface
to the *Repressor*, R. S., 1860, p. xlvi) "stood for a few moments in motion-
less silence, not knowing what to answer.   He then replied as follows :
' I am in a strait betwixt two, and hesitate in despair as to what I shall
choose.   If I defend my opinions and positions, I must be burned
to death : if I do not, I shall be a byword and a reproach.   Yet it is
better to incur the taunts of the people, than to forsake the law of faith
and to depart after death into hell-fire and the place of torment.   I choose,
therefore, to make an abjuration, and intend for the future so to live that
no suspicion shall arise against me all the days of my life.'   He then and
there made, as a preliminary to his abjuration, a confession in presence
of the archbishop and the assembly, and retracted in general all the
heretical positions which were contained in his various books."   The
following two extracts give a fair idea of the stress which Pecock laid
upon reason, and the offence which his *Repressor* was certain to give
among the conservative theologians of his day.

---

[1] either.   [2] disputing.   [3] hitherto.   [4] anon.   [5] wound.
[6] barked.   [7] died.

(*a*) Vol. I. p. 25.

Of whiche first principal conclusioun thus proved folewith ferther this corelarie, that, whanne evere and where evere in Holi Scripture or out of Holi Scripture be writen eny point or eny governaunce of the seide lawe of kinde[1], it is more verrili writen in the book of mannis soule than in the outward book of parchemyn or of velym ; and if eny semyng discorde be bitwixe the wordis writen in the outward book of Holi Scripture, and the doom[2] of resoun write in mannis soule and herte, the wordis so writen withoutforth[3] oughten be expowned and be interpretid and brought forto accorde with the doom of resoun in thilk mater ; and the doom of resoun oughte not forto be expowned, glosid, interpretid, and broughte for to accorde with the seid outward writing in Holi Scripture of the Bible, or oughwhere ellis out of the Bible.

(*b*) *Ibid.*, p. 98. Pecock is arguing against the third position of Lollards, that, when the true sense of Scripture has been discovered by the religious enquirer with the aid of his inner light, he should listen to no contrary arguments advanced by the clergy.

That the iij[e]. opinioun is also agens reson, y mai schewe thus :...the more eny treuthe, whether he be of feith or of no feith, be brought in to examinacioun of arguyng, the more trewe and the more cleerli trewe he schal be seen ; and if he be not trewe, but seme trewe eer he come into triyng of argumentis, the lenger he abidith the examynacioun of arguyng, the more untrewe and the more cleerli vntrewe he schal be seen ; right as good trewe gold, the more it suffrith the fier, the more cleerli he is seen to be trewe gold ; and if he be not but countirfeet gold, certis the lenger he abidith the examynacion of fier, the more cleerli it schal be seen that he is fals and not trewe gold. And therfore, Goddis forbode that any Cristen man schulde thinke and trowe [it] to be a trewe and a good governance forto kepe hise feithis and his othere opiniouns privey, and lete hem not come into what ever examynacioun of argumentis whiche mowe[4] be mad ther upon ; namelich[5] whanne and where the holder of tho feithis

---

[1] nature.   [2] judgment.   [3] outwardly.   [4] may.
[5] especially.

and of hise othere opinions mai be sikir[1] forto come and go
and speke and argue and answere withoute eny bodili harme,
and with out eny losse of his ricches or of his fame. Certis,
if eny man dare not (in the now seid casis) suffre his feith and
his othere opiniouns be brought into light and into fier of
argumentis, to be at uttrist[2] examyned, he oughte be trowid
that, in that, he hath untrewe chaffar[3] and untrewe gold, which
mai not abide light and fier.

Also that this iij[e]. opinioun is agens resoun it is evydent
herbi : He is lijk to the lawe of Macomet and of Sarezenis
in thilk[4] point in which her lawe is moost unresonable. Forwhi[5]
the lawe of Macomet biddith, undir greet peyne of horrible
deeth suffring, that no man aftir he hath receyved the feith of
thilk lawe dispute or argue with eny other man upon eny
point, article, or conclusioun of thilk lawe : and bi this wrecchid
and cursid maundement the peple of thilk secte ben so miche
lockid up undir boond, that manie mo of hem myghten be
convertid into trewe feith than yit ben, if thilk so unresonable
maundement of the same lawe ne were. And if any Cristen
men wolen locke hem-silf so up, in her feithis and othere
opiniouns of Cristis lawe, fro arguyng and disputing ther upon
with othere men, (as y have knowe bi reporting of ful trewe
persoones that thei so doon), certis therin thei doon foul
vilonie to Cristis lawe of feith and [to] lawe of kinde, making
as though Cristis seide lawe were so feble chaffare and so
countirfetid and so untrewe, that it durst not save his worschip
if he were thriftili[6] examyned. And thei doon also ful
periloseli to hem silf for to make hem so sikir in a feith, eer
it be sufficientli tried and proved forto be holde[n] worthi
a trewe feith or no. And therfore the thridde bifore-sett
opinioun in the first chapiter of this book is unresonable.

---

[1] sure.　　[2] uttermost.　　[3] wares for sale.　　[4] that.　　[5] because.
[6] carefully.

35   LATIMER'S CONVERSION

Hugh Latimer was born about 1490 at Thurcaston near Leicester. He went up to Cambridge at the age of 14, and was converted to Protestantism about 1521, when he was proceeding to the degree of B.D. He became Bishop of Worcester in 1535, and was burned in 1555.

The First Sermon upon the Lordes Prayer.

Here I have occasion to tell you a story which happened at Cambridge. Maister Bylney (or rather Saint Bilney that suffred death for Gods worde sake) the same Bylney was the instrument whereby God called me to knowledge, for I may thanke hym, next to God, for that knowledge that I have in the worde of God. For I was as obstinate a Papist as any was in England, in so much that when I should bee made Bacheler of Divinitie, my whole Oration went agaynst Philip Melancthon, and agaynst his opinions. Bilney heard me at that tyme, and perceived that I was zelous without knowledge, and he came to me afterward in my studie, and desired me for Gods sake to heare his confession. I did so. And to say the trueth, by his confession I learned more then before in many yeares. So from that tyme forward I began to smell the word of God, and forsooke the Schoole Doctoures and such fooleries.

Now after I had beene acquainted with him, I went with him to visite the prisoners in the tower at Cambridge, for he was ever visiting prisoners and sicke folke. So wee went together, and exhorted them as well as we were able to doe, moving them to patience, and to acknowledge their faultes.

36   UTOPIAN MONKS AND CLERGY

More's *Utopia*, tr. Ralph Robinson, 1551 (ed. Lumby, 1879, p. 150). Compare More's satire on monks and friars on pp. 45, 81 of the same edition.

They [the Utopians] thinke that the contemplation of nature, and the prayse thereof comminge, is to God a very acceptable honoure. Yet there be many so earnestlye bent and affectioned to religion, that they passe no thing for lern-ing, nor geve their mindes to any knowledge of thinges. But ydelnes they utterly forsake and eschue, thinking felicitie after this life to be gotten and obteined by busie labors and good exercises. Some therfore of them attende upon the sicke, some amende high waies, clense ditches, repaire bridges, digge turfes, gravell and stones, fel and cleave wood, bring wood, corne and other thinges into the cities in cartes, and serve not onelye in commen woorkes, but also in private laboures as servauntes, yea, more then bondmen. For what so ever unpleasaunt, harde and vile worke is anye where, from the whiche labour, lothsomnes and desperation doth fray other, al that they take upon them willingly and gladly, procuring quiete and rest to other, remaininge in continual woorke and labour themselves, not embraidinge[1] others therewith. They neither reprove other mens lives, nor glorie in theire owne. These men, the more serviceable they behave themselves, the more they be honoured of all men. Yet they be divided into two sectes. The one is of them that live single and chast, absteining not onely from the companie of women, but also from eating of fleshe, and some of them from all maner of beastes. Whiche utterly rejecting the pleasures of this present life as hurtfull, be all 'wholye set upon the desier of the lyfe to come, by watchynge and sweatynge hoopinge shortly to obtaine it, being in the meane season merie and lustie. The other secte is no lesse desirous of laboure, but they embrace matrimonye, not despisynge the solace therof, thinking that they can not be discharged of their bounden duties towardes nature without labour and toyle, nor towardes their native countrey without procreation of children. They abstaine from no pleasure that doeth nothinge hinder them from laboure. They love the flesh of foure footed beastes, bicause they beleve that by that meate they be made hardier and stronger to woorke. The Utopians counte this secte the wiser, but the other the holier. Which in that they preferre single life before matrimony, and that sharp life before an easier life, if herein they grounded upon reason they would mock them. But now forasmuch as they say they be led to it by religion, they honor

---

[1] upbraiding.

and worship them. And these be they whom in their language
by a peculiar name, they cal Buthrescas, the which woord by
interpretation signifieth to us men of religion or religious
men. They have priestes of exceding holines, and therefore
very few....The priestes, onles they be women (for that kinde
is not excluded from priest-hoode, howbeit fewe be chosen, and
none but widdowes and old women) the men priestes, I saye,
take to their wifes the chiefest women in all their countreye.

SECTION V

KINGS, KNIGHTS AND WAR

1   THE CONQUEROR'S CHARACTER

It is impossible, within any reasonable space, to do justice to the picturesque side of this section ; but here the reader has many first-rate authorities easily accessible ; e.g. Berners's *Froissart* (Globe Edition, abbreviated), *Adam of Usk* (tr. Maunde Thompson, 1904), Sir Thomas Gray's *Scalacronica* (tr. Stirling-Maxwell, 1907), Malory's *Morte d'Arthur*, and Bohn's translations of Matthew Paris and many other chronicles. Apart, therefore, from a few extracts illustrating the relations between king and people, the reader will here find only documents which he would be less likely to meet with independently.

Trevisa's *Higden*, vol. VII. p. 315.

This William Conquerour was a wise man and a gileful, riche and coveitous, glorious, and loved wel greet loos[1] ; faire spekere with Goddes servauntes, and sturne to them that wolde them withstonde.   In the province of Hamptoun, in the newe forest, in the space of thritty myle, he threw doun cherches and townes, and put there wilde bestes.   So that who took there a wilde best schulde lese his oon yghe ;... Kyng William was of skilful[2] stature, to[3] greet and fat of body, and sturne of face, bare of forheed, greet of strengthe in brawne and armes, so that unnethe[4] eny man myght bende his bowe ; bote[5] he wolde on his hors strecche forth his senewes and bende hit esiliche ynow uppon his owne foot.   He had skilful strengthe and gaf hym self to moche to hontynge, so that he threwe doun cherches and townes to make wodes. He made grete festes and revelles in the highe feestes of the yere.   He hilde his mydwynter tide at Glowcestre, his Esterne

---

[1] fame   [2] reasonable.   [3] too.   [4] scarcely.   [5] but.

at Wynchestre, Witsonday at Westmynster, whan he was in Engelond. But he passede and overdede[1] in gadringe of money of the people, other to withstonde his enemyes, other to make hym a greet name, other to cese[2] his covetise.

2   THE DEATH OF RUFUS

The Brut, E.E.T.S., 1906, Part I. p. 138.

And this Kyng made the new Forest, and caste doun and destroiede xxvj tounes and xxiiij house[s] of religion, al forto make his foreste longer and broder, and bicome wonder glade and prout of his wode and of his Forest, and of the wilde bestes that wer therin, that it was mervailous forto wete[3], so that men callede him "keper of wodes and of pastures." And the lenger that he levede, the more wikkede he bicome, bothe to God and to holy cherche, and to alle his men. And this kyng lete make the grete halle of Westmynstre ; and so oppon a Whitsonday he helde therin his ferste feste, he lokede aboute him, and saide that the halle was to litel by halvendele. And at the laste he bicome so contrarious, that al thing that plesede God, displesede him ; and al thing that gode men lovede, he hatede dedly. And so hit befel that he dremede and mette[4] oppon a nyght, bifore a litil or that he deide, that he was [let] bloode, and bledde a grete quantite of bloode, and a streme of blode lepte an hye toward Heven more than an hundred [fathom?] ; and the clerenesse of the day was turnede al to derkenesse, and the firmament also. And when he awoke, he hade grete drede, so that he nyste[5] what to done ; and tolde his dreme to meny of his conseile, and saide that he hade grete drede, and supposede that him was some meschaunce to come. And the secunde nyght bifore, a monke dremed of the houshald, that the kyng went into a cherche with miche peple ; and he was so prout that he despisede al the peple that was with him ; and so he toke the ymage of the crucifixe, and shamefully bote[6] hit with his teith ; and the crucifix mekely soffrede al that he dede ; but the

---

[1] excceded.   [2] allay.   [3] know.   [4] dreamed.
[5] wist not.   [6] bit.

kyng, as a wode[1] man, rent of[f] the armys of the crucifixe and caste it under his feete, and defoulede it and threwe it al [a]brode; and a grete flame of fire come out of the crucifixez mouthe; of the whiche dreem, meny a man hade grete wonder. The gode man that dremede this dreem tolde it to a knyght that tho[2] was moste prive with the Kyng of al men; and the knyght me[n] callede Hamundus sone; and the monke and he tolde the dreem to the Kyng, and saide that it shulde bitoken othere thing than gode. And nothelesse the Kyng laughede therat ij or iij, and litil sette therof; and thought that he wolde gone hunte and pleye in the forest; and his men conseiled him that he shulde nought that day, for no maner thing, come in the wode, so that he abode at home bifore mete. But anone as he hade eten, nothing might him lette but he wolde go to the wode forto have his disporte. And so hit bifelle that one of his knyghtes, that hight Walter Tyrel, wolde have shotte to an herte; and his arwe glasede oppon a braunche, and through misaventure smote the Kyng to the hert; and so he felle doune dede to the grounde, withouten eny worde spekyng, and so he endede his lif.

3   HENRY II AND HIS SONS

Trevisa's *Higden*, VIII. 37.

It happede in a tyme at Wynchestre in this kyng Henries chambre, that was dyversliche i-peynted, that one place was lefte unpaynted by the kynges heste[3], there the kyng heet[4] afterward peynte an egle with foure briddes[5]; the thre briddes cracched[6] and rent the fader with billes and with clawes, bote the fourthe bridde besied hym faste to cracche out his fader eyghen. Me[n] axede of the kyng what this wolde mene. "These foure bryddes," quoth the kyng, "beeth myn foure sones, that wil not cese to pursewe me anon to the deeth, and nameliche[7] this laste John, whom I loved now moost, schal most scharpliche awayte and caste for my deeth."

---

[1] mad.   [2] then.   [3] command.   [4] bade.   [5] birds.   [6] scratched.
[7] especially.

4 THE DAUGHTERS OF RICHARD I

Trevisa's *Higden*, VIII. 159.

That tyme oon Fulco, an holy preost in Gallia, cam to kyng Richard and seide, "Kyng, to the[1] I seie in the name of God Almyghti that thou marie sone[2] thy thre evel doughtres, leste som worse hap by the falle." "Thou lyest, ypocrite," quod the kyng, "for doughter have I none." "Yis," quoth he, "for thou hast pride, covetise, and leccherie." The kyng had [his] lordes to gidres[3], and seide, "I geve my pride to the Templeres and Hospitalers, my covetise to white monkes, and my leccherie to prelates of holy cherches."

5 JOHN'S DEATH

The Brut, E.E.T.S., 1906, p. 169. Several chroniclers tell this story. The most deadly poisons, according to medieval ideas, were those secreted by toads and spiders.

And in the same tyme the Pope sent into Englond a legate that me[n] callede Walo, and he was prest Cardinal of Rome, forto mayntene Kyng Johnes cause agheyngh the barons of Engeland; but the barons hade so huge partye and help through Lowys, the Kyngus sone of Fraunce, that Kyng John wist nought whider forto turne ne go. And so it bifel, that he wold have gon to [Lincoln]; and as he went thiderward, he come by the Abbay of Swyneshede, and there he abode ij dayes. And as he satte at the mete, he axede a monk of the hous, 'how miche a lofe was worth, that was sette bifore him oppon the table.' And the monk saide that 'the lof was worth but an halpeny.' "O," quod he, "tho[4] here is grete chepe of brede. Now," quod the Kyng, "and y may leve[5], soche a lof shal bene worth xx s., or halfe yere be gone." And when he hade saide this word, michel he thought, and ofte-tyme sichede[6], and toke and ete of the brede, and saide: "by God, the worde that y have saide, hit shal ben soth." The monk, that stode bifore the Kyng, for this word was ful sory in hert, and thought, rather he wolde him-self soffre pitouse deth, and thought to ordeyn therfor somme maner remedy. And anone the monk

---

[1] thee. [2] soon. [3] together. [4] then. [5] if I may live. [6] sighed.

went to his Abbot, and was shryven of him, and tolde the Abbot al that the Kyng saide, and praiede his Abbot forto assoile[1] him, for he wolde geve the Kyng soche a wassaile that al Engeland shall be therof glade and joyful. Tho[2] went the monk into a gardeyn, and founde a grete tode therin, and tok her up, and put here in a coppe, and prickede the tode through with a broche[3] meny tymes, til that the venyme come out on everyche side into the coppe. And tho tok he the coppe, and fellede hit with god ale, and brought hit bifore the Kyng, and knelyng saide: " Sir," quod he, " Wassaile! for never, dayes of your lyve, dranke ye of soche a coppe." " Bygynne, monk," quod the Kyng, and the monk dranke a grete draught, and toke the Kyng the coppe ; and the Kyng drank also a grete draughte, and sette doune the coppe. The monk anone right went into the fermory[4], and there deide anon, on whos soule God have mercy, Amen! and v monkes singeth for his soule, and shal whiles that Abbay stant. The Kyng aros up anone ful evel at ese, and commanded anon to remeve the table, and axede after the monk ; and men tolde him that he was dede, for his wombe[5] was broken in sondre. When the Kyng herde this tidynges, he comandede forto trusse[6] ; but al it was for nought, for his bely biganne to swelle, for the drynk that he drank, that he deide within ij daies, the morwe after Seynt Lukes day.

6   COURT AND CITY

The Brut, E.E.T.S., 1908, p. 345.

And yn the xvj yere of Kyng Richard his regne, John Hende beyng that tyme Maire of London, and John Walworth and Henry Vannere beyng scherreffes of London, that tyme a bakers man bare a basket of horsbred yn to Flet-strete, toward an ostrye hous[7] ; and there come a yemon of the Bischoppis of Salysbury, that was callyd Romayn, and he tok an horsloff out of the basket of the baker ; and he askyd hym 'whi he dede so.' And this Romayn turned ayen, and brak the bakers hedde ; and neybourez come out, and wolde have

---

[1] absolve.   [2] then.   [3] spit.   [4] infirmary.   [5] belly.

[6] pack up.   [7] hostelry.

restid this Romayne; and he brak from ham and fledde yn-to
the lordez place. And the counstablis wolde have hadde hym
out; but the Bischoppez men schitte the gatis fast, and kept
the place that no man myghte entre. And thanne moch more
pepil gadryd thedir[1], and saide that ' thai wolde have hym out,
or ellis thei wolde brenne up the place, and alle that were
with-ynne.' And thanne come the Maire and Schereffez, with
othir myche pepill, and cecid[2] the malice of the comynez, and
made every man go hom to his hous, and kepe the peez.
Thanne thez Romaynes lorde, the Bischop of Salusbery, Ser
John Waltam (that was that tyme treserer of Engelond) went
to Ser Thomas Arundel, Archebischop of York, and also
Chaunceler of Engelonde, and to hym made his complaynt
upon the peple of the cite of London. And thanne theze ij
Bischopez, of grete malice and vengeaunce, comyn unto the
King to Wyndesore, and made a grete complaynte upon the
Maire and the Schereffes; and anon aftirward alle the cite
was before the King and his consel....And anon sodenly the
King sent for the Maire of London and for the ij scherreffez;
and thai cam to hym to the Castell of Wyndesore. And the
King rebukyd the Maire and the scherreves fulle foule, for
the offens that thai hadde do ayens hym and his officers, yn
his chaumbir of London. Wherfore he deposid and put out
the Mayre of London and the ij Scherrevez; and this was
don xiiij dayez afore the Fest of saint John the Baptist. And
thanne the King callyd to hym a knight that me[n] called Ser
Edward [D]alyngrigge, and made hym warden and governoure
of the cite, and Chaumbyr of London, and ovyr alle his pepil
thereynne; and so he kept that office but iiij wokis, because
he was so tendir and gentill un-to the cetezens of London;
wherfore the King deposyd hym, and made Ser Bawdewyn
Radyngton, knyght, that was Countroller of the Kingis Housholde, wardeyne and governoure of his chaumbyr, and of his
peple therynne; and chese unto hym to worthi men of the
cite to be Schereviz with hym, for to governe and kepe the
kingez lawez yn the cite....And thanne the King and his
Counsel, for grete malice of the Cite of London, and despite,

---

[1] thither.   [2] stayed.

remevid alle his Courtez fro Westmynstre un-to the cete of
Yorke, that is to say, the Chauncerie, the Cheker, the Kingez
Bench, and also the Comyn Place, and there thay hilde alle
her Courtis of Law fro mydsomer un-to the fest of Cristismesse
next comyng.   And thanne the King and his counsel sawe it
not so profitable there, as it was at London ; thanne anon he
removid hit ayen to London, and so to Westmynstre, for gret
ese of his officers and avauntage of the King and of alle the
comyns of the Reme.

And whenne the peple of London sawe and knew that
these courtis were come ayen[1], and the King and his peple also,
thanne the Maire and the Aldermen, with the Cheff comyns,
let gadir a grete summe of goolde of alle the comyns of the
cite, and ordeyned and made grete rialte[2] ayens his comyng
to London, for to have his grace and gode lordeschip, and
also her[3] liberteis and Fraunchezes graunted unto ham ayen
as thai afore tyme hadde.   And thann, by grete instaunce and
praier of Quene Anne, and of other lordez and ladez, the King
graunted hem grace....And than the King with-ynne ij dayez
aftir, com to London ; and the Maire of London, scherevez, aldre-
men, and alle the worthi cite aftirward, redyn ayens the King
yn gode araye unto the heth[4] on this syde the maner of Schene,
submittyng humyly hem self, and mekely, with al maner of
obeysauncez un-to hym, as thay owed to do.   And thus thai
brought the King and the Quene to London.   And whanne
the King come to the gate of the Brygge of London, there
thay presentid hym with a mylke-white stede, sadelled and
brydilled, and trapped with white cloth of golde and red parted
togadir, and the Quene a palfraye alle white, trappid yn the
same aray with white and rede, and the conditez[5] of London
ronnen white wyne and rede, for al maner pepill to drynke
of.   And betuene Seint Poulez and the Cros yn Chepe, there
was made a stage, a ryalle, stondyng upon hygh ; and therynne
were mony angelis, with dyvers melodiez and songe ; and an
aungell come doun fro the stage on high, by a vice[6], and sette
a croune of golde and precious stonez and perlez apon the

---

[1] again.   [2] royalty.   [3] their.   [4] heath.
[5] conduits.   [6] winding stair.

Kingez hed, and another on the Quenez hed; and so the citezenys brought the King and the Quene unto Westmynstre, yn-to his palice at Westmynstre, and presentyd hym with ij basyns of sylver, and ovirgilte, fulle of coyned golde, the summa of xx m^s li, prayng hym, of his mercy and lordschip and specialle grace, that thay myght have his gode love, and liberteez and fraunchezes like as they hadde before tymez, and by his lettrez patentez confermed. And the Quene, and other worthi lordez and ladiez, ffillyn on hir kneys, and besought the King of grace to conferme this. Thanne the King toke up the Quene, and grauntyd hir alle hir askyng, and thanne thei thanked the King and the Quene and went home ayene.

7 KNIGHTLY IDEALS AND REALITIES

To understand both sides of knighthood we can find no better guide than Froissart, remembering always that the military and political power of this institution was already decaying in his time. Léon Gautier puts its zenith at the end of the twelfth century; and from this period we have two different lines of evidence in the writings of John of Salisbury and Peter of Blois, archdeacon of Bath. The former, while defining the ideal admirably in his *Policraticus* (lib. VI. c. 8), more than hints that exceptions were common in practice (*ib.* c. 3, 13). The latter, it will be seen, writing as a satirist, emphasizes the darker side; but his sneer as to the bloodless character of many battles is borne out by statistics; see p. 199 of my *Chaucer and his England*.

(*a*) *Policraticus* (Migne, *P. L.*, vol. 199, col. 600; cf. *Piers Plowman* B, *prol.* 112 ff. and VI. 25 ff.).

But what is the function of orderly knighthood? To protect the church, to fight against treachery, to reverence the priesthood, to fend off injustice from the poor, to make peace in your own province, to shed your blood for your brethren, and, if needs must, to lay down your life.

(*b*) Petrus Blesensis, *Epistolae*, No. XCIV. To John the Archdeacon.

I cannot bear the vaunting and vainglory of the knights your nephews....The Order of Knighthood, in these days of ours, is mere disorder. For he whose mouth is defiled with the foulest words, whose oaths are most detestable, who least fears God, who vilifies God's ministers, who feareth not the church—that man nowadays is reputed bravest and most renowned of the knightly band....The knights of old were wont to bind themselves by an oath to maintain the state, never to flee in battle, and to set the common weal before their own life. Nay, even nowadays aspirants receive their swords from the altar in order that they may profess themselves sons of the church, acknowledging themselves to have received their weapons for the honour of the priesthood, the defence of the poor, the avenging of wrongs and the freedom of their country. Yet in practice they do the contrary.... These men, who should have used their strength against the enemies of the cross of Christ, contend in wassail and drunkenness; they stagnate in sluggardy and rot in riotous living; dragging through their degenerate lives in uncleanness, they dishonour the name and order of knighthood.... If these knights of ours are sometimes constrained to take the field, then their sumpter-beasts are laden not with steel but with wine, not with spears but with cheeses, not with swords but with wine-skins, not with javelins but with spits. You would think they were on their way to feast, and not to fight. They bear shields bright with beaten gold, as who should hope rather for prey than for hard fighting; and in truth these same shields (if I may so say) come back intact in their virginity. Nevertheless they embroider their saddles and blazon their shields with scenes of battle and tourney, delighting in a certain imagination of those wars which, in very deed, they dare not mingle in or behold.

8   THE MAKING OF A LORD

John Hardyng was born in 1378, was admitted at the age of 12 to the family of Sir Henry Percy (Hotspur) and fought at Homildon Hill and Shrewsbury. In 1403 he received the royal pardon and enlisted under Sir Robert Umfraville, Warden of the Northern Marches, who in 1405 made Hardyng warden of his castle of Warkworth. His rhymed *Chronicle* is poor poetry, but sometimes gives us original matter of real value. He brought it down to 1464, and must, therefore, have lived at least to 86. But he had finished an earlier version in 1457 for Henry VI.; and it is from this unprinted version that Ellis published the following three stanzas in his edition of the *Chronicle* (1812, introd. p. i).

And as lordes sonnes bene sette, at foure yere age,
To scole [to] lerne the doctryne of lettrure,
And after at sex to have thaym in language,
And sette[1] at mete semely in alle nurture;
At ten and twelve to revelle is thair cure,
To daunse and synge, and speke of gentelnesse;
At fourtene yere they shalle to felde I sure[2],
[To] hunte the dere, and catch an hardynesse.

For dere to hunte and slea, and se them blede,
Ane hardyment gyffith to his corage,
And also in his wytte he takyth hede
Ymagynynge to take thaym at avauntage.
A[t] sextene yere, to werray[3] and to wage,
To juste[4] and ryde, and castels to assayle,
To scarmyse[5] als, and make sykyr[6] scurage[7],
And sette his wache for perile nocturnayle;

And every day his armure to assay
In fete of armes with some of his meyne[8],
His might to preve[9], and what that he do may
Iff that he were in suche a juperte[10]
Of werre[11], by falle, that by necessite
He might algates[12] with wapyns[13] hym defende:
Thus shuld he lerne in his priorite[14]
His wapyns alle in an armes[15] to dispende[16].

9   A VERRAY PARFIT GENTIL KNYGHT

From the chronicler Hardyng's first description of his master Sir
Robert Umfraville, Warden of the Northern Marches, printed from the
MS. by Mr C. L. Kingsford in *The English Historical Review* for Oct.
1912, pp. 746 ff.

Thof[17] my body here be a symple wyght
Abydynge at the wyll omnipotent,
My herte with hym shalbe bothe day and nyght
To pray for hym with all my hole intent.

---

[1] sit.   [2] assure.   [3] make war.   [4] joust.   [5] skirmish.
[6] sure.   [7] scouting.   [8] meinie.   [9] prove.   [10] jeopardy.
[11] war.   [12] altogether.   [13] weapons.   [14] early days.
[15] in full armour.   [16] employ.   [17] though.

A beter lorde I trow God never yit sent
Into the north, of all gode sapience,
Ne so helply with knyghtly diligence.

Ne contekour[1] he was in his Cuntre,
Nor never drewe swerde ne knyfe to Englyshman,
Ne Riotour, ner never made assemble
Agayn neyghbour that any man tell kan.
The Comonté[2] he halpe and never over ran;
A trew Justyse of pese in his Cuntré
He was alway withouten partyalté.

A beter knyght was never in that Cuntré
To kepe the trewes[3] whils that it dyd endure;
With costage[4] grete eche wouke[5] in sertaynté
Days of redresse to every creature,
To Scottes he helde, and Englyssh also full sure;
Who so complaynde of ought it was refourmed,
So godelyly to pese[6] he hym conformed.

In so ferr forth[7] his Jugementes wer approved
That Scottes feel[8] byyonde the Scottysshe see
Thar own Jugges forsoke as hole[9] reproved,
And by assent to Berwyke came, I se;
And bonde thaym[10] thar to stonde to his decre,
And plesed were with all his jugymentes,
So rightwyse was his reule and Regymentes.

Bot noght-forthy[11] whan enmyse gafe up pese,
And it away with werre[12] had hole exilde[13],
As lyon fell he putte hym forth in prese[14],
The werre maynteynde, and kepte hym unrevylde.
What so men gat, covetyse noght hym fylde[15],
The wynners had it all withoute surpryse;
For whiche the folke wer glad to his servyse.

---

[1] quarreler.   [2] common people.   [3] truce.   [4] cost.   [5] week.
[6] peace.   [7] to such an extent.   [8] many.   [9] wholly.
[10] bound themselves.   [11] nevertheless.   [12] war.   [13] driven.
[14] into the press.   [15] filled.

Of the Garter full eght and thretty yere
He was a knyght electe for worthihode,
Whan his lyfelode[1] exceded noght, all clere,
An hundreth marke to leve[2] upon in dede,
Bot oonly of the werres[3] thurgh his manhede;
Yit helde he than a countenaunce[4] and estate
With hym that was a baron nomynate.

His servantes wolde he noght rebuke ne chide,
Bot softely say to hym in pryvyte
All his defaute, and as his preest it hide;
And whan they stale[5] his gode that he dyd se,
He wolde it layne[6] fro his other maynee,
And noght repreve hym more in any wyse,
So was he kynde withouten covetyse.

A clenner knyght of his levynge was none
In all degre withouten vice detecte,
And as of treuth he myght be sette allone;
His worde so sadde[7] was wele and ever protecte,
With variance yit that it was never infecte;
In so ferre forthe his fose had delectacion
Mor in his worde than neyghbours obligacion.

Of sapyence and verry gentylnesse,
Of lyberall herte and knyghtly governaunce,
Of hardyment, of treuth and grete gladnesse,
Of honest myrth withoute any grevaunce,
Of gentyll bourdes[8] and knyghtly daliaunce
He hath no make[9]: I darr right wele avowe;
Now is he gone, I may not glose[10] hym nowe.

---

[1] income. [2] live. [3] except what he got from the wars.
[4] appearance. [5] stole. [6] conceal. [7] steadfast.
[8] jests. [9] peer. [10] flatter.

10   THE SQUIRE IN HALL AND BOWER

"Curteis he was, lowely and servysable
And carf biforn his fader at the table."

Perhaps, the best commentary on this Chaucerian description of a squire's social duties is the following, from the thirteenth century romance, *Blonde of Oxford* (Camden Soc. 1858). The hero, Jehan de Dammartin, is squire to the Earl of Oxford. (p. 14, l. 371.)

Fair, and fairer still than I can say, was Blonde the Earl's daughter. She sat at dinner, and was served by Jehan, fair and free of body, who pained himself much to earn all men's grace by his courteous service. He waited not on his lady alone, but up and down throughout the hall; knight and lady, squire and page, groom and messenger, all he served according to their desire, and thus from all he earned good-will He knew well to seize the moment for serving and honouring each guest, so that Blonde, the fair and shapely, found her needs none the worse supplied.

After the dinner they washed their hands, and went to play, each as he would, up in the forest or down by the river or in some other sort of pastime. Jehan went with whom he would; and, on his return, oftentimes would he go to play in the countess's bower, wherein the ladies, as it were by main force[1], kept him to teach them French. He, as a courteous youth, did and said ever according to their prayer, as one who well knew how to comport himself. Well he knew all chamber-games— chess and tables[2] and dice, wherewith he diverted the lady Blonde; often said he *check* and *mate* to her. Many other games he taught her; and taught her a better French than she had known before his coming; wherefore she held him full dear....

One day, as Blonde sat at table, it was for Jehan to carve before her....By chance he cast his eyes on her; yet he had seen her daily these eighteen weeks past....From this look such thoughts came into his head, that on his carving he thought no more. Blonde, who marked his thoughts astray,

---

[1] This seems the meaning of the phrase *qui en destrèce.*

[2] A sort of backgammon, which, like chess, led to much gambling in the Middle Ages and therefore was forbidden to clerics and university students.

THE SQUIRE AT TABLE

A Medieval Shop

took upon her to rebuke him therefore, and bade him think on his carving without delay. Seeing then that Jehan heard her not for the moment, then spake she again, " Carve, Jehan ! are you sleeping or dreaming here ? I pray you, give me now to eat; of your courtesy, dream now no more." At this word Jehan heard her voice; therewith he started as one who is shaken suddenly from his sleep. He marvelled at this adventure; he seized the knife as a man in a dream, and thought to carve well and fair, but so distraught was he that he cut deep into two fingers : forth sprang the blood as he rose from table, and sad was Blonde at that sight. Jehan prayed another squire to carve before his lady, and went forthwith to his own chamber.

11   CRUSADERS' REDEMPTIONS

The Crusades, like many other ideal movements, drifted into the hands of practical politicians. Just as money payments gradually took the place, to a great extent, of the older ecclesiastical penances, so the Crusader's vow was often redeemed for a fine, especially after it became common for confessors to enjoin the vow upon their penitents. Archbishop Giffard of York enregistered a number of these commutations between the years 1267 and 1276 : the first is here translated in full. (Giffard's *Register*, Surtees Soc., 1904, pp. 277 ff.)

[Archbishop Giffard to the official of the Archdeacon
of Cleveland.]

John de Ellerby, the bearer of these present letters, appeared before us and related how, having set aside the fear of God and laid rash and violent hands upon Roger de Newton, Priest, he had afterwards competently satisfied the aforesaid priest for that injury; in proof of which satisfaction he exhibited letters patent from the said priest[1]. And seeing that the said John hath thus earned the penalty of being signed with the cross by us, and that the assault was slight and small, by the Apostolic authority granted to us in this matter of the Crusade we have thought fit to absolve him in due form of law, sending him to you as thus absolved; and the said John must spend of his own goods in succour of the Holy Land, to wit, the sum of five shillings sterling, whensoever this be demanded of him

[1] See above, Section II no. 19.

on the part of the Pope. Wherefore we command you to permit no man to molest or trouble him further in this matter.

The list proceeds as follows :

(2) For assaulting a priest; Culprit to go on the crusade or make fine by payment of one-third of his property. (3) Assault on priest, 2s. (4 to 16) Clergy who had got ordained by other bishops without licence from their own diocesan, redemptions varying from 3s. 4d. to £1. (17) A knight, for assault on priest, £6. 13s. 4d. (18 to 56) Thirty-eight clerics irregularly ordained as above, fines from 3s. to 11s. 4d.

Out of the 300 redemptions recorded in the register, the enormous majority are thus levied from irregularly-ordained clerics. In eleven cases, however, the victims are recorded to have taken the cross *ex devotione*, i.e. of their own accord, and not as penance for any particular transgression ; these redemptions range from 2s. to £2. 10s. (£5 for a knight and his wife). One of these is interesting : "to our beloved daughters in God, Helewysa Palma and Isabella her daughter, greeting etc. As we hear from your own confession, ye have made a vow some time since to go on a pilgrimage to St James of Compostella, but because ye cannot fulfil the said vow on the plea of poverty [*pretextu paupertatis*], at your own urgent request we, by our Apostolic authority, have thought fit to convert your vow into a subsidy for the Holy Land, granting you the cross and enjoining that ye pay two shillings sterling in succour of the Land aforesaid, whensoever the collectors specially deputed for this work shall demand it of you." Two penitents, again, had "unjustly imprisoned clerks" ; several more had assaulted clerks ; in one case a priest had committed an assault, presumably upon a fellow-cleric. One knight, for adultery with the wife of another knight, bound himself to pay £100 in case of relapse ; "and we, pondering in our heart his contrition and mitigating the rigour of the penalty as best we may, have here given him the cross, that he may go to the Holy Land in his own person, or send a fit man of war at his own expense in atonement for this crime." The expedition for which these sums were collected was, in fact, never carried into effect ; our own Edward I was "the last Crusader of the last Crusade" in 1270.

12   CRUSADE VOWS BROKEN

From the so-called *Revelation to the Monk of Evesham* (see Section IV., no. 18), in Arber's *English Reprints*, p. 74.

Amonge hem[1] that brake her vowys y sawe a yong knyght brennyng in the myddys of fyre whome y knewe sumtyme ful wele. And as y enquyred of him why he was putte in so grete peynes, thys he tolde me. My lyfe (he seyde) that y levyd was

---

[1] them.

but baren and vayne and also vycyous. For y was insolent and nyse[1] in pryde and elacyon, and foule and unclene by the vyce of lecherye. Not withstonding for thys y am nowe specyally ponysht, by cause y caste aweye fro me the sygne of the holy crosse the whyche y hadde takyn apone me in a vowe that y made to goo to the holy lond, howe be yt that y toke the crosse not for devocyon but for vayne glorye, the whiche y loved to have hadde of the lorde yat y servyd. Trewely every nyght y labur in going, as mekyl as y maye, to make an ende of that pilgremage. But, what for febulnes of strenthe and contraryusnes of the wedyr and also scharpnes of the waye, y am lettyd gretly, that onethe[2] y may goo at on tyme a full lytyl dayes journey. Sothely, whenne the mornyng begynneth, fleyn to me wykyd spirytys, beyng wodde[3] yn al cruelnes, and drawyn me ageyne to the place of my peynys, where ever more al the days tyme y am gretly peynde yn fyre. Nevertheles wyth a certen amendement of lessur dyssese[4], thawght[5] hyt be lytyl. And ageyne when nyghte comythe y am restoryd to the place where y lefte laste my journey; and so y go forthe on my pylgrimage, and when the mornyng ys cumme y am drawyn ageyne and caste to peynys. And al that have vowyd to go to the holy londe, and aftyr dyd caste fro hem her crosse, and whent not dedyr[6], yn lyke wyse as y go they be compellyd to do her pylgrymage, so yf they may have the grace of god yn her laste ende to repente hem, as y had to repente me for brekyng of my vowe; and than by the holsum remedy of confession thys synne that was dedly synne may be changed to a venyal synne. Othyr wyse al that breke that same vowe be put to eternalle dampnacion.

13 CRUSADER AND WIFE

An Alphabet of Tales, E.E.T.S., 1904, p. 159 (Tale CCXXIX.).

Jacobus de Vetriaco tellis of hym selfe and says; "On a tyme as I was in a town prechand, ther was a man that durste not com unto the sermon for his wyfe, not in-to the kurk. And he come to a wyndow and harde the sermon; and when

---

[1] foolish. [2] scarcely. [3] furious. [4] discomfort. [5] though. [6] thither.

he had hard of the indulgence [th]at longis unto thaim [th]at
er merkid[1] with the cros, for als mekull[2] as he durste not com
in att the dure for his wyfe, he crope in att the wyndow in
myddeste the peple, and tuke the cros as thai did."

14   A CRUSADER'S FALSEHOOD

Ibid. p. 160 (Tale ccxxxi.).

Cesarius tellis how that in the bisshoppryk of [Utrecht],
ane userer tuke the cros and lete as he wald go unto the Holie
Land. And when he sulde go furth, he fenyd hym selfe seke
and wayke[3], and sayd he myght not go, and hyrid anoder to
go for hym, and gaff hym bod[4] v marcis[5], thuf-all[6] he myght
have giffen hym xl[ti] marcis. So afterward when thai [th]at wer
burnyd[7] wer bown[8] furth, he satt with thaim in the tavern and
sayde unto thaim ; "ye wrichis, now ye forsake your wyvis
and your childer, and your frendis, and all your other gudis,
and puttis your bodis in perels be-yond the see ; and I sitt
att home with my wyfe and my childer, and with all my gudis,
and for v marke have als mekull[9] perdon as ye hafe." Bod[10]
almyghti God, [th]att is rightwus, shewyng how mekull the
labur and expensis of pylgramys plesis hym, and how mekull
desayte[11] and blasfeme of bakbyters displesis hym, sufferd thatt,
on the night after, the devull come unto hym in liknes of a
servand of his awn, and broght with hym ij grete blak hors[es],
and bad hym faste caste of[f] his uppermest clothe, and go with
hym and lope[12] on one of thies hors. And the cross [th]at he
had takyn was sewid opon his overmeste clothe, and so he umthoght hym that he mott[13] not esskape, and keste[14] away his
overmeste clothe and onone[15] lepid on the to hors, and the
devull lepid on the tother ; and with-in a while thai war led
ther[16] dyvers paynys wer. And the devull shewid hym the
seatt ther he sulde sytt in paynys, and the devull sayd unto
hym ; "Now thou sall turn agayn into thy howse, bod with-in
iij days thou sall dy, and turn agayn." And than he was
broght agayn, and men askid hym whar he had bene ; and

---

[1] marked.   [2] forasmuch.   [3] weak.   [4] but.   [5] marks.   [6] although.
[7] armed.   [8] bound.   [9] mickle.   [10] but.   [11] deceit.   [12] leap.
[13] could.   [14] cast.   [15] anon.   [16] where.

he tolde thaim all as is afor sayd. And than a preste was broght unto hym, that counceld hym to shryfe hym and do penance for his syn. And he wold nott, bod fell in despar and dyed withouten owder[1] shrift or howsill[2] or contricion, and was berid in hell.

15   SPECULATION IN RANSOMS

H. T. Riley, *Memorials of London*, 1868, p. 392.

A.D. 1376. To all persons who these letters shall see or hear, William de Beauchaumpe, greeting. Whereas Messire Thomas de Feltone is bound unto me, and obligated, in 4000 silver marks, by reason of the purchase of Messire Berard de la Bret, my prisoner, I do will and grant that the said Messire Thomas, his heirs, and his executors, shall be acquitted and discharged by these present letters; and that I myself, my heirs, and my executors, be ousted for ever hereby from all manner of action by reason of the said Statute, or by reason of the purchase of the said Messire Berard, my prisoner.

16   "THEY BLUSTREDEN FORTH AS BESTËS, OVER BANKES AND HILLES"

Edward III.'s first campaign against the Scots, in 1327, was, perhaps, the last English campaign conducted mainly on the traditional feudal lines. After great sufferings, Edward's army never even came to battle with the Scots, who had ravaged Durham and retired unscathed. In later campaigns, such as those of Crécy and Poitiers, Edward's army resembled far more nearly a modern conscript army, drawn from all classes of the country and stiffened by a nucleus of professional soldiers; see the present compiler's *Chaucer and his England*, chap. XVIII. The following is from Berners's *Froissart* (ed. Ellis, 1812), chap. XVII. pp. 18 ff.

These Scottysshe men are right hardy, and sore travelyng in harneys and in warres; for whan they wyll entre into Ingland, within a daye and a nyght, they wyll dryve theyr hole host xxiiii. myle, for they are all a horsbacke, without it be the traundals[3] and laggers of the [h]ost, who folow after, a foote. The knyghtis and squiers are well horsed, and the comon people and other, on litell hakeneys and geldyngis; and they carey with them no cartis, nor chariettis, for the diversities of

---

[1] either.   [2] communion.   [3] camp-followers.

the mountaignes that they must passe through, in the countrey
of Northumbrelande.   They take with them noo purveyaunce
of brede nor wyne, for their usage and sobrenes is suche in
tyme of warre, that they wyll passe in the journey a great
long tyme, with flesshe halfe soden, without brede, and drynke
of the ryver water without wyne : and they nother[1] care for
pottis, nor pannis, for they seeth[e] beastis in their owne
skynnes.   They are ever sure to fynde plenty of beastis in the
countrey that they wyll passe throughe.   Therfore they cary
with them none other purveyaunce, but on their horse, bitwene
the saddyll and the pannell[2], they trusse a brode plate of metall,
and behynde the saddyl, they wyll have a lytle sacke full of
ootemele, to the entent that whan they have eaten of the
sodden flesshe, than they ley this plate on the fyre, and tempre
a lytle of the ootemele : and whan the plate is hote, they cast
of the thyn paste theron, and so make a lytle cake in maner
of a crakenell, or bysket, and that they eate to comfort with
all theyr stomakis.   Wherfore it is no great merveile, though
they make greatter journeys than other pepple do.   And in
this maner were the Scottis entred into the sayd countrey,
and wasted and brent all about as they went, and toke great
nombre of bestis.   They were to the nombre of iiii. M. men
of armes, knightis and squiers, mounted on good horses, and
other x. M. men of warre were armed after their gyse, right
hardy and firse[3], mounted on lytle hakeneys, the whiche were
never tyed nor kept at hard meate, but lette go to pasture in
the feldis and busshes....

Whan the kyng of Ingland and his oste had sene and h[e]ard
of the fyers that the Scottis had made in Inglande, incontynent
was cryed alarme, and every man commaunded to dislodge,
and folowe after the marshals baners....   And whan they were
over [the Tyne], they lodged theym that nyght by the ryver
syde ; and by that tyme the son was goon to reste, and there
was but fewe among them that had other[4] axe or hoke[5], or any
instrument to cutte downe any woodde to make their lodgyngis
withal ; and there were many that had loste there owne company, and wist nat where they were.   Some of the footemen

---

[1] neither.   [2] saddle-cloth.   [3] fierce.   [4] either.   [5] bill-hook.

were farre behynde, and wyst nat well what way to take : but suche as knewe beste the country, sayd playnly, they hadde rydden the same daye xxiiii. englysshe myles : for they roode as faste as they might without any rest, but at suche passages as they coulde nat chese[1].... Thus theyr horses dyd eate no meate of all that nyght nor day before ; they had nother ootes for forage for them : nor the people of the oste had no sustenaunce of all that day nor nyght, but every man his loffe[2] that he hadde caryed behynde hym, the whiche was sore wette with the swette of the horses. Nor they dranke none other drynke but the water of the ryver, withowte it were some of the lordis that had caryed botels with them : nor they had no fyer nor lyght, for they had nothyng to make lyght withall, without it were some of the lordes that had torches brought with them.... And about noone some poore folkis of the countrey were founde, and they said howe they were as than xiiii. myle from Newcastell upon Tyne, and xi. myle from Carlyle, and that there was no towne nerer to them, wherein they might fynde any thyng to do theym ease withall. And whan this was shewed to the kyng, and to the lordes of his counsell, incontinent were sent thither horses and sompters, to fetche thens some purveyance ; and there was a crye in the kyngis name made in the towne of Newcastell, that who so ever wolde bryng brede, or wyne, or any other vitaile, shulde be payd therfor incontinent at a good price.... Thus iii. dayes and iii. nyghtis, they were in maner withowte brede, wyne, candel, or lyght, foder, or forage, or any maner of purveyaunce, other for horse or man : and after the space of iiii. dayes, a loffe of brede was solde for vi. d. the whiche was worthe but i. d. And a gallon of wyne for vi. grootis, that was worth but vi. d. And yet for all that, there was suche rage of famin, that eche toke vitailes out of others handis, wherby there rose divers batels and stryffes bitwene sondry companyons....

---

[1] choose.   [2] loaf.

17　THE FIGHT OF THE THIRTY

Unfortunately this most picturesque episode was lacking in the MS. of Froissart used by Lord Berners ; so that it does not appear in the Globe edition. In Buchon's edition it forms the 7th chapter of Bk I. pt ii. (2nd edn, vol. I., p. 293). A fuller and even more picturesque account of the fight may be found in the contemporary poem published by Buchon with the first edition of his Froissart (1826 : *Collection de Chroniques* etc. tom. XIV. p. 301). Froissart substantiates all essential details of the poem, and adds "their captors put them most courteously to ransom afterwards, when they were healed of their wounds, for there was none who was not sore hurt, whether of the French or of the English. And in later days I saw at the table of King Charles of France a Breton knight who had been in that battle, Sir Yvain Charruel ; but his face was so sore cut and scarred that it showed plainly how rough the fight had been." The poem runs to 6000 lines, full of epic repetitions ; I have therefore been compelled to abbreviate severely in this translation. The fight here commemorated was one of the last flickers of the old lamp of feudal chivalry : most of the Hundred Years' War was fought, by the English at least, on predominantly business lines.

Lordings, give ear ; true is my story and noble my matter ; for I tell how thirty English, brave as lions, fought one day with thirty Bretons ; nobles and clerks will rehearse the tale in hall and bower for a hundred years to come.

When Dagworth died—he fell before the stronghold of Auray ; God of His holy pity have mercy upon the Breton lords who fell on that day ! in his lifetime he had ordained that the small folk of the township who till the corn should no more be warred upon nor taken by the English—when that lord, I say, was dead, his ordinance was forthwith forgotten. For after him came Brambro, who swore by St Thomas that he would be well avenged ; then he overran the country and wasted the land and took Ploërmel by vile craft. Then wrought he all his will in Brittany, until that day when, as God would have it, the good Beaumanoir [Captain of Château-Josselin] whom men praised so high, and my lord John, the wise and brave and prudent, went to the English to speak with them under safe-conduct. There they saw poor folk in torments, that it was great pity ; some in the stocks and others in irons ; some gyved and others in secret dungeons, all bound by twos and threes like kine or oxen that men take to market. When

Beaumanoir saw this, deep from his heart he sighed; then said he to Brambro in great and haughty words, "O knight of England, you sin grievously in that you pain these poor folk who sow the corn, and from whose tillage we have flesh and wine. If there were no labourers in the land (I tell you the thought of my heart) then must we nobles labour in the fields with flail and hoe, and suffer poverty, which is great pain to such as are not to the manner born. Let such have peace henceforward, for sore have they suffered; Dagworth's testament is soon forgotten." Then answered Brambro in great and proud words, "Beaumanoir, hold your peace! let us hear no more of this! Edward shall be crowned king of France, and the English shall have power and mastery on every side, in spite of all Frenchmen and all that fight on their behalf." Then answered Beaumanoir with great humility, "Dream another dream, for this is ill-dreamt; all your boasting is of no avail. Now, Brambro" (said he), "let it please you to order this matter wisely; let us fight together on a chosen day with sixty companions, or fourscore or a hundred; then shall we be assured, without further parley, which of us hath the right or the wrong." Thus was the battle sworn; that each should bring thirty fellows in his train.

Brambro, however, was not able to raise more than 20 English and made up the number with 6 Germans and 4 Brabançons (or, according to another account, 6 Flemings and 4 Bretons of the English faction). The Bretons heard mass and confessed themselves; Brambro encouraged his party by quoting the prophecies of Merlin.

Then the sixty fell upon each other with one accord; at the first shock great was our discomfiture; Charruel was taken, Mellont was slain, and the valiant Tristan, so great and strong, was sore stricken with a mace; Sir Jehan Rousselot was wounded almost to death. If Jesus Christ, Who guideth all things well, think not upon us now, the Bretons will surely have the under hand.

Sore was the battle on that grassy field; Caron de Bosc de Gas was smitten with a mace, Mellont and Tristan were wounded to death; then he [*sic*] cried aloud "Beaumanoir, where art thou? The English bear me off wounded and

broken; I had no fear that day that I saw thee; yet, if the
true God think not on me now in His holy strength, these
English will bear me off and thou wilt have lost me." Then
sware Beaumanoir, by God who hung on the cross, that many
a sore stroke should first be stricken, and many a lance broken,
and many a shield pierced. With these words he grasped his
fair keen spear; all whom he smote were slain or stricken
down; yet stoutly did the English defend their own part; for
all his power they cared not a straw.

Sore was the fight, and fierce the affray; men fought on
either side like lions; and all, with one consent, besought a
truce to go drink without hindrance, each from his own bottle;
good was that wine of Anjou, I trow! When all had thus
drunken with one accord, then they returned without further
tarrying to the fight.

Sore was that battle in the midst of the mead, and horrible
the affray and wild the storm on either hand! The Bretons
had the worst, I will not lie, for two are slain and three are
prisoners, God stand their help! Now they are but five and
twenty in battle-array. But Geoffroy de la Roche demanded
his knighthood; a right noble squire of great ancestry. Then
Beaumanoir dubbed him in Saint Mary's name, saying "Fair
sweet son, now spare not thine own body; bethink thee of
him who, for honour of knighthood, fought alone and unaided
at Constantinople; and I swear by God who ruleth all that
the English shall find thy worth ere the bell ring for even-
song!"

Brambro heard that word; he prized all their puissance
and lordship at one clove of garlic. Then cried he to Beaumanoir, "Slay thee I will not, but I will give thee for a gift
to my leman; for I have promised her (I lie not) that to-day
I would bring thee to her fair bower." Then answered Beaumanoir, "I defy thee, so please it God and Saint Mary and the
good Saint Yves in whom I trust so well; cast now the die
without blenching; on thee shall be the hazard, short shall be
thy life." Alain de Carroumois lost no word of this; "False
faitour," cried he to Brambro, "what dreamest thou there?
thinkest thou to take a man of such valour? With my body

I defy thee as from him; with my keen spear will I smite thee now." So spake Alain, and smote him fair and full with the sharp steel of his lance; full and fair in the face, in all men's sight, so that the iron clave even unto his brain; with that lance-thrust Brambro fell to earth. Yet he rose to his feet and thought to grapple with his foe; but Sir Geoffroy de Boves marked that well, and struck him down again with his lance, so that Brambro fell dead to earth. Then cried Boves, "Beaumanoir, where art thou? dost hold thyself well avenged? here lies he dead!" Beaumanoir heard that well, and made answer, "Lords, quit you like men, for our time is come; let him lie there, for God's sake, and fall upon the rest!"

Now saw the English that Brambro was gone, and all his pride and boasting with him. Then cried Croquart, a felon German, "Lords, know for truth that Brambro hath brought us hither and failed us in our need; all his books of Merlin whereby he set so great store have not been worth two pence! there lies he dead, gaping open-mouthed at the sky. Wherefore I pray you, fair lords, do as men of sense; keep ye serried close side by side, that he who falleth upon us may be smitten or slain."

At these words Charruel arose, and the valiant Tristan, sore wounded as he was, and Caron de Bosc de Gas, the valiant and renowned; all three were prisoners to the felon Brambro, but his death hath acquitted all. Each seizes in his fist the good sharp spear, and foins with right good-will upon the Englishmen.

After the death of the bold Brambro, great was the battle and grievous the stowre; horrible and marvellous and sore was the affray. For there still stood Sir Croquart the German; and Thomas Beaufort who fought like a giant, smiting with a grievous mace of steel; and Hugh de Calverley as terrible as he; and Sir Robert Knolles full of all craft of war, and all their companions, each in his degree. Then English and Germans spake words of cheer one to another, saying, "Let us avenge Brambro our loyal friend; let us slay all and spare none, for the battle shall be ours ere sundown!" But noble Beaumanoir faced them stoutly, he and his beloved companions; then began a sore and sad affray, that the strokes might be heard for a quarter of a league around, the sore strokes that were dealt upon the headpieces on either side. There died two Englishmen and one stout German; there too Dardaine of Rennes was slain, and Geoffroy Poulart slept his last sleep, and the bold Beaumanoir was wounded. If Jesus Christ, the almighty Father, bring not some remedy, no living soul will be left on either side!

Sore was the fight, and long it endured; sore was the heat, that the earth ran with sweat and blood. That holy Saturday Beaumanoir had fasted; sore he thirsted now, that good lord, and yearned for drink. But Geoffroy de Boves made answer, " Drink thine own blood, Beaumanoir, and thy thirst will pass : this day we shall all gain such honour that our valiant renown shall never die ! " Then the brave Beaumanoir took heart again ; such was his wrath and grief that his thirst was gone ; then again began the fray on either side ; men fell dead or sore hurt; scarce one will be left alive. Sore was that battle and mortal that affray, halfway between Josselin and the castle of Ploërmel, in a fair meadow on a sloping ground ; *the Half-way Oak*, men call it, alongside a thicket of broom that groweth green and fair. There were the English in a serried ring, the valiant Calverley, that hardy warrior, and Thomas Beaufort with his mace; he who feeleth that mace upon his chine will never eat of loaf or cake again....

Sore was the fight; never will ye hear of such another. Stout and close the English stand, no man can press among them but he is forthwith hurt or slain, all stand in one throng as though they were bound man to man. Then Guillaume de Montauban, the valiant and renowned, stood forth from the stowre and looked upon the foe. High swelled his heart ; and he prayed to Jesus Christ, who was pained upon the cross, that, if he might mount a horse that would do his will, he would break up that band, to its shame and dishonour[1].

[1] Froissart writes that all had dismounted for the fight, except that "some relate how five of the Bretons remained on horseback at the edge of the field, and the rest dismounted as the English had done.... Finally the English were worsted ; for, as I have heard tell, one of the Frenchmen who had remained on horseback broke their ranks and trod them miserably underfoot."

Then bound he good sharp spurs to his feet and mounted a proud charger, and took a lance with right square steel ; then he feigned himself, the crafty squire, as though he would have fled. Beaumanoir saw this and rebuked him, saying, " Friend William, what thinkest thou, how dost thou flee like a false recreant ? thou and thine heirs shall ever bear this shame." Then laughed Guillaume a loud laugh, and cried aloud, that his voice was well heard, " Do thine own work, Beaumanoir the frank and prudent knight ; for I will do well mine ; I have mine own thoughts."

Then set he spurs to his horse, pricking on flank and on rib, that the crimson blood ran down upon the mead. Right on the English he fell, seven hath he overthrown, all have lost heart, I lie not ; whoso would, might then take them and receive their oath of captivity. Loud spake Montauban when he saw this ; "*Montjoie!* he cried, now smite in, my lords ! All you my comrades, God so prosper you as ye avenge you now of these English whom ye have at your will ! "

Sore was the battle, and wondrous the affray ; the good Tintiniac was first, and with him the far-famed Beaumanoir, for this feat shall men ever praise his name. Then had the Bretons their force and will of the Englishmen ; some cried mercy and the rest were taken. Knolles and Calverley are in great danger, and Thomas Beaufort had nought but his own wrath—he and all his companions who came so blithely to this field—for that emprise of Brambro the hardy and the proud ! Sir John Plessington, the warlike Ridele, Helcoy and his brother, Ripefort the valiant and the proud Richard of Ireland, are led forthwith to Château-Josselin.

Oftentimes will ye hear tell of this great battle ; for men know it well, and it is noised abroad in song and written and painted in tapestry through all the realms on this side the Great Sea ; three hundred years hence, men will still sing of this Fight of the Thirty that had no peer. Sore was the fight, know ye that for sure ; discomfited were the English who strove to have dominion and lordship over the Bretons ; but all their pride was turned to folly. Pray ye therefore to God the Son of Mary for all those who were in that company; be they Bretons or English, beseech God in every place that they be not damned at the Day of Doom. May Saints Michael and Gabriel stand by them on that day : say ye all *Amen*, that God may grant thee grace !

Here endeth the Battle of Thirty English and Thirty Bretons, which was fought in Brittany in the year of grace 1350 *and the Saturday before Laetare Jerusalem.* [*4th Sunday in Lent.*]

SECTION VI

MANOR AND COTTAGE

This subject is so vast that we must restrict ourselves to a few documents which may supply some real historical background for Chaucer's *Nun's Priest's Tale* and for *Piers Plowman*.

1   A MODEL MANOR

Léopold Delisle, in his exhaustive *Condition de la Classe Agricole en Normandie au Moyen-Age*, laments that France possesses no such medieval treatises on rural economy as we possessed already in the 13th century. Perhaps the best of these is *Fleta*, edited by John Selden in 1647, from which the following extracts are translated: similar matter may be found in Walter of Henley (ed. Lamond and Cunningham, 1890) and in the *Bibliothèque de l'École des Chartes*, 1856, pp. 123 ff. The author of *Fleta* describes the model servant in the same Utopian spirit in which monastic custumaries sometimes describe the ideal of a conventual administrator. A duchess of the Ancien Régime is said to have replied to a friend who besought her to procure a *chef* answering to a long list of transcendental qualities; " My dear, if I could ever find a man like that, I would marry him!" Her ancestress of the 13th century might almost have said the same of *Fleta's* Seneschal, or Steward. The reader will hardly need to be reminded that Malvolio was Olivia's seneschal.

(p. 159.) Let the lord then procure a *Seneschal*; a man circumspect and faithful, provident, discreet and gracious, humble and chaste and peaceful and modest, learned in the laws and customs of his province and in the duties of a Seneschal; one who will devote himself to guard his lord's rights in all matters, and who knoweth how to teach and instruct his master's under-bailiffs in their doubts and their errors; merciful to the poor, turning aside from the path of justice neither for prayers nor for bribes....Let the Seneschal see to it that, in every manor, he measure clearly and openly with the common rod how many acres of arable land it may contain, and learn how much seed is needed, of every sort, for the ploughland, lest cunning reeves should reckon too much in their computations. Let him heed again that all offices be securely locked; for an easy access oftentimes tempteth the weaker brethren to sin, and men say in the vulgar tongue 𝕺𝖋𝖙𝖊 𝖋[𝖆]𝖘𝖙𝖊 𝖑𝖔𝖐𝖊𝖘 𝖒𝖆𝖐𝖊𝖙𝖍 𝖙𝖗𝖊𝖜𝖊 𝖍𝖞𝖓𝖓𝖊𝖓, which is as much as to say "fast locks make true hinds."...Let him also enquire concerning the bailiffs or sergeants of each manor, and of their underlings, how they have borne and demeaned themselves towards their neighbours and the lord's tenants and other folk; and let them be removed from the room during this inquisition, lest the truth be suppressed through fear. Let him enquire whether they have meddled with disseisins[1] of any kind, or blows or scuffles or wrestlings; or if they neglect their duties to haunt taverns and wakes by night, whereby the lord may suffer loss....Again, he must know the wardships and marriages, at what time they fall into his lord's hands, and what is their yearly value....Moreover, he must forbid, both in general and in especial, the flaying of any sheep or other beast until it have been seen by the bailiff and reeve or other trustworthy witnesses competent to judge of the manner of its death, whether it have been slain of set purpose...or by chance and evil fortune....Again, he must compute for the household expenses every night, whether in person or by deputy, on the lord's account, with the marketer, the mareschal [chief groom], the cook, the spencer[2], and the other officials; and he must make out the sum of expenses for that day. So must he also compute with the larderer, according as each kind of flesh or fish be received by tally; and the carving must be done in his presence, and he must reckon up the joints with the cook and receive a reasonable account thereof. He must know exactly how many halfpenny-loaves are to be made from a quarter of corn, that the baker may deliver the due tale to the pantler; also, how many dishes are needed for the household in themselves [apart from guests] on common days....And all the servants, severally and collectively, are bound to answer for their offices

---

[1] unlawful evictions. [2] keeper of the provisions.

to the Seneschal, who for his part is bound to report of their behaviour to his lord.

(p. 161.) The *Bailiff* of every manor should be truthful in word, diligent and faithful in deed....Let him beware of blame for sloth; therefore let him arise betimes in the morning, lest he seem but lukewarm and remiss. Let him first see to the plough-yoking, and then go round to survey the fields, woods, meadows and pastures, lest damage be done there at dawn....Let him see that the ploughmen do their work diligently and well; and, so soon as the ploughs be unyoked, let him measure forthwith the work that hath been done that day; for, unless the ploughmen can give reasonable excuse, they are bound to be accountable for the whole day's ploughing. Nevertheless he must watch their labour and their shortcomings over and over again, and make sure through the Hayward that such defaults be visited with due correction and punishment.

(p. 164.) The *Reeve*, elected by the township to that office as the best manager and tiller, must be presented to the lord or to his Seneschal, who should invest him forthwith with his office. Let him therefore not be slothful or sleepy, but let him effectually and unceasingly strive for his lord's profit....When the dung is to be carried to the fields, let the Reeve abide all day with the carters, that they may labour and finish their day's work without subterfuge....Let the Reeve cause the beasts and horses to be daily fed by daylight in his own or the Hayward's presence...by daylight, I say, lest under cover of night their keepers steal their provender....Let the forage be given in small quantities at a time; if they be too profusely supplied, they will low over it in their fulness, and tread the residue under foot, and blow upon it with their nostrils, whereby they will take it in great disfavour and count it as unclean. Moreover it profiteth at times to wash the beasts and comb them when they are dry; it is good also to rub down the oxen twice daily with a wisp of straw, that they may more lovingly lick themselves....When, in time of pasture, the milch-cows are parted from the rest, and the good are sent to saltmarsh pasture, then the milk of two such heifers should, by common custom, answer for one weight of cheese in four-and-twenty weeks, and half a gallon of butter weekly. But if they be fed in the woods or mown meadows, or in stubble after harvest, then three kine shall answer for as much as the two aforesaid...and whatsoever we say of these three kine may be said also of a score of well-kept milch-ewes...(p. 170.) Let the threshers and winnowing-women be closely spied upon, lest they steal corn in their shoes, gloves, wallets, scrips, bags, or satchels hidden near the barn. Let no Reeve remain in office beyond the year, unless he be approved as faithful and excellent; and, so long as he be Reeve, let him look closely to all defaults on the farm...for that which may be amended to-day for one penny may chance not to be amended in a year's time for twelvepence....Let no hedges be made of apples, pears, cherries, or plums, but of willow or whitethorn....Let him suffer neither man nor woman to have access to the dairy or carry thence cheese, milk, butter or the like, which might well profit a small household to the loss of the [lord's] cheese or butter or dairy-stuff. Nor let him suffer any servant of the manor to hold, by night or by day, fairs, markets or disseisins, nor to haunt wakes or taverns; but let him compel all to attend unceasingly to their own duties.... Let him permit no fire to be brought to the stable or cowshed, nor any lighted candle except in case of necessity, when it shall be borne by two men at least.

(p. 166.) The *Plough-driver's* art consisteth herein, that he drive the yoked oxen evenly, neither smiting nor pricking nor grieving them. Such should not be melancholy or wrathful, but cheerful, jocund and full of song, that by their melody and song the oxen may in a manner rejoice in their labour. Such a ploughman should bring the fodder with his own hands, and love his oxen and sleep with them by night, tickling and combing and rubbing them with straw; keeping them well in all respects, and guarding their forage or provender from theft....If he find other beasts in their pasture, he must impound them. He and the hinds, when plough-time is over, must dike and delve, thresh, fence, clean the watercourses, and do other such-like profitable works.

(p. 167.) It profiteth the lord to have discreet *Shepherds*, watchful and kindly, so that the sheep be not tormented by their wrath, but crop their pasture in peace and joyfulness; for it is a token of the shepherd's kindliness if the sheep be not scattered abroad, but browse around him in a company. Wherefore each Shepherd shall find surety for his praise-worthy conduct in all that appertaineth to his office.   Let him provide himself with a good barkable dog [*de bono cane latrabili*], and lie nightly with his flock....Let him not suffer them to feed in miry places or marshes or sloughs or bogs, nor to browse unwholesome herbs, lest by such neglect they rot and perish, for which he will be held to account and penalty.... Some circumspect householders, if a sheep die of murrain, will plunge the carcase into water from noon to vespertide, and then hang it up until the water run off; after which it is salted and dried and valued at a price, and expended among the workfolk and the household[1].

(p. 171.) The *Baker* may expend no bran (as for example to feed the dogs, or for the bread of the grooms or the poor, or for any other use) until the Reeve have received it from him, and rendered it again by tally.

(p. 172.) The *Hayward* should be fortified with the virtues of strength, health, sternness and fidelity.   Late and early he must range round and spy upon the woods, the farm, the meadows and fields, and all that appertaineth unto the manor; all cattle found to his lord's damage must be impounded; and if a lawsuit ensue he must give security to prosecute the quarrel.

(*ibid.*) The *Carter* must be constant, skilful, modest, not given to wrath, learned and expert in the arts of lading, pitching and carrying.   Let him love his horses, not over-

---

[1] Compare the similar advice given 250 years later by Thomas Tusser in his *Five Hundred Points of Good Husbandry* (Southey, *British Poets*, 1831, p. 156) § 37 :

> Thy measelèd bacon-hog, sow, or thy boar,
> Shut up for to heal, for infecting thy store;
> Or kill it for bacon, or souse it to sell
> For Flemming that loves it so daintily well.

Also the Oxford ordinance for giving meat, condemned as putrid in the open market, to the leper-hospital (Section XIV., no. 12, below).

burdening them but keeping them in his power, lest they perish from too great load or labour. He should know how to prepare and mend the traces, trappings and small harness appertaining to his carts; and every carter should lie by night with his horses. Let us say the same of the carter with his horses as of the oxherd with his oxen, lest they evade responsibility for the beasts committed to their charge and lost by evil custody.

(*ibid.*) The *Dairymaid* should be chaste and honest, faithful and laborious in her dairy-work, wise and neat-handed, not lavish, but of a saving temper; for she shall suffer neither man nor woman to come to her dairy and bear aught away which might disparage that for which she must make account....Her office is to take the milk by tally, to make cheese and butter according to the tale of the gallons, and to care for the poultry-yard[1]. For these outgoings and incomings she must give frequent account to the Bailiff and the Reeve; and note that some auditors of accounts will not suffer the dairy to allow less than twelvepence yearly for the profit of a goose, and fourpence for a hen. Moreover, it is her duty to winnow and to make packages, to cover over the fire, and to do suchlike small works whereunto her leisure may extend.

2   THE MANORIAL COURT

A few selected presentments from the opening pages of F. W. Maitland, *Select Pleas in Manorial Courts* (Selden Soc. 1889). All these courts were held in the years 1246–9; they throw much light on the life and status of English serfs at that time.

(p. 7.) John Sperling complains that Richard of Newmere on the Sunday next before S. Bartholomew's day last past with his cattle, horses, and pigs wrongfully destroyed the corn on his [John's] land to his damage to the extent of one thrave of wheat, and to his dishonour to the extent of two shillings; and of this he produces suit. And Richard comes and defends all of it. Therefore let him go to the law six handed[2]. His pledges, Simon Combe and Hugh Frith.

---

[1] Cf. Chaucer, *Nun's Priest's Tale*, where the old woman who keeps three kine and a few poultry is described as a sort of "deye," or dairy woman.

[2] He must bring five "compurgators," i.e. five neighbours who will support his

(p. 9.) Hugh Free in mercy for his beast caught in the lord's garden. Pledges, Walter Hill and William Slipper. Fine 6*d.*

(*ibid.*) [The] twelve jurors say that Hugh Cross has right in the bank and hedge about which there was a dispute between him and William White. Therefore let him hold in peace and let William be distrained for his many trespasses. (Afterwards he made fine for 12*d.*)

(*ibid.*) Roger Pleader is at his law against Nicholas Croke [to prove] that neither he [Roger] nor his killed [Nicholas's] peacock. Pledges, Ringer and Jordan. Afterwards he made his law and therefore is quit.

From the whole township of Little Ogbourne, except seven, for not coming to wash the lord's sheep, 6*s.* 8*d.*

(p. 12.) Gilbert Richard's son gives 5*s.* for licence to marry a wife. Pledge, Seaman. Term [for payment,] the Purification.

William Jordan in mercy for bad ploughing on the lord's land. Pledge, Arthur. Fine, 6*d.*

The parson of the Church is in mercy for his cow caught in the lord's meadow. Pledges, Thomas Ymer and William Coke.

From Martin Shepherd 6*d.* for the wound that he gave Pekin.

Ragenhilda of Bec gives 2*s.* for having married without licence. Pledge, William of Primer.

(p. 16.) Walter Hull gives 13*s.* 4*d.* for licence to dwell on the land of the Prior of Harmondsworth so long as he shall live and as a condition finds pledges, to wit, William Slipper, John Bisuthe, Gilbert Bisuthe, Hugh Tree, William Johnson, John Hulle, who undertake that the said Walter shall do to the lord all the services and customs which he would do if he dwelt on the lord's land, and that his heriot[1] shall be secured to the lord in case he dies there [i.e. at Harmondsworth].

The Court presented that William Noah's son is the born

oath of innocence by swearing on their part that they believe him. See F. W. Maitland, *Collected Papers*, vol. II. p. 446.

[1] See Section VIII., no. 12.

bondman of the lord and a fugitive and dwells at Dodford. Therefore he must be sought. They say also that William Askil, John Parsons and Godfrey Green have furtively carried off four geese from the vill of Horepoll.

(p. 19.)   It was presented that Robert Carter's son by night invaded the house of Peter Burgess and in felony threw stones at his door so that the said Peter raised the hue. Therefore let the said Robert be committed to prison. Afterwards he made fine with 2*s.*

All the ploughmen of Great Ogbourne are convicted by the oath of twelve men...because by reason of their default [the land] of the lord was ill-ploughed whereby the lord is damaged to the amount of 9*s.*....And Walter Reaper is in mercy for concealing [i.e. not giving information as to] the said bad ploughing. Afterwards he made fine with the lord with 1 mark.

3   THE PEASANT'S FARE

Piers Plowman, B, VI. 282, p. 220.

" I have no peny," quod Peres "poletes[1] forto bigge[2],
Ne neyther gees ne grys[3], but two grene[4] cheses,
A fewe cruddes[5] and creem and an haver[6] cake,
And two loves of benes and bran y-bake for my fauntis.
And yet I sey, by my soule, I have no salt bacoun,
Ne no kokeney[7], bi Cryst, coloppes[8] forto maken.
Ac[9] I have percil[10] and porettes[11] and many kole-plantes[12],
And eke a cow and a kaf and a cart-mare
To drawe a-felde my donge the while the drought lasteth.
And bi this lyflode we mot lyve til Lammasse tyme ;
And bi that, I hope to have hervest in my croft ;
And thanne may I dighte thi dyner as me dere liketh."

Skeat refers to the very similar catalogue of shepherds' fare, on a festive occasion, at the beginning of the Chester *Shepherds' Play* (ed. T. Wright, p. 123).

[1] pullets.   [2] buy.   [3] pigs.   [4] fresh.   [5] curds.   [6] oaten.
[7] big eggs.   [8] eggs and bacon.   [9] but.   [10] parsley.   [11] leeks.
[12] cabbages.

4   INCIDENTS OF THE COUNTRYSIDE

From different proofs of age, in *Calendar of Inquisitiones Post Mortem*, vol. VII.

(p. 380.)   7 Edw. III.

Maud Gerounde.

Nicholas de Mesendene, aged 42 years, says the same and knows it because the same day and year he made a hedge round his close.

Robert le Hemt, aged 44 years, says the same and knows it because on the same day and year he made a fishery in his close.

(p. 384.)   7 Edw. III.

Isabel de Wolryngton.

Geoffrey le White, of Eton, aged 50 years and more, says the like and knows it because on the morrow of the Purification, 10 Edw. II., he had an oast house with three quarters of malt burnt through the fault of Cecily his maid, 16 years ago.

(p. 440.)   8 Edw. III.

William Loveday.

John Derby, Edmund de Holme, Edmund atte Brugge, Henry Palmere, Richard Lord, William atte Churchegate and Gilbert Godwyne, each aged 40 years and more, agree, and know it because on the same day, time and year, they were with the prior of Bernewell at Drayton, at a feast, and a messenger came publicly announcing the birth of the said William.

(p. 492.)   9 Edw. III.

Peter Bekard or Bocard.

Adam de Hayton, aged 66 years, says the like and knows it because in the same year that the said Peter was born, his brother, named William, in going towards the Schools of Oxford was killed by misadventure, and from that time 21 years and more have elapsed.

5 ESSEX PLOUGHBOYS

Sir Anthony Fitzherbert was born in 1470, knighted 1516 and raised to the Bench in 1523; he died in 1538. His *Book of Husbandry* (ed. W. W. Skeat, 1882) is of great value; but with him, as with almost all old writers, we must make considerable allowance for the tendency to depreciate the present in comparison with the past : e.g. his remarks on costume in Section IX., no. 8 (*c*), below.

In Essex they use to have a chylde, to go in the forowe[1] before the horses or oxen, with a bagge or hopper full of corne ; and he taketh his hande full of corne, and by lyttel and lytel casteth it in the sayd forowe. Me semeth, that chylde oughte to have moche dyscretion.

6 THE MILLER'S TRICKS

The Coventry Leet Book, E.E.T.S., Part II. p. 397 ; ordinances for the Town Millers.

Nother that he water nother chaung[e] no manners corne, to geve hym the wers for the better ; nother he schall have no hogges, Gees ne duckys at hys Mille, nor no maner of Pultre, but iij hennes and on[e] Cokke ; and if he do the contrary to any of [these] his fyne is at every tyme xl *d.* ; and if he will not be war by iij warnynges, the iij[de] tyme he to be juged to the Pillory.

7 DECAY OF YEOMANRY

Latimer, *First Sermon before King Edward* [*VI.*].

Furthermore, if the kinges honour (as some men say) standeth in the great multitude of people, then these grasiers, inclosers and rentrearers, are hinderers of the kinges honor. For where as have bene a great many of housholders and inhabitauntes, there is now but a shepeheard and his dogge, so they hynder the kynges honour most of all. My Lordes and maysters, I say also, that all such proceedinges which are agaynst the kynges honour (as I have a parte declared before) and as far as I can perceive, doe intend plainly, to make the yomanry slavery, and the clergy shavery. For such workes are all singular, private wealth and commodity. We

---

[1] furrow.

of the clergy had to much, but that is taken away, and now we have to little. But for myne owne parte, I have no cause to complaine, for I thanke God and the king, I have sufficient. And God is my judge I came not to crave of any man, any thing, but I know them that have too little. There lyeth a great matter by these appropriations, great reformation is to be had in them. I know where is a great market towne with divers hamelets and inhabitantes, where doe rise yearely of theyr laboures to the value of fifty pound, and the Vicar that serveth (being so great a cure) hath but xij. or xiiij. markes by yeare, so that of this pension he is not able to buy him bookes, nor geve his neighbour drinke; all the great gayne goeth an other way.

My father was a yoman, and had no landes of hys owne; onely he had a farme of iij. or iiij. pound by yeare at the uttermost, and hereupon he tilled so muche as kept halfe a dosson men. He had walke for an hundred sheepe, and my mother milked xxx. kyne. He was able, and did finde the king a harnesse, with him selfe and his horse, while he came to the place that he should receyve the kinges wages. I can remember, that I buckled his harnesse, when he went unto Blacke heath fielde. He kept me to schole, or els I had not bene able to have preached before the kinges majestie now. He maryed my sisters with five pound, or xx. nobles[1] apiece, so that he brought them up in godlinesse, and feare of God. He kept hospitality for his poore neighboures. And some almes he gave to the poore, and all thys did he of the sayde farme. Where he that now hath it, payeth xvj. pound by the yeare or more, and is not able to doe any thyng for hys prince, for him selfe, nor for his children, or geve a cup of drinke to the poore.

Thus all the enhaunsing and rearing goeth to your private commoditie and wealth. So that where ye had a single too much, you have that: and since the same, ye have enhaunced the rent, and so have encreased an other too much: so now ye have double too much, which is to[o] too much. But let the preacher preach till his tongue be worne to the stompes,

[1] *6s. 8d.*

nothyng is amended. We have good statutes made for the common wealth as touching commoners and enclosers, many meetings, and sessions, but in the ende of the matter, there commeth nothing foorth. Well, well, this is one thing I will say unto you, from whence it commeth I knowe, even from the devil. I know his entent in it. For if ye bring it to passe, that the yeomanry be not able to put theyr sonnes to schole (as in deede universities doe wonderously decay already) and that they be not able to marry theyr daughters to the avoyding of whoredome, I say ye plucke salvation from the people, and utterly destroy the realme. For by yomens sonnes, the faith of Christ is, and hath beene maintained chiefly. Is this realme taught by rich mens sonnes? no, no. Read the chronicles : ye shall find sometime noble mens sonnes, which have beene unpreaching bishops and prelates, but ye shall finde none of them learned men : but verily, they that should looke to the redresse of these thinges, be the greatest against them. In this realme are a great many folkes, and amongest many, I knowe but one of tender zeale, [who,] at the motion of his poore tenantes, hath let downe his landes to the old rentes for theyr relife. For Gods love, let not him be a phenix, let him not be alone, let him not be an heremite closed in a wall ; some good man folowe him, and do as he geveth example.

8   DECAY OF HUSBANDRY

Sir T. More, *Utopia* etc., Ralph Robinson, 1551 (ed. Lumby, 1879), p. 32.

But yet this is not only the necessary cause of stealing. There is an other, whych, as I suppose, is proper and peculiar to you Englishmen alone. What is that, quod the Cardinal ? Forsoth my lorde (quod I) your shepe that were wont to be so meke and tame, and so smal eaters, now, as I heare saye be become so great devowerers and so wylde, that they eate up, and swallow downe the very men them selfes. They consume, destroye, and devoure whole fieldes, howses, and cities. For looke in what partes of the realme doth growe the fynest and therfore dearest woll, there noblemen and gentlemen, yea and certeyn abbottes, holy men no doubt—not contenting them

selfes with the yearely revenues and profytes that were wont
to grow to theyr forefathers and predecessours of their landes,
nor beynge content that they live in rest and pleasure nothinge
profiting, yea much noyinge the weale publique—leave no
grounde for tillage, thei inclose al into pastures; thei throw
doune houses; they plucke downe townes, and leave nothing
standynge, but only the churche to be made a shepehowse.
And, as thoughe you loste no small quantity of grounde by
forestes, chases, laundes and parkes, those good holy men
turne all dwellinge places and all glebeland into desolation
and wildernes. Therfore that on[e] covetous and unsatiable
cormaraunte, and, very plage of his natyve contrey, maye com-
passe aboute and inclose many thousand akers of grounde
together within one pale or hedge; the husbandmen be thrust
owte of their owne, or els either by coveyne and fraude, or by
violent oppression they be put besydes it, or by wronges and
injuries thei be so weried, that they be compelled to sell all:
by one meanes therfore or by other, either by hooke or crooke
they muste needes departe awaye, poore, selye¹, wretched soules,
men, women, husbands, wives, fatherlesse children, widowes,
wofull mothers, with their yonge babes, and their whole houshold smal in substance and muche in numbre, as husbandrye
requireth manye handes. Awaye thei trudge, I say, out of
their knowen and accustomed houses, fyndynge no place to
reste in. All their housholdestuffe, whiche is verye litle woorthe,
thoughe it myght well abide the sale, yet, beeynge sodainely
thruste oute, they be constrayned to sell it for a thing of
nought. And when they have wandered abrode tyll that be
spent, what can they then els doo but steale, and then justly
pardy² be hanged, or els go about a beggyng. And yet then
also they be caste in prison as vagaboundes, because they go
aboute and worke not: whom no man wyl set a-worke, though
thei never so willyngly profre themselves therto. For one
shephearde or heardman is ynoughe to eate up that grounde
with cattel, to the occupiyng wherof aboute husbandrye manye
handes were requisite. And this is also the cause why victualles
be now in many places dearer. Yea, besides this, the price of

¹ helpless.　² pardieu!

wolle is so rysen, that poore folkes, which were wont to worke it and make cloth therof, be nowe hable to bye none at all. And by thys meanes verye manye be forced to forsake worke, and to geve them selves to idelnesse. For, after that so much grounde was inclosed for pasture, an infinite multitude of shepe dyed of the rotte, suche vengeaunce God toke of their inordinate and unsaciable covetousnes, sendinge amonge the shepe that pestiferous morrein, whiche much more justely shoulde have fallen on the shepemasters owne heades. And though the number of shepe increase never so faste, yet the price falleth not one myte, because there be so fewe sellers. For they be almooste all comen into a fewe riche mennes handes, whome no neade forceth to sell before they lust, and they luste not before they maye sell as deare as they luste. Now the same cause bringeth in like dearth of the other kindes of cattell ; yea and that so much the more, bicause that, after fermes plucked downe and husbandry decaied, there is no man that passethe for the breadynge of younge stoore. For these riche men brynge not up the yonge ones of greate cattel as they do lambes. But first they bie them abrode verie chepe ; and after-ward, when they be fatted in their pastures, they sell them agayne excedynge deare. And therefore (as I suppose) the whole incommoditie hereof is not yet felte. For yet they make dearth onely in those places where they sell. But when they shall fetche them away from thence wheare they be bredde faster then they can be broughte up, then shall there also be felte greate dearth, stoore beginning there to faile where the ware is boughte. Thus the unreasonable covetous-nes of a few hath turned that thing to the utter undoing of your ylande, in the whiche thynge the cheife felicitie of your realme did consist. For this greate dearth of victualles causeth men to kepe as litle houses and as smale hospitalitie as they possible maye, and to put away their servauntes : wh[i]ther, I pray you, but a-beggynge : or elles (whyche these gentell bloudes and stoute stomackes wyll sooner set their myndes unto) a-stealing[1] ?

---

[1] Cf. Fortescue in Section XIV., no. 14.

SECTION VII

TOWN LIFE

The large majority of the following extracts are taken from London records, which are fuller, more interesting, and more accessible than those of any other British town: moreover, such concentration gives much more unity to the general picture. Readers who wish to pursue the subject further should read Dr R. R. Sharpe's *Calendars* of London Letterbooks, Wills and Inquests; Prof. G. Unwin's *London Gilds and Companies*; Miss Bateson's editions (with translations) of the Leicester and Northampton Borough Records; and Miss Maud Sellers's *York Memorandum Book* (Surtees Soc., 2 vols.).

1   LONDON FOLK-MOTE

From *Liber de Antiquis Legibus*, in *Chronicles of Old London*, tr. Riley, 1863, pp. 34, 38, 48. (A very useful translation of the *Liber de Antiquis Legibus*, written about 1274, with later additions, and of the *French Chronicle of London*, written about 1360.) For a description of the medieval mote see F. W. Maitland's article in Chapter III. of H. D. Traill's *Social England*.

[A.D. 1257.] Afterwards on the Vigil of the Purification, the Mayor and a countless multitude meeting in the Guildhall, Michael Tovy and Adam de Basing were sent thither by his lordship the King, to say that the King was willing to preserve all their franchises unimpaired; but that, for the benefit of the City, he was wishful that inquisition should be made, and that too upon oath, by what persons his commons had been so aggrieved in reference to tallages and other instances of transgression; as also, that no one should be punished unless he had offended, and that too, without detriment to the community. In the same words John Maunsel and the others, sent by the King, made affirmation; and so, by reason of such words and pleasant promises, the populace gave assent, crying aloud, "Ya, ya," to taking the oath, in disparagement of their own franchises; which in fact these same wretched creatures had not been the persons to secure....

[After a long inquiry] John Maunsel and the others who had been sent by his lordship the King, came to Saint Paul's Cross; and one of them, using bland words, and, as it were, preaching unto the populace, while promising them that all their rights and liberties should be preserved unimpaired by his lordship the King, further said;—"Supposing that any bailiff or bailiffs of theirs should have treated them unjustly, and have inflicted many evils and hardships upon them and upon the City—supposing such a case, ought they, according to the law of the City, to defend themselves as against the King, upon his making suit, by the oaths of twelve men, and as against their fellow citizens by the oaths of six, and so be acquitted of all the consequences of such an offence?" To which enquiry (no conference being first held among the discreet men of the City, as is usually the practice), answer was made by some of the populace, sons of divers mothers, many of them born without the City, and many of servile condition, with loud shouts of "Nay, nay, nay," in contravention of the privilege of the franchises that had been granted unto the City of old, and by their predecessors, citizens of blessed memory, obtained, and, until that time, strictly observed. And thus and in such manner, without any shape of reason, were all the Aldermen of the City disavowed....

The same year [1260], after the Purification of the Blessed Mary [2 February] the King came to London, and afterwards, on the Sunday before the Feast of Saint Valentine, had the Folkmote summoned at Saint Paul's Cross, whither he himself came, and the King of Almaine, the Archbishop of Canterbury, John Maunsel, and many others. The King also commanded that all persons of the age of twelve years and upwards should make oath before their Alderman, in every Ward, that they would be faithful unto him, so long as he should live, and, after his death, to his heir; which was accordingly done. Then all the Gates of the City were shut, night and day, by the King's command, the Bridge Gate, and the Gates of Ludgate and Aldgate, excepted, which were open by day, and well fortified with armed men.

2 AN UNPARDONABLE WORD

H. T. Riley's *Memorials of London and London Life* (1868) is a very valuable collection of translations from the medieval French and Latin documents in the city records. I have drawn very freely from this source, not only because London was so much more important than any other town, but also because we get a more concentrated and clearer picture by focussing our attention as much as possible upon one community.

1291. (p. 27.) Roger de Portlaunde, clerk of the Sheriff of London, made plaint to Ralph de Sandwich, Warden of the City of London, and Henry le Waleys, and others, Aldermen of the City aforesaid, that Robert de Suttone, in the full Court of Thomas Romeyn, Sheriff of the same city, which the said Roger was then holding in the name of his master aforesaid, on Thursday the morrow of St James the Apostle [25 July], in the 19th year of the reign of King Edward, cast vile contempt upon him, the said Roger, in contempt of our Lord the King, by saying these words in English,—[1] "*Tprhurt, Tprhurt*"; because he would not allow him, the said Robert, to plead in his Court, before he had reformed his conduct towards the Warden of the city aforesaid, by whom he had been before suspended for certain trespasses alleged against him ; and because he would not submit to being forbidden by the said Roger; and thereupon uttered the aforesaid words,—"*Tprhurt, Tprhurt,* [2] *Tphurt,*" to his damnifying, and in manifest contempt of our Lord the King.

And the said Robert, who is present, appears and denies whatever [is alleged against him], and says that he did nothing at all, nor did he say the aforesaid words in contempt of our Lord the King ; nor did he proffer to do so to the Court aforesaid, as the said Roger imputes to him : and he places himself

---

[1] An expression of contempt. Compare, later, Section XV., no. 14. In Wright's *Political Songs* (Camd. Soc. 1839, pp. 223, 381) it appears under the form "*Tprot*". For a similar scene in court, see Riley, p. 275 below.

[2] These variations in the form of the word occur in the original.

upon the record of the four benches of the Court aforesaid, and the said Roger does the same.

And the assessors of the four benches of the said Court appeared, upon whose verdict the parties aforesaid had put themselves ; who say that the said Robert did say in full Court that he would care nothing, for all the forbidding of the said Roger ; also, still further speaking in manifest contempt, he uttered these words in English,—" *Tphurpt, Tphurt*[1]," at the same time raising his thumb, in contempt for his suspension aforesaid.   Therefore, he was to be committed to prison for the contempt aforesaid.

3　　TOWN AND FIRE

1302.   (p. 46.)   Thomas Bat came before John le Blund, Mayor of London, and the Aldermen, and bound himself, and all his rents, lands, and tenements, to keep the City of London indemnified from peril of fire and other losses which might arise from his houses covered with thatch, in the Parish of St Laurence Candelwykstrete ; and he agreed that he would have the said houses covered with tiles about the Feast of Pentecost then next ensuing.   And in case he should not do the same, he granted that the Mayor, Sheriffs, and bailiffs, of London, should cause the said houses to be roofed with tiles out of the issues of his rents aforesaid.

4　　A LONDON GARDEN

1315.   (p. 117.)   Be it remembered, that, by John de Gisorz, Mayor, and other Aldermen there was granted to Sir Gilbert de Hardyngham a certain hermitage near the King's garden, on London Wall, with all the appurtenances, to have and to hold to the same Sir Gilbert for the whole of his life, provided always that he shall properly behave himself; he rendering to the commonalty one half mark per annum, at the four terms of the year, for the same.

[1] *Sic.*

5   OLD ST PAUL'S

From *Liber de Ant. Legibus*, in H. T. Riley, *Chronicles of Old London*, 1863.

(*a*) p. 215, 1313 A.D.

Memorandum,—that in the eighth year of King Edward the cross with the ball[1], all gilt, was raised upon the belfry of St Paul's; and the Bishop of London, Gilbert of Segrave, deposited many precious things in the said cross on the belfry, on the Friday next after St Michael in the following year.

(*b*) *Ibid.* p. 257.

In this year the cross of the belfry of Saint Paul's was taken down and repaired; and in the old cross certain relics were found, that is to say, a corporal with which they sing mass, white and entire, without any defect; and in this corporal was found a part of the wood of the cross of our Lord Jesus Christ, wrought in the form of a cross; a stone of the Sepulchre of our Lord; and another stone from the place where God stood when he ascended into heaven; and another stone from Mount Calvary, where the Cross of our Lord was erected.   There was also found a purse, and in this purse a piece of red sendal[2], in which were wrapped some bones of the Eleven Thousand Virgins and other relics, the names of which were unknown.   These relics Master Robert of Clothale shewed to the people during his preaching on the Sunday before the Feast of Saint Botolph [17 June]; and, after the same, the relics were replaced in the Cross, and many other new ones as well, on the Day of Saint Francis [16 July].

(*c*) Riley, *Memorials*, p. 580.

1411.   (p. 580.)   Proclamation made on the Friday next before the Feast of St Bartholomew:

" That no manere man ne child, of what estate or condicioun that he be, be so hardy to wrestell, or make ony wrestlyng, within the Seintuary[3] ne the boundes of Poules, ne in non other

---

[1] "From other sources we learn that this *pomel*, or ball, was of sufficient capacity to hold 10 bushels of corn, the cross being 15 feet in height."   Riley.
[2] a fine silken stuff.   [3] churchyard.

open place within the Citee of Londone, up peyne of emprisonement of fourty dayes, and makyng fyn unto the Chaumbre, after the discrecioun of the Mair and Aldermen."

Compare the similar prohibitions for medieval college chapels, **e.g.** Section II., no. 20 of this book.

6 FORBIDDEN SPORTS

1351. (p. 269.) It is forbidden on behalf of our Lord the King and the Council, on pain of imprisonment, that any child, or other person, shall play in any place of the Palace of Westminster, during the Parliament which is summoned thereto, at bars, or at other games not befitting, and such as taking off the hoods of people, or laying hands upon them ; or in other way causing hindrance, whereby each person may not peaceably follow his business.

7 THE TOWN PEACE

H. T. Riley, *French Chronicles of Old London*, p. 253.

In this year [1319] swords were forbidden, so that no one was to wear them ; by reason of which, many swords were taken and hung up beneath Ludgate, within and without. At this time many of the people of the trades of London were arrayed in livery, and a good time was about to begin....In this year [1320] the Mayoralty of London was forfeited, by reason of an offence which John Gysors had committed in the time when he was Mayor, in having admitted Henry de Braundeston, a felon to the king, to enjoy the franchise of London after such felony committed. For this Henry had slain a man in Holy Church, at Our Lady atte Hill....In this year a woman, Isabele de Bury by name, slew the clerk of the Church of Allhallows near London Wall ; and kept herself within the same church for five days, until the Bishop of London sent his letters to the effect that the Church would not save her ; whereupon, she was carried out of the church to Neugate, and the third day after was hanged.

8   CITY VAGRANTS

H. T. Riley, *Memorials.*

1359. (p. 304.) "Forasmuch as many men and women, and others, of divers Counties, who might work, to the help of the common people, have betaken themselves from out of their own country to the City of London, and do go about begging there, so as to have their own ease and repose, not wishing to labour or work for their sustenance, to the great damage of such the common people ; and also, do waste divers alms, which would otherwise be given to many poor folks, such as lepers, blind, halt, and persons oppressed with old age and divers other maladies, to the destruction of the support of the same :— we do therefore command, on behalf of our Lord the King, whom may God preserve and bless, that all those who go about begging in the said city, and who are able to labour and work, for the profit of the common people, shall quit the said city between now and Monday next ensuing. And if any such shall be found begging after the day aforesaid, the same shall be taken and put in the stocks on Cornhulle, for half a day the first time ; and the second time, he shall remain in the stocks one whole day ; and the third time, he shall be taken, and shall remain in prison for 40 days, and shall then forswear the said city for ever."

9   CORRUPT WINE

1364. (p. 318.) John de Brykelesworthe, who prosecuted for the King and the Commonalty of the City of London, said that the same John Ryghtwys and John Penrose sold red wine to all who came there, unsound and unwholesome for man, in deceit of the common people, and in contempt of our Lord the King, and to the shameful disgrace of the officers of the City ; to the grievous damage of the Commonalty etc. [The judgment was] that the said John Penrose shall drink a draught of the same wine which he sold to the common people ; and the remainder of such wine shall then be poured on the head of the same John ; and that he shall forswear the calling of a vintner in the City of London for ever, unless he can obtain the favour of our Lord the King as to the same.

C.

10   FRAUDULENT TRADERS

(*a*)   H. T. Riley, *Chronicles of Old London*, 1863, pp. 150, 151.

Throughout all this year [1272], no punishment was inflicted upon the bakers; but they made loaves at their own will; so much so, that each loaf was deficient one-third in weight, or one fourth at least.

(*b*)   *Ibid.* p. 251.

In this year [1314], upon the Day of Saint James [25 July] before August there was one baker drawn upon the hurdle alone; and because another baker did not have the same sentence carried out, the same day the Mayor before-mentioned was reviled by the people and called a rogue; for which many persons were imprisoned and impoverished, through the malice and false compassing of the said John Gisors, the Mayor.

(*c*)   *Piers Plowman*, B, III. 69, p. 68.

For-thi[1] I lere[2] yow, lordes....
Meires and maceres[3], that menes[4] ben bitwene
The kynge and the comune to kepe the lawes,
To punyschen on pillories and pynynge-stoles[5]
Brewesteres and bakesteres, bocheres and cokes;
For thise aren men on this molde[6] that moste harme worcheth[7]
To the pore peple that parcel-mele buggen[8].
For they poysoun the peple priveliche and oft,
Thei rychen thorw regraterye[9], and rentes hem[10] buggen
With that the pore people shulde put in here wombe[11];
For, toke thei on trewly, thei tymbred nought so heighe,
Ne boughte non burgages[12], be ye ful certeyne.

(*d*)   H. T. Riley, *Memorials*.

1365.   (p. 320.) John de Alleford, of the County of Surrey, went to the Prioress of the House of St Mary at Clerkenwell, bearing a white wand in his hand, as a token of his office etc.

---

[1] therefore.   [2] teach.   [3] officers of justice.   [4] intermediaries.
[5] stools of penance.   [6] earth.   [7] work.   [8] buy in small quantities.
[9] buying cheap and selling dear.   [10] for themselves.   [11] belly.
[12] If they had made only honest gains, they would not have built such high houses, nor bought tenements.

A RICH CITIZEN

A FORESTALLER IN THE PILLORY

And he then told the said Prioress, that Simon, by Divine permission, Archbishop of Canterbury, had now become so stricken with old age, and afflicted with divers other infirmities, that he could not make visitation in person throughout his Province. And he was asked by the Court for what reason he so went to the Prioress as aforesaid ; whereupon he said, for the sake of getting some money from her. And as it seemed to the Mayor and Aldermen, that the things aforesaid were done in contempt of our Lord the King, and to the injury of the estate of the said Lord Archbishop, so worthy a prelate, and him too, the Primate of all England etc., it was adjudged that the said John should have the punishment of the pillory, to stand two hours thereon, the reason for such punishment being there publicly proclaimed. And after judgment should have been so executed, the same John was to be taken back to the Prison of Newgate, until our Lord the King should of his grace give precept for his release.

(*e*) 1365. (p. 328.) John de Briclesworthe, who prosecutes for the Commonalty aforesaid, says that the same John Russelle, on the 15th day of September in the 39th year etc., at Billyngesgate, exposed 37 pigeons for sale, putrid, rotten, stinking, and abominable to the human race, to the scandal, contempt, and disgrace of all the City. And this for the Commonalty he makes offers to prove etc. And the said John Russelle says that the same pigeons are good and proper for sale to mankind, and he offers to prove the same etc. And hereupon, John Vygerous, Thomas de Wynchestre, *pye-bakeres*, John Wenge, Geoffrey Colman, John Lowe, Thomas Colman, and Richard de Daventre, cooks, being sworn to inspect and examine whether the said pigeons are good and proper or not etc.; say upon their oath, that the said pigeons are not good or wholesome for mankind, but rather to the corruption of man etc. Therefore he is to have judgment of the pillory, and the said pigeons are to be burnt beneath the pillory, and the cause of his punishment is to be there proclaimed.

(*f*) 1366. (p. 332.) John Edmond, of Esthamme, *cornmongere*, of the County of Essex, was brought before John Lovekyn, Mayor, and the Aldermen, at the Guildhall, for that he had exposed for sale at Grascherche one quarter of oats in a sack, and had put a bushel of good oats at the mouth of the sack, all the rest therein being corn of worse quality, and of no value, in deceit of the common people. Being questioned as to which falsity, how he would acquit himself thereof, the same John did not gainsay the same. Therefore it was adjudged that he should have the punishment of the pillory, to stand upon the same for one hour of the day.

11   SEA-COAL

1369. (p. 338.) John Wirhale, Roger Cooke, Henry Cornewaille, and Geoffrey Prudhomme, were chosen to hold the office of Meters of sea-coal coming into the City of London; and sworn that they would well and trustily make measure of coals so coming thither, taking for their trouble as from of old they were wont.

12   THE LIAR'S REWARD

1371. (p. 352.) Nicholas Mollere, servant of John Toppesfeld, *smythe*, was brought before the Mayor and Aldermen, to make answer for that—whereas by Statute it is ordained that no one shall presume to publish or spread false news, or to invent the same, whereby dissension, or tendency to dissension or scandal, may be produced between the King and the people, or other nobles of his realm, on pain of imprisonment etc.—the same Nicholas, on the Friday last past, at the Guildhall of London, openly asserted that on the said Saturday it was to be publicly proclaimed throughout the whole of the city aforesaid, that all merchants alien might come to buy and sell all manner of merchandize in the same city, as freely as the freemen of the same. And that all the prisoners in Neugate were to be taken to the Tower of London, and there was no longer to be any prison at Neugate. Which news the same Nicholas published, to the injury of the franchise; and to the scandal of the city aforesaid, as it is alleged etc. And the said Nicholas, being questioned hereupon, acknowledged that he did tell and publish the news aforesaid. And he said that he heard a certain esquire of our Lord the Prince telling the same in the shop of John, his master, before-mentioned. And afterwards, being diligently examined hereupon, as to whether he had any knowledge of this esquire, he said that he had no knowledge of his person, nor did he hear such esquire relate the said news, as he had before alleged. But he said that he heard one Alan Grygge, *chaundeler*, relating the said news in manner aforesaid, by the shop of the said John, his master.... And the jury, by assent of the parties chosen, by John Rygge and eleven others, said upon their oath, that the said Alan Grygge did not utter the words aforesaid, or say as the said Nicholas above imputed to him. Therefore it was adjudged that the same Alan should go acquitted thereof; and that the said Nicholas, for the lie of which he was so convicted, and by him maliciously invented, should have the punishment of the pillory; to stand thereon for one hour of the day, and to have the whetstone hung from his neck, for such liars, according to the custom of the City, provided.

13   CHILD-STEALING

1373. (p. 368.) Alice de Salesbury, a beggar, was adjudged to the pillory called the "*thewe*," for women ordained, by award of the Mayor and Aldermen, there to stand for one hour in the day; for that, on the Sunday before, she had taken one Margaret, daughter of John Oxwyke, grocer, in the Ropery, in London, and had carried her away, and stripped her of her clothes, that she might not be recognized by her family; that so, she might go begging with the same Alice, and gain might be made thereby.

14   CHAUCER'S LEASE

1374. (p. 377.) "To all persons to whom this present writing indented shall come, Adam de Bury, Mayor, the Aldermen, and the Commonalty of the City of London, greeting. Know ye that we, with unanimous will and assent, have granted and released by these presents unto Geoffrey Chaucer the whole of the dwelling-house above the Gate of Aldgate, with the rooms built over, and a certain cellar beneath the same gate, on the South side of that gate, and the appurtenances thereof; to have and to hold the whole of the house aforesaid, with the rooms so built over, and the said cellar, and the appurtenances thereof, unto the aforesaid Geoffrey, for the whole life of him, the same Geoffrey. And the said Geoffrey shall maintain and repair the whole of the house aforesaid, and the rooms thereof, so often as shall be requisite, in all things necessary thereto, competently and sufficiently, at the expense of the same Geoffrey, throughout the whole life of him, the same Geoffrey. And it shall be lawful for the Chamberlain of the Guildhall of London, for the time being, so often as he shall see fit, to enter the house and rooms aforesaid, with their appurtenances, to see that the same are well and competently and sufficiently maintained and repaired, as aforesaid. And if the said Geoffrey shall not have maintained or repaired the aforesaid house and rooms competently and sufficiently, as is before stated, within forty days after the time when by the same Chamberlain he shall have been required so to do, it shall be lawful for the said Chamberlain wholly to oust the before-named Geoffrey therefrom, and to re-seise and resume the same house, rooms, and cellar, with their appurtenances, into the hand of the City, to the use of the Commonalty aforesaid ; and to hold the same in their former state to the use of the same Commonalty, without any gainsaying whatsoever thereof. And it shall not be lawful for the said Geoffrey to let the house, rooms, and cellar, aforesaid, or any part thereof, or his interest therein, to any person whatsoever. And we, the Mayor, Aldermen, and Commonalty aforesaid, will not cause any gaol to be made thereof, for the safe-keeping of prisoners therein, during the life of the said Geoffrey ; but we and our successors will warrant the same house, rooms, and cellar, with their appurtenances, unto the before-named Geoffrey, for the whole life of him, the same Geoffrey, in form aforesaid : this however excepted, that in time of defence of the city aforesaid, so often as it shall be necessary, it shall be lawful for us and our successors to enter the said house and rooms, and to order and dispose of the same, for such time, and in such manner, as shall then seem to us to be most expedient. And after the decease of the same Geoffrey, the house, rooms, and cellar aforesaid, with their appurtenances, shall wholly revert unto us and our successors. In witness whereof, as well the Common Seal of the City aforesaid as the seal of the said Geoffrey, have been to these present indentures interchangeably appended. Given in the Chamber of the Guildhall of the city aforesaid, the 10th day of May, in the 48th year of the reign of King Edward, after the Conquest the Third."

15   COOK-SHOPS

(*a*) 1378. (p. 426.) The Ordinance of the Cooks, ordered by the Mayor and Aldermen, as to divers flesh-meat and poultry, as well roasted as baked in pasties:—

"The best roast pig, for 8*d*. Best roast goose, 7*d*. Best roast capon, 6*d*. Best roast hen, 4*d*. Best roast pullet, 2½*d*. Best roast rabbit, 4*d*. Best roast river mallard, 4½*d*. Best roast dunghill mallard, 3½*d*. Best roast teal, 2½*d*. Best roast *snyte*[1], 1½*d*. Five roast larks, 1½*d*. Best roast *wodecok*, 2½*d*. Best roast partridge, 3½*d*. Best roast plover, 2½*d*. Best roast pheasant, 13*d*. Best roast curlew, 6½*d*. Three roast thrushes, 2*d*. Ten roast finches, 1*d*. Best roast heron, 18*d*. Best roast bittern, 20*d*. Three roast pigeons, 2½*d*. Ten eggs, one penny. For the paste, fire, and trouble upon a capon, 1½*d*. For the paste, fire, and trouble upon a goose, 2*d*. The best capon baked in a pasty, 8*d*. The best hen baked in a pasty, 5*d*. The best lamb, roasted, 7*d*."

(*b*) 1379. (p. 438.) "Because that the Pastelers of the City of London have heretofore baked in pasties rabbits, geese, and garbage[2], not befitting, and sometimes stinking, in deceit of the people; and also, have baked beef in pasties, and sold the same for venison, in deceit of the people; therefore, by assent of the four Master Pastelers, and at their prayer, it is ordered and assented to.—

"In the first place,—that no one of the said trade shall bake rabbits in pasties for sale, on pain of paying, the first time, if found guilty thereof, 6*s*. 8*d*., to the use of the Chamber, and of

---

[1] snipe.   [2] Compare Chaucer, *Cook's Tale*, Prologue. (Group A, l. 4346.)

going bodily to prison, at the will of the Mayor; the second time, 13s. 4d. to the use of the Chamber, and of going etc.; and the third time, 20s. to the use of the Chamber, and of going etc.

" Also,—that no one of the said trade shall buy of any cook of Bredestret, or, at the hostels of the great lords, of the cooks of such lords, any garbage from capons, hens, or geese, to bake in a pasty, and sell, under the same penalty.

" Also,—that no one shall bake beef in a pasty for sale, and sell it as venison, under the same penalty.

" Also,—that no one of the said trade shall bake either whole geese in a pasty, halves of geese, or quarters of geese, for sale, on the pain aforesaid."

16   TRADE TRICKS

1387. (p. 498.) Robert Porter, servant of John Gibbe, baker of Stratforde, was brought here, into the Guildhall of London, before Nicholas Extone, Mayor of the said city, John Hadle, and other Aldermen, and questioned for that, when the same Mayor on that day went into Chepe, to make assay there of bread, according to the custom of the City, he, the said Robert, knowing that the bread of his master, in a certain cart there, was not of full weight, took a penny loaf, and in it falsely and fraudulently inserted a piece of iron, weighing about 6s. 8d.[1]; with intent to make the said loaf weigh more, in deceit of the people etc.

Wherefore, enquiry was made of the same Robert, how he would acquit himself thereof; upon which, he acknowledged that he had done in manner aforesaid. And for his said falsity and deceit, it was adjudged that he should be taken from thence to Cornhulle, and be put upon the pillory there, to remain upon the same for one hour of the day, the said loaf and piece of iron being hung about his neck. And precept was given to the Sheriffs, to have the reason for such punishment publicly proclaimed.

---

[1] i.e. about ⅓ of a pound. The pound sterling was not a coin in medieval England, but a weight of metal, coined or otherwise; it is therefore common to find fractions of a pound-weight expressed in shillings and pence.

17   THE PLAIN-SPOKEN BUTCHER

1388. (p. 502.) William Wottone, Alderman of the Ward
of Dovegate, on Saturday, the Eve of Pentecost, in the 11th
year etc., went to the Shambles of St Nicholas in London, and
seeing divers pieces of meat lying for sale at the shambles there
of Richard Bole, butcher, asked the said Richard at what price
he sold the same ; to which he made answer, that 4 shillings
was the price.   Whereupon, the Alderman said that the meat
was too dear ; to which the said Richard made reply ;—" I do
verily believe that the meat is too dear for thee ; who, I suppose, never bought as much meat as that, for thine own use."
And thereupon, the said Richard immediately observing that
William aforesaid was wearing a hood of the Aldermen's
pattern, and so knowing thereby that he was an Alderman, he
further said to him,—" Art thou an Alderman ? " to which the
other answered,—" Yea ; why askest thou ? " whereupon he
said,—" It is a good thing for thee and thy fellows, the Aldermen, to be so wise and wary, who make but light of riding on
the pavement, as some among ye have been doing."

For which words so uttered,...after due consideration had
upon the matter, because that the same words were expressly
uttered in disparagement of our Lord the King, as well as to
the scandal and dishonour of the said Mayor, Sheriffs, and
Aldermen, and all other the officers of the city aforesaid, it
was adjudged that the said Richard should be imprisoned in
Neugate for the next half year ; and that, on his leaving prison,
with his head uncovered, and bare legs and feet, he should carry
in his hand a wax torch, weighing one pound, and lighted, from
Neugate through the Shambles aforesaid, and so straight
through Chepe as far as St Laurence Lane, and through that
lane to the Chapel of the Guildhall, and there make offering of
the same ; unless he should meet with increased favour in the
meantime.

Afterwards however, on the same day, as well at the
instance of the Archbishop of Armagh, Primate of Ireland,
who entreated the Mayor and Aldermen in behalf of the same
Richard, as at the entreaty of the reputable men of the said

trade of butchers, the imprisonment for half a year was remitted unto him ; on the understanding that on the same day he was to be taken back to Neugate aforesaid etc., and there make offering of the same ; which done, he was to be released.

18   TOWN SANITATION

This Act of 1388 (12 Rich. II. c. 13) is said to be the first Urban Sanitary Act in English history, as distinguished from the local ordinances of different boroughs, which occur a little earlier ; the earliest London ordinance is here added in small type. It is suggested, with considerable probability, that the Act was suggested to this Parliament, which sat at Cambridge, by the observed state of the streets in that royal borough. Certain it is that, a few weeks before, the Chancellor of the University had been required by royal writ " to remove from the streets and lanes of the town all swine, and all dirt, dung, filth and branches of trees ; and to cause the streets and lanes to be kept clean for the future." (Cooper, *Annals of Cambridge*, I. 134.)

Cap. XIII.

The punishment of them which cause corruption near a City or great town to corrupt the Air.

Item. For that so much Dung and Filth of the Garbage and Intrails as well of Beasts killed, as of other Corruptions, be cast and put in Ditches, Rivers and other Waters, and also within many other Places, within, about and nigh unto divers Cities, Boroughs, and Towns of the Realm, and the suburbs of them, that the air there is greatly corrupt and infect, and many Maladies and other intolerable Diseases do daily happen, as well to the Inhabitants, and those that are conversant in the said Cities, Boroughs, Towns, and Suburbs, as to other repairing and travelling thither, to the great Annoyance, Damage, and Peril of the Inhabitants, Dwellers, Repairers, and Travellers aforesaid : It is accorded and assented, That Proclamation be made as well in the City of London, as in other Cities, Boroughs, and Towns through the Realm of England, where it shall be needful, as well within Franchises as without, that all they which do cast and lay all such Annoyances, Dung, Garbages, Intrails, and other Ordure in Ditches, Rivers, Waters, and other Places aforesaid, shall cause them utterly to be removed, avoided, and carried away betwixt this and the Feast of St Michael next ensuing after the end of this present Parliament, every one upon Pain to lose and forfeit to our Lord the King xx li.

And that the Mayors and Bailiffs of every such City, Borough, or Town, and also the Bailiffs of Franchises, shall compel the same to be done upon like Pain. And if any feel himself grieved that it be not done in the manner aforesaid, and will thereupon complain him to the Chancellor after the said Feast of S. Michael, he shall have a writ to make him of whom he will complain to come into the Chancery, there to shew why the said Penalty should not be levied of him. And moreover Proclamation shall be made, as well in the City of London, as in other Cities, Boroughs, and Towns as afore, that none, of what condition soever he be, cause to be cast or thrown from henceforth any such Annoyance, Garbage, Dung, Intrails, or any other Ordure into the Ditches, Rivers, Waters, and other Places aforesaid ; and if any do, he shall be called by writ before the Chancellor, at his Suit that will complain ; and if he be found guilty, he shall be punished after the Discretion of the Chancellor.

From Letter-Book A of the City of London (H. T. Riley, *Memorials of London*, p. 20), date 1281.

It is provided and commanded, that no woman of the City shall from henceforth go to market, or in the King's highway, out of her house, with a hood furred with other than lambskin or rabbit-skin, on pain of losing her hood to the use of the Sheriffs ; save only those ladies who wear furred capes, the hoods of which may have such furs as they may think proper. And this because that regratresses[1], nurses and other servants, and women of loose life, bedizen themselves, and wear hoods furred with gros vair[2] and with minever, in guise of good ladies.

And further, that no swine, and no stands[3] or timber lying, shall from henceforth be found in the streets, after Monday next.

[And as to swine so found] let them be killed, and redeemed of him who shall so kill them, for four pence each ; and let the stands and timber be forfeited to the use of the Sheriffs ; hay also, and fodder, belonging to persons, found in West Chepe.

---

[1] Females who sold articles by retail.

[2] *Gros vair*, or simply vair, was a precious fur of alternate backs and bellies of some rodent sewn together ; *menu vair*, or miniver, was ermine.

[3] Boxes placed in the streets, for the sale of wares.

19　CHRISTMASTIDE

1405. (p. 561.) "We do command and charge you...that you do order good and sufficient watch of folks, properly armed and arrayed, to be kept in your Ward every night during this solemn Feast of Christmas; going always, and passing, through all the streets and lanes in your said Ward, in manner as heretofore has been wont to be done. And that no persons shall go in the said city, or in the suburbs thereof, with visors or false faces, on the pain that awaits the same. And that on the outside of every house that is upon the high streets and lanes of the said city, every night during the solemn Feast aforesaid, a lantern shall be hung, with a lighted candle therein, the same to burn so long as it may last; on pain of paying four pence to the Chamber of the Guildhall, every time that default in such light shall be made. And this you are in no manner to omit."

20　HOCK DAYS

These were the 3rd Monday and Tuesday after Easter. See Strutt, *Sports and Pastimes*, Bk IV. ch. iii. § 14.

1409. (p. 571.) "Let proclamation be made, that no person within the City of London, or in the suburbs thereof, of whatsoever estate or condition such person may be, whether man or woman, shall, in any street or lane thereof, take hold or, or constrain, any person, of whatsoever estate or condition he may be, within house or without, for *hokkyng*, on the Monday or Tuesday next, called '*Hokkedayes.*' And that no person shall levy money, or cause it to be levied, for the games called '*foteballe*' and '*cokthresshyng,*' because of marriages that have recently taken place in the said city, or the suburbs thereof; on pain of imprisonment, and of making fine at the discretion of the Mayor and Aldermen."

21　PROFITEERING

1416. (p. 643.) The wife of Hildy, the poulterer, and the wife of John Mede, were committed to prison, for that, against the proclamation of the Mayor, the wife of Hildy sold four *wodecokes* for 20 pence, and the wife of John Mede refused to take 12 pence for two partridges.

On Saturday, the 14th day of November, the wife of Hildy and the wife of Mede were released from prison; and they were enjoined that in future they must sell their fowl according to the assize, on pain of imprisonment; from which without great chastisement they should not escape.

This was a breach of the tariffs fixed by proclamation, for which see Riley, pp. 312, 347. The current tariff was apparently still that of 1343, which priced a woodcock at 3*d.* and a partridge at 5*d.*

22   TOWN AND FOREST

John Stow's *Survey* shows us how much heath and moor and forest could be found just outside medieval London; it is interesting to parallel this by a brief extract from the Leicester records (Ch. Bémont, *Simon de Montfort*, p. 362; Miss Bateson, *Records of Leicester*, I. 43).

1253 A.D.   The jury say, upon oath, that [in 1118] the forest of Leicester was so great and thick and wide that a man could scarce go by the wood-ways for the multitude of dead wood and wind-fallen boughs; and then, by assent and will of the Earl and his council, it was granted that all might fetch dead wood at six cartloads for a penny, and a horseload every week for a half-penny [a year], and a man's load weekly for a farthing.

23   WILD BIRDS AT CHARING CROSS

The Brut, E.E.T.S., 1908, p. 604.

And aftyr that [about 1471], ther bred a Raven on Charyng Crosse at Londen; and never was seen noone brede there before. And aftyr that, cam a gret dethe of Pestilence, that lastyd iij. yer; and peple dyed myhtely in every place, man, woman and chylde; on whois soulys God have mercy! Amen!

24   THROUGH ITALIAN EYES

Italian Relation of England, A.D. 1500 (Camden Soc. 1847), p. 41. The reader has already been cautioned against this writer's picturesque exaggerations: e.g. though the London of 1500 was probably larger than any other four towns in the kingdom, it was far from monopolizing "all the beauty of the island," even from the point of view of an average traveller of that time; nor was it so populous as Florence or Rome, by a long way. But, with all its defects, this *Relation* is of great value.

There are scarcely any towns of importance in the kingdom, excepting these two: Bristol, a seaport to the west, and Boraco (Eboracum) otherwise York, which is on the borders of Scotland; besides London to the south. Eboracum was in ancient times the principal city of the island, and was adorned with many buildings by the Romans, in their elegant style; but, having been sacked and burnt in the reign of King William the Conqueror, she never afterwards could recover her former splendour; so that, at present, all the beauty of this island is confined to London; which, although sixty miles distant from the sea, possesses all the advantages to be desired in a maritime town; being situated on the river Thames, which is very much affected by the tide, for many miles (I do not know the exact number) above it: and London is so much benefited by this ebb and flow of the river, that vessels of 100 tons burden can come up to the city, and ships of any size to within five miles of it; yet the water in this river is fresh for twenty miles below London. Although this city has no buildings in the Italian style, but of timber or brick like the French, the Londoners live comfortably, and, it appears to me, that there are not fewer inhabitants than at Florence or Rome. It abounds with every article of luxury, as well as with the necessaries of life: but the most remarkable thing in London is the wonderful quantity of wrought silver. I do not allude to that in private houses, (though the landlord of the house in which the Milanese ambassador lived, had plate to the amount of 100 crowns), but to the shops of London. In one single street, named the Strand, leading to St Paul's, there are fifty-two goldsmith's shops, so rich and full of silver vessels, great and small, that in all the shops in Milan, Rome, Venice, and Florence put together, I do not think there would be found so many of the magnificence that are to be seen in London. And these vessels are all either salt cellars, or drinking cups, or basins to hold water for the hands; for they eat off that fine tin, which is little inferior to silver (pewter). These great riches of London are not occasioned by its inhabitants being noblemen or gentlemen; being all, on the contrary, persons of low degree, and artificers who have congregated there from all parts of the island, and from Flanders, and from every other place. No one can be mayor or alderman of London, who has not been an apprentice in his youth; that is, who has not passed the seven or nine years in that hard service described before. Still, the citizens of London are thought quite as highly of there, as the Venetian gentlemen are at Venice, as I think your Magnificence may have perceived. The city is divided into several wards, each of which has six officers; but superior to these, are twenty-four gentlemen who they call aldermen, which in their language signifies old or experienced men; and, of these aldermen, one is elected every year by themselves, to be a magistrate named the mayor, who is in no less estimation with the Londoners, than the person of our most serene lord (the Doge) is with us, or than the Gonfaloniero at Florence; and the day on which he enters upon his office, he is obliged to give a sumptuous entertainment to all the principal people in London, as well as to foreigners of distinction; and I, being one of the guests, together with your Magnificence, carefully observed every room and hall, and the court, where the company were all seated, and was of opinion that there must have been 1000 or more persons at table. This dinner lasted four hours or more; but it is true that the dishes were not served with that assiduity and frequency that is the custom with us in Italy; there being long pauses between each course, the company conversing the while. A no less magnificent banquet is given when two other officers named *sheriffs* are appointed; to which I went, being anxious to see every thing well; your Magnificence also was invited, but did not go in consequence of the invitation having come from the Lord Privy Seal. At this feast, I observed the infinite profusion of victuals, and of plate, which was for the most part gilt; and amongst other things, I noticed how punctiliously they sat in their order, and the extraordinary silence of every one, insomuch that I could have imagined it one of those public repasts of the Lacedemonians that I have read of.

SECTION VIII

RICH AND POOR

The medieval Church often succeeded admirably in patriarchal government; but, in the later Middle Ages, two defects rendered her incapable of solving the social problem in any true sense. First, she justified servitude, both in theory and in practice. St Gregory the Great, in a letter often quoted by apologists (lib. VI. ep. 2), wrote in words of lofty generosity concerning two slaves whom he was setting free; but we must remember also that Gregory's papal estates were tilled by thousands of others whom he never attempted to liberate; and in a later letter (lib. IX. ep. 102) we find him actually exerting himself to recover a slave of his own brother, who had escaped with his wife and child and small belongings. St Thomas Aquinas expressly defends servitude as economically expedient (*Summa Theol.* I*2*ᵃᵉ, quaest. 94. art. 5, iii.). Servitude was recognised and enforced by Canon Law; e.g. Gratian, *Decretum*, Causa X. Quaest. ii. c. 3 and Causa XII. Q. ii. c. 39, in which latter case bishops are severely condemned for freeing serfs of the Church. For churchmen, especially monks, were always among the richest holders of serfs; when Theodore of Tarsus came to the Archbishop of Canterbury, he noted that whereas "Greek monks keep no serfs, Roman monks possess them" (*Poenitentiale*, cap. viii.; Migne, *P.L.* vol. XCIX. col. 931 C). Nor were churchmen more willing than others to free their bondmen, except on business terms; see, for instance, Fournier's paper in *Revue Historique*, vol. XXI. (1883). When Cardinal Gasquet claims that the English episcopal registers contain many records of the liberation of serfs, he is apparently copying a curious blunder of Dr Cutts, who mistook dispensations granted to illegitimates (*de defectu natalium*) for servile manumissions. Actual manumissions are very rare in the registers.

Secondly, the medieval Church put itself in an almost equally difficult position by its condemnation of usury; a condemnation which the Roman See has never legally revoked, though since 1830 confessors have been officially warned not to trouble penitents on this subject in the confessional. Capitalism and banking on a large scale developed long before the Reformation; already St Thomas Aquinas drew fine but important distinctions—not officially sanctioned—between lawful and unlawful interest for capital; and Canonists in the great Italian and German cities tried to legalize interest still further; but there were no pronouncements that could be called authoritative, and the gulf between commercial and religious thought necessarily widened. While the open usurer felt that "he might as well be hanged for a horse as a sheep," there grew up a whole system of fictitious bargains which were really covert usury, under the name chevisance—see Chaucer, Gower and *Piers Plowman*. It seems better, therefore, to begin this section with a few extracts illustrating these two points.

SERVITUDE

1   THE ORTHODOX THEORY OF BONDAGE

St Anselm, *De Conceptu Virginali*, cap. xxviii. (*Opera*, ed. Gerberon, 1721, p. 106). This is quoted with approval by St Bonaventura in a discussion on the theory of servitude (*In Sententias*, Lib. II. Dist. xxxii. Art. 3. q. 2, ed. Quaracchi, vol. III. p. 773 *a*).

There are some whose minds refuse to accept the teaching that [unbaptized] infants must be damned for the sole unrighteousness whereof I have spoken [i.e. original sin].... Yet even this judgment of God, whereby infants are damned, differeth much from the judgment of man. For if any man and his wife, promoted by no merit of their own but by grace alone, commit in partnership a grievous and inexcusable fault, for which they are justly degraded and reduced to servitude, who would assert that their children whom they beget after their condemnation should not be subject to the same servitude, but rather should be restored of grace to the goods which their parents have justly lost?

2   THE UNORTHODOX THEORY

The only great Schoolman, so far as I know, who disapproved on principle of hereditary bondage is John Wyclif (*De Civili Dominio*, lib. I. c. xxxiv., Wyclif Soc. 1885, p. 240). It must be noted, however, that an English tract attributed to him, written after the Peasants' Revolt, expressly denies the right of serfs to rebel against their lords. (*English Works*, E.E.T.S., 1880, p. 227.)

We must further question whether the civil laws enforcing hereditary servitude are conformable to the law of Christ; and it would seem that they are not: for it is written, "The son shall not bear the iniquity of the father"...therefore this law of hereditary servitude savoureth of injustice. Moreover, as we have proved in the foregoing chapter, there could be no hereditary servitude unless a father might lawfully sell his own offspring; which he cannot; therefore such servitude doth not proceed as a matter of course from descent by blood[1]. [Certain unequal bargains are stigmatized by the law as unjust]; but how much greater is the injustice when that person is sold for a vile price, for whose redemption Christ was content to give His life? nor doth it avail to contend that the child born of a serf is naturally a serf from his cradle; for that is common to all mankind in our fallen state....

They argue against us: "A man is lord of his whole body, and therefore of his offspring, which is part of his body."... Again: "Many holy lords of temporal possessions have made use of hereditary servitude; therefore it is lawful."...(p. 247) But it is their lust of dominion; it is their neglect of consulting God's law; it is the blindness of their belief in the principle of the state—such are the causes which persuade these mighty ones that it is as just and natural for their whole tribe of serfs to be in bondage to them and theirs, by the law of the state, as it is natural for fire to burn.

3 THE SERF'S LEGAL STATUS

Glanvill, *De Legibus Angliae*, Lib. v. c. 5, quoted in W. Stubbs's *Select Charters*, 1890, p. 162. Glanvill, who wrote about 1181, was one of Henry II.'s greatest ministers: his work is the earliest treatise on English law. The harshness of this theory, however, was considerably modified in practice as time went on. "The serf's condition seems better described as unprotectedness than as rightlessness," Pollock and Maitland, *Hist. of Eng. Law*, 1898, vol. I. p. 417.

This must be noted, that no man who is in serfdom can buy his liberty with his own money; for, even if he had paid the price, he might be recalled to villenage by his lord ac-

---

[1] Contrast this with the orthodox scholastic view, as expressed by St Bonaventura, in which the theologians accepted and justified the principles of Roman Civil Law: "We must say that children must not and cannot be sold [into serfdom] without any fault of their own, except under necessity of poverty or famine, in which case the mother also must consent....That in time of famine or necessity they may be so sold, is proved by II. Esdras v. 5 'Behold, we bring into bondage our sons and our daughters, etc.'...and by the Code of Justinian, c. IV. tit. 43." (Bonaventura *In Sent*. l. IV. dist. xxxvi. dub. 2, 3.)

cording to the law and custom of this land; for all the chattels of all serfs are understood to be so far within the power of his lord, that he cannot redeem himself from his lord by any money of his own....

And this also, that a man may free his serf, so far as regards his own person or his own heirs, but not as regards others. For if any serf thus freed were brought into court to make suit against any other man, or to make any law of the land, then he might justly be removed, if his former state of serfdom were objected and proved against him; and this would be so, even though the man thus freed from villenage had been dubbed a knight.

Item, if any serf shall have dwelt unclaimed for a whole year and a day in any chartered town, so that he hath been received into the community or gild of that town as a citizen, then that single fact shall free him from villenage.

4 THE SERVANT'S LOT

Trevisa, *Bartholomew*, Lib. VI. cc. 12 and 15.

A servaunt woman is ordeyned [for] to lerne the wyves rule and is put to offyce and werke of traveylle, toylynge and slubberynge[1]. And is fedde with grosse mete and symple, and is clothed with clothes and kepte lowe under the yoeke of thraldom and of servage; and, if she conceyve a chylde, it is thralle or it be borne, and is taken frome the mothers wombe to servage. Also if a servynge woman be of bonde condicion she is not suffred to take a husbonde at her owne wylle; and he that weddyth her, if he be free afore, he is made bonde after the contracte. A bonde servaunt woman is bought and solde lyke a beeste[2]. And if a bonde servaunt man or woman

---

[1] drudging at dirty work.

[2] The author's words are not applicable in their most invidious sense to 13th century England, where actual slavery no longer existed, and the villein, though sold with the land, could seldom be the victim of a separate sale. On the Continent, heathen slaves were frequently bought all through the Middle Ages; and conditions had long since been laid down in Canon Law which admitted the legality of such transactions (Gratian, *Decretum*, Pars I. Dist. liv. cc. 13–18). Nor did an English freeman become bond by marriage with a serf, though Canon Law declared his issue to be unfree and English Civil Law often took the same invidious view. (Pollock and Maitland, *l.c.* pp. 414, 422–3.)

be made free, and afterwarde be unkynde[1], he shall be callyd
and brought again into charge of bondage and of thraldom.
Also a bonde servaunt sufferith many wronges, and is bete
with roddes, and constreyned and holde lowe with diverse and
contrarye charges and travayles amonges wretchydnes and
woo. Oneth[2] he is suffered to reste or to take brethe. And
therefore amonge all wretchydnesse and woo the condicion of
bondage and thraldom is moost wretchid, as sayth Rabanus
expownynge this worde, Jher. ix. ye shall serve strange
goddys, that shal not suffre you to reste day ne nyghte. It is
one proprete of bonde servynge women, and of them that be
of bonde condition, to grudge and to be rebell and unbouxom[3]
to theyr lordes and ladyes, as saieth Rabanus. And whan they
ben not holde lowe with drede, theyr hartes swelle, and wax
stoute and proude ayenst the commaundementes of theyr sover-
aynes; as it farid of[4] Agar, a woman of Egypt, servaunt of
Sarra; for whan she sawe that she had conceyved and was
with chylde, she dispysed her owne lady, Gen. xvi. and wolde
not amende her, but than her lady putte her to be scourged
and beten. And so it is wrytte that Sarra chastysyd her, and
bete her, etc. Drede makyth bonde men and women meke
and lowe, and goodly love makyth theym prowde and stoute,
and dyspiteous, as it is sayd there. And it is written: He
that nourysshyth his servaunte delycatly, shal finde hym rebel
at th'ende....A servant hyghte *servus* in latyne, and hath that
name of *servare* to kepe: for sometyme prisoners were kepte
eyther to be byheded, or to be raunsomed as sayth Isydore.
Or els they have that name of *servire* to serve: for they be put
to vyle servyce of offyce, that ben not covenable to lordes, nor
for theyr chyldren. And Isidore sayth, that there bene iii
maner of servantes: Some servantes ben bonde and bore in
bondage, and suche have many peynes by lawe, for they may
not selle nor geve away theyr owne good and cattell, nother
make contractes, nother take office of dignitie, nother bere
witness without leve of their lordis. Wherfore, though they
ben not in chyldhode, they ben ofte punyshed with peynes of
chyldehode. Other servauntes there be that hyght Empticii,

[1] illbehaved.   [2] scarcely.   [3] disobedient.   [4] fared with.

the whiche, beinge taken with straungers and aliens and with
ennemyes, bene boughte and solde and holde[n] lowe under the
yocke of thraldom. The thyrde maner of servantes ben bounde
freely by theyr owne good will, and serve for rewarde and for
hyre. And these comynly bene called Famuli.

5   MONASTIC SERFS

Dugdale-Caley, *Monasticon*, vol. III. p. 26.

I Gunyora de la Mare, in my lawful widowhood, have given
to the monks [of Eynsham] the half-hide of land in Eston
which Roger the Palmer of Eston held of me, together with
the same Roger and all his brood[1], at the burial of Geoffrey
of Elfeistone my late husband [in the Abbey]....

I William of Dives have given to the monks of Eynsham
Richard Rowland of Wealde, who was my born serf, with all
his brood.

6   THE SERF AT THE CONFESSIONAL

The *Pupilla Oculi* is one of the most popular of the medieval parsons'
handbooks. It was written by John de Burgo, Chancellor of Cambridge
University in 1385, and a strong anti-Wycliffite, to instruct the clergy in
the duties of their profession. I translate here from Part v. c. ix. § F.

Let peasants and serfs be questioned [in the confessional]
whether they have defrauded by withholding or diminishing
their tithes, either of produce or of personal labour : whether
they have failed in reverence to their lords, or have not provided
for them in their necessity : whether they have withheld their
bounden service to their lords : whether they have unjustly
procured the help of other great men against their lords, or in
any way have been rebellious to the same : whether they have
held markets, or done any servile work, on holy days, against
the precept of the Church :...whether they have encroached
on their neighbours' ground with plough or with cattle. Moreover both peasants and serfs and artisans commonly sin in
this : that they will labour fervently before a man's face, but

---

[1] *sequela,* a term used for the litter of a domestic animal or of a serf. Cf.
I. Leadam's *Star Chamber,* p. 119, note 7.

feebly and remissly behind his back; and then, if they be rebuked, they will murmur or withdraw from the work or labour all the worse.

USURY

This very complicated subject is treated at length, and with great sympathy, by Sir William Ashley in his *Economic History*, 3rd ed. vol. I., Pt I. pp. 195 ff. and Pt II. pp. 395 ff. He there defends the medieval Church against many unjust reproaches, but leaves us still regretting that the Popes and the hierarchy, who had so much power, showed an imperfect appreciation of the inevitable and legitimate tendencies of finance. The Papal theory of usury, though undoubtedly not only benevolent but (as Sir William Ashley has shown) in many ways beneficent during the earlier times, was built up piecemeal. The authorities, instead of anticipating practical difficulties, generally stepped in officially only when the trend of actual events had practically decided the debate. Meanwhile business men were subject to Canon Law regulations which were often very difficult to keep; and, as the 14th century professor Benvenuto da Imola puts it, "he who practiseth usury goeth to hell, and he who practiseth it not tendeth to destitution" (*Comentum Super Dantis Comoediam*, ed. Lacaita 1887, vol. I. p. 579). The most promising solution of the problem from the ecclesiastical and charitable point of view—the establishment of *Montes Pietatis*, or lending-banks for the poor—was due to private initiative; it met with strong opposition from one theological faction, and was not officially approved by the papacy until half a century had elapsed. (See Ashley, *l.c.* II. 449–51.) Moreover the Popes, as well by their own financial operations as by their practice of demanding enormous sums from prelates on their appointment, rendered the usurer a necessary, though abhorred, member of society. The following extracts give first the point of view of an able contemporary historian, and secondly the actual experience of one of our best medieval Archbishops. Usurers were very commonly called *Caursini*, or *Lombards*, because Cahors and other towns in South France vied with those of North Italy in this practice.

7   USURERS IN ENGLAND

Matthew Paris, *Chron. Major.*, R. S., vol. III. p. 328.

In these days [A.D. 1235] the abominable plague of Caursins raged so fiercely that there was scarce any man in all England, especially among the prelates, who was not entangled in their nets. The King himself also was in debt to them for an incalculable amount. They circumvented the indigent in their necessities, cloaking their usury under the pretence of trade, and feigning not to know that whatsoever payment is added to the principal is usury, under whatsoever name it be called...That same year Roger, Bishop of London, a learned and religious man, when he saw how these Caursins practised their usury publicly and unabashed, and led a most unclean life, and harried Religious folk with divers injustices, cunningly amassing money and compelling many folk under their yoke, he was moved to wrath. Then, kindled with righteous zeal, he admonished them all, as schismatics, to cease from these enormities as they loved the salvation of their own souls, and to do penance for the past. They for their part scorned his words with mockery and derision and threats; wherefore the Bishop girded on his weapons of spiritual justice and involved them all under a general anathema; moreover, he strictly and expressly ordered that all such should be removed from the city of London, which had hitherto been free from this plague, lest his diocese should be infected therewith. But the usurers were proud and puffed-up, as men who trusted in the Pope's protection; and indeed, without difficulty or delay, they obtained their own will at the Court of Rome. The Bishop— an old man, weak and failing in health—was peremptorily cited to cross the sea and appear at Rome before certain judges, friends of the Caursins, whom they themselves had chosen at their will, and to answer for the injury done to the Pope's merchants. The Bishop, willing rather to follow Shem in covering his father's shame than to discover it with Ham, appeased the tumult by peaceful methods, dissembling and passing on. For he commended this arduous cause to his patron St Paul, who had himself written in defence of the strict faith and righteousness "Though an angel from heaven preach the contrary of these things, let him be accursed."

Ibid. v. 405, A.D. 1253. (Grosseteste's complaints on his deathbed against the then Pope, Innocent IV.)

Moreover, though many other Popes have afflicted the Church, this one hath oppressed her with a more grievous servitude, and hath multiplied injustices. For the Caursins are manifest usurers; and they have been cast forth from

France (for this plague was then unknown in England) by
holy fathers and teachers whom we have seen and known
personally—by that most excellent preacher in France, the
Abbot of Fly, Master Jacques de Vitry, archbishop Stephen
of Canterbury when he was in exile, and Master Robert de
Courçon. Notwithstanding, this Pope hath raised them up
and protected them in their high place ; and, if any man speak
against them, he is wearied with loss and labour, as we have
seen in the case of Bishop Roger of London. The whole
world knoweth that usury is held in detestation in the Old
and New Testament, and is forbidden by God. Yet now the
lord Pope's merchants or money changers practise their usury
publicly in London, to the disgust of the Jews. They plot
divers and grievous machinations against men of Holy Church,
and especially Religious, compelling men under pressure of
penury to lie, and to append their signs-manual to false deeds[1];
which is as it were to commit idolatry and to renounce Truth,
that is, God. For instance, I borrow a hundred marks for a
hundred pounds [which I am to pay at the end of the term] ;
I am compelled to execute and sign a deed wherein I confess
that I have received a loan of a hundred pounds, which I will
repay at the end of the year. And if, by chance, thou wilt
pay the Papal usurer the principal of the money, which thou
hast now in possession, within a month or less [of the day of
borrowing], he will not accept it unless thou pay him the whole
hundred pounds. This is worse than a Jew's conditions ; for
the Jew will receive the principal courteously whensoever thou
shalt return it, with only so much interest as is proportionate
to the time for which thou hast had it in hand[2].

---

[1] Usurious transactions were carried on under cloak of legal fictions—fictitious
sales, etc.—to save the letter of the law.

[2] For this particular usurer's trick see Matthew Paris III. 331 and Ashley
(*l.c.* I. 200), who points out that this odious contrast between Papal and Jewish
usurers is literally true.

8   AN ARCHBISHOP EXCOMMUNICATED

Registrum Epistolarum J. Peckham, R. S., 1882, vol. I. p. 18.   July 11, 1279.   Abp Peckham to Pope Nicholas III.

To the most holy father and lord in Christ Nicholas, by divine providence supreme pontiff of the holy Roman Church, his poor little brother John, priest of Canterbury, sendeth greeting, falling down with all reverence and kissing his holy feet....There hath lately reached me a letter of execution, horrible to see and terrible to hear, whereof the final purport is this : that unless, within a month from the feast of Michaelmas next coming, I pay fully and completely to the merchants of Lucca, from whom I borrowed [it] at the Court of Rome, the sum of four thousand marks[1], I shall be forthwith involved in the sentence of excommunication, and shall be denounced as excommunicate in my own and other cathedral churches, with bell, book and candle, on every Sunday and holy-day... And this though, according to the contract which I signed, I might have secured freedom to myself and my church for an indefinite time, so long as I paid the damages and interest to the aforesaid merchants, in consideration of the losses they would incur by my delay....Therefore, most holy Father, may it please your most merciful Holiness to reach me the right hand of succour and to revoke this cruel letter...otherwise, I see no other refuge but two.   I may, indeed, leave this prelacy committed to me, disperse my household or flock, and depart as an exile into some distant land, where I may lurk alone in some monastery and bear this anathema with humility until, as God shall give occasion, I shall have succeeded in satisfying the aforesaid merchants from the revenues of my see, as they can be raised from time to time.   Or, again, I may borrow further from these merchants, and, as a borrower, fawn upon them and bear with patience their base speech (though, by your holiness's special mandate, it would be my duty to take strong measures against such lenders) since in these days no other men can be found in England who have money enough; nor, in the face of the present change and clipping of coinage, could I borrow elsewhere [than from these merchants of Lucca].

[1] Equivalent to £40,000 or more in modern currency.

9   THE CORROSION OF USURY

An Alphabet of Tales, E.E.T.S., 1904, p. 181 (Tale CCLX.).

Cesarius tellis how some tyme ther was ane usurer that lent a certayn of mony unto a selerer of the Ceustus[1] ordur ; and he selid it and layd it in a kyste[2] besyde a certan money of ther awn. So afterward this usurar askid it agayn ; and the monke went unto the kiste, and he fand nowder ther awn money nor itt. And he lukid and saw [th]at no bodie had tuchid the lokk bod[3] hym selfe, and the selis of the sakettis[4] safe, [th]at he mot know no suspecion of thifte. Than he conseyvid in his mynd that the mony of the usuraris had devowrid and distroyed the money of ther monasterie.

10   A MONT DE PIÉTÉ

W. H. Bliss, *Calendar of Papal Letters*, vol. I. 1893, p. 267 (1251 A.D.). Though these charitable banks were never systematized here as on the Continent, yet this extract testifies to an enterprise of the kind in England, which seems gradually to have died out. College and University "Chests," which did the same work on a small scale, were as common in England as elsewhere : see Section II., no. 20, and Rashdall, *Universities of Europe* II. 350 and 660 *note*.

[Papal] confirmation to the bishops of Bath and Wells and Salisbury of the ordinance by which many burgesses of cities and places in England have set aside a certain sum of money to be lent to the poor without interest, by trustworthy persons, that they may not be oppressed or devoured by usury ; with mandate to the same not to allow any interference with the said ordinance.

11   FINES AND BRIBES

A small selection from typical entries chosen from manor-rolls by the late Prof. Rogers will show, more plainly than any other document of the kind, how heavily the serfs and the lower middle classes had to pay for liberties which seem to us so natural. They will explain the attitude of thinking men towards social reform, from *Piers Plowman* to Fortescue and Sir Thomas More (J. E. T. Rogers, *Hist. Ag. and Prices*, vol. II. 1866, pp. 608 ff.).

CAMBRIDGE. 1325. Expenses of 6 men going about the country and to London to seek stolen oxen, for 6 days, 1ˢ 4ᵈ ;

---

[1] Cellarer of the Cistercian.   [2] chest.   [3] but.   [4] money-sacks.

given to the King's servants, lest they should do greater damage, 8ᵈ.

1328. To the King's servants, that they should not carry corn away, 2ˢ.

1331. To the Earl of Lancaster, to have his succour, 5ˢ.

1333. To the King's servants, that they should not carry away horses and carts, 1ˢ.

1338. To Sir William de Wallingford taking corn and other victuals for the lord King, that he might not carry off 7 quarters of wheat and 14 quarters of oats and other corn which he had seized, 7ˢ 2ᵈ.

1341. To the King's servants taking beasts to carry fish from Swavesey to London, that they might not take the beasts on our manor, 2ˢ.

1347. To the servants of Lionel of Antwerp, the King's son[1], that they might not seize our corn, 2ˢ 1ᵈ.

GAMLINGAY. 1281. To the Lord Robert Fitzwalter, a serf pays for licence to give his own daughter in marriage, 10 shillings.

1322. For a groom [*garcio*] carrying a letter to Oxford to ask counsel of the Masters about the taking of corn for the King's use, 6ᵈ.

1334. To the King's bailiff, that he should not take away corn to the Lord King, 3ˢ 4ᵈ.

1344. To divers persons of the said panel [i.e. jury] who came on the part of the lords, that they might be inclined to the will of the guardian [of the manor], and on his side, 17ˢ 4ᵈ.

WOBRIDESTON. 1335. William at Water pays for licence to promote his younger son William to holy orders, 10ˢ; Richard Kynne for licence of his daughter's marriage, 6ᵈ.

1336. Thomas Att Hull fines in 6ˢ 8ᵈ, that he may be ordained to any order in the church and depart from his lord and live wheresoever he will without being claimed by his lord[2].

---

[1] i.e. Chaucer's first royal patron.

[2] The rigour of the law of redemption, as stated by Glanvill (extract 3 here above), is by this time much relaxed.

1338. Margery Jordan fines for licence of marriage, 1ˢ.

1342. William Atte Hull for privilege to marry his daughter pays 2ˢ.

1359. Edith at Sherde, for licence to marry and quit the manor, 5ˢ.

STOCKTON. 1286. Robert Palmer married against the Bailiff's licence ; fine 1ˢ 6ᵈ.

12   PRIESTS OF PREY

As tithes were a natural and constant source of friction between priests and people, so also was the mortuary system, which will be sufficiently intelligible from the following extract, but which is dealt with at greater length in the 8th of my *Medieval Studies.*

Lyndwood's *Provinciale,* 1679, p. 19. (Statute of Abp Langham, in synod, for the diocese of Canterbury.)

Seeing that, by occasion of this statute, quarrels too frequently [*frequentius*] arise, therefore we have thought good to declare and interpret it as follows in this synod : that if a man die leaving among his goods three or more of any kind of beast, the best shall be reserved to him who may lawfully claim it [as a heriot[1]]. The second best beast must then be set aside, without any fraud, sleight or contradiction whatsoever, for the church wherein he was wont to receive the sacrament while he yet lived ; and it must be delivered over to that his church, after his death, for the good of his soul, as an indemnity for the withholding of personal tithes and oblations. If, however, the deceased leave only two beasts, then let the Church, in her mercy, remit every sort of exaction under this name of mortuary. But if the woman die before her husband, let him not be compelled to pay a mortuary. If, however, a widow live a year after her husband, ruling her family in the same house, she shall be liable to a mortuary according to the above form. But by this interpretation we will not in any way prejudice the laudable custom of mortuaries observed in times past in our pro-

---

[1] As a rule, the Lord of the Manor could claim the deceased man's best beast ; this privilege of the lay lord is also called *mortuary* sometimes, but more commonly *heriot.*

vince; nay, whether the party deceased have possessed this
number of beasts or not—or, again, whether the man or wife
die sooner or later—let the Church custom of payment of
mortuary be kept. And we decree that all recalcitrants be
compelled by excommunication through the Ordinaries.

Lyndwood's notes.

Of any kind, whether of horses, bulls, oxen, cows, sheep, swine, or
any other such. Therefore, to bring him under this debt of mortuary,
it sufficeth that there should be three beasts of the same kind, as three
horses or cows; or again that there should be two of the same kind, as
two horses, and a third of another kind, as a cow. And the same will
hold good if they be three beasts of diverse kinds, as one horse, one ox,
and one sheep.

Beasts.... Do the words here written apply to animals of all sorts,
whether tame or wild? It would seem that we must say *yes,* especially of
those which we are able to govern....Wherefore it would seem that, if the
deceased man had three or more beasts, whether four-footed beasts or fowls
or fishes, this statute will take effect....Yet we must add that this general
term *beasts* should be restricted by what is customarily done; wherefore
we must take it only of four-footed beasts fit for food (as swine and sheep
and the like) or proper for man's use, as horses, oxen, asses and the like.

Fraud...: as for example, a man sick of his last sickness, and pos-
sessing three or more beasts, alienates all his beasts without any necessity :
here is a presumption of fraud.

After his death. What then if the father of the family, while yet
alive, but taken with the sickness whereof he died, should sell any of his
beasts through necessity and as a relief to his poverty or indigence, so
that after his death there remaineth nought wherefrom the mortuary can
be paid, what is the Church to do? We must say, I think, that if such
alienation be made without fraud or guile, then the Church will have
nothing.

For the good of his soul, which consisteth in the remission of sins;
which are not remitted unless restitution be made.

Withholding: supply '*in ignorance*'; for, if he shall have knowingly
and wilfully withheld personal tithes or oblations due to the Church, and
these tithes or oblations were in great quantity, beyond the value of his
second beast, then it would be no just compensation.

In her mercy.... For it would be very rigorous, when there are but
two beasts, and one is perchance due to the lord of the manor or some
other man, by law or custom, that the Church should take the second best
beast, leaving nothing to the widow or children; especially if they be poor
and needy.

Laudable custom, whereunto even the unwilling may be compelled to
conform....Hostiensis giveth as example the custom of Venice, where at
a man's death the tenth of all his movable goods is paid to the Church;
and in Brittany the third part so paid. And we may call *laudable customs*

all such as are not against faith or morals, and which are pious to God and the Church....Wherefore in some places it is customary that the Church should have the dead man's bed or his garments[1].

13   THE POOR LAW ANTICIPATED

Roger Bacon, *Opus Majus*, ed. Bridges, II. 251.

Therefore, as saith Avicenna, it behoves the Prince to forbid idleness and sloth on the part of the people. Those, therefore, who cannot be disciplined by compulsion, should be expelled from the state, unless the cause of their idleness be sickness or old age; for which cases a house should be founded wherein such may live, and a guardian should be deputed for them. For the state should possess a certain common and public fund composed partly from the law of contracts, partly from pecuniary amercements, partly from the estates or confiscations of rebels, and partly from other sources; and this fund should be devoted partly to such as are hindered of their livelihood by sickness or age, partly to doctors of medicine and law, and partly to common uses.

14   THE FIRST STATUTES OF LABOURERS

Translations and summaries from *Statutes of the Realm*, 1735, p. 234. These documents make Wat Tyler's revolt, on the one hand, and the attitude of *Piers Plowman* towards the social problem on the other, immediately intelligible.

(*a*) Edward by the Grace of God, etc. to the Reverend Father in Christ, William, by the same Grace Archbishop of Canterbury, Primate of all England, Greeting. Because a great part of the People, and especially of Workmen and Servants, late died of the Pestilence, and many (seeing the necessity of Masters, and great Scarcity of Servants) will not serve unless they may receive excessive Wages; and some [are] rather willing to beg in Idleness than by Labour to get their Living; We, considering the grievous Discommodity, which of the lack

[1] A concrete instance of this kind from a contemporary document is translated in my *Medieval Garner*, p. 593. Again, the Prior of Walsingham, as Rector of the parish church, "had a mortuary of every parishioner in Walsingham, of the second best animal, and if there was but one, then of that." Blomefield's *Norfolk*, 1810, vol. IX. p. 277.

especially of Ploughmen and such Labourers may hereafter come, have upon Deliberation and Treaty with the Prelates and the Nobles, and Learned Men assisting us, of their mutual Counsel ordained :

CAP. I.

Every Person able in Body under the Age of Sixty Years, not having [wherewith] to live, being required shall be bound to serve him that doth require him, or else committed to the Gaol, until he find Surety to serve.

CAP. II.

If a Workman or Servant depart from service before the time agreed upon, he shall be imprisoned.

CAP. III.

The old Wages, and no more, shall be given to Servants.

CAP. IV.

If the Lord of a Town or Manor do offend against this Statute in any point, he shall forfeit the treble Value.

CAP. V.

If any Artificer or Workman take more Wages than were wont to be paid, he shall be committed to the Gaol.

CAP. VI.

Victuals shall be sold at reasonable Prices.

CAP. VII.

No person shall give anything to a Begger, that is able to labour.

CAP. VIII.

He that taketh more Wages than is accustomably given, shall pay the surplusage to the Town where he dwelleth, towards a Payment to the King of a Tenth and Fifteenth granted to him.

(*b*) A Statute of Labourers, made Anno 25 Edw. III. Stat. I. and A.D. 1350.

Whereas late against the Malice of Servants, which were idle, and not willing to serve after the Pestilence, without taking excessive Wages, it was ordained by our Lord the King, and by assent of the Prelates, Earls, Barons, and other of his Council, that such manner of Servants, as well Men as Women, shall be bound to serve, receiving [such] Salary and Wages [as were] accustomed in the Places where they ought to serve, in the Twentieth Year of the reign of the King that now is, or five or six Years before; and that the same Servants refusing to serve in such manner should be punished by Imprisonment of their Bodies, as in the said Statute is more plainly contained ; Whereupon Commissions were made to divers People in every County to enquire and punish all them which offend against the same. And now for as much as it is given to the King to understand in this present Parliament, by the Petition of the Commonalty, that the said Servants, having no regard to the said Ordinance, but to their Ease and singular Covetise, do withdraw themselves to serve Great Men and other, unless they have Livery and Wages to the double or treble of that they were wont to take the said Twentith Year, and before, to the great Damage of the Great Men, and impoverishing of all the said Commonalty, whereof the said Commonalty prayeth Remedy ; Wherefore in the same Parliament, by the Assent of the said Prelates, Earls, Barons and other Great Men of the same Commonalty there assembled, to refrain the Malice of the said Servants, be ordained and established the things under-written :

CAP. I.
The Year and Day Wages of Servants and Labourers in Husbandry.

CAP. II.
How much shall be given for Threshing all sorts of Corn by the Quarter.

CAP. III.
The several Wages of several sorts of Artificers and Labourers.

CAP. IV.
Shoes and Boots shall be sold as they were the 20th Year of King Edward the Third.

Artificers sworn to use their crafts as they did in the 20th Year of the same King.

CAP. V.
The several Punishments of several Persons offending against this Statute.

CAP. VI.
[No] Sheriffs, Constables, Bailiffs, Gaolers, nor other Officers, shall exact anything of the same Servants.

CAP. VII.

The Justices shall hold their Sessions four times a Year, and at all times needful.

Servants which flee from one Country to another, shall be committed to Prison.

15   THE RISING TIDE

J. Gower, *Mirour de l'Omme*, ll. 26, 437 ff.   Gower was of the upper middle class, but far from a hide-bound conservative. He was quite willing to air democratic opinions so long as they were not too definitely interpreted in practice ; cf. ll. 17, 333 ff., where he combats the exclusive ideas of high-born ladies by reminding them that Eve had no chance of marrying a gentleman. The present passage is all the more interesting because it was written before Wat Tyler's revolt—probably about 1375.

The world goeth fast from bad to worse, when shepherd and cowherd for their part demand more for their labour than the master-bailiff was wont to take in days gone by. Labour is now at so high a price that he who will order his business aright must pay five or six shillings now for what cost two in former times. Labourers of old were not wont to eat of wheaten bread ; their meat was of beans or coarser corn, and their drink of water alone. Cheese and milk were a feast to them, and rarely ate they of other dainties ; their dress was of hodden grey ; then was the world ordered aright for folk of this sort....

Three things, all of the same sort, are merciless when they get the upper hand ; a water-flood, a wasting fire, and the common multitude of small folk. For these will never be checked by reason or discipline ; and therefore, to speak in brief, the present world is so troubled by them that it is well to set a remedy thereunto. Ha! age of ours, whither turnest thou ? for the poor and small folk, who should cleave to their labour, demand to be better fed than their masters. Moreover, they bedeck themselves in fine colours and fine attire, whereas (were it not for their pride and their privy conspiracies) they would be clad in sackcloth as of old....Ha! age of ours, I know not what to say ; but of all the estates that I see, from the highest to the lowest, each decayeth in its own degree. Poor man or lord, all alike are full of vanity ; I see the poor folk more haughty than their lords ; each draweth whither he pleaseth.

16   INSTIGATIONS TO REVOLT

Sir E. Dudley, *Tree of the Commonwealth*, ed. 1859, p. 51.

The name of the second messenger [of the Devil] is Arro-gancye.   His nature and propertie is to entice to enable yourself to such thinges as nothing beseemeth, or to doe such thinges as you can nothing skill on.   He will shewe you that you be made of the same moulde and metall that the gentiles be made of.   Whie then should they sporte and plaie, and you labour and tyll?   He will tell you also that at your birthes and at your deathes your riches is indifferent.   Why should they have soe much of the prosperitie and treasour of this world, and ye soe little?   Besides that, he will tell you that ye be the children and right inheritours to Adam, as well as they.   Whie should they have this great honour, royall castells and mannors with soe much landes and possessions, and you but poore tenementes and cotages?   He will shewe you also whie that Christ bought as derely you as them, and with one man-ner of price, which was his precious blood.   Whie then should you be of soe poore estate, and they of soe hie degree?   Or whie should you doe them soe much honour and reverence with crowching and kneeling, and they take it soe high and statelie on them?   And percase[1] he will informe you howe your soules and theires (which maketh you all to be men, for els ye were all but beastes, whereby god created in you one manner of noblenes without any adversity[2]), and that your soules be as precious to god as theires.   Whie then should they have of you so great authority and poure to commyt to prison, to ponishe and to judge you?

But you, good commoners, in any wise utterlie refuse this messenger ; for, though he shewe the truth to you, he meaneth ful falslie, as afterwardes you shall well knowe ; and if you once savor in these thinges, then cometh your lewde enterprise, the core of your fruite of tranquillitie, and he will you en-couradge to play the man, and bid you remember well the

---

[1] perchance.

[2] Probably a slip for *diversity*; the text is obviously corrupt in places, and either author or transcriber has made an ungrammatical sentence here.

monstracions or shewinges of the messenger Arrogancy. He will bid you leave[1] to ymploie yourselves to labour and to tyll like beastes, nor suffer yourselves to be subdued of your fellowes. He will promise to set you on high and to be lordes and governours, and noe longer to be churles as you were before; or at the leaste he will promise you to make you fellowes in bodyes, as god made you in soules, and then shall there be a Royall rule in this realme. And to put you in a further comfort he will assure you that some of the Chevalrie will take your parte openly and privilie, or at the least to give you sufferaunce, prove as you maye. He will also displaye unto you his banner of insurreccion and saie to you, "nowe set forwarde; your tyme is right good." But woe be unto that man that will fight thereunder. He will promise you to wante noe treasour to performe your purpose, for he will saie some of the clergie will comfort you right well and lardglie with mony, for they have looked therefore many a daye. The merchauntes, the ffarmours, the grasiers that be rich, into this market will bring their bages that they have kept so long. And as for the widowes and the wyves also, they will ransacke their forcers[2] and their knotted cloutes to the last penny that they can finde, and rather then faile, their girdles, their beades, and their weddinge ringes, thus wisely they will them bestowe. And as for men, he promiseth you ynnumerable. But ye good Commoners, for your owne ease, deale not with this false core, but be contented with the fruite of tranquillity....Let us all consider that god hath set a due order by grace between himself and anngells, and between ang[el] and angell, and by reason betwene Aungell and man, and betwene man and man, and man and beast, and by nature only betwene beaste and beaste, whiche order from the highest pointe to the loweste, god willeth us fervently to kepe, without any enterprise to the contrary.

The whole of this passage should be compared with John Ball's speech in the *Globe* Froissart, p. 251.

[1] cease.   [2] chests.

17   A PREMATURE REVOLT

William Fitzosbert or Longbeard was drawn and hanged in 1194, for
a revolt of which we know little more than Higden has here gathered
from other chroniclers.

Trevisa's *Higden*, VIII. 145.

Men sayn that this William was i-bore at Londoun, and
hadde his surname of his longe berde that he usede, and was
y-cleped William with the longe berde.   He usede that long
berd for he wolde seme the more worthy and semelich in
speche, and gaderynge[1] of many men.   He was scharp of witte
and somwhat i-lettred, and over mesure a greet speker, and by
a manere kyndeliche rabbischnesse[2] of wit and of thewes[3] he
wolde gete hym a greet name, and caste hym to doo newe
dedes, and bygan to hyre[4] greet doynge and dedes.   Also his
wrecched and shameliche dedes agenst his owne brother was
signe and tokene of his woodnes[5] in his other dedes; for he
accused his owne brother of tresoun to the kyng, for he gaf
hym nought more large spens[6] of solas and cost than he was
i-woned[7].   His brother was a burgeys of Londoun, and hadde
i-founde hym to scole.   He was scorned of the prince for that
dede, and yit by favour of som men he had place among the
grete of Londoun ; also among the peple he blamede venym-
liche the prive dedes and the outrage of riche men, that
misferde[8] with pore men ; and so he excitede hugeliche the
mene men to love and desire fredom out of mesure, so that he
socied[9] meny to hym as though they were bewicched right with
wichcraft.   For there he hadde tendaunt to his hestes[10] fifty
and two thowsand men of Londoun, as it were to the comoun
provyour[11] of alle.   Whan he hadde so many fautours[12], as he
that wolde stonde for the pore peple and for the kynges profite,
he wolde in everiche gadrynge and counsaile withstonde gentil
men, and segge[13] that by there fraude the kyng loste meny
enchetes[14]; they grucched agens hym therfore, and he seilled[15]
to the kyng, and seide hym that riche men dede hym greet

---

[1] gathering.   [2] natural unruliness.   [3] character.   [4] hear.
[5] madness.   [6] expense.   [7] accustomed.   [8] dealt ill.   [9] associated.
[10] attending on his behests.   [11] provider.   [12] abettors.   [13] say.
[14] revenues.   [15] sailed.

wrong, for he was trewe to hym. Than he cam agen and gan to worche¹ with fraude, as he was i-wonde², more besiliche and more tristeliche³, and conforted his fautours as it were by favour of the kyng. Noyse and tydinges of this conspiracie sprang out, and Hubert archebisshop of Canturbury, that hadde the rule of the rewme⁴, herde therof, and sente for the peple, and rehersed how it was i-tolde ; and, forto putte of[f] all evel suspeccioun, he prayed wel faire, and axede plegges. The pepil was i-plesed with his faire speche, and gaf and delivered hym plegges ; bote this William helde forth as he hadde by-gonne, and hadde moche folk aboute him, and wente with greet boost and array, and made openliche conventicles and counsailes and gadrynge of men, and cleped hym self the sa-vyour of pore men, and made greet boost and brag, and seide that the frowardnesse and outrage of myghti men schulde be aleyde⁵, and that in a schort tyme ; and he took a theme of holy writt, and gan to preche in this manere: "Haurietis aquas in gaudio de fontibus salvatoris" [Is. xii. 3]; that is Kecheth⁶ up water with joye of the savyour his welles. "I am," quoth he, "the savyour of pore men ; ye beeth pore men, and haveth assayed the hard bondes of ryche men, and now kecheth and laveth⁷ up water of hulful⁸ lore up of my welles, and that with joye, for the tyme of youre visitacioun is y-come. Y schal," quod he, "departe and to-dele¹⁹ watres from watres. The peple is water : thanne y schal to-dele and departe the peple that is trewe and meke from the peple that is false and proude ; y schalde parte good men from evel men, as lyght from derke-nesse." Thanne by counsaile of lordes this Hewbert sente for William, for he schulde stonde and answere to that me[n] schulde putte agenst hym. He com at the tyme as he was sommed¹⁰, but he hadde so moche folk aboute hym, that he that had i-sent for hym was aferd, and the nysechere¹¹ in his doynge, and put of the dome¹² for that tyme. Afterward opor-tunite was aspied by twene burgeys of Londoun whan he myghte be founde allone with oute peple aboute hym, and men

---

¹ work. ² wont. ³ confidently. ⁴ realm. ⁵ allayed. ⁶ draw.
⁷ bring. ⁸ healthful. ⁹ part and divide. ¹⁰ summoned. ¹¹ more lenient.
¹² judgment.

of armes were i-sende for to take hym. Bote[1] William with his ax slow oon[2] the burgeys that hadde aspied hym. Anon William with fewe of his men, and with his concubyne that wolde nevere from hym, wente into a cherche that was there faste by, that is Seint Marie cherche at the bowe. There he wolde nought defende hym not as it were in a cherche, bote as it were in a castel with strengthe, and hopede in vayn that his peple wolde come and delivere hym. The peple was sory for the peril that he was ynne, and is no wonder; bote by cause of the plegges that they hadde i-geve, and for drede of the knyghtes that they sigh[3] i-armed, thei com nought to his delyveraunce. Thanne William was i-hote[4] to come out, bute wolde nought ; than he was compelled with fuyre[5] and with smoke to come out maugre his teeth[6]. Whanne he come out, the burgeys sone that he had i-slawe forkutte his wombe[7] with a knyf; but by dome of the court whan he was i-take he was firste to-draw with hors, and than he was an honged with nyne felawes that wold nevere leve hym. But fautoures diffamed the archebisshop as a man-sleere ; and nought onliche that, bote also for to wype awey the schame of her owne conspiracie, and for to preve that they that dampned William were wikked men and evel doers, by craft and by fraude and gyle they fondede[8] to make William have the name and worschip of a martir. Also men seyn that a preost[9] of William his kyn, leyde the chayne that William was with i-bounde under a manis heed that was sike in the feveres, and preched opounliche that the man was hool[10] anon rightes. This sprang out among the peple, and the peple com theefliche[11] be nyghte, and took awey his gybet, and pared awey litel and litel the erthe that was by-bled with his blood, and made a grete diche, and kepte the erthe as it were holy relikes to hele with[12] sike men. Name and tidinges hereof sprang wel wide, and greet companyes bothe of sly men and of fooles come to the place, and wook[13] there be nyghte; alwey come thider greet multitude of lewed men and of fooles, and as moche worschippe as thei dede that man, so moche vilenye

---

[1] but. [2] one of. [3] saw. [4] bidden. [5] fire. [6] against his will.
[7] that he had slain ripped up his belly. [8] strove. [9] priest. [10] whole.
[11] furtively. [12] wherewith to heal. [13] watched.

they putte upon hym that hym hadde i-dampned. This error hadde so his forth[1] whan it was bygunne that it wolde have bewicched wys men and redy[2], ne hadde thei rediliche i-take hede to the doynge that thei knewe of this William his dedes ; for he slow a man a litel tofore his takynge, and that is ynow for a wise man to knowe that he schulde not be worschipped for a martir ; and yit his laste confessioun that he made whanne he schulde deie schulde schame alle that worschipped hym for a martir....Also, for his men come nought at his wille to de-lyvere hym, he forsook Mary sone, and cleped the devel to help, and prayde that he wolde delyvere hym. William his fautores denyed al this, and seide that it was falsliche i-feyned. Also the vanyte of this tale [of the miracles] fil[3] downe sone, and durede but awhile, and aleyde the strif ; for the soothnes is stedefast and is streng in long tyme, but fal[s]nes i-feyned vanscheth awey in schort tyme. Than Hubert the arche-bisshop, ruler of the reame, cursede that preost, and sette men of armes to kepe that place, for men schulde not come thider a-pilgrymage ; and so the sleythe[4] that was i-feyned fil away in schort tyme, and the opinioun of the peple gan forto reste.

18   THE CRY OF INTERNATIONALISM

(a) *From Shire to Shire.*

Thos. de Walsingham, *Historia Brevis*, A.D. 1381, from the edition of 1574, p. 293, in which the spelling is partly modernized.

John Schep sometime Seint Mary priest of Yorke, and now of Colchester, greeteth well John Namelesse, and John the Miller, and John Carter, and biddeth them that they be-ware of guyle in borough, and stand together in God's name, and biddeth Piers Ploweman goe to his werke, and chastise well Hob the robber, and take with you John Trewman, and all his fellows, and no moe.

John the Miller hath ground small, small, small :
The Kings sonne of heaven shal pay for all.
Beware or ye be woe,
Know your frende fro your foe,

[1] progressed so rapidly.   [2] prudent.   [3] fell.   [4] sleight.

Have ynough, and say *hoe*!
And do wel and better, and flee sinne,
And seeke peace and holde you therin,
And forbiddeth[1] John Trewman and all his fellowes.

(b) From Paris to Flanders.

F. T. Perrens, *Étienne Marcel*, Paris, 1874, p. 280. The Parisians, desperate under misgovernment and evil taxes after Poitiers, had set up practically a republic under Étienne Marcel in 1357; the peasants had revolted independently (*Jacquerie*) but had been put down with indiscriminate slaughter. As a last resource, Marcel sent his *Letter to the Good Towns*, not only of France but also of Flanders, where democratic ideas were far stronger. The story is told at some length by Froissart (cf. Globe *Froissart*, pp. 133-9). Perrens gives the whole of the original letter, from which the following extract is translated.

Beloved lords and great friends, we think that ye have surely heard tell how a great multitude of nobles, not only of your own countries of Flanders, Artois, Boulogne, Guisnes, Ponthieu, Hainault, Corbie, Beauvais and Vermandois, but also of many other parts, after the universal fashion of nobles dealing with commoners, without making any distinction between innocent or guilty, good or evil, came in arms and in fashion of war, murder and robbery, beyond the waters of Somme and Oise; and, notwithstanding that many of them had suffered no wrong, yet did they all burn towns, slay the good folk of the country without pity or mercy, rob and despoil all that they found—men, children, priests, men of religion—and put their victims to cruel torments to discover and rob their possessions; moreover, many have died in such torments, churches have been robbed,...the celebrating priests taken and their chalices torn from them, our Lord's Body cast to their varlets, His Blood cast against the wall, the vessels stolen wherein His Body and Blood were kept, abbeys, priories and parish churches either set to ransom or burned. So also with the persons of Holy Church; maidens and wives defoiled under the eyes of their husbands; and, in brief, more and more inhuman cruelties wrought than ever Vandals did or Saracens....Every commoner of the good towns or the open country, and all the labourers, have been put to death or

---

[1] pray for.

robbed; five-and-forty mules laden with cloth of Flanders and elsewhere have been seized, and the merchants that led them have been pillaged....

Beloved lords and very dear friends, all these things aforesaid we write unto you, for we are assured that ye have ever loved, and love still, the good town of Paris, and her good merchants, and the other good towns; the good commonalty and the good country folk ye love and have ever loved; and for three causes we now write unto you. The first is, that ye may see the good reason and justice that is on our side, and the great wrong, disloyalty and injustice that these others have towards us and the commonalty. The second, to have your counsel and succour; for these things are great, perilous and weighty, not only to us and to the countries that are wasted, but also to you and to all other parts where merchandise should go freely, and whither the corn and wine should have been brought which these men have so spoiled without reason; and ye may well see that, if they waste the country of Laon even as they have wasted Beauvais, then the whole land beyond the Oise would be destroyed, which serveth with wine the good provinces of Flanders and Hainault and Cambrai; whereof great damage would ensue to the whole countryside. The third is, that ye may deal with many nobles of Flanders and of the aforesaid provinces who have done the aforesaid robberies, in these same parts, by taking from them all their goods which ye see to lie in your land and power, and by seizing them into your hand for a security against them....

Well-beloved lords and good friends, pardon us and have us excused if we have written at so great length concerning these matters; for the roads were very perilous and unsafe, and these nobles beset all the roads and the whole countryside. Yet ye must know that, albeit many nobles and men at arms lie now before Paris in the Duke's host, yet we and our whole commonalty are of one mind to defend the city; and, God be thanked! we are well ordered and have great abundance of victual. Moreover, in defence of the honour of the good city of Paris, lest we, who have ever been freemen, should fall into such servitude whereunto these gentlefolk would constrain us—nay, rather villains than gentlefolk—we would rather adventure our bodies and our goods, as willing rather to die than to be brought into slavery. For they boast, against us and their other adversaries, that they will strip us of all save a rug of serge, and will make us draw at the plough with their horses....And we pray you that, when ye have seen and read this present scroll, it may please you to send it to some of the good towns of Flanders for the good folk and commonalty thereof, whom we pray and beseech, even as we beseech you, to give us the succour aforesaid.

May the Holy Spirit of His grace save and guard you all ! On all matters whereof we here write, we desire earnestly to have tidings and answer from you ; wherefore we beseech that it may please you to make reply as hastily as ye may well write. Written from Paris this 11th day of July in the year LXVIII.

19   TRADE-UNIONS

H. T. Riley, *Memorials of London*, 1868, p. 495.   (A.D. 1387.)

1387.   John Clerk, Henry Duntone, and John Hychene, were attached on the 17th day of August, in the 11th year etc., at the suit of Robert de York, Thomas Bryel, Thomas Gloucestre, and William Mildenhale, overseers of the trade of Cordwainers, and other reputable men of the same trade, appearing before Nicholas Extone, Mayor, and the Aldermen, in the Chamber of the Guildhall of London ; and were charged by the said prosecutors, for that—whereas it was enacted and proclaimed in the said city, on behalf of our Lord the King, that no person should make congregations, alliances, or [compacts] of the people, privily or openly; and that those belonging to the trades, more than other men, should not, without leave of the Mayor, make alliances, confederacies, or conspiracies—the aforesaid John Clerk, Henry Duntone, and John Hychene, serving-men of the said trade of Cordwainers, together with other their accomplices, on the Feast of the Assumption of the Blessed Virgin [15 August] last past, at the Friars Preachers in the said city, brought together a great congregation of men like unto themselves, and there did conspire and confederate to hold together; to the damage of the commonalty, and the prejudice of the trade before mentioned, and in rebellion against the overseers aforesaid; and there, because that Richard Bonet, of the trade aforesaid, would not agree with them, made assault upon him, so that he hardly escaped with his life; to the great disturbance of the peace of our Lord the King, and to the alarm of the neighbours there, and against the oath by which they had before been bound, not to make such congregations, or unions, or sects, for avoiding the dangers resulting therefrom.

And the said persons, being examined and interrogated thereon, could not deny the same; but they further confessed that a certain Friar Preacher, 'Brother William Bartone' by name, had made an agreement with their companions, and had given security to them, that he would make suit in the Court of Rome for confirmation of that fraternity by the Pope; so that, on pain of excommunication, and of still more grievous sentence afterwards to be fulminated, no man should dare to interfere with the well-being of the fraternity. For doing the which, he had received a certain sum of money, which had been collected among their said companions: a deed which notoriously redounds to the weakening of the liberties of the said city, and of the power of the officers of the same. Wherefore, by award of the said Mayor and Aldermen, it was determined that the said John Clerk, Henry Duntone, and John Hychene, should be confined in the Prison of Neugate, until they should have been better advised what further ought to be done with them.

20   THE BAKERS' STRIKE

The Coventry Leet Book, E.E.T.S., 1908, p. 519. (A.D. 1484.)

Mem. that in the moneth of Decembre the yere aforesaid the Bakers of the sede Citie in gret nombre riottesly disposed assembled theym and unlawefully confedered, intendyng of hight wille the reproche of the seid Maire, sodenly departed oute of the seid Cite unto Bakynton, levyng the seid Cite destitute of bred; wherthorough not only straungers re-

sortyng to the seid Cite and the Inhabitauntes of the same
were unvittailled, in gretly noysyng[1] the seid Cite and villany
and reproche of the seid Maire and all the officers therof.
Of which riotte divers of the seid Bakers were indited, as
appereth of recorde in the seid Cite etc. Whech seid Bakers
callyng theym to theymself[2], resorted and came unto the seid
Maire and humbly submytted theym-self unto his correccion.
Wheruppon they were commytte[d] to warde, and their ffyn
[as]sessed bi the seid Maire and other Justices of pease within
the seid Cite at xx li.; of which somme x li. was yffen[3] to
theym ageyn etc., the other x li. was resceyved...[and to give
surety to obey the Mayor's orders and keep the assize for the
future, or pay 20s. fine].

21 DIVES AND LAZARUS

R. of Brunne, *Handlyng Synne*, E.E.T.S., 1901, p. 218. The passage
is interesting not only as a picture of fourteenth century oppression
(cf. *Piers Plowman*, B, IV. 147), but also as showing the limitations of
Robert's own Bible knowledge, though he was a monk of Sempringham.

Why was God moste wyth hym [*Dives*] wroth?
For he dyd the pore man loth[4],
And for he dyd hys houndes oute latc[5]
To byte the Lazare at the gate;...
For ful comunly shalt thou fynde
Oftë rychë men unkynde.

Lorde! how shul these robbers fare,
That the pore pepyl pelyn[6] ful bare,—
Erlës, knyghtës, and barouns,
And outher lordyngës of tounnes;
Justyses, shryves, and baylyvys,
That the lawës alle to-ryves[7],
And the pore men alle to-pyle[8];
To ryche men do they but as they wylle.
Thys ryche man, as the gospel seys,
Was but to [one] man uncurteys,

---

[1] harming.   [2] coming to a right mind.   [3] given.   [4] injury.   [5] let.
[6] pillage.   [7] tear to pieces.   [8] pillage.

And hadde so mochë pyne tharfore;
On hem wyl fallë mochë more
That many pore men pyle and bete,...
He dyde but lete an hounde hym to;
Ye rychë men, we[l]l wers ye do!
Ye wyl noun houndës to them lete,
But, ye self, hem sle[1] and bete.
He ne dyd but werned[2] hym of hys mete;
And ye, robbe al that ye mow[3] gete.

22   THE KNIGHT REBUKED

R. of Brunne, *Handlyng Synne*, E.E.T.S., 1901, p. 273. This anecdote, again, is the more valuable for being from the author's own stock.

Yn Northfolk, yn a toune,
Wonede[4] a knyght besyde a persone[5];
Fyl hyt so[6], the knygtes manere
Was nat fro the cherche ful fere;
And was hyt than, as oftyn falles,
Brokë were the cherche-yerde walles.
    The lordës hyrdës[7] often lete
Hys bestys yn-to the cherche yerde and ete;
The bestys dyd as they mote nede[8],
Fyled[9] overal there they gede[10].
A bondman say[11] that, and was wo
That the bestys shuld there go;
He com to the lorde, and seyd hym thys:—
"Lorde," he seyde, "youre bestys go mys;
Youre hyrde doth wrong, and yourë knavys,
That late[12] youre bestys fyle thus these gravys;
There mennys bonys shuldë lye,
Bestës shuld do no vyleynye."
    The lordes answere was sumwhat vyle,
And that falleth evyl to a man gentyle;
"Weyl were hyt do rygt for the nones
To wurschyth swych[ë] cherlës bones[13];

---

[1] slay.   [2] refuse.   [3] can.   [4] dwelt.   [5] parson.   [6] it so befel.
[7] herdsmen.   [8] must needs.   [9] defiled.   [10] went.   [11] saw.   [12] let.
[13] A pretty thing, now, to pay honour to such churls' bones!

What wurschyp shuld men make
Aboute swych cherlës bodyes blake[1]?'
The bonde man answerëd, and seyd
Wurdys[2] to-gedyr ful weyl leyd:
" The lorde that made of erthë, erles,
Of the same erthe made he cherles;
Erlës mygt, and lordës stut[3],
As cherlës shal yn erthe be put;
Erlës, cherlës, alle at ones,
Shal none knowe youre, fro oure, bones."
The lorde lestened the wurdës weyl
And recorded them every deyl[4];
No morë to hym wulde he seye,
But, lete hym go furthe hys weye;
He seyd the bestys schulde no more,
By hys wyl, comë thore.
Sethen[5] he closed the chercheyerde so
That no best mygt come tharto
For to ete, ne fyle ther-ynne;
So thogt hym[6] sethen, that hyt was synne.
Thyr are but fewë lordës now
That turne a w[o]rde so wel to prow[7];
But, who[so] seyth hem any skylle[8],
Mysseye agen foul[l]y they wylle.
Lordynges, thyr are ynow of tho[9]!
Of gentyl men, thyr are but fo[10].
Hyt ys defended[11] yn the decre[12],
That none yn cherche shal beryed be,
But bysshope, or abbot of relygyun,
Or prest that ys of gode renoun....
Gyf the soulë be not wurthy
That the body lygge so solempny,
Than hath the soule morë peyne;
That men wurschyp the body, ys veyne.
Wykked men and userers,
Lechours, and lordys of foule man[n]ers,

---

[1] black. [2] words. [3] stout. [4] deal. [5] then. [6] he thought.
[7] profit. [8] reason. [9] them. [10] few. [11] forbidden. [12] Canon Law.

That mow gyve pens ful godë wone[1],
They shul be leyde in toumbe of stone,
And hys ymáge ful feyre depeynte[2],
Rygt as hé were a cors seynt[3];
The wrecched soule, the sothe to seye,
Shal a-bye[4] alle the noblye[5].

23   THE POWER OF MONEY

Rel. Ant., vol. II. p. 108, from MS. Moore, 147, in the Library of Caius College, Cambridge, written in the 15th century. A longer version of the 14th century is printed in the second edition of Ritson's *Ancient Popular Poetry*; and, with two other variants, on p. 359 of *Poems of Walter Mapes*. (Camden Soc. 1841.) Complaints of the power of money are just as common in medieval as in modern literature; and it is difficult to deny that they have at least equal justification.

SYR PENY

In erth there ys a lityll thyng,
That reynes as a grete kyng
There he is knowen in londe;
Peny is hys name callydde,
Ffor he makyth both yong and olde
To bowe unto hys hande.

Pope, kyng, and emperoure,
Byschope, abbot and prioure,
Parson, preste, and knygt,
Duke, erle, and baron,
To serve syr Peny are they boen[6]
Both be day and nygth.

Peny chaungeth ofte menys mode[7],
And garreth[8] them do of[f] ther hode
And ryse[9] hym ageyn.
Men doth hym all obedyens,
And full grete reverens,
That lytyll roende swayn[10].

---

[1] can give good plenty of pence.   [2] carved (*or* painted).   [3] saint's body.
[4] suffer for.   [5] pomp.   [6] bound.   [7] mood.   [8] maketh.   [9] raise.
[10] round fellow.

In a courte hit is no bote[1]
Ageyn syr Peny for to mote[2],
 Ffor hys mekyll mygth;
He is so wyse and so strange[3],
Were hit never so mekyll wrang,
 He wyll make hit rygth.

With Peny men may women tyll,
Be they never so strong of wyll,
 So ofte hyt may be sene,
Ageyn hym they wyll not chyde,
Ffor he may gar them trayle syde[4]
 In burnet[5] and in grene.

When Peny begynnys to spelle[6],
He makyth them meke that are fell[7],
 Fful ofte hit is i-sene;
The nedes are fulle sone spedde,
Both without borow or wedde[8],
 There Peny goeth betwene.

Peny may be[9] both hevyn and helle,
And alle thyng that is to selle,
 In erth hath he that grace;
Ffor he may both lose[10] and bynde,
The pore is ay set behynde,
 There Peny comes in place.

Peny is set on hye dese[11],
And servd at the best messe,
 And the hygh borde;
Men honoure hym as a man;
Iff he litell gode can,
 Gyt[12] he is in horde.

Peny doth gyt well mare[13],
He makyth men have moch care,
 Hym to get and wynne;

---

[1] good.   [2] plead.   [3] strong.   [4] flaunt ample robes.
[5] fine brown cloth.   [6] speak.   [7] fierce.   [8] pledge or pawn.   [9] buy.
[10] loose.   [11] dais.   [12] yet.   [13] more.

He garrith men be forsworen,
Soule and lyfe be forloren,
　Ffor covetyse of syn.

The dede that Peny wyll have done,
Without let hyt spedys sone[1]
　At his owen[2] wylle.
Peny may both reve[3] and gyffe,
He may gar sle[4], he may gar lyfe,
　Both gode and ylle.

Be he nevyr so strang a thefe,
Peny, that is man fulle lefe[5],
　May bowwe[6] hym to lyfe;
Peny is a gode felowe,
Both with hygh and with lowe,
　And councell for to gyffe.

He is a redy massyngere,
When he comes far or nere;
　An errand for to do,
Come he erly or late,
Hym is warned[7] nor dore ne gate,
　That he comes onto....

Peny hath do alle treson,
Both in cité and in toen[8],
　In castelle and in coure[9].
When Peny comyth with schylde and spere,
He wynnys the gre[10] in ylke a were[11],
　And in ylke a bowre—

With reson may ye wele se,
That Peny wyll mayster be,
　Prove nowe man of mode;
Peny rydys troen be troen[12],
Ovyr all in ylke a toen,
　On land and eke on flode.

[1] soon.　[2] own.　[3] rob.　[4] slay.　[5] dear.　[6] buy.
[7] refused.　[8] town.　[9] court.　[10] prize.　[11] war.
[12] throne by throne (there is, perhaps, some corruption in the text).
C.　　　　　　　　　　　　　　　　　　24

He makyth the fals to be soende[1],
And ryght puttys to the grounde,
    And fals lawys ryse.
This may ye find yf ye wyll loke,
Wretyn ill, without the boke,
    Ryght on this wyse.

[1] sound.

LADIES HUNTING

SECTION IX

HOUSE, DRESS AND MEALS

1   THE CAT

Trevisa's *Bartholomew*, Lib. XVIII. c. 76.

The catte is a beaste of uncerten heare[1] and colour; for some catte is white, some rede, some blacke, some skewed[2] and speckled in the fete and in the face and in the eares.... And he is a ful lecherous beste in youth, swyfte, plyaunte, and mery, and lepeth and reseth[3] on all thynge that is to-fore him; and is led by a strawe and playeth therwith. And is a right hevy beast in aege, and ful slepy, and lyeth slily in wait for myce; and is waare where they ben more by smelle than by sight; and hunteth and reseth on them in prevye places; and whan he taketh a mous he playeth therwith, and eateth him after the play. And is as it were wilde, and gothe about amonge cattes. In tyme of love is harde fightyng for wives, and one cratchethe and rentethe the other grevously with bytyng and with clawes. And he maketh a ruthefull noyse and gastfull, whan one proffreth to fyghte with another...and falleth on his owne fete whan he falleth out of hye places.

2   THE DOG

Trevisa's *Bartholomew*, Lib. XVIII. cc. 25-8.

Nothing is more besy and wittyer than an hound, for he hath more wit than other bestis. And houndes knowe theyr owne names, and love their maisters, and defend the houses of their maisters, and put themselfe wilfullye in peryll of deth for their maisters, and ren[4] to take proies[5] for their maisters

---

[1] hair.   [2] piebald.   [3] rusheth.   [4] run.   [5] prey.

and forsake not the deed bodyes of theyr maysters. And houndes pursue the fote[1] of proie by smel of blode, and love company of men, and maye nat be withoute men....Amonge beastes that dwell with us, houndes and horses ben mooste gracious. We have knowen that houndes faught for theyr lordes agaynst theves and were sore wounded, and that they kept away beastes and foules fro theyr maysters bodyes deed. And that an hounde compelled the sleer[2] of his master with berkynge and bytynge to knowlege his trespas and gylte.... The cruelness of an hound abateth to a meke man.

Houndes have other proprites that ben not ful good, for houndes have contynualle Bolisme[3], that is immoderate appetyte....Also an hounde is wrathefull and malycyous, soo that, for to awreke hym selfe, he bytethe ofte the stoon that is throwen to hym, and byteth the ston with gret wodnesse[4] that he breketh his owne teethe and greveth not the stone, but his owne teethe full sore. Also he is gylefull and dysceyvable, and so ofte he fyckelythe[5] and fawneth with his taylle on menne that passethe by the waye, as though he weere a frende; and byteth them sore, (yf they take none hede) bakwarde....Also he is covetous and glotonous...and he gadryth[6] herbes prively, by whom he purgeth hymselfe, and hathe envye and is ryghte sorye if any man knowith the vertu of those herbes. And is also evyll-apayd[7] if any straunge houndes and unknowen come in to the place there he dwellethe, and dredeth lest he shulde fare the worse for the other houndes presence, and fyghteth with hym therfore. Also he is covetous and scarse[8] and besy to laye up and to hyde the releyf[9] that he leveth. And therfore he comyneth[10] not ne yeveth[11] fleshe and mariboones[12], that he may not devour, to other houndes, but layeth them uppe besyly and hydeth them untyl he hungreth ayen[13]....Aristotle sayth,that houndes in age have the podagre[14], and fewe of them scape that evil, and therefore they slepe in daye time....And though [the flies] bite and perce somtyme the houndes eares, yet for slouth he taketh no comforte and

---

[1] foot.   [2] slayer.   [3] βουλιμία.   [4] madness.   [5] flattereth.
[6] gathereth.   [7] ill-pleased.   [8] miserly.
[9] remnants ; cf. Section IV., no. 27 and IX. 4.   [10] shareth.
[11] giveth.   [12] marrow-bones.   [13] again.   [14] gout.

strength to chace and dryve them awaye, but unneth[1] whan
they fle ayenst his face he snatcheth at them with his mouthe,
and besiethe to bite them with his teethe. And at the laste
the scabbed hounde is vyolently drawen out of the dounghyl
with a rope or with a whyp bounde abowt his necke, and is
drowned in the ryver, or in some other water, and so he endeth
his wretched lyfe. And his skynne is not take of[2], nor his
fleshe is not eate nor buryed, but left finally to flyes and to
other dyvers wormes....Houndes that ben ordeyned to kepyng
of houses sholde be closed and bounde in a derke place by
daye, and soo they benne the stronger by nyght, and the more
cruell ayenste theves.

3 A FAMILIAR BEAST TO MAN

(*a*) Trevisa's *Bartholomew*, Lib. XVIII. c. 89 compressed.

The flee is a lyttell worme, and greveth men mooste ; and
scapeth and voideth peril with lepynge and not with rennynge,
and wexeth slowe and fayleth in colde tyme, and in somer
tyme it wexeth quiver[3] and swyft; and spareth not kynges.

(*b*) G. Gascoigne's *Good-Night* (Southey's *British Poets*, 1831, p. 202).
The poet, going to bed, moralizes on the resemblance between sleep and
death :—

My bed itself is like the grave, my sheetes the winding-sheete,
My clothes the mould that I must have, to cover me most
    meete ;
The hungry fleas which friske so freshe, to wormes I can
    compare,
Which greedily shall gnaw my fleshe, and leave the bones
    ful bare.

Cf. *Registrum Johannis Peckham*, R. S., 1882, vol. I. introd. p. l.

4 DINNER AND SUPPER

Trevisa's *Bartholomew*, Lib. VI. cc. 23 and 24 (Ed. 1536, f. 81 *a*).

Of Dyner and festynge.

Meate and drynke ben ordeined and conveniente to dyners
and to feastes, for atte feastes fyrste meat is preparyd and

---

[1] scarcely.   [2] taken off.   [3] alert

arayed; guestes ben called togyders[1]; formes and stoles[2] ben
set in the halle; and tables, clothes and towalles ben ordeynyd,
disposyd, and made redy. Guestes ben sette with the lorde
in the chefe place of the borde, and they sitte not down at the
borde before the guestes washe theyr hondes. Chyldren ben
sette in theyr place, and servauntes at a table by them selfe.
Fyrst knyves, spones, and saltes bene sette on the borde, and
than brede and drynke, and many divers messes. Housholde
servauntes besyly helpe eche other to every thinge diligently
and talke merily togider. The guestes ben gladded with lutes
and harpes. Nowe wine and nowe messes of meate ben
brought forth and departed[3]. At the laste comyth frute and
spyces, and wher they have ete, bord clothes and relyf[4] ben
borne awaye, and guestes wasshe and wype theyr hondes
agayne. Then graces ben sayd and guestes thank the lorde.
Than for gladdenesse and comforte drynke is broughte yet
agayne. Whan al this is done, atte mere[5] men take theyre
leve, and some goon to bedde and slepe and some goo home
to theyr one lodgynges.

Of the Suppar.

All that is reherced afore of dyners and of feastes accordeth
to the supper also. Many thynges bene necessarye and
worshyppe[6] the supper, and were al in Assuerus feastes, as it
is written, Hest. 1.[7]

The first is convenable time : For it is convenient that a
supper be made in dewe time, not to erly nor to late. The
seconde is convenable place, large, plesant, and siker[8]. Therefore
it is said of Assuerus, that he made his fest tofore an orchard,
whiche was hewen downe. The thirde is the herte and glade
chere of him that maketh the fest. The supper is not worthy
to be praised, if the lorde of the hous be hevy cheryd[9] (Hest. 1.
Whan he wexeth hote, etc.). The fourth is many dyverse
messes. So that who that woll not of one, maye taste of a
nother (Hest. 1. There were brought in dysshe upon dysshe).

---

[1] together.   [2] stools.   [3] divided.   [4] remnants.   [5] at the end.
[6] honour.   [7] In the 1st chapter of the book of Esther.
[8] sure.   [9] melancholy.

A Norman Feast

A Feast with Mummers

The fyfth bene dyvers wynes and drynkes (Hester 1. Wyne was broughte, etc.). The VI is curtese and honestie of servantes (Hester 1. He ordeyned of his prynces to be maysters over the bordes, etc.). The seventhe is kynde frendeshyp and company of them that sytte at the supper (Hest. 1. He made a feaste unto al the Medes). The VIII is myrthe of songe and of Instrumentes of musike. Noble men use not to make suppers without harpe or symphony (Luk. 15, 25. Whan he herde the symphony and cornemuse, etc.). The IX is plente of lyghte of candels and of pryckettes[1], and of torches. For it is shame to suppe in darknes, and perillous also for flyes and other fylthe. Therfore candels, and pryckettes ben sette on candelstickes and chaundelars, lanterns and laumpes ben necessarye to brenne[2]. The X is the delycyousnes of al that is sette on the borde. For hit is not used at supper to serve men with greate meate and comin[3], as it is used at dyner, but with specyall lyghte meate and delycyouse, and namely in lordes courtes. The XI is longe durynge of the soupper. For menne use, after full ende of werke and of traveyle to sytte longe at the supper. For meate eten to hastely, grevethe ayenste nyghte[4]. Therfore at the soupper men schulde eate by leyser[5] and not to hastely. Therfore Assuerus feaste duryd[6] by the space of C.L. dayes. The XII is surenesse. For without harm and domage every man shall be prayed[7] to the supper. After supper that is freely yeve[8] it is not honest to compell a man to paye his scot[9]. The XIII is softnes and lykynge of reste and of slepe. After supper men shal reste, for then slepe is swete and lykynge. And therfore beddes of yvory and of gold were spred uppon the pavement in Assuerus palaice, as it is sayde, Hester 1. For, as Constantyne saith, whan smoke of meate cometh in to the brayne, men slepe easely.

---

[1] tapers.   [2] burn.   [3] common.   [4] is harmful when the night comes.
[5] leisure.   [6] lasted.   [7] invited.   [8] given.   [9] reckoning.

5   BREAD RATIONS

Coventry in 1520 was one of our most important towns; and the following document is of extraordinary interest even on the surface. It is perhaps the only surviving early record of the exact census of any urban population in Britain; and, again, it admirably exemplifies the paternal solicitude of the government in a well-ordered and progressive municipality. But still more interesting are the statistics of food and drink deducible from it. The *Northumberland Houshold Book* shows that early 16th century brewers made 83 gallons of beer from a quarter of malt. This, comments Hume, "would not be very strong beer"; but Hume's was a hard-drinking age. Modern British brewers reckon that a quarter produces 76 gallons of strong beer or 150 of mild; we should therefore call the Northumberland beer decidedly strong in these days. At that rate, the Coventry consumption would be 12,118 gallons a week, or almost exactly a quart per diem per soul, man woman and child. Miss Bateson, in her *Medieval England* p. 314, halves the actual rations of beer for Dover garrison; the actual allowance was two quarts per diem, and this in siege-time. The monastic allowance, where definitely specified, is seldom or never less than a gallon per monk per diem. The Northumberland household, in 1512, had a quart per person per meal; "my Lord Percy and Master Percy," aged about 10 and 8, had their quart-allowance each for breakfast. The bread ration is almost as interesting. A good deal of the rye and beans doubtless went to horse-bread; but, taking the wheat only, we get 9·3 lbs. per week per head; this, making allowance for all the coarser stuff used, would probably mean a consumption of 12 lbs. weekly, or even more. Of course our ancestors had far less of other foods. The document is printed in *The Coventry Leet Book*, E.E.T.S., 1909, p. 674.

[A.D. 1520.]   Memorandum That the xth day of Octobre and in the yer of the Raigne of Kyng Henry the Viij^th, then Maister Joh. Bonde beyng Maier of the Cite of Coventre, The price of all maner of Corne and graynes be-ganne to a-Ryse, wheruppon a veu¹ was takon by the said Maier and his brethern what stores of all Maner of Corne, and what nombre of people was then whithin the said Cite, men, women and Childern, etc.

Nomber of people   The nomber of Greynes
in every warde.   of all Maner of Cornes.

Summa:

c

Erle-strete warde.   ⎧ In Malt, iiij liiij quarter,
vij C and vij persones. ⎨ In Rie, xxxvj stryke dim.²
                         ⎩ In whete, xvij quarter ij stryk.

---

¹ view.   ² and a half.

[The rest may be given in a brief summary: *Smithford Street ward.* 406 persons; malt and barley, 220 qrs.; rye, 15 qrs. 2 strike; wheat, 2½ qrs.; "ottes," 27 qrs.; "pese," 7½ qrs. *Gosford Street ward.* 875 persons; malt, 456 qrs.; "whet and Rye," 16 qrs.; peas, 1 qr. *Much Park Street ward.* 719 persons; malt, 287 qrs.; wheat, 14½ qrs. 1 strike; peas, 7 qrs. *Bishop Street ward.* 1018 persons. *Bayly Lane ward.* 459 persons. "*Brodyate warde.*" 552 persons. *Cross-Cheaping ward.* 884 persons. *Jordan Well ward.* 354 persons. *Spon Street ward.* 627 persons.]

Summa totalis of the numbre of the people then beying within the Cyte, of men, women and Childern.

Summa totalys.

vj M^li vjC and j.

In Malt, ij M^li iij^C v^xx and v quarter,

In Rye and Mastlin jC quarter, j stryk,

In whet, xlvij quarter,

In ottes, xxxix quarter, ij stryk,

In pese, xviij quarter, ij stryk.

Also a veu by hym takon what supstance of malt was then brewede within the Cyte wokly[1] by the comyn brewers that brewed to sell and fyll furthe by the Sesters[2]; the nombre of the comyn brewers in all the Cyte ys......................iij^xx viij

Item, they brewid wekly in malt vij^xx vj quarter, j bus

[1] weekly.

[2] Sextary, a large liquid measure used mainly for wholesale purposes. The royal sextary contained 4 gallons: see *Fleta* II. 12, § 11 (ed. Selden, p. 73), and the Introduction to J. Nichols' *Illustrations of Manners, etc.*, 1797. The same is also clearly implied in Topham, *Liber Quotidianus of Ed. I.*, 1787, pp. 15, 109; in J. E. T. Rogers, *Hist. Ag. and Prices*, vol. II. pp. 548–90, and in Dugdale's *Monasticon*, ed. Caley, vol. III. p. 162. It is also the only possible theory on which we can work out the Buckingham Household Accounts (*Archaeologia*, vol. xxv. pp. 319–35: the editor's notes on p. 318 are valueless; the *pitcher* of these, as of other accounts, is one gallon). The German *sester* was also apparently of the same capacity: see Miss F. E. Harmer's *Select Historical Documents*, p. 80. At Coventry, however, the *Leet Book* expressly puts the sester at 14 (or 13) gallons (see pp. 696, 772, and cf. 25, 530–2 and Editor's note p. 848). Variations so great, in civilized parts of England, are very rare; and it is difficult not to suspect some corruption in the MS.

Mem. that ther was brought into this said Cyte the ffryday before Crystmas day in the yer of the said Joh. Bonde then beying mayer, by his labour and his ffrendys, to helpe to susteyne the Cyte with corne of all maner of greyne.

Summa iiij and xvij quarter and vj stryke.

Mem. that ther was at that tyme xliij bakers within the Cyte, the wiche dyd bake wekly a-mongest all vj [six score] quarter of whet and xij, besydes pese and Rye.

6   BEER AND GOD'S LAW

Teetotalism was extremely rare in the Middle Ages, as we might already surmise from the fact that *Drinkwater* and *Boileau* were distinctive and not very common surnames. Even among monks and professional ascetics only an insignificant fraction avoided intoxicants; for temperance drinks were practically unknown. This lends special interest to the following illustration from Pecock's *Repressor*, R. S., I. 120. Pecock is combating the Lollard contention that Scripture is the sole guide of conduct.

Where is it expressid bi word or bi eny persoonys ensaumpling in Holi Scripture that men schulden make ale or beer? of whiche so myche horrible synne cometh, myche more than of setting up of ymagis, or of pilgrymagis; and the defautis doon aboute ymagis and pilgrimagis ben muche lighter and esier to be amendid, than the defautis comyng bi making of ale and of beer. And also here with, it is trewe that without ale and bere, and without sidir[1] and wijn and meeth[2], men and wommen myghte lyve ful long, and lenger than thei doon now, and in lasse jolite and cherte of herte forto bringe hem into horrible grete synnes. And yit thou wolte seie that forto make ale and beer and forto drinke hem is the service of God, and is merytorie, and therfore is the lawe of God.

7   A FRIAR'S PRAISE OF WINE

Trevisa's *Bartholomew*, Lib. XVII. c. 184.

The worthynes and praysynge of wyne might not Bacchus him self discryve at the fulle, though he were alyve. For among all lycours and juys of trees, wyne bearethe the pryce; for, passynge all lycours, wyne moderately dronken mooste com-

---

[1] cider.   [2] mead.

forteth the body, and gladdeth the harte, and healeth and sa[l]veth woundes and evylles. Therof spekethe Isaac in dietis ultimo[1], and saith, that wyne yeveth good nourishing to the body, and restoreth hele that was loste, and conforteth and encreceth kynde[2] heate passinge all other meate and drynke, and that for lykenes and companye that wyne hathe with kynde. And so wyne bredethe mooste pure bloudde, and pirsueth and clenseth trowbly and thycke bloudde, and openeth and clenseth the mouth of the veynes and cometh inwarde by his subtyltie to clense and to pourge the inner partyes.

8 EXTRAVAGANT COSTUME

The *locus classicus* here is of course Chaucer's *Parson's Tale*, which may be illustrated by the following three extracts.

(*a*) *The Brut* (E.E.T.S., 1906), p. 249.

And at that tyme [1337] the Englisshe-men were clothede alle in cotes and hodes, peyntede with lettres and wlth floures ful semely, with long berdes ; and therfore the Scotes made a bille that was fastenede oppon the cherche dores of Seint Petre toward Stangate. And thus saide the scripture in despite of the Englisshe-men :

> Longe berde hertles[3],
> Peyntede Hode witles[4],
> Gay cote graceles,
> Maketh Englond thriftless[5].

(*b*) *Ibid.* p. 296.

In this tyme [about 1345] Englisshe men so muche haunted and clevyd to the wodnes[6] and foley of the strangers, that fro the tyme of the comyng of the Henauderns[7], xviij yere passid, they ordeyned and chaungyd tham every yere divers schappis of disgynges[8] of clothing of long large and wyde clothis, destitu and desert fram al old honeste and good usage ; and another tyme schorte clothis and stret-wasted[9], dragged

---

[1] In the last chapter of his book on Diet. [2] natural.
[3] faint-hearted. [4] witless.
[5] There is a similar rhyme in *Reliquiae Antiquae*, I. 316 ; and another of the same type is scratched on a pillar in Steeple Bumstead Church, Essex.
[6] madness. [7] Hainaulters. [8] shapes of disguisings. [9] tight-waisted.

and ket[1], and on every side desslatered and boned[2], with sleves
and tapets[3] of sircotys and hodes[4] overe longe and large, and
overmuche hangynde; that, if y soth schal say, they were more
liche to turmentours and devels, in thire clothing and schewyng
and other arraye, then comen[5]. And the wemmen more
[n]yseli[6] yet pasted[7] the men in array, and cureslicher[8]; for
they were so strete clothed that they lete hange fox tailes
sawyd[9] benethe withinforth thire clothis,...the whiche dis-
gysenges and pride peraventure afterward broughte forthe
and encausid many mys-happis and mischevys in the reaume
of Engelond.

(c)　After the end of the 14th century, the most extravagant period of
English costume was probably the first part of Henry VIII.'s reign.

Fitzherbert, *Book of Husbandry*, ed. Skeat, 1882, p. 102.

I have seen bokes of accompte of the yomen of the ward-
ropes of noble men, and also inventorys made after theyr
decease of their apparell, and I doubte not but at this day, it
is xx tymes more in value, than it was to suche a man of
degree as he was an C yere a-go. And many tymes it is gyven
away, or[10] it be halfe worne, to a symple man, the whiche causeth
hym to weare the same; and an other symple man, or a lyttell
better, seynge him to weare suche rayment, thynketh in his
mynde, that he maye were as good rayment as he, and so
causeth hym to bye suche other, to his great coste and charge,
above measure, and an yll ensample to all other. And also to
see mens servantes so abused in theyr aray, theyr cotes be so
syde[11], that they be fayne to tucke them up whan they ryde, as
women do theyr kyrtels whan they go to the market or other
places, the whiche is an unconvenient syght. And ferther-
more, they have suche pleytes[12] upon theyr brestes, and ruffes
uppon theyr sleves, above theyr elbowes, that, yf theyr mayster
or theym-selfe hadde never so greatte nede, they coude not
shoote one shote to hurte theyr ennemyes, tyll they hadde
caste of theyr cotes, or cut of theyr sleves.

---

[1] cut.　　　　　[2] slashed and loose, cf. N.E.D. *Bone*, v[1]. 2.　　　　[3] tippets.
[4] hoods.　　　[5] common men.　　　[6] foolishly.　　　[7] surpassed.
[8] more cursedly.　　[9] sewed.　　　[10] ere.　　[11] wide.　　[12] pleats.

9   BUYING A NEW SUIT

From Caxton's *Dialogues in French and English* (E.E.T.S., Extra Series, 1900), p. 14 : a few mistranslations corrected.

Of othir thinge withoute taryeng, whiles that I remembre, I wyll to you devise and teche. Yf ye wyll bergayne wullen cloth or othir marchandise, so goo to the halle whiche is yn the market. So goo upon the steyres[1]; there shall ye fynde the clothes: clothes medleyed, red cloth or grene, blyew y-asured[2], yelow, reed, sad blew[3], morreey[4], raye[5], chekeryd, saye[6] white and blew, scarlet in grayne.

So may ye begynne by suche gretyng as it is in the first chapitre. "Dame, what hold ye the elle of this cloth ? Or what is worth the cloth hole ? In shorte to speke, how moche th'elle ?" "Syre, resone; I shall doo to you resone; ye shall have it good cheep." "Ye[a], truly, for catell, Dame, me must wynne[7]. Take hede what I shall paye." "Four shelynges for the elle yf it [so] plese you." "Hit ne were no wysedom. For so moche wold I have good scarlete !" "Ye have right, yf ye maye. But I have yet somme which is not of the beste, which I wold not yeve[8] for seven shelynges." "I you bileve well; but this is no suche cloth of so moche money, that knowe ye well! This that ye shall [abate of the price] shall [make it possible to] be solde." "Syre, what is it worth?" "Dame, it were worth to me well thre shellyngs." "That is evyll boden[9], or to moche axed; yet had I lever that [there] were gold in your cheste." "Damoyselle, ye shold not lese[10] theron never a crosse[11], but saye certainly how shall I have it withoute thyng to [abate]." "I shall gyve it you at one worde: certaynly, if ye have it, ye shall paye fyve shellyngs for so many elles whiche ye shall take; for I wyll abate no thyng." "Dame, what shall avaylle thenne longe wordes? Cutte for me a pair of gounes." "How moche shall I cutte ?" "Also[12] moche as ye wene as me shall nede for a surcote, for a cote, for an

---

[1] steps.   [2] azure blue.   [3] dark blue.   [4] mulberry-coloured.
[5] striped.   [6] usually "fine silk " : but here apparently "fine woollen."
[7] I must earn money, Dame.   [8] give.   [9] offered.   [10] lose.
[11] farthing.   [12] as.

hewke[1], for a pair hosen." "Sir, it you behoveth wel fiften elles." "In goddes name, cutte them. Of what brede is it?" "Of two ellis and an half." "That is good brede. Cutte at that othir ende." "Hit is all one, by my soule! But I shall doo it gladly." "Dame, mete well." "Sire, I shall never shrive me therof of that I shall with-holde yow." "Dame, that knowe I well; if I had not trusted you I had called the metar[2]." "Sire, yf it plese you, he shall be called." "Nay truly, dame, I holde me well content with you; for me semeth that ye have to me well done. Folde it up in goddes name." "I shall not, sauf your grace; I wyll that ye mete it." "Dame, syth that I me holde playnly content, and sith it well me suffyseth, it is no nede to mete it agayn. Holde thou, boye, and bere it; thou shalt have an half-peny. Now, dame, how moche cometh it to, this that I have of you?" "Syre, yf ye gyve to me xix shellyngs, ye shall paye me well; so moche ye owe me." "Damoyselle, holde, telle[3]." "What moneye gyve ye to me?" "Good moneye; thise ben grotes of englond;...the olde grotes of englond which be worth v pens; the newe be worth foure pens; ye ought well to knowe, that so moche moneye receyve." "Ye saye trouthe, sire....This is all good moneye; ye[4], and I may gyve it oute?" "Yes, ye shall gyve it oute well within the towne and all aboute the contre, in all penyworthes, in all marchandyses." "Fair sire, I am well plesyd with you; were it so that ye failled[5] ony ware of whiche I medle with, or that I have under hande, ye may bere it a-waye withoute halpeny or peny; so well have ye me payd." "Right grete gramercy. Wyte ye that my silver ye shall have tofore an othir. Hit were right for your goodlynes, for the courtosye that is in you. It ne is not the last silver that ye shal have of me, how be it that this is the first."

---

[1] cloak. [2] official measurer. [3] here it is, count it. [4] yea.
[5] lacked.

10   BARONIAL BREAKFASTS

The *Northumberland Houshold Book* contains a series of regulations drawn up in 1512 for the household of Henry Algernon, fifth earl of Northumberland ; it is of the greatest value for the social history of that time. The following extracts tell their own tale except for one personal note. "My Lorde Percy" of these breakfasts is the eldest son Henry, then in his 11th year, who in later years was the lover, and possibly even the betrothed lover, of Anne Boleyn before she attracted the king's attention. Wolsey and the old earl separated the pair with an inconsiderate brutality which is recorded at length in Cavendish's *Life of Wolsey*: and Henry Percy never recovered from the effect of these early misfortunes. The whole of this shabby-genteel romance may be found in E. V. Fonblanque, *Annals of the House of Percy*, 1887. My references are to the first edition of the *Houshold Book*, edited by Bp Percy in 1770.

(p. 73.) THIS IS THE ORDRE of all suche BRAIKFASTIS as shal be allowid daily in my Lordis hous EVERY LENT begynnynge at Shroftide and endyng at Estur, And what they shall have at theire Braikfasts as to say SONDAY TEWISDAY THURSDAY and SETTERDAY, Except my Lordis Childeryn, which shall have Braikfasts every day in the weik in Lent; As the names of the Persons, and What they be And What they shall have the said days allowid theym, hereafter follouyth in this Book.

BRAIKFASTE for my Lorde and my Lady. FURST a Loif of Brede in Trenchors[1] ij Manchetts[2] a Quart of Bere a Quart of Wyne ij Pecys of Saltfisch vj Baconn'd Herryng iij White Herryng or a Dysche of Sproits[3].

BRAIKFASTE for my Lorde Percy and maister Thomas Percy. ITEM half a Loif of houshold Brede a Manchet a Potell of Bere a Dysch of Butter a Pece of Saltfish a Dysch of Sproits or iij White Herrynge.

BRAIKFAST for the Nurcy for my Lady Margaret and maister Ingeram Percy. ITEM a Manchet a Quarte of Bere a Dysch of Butter a Pece of Saltfisch a Dysch of Sproitts or iij White Herryng.

BRAIKFAST for my Ladis Gentyllwomen. ITEM a Loof

---

[1] *Trenchers* were slices of bread which our ancestors used as plates, eating their meal upon them and leaving them as remnants for the poor or for their dogs.
[2] fine white loaf.   [3] sprats.

of Brede a Pottell of Bere a Pece of Saltfische or iij White
Herryng.

BRAIKFASTS for my Lords Breder and Hede Officers of
Houshold. ITEM ij Loofs of Brede a manchet a Gallon of
Bere ij Peces of Saltfisch and iiij White Herrynge.

(p. *75*.) THIS IS THE ORDRE of all suche BRAIKFASTS
that shal be lowable[1] dayly in my Lordis hous THOROWTE
THE YERE from Michaelmas unto Michaelmas, and What
they shall have to their Braikfasts as well as on FLESCHE
DAYS as FYSCH DAYS in Lent and out of Lent. As the
Namys of the Persons and What they be and What they
shall have allowid theym to their Briekfastis hereafter follouyth in this Book, Begynnynge on Sonday the second day
of February which was Candlemas day last past in the secund
Yere of the reign of our Sovereigne Lorde Kyng Henry the
viij[th], That be daily in the hous.

BRAIKFASTIS OF FLESCH DAYS DAYLY
THOROWTE THE YERE

BRAIKFASTIS for my lorde and my lady. FURST a Loof
of Brede in Trenchors ij Manchetts j Quart of Bere a Quart
of Wyne half a Chyne of Muton or ells a Chyne of Beif
Boilid.

BRAIKFASTIS for my Lorde Percy and Mr Thomas Percy.
ITEM Half a Lo if of houshold Breide. A Manchett j Potell[2]
of Bere a Chekynge[3] or ells iij Muton Bonys boyled.

BRAIKFASTS for the Nurcy for my Lady Margaret and
Mr Yngram Percy. ITEM a Manchet j Quarte of Bere and
iij Muton Bonys boiled.

BRAIKFASTS for my Ladys Gentylwomen. ITEM a loif
of Houshold Breid a Pottell of Beire and iiij Muton Bonys
boyled or ells a Pece of Beif Boilid.

BRAIKFASTS for my Lords Breder his Hede Officers of
Houshold and Counsaill. ITEM ij. Loofs of Houshold Briede
a Manchet a Gallon of Bere ij Muton Bonys and ij Peces of
Beif Boilid.

---

[1] allowed.   [2] two quarts.   [3] chicken.

11 EXTRAVAGANT FOOD

Fitzherbert, *Book of Husbandry*, ed. Skeat, 1882, p. 103.

Howe costely are the charges of delycious meates and drynkes, that be nowe most commonly used, over that it hath ben in tymes paste, and howe fer[1] above measure? For I have seen bokes of accompte of householde, and brumentes[2] upon the same, and I doubte not, but in delycyous meates, drinkes, and spyces, there is at this daye foure tymes so moche spent, as was at these dayes, to a lyke man in degree; and yet at that tyme there was as moche befe and mutton spent as is nowe, and as many good householders kept, and as many yomenne wayters therin as be nowe.

12 BY THE EVENING FIRE

Ibid. p. 101. The medieval moralist often deprecates sitting up by the fire, as likely to lead to drinking (e.g. Section II., no. 20); Fitzherbert attacks it from the business point of view. Medieval cattle, it must be remembered, were difficult to fatten: it is frequent to find tallow costing four times the price of lean meat.

One thinge I wyl advise the to remembre, and specially in wynter-tyme, whan thou sytteste by the fyre, and hast supped, to consyder in thy mynde, whether the warkes, that thou, thy wyfe, and thy servantes shall do, be more avauntage to the[3] than the fyre, and candell-lyghte, meate and drynke that they shall spende, and if it be more avantage, than syt styll: and if it be not, than go to thy bedde and slepe, and be uppe betyme, and breake thy faste before day, that thou mayste be all the shorte wynters day about thy busynes.

13 THE DRUDGING GOBLIN

From Gervase of Tilbury, *Otia Imperialia*, selections edited by Felix Liebrecht, Hanover, 1856. The author was for some time in the service of King John's relation and ally, the emperor Otto IV., who made him Marshal of the Kingdom of Arles, and for whom he wrote his book in 1211. p. 29, cap. LXI.

Even as Nature produceth certain freaks among men, so do spirits also play their pranks in those unsubstantial bodies which they assume by God's permission. For England hath

---

[1] far.   [2] entries (brevements).   [3] thee.

certain goblins...which the people call *Portunos* [Brownies?].
It is the wont of such elves to take advantage of the simplicity
of well-to-do peasants; when these sit up at night to work, as
soon as the doors are shut the goblins warm themselves at
the fire, and take frogs from their bosom which they roast on
the embers and proceed to eat. Their faces are wrinkled as
with extreme age; their stature is small, not half an inch in
length. They are clothed in patched garments; and, if there
is any business in the house or any work of great labour, they
join in with the rest and perform it more swiftly than any
hand of man. It is their nature to give succour; nor can
they harm us save in one little thing. For at times, when
Englishmen ride abroad in the darkness of night, an unseen
Portunus will join company with the wayfarer; and, after
riding awhile by his side, will at length seize his reins and
lead his horse into the slough, wherein he will stick and
wallow while the Portunus departs with mocking laughter,
thus making sport of man's simplicity.

14   ECONOMY IN BEDDING

The Percies, like most other great lords, could only live by moving from
house to house, where they rapidly ate up the year's stores and then passed
on. Henry Algernon had a score or more of such castles, all in the north. At
each "flitting" a great deal of the furniture was carried away with the household; the routine was minutely prescribed by the *Houshold Book*, pp. 386
ff. These prescriptions reveal that most of the servants, clergy included,
had to be content with only a fraction of a bed.

p. 389. ITEM. Yt is Ordynyd at every Remevall that
the Deyn Sub-dean Prestes Gentilmen and Children of my
Lordes Chapell with the Yoman and Grome of the Vestrey
shall have apontid theime ij cariadges at every Remevall: Viz.
One for ther Beddes Viz. For vj Prests, iij Beddes after ij to
a Bedde. For x Gentillmen of the Chapell, v Beddes ij to a
Bedde. And for vj Children, ij Beddes after iij to a Bedde.
And a Bedde for the Yoman and Grom o' th Vestry. In all
xj Beddes for the furst Cariage. And the ij Cariage for ther
Aparells and all outher ther Stuff. And to have no mo
Cariage allowed them, but onely the said ij Cariages allowid
theime.

SECTION X

SPORTS AND PASTIMES

In this section also, it would be superfluous to retrace again all the ground which has been covered by J. Strutt in his *Sports and Pastimes of the English People* (cheap edition by Chatto and Windus, 1898). Here again, it has seemed best to concentrate mainly upon London.

1   LONDON PASTIMES

John Stow understood medieval London life so well, and formed his opinions on so careful and exhaustive a study of original documents (many of which he uses textually), that it needs no further apology for including his own description of London revels and pageants in this collection of authentic medieval documents (*A Survey of London*, 1603, chap. XI. p. 92). A considerable portion of this chapter is translated textually from Fitzstephen's twelfth-century description of London, which has been printed in *Materials for the History of Thomas Becket*, R.S., vol. III.

SPORTS AND PASTIMES OF OLD TIMES USED IN THIS CITIE.

Let us now (saith Fitzstephen) come to the sports and pastimes, seeing it is fit that a Citie should not only be commodious and serious, but also merrie and sportful.... But London, for the shews upon Theaters, and Comicall pastimes, hath holy playes—representations of myracles which holy Confessours have wrought, or representations of torments wherein the constancie of Martyrs appeared. Every yeare also at Shrovetuesday, (that we may begin with childrens sports, seeing we al have beene children,) the schoole boyes do bring Cockes of the game to their Master, and all the forenoone delight themselves in Cockfighting : after dinner all the youthes go into the fields to play at the bal. The schollers of every schoole have their ball, or [staff], in their hands: the

auncient and wealthy men of the Citie come foorth on horsebacke to see the sport of the yong men, and to take part of
the pleasure in beholding their agilitie. Every Fryday in
Lent a fresh company of young men comes into the field on
horsebacke, and the best horsm[a]n conducteth the rest. Then
march forth the citizens sons, and other yong men with disarmed launces and shields, and there they practise feates of
warre. Many Courtiers likewise, when the king lieth nere,
and attendants of noblemen doe repaire to these exercises;
and, while the hope of victorie doth inflame their minds, do
shew good proofe how serviceable they would be in martiall
affayres. In Easter holydayes they fight battailes on the
water. A shield is hanged upon a pole, fixed in the midst of
the stream; a boat is prepared without oares to bee caried by
violence of the water, and in the fore part thereof standeth a
young man readie to give charge upon the shield with his
launce; if so be hee breaketh his launce against the shield,
and doth not fall, he is thought to have performed a worthy
deed. If so be without breaking his launce he runneth
strongly against the shield, downe he falleth into the water,
for the boat is violently forced with the tide; but on each side
of the shield ride two boates, furnished with yong men, which
recover him that falleth as soone as they may. Upon the
bridge, wharfes, and houses, by the rivers side stand great
numbers to see, and laugh therat. In the holy dayes all the
Somer the youths are exercised in leaping, dancing, shooting,
wrastling, casting the stone, and practising their shields: the
Maidens trip in their Timbrels, and daunce as long as they
can well see. In Winter, every holy day before dinner, the
Boares prepared for brawne are set to fight, or else Buls and
Beares are bayted.

When the great fenne or Moore, which watreth the wals of
the Citie on the Northside, is frozen, many yong men play
upon the yce; some, striding as wide as they may, do slide
swiftly: others make themselves seates of ice, as great as
Milstones: one sits downe, many hand in hand doe draw him,
and, one slipping on a sudden, all fall togither: some tie
bones to their feete, and under their heeles, and shoving them-

selves by a little picked staffe, doe slide as swiftly as a bird flieth in the ayre, or an arrow out of a Crossebow. Sometime two runne togither with Poles, and, hitting one the other, eyther one or both doe fall, not without hurt: some breake their armes, some their legges, but youth desirus of glorie in this sort exerciseth it selfe agaynst the time of warre. Many of the Citizens doe delight themselves in Hawkes, and houndes, for they have libertie of hunting in Middlesex, Hartfordshire, all Chiltron, and in Kent to the water of Cray—thus farre Fitstephen of Sportes....

The marching forth of Citizens sonnes, and other yong men on horsebacke, with disarmed Launces and Shieldes, there to practise feates of warre, man agaynst man, hath long since be left of[f], but in their Citie, they have used on horsebacke, to runne at a dead marke, called a Quinten. For note whereof I reade that in the yeare of Christ 1253, the 38. of Henrie the third, the youthfull Citizens, for an exercise of their activitie, set forth a game to runne at the Quinten, and whosoever did best, should have a Peacocke, which they had prepared as a prise: certaine of the kings servants (because the Court lay then at Westminster) came as it were in spite of the Citizens, to that game, and giving reprochfull names to the Londoners, which for the dignitie of the Citie, and auncient priviledge which they ought to have enjoyed, were called Barons: the said Londoners, not able to beare so to be misused, fell upon the kings servants, and bet them shrewdly, so that upon complaint to the king, he fined the Citizens to pay a thousand Markes. This exercise of running at the Quinten was practised by the youthful Citizens, as well in Sommer as in Winter, namely[1], in the feast of Christmasse. I have seene a Quinten set upon Cornehill, by the Leaden Hall, where the attendantes on the Lords of merrie disports have runne, and made great pastime; for he that hit not the brode end of the Quinten, was of all men laughed to scorne, and he that hit it full, if he rid not the faste[r], had a sound blow in his necke, with a bagge full of sand hanged on the other end. I have also in the Sommer season seene some upon the river of

[1] especially.

Thames rowed in whirries, with staves in their hands, flat at
the fore end, running against one another, and, for the most
part, one or both overthrowne, and well dowked.

On the Holy dayes in Sommer, the youthes of this Citie
have in the field exercised themselves in leaping, dauncing,
shooting, wrestling, casting of the stone or ball, etc.

And for defence and use of the weapon, there is a
speciall profession of men that teach it. Ye may reade in
mine Annales, how that in the yeare 1222, the Citizens kept
games of defence and wrestlings neare unto the Hospitall of
Saint Giles in the field ; where they chalenged, and had the
mastrie of, the men in the Suburbs, and other commoners, etc.
Also in the yeare 1453, of a tumult made agaynst the Prior,
at the wrestling besides Clearkeswell, etc. which [is] sufficient to
prove that of olde time the exercising of wrestling, and such
like, hath beene much more used then of late yeares. The
youthes of this Citie also have used on holy dayes after Evening prayer, at the Maisters doores, to exercise their Wasters[1]
and Bucklers : and the Maidens, one of them playing on a
Timbrell, in sight of their Maisters and Dames, to daunce for
garlandes hanged thwart the streetes, which open pastimes in
my youth being now suppressed, worser practises within
doores are to be feared ; as for the bayting of Bulles and
Beares, they are till this day much frequented, namely in
Bearegardens on the Banks side, wherein be prepared scaffolds
for beholders to stand upon. Sliding upon the Ice is now
but childrens play : but in hawking and hunting many grave
citizens at this present have great delight, and doe rather want
leysure then goodwill to follow it.

Of triumphant shewes made by the Citizens of London, yee
may read in the yere 1236. the 20. of Henrie the third, Andrew
Bockwell then being Maior, how Helianor daughter to Raymond
Earle of Provance, riding through the Citie towardes Westminster, there to be crowned Queene of England, the Citie
was adorned with silkes, and in the night with Lamps, Cressets,
and other lights without number, besides many Pageants, and
straunge devises there presented. The Citizens also rode to meet

---

[1] fencing-cudgels.

the King and Queene, clothed in long garments embrodered about with gold and silks of diverse colours, their horses gallantly trapped to the number of 360, every man bearing a cup of gold or silver in his hand, and the kings trumpetters sounding before them. These Citizens did minister wine, as Bottelers, which is their service at their coronation. More, in the yeare 1298, for victorie obtained by Edward the first agaynst the Scots, every Citizen according to their severall trade made their severall shew, but specially the Fishmongers, which in a solemne Procession passed through the Citie, having, amongest other Pageants and shews, foure Sturgeons guilt, caried on four horses: then foure Salmons of silver on foure horses, and after them five and fortie armed knights riding on horses, made like Luces of the sea[1], and then one representing Saint Magnes, because it was upon St Magnes day, with a thousand horsemen, etc.

One other shew in the year 1377, made by the Citizens for Disport of the yong prince Richard, son to the blacke prince, in the feast of Christmas, in this manner. On the Sonday before Candlemas in the night, one hundred and thirty Citizens, disguised and well horsed in a mummerie, with sound of Trumpets, Shackbuts, Cornets, Shalmes, and other Minstrels, and innumerable torch lights of Waxe, rode from Newgate through Cheape over the bridge, through Southwarke, and so to Kennington besides Lambhith, where the Young Prince remayned with his mother and the Duke of Lancaster his uncle, [the] Earles of Cambridge, Hertford, Warwicke and Suffolke, with divers other Lordes. In the first ranke did ride 48. in the likenes and habite of Esquires, two and two together cloathed in redde coates and gownes of Say or Sandall[2], with comely visors on their faces: after them came riding 48. knightes in the same livery, of colour and stuffe. Then followed one richly arrayed like an Emperour, and after him some distance, one stately tyred like a Pope, whom followed 24 Cardinals, and after them eight or tenne with black visors not amiable, as if they had beene Legates from some forain Princes. These maskers, after they had entered

---

[1] hake.   [2] two different kinds of silk-stuff.

the Mannor of Kenington, alighted from their horses, and entered the hall on foot; which done, the Prince his mother and the Lordes came out of the Chamber into the hall, whome the saide mummers did salute : shewing by a paire of dice upon the table their desire to play with the Prince, which they so handled, that the Prince did alwayes winne when hee cast them. Then the mummers set to the Prince three Jewels, one after another, which were a boule[1] of gold, a cup of gold, and a ring of gold, which the Prince wanne at three casts. Then they set to the Princes mother, the Duke, the Earles, and other Lordes, to every one a ring of gold, which they did also win. After which they were feasted, and the musicke sounded; the prince and Lords daunced on the one part with the mummers, which did also daunce : which jolitie being ended, they were againe made to drinke, and then departed in order as they came.

The like was to Henry the fourth in the 2 of his raigne ; hee then keeping his Christmas at Eltham, vij Aldermen of London and their sonnes rode in a mummery, and had great thanks.

Thus much for sportfull shewes in Triumphs may suffice : now for sportes and pastimes yearely used. First, in the feaste of Christmas, there was in the kinges house, wheresoever hee was lodged, a Lord of Misrule, or Maister of merry disports, and the like had yee in the house of every noble man of honor, or good worshippe, were he spirituall or temporall. Amongst the which the Mayor of London and eyther of the shiriffes had their severall Lordes of Misrule, ever contending without quarrel or offence, who should make the rarest pastimes to delight the Beholders. These Lordes, beginning their rule on Alhollon[2] Eve, continued the same till the morrow after the Feast of the Purification, commonlie called Candlemas day [Feb. 2]: In all which space there were fine and subtle disguisinges; Masks and Mummeries, with playing at Cardes for Counters, Nayles and pointes in every house, more for pastime than for gaine. Against the feast of Christmas, every mans house, as also their parish churches, were decked with

---

[1] bowl. [2] Allhallows'.

holme¹, Ivie, Bayes, and whatsoever the season of the yeare aforded to be greene. The Conduits and Standardes in the streetes were likewise garnished, amongst the which I reade in the yeare 1444 that, by tempest of thunder and lightning, on the first of Februarie at night, Powles steeple was fired, but with great labour quenched; and toward the morninge of Candlemas day, at the Leaden Hall in Cornhill, a Standarde of tree being set up in the midst of the pavement fast in the ground, nayled ful of Holme and Ivie, for disport of Christmas to the people, was torne up, and cast downe by the malignant spirit (as was thought) and the stones of the pavement all aboute were cast in the streetes, and into divers houses, so that the people were sore agast of the great tempests.

In the weeke before Easter, had ye great shewes made for the fetching in of a twisted tree, or "With," as they termed it, out of the Woods into the Kinges house, and the like unto every mans house of Honor or Worship.

In the moneth of May, namely on Mayday in the morning, every man, except impediment, would walke into the sweete meadows and greene woods, there to rejoyce their spirites with the beauty and savour of sweete flowers, and with the harmony of birds praysing God in their kind. And for example hereof Edward Hall hath note, that Henry the eight, as in the 3. of his raigne and divers other yeares, so namely in the seaventh of his raigne on May day in the morning, with the Queene Katheren his wife, accompanied with many Lords and Ladies, rode a maying from Greenwitch to the high ground of Shooters hill, where as they passed by the way, they espied a companie of tall yeomen cloathed all in Greene, with greene hoodes, and with bowes and arrowes, to the number of 200. One, being their chieftaine, was called Robin Hoode, who required the king and his companie to stay and see his men shoote ; whereunto the king graunting, Robin Hoode whistled; and all the 200 Archers shot of[f], loosing all at once, and when he whistled againe, they likewise shot againe. Their arrowes whistled by craft of the head, so that the noyse

¹ ilex.

was straunge and loude, which greatly delighted the King, Queene, and their Companie. Moreover, this Robin Hoode desired the King and Queene with their retinue to enter the greene wood, where, in harbours made of boughs, and decked with flowers, they were set and served plentifully with venison and wine, by Robin Hoode and his meynie, to their great contentment, and had other Pageants and pastimes; as ye may reade in my saide Authour. I find also that in the moneth of May, the Citizens of London of all estates, lightly[1] in every Parish, or sometimes two or three parishes joyning togither, had their severall mayings, and did fetch in May-poles, with diverse warlike shewes, with good Archers, Morice dauncers, and other devices for pastimes all the day long. And towards the Evening they had stage playes, and Bonefiers in the streetes. Of these Mayings, we reade, in the raigne of Henry the sixt, that the Aldermen and Sheriffes of London being on Mayday at the Bishop of Londons Wood in the parish of Stebunheath[2], and having there a worshipfull dinner for themselves and other commers, Lydgate, the Poet, that was a Monke of Bery, sent to them by a Pursivant a Joyfull commendation of that Season containing 16. staves in meter Royall, beginning thus—

    Mightie Flora, Goddesse of fresh flowers,
      which clothed hath the Soyle in lustie greene....

These great Mayings and Maygames made by the governors and Maisters of this Citie, with the triumphant setting up of the great shaft (a principal May-pole in Cornehill, before the Parish Church of S. Andrew therefore called Anderschaft,) by meane[3] of an insurrection of youthes against Aliens on may day, 1517, the ninth of Henry the 8., have not beene so freely used as afore ; and therefore I leave them, and wil some what touche of watches, as also of shewes in the night.

---

[1] usually.   [2] Stepney.   [3] on account.

2 HAWKING

(a) Giraldus Cambrensis, *Gemma Ecclesiastica*, D. i. c. 54. (R. S., vol. II. p. 161.)

King Henry the Second of England (or his son Richard; I name both, but shun to distinguish clearly since my tale is to his dishonour) in the early days of his reign cast off his best falcon at a heron, for the sake of that cruel pastime. The heron circled higher and higher; but the falcon, being swifter, had already wellnigh overtaken him, when the king felt certain of victory and cried aloud, "By God's eyes or His gorge..., that bird shall not now escape, even though God Himself had sworn it!" (for they had learned thus to swear in their youthful insolence; and such habits may scarce be unlearnt; even as Henry II.'s grandfather, Henry I., was wont to swear *By God's Death*.) At these words the heron turned forthwith to bay; and, by a most miraculous change from victim to tormentor, stuck his beak into the falcon's head, dashed out his brains, and (himself whole and unhurt) cast the dying bird to the earth at the king's very feet.

(b) *Statutes at Large*, A.D. 1360. (35 Edward III. cap. 22.)

Item it is acorded in this present Parliament, That every person which findeth a Faulcon, Tercelet, Laner or Laneret, or other Hawke, that is lost of their Lord, that presently he bring the same to the Sheriff of the County, and that the Sheriff make Proclamation in all the good Towns in the County, that he hath such a Hawk in his Custody. And if the Lord which lost the same, or any of his people, come to challenge it, and proveth reasonably that the same is his Lord's, let him pay for the Costs, and have the Hawk. And if none come within four Months to challenge it, that then the Sheriff have the Hawk, making gree[1] to him that did take him, if he be a simple man; and if he be a Gentleman, and of Estate to have the Hawk, that then the Sheriff redeliver to him the Hawk, taking of him reasonable Costs for the time that he had him in his Custody. And

[1] a gratuity.

if any man take such Hawk, and the same conceal from the
Lord whose it was, or from his Faulconers; or whosoever
taketh him from the Lord, and thereof be attainted, shall
have Imprisonment of two Years, and yield to the Lord the
Price of the Hawk so concealed and carried away, if he have
whereof; and, if not, he shall the longer abide in Prison.

(*c*) From the household accounts of Nicholas de Litlington, Abbot
of Westminster 1362–86, extracted from *West. Munim.* 24, 512, by Dr
J. Armitage Robinson on p. 10 of *The Abbot's House at Westminster*,
1911. Compare Margaret Paston's offering of an image of wax of the
weight of her sick husband to Our Lady of Walsingham : Section XII.,
no. 12.

1368 *Item*, for a waxen image of a falcon bought to offer
[at the altar] for a sick falcon, 6*d*.

1368/9 *Item*, for a collar bought at the lord Abbot's bidding
for his greyhound Sturdy, 3*d*.

3   SPORT AND CHURCH

(*a*) The *Ménagier de Paris* was written between 1392 and 1394 by a
Parisian citizen, to instruct his young wife in her domestic, social and
religious duties.   It has a good many affinities with English treatises on
deportment of about the same date.   Ed. 1846, p. 296.

At this stage of training your hawk, you must keep him on
your fist more than ever before, taking him to law-courts and
among folk assembled in church or elsewhere, and into the
streets.   Keep him thus as long as you can, by day or night;
and sometimes perch him in the streets, that he may see and
accustom himself to men, horses, carts, hounds, and all other
things.

(*b*) Johann Geiler of Kaysersberg was one of the most distinguished
German churchmen, in character and intellect, during the early 16th century.   The following passage from his satirical "Ship of Fools" is quoted
by Abbé L. Dacheux.   *Jean Geiler*, 1876, p. 67, n. z.

Some men go to church in the guise of huntsmen, bearing
on their fist a hawk and bells, with a pack of dogs barking at
their heels, to the disturbance of divine service....Such conduct
is very blameworthy in all men, but most blameworthy in the
clergy, though some would fain excuse themselves on the plea
of noble birth.

(c) Injunctions of Bp Wykeham to the three great nunneries of Romsey, Wherwell, and St Mary's, Winchester, after his visitation in 1387. (Communicated by Miss E. E. Power from the MS. at New Coll. Oxford. f. 88 a and 88 b.)

Item—whereas we have convinced ourselves by clear proofs that some of the nuns of your house bring with them to church birds, rabbits, hounds, and such like frivolous things, whereunto they give more heed than to the offices of the church, with frequent hindrance to their own psalmody and that of their fellow-nuns, and to the grievous peril of their souls—therefore we strictly forbid you all and several, in virtue of the obedience due unto Us, that ye presume henceforward to bring to church no birds, hounds, rabbits or other frivolous things that promote indiscipline....

Item—whereas, through hunting-dogs and other hounds abiding within your monastic precincts, the alms that should be given to the poor are devoured, and the church and cloister and other places set apart for divine and secular services are foully defiled, contrary to all honesty—and whereas, through their inordinate noise, divine service is frequently troubled—therefore we strictly command and enjoin you, Lady Abbess, that you remove these dogs altogether, and that you suffer them never henceforth, nor any other such hounds, to abide within the precincts of your nunnery.

4   THE ENGLISH LONGBOW

(a) Froissart, ed. S. Luce, vol. I. (1869), p. 402.

Again, [in this year 1337] it was advised and decreed that, throughout the realms of England, no man should use any play or pastime save only the longbow and arrows, on pain of death ; and that every bowyer and fletcher should be made quit of all his debts.

(b) *Rotuli Parliamentorum*, VI. p. 188. A petition of the Commons in 1477.

To the King oure Liege Lord ; Pray we the Comons in this present Parlement assembled, That where[as], after the Lawes of this Lond, no persone shuld use any unlawfull Pleys, as Dise, Coyte, Foteball, and such like Pleys, but that every persone myghty and able in bodie shuld use his Bowe, by cause that the defense of this Lond stondeth moche by Archers...

Pleas it therefore your Hignes...to ordeyne and establish that, from the fest of Ester next comyng, no person Occupiour nor Governor of any Messuage, Tenement, Gardyn or other place within this Realme, voluntarily suffre any person to occupie or playe any of the said Pleys....

Le Roi le voet[1].

(c) *Statutes of the Realm*, 3rd Henry VIII. c. 3.

The Kyng our Sovereign Lord, (callyng to his most noble and gracious remembraunce that by the feate and exercise of the Subgiettes of this Realme in shotyng in long bowes there hath continually growen and ben within the same gret nombre and multitude of good Archers....And also, by meanes and occasion of custumable usage of Teynes-Play, Bowles, Classhe[2] and other unlawfull games, prohibetted by many good and beneficiall estatutes by auctorite of parliament in that behalf provided and made, grete impoverisshement hath ensued, and many heynous Murders Roberies and Feloun[i]es be committed and done, and also the devyne [service] by suche missedoers on holy and festivall days not herd or solempnised, to the high displeasure of Almyghty God)...hath ordeyned...that every man, being the Kynges subgiett, not lame decrepute or maymed, nor havyng any other lawfull or resonable cause or impediment, beyng withyn the age of LX yeres, (except to tho men, spirituall men, Justices of the one benche and of the other, Justices of Assise and Barons of the Escequere,) do use and exercise shotyng in longbowes, and also to have a bowe and arrowes redy contynually in his house to use hymself, and do use hymself in shotyng; And also that the father[s], governours and rulers of such as be of tendre age do teche and bring uppe theym in the knowledge of the same shotyng. ...And that all Statutes heretofore made agenst theym that use unlaufull games be duely putt in execucion.

---

[1] formula of assent.   [2] skittles.

ARCHERY PRACTICE

An English Archer

(*d*)   Latimer, *Sixth Sermon before King Edward* [*VI.*].

(p. 70.)   There is such dycing houses also, they say, as hath
not bene wont to be, where young gentlemen dice away theyr
thrift, and, where dycing is, there are other follies also.   For
the love of God let remedy be had, let us wrastle and stryve
against sinne.   Men of England in tymes past, when they
would exercise themselves (for we must needes have some
recreation, our bodies can not endure without some exercise)
they were wont to goe abroad in the fieldes a Shooting, but
now it is turned into glossing[1], gulling, and whooring within
the house.   The Arte of Shooting hath bene in times past
much esteemed in this realme, it is a gift of God that he hath
geve us to excell all other nations withall, it hath bene Gods
instrument wherby he hath geven us many victories against
our enemyes.   But now we have taken up whooring in townes,
in stead of Shooting in the fieldes.   A wonderous thing, that
so excellent a gift of God should be so little esteemed.   I
desire you my Lordes, even as ye love the honour and glory
of God, and entend to remove his indignation, let there be
sent forth some proclamation, some sharpe proclamation to
the Justices of peace, for they doe not their duetie.   Justices
now be no Justices; there bee many good actes made for this
matter already.   Charge them upon their allegiance, that this
singular benefite of God may be practised, and that it be not
turned into bolling[2], glossing, and whooring within the townes:
for they be negligent in executing these lawes of Shooting.
In my time, my poore father was as diligent to teach me to
Shoote, as to learne me any other thing, and so I thinke other
men did their children.   He taught me how to draw, how to
lay my body in my bowe, and not to draw with strength of
armes as other nations doe, but with strength of the body.   I
had my bowes bought me, according to my age and strength :
as I encreased in them, so my bowes were made bigger and
bigger : for men shall never Shoote well, except they be
brought up in it.   It is a goodly Arte, a wholesome kinde
of exercise, and much commended in Phisicke.   Marcilius
Phicinus in hys booke *de triplici vita* (it is a great whyle since

[1] cheating.   [2] bowling.

I read him now) but I remember he commendeth this kynde of exercise, and sayth, that it wrestleth agaynst many kindes of diseases.   In the · reverence of God let it be continued. Let a proclamation goe forth, charging the Justices of peace, that they see such Actes and Statutes kept, as were made for this purpose.

5   FOOTBALL

W. H. Bliss, *Calendar of Papal Letters*, vol. II. (1895) p. 214.   A.D. 1321. Papal grace to a canon of Shouldham.

To William de Spalding, canon of Sculdham, of the order of Sempingham.   During a game of ball [*ad pilam*], as he kicked the ball [*cum pede*], a lay friend of his, also called William, ran against him and wounded himself on a sheathed knife carried by the canon, so severely that he died within six days.   Dispensation is granted, as no blame is attached to William de Spalding, who feeling deeply the death of his friend, and, fearing what might be said by his enemies, has applied to the Pope.

6   FORBIDDEN TOURNEYS

Few things are more surprising to the casual reader of medieval documents than to find that tournaments were always forbidden by the Church, and frequently by the State.   As Léon Gautier puts it (*La Chevalerie*, pp. 681, 683), "From Innocent II. to Clement V. (i.e. 1143 to 1314) we get a long series of anathemas and papal thunderbolts.... Philippe-Auguste once made his children swear to take no part in any tourney...But Popes and Kings were impotent here, and men laughed at their prohibitions."   C. H. Cooper's *Annals of Cambridge* contains several prohibitions on the part of Henry III. of tourneys about to be held in that royal borough, e.g. under the years 1234, 1236, 1245, 1251.   During the Hundred Years' War, tourneys were often encouraged by the French Kings, but far less often permitted by the more business-like English sovereigns.

With Miracle-Plays, as with Church Ales and a good many similar festivals, the Church began with prohibition, but finally accepted the *fait accompli* and attempted to regulate it.   Dancing is almost universally condemned by the medieval moralist : see my *Chaucer and his England*, p. 108.

(*a*)   Trevisa's *Higden*, VIII. 133.   A.D. 1195.

For use of yonge knyghtes, as it were to make them alle to fighte in bataile, that tyme tournamentis, that were left of

longe tyme, were i-made and i-used agen, nought withstondynge
the popes forbedynge.

(*b*)   Robert of Brunne's *Handlyng Synne*, E.E.T.S., 1901, p. 153.

Of tournamentys that are forbede
Yn holy cherchë, as men rede,
Of tournamentys y preve[1] therynne,
Sevene poyntës of dedly synne :

(1)   Fyrst, ys pryde, as thou wel wost, ...
(2)   Wete thou wel ther ys envye
        Whan one seeth another do maystrye, ...
(3)   Yre and wraththe may they nat late[2] ;
        Ofte are tournamentys made for hate.
        Gyf every knygt lovede other weyl,
        Tournaments shulde be never a deyl ;
(4)   And certys they falle yn sloghnes[3],
        They love hyt more than God other messe[4] ; ...
        And yyt may nat, on no wyse,
(5)   Be forgete dame covetyse,
        For she shal fonde[5], on allë wyse,
        To wynnë hors, and harnyse.
        And yyt shal he make sum robbery,
        Or bygyle hys hoste ther he shal lye.
(6)   Glotonye also ys them among.
        Delycyus metes to make them strong ;
        And drynke the wyne that he were lyght[6],
        Wyth glotonye to make hym wyght[7].
(7)   Yyt ys there dame lecherye ;
        Of here cumth allë here maystrye.
        Many tymes, for wymmen sake,
        Knyghteys tournamentys make ;
        And whan he wendyth to the tournament
        She sendyth hym sum pryvy present,
        And byt[8] hym do for hys lemman
        Yn vasshelage alle that he kan ;
        So ys he bete there, for here love,
        That he ne may sytte hys hors above,

---

[1] prove.   [2] leave.   [3] sloth.   [4] or mass.   [5] strive.   [6] easy.
[7] doughty.   [8] bids.

That peraventure, yn alle hys lyve
Shal he never aftyr thryve[1].
Loke now whedyr swyche tournours
Mow be kallëd turmentours?
For they turmente alle with synne;
There tourment ys, ther shul they ynne[2],
But they levë swyche[3] myschaunce,
And for here[4] synne do penaunce....

Hyt ys forbode hym, yn the decre,
Myracles[5] for to make or se;
For, myracles gyf thou bygynne,
Hyt ys a gaderyng[6], a syght of synne.

He may yn the cherche, thurgh thys resun,
Pley the resurreccyun,—
That ys to seyë, how God ros,
God and man yn mygt and los[7],—
To make men be yn belevë gode[8]
That he ros with flesshe and blode;
And he may pleye, withoutyn plyght[9],
Howe God was bore yn golë[10] nyght,
To make men to beleve stedfastly
That he lyght yn the vyrgyne Mary.

Gif thou do hyt yn weyys or grevys[11],
A syght of synne truly hyt semys....

Gyf prest or clerk lene[12] vestëment
That halwed ys thurgh sacrament;
More than outher[13] they are to blame,
Of sacrylege they have the fame....

Daunces, karols, somour games,
Of many swych come many shames;
Whan thou stodyst[14] to makë thyse,
Thou art slogh[15] yn Goddys servyse;
And [they] that synnen yn swych thurgh the[e],
For them thou shalt a-couped[16] be.

---

[1] be well.   [2] they (who practise them) shall go to the place of torment.
[3] such.   [4] their.   [5] miracle-plays.   [6] gathering.   [7] praise.
[8] faith of God.   [9] peril.   [10] Yule.   [11] roads or groves.   [12] lend.
[13] others.   [14] studiest.   [15] slow.   [16] condemned.

What seye ye by every mynstral,
That yn swyche thynges delyte them alle?
Here[1] doyng ys ful perylous,
Hyt loveth nother[2] God ne goddys house;
Them were lever here of a daunce,
Of bost, and of olypraunce[3],
Than any gode of God of hevene,
Or other wysdom that were to nevene[4].
Yn folys[5] ys allë that they gete,
Here cloth, here drynkë, and here mete.

7 THE ACTOR'S STATUS

Thomas de Chabham, who was sub-dean of Salisbury in 1214 and 1220, compiled a *Penitential*, or guide-book for confessors, from which the following extract is translated. Mr E. K. Chambers, who prints the Latin (*Medieval Stage*, II. 262), notes that the doctrine here laid down about minstrels is often repeated in later treatises of the kind. Grosseteste took the same view (R. of Brunne, *Handlyng Synne*, E.E.T.S., 1901, p. 158).

There are three kinds of play-actors [*histrionum*]. Some transform and transfigure their own bodies by base contortions and base gestures, or by basely denuding themselves, or by wearing horrible masks; and all such are to be damned unless they abandon their calling. Others, again, do no work, but commit criminal deeds, having no fixed abode, but haunting the courts of great men and backbiting the absent opprobriously and ignominiously in order to please others. Such men also are to be damned; for the Apostle bids us take no food with such men as this; and such men are called wandering buffoons, for they are good for nothing but gluttony and backbiting. There is also a third kind of actors who have musical instruments for men's delight; and such are of two kinds. Some haunt public drinkings and wanton assemblies, where they sing divers songs to move men to wantonness; and such are to be damned like the rest. But there are others called jougleurs [*joculatores*], who sing the deeds of princes and the lives of the saints, and solace men in their sickness or in their anguish, and do not those innumerable base deeds

---

[1] their. [2] neither. [3] ostentation. [4] name. [5] fools.

which are done by dancing-men and dancing-women and others who play in indecent figures, and make men see a certain show of phantasms by enchantment or in any other way. If, then, these do no such thing, but sing to their instruments of the deeds of princes and other such profitable things, for the solace of their even-Christians, as is aforesaid, then such may well be borne with, as was said by pope Alexander [III.?]. For, when a jougleur asked of him whether he could save his soul in that calling, the Pope asked him whether he knew any other work for his livelihood ; and he made answer that he knew none. Then the Pope permitted him to live by that calling, so long as he abstained from the aforesaid base and wanton practices. And it must be noted that all commit mortal sin who give any of their goods to buffoons or jesters or the aforesaid play-actors ; for to give to play-actors is no other than to throw our money away.

8　KING AND MINSTREL

An Alphabet of Tales, E.E.T.S., p. 245, § 356.

We rede in " Gestis Francorum " how Philypp, [th]at som tyme was kyng of France, on a tyme when he saw mynstrallis and jogullurs hafe gay clothyng and grete giftis giffen thaim oute of courte ; and he promysid with all his harte, that als lang as he liffid, ther sulde no mynstrall were no clothe [th]at langed[1] unto his bakk. For, he said, hym had levur clethe[2] Criste ther-with, or pure men, than for to giff thaim to mynstrallis. " For," he said, " it was no noder[3] to giff to mystrals bod[4] for to offyr to fendis[5]."

9　A MINSTREL'S TRICK

Ibid. § 357.

Jacobus de Vetriaco tellis how som tyme ther was ane abbott of Ceustus[6] ordur ; and when he was a monke, he was a passand[7] hard man, and a sparand[8]. So hym happynd be made hosteler, to kepe gestis in ther ostrie[9], afor he was made

---

[1] belonged.　　[2] clothe.　　[3] nothing else.　　[4] but.　　[5] fiends.
[6] Cistercian.　　[7] passing.　　[8] miserly.　　[9] guesten-house.

abbott. So on a tyme ther come unto this abbay on a day a mynstrall, and was sett in the ostrie att dyner. And this monke servid hym of passand gray bread, and thyn potage, and a little salte; and he had no drynk bod[1] watir. And at evyn he was layd in a vyll[2] bedd, and a hard. And opon the morn this mynstrall was ill plesid, and umthoght[3] him how thatt he mott venge hym on this monke [th]at had servid hym so evull. So, as he went furth of his chamber ther he lay, hym happend to mete with the abbot; and this mynstrall come unto hym and haylsid[4] hym, and said; " My lord, I thanke you and your wurthie covent of grete cher at I hafe had here, and of grete coste that I hafe taken of you ; ffor yone gude liberall monke, your hostley, servid me yistrevyn[5] at my supper wur- thelie, with many dyvers costious mece[6] of ffissh, and I drank passand gude wyne. And now, when [th]at I went, he gaff me a payr of new butis[7], and a gude payr of new knyvis, and a poynt to [bynd] thaim with[8]." And when the abbott had hard this, onone[9] he went unto the closter, and callid this monke befor all his covent, and betid hym grevuslie here-for, and putt hym furth of his offes[10].

10   GOD'S MINSTRELS

Piers Plowman, C, VIII. 82, p. 175.

Ye lordes and ladyes and legates of holy churche,
That feden fool sages[11], flaterers and lyers,
And han lykynge to lythen[12] hem in hope to do yow lawghe[13]...:
And geveth suche mede[14] and mete, and poure men refusen
In youre deth-deynge ich drede me sore
Lest tho manere men to moche sorwe yow brynge ;...
Clerkus and knyghtes welcometh kynges mynstrales,
And for love of here[15] lordes lithen hem at festes ;
Muche more, me thenketh, riche men auhte[16]

---

[1] but.   [2] vile.   [3] bethought.   [4] saluted.   [5] yestreen.
[6] messes.   [7] boots.
[8] What Vitry really says is "a girdle." (*Exempla*, ed. Crane, 1890, p. 28.)
[9] anon.   [10] office.   [11] wise fools (i.e. professional fools).
[12] listen to.   [13] make you laugh.   [14] reward.   [15] their.   [16] ought to.

Have beggers by-fore hem, whiche beth godes mynstrales,
As he seith hym-self, seynt Johan bereth witnesse,
 Qui vos spernit, me eciam spernit[1].
Ther-for ich rede[2] yow riche, reveles when ye maken,
For to solace youre soules suche mynstrales to have;
The poure, for a fol sage, syttynge at thy table,
With a lered[3] man, to lere[4] the what oure lord suffrede
For to savy thy saule fram Satan thyn enemye,
And fithele[5] the, with-oute flateryng, of goode Fryday the
 geste[6];
And a blynde man for a bordiour[7], other[8] a bedreden womman
To crye a largesse by-fore oure lorde, your goode loos[9] to
 shewe.
Thuse thre manere mynstrales maken a man to lauhe;
In hus deth-deynge thei don hym gret comfort....
Ther[10] flaterers and foles, with here foule wordes,
Leden tho that lithen hem to Luciferes feste,
With *turpiloquio*[11], a lay of sorwe, and Lucifers fithele,
To perpetuel peyne, other purgatorye as wykke[12];
For he litheth and loveth that [which] godes lawe despiceth;
 Qui histrionibus dat, demonibus sacrificat[13].

11 A MINSTREL'S WHIM

Chronicles of Old London, etc., 1863, p. 258.

[1323.] On the first Sunday in Lent, after this, a minstrel,
Roger Wade by name, a crowder[14], solemnly celebrated his
own interment, as though he had been dead, and had masses
sung for his soul, both he himself and others in his company
making offering, so that many persons marvelled thereat.
And this he did, because he put no trust in executors; but by

---

[1] "He that despiseth you despiseth me" (not John, but Luke x. 16).
[2] counsel. [3] learned. [4] teach. [5] fiddle. [6] story. [7] jester.
[8] or. [9] fame. [10] whereas. [11] evil-speaking. [12] bad.
[13] "He who giveth to play-actors, sacrificeth to demons." This is not, as the
context seems to imply, a direct quotation from Canon Law, but the substance is
there; "to give one's goods to play-actors is no virtue, but a most grievous fault "
[*vitium immane*]—Gratian, *Decretum*, Pars I. Dist. lxxxvi. c. 7.
[14] The *crowd* was a kind of fiddle, much used in Wales.

reason of this act, some persons of the religious orders would have withdrawn from him his livery[1], which he had bought from them for the term of his life; he himself however died soon after Easter.

12   MIRACLE-PLAY AND MIRACLES

John of Beverley was Bishop of York from 705 to 718: he became the tutelar saint of Beverley Minster. The following translation is from a book of his miracles written towards the end of the 13th century (*Historians of the Ch. of York*, R. S., 1879, vol. I. p. 328).

It befel one summer day that the masked players [*larvati*] played and acted, after their wont, a certain play of the Lord's Resurrection within the churchyard of St John. Thither were gathered together a great multitude of both sexes, moved by divers causes; some for pleasure, some for wonder, and some for the holy purpose of arousing devotion. In this dense crowd that gathered round the players, there were many (and especially of small stature) who failed to gain the access which they desired; wherefore very many entered into the church, either to pray or to look at the pictures or to beguile the weariness of this day by some kind of recreation and solace. Certain youths, therefore, entering the church precincts, found by chance a half-opened door leading to the stairs which ascend to the top of the walls. Thither they hastened with boyish levity, and began to climb, step by step, to the stone vault of the church, intending either to peep through the lofty loopholes of the turrets, or through any holes they might find in the glass windows, that thus they might see more clearly the dress and gestures of the actors, and hear their dialogues with greater distinctness; wherein they imitated Zacchaeus, who, because he was little of stature, climbed up into a sycamore tree to see Jesus. But behold! men told to the custodians what these youths were doing; and they (fearing lest the boys should break or in some way harm the glass windows in their eagerness to see the performances in this miracle play) followed swiftly after them; and, rebuking their temerity, buffeted them soundly with the palms of their hands and drove them down again.

[1] i.e. *corrody*; a daily allowance of the necessaries of life.

Meanwhile one of the boys, beholding how ill his fellows fared, and fearing to fall into the pursuers' hands, ran aside among the upper parts of the church, until he had come in his hasty course to a spot beyond the great cross, which then stood by St Martin's altar. Standing there and looking down, he rashly set foot upon a certain squared stone which broke away from the wall and fell down with a crash to the stone pavement, with such force that, notwithstanding its hardness, it was dashed to a thousand pieces. The youth, lacking all support, and struck with fear and horror, fell also, lying there as one dead for some time afterwards. A crowd gathered round, sighing grievously and wailing miserably over this misfortune and venting their grief with gushing tears. His parents shrieked and tore their hair, while frequent sobs interrupted their cries of sorrow; for they knew not that their mourning was destined soon to be turned to laughter, and their sadness to joy, by God's good providence. For the Lord suffered not that the church, built in His honour and in that of His confessor [St John of Beverley], should be polluted as with a man's death; but, desiring it to be held in even greater reverence for the future, and desiring also to give a testimonial of veracity to that representation of His own resurrection which was meanwhile being played, He raised up in the sight of all men safe and sound, that youth who was believed to be dead, so that no hurt whatever could be found in his whole body. Thus it came to pass that those who, for the greatness of the press, were unable to witness the stage-play outside the church, became witnesses of a more marvellous proof of resurrection within the sacred building— nay, not only of our Lord's resurrection, but of His passion also. For the cutting-away of that stone, which fell away from the wall without touch of human hand, was a plain indication of the Lord's Incarnation of a pure virgin without knowledge of man; and the fall of those two, the stone and the boy, was a type of His passion, who was both God and man. Yet the stone, dashed to pieces by its fall, was again a type of the ram that was slain, while the youth was a type of Isaac who remained unhurt. Wherefore, as this fall was a symbol of His passion, in human flesh, so the youth's miraculous raising-again was a symbol of His resurrection in the Godhead.

13 DANCE AND SONG FOR BANNOCKBURN

The Brut, E.E.T.S., 1906, vol. I. p. 208.

And also, for that [king Edward] was discomfited at Bannokesbourne, therefore maidenes made a songe therof, in that contre, of kyng Edward of Engeland ; and in this maner thai songe :

Maydenes of Engelande, sare may ye morne,
For tynt[1] ye have youre lemmans at Bannokesborn,
    With hevalogh[2].
What wende[3] the Kyng of Engeland
To have ygete Scotlande,
    With rombylogh[4].

14 THE DEMAUNDES JOYOUS

Reliquiae Antiquae, vol. II. p. 72, where it is described as "From a unique copy in the Public Library of the University of Cambridge, printed by Wynken de Worde." It is a fair specimen of medieval amusements over the evening fire, when the Scholars and Fellows of Colleges were writing "poems, chronicles of realms, and the wonders of this world" (Sect. II., no. 20).

Demaunde. Who bare the best burden that ever was borne? *R.* That bare the asse when our lady fled with our lorde into Egypte. *Demaunde.* Where became the asse that our lady rode upon ? *R.* Adams moder dede ete her. *D.* Who was Adams moder ? *R.* The erthe. *D.* What space is from the hyest space of the se to the depest ? *R.* But a stones cast.... *D.* What thynge is it that never was nor never shall be ? *R.* Never mouse made her nest in a cattes ere. *D.* Why dryve men dogges out of the chyrche ? *R.* Because they come not up and offre. *D.* Why come dogges so often to the chyrche ? *R.* Because, whan they se the aulters covered, they wene theyr maysters goo thydere to dyner. *D.* Why dooth a dogge tourne hym thryes aboute or that he lyeth hym downe ? *R.* Bycause he knoweth not his beddes hede from

---

[1] lost.   [2] heave-alow.   [3] weened.   [4] rumbelow.

the fete. *D.* Why doo men make an oven in the towne?
R. For bycause they can not make the towne in the oven....
D. What almes is worst bestowed that men gyve? *R.* That
is to a blynde man, for as he hathe ony thynge gyven hym, he
wolde with good wyll se hym hanged by the necke that gave
it hym. *D.* Wherfore set they upon chyrche steples more a
cocke than a henne? *R.* Yf men shold sette there a henne,
she wolde laye egges, and they wolde fall upon mennes hedes.
D. What thyng is it that hath none ende? *R.* A bowle.
D. What wode is it that never flyes reste upon? *R.* The
claper of a lazers dysshe[1]....*D.* Whiche ben the moost profyt-
able sayntes in the chyrche? *R.* They that stonde in the
glasse windowes, for they kepe out the wynde for wastynge of
the lyghte. *D.* What people be they that never go a procession? *R.* They be those that rynge the belles in the
meane season. *D.* What is it that freseth never? *R.* That
is hote water. *D.* What thynge is that, that is moost lykest
unto a hors? *R.* That is a mare. *D.* Wherefore be there
not as many women conteyned in the daunce of poules[2] as
there be men? *R.* Bycause a woman is so ferefull of herte
that she had lever daunce amonge quycke folke than dede....
D. What thyng is it, the lesse it is the more it is dredde?
R. A brydge....*D.* What is it that is a wryte[3], and is no man,
and he dothe that no man can, and yet it serveth both God
and man? *R.* That is a be. *D.* What people be they that
love not in no wyse to be prayed for? *R.* They be beggers
and poore people, whan men say, God helpe them! whan they
aske almes. *D.* Howe many strawes go to gose[4] nest?
R. None, for lack of fete....*D.* What was he that slewe the
fourthe parte of the worlde? *R.* Cayne, whan he slewe his
broder Abell, in the whyche tyme was but foure persons in the
worlde....*D.* What is the aege of a feld mous? *R.* A yere,
and a hedge may stande thre mous lyves, and the lyfe of a
dogge is the terme of thre hedges standynge, and the lyf of a

[1] Lepers had a wooden dish with a clapper-lid, which served the double duty
of warning the public and receiving alms.
[2] A famous Dance of Death painted in the north cloister of Old St Paul's, and
destroyed in 1549.
[3] carpenter. [4] a goose's.

horse is thre dogges lyves, and the lyf of a man is thre hors
lyves, and the lyf of a gose is thre mennes lyves, and the lyfe
of a swanne thre gose lyves, and the lyfe of a swalowe is three
swanne lyves, and the lyfe of an egle is thre swalowes lyves,
and the lyfe of a serpent is thre egles lyves, and the lyfe of a
raven is thre serpentes lyves, and the lyfe of a harte is thre
ravens lyves, and an oke groweth fyve hondreth yere, and it
fadeth fyve hondreth yere, besyde the rote[1], whyche doubleth
three tymes everyche of the three ages aforesayd.

15   SWIMMING

Elyot, *The Governour*, ed. Croft, 1880, p. 176.   The cold bath was not
a medieval institution, in any form : hot baths were frequent enough among
the well-to-do as a luxury, but were more or less absolutely forbidden as
such by ascetic disciplinarians.

There is an exercise which is right profitable in exstreme
daunger of warres, but by cause there semeth to be some perile
in the lernynge therof, and also it hath nat bene of longe tyme
moche used, specially amonge noble men, perchan[c]e some
reder wyll litle esteme it, I meane swymmynge.   But nat-
withstandyng, if they revolve the imbecilitie of our nature,
the hasardes and daungers of batayle, with the examples which
shall herafter be showed, they wyll (I doubt nat) thinke it as
necessary to a capitayne or man of armes, as any that I have
yet rehersed.

Mr Croft notes "Probably the earliest treatise devoted specially to
this subject is the one called *De Arte Natandi*, by Everard Digby, which
was published in 1587.   The Author, a Cambridge Master of Arts,...ex-
plains that the number of deaths amongst the undergraduates by drowning
in the Cam warrants him in recommending the scientific teaching of
swimming."

[1] root.

SECTION XI

WAYFARING AND FOREIGN TRAVEL

1   THE GREATEST CITY IN EUROPE

The first extract is from Rabbi Benjamin of Tudela's Travels in 1160–73 and the second from Geoffroy de Villehardouin's *Chronicle*. Villehardouin was one of the principal captains of the Fourth Crusade. He was born about 1150, started on the Crusade in 1202, and wrote only a few years after the events which he records.

(*a*)   Benjamin of Tudela.   (Thos. Wright, *Early Travels in Palestine*, Bohn, 1848, p. 74.)

The circumference of the city of Constantinople is eighteen miles....Great stir and bustle prevails at Constantinople in consequence of the conflux of many merchants, who resort thither, both by land and by sea, from all parts of the world for purposes of trade.   In this respect the city is equalled only by Bagdad, the metropolis of the Mohammedans.   At Constantinople is the place of worship called St Sophia, and the metropolitan seat of the pope of the Greeks, who are at variance with the pope of Rome.   It contains as many altars as there are days of the year, and possesses innumerable riches, which are augmented every year by the contributions of the two islands and of the adjacent towns and villages.   All the other places of worship in the whole world do not equal St Sophia in riches.   It is ornamented with pillars of gold and silver, and with innumerable lamps of the same precious materials.   The Hippodrome is a public place near the wall of the palace, set aside for the king's sports.   Every year the birthday of Jesus the Nazarene is celebrated there with public rejoicings.   On these occasions you may see there representations of all the nations who inhabit the different parts of the world, with surprising feats of jugglery. Lions, bears, leopards, and wild asses, as well as birds, which have been trained to fight each other, are also exhibited. All this sport, the equal of which is nowhere to be met with, is carried on in the presence of the king and the queen.

King Manuel has built a large palace for his residence on the sea-shore, near the palace built by his predecessors: and to this edifice is given the name of Blachernes. The pillars and walls are covered with pure gold, and all the wars of the ancients, as well as his own wars, are represented in pictures. The throne in this palace is of gold, and ornamented with precious stones; a golden crown hangs over it, suspended on a chain of the same material, the length of which exactly admits the emperor to sit under it. This crown is ornamented with precious stones of inestimable value. Such is the lustre of these diamonds that, even without any other light, they illumine the room in which they are kept. Other objects of curiosity are met with here which it would be impossible to describe adequately.

The tribute which is brought to Constantinople every year from all parts of Greece, consisting of silks, and purple cloths, and gold, fills many towers. These riches and buildings are equalled nowhere in the world. They say that the tribute of the city alone amounts every day to twenty thousand florins, arising from rents of hostelries and bazaars, and from the duties paid by merchants who arrive by sea and by land. The Greeks who inhabit the country are extremely rich, and possess great wealth in gold and precious stones. They dress in garments of silk, ornamented with gold and other valuable materials. They ride upon horses, and in their appearance they are like princes. The country is rich, producing all sorts of delicacies, as well as abundance of bread, meat, and wine. They are well skilled in the Greek sciences, and live comfortably, "every man under his vine and his fig tree." The Greeks hire soldiers of all nations, whom they call barbarians, for the purpose of carrying on their wars with the sultan of the Thogarmim, who are called Turks. They have no martial

spirit themselves, and, like women, are unfit for warlike enter-
prises. No Jews dwell in the city with them ; they are obliged
to reside beyond the one arm of the sea, where they are shut
in by the channel of Sophia on one side, and they can reach
the city by water only, when they want to visit it for purposes
of trade. The number of Jews at Constantinople amounts to
two thousand Rabbanites and five hundred Caraites, who live
on one spot, but divided by a wall....Many of them are manu-
facturers of silk cloth, many others are merchants, some being
extremely rich ; but no Jew is allowed to ride upon a horse,
except R. Solomon Hamitsri, who is the king's physician,
and by whose influence the Jews enjoy many advantages even
in their state of oppression, which is very severely felt by
them ; and the hatred against them is increased by the
practice of the tanners, who pour out their filthy water in the
streets and even before the very doors of the Jews, who, being
thus defiled, become objects of contempt to the Greeks.
Their yoke is severely felt by the Jews, both good and bad ;
for they are exposed to be beaten in the streets, and must
submit to all sorts of bad treatment. Still the Jews are rich,
good, benevolent, and religious men, who bear the misfortunes
of their exile with humility. The quarter inhabited by the
Jews is called Pera.

    (*b*) Villehardouin, ed. N. de Wailly, 1887, p. 44.

On St John's Eve (June 23, 1203) the Crusaders came by
ship to St Stephen's Abbey, three leagues from Constantinople. There they had the city in full view, and drew to land,
and anchored their ships. And you may be assured that
those who had never seen Constantinople opened wide eyes
now ; for they could not believe that so rich a city could be
in the whole world, when they saw her lofty walls and her
stately towers wherewith she was encompassed, and these
stately palaces and lofty churches, so many in number as no
man might believe who had not seen them, and the length
and breadth of this town which was sovereign over all others.
And know that there was no man among us so bold but that
his flesh crept at the sight ; and therein was no marvel ; for

never did any men undertake so great a business as this assault of ours, since the beginning of the world.

p. 69. [When the Greek Emperor had surrendered the city], you may be assured that many of our army went to see this city of Constantinople, and the rich palaces and churches that were so many. Of relics I speak not; for at that time [before the sack of the city] there were as many here as in all the rest of the world.

p. 94. [When we had sacked the city], the chattels and the spoils were brought together....Rest assured that much riches were there; for, without counting all that was stolen, or the equal share given to the Venetians, four hundred thousand silver marks were brought together, and a good ten thousand horses and mules.

2   A MERCHANT ADVENTURER

The *Life of St Godric* is one of those real biographies which are too seldom met with among the mass of conventional Saints' Lives. It was composed by his younger contemporary, Reginald, a monk of Durham, and was written before the Saint's death in 1170. The author, as Boswell in like case, had often taken notes of St Godric's words on the very day on which they were uttered (p. 315). It exists in three recensions, each fuller than its predecessor. The Surtees Society edition (1847) follows the latest of these, but gives interesting variations in the notes. The following translation is based mainly upon the briefer variants, but with occasional substitution of the longer text. The unique interest of the book is that Godric, before retiring to his hermitage, was a "mercator"; and that, thanks to Reginald's fidelity, we have here what is practically the autobiography of a "Marchant with a forkèd berd" in the 12th century.

p. 21. This holy man's father was named Ailward, and his mother Edwenna; both of slender rank and wealth, but abundant in righteousness and virtue. They were born in Norfolk, and had long lived in the township called Walpole....When the boy had passed his childish years quietly at home; then, as he began to grow to manhood, he began to follow more prudent ways of life, and to learn carefully and persistently the teachings of worldly forethought. Wherefore he chose not to follow the life of a husbandman, but rather to study, learn and exercise the rudiments of more subtle conceptions. For this reason, aspiring to the merchant's trade, he began to follow the chapman's way of life, first learning how to gain in small bargains and things of insignificant price ; and thence, while yet a youth, his mind advanced little by little to buy and sell and gain from things of greater expense. For, in his beginnings, he was wont to wander with small wares around the villages and farmsteads of his own neighbourhood ; but, in process of time, he gradually associated himself by compact with city merchants. Hence, within a brief space of time, the youth who had trudged for many weary hours from village to village, from farm to farm, did so profit by his increase of age and wisdom as to travel with associates of his own age through towns and boroughs, fortresses and cities, to fairs and to all the various booths of the market-place, in pursuit of his public chaffer. He went along the high-way, neither puffed up by the good testimony of his conscience nor downcast in the nobler part of his soul by the reproach of poverty....

p. 26. Seeing that he then dwelt by the sea-shore, he went down one day to the strand to seek for some means of livelihood....The place is called Wellstream, hard by the town of Spalding ; there, when the tide was out, the country-folk were wont to scour and explore the stretches of sand, discovering and converting to their own use whatever wreckage or drift the sea might have brought to shore ; for hence they sometimes get wealth, since they are free to seize there upon whatsoever goods or commodities they may find by the shore. The saint, then, inspired by such hopes, roamed one day over these stretches of foreshore ; and, finding nothing at first, he followed on and on to a distance of three miles, where he found three porpoises lying high and dry, either cast upon the sands by the waves or left there by the ebb-tide. Two were still alive and struggling : the third, in the midst, was dead or dying. Moved with pity, he left the living untouched, cut a portion from the dead fish, and began carrying this away upon his back[1]. But the tide soon began to flow ; and Godric, halting under his burden, was overtaken by the waves ; first they wet his feet, then his legs ; then his upper body was compassed about

---

[1] Fats were rare and costly in the Middle Ages ; therefore porpoise was highly esteemed and always fetched a considerable price.

by the deep ; at length the waters went even over his head ; yet Godric, strong in faith, bare his burden onwards even under the waves, until, by God's help, he struggled out upon the very shore from which he had gone forth.   Then, bringing the fish to his parents, he told them the whole tale, and exhorted them to declare the glory of God.

p. 28. Yet in all things he walked with simplicity; and, in so far as he yet knew how, it was ever his pleasure to follow in the footsteps of the truth. For, having learned the Lord's Prayer and the Creed from his very cradle, he oftentimes turned them over in his mind, even as he went alone on his longer journeys; and, in so far as the truth was revealed to his mind, he clung thereunto most devoutly in all his thoughts concerning God.   At first, he lived as a chapman for four years in Lincolnshire, going on foot and carrying the smallest wares ; then he travelled abroad, first to St Andrews in Scotland and then for the first time to Rome. On his return, having formed a familiar friendship with certain other young men who were eager for merchandise, he began to launch upon bolder courses, and to coast frequently by sea to the foreign lands that lay around him.   Thus, sailing often to and fro between Scotland and Britain, he traded in many divers wares and, amid these occupations, learned much worldly wisdom....He fell into many perils of the sea, yet by God's mercy he was never wrecked ; for He who had upheld St Peter as he walked upon the waves, by that same strong right arm kept this His chosen vessel from all misfortune amid these perils.   Thus, having learned by frequent experience his wretchedness amid such dangers, he began to worship certain of the Saints with more ardent zeal, venerating and calling upon their shrines, and giving himself up by wholehearted service to those holy names.   In such invocations his prayers were oftentimes answered by prompt consolation ; some of which prayers he learned from his fellows with whom he shared these frequent perils ; others he collected from faithful hearsay ; others again from the custom of the place, for he saw and visited such holy places with frequent assiduity.   Thus aspiring ever higher and higher, and yearning upward with his whole heart, at length his great

c.

labours and cares bore much fruit of worldly gain. For he laboured not only as a merchant but also as a shipman...to Denmark and Flanders and Scotland; in all which lands he found certain rare, and therefore more precious, wares, which he carried to other parts wherein he knew them to be least familiar, and coveted by the inhabitants beyond the price of gold itself; wherefore he exchanged these wares for others coveted by men of other lands; and thus he chaffered most freely and assiduously. Hence he made great profit in all his bargains, and gathered much wealth in the sweat of his brow; for he sold dear in one place the wares which he had bought elsewhere at a small price.

Then he purchased the half of a merchant-ship with certain of his partners in the trade; and again by his prudence he bought the fourth part of another ship. At length, by his skill in navigation, wherein he excelled all his fellows, he earned promotion to the post of steersman....

p. 30. For he was vigorous and strenuous in mind, whole of limb and strong in body. He was of middle stature, broad-shouldered and deep-chested, with a long face, grey eyes most clear and piercing, bushy brows, a broad forehead, long and open nostrils, a nose of comely curve, and a pointed chin. His beard was thick, and longer than the ordinary, his mouth well-shaped, with lips of moderate thickness; in youth his hair was black, in age as white as snow; his neck was short and thick, knotted with veins and sinews; his legs were somewhat slender, his instep high, his knees hardened and horny with frequent kneeling; his whole skin rough beyond the ordinary, until all this roughness was softened by old age.... In labour he was strenuous, assiduous above all men; and, when by chance his bodily strength proved insufficient, he compassed his ends with great ease by the skill which his daily labours had given, and by a prudence born of long experience....He knew, from the aspect of sea and stars, how to foretell fair or foul weather. In his various voyages he visited many saints' shrines, to whose protection he was wont most devoutly to commend himself; more especially the church of St Andrew in Scotland, where he most frequently made and paid his vows. On the way thither, he oftentimes touched at the island of Lindisfarne, wherein St Cuthbert had been bishop, and at the isle of Farne, where that Saint had lived as an anchoret, and where St Godric (as he himself would tell afterwards) would meditate on the Saint's life with abundant tears. Thence he began to yearn for solitude, and to hold his merchandise in less esteem than heretofore....

p. 36. And now he had lived sixteen years as a merchant, and began to think of spending on charity, to God's honour and service, the goods which he had so laboriously acquired. He therefore took the cross as a pilgrim to Jerusalem, and, having visited the Holy Sepulchre, came back to England by way of St James [of Compostella]. Not long afterwards he became steward to a certain rich man of his own country, with the care of his whole house and household. But certain of the younger household were men of iniquity, who stole their neighbours' cattle and thus held luxurious feasts, whereat Godric, in his ignorance, was sometimes present. Afterwards, discovering the truth, he rebuked and admonished them to cease; but they made no account of his warnings; wherefore he concealed not their iniquity, but disclosed it to the lord of the household, who, however, slighted his advice. Wherefore he begged to be dismissed and went on a pilgrimage, first to St Gilles and thence to Rome the abode of the Apostles, that thus he might knowingly pay the penalty for those misdeeds wherein he had ignorantly partaken. I have often seen him, even in his old age, weeping for this unknowing transgression....

p. 38. On his return from Rome, he abode awhile in his father's house; until, inflamed again with holy zeal, he purposed to revisit the abode of the Apostles and made his desire known unto his parents. Not only did they approve his purpose, but his mother besought his leave to bear him company on this pilgrimage; which he gladly granted, and willingly paid her every filial service that was her due. They came therefore to London; and they had scarcely departed from thence when his mother took off her shoes, going thus barefooted to Rome and back to London. Godric, humbly serving his parent, was wont to bear her on his shoulders....

p. 41. Godric, when he had restored his mother safe to his father's arms, abode but a brief while at home ; for he was now already firmly purposed to give himself entirely to God's service. Wherefore, that he might follow Christ the more freely, he sold all his possessions and distributed them among the poor. Then, telling his parents of this purpose and receiving their blessing, he went forth to no certain abode, but whithersoever the Lord should deign to lead him ; for above all things he coveted the life of a hermit.

He finally settled at Finchale near Durham ; but it was forty years before he was able finally to conquer his passions and to attain peace in his new life (p. 90). The Virgin Mary, who had already deigned to join Godric and his mother as their daily companion on the Roman pilgrimage, was his constant consoler in this cell ; and it was she (he insisted) who taught him what is probably the earliest piece of noted middle English song which has come down to us (p. 288).

einte   Ma-rie   vir-gi-ne   moder   Jesu   Cristes   Naza-re-

-ne   onfong   schild   help   thine   Go - dric   on-fong   bring

heglic   with   The   in   godes   ric[1].

He died in 1170 ; for the last eight years he had been bedridden and beset by devils in visible form (pp. 311–12) almost to the day of his death (p. 313). His actual passing was in physical struggle and inward peace (pp. 322–6).

3   A JOURNEY TO AVIGNON

From J. E. T. Rogers, *Hist. Ag. and Prices*, vol. II. (1866), p. 631. Itinerary of a Fellow of Merton and his servant. The items should be multiplied by about 15 to bring them into terms of the purchasing power of modern money.

The account of John de Middelton, of receipts and expenses in the business of procuring the appropriation of

---

[1] Text partly corrected from *Englische Studien*, vol. XI. (1888), p. 423. *Onfong*=receive ; *schild*=shield ; *heglic*=gloriously ; *ric*=kingdom.

Emeldon Church [to our College], going to the Papal Court at Avignon and returning to Oxford, from Monday, Jan. 21, 1331 to Aug. 24 of the same year.

Receipts. £10 from Harinton, the Bursar. For his horse, sold at the Court, £3. 10. Sale of his long gown, 6s 8d. Sale of fur from his supertunic 2s. Gain on a certain horse sold at Amiens, 3s 5½d. Received from the Bailiff of Elham, £1.

Total £16. 2s 1½d.

Expenses. Monday, at Thame, 1½d. Tuesday, Uxbridge [Wuksebrug] and Acton, 5½d, and that night and the 3 following at London with the Warden. Saturday, Newton [*hiatus in MS.*]. Sunday, Canterbury and Dover 1s 7¼d. Monday, customs on the sea and a mantle, 1s: offerings at St Nicholas' shrine 1d; that night at Calais 1s 3d. Tuesday, to and at Boulogne, 1s 4d. Wednesday, to and at Crécy, 1s 6d. Thursday, to and at Poix, 1s 10d. Friday, to and at Tillart, 1s 8d. Saturday, to and at Paris, 1s 8d. Sunday and Monday, at Paris, 5s 9½d. Tuesday at Essonne, 1s 3d. [Here he stayed the next 3 days and spent 4s 5½d.] Saturday, at [Esmans?] 1s 11d. Sunday, at *la Male Taverne*, 1s 11d. Monday at Cosne, 1s 10½d. Tuesday, Nevers, 1s 9d. Wednesday, being Ash Wednesday, at Nevers also, 2s 3d. Thursday, at [Cercy?], 1s 11d. Friday, at Forges [St Forgeux?], 1s 4d. Saturday, at Thoissey, 1s 8d. Sunday, at Lyons, 1s 7½d. Monday, also at Lyons, 2s 2d. Tuesday, Vienne 2s 1½d. Wednesday, at Champagne, 1s 3d Thursday, at Voulte-s-Rhône, 1s 7d. Friday, at Bourg-St-Andéol 1s 1d. Saturday and Sunday, at Avignon, 2s 2d Monday 10d, Tuesday 10d, Wednesday and Thursday 1s 7d, Friday 10d.

Total £2. 15s 1½d.

Then, for the third week of Lent, my commons cost 1s 8d; my servant's commons 1s 1¼d. The next week, my commons 1s 11½d; my servant's [*and so on from week to week*]. Item, on a feast for my companions because the grace was granted, 3s 3½d. *Item* for the use of the hall and kitchen, and bacon from the larder, and vessels, 2s 3d [for the whole 21½ weeks].

Item to the common servants 2ˢ 4ᵈ. *Item* to the barber 6ᵈ. Item to the washerwoman 6ᵈ.

Total £3. o. 10.

A few items from the homeward journey:
One horse was sold at Avignon. On the way home William the servant fell ill, and needed an extra horse (for a litter?); this was hired for 10½ᵈ a day. At Amiens the servant's horse was sold; a hired horse took him to Wissant for 2ˢ. Another, which had been bought for him, "died through the tempest"; a loss of 9ˢ. The passage from Wissant to Dover cost 3ˢ 6ᵈ. They carried their own bedding with them; this was a common practice. Arrived at Canterbury, they offered to St Thomas "iiijᵈ sterling," and finally feasted their successful journey at Oxford at an expense of 3ˢ 6½ᵈ.

They had taken 34 days to get to Avignon, staying here and there on the way. The return journey was more expeditious: they seem to have reached Wissant on the fourteenth day after leaving Avignon. Middleton must have been a good man of business; he lost only 7ᵈ in false money, though he had to deal with four different currencies. The College sent him next year on a similar mission to Northumberland, to procure the appropriation of the great tithes of Embleton (*Hist. Ag. and Prices*, II. 635); and it is pleasant to think that he is probably the Midelton of the Merton Scrutinies (*ibid.* p. 670 ff.: see Section II., no. 21).

4 TRAVEL PRICES

Northumberland Houshold Book, p. 117: cf. the contemporary *Lestrange Household Book* in *Archaeologia*, vol. XXV. pp. 411 ff.

Whensoever any of his Lordship Servauntes be comaunded to ride on message in Winter...that every of theym be allowed for the tyme for his being furth in his jornay... ijᵈ for every meall and *ob* [½ᵈ] for every his baiting; and for his Hors every day and night of his saide jornay iiijᵈ, *viz.* a penny for his baiting ande iijᵈ at night for his provounder. The whiche is in all for a Man and his Hors in the Daie in Winter viijᵈ if it be Etting-Daye; and, if it be Fasting-Daie, than ijᵈ to be abated; the which is vjᵈ on a Fasting-Day.

[In summer, the man's expenses are the same, but the horse's only 1½ᵈ: total 5½ᵈ per eating-day and 3½ᵈ per fast-day. The halfpenny for the man's "baiting" is mysterious; it is not counted in the addition either of the winter or of the summer total. A London ordinance of 1371 fixed 2½ᵈ as maximum price for "hay for the feeding of one horse a day and a night." Riley, *Memorials*, p. 347.]

5   THE TRAVELLER'S GEAR

Fitzherbert, *Book of Husbandry*, ed. W. W. Skeat, 1882, p. 93.

A lesson made in Englisshe verses, to teache a gentyl-mans servaunt, to saye at every tyme whan he taketh his horse, for his remembraunce, that he shall not forget his gere in his inne behynde hym.

Purse, dagger, cloke, nyght-cap, kerchef, shoyng-horne, boget[1] and shoes.

Spere, male, hode, halter, sadelclothe, spores, hatte, with thy horse-combe.

Bowe, arrowes, sworde, bukler, horne, leisshe[2], gloves, stringe, and thy bracer[3].

Penne, paper, inke, parchmente, reedwaxe, pommes[4], bokes, thou remember.

Penknyfe, combe, thimble, nedle, threde, poynte, leste that thy gurthe breake.

Bodkyn, knyfe, lyngel[5], gyve thy horse meate, se he be showed[6] well.

Make mery, synge and thou can; take hede to thy gere, that thou lose none.

6   TRAVELLERS' TALES

Riley, *Memorials of London*, 1868, p. 445.

A.D. 1380. John Warde, of the County of York, and Richard Lynham, of the County of Somerset, two impostors, were brought to the Hall of the Guildhall of London, before John Hadlee, Mayor, the Aldermen, and the Sheriffs, and questioned for that, whereas they were stout enough to work for their food and raiment, and had their tongues to talk with, they, the same John Warde and Richard Lynham, did there pretend that they were mutes, and had been deprived of their tongues; and went about in divers places of the city afore-said, carrying in their hands two ell measures, an iron hook and pincers, and a piece of leather, in shape like part of a tongue, edged with silver, and with writing around it, to this

---

[1] budget.   [2] leash.   [3] arm-guard for bow-shooting.   [4] pumice.
[5] shoemaker's thread.   [6] shoed.

effect, "*This is the tongue of John Warde*"; with which instruments, and by means of divers signs, they gave many persons to understand that they were traders, in token whereof they carried the said ell measures; and that they had been plundered by robbers of their goods; and that their tongues had also been drawn out with the said hook, and then cut off with the pincers; they making a horrible noise, like unto a roaring, and opening their mouths; where it seemed to all who examined the same, that their tongues had been cut off: to the defrauding of other poor and infirm persons, and in manifest deceit of the whole of the people, etc. Wherefore, they were asked how they would acquit themselves thereof; upon which, they acknowledged that they had done all the things above imputed to them; it was awarded that they should be put upon the pillory on three different days, each time for one hour in the day; the said instruments being hung about their necks each day.

7   THE WAYFARING FRIAR

For this Walter of Maddeley see Section II., no. 14. The anecdote is related by Eccleston (*Monumenta Franciscana*, R. S., vol. i. p. 28) who, writing about 1260, implies that Walter was by that time dead. Franciscans sometimes went quite barefoot, but generally wore sandals in cold climates.

[In early days] the Brethren did not even wear socks, save only the rich or ailing; and even then only by special licence. It came to pass that brother Walter of Maddeley, of pious memory, found two socks, and put them on when he went to matins; during which service, as he thought, he felt better than was his wont. But afterwards, when he went to bed and slept, he dreamed that he must needs pass through a certain perilous pass betwixt Oxford and Gloucester called Boys-aliz, which was haunted by robbers; and, as he went down into a deep dale, they came upon him from every hand, crying *Kill*, *Kill!* Whereat he feared greatly, and cried that he was a Friar Minor. "Thou liest," said they, "for thou goest not unshod!" But he, believing himself to be unshod as was his wont, cried "Nay, but I walk unshod," and confidently thrust forward his foot; whereupon he found himself shod, under

A Medieval Inn

THE BLIND WAYFARER

CROWLAND BRIDGE

their very eyes, with the socks aforesaid ; and, overcome with confusion, he forthwith awaked from sleep and cast the socks into the midst of the cloister-garth.

8   THE BLIND MAN'S WAYFARING

Trevisa's *Bartholomew*, Lib. VII. c. 20.

The blinde mannes wretchednes is so moche, that it maketh hym not onlye subgette to a chylde, or to a servaunte, for rulynge and ledynge, but also to an hounde.   And the blynde is ofte broughte to so greate nede, that to passe and scape the peryll of a brydge or of a fourde he is compelled to truste in an hounde more than to himselfe.   Also oft in perils, where al men doubte or drede, the blynde man, for he seeth no perill, is syker[1]....Also sometyme the blind beteth and smiteth and greveth the child that ledeth him, and shal soone repent the beting by doinge of the child.   For the child hath mind of the beting, and forsaketh him and leveth him alone in the myddle of a brydg, or in some other peril, and techeth him not the way to void the peril.

9   FOREST WAYS

Ibid., Lib. XVII. c. 142, f. 285 *b*.

Then saltus, silva, and nemus [*i.e. different kinds of woods*] ben wyde places, waste, and desolate, that many trees growen in without fruyte and also fewe havyng fruyte.   And those trees whiche ben bareyn and bearen no maner frute ben alway generally more and hyer than that with fruyte, fewe oute taken[2], as oke and beche.   In these woods be oft wylde beastes and foules ; therin groweth herbes grasse lees and pasture, and namelye[3] medycynall herbes in woodes be founde. In somer wodes ben bewtyed with bowes and braunches, with herbes and gras.

In woodes is place of disceyte and of huntynge.   For therin wylde beastes ben hunted, and watches and disceytes be ordeined and set of houndes and of hunters.   There is place of hyding and of lurking : for oft in woodes theves ben hyd and oft in theyr awaytes and disceytes passinge men comethe

[1] sure.   [2] excepted.   [3] especially.

and ben spoyled and robbed, and oft slayne. And soo, for many and dyvers wayes and uncerten, strange men ofte erre and go out of the waye: and take uncerten waye and the way that is unknowe, tofore the way that is knowen: and come ofte to the place there theves lye in awayte, and not without peryll. Therfore ben ofte knottes made on trees and in bushes, in bowes[1] and in braunches of trees: in token and marke of the highe waye, to shewe the certen and sure way, to wayfaring men: but oft the theves, in tornynge and metynge of waies, change suche knottes and signes, and begyle many men, and brynge them out of the right waye by false tokens and sygnes. Birdes, foules, and bein fleeth to wod: Byrdes to make nestes, and bein to gader hony.

10　A TRAP FOR TRAVELLERS

From the treatise on the Fistula by John Arderne, the earliest known of our great British surgeons, about A.D. 1370 (E.E.T.S., 1910, p. 100). Compare Chaucer, *C. T.* B, 4,174 ff.; also the very picturesque story which is recorded in Abbot Islip's diary [about 1498] and summarized in *The Church Quarterly*, Ap. 1907, p. 67, of the priest who discovered two corpses under the straw at a lonely inn.

[Powder] for to make a man sleep agaynz his wille, after maner of Ribaldez and trowans[2] in fraunce, that felawshypeth tham[3] by the waiez to pilgrimez that thai may robbe tham of thair silver when thai ar aslepe. *Recipe* [Henbane, darnel, black poppy and bryony root]; brek al-togidre in a brasen morter into ful smal poudre, of which poudre giffe hym in his potage or in a kake of whete or in drynk; and he schal slepe alsone[4], wille he wil he noght, al-aday or more, after the quantite that he hathe taken.

11　PITS IN THE HIGH ROAD

The Coventry Leet Book, E.E.T.S., 1908, p. 338. How necessary the prohibition was, may be gathered from an incident told by Mrs Green, *Town Life in the 15th Century*, 1894, vol. II. p. 31. An Aylesbury miller, in 1499, dug a clay pit in the highway, 10 feet long, 8 feet broad and 8 deep, in which a travelling glove-merchant was drowned one night. The local jury acquitted the miller, on the ground that he had nowhere else to get the particular clay he needed.

---

[1] boughs.　　[2] tramps (*truand*).　　[3] associate themselves.　　[4] at once.

Also that no man fro hensfurth digge cley uppon Cheyles-more Grene nor in the high-weye betwixt Somerlesve buttis and Spon market, up[on] the peyn of xl d.

12   A STORMY CROSSING
The Brut, E.E.T.S., 1908, p. 295. Cf. T. Blount, *Antient Tenures*, 1679, pp. 61, 63.

And in the xvj yere of his regne folwynge [1343] in the wynter tyme, the king...dressid hym over see [from France] into Engelond warde. And as he sayled toward Engelond, in the hye see, the moste mishappes, stormes and tempeste, thundres and lightnyngez, fil to hym in the see, the whiche was seyd that it was done and areysed[1] thorugh evel spirites made by sorcery and Nigromancye of them of Fraunce. Wherfore the Kingez hert was ful of sorwe and angwysshe, weyling and sighyng, and said unto oure lady on this wyse. "O blessid lady, sent Marye! what is the cause that ever-more, goyng into Fraunce, al thinges and wederes[2] fallyn to me joyful and likyng and gladsome, and as y wolde have [them]; but alwey turnyng into Engelond ward, al thinges fallen unprofitable and harmfull?" Never the latter, he, scapyng alle the perilles of the see, as God wolde, come by nyght to the Tour of London....

13   THE PILGRIMS' SEA VOYAGE
From E.E.T.S., vol. xxv. (1867), *The Stacions of Rome, etc.* p. 37.

> Men may leve alle gamys,
> That saylen to seynt Jamys!
> Ffor many a man hit gramys[3],
>   When they begyn to sayle.
> Ffor when they have take the see,
> At Sandwyche, or at Wynchylsee,
> At Brystow, or where that hit bee,
>   Theyr hertes begyn to fayle.
> Anone the mastyr commaundeth fast
> To hys shyp-men, in alle the hast,
> To dresse hem[4] sone about the mast,
>   Theyr takelyng[5] to make.

---

[1] aroused.   [2] weathers.   [3] grieves.   [4] busy themselves.   [5] tackling.

With "howe! hissa!" then they cry,
"What, howe, mate! thow stondyst to ny,
Thy felow may nat hale the by[1]";
    Thus they begyn to crake[2].

A boy or tweyn anone up styen[3],
And overthwart the sayle-yerde lyen;—
"Y how! taylia!" the remenaunt cryen,
    And pulle with alle theyr myght.
"Bestowe the boote[4], Bote-swayne, anon,
That our pylgryms may pley theron;
For som ar lyke to cowgh and grone
    Or[5] hit be full mydnyght.

"Hale the bowelyne! now, vere the shete!—
Cooke, make redy anoon our mete,
Our pylgryms have no lust to ete,
    I pray god yeve[6] hem rest!"
"Go to the helm! what, howe! no nere[7]?
Steward, felow! A pot of bere!"
"Ye shalle have, sir, with good chere,
    Anon alle of the best."

"Y howe! trussa! hale in the brayles[8]!
Thow halyst nat, be god, thow fayles[9]!
O se howe welle owre good shyp sayles!"
    And thus they say among.
"Hale in the wartake[10]!" "hit shal be done."
"Steward! cover the boorde anone,
And set bred and salt therone,
    And tary nat to long."

Then cometh oone and seyth, "be mery;
Ye shall have a storme or a pery[11]."
"Holde thow thy pese! thow canst no whery[12],
    Thow medlyst wondyr sore."

---

[1] haul past thee.   [2] cry.   [3] climb.   [4] stow the boat.   [5] ere.
[6] give.   [7] no nearer to the wind?   [8] furling ropes.   [9] slackest off.
[10] a kind of rope.   [11] squall (usually *pirrie*).   [12] curse?

Thys mene whyle the pylgryms ly,
And have theyr bowlys fast theym by,
And cry aftyr hote maluesy¹,
  Thow helpe² for to restore.

And some wold have a saltyd tost,
Ffor they myght ete neyther sode ne rost³;
A man myght sone pay for theyr cost,
  As for oo⁴ day or twayne.
Som layde theyr bookys on theyr kne,
And rad⁵ so long they myght nat se ;—
" Allas ! myne hede wolle cleve on thre⁶ ! "
  Thus seyth another certayne.

Then commeth owre owner lyke a lorde,
And speketh many A Royall worde,
And dresseth hym to the hygh borde,
  To see alle thyng be welle.
Anone he calleth a carpentere,
And byddyth hym bryng with hym hys gere,
To make the cabans here and there,
  With many a febylle⁷ celle ;

A sak of strawe were there ryght good,
Ffor som must lyg theym⁸ in theyr hood ;
I had as lefe be in the wood,
  Without mete or drynk ;
For when that we shall go to bedde,
The pumpe was nygh oure beddes hede,
A man were as good to be dede
  As smell thereof the stynk !

---

¹ malmsey. ² their health ? ⁵ boiled nor roast. ⁴ one. ⁵ read.
 ⁶ split in three. ⁷ ramshackle. ⁸ lie down.

14   A TRAVELLERS' GUIDE

A little work of *Dialogues in French and English* was printed by Caxton about 1483. He took the French portion from a French-Flemish phrase-book compiled at Bruges, probably in the first half of the 14th century: this he printed side by side with an English translation of his own for the use of travellers; the English alone is here printed, from the edition published by the E.E.T.S. (Extra Series, 1900), p. 48.

Yf ye owe ony pylgremages, so paye them hastely. Whan ye be mevyd[1] for to goo your viage, and ye knowe not the waye, so axe it thus, in comending the peple to god: " To god, goode peple; I goo to Saynt James, ([or], to our lady of Boloyne). At whiche gate shall I goo out, and at whiche hande shall I take my way?"   "On the right hande, whan ye come to a brigge, so goo ther over; ye shall fynde a lytill waye on the lyfte honde, whiche shall brynge you in a contre there shall ye see upon a chirche two hye steples; fro thens shall [y]e have but four myle unto your loggyng. There shall ye be well easyd for your money, and ye shall have a good Jorne[2]."

"Dame, god be here!"   "Felaw, ye be welcome."   "May I have a bedde here withinne?—May I here be logged?" "Ye[3], well and clenly, alle[4] were ye twelve, alle on horseback." "Nay, but we thre. Is there to ete here within?"   "Ye, ynough, god be thanked."   " Brynge it to us. Gyve heye to the hors, and strawe them well; but [see] that they be watred."

"Dame, what owe we?   We have ben well easyd."   "We shall rekene to morow, and shall paye also, that ye shall hold you plesid." "Brynge us to slepe; we ben [w]ery." "Well, I goo, ye shall reste. Jenette, lyghte the candell; and lede them ther above in the solere[5] tofore; and bere them hoot watre for to wasshe their feet; and covere them with quysshons[6]; se that the stable be well shette[7]."

"Dame, may men goo by ship from hens to Boloyne?"   "Ye, now ther is a shippe redy ful of peple. God wel them conduyte[8]! God brynge them in savete!"

---

[1] stirred.   [2] journey.   [3] yea.   [4] even though.   [5] upper room.
[6] cushions.   [7] shut.   [8] conduct.

15   BECKET ON A JOURNEY

Description by his chaplain, William Fitzstephen. (*Materials for the History of Becket*, R. S., vol. III. 1877, 27 ff.)   Becket, Archdeacon and Chancellor, but not yet Archbishop, was sent in 1158 to demand a French princess in marriage for prince Henry.

He prepared lavishly to display the wealth of English luxury, that all men might honour the king's person in his ambassador, and Becket's in his own self.   He had some 200 servants on horseback, knights, clerks, stewards, servants, esquires, and noble youths serving their knightly apprenticeship in his household, all in orderly array.   This whole household, with all their followers, glittered in new and splendid attire, each after his own fashion, for this festal journey.   He himself had four-and-twenty changes of raiment....With him were hounds and all kinds of hawks that kings and rich men nourish.   In his train were eight splendid chariots, each drawn by five horses no less strong and shapely than war-horses ; each horse had a stout young man to lead him, clad in a new coat and walking by his side ; moreover, each chariot had its own driver and guardian.   Two of these chariots were laden solely with iron-bound barrels of ale, decocted from choice fat grain, as a gift for the French, who wondered at such an invention—a drink most wholesome, clear of all dregs, rivalling wine in colour and surpassing it in savour.   The Chancellor's chapel had its own chariot, as likewise had his exchequer, his pantry, his kitchen ; others bore loads of meat and drink, others cushions, rugs and tapestry, others the bags of bedclothes, the packs, and the various furniture.   He had also twelve packhorses, eight chests containing the Chancellor's gold and silver plate, vats, earthen pans, dishes, cups, goblets, kettles and cauldrons, basins, salt-cellars, spoons, plates and chargers.   Others of his coffers and chests contained his treasury ; a rich store of coin for his daily expenses and gifts, and his raiment, with a few books and other such gear.   One packhorse, that went before the rest, bore the sacred vessels and ornaments and books of his chapel.   Each packhorse had his sufficient and well-trained groom.   Each chariot, again, had its watch-dog bound above or beneath ; great hounds and weighty and fierce, such as might seem fit to strangle a bear or a lion. On each of the sumpter-beasts was perched either a long-tailed she-ape or (as saith the poet) " a he-ape that mimics the face of man."

When he entered into any village or town of France, first came the grooms on foot, " born to consume the fruits of the earth," to the number of some two hundred and fifty. These went in bands of six or ten, chanting some song of their own land in their native fashion. Then, after a space, came the coupled hounds, and the greyhounds in their slips and leashes, and all other kinds of hounds, with their own runners and attendants. Then, after a moderate distance, these iron-bound chariots came creaking over the stones of the streets, covered with great skins sewn together. After another small space came the sumpter-beasts, ridden by the grooms who knelt on the horses' rumps. Some of the French, coming forth from their doors at this noise, would ask who came here, with all this household. "The English Chancellor," men would answer, " sent on a mission to the King of France." Then said these French, "Marvellous is this English king, who hath such a Chancellor to journey in such state as this !" After a while behind the packhorses came the squires bearing the knights' shields and leading their chargers ; then other squires ; then the noble youths ; then the falconers with their birds ; then the stewards and masters and servants of the Chancellor's household ; then the knights and clerks, riding two and two ; last of all, the Chancellor himself, with a few familiars riding around him.

SECTION XII

WOMEN'S LIFE

A storehouse of peculiarly medieval ideas on this subject is *The Book of the Knight of La Tour-Landry*. It was French in origin, but was adopted in many other countries through medieval translations and early printed editions. The book, however, is so easily accessible (E.E.T.S., 1868, reprinted 1915; another edition 1902, ed. G. B. Rawlings) that it seems better to draw here almost exclusively from other sources.

1 THE THIRTEENTH CENTURY GIRL

Trevisa's *Bartholomew*, Lib. VI. c. 7.

Men byhove to take hede of maydens; for they ben hote and tendre of complexion[1], smale, pliaunt and fayre of disposicion of body: shamfaste, ferdefull[2], and mery[3] touchynge the affeccion of the mynde. Touchynge outwarde disposicion they be well nurtured, demure and softe of speche, and well ware of what they say: and delycate in theyr apparell.... Their hondes and the uttermeste party of their membres ben ful subtyll and plyaunt, theyr voyce small, theyr speche easy and shorte; lyght in goynge[4], and shorte steppes, and lyght wit and heed[5]; they ben sone[6] angry, and they ben mercyable and envyous, bytter, gylefull, able to lerne....And, for a woman is more meker than a man, she wepeth soner. And is more envyousse, and more laughinge, and lovinge, and the malice of the soule is more in a woman than in a man. And she is of feble kinde[7], and she makith more lesynges[8], and is more shamefaste and more slowe in werkynge and in mevynge[9], than is a man, as sayth Aristotle lib. 8.

[1] constitution.   [2] timid.   [3] merry.   [4] gait.   [5] head.
[6] soon.   [7] nature.   [8] lies.   [9] moving.

2　WOMEN'S EDUCATION

The Book of the Knight of La Tour-Landry (E.E.T.S., 1868, p. 118) voices the general view of reasonable men in the Middle Ages—that there was no harm in educating a girl well enough to enable her to read her Psalter and write her own letters.

And therfor this is a good ensaumple to putte yonge children unto the scole, and to make hem[1] bokys[2] of wisdom and of science, and bokes of vertu and profitable ensaumples, whereby they may see the savement of the soule and of the body by the ensaumples of good levinge[3] of the holy faderes before us, and not forto studie in the bokis that speke of love fables, and of other wor[l]dely vanitees. For it is beter and more noble thinge to here speke of good ensaumples, and of vertuous levinge of seintes, whiche profitethe to oure sowles and body, thanne forto studie or to rede of fayned stories and fables, suche as may not cause encrese of science, and is inprofitable unto the soule. How be it there be suche men that have opynion that thei wolde not that her[4] wyves nor her doughtres shulde knowe no thinge of the scripture; as touchinge unto the hcly scripture, it is no force[5] thoughe women medille not nor knowe but litelle therof but forto rede, everi woman it is the beter that canne rede and have knowinge of the lawe of God, and forto have be[en] lerned to have vertu and science to withstonde the perilles of the sowle, and forto use and excer[ci]se the werkys of thaire savement, for that is thinge aproved and necessarie to alle women.

3　PRECOCIOUS JEALOUSY

An Alphabet of Tales, E.E.T.S., 1904, p. 272 (Tale cccxcvi.).

Cesarius tellis how that in Freseland in a nonrie[6] ther was ij little maydens that lernyd on the buke, and ever thai strafe[7] whethur of thaim shulde lerne mor than the toder[8]. So the tane[9] of thaim happend to fall seke, and sho garte[10] call the Priores unto hur and sayd; "Gude ladie! suffre nott my felow to lern unto I cover[11] of my sekenes, and I sall pray my moder to gif me vj*d*, and that I sall giff you and ye do so; ffor I drede that, whils I am seke, that sho[12] sall pas me in lernyng, and that I wolde not [th]at sho did."

---

[1] them.　　[2] books.　　[3] living.　　[4] their.　　[5] it matters not.　　[6] nunnery.
[7] strove.　　[8] other.　　[9] one.　　[10] caused.　　[11] till I recover.　　[12] she.

4 THE SPINSTER'S LOT

Paston Letters, ed. 1900, vol. I. p. 89 : to John Paston.

Cosyn, I lete zow wete[1] that Scrope hath be[en] in this cuntre to se my cosyn zoure sustyr, and he hath spoken with my
cosyn zoure moder, and sche desyreth of hym that he schuld
schewe zow the endentures mad betwen the knyght that hath
his dowter and hym, whethir that Skrop, if he were maried
and fortuned to have children, if tho children schuld enheryte
his lond, or his dowter, the wheche is maried.

Cosyn,...Scrop seith to me, if he be maried and have a sone
an[d] eyre, his dowter that is maried schal have of his liflode[2]
fifty marke and no more; and therfore, cosyn, me semeth he
were good for my cosyn zowre sustyr, with[out] that ye myght
gete her a bettyr. And if ze can gete a better, I wold avyse
zow to labour it in as schort tyme as ze may goodly, for sche
was never in so gret sorow as sche is now a dayes; for sche
may not speke with no man, hosoever come, ne not may se
ne speke with my man, ne with servauntes of hir moderys[3] but
that sche bereth hire an hand otherwyse than she menyth[4].
And sche hath sen[5] Esterne the most part be betyn onys[6] in
the weke or twyes, and som tyme twyes on o day, and hir hed
broken in to or thre places. Wherfor, cosyn, sche hath sent
to me by Frere Newton in gret counsell, and preyeth me that
I wold send to zow a letter of hir hevynes[7], and prey yow to
be hir good brothyr, as hir trost is in zow; and sche seith, if
ze may se be[8] his [*Scrope's*] evydences that his childern and
hire[9] may enheryten, and sche to have resonable joynture, sche
hath herd so mech of his birth and his condicions, that, and ze
will, sche will have hym, whethyr that hir moder wil or wil
not, not withstandyng it is tolde hir his persone is symple, for
sche seyth men shull have the more deyute[10] of hire if sche
rewle hire to hym as sche awte to do.

Cosyn, it is told met her is a goodly man in yowre Inne[11],

---

[1] let you know. [2] income. [3] mother's.
[4] misconstrues her intentions. [5] since. [6] been beaten once.
[7] heaviness. [8] by. [9] hers. [10] duty.
[11] i.e. a fellow-lawyer in London.

of the qweche the fadyr deyed litte[1], and if ze thynk that he were better for hir than Scroop, it wold be laboured, and yif[2] Scroop a goodly answere that he be not put of[f] tyl ze be sure of a bettyr; for he seid whan he was with me, but if[3] he have som counfortable answer of zow, he wil no more laboure in this mater, be cause he myght not se my cosyn zoure sustyr....Wherfore, cosyn, thynk on this mateer, for sorow oftyn tyme causeth women to beset hem[4] otherwyse than thei schuld do, and if sche where in that case, I wot weel ze wold be sory. Cosyn, I prey zow brenne this letter, that zoure men ne non other man se it; for and my cosyn zowre moder knew that I had sent yow this letter, sche shuld never love me. No more I wrighte to zow at this tyme, but Holy Gost have zow in kepyng. Wretyn in hast, on Seynt Peterys day, be candel lyght.

Be youre Cosyn, ELIZABETH CLERE.

5 THE CORROSIVE DOWRY

Sir Thomas Elyot to Cromwell (*Cromwell Correspondence*, vol. x. no. 59).

Notwithstanding with his industry in provision for his householde, without ferme, grasing of catell, or regrating, he kepith an honest port, and findeth many sones to skoole, which by his education be very towardly. And moreover he hath many doughters for to sett furth in mariage, which, as ye well know, be grete corrosives of a litle substance.

6 THE LAW OF MARRIAGE

The Marriage Law of the Medieval Church was a heterogeneous compound of Roman and Feudal, Christian and Jewish traditions. For two very different views as to the responsibility of the Church in this matter, the reader may refer to the chapter on Family Law in Pollock and Maitland's *History of English Law* (2nd ed. 1898) and to Chap. II. of Mr A. L. Smith's *Church and State in the Middle Ages* (1913). The following extract is from Lyndwood's *Provinciale*, 1679, p. 271 ; the first text is a constitution of Abp Walter Reynold of Canterbury at the Synod of Oxford in 1322: the second emanates from St Edmund Rich (1236). The comments (abbreviated) are those of Bp Lyndwood, whose book was accepted as the standard for Canon Law in England during the century before the Reformation.

[1] whose father died lately.   [2] give.   [3] unless.   [4] behave.

A Lady Artist

(*a*) *Text.* Let Matrimony, like other sacraments, be celebrated with honour and reverence, in the daytime and in face of the Church, not with laughter and jest and contempt. Moreover, when matrimony is being contracted, let the priests always enquire thrice, on three Sundays or holydays at intervals, whether the contracting parties are free to marry. If any priest observe not this rule of Banns, let him not escape the penalty lately decreed in Council for this offence. Again, let priests frequently proclaim to those who are about to marry, under pain of excommunication, that they plight not their mutual faith except in some open place, publicly, and in the presence of several persons assembled for that purpose.

(*b*) *Text.* Where mutual consent is not, there is no marriage; therefore, those who give in marriage boys and girls in their cradles effect nothing, unless each of the children, having come to years of discretion, consent to the union. Thus, by the authority of this decree, we do henceforth prohibit the conjunction of children so long as either or both be not arrived at the age determined by Civil Law and decreed by Canon Law, unless such an alliance be tolerated under urgent necessity, for the blessing of peace.

(*c*) *Comment:* ¶ *Boys:* by this word those are properly understood who are between the ages of 7 and 14; but here the word is used of younger children, as appeareth from the words *in their cradles.* ¶ *Girls*, who, the more they grow, the more expense they cause to their parents. ¶ *In their cradles.* Such espousals are null, since consent is impossible. ¶ *Effect nothing*, that is, so far as matrimony is concerned, nor even towards espousal, unless, when both are past their 7th year, it shall appear in word or in deed that they remain in this intention; for after that time, through such will or consent, espousals do in fact begin. ¶ *Years of discretion.* This must be understood of the bond of matrimony; for the espousal would be valid if each of them should remain of the same mind after the completion of the 7th year. ¶ *Age.* This, for espousal, is seven years, at which time infancy endeth for both sexes; for matrimony, the girl must be 12 and the boy 14. But why is a different age fixed for the two sexes? Placentinus[1] giveth as a reason, that ill weeds grow apace. ¶ *The conjunction.* The reason of this is, that such affianced folk oftentimes prove recalcitrant and repent of their troth and leave each other, as they legally may; yet there still remaineth a certain bond or knot, whereby all of the kindred of the boy are prohibited from marrying the girl thus repudiated, nor can the boy marry any of the girl's kinsfolk. Another reason is, that it is prejudicial to the State for so many persons to be involved in matrimonial impediments by such dissolutions of espousals at the will of the parties. ¶ *Urgent necessity,* whereby other forbidden things are conceded. But who is to judge of such necessity? The Diocesan, according to Joannes Andreae. These precautions are all the more necessary when one of the parties is a stranger newly come to the city; therefore the priest should beware of espousing a girl of his parish to any stranger without consulting the priest of that stranger's parish. For each shepherd should know his sheep, and care for his own rather than for strangers; which, however, (as Hostiensis saith,) is a truth ill taught and worse kept. ¶ *The blessing of peace,* which is one of the secondary causes of matrimony, whereof there are many, *viz.* personal alliances, the acquisition of friends and wealth, the reformation of peace, the wife's beauty, and other like causes.

7 A MARRIAGE ARRANGED

Calendar of Inq. Post Mortem, vol. VII. p. 352.
Easter fell March 31 that year: for a case of equally expeditious marriage arrangements, see *ibid.* p. 489.

William de Kyvele, aged 60 years and more, says [that Philip Maubank was born March 12, 1331], and recollects it because on the same day a marriage was arranged for Alice his daughter, who was married to John de Shirburn within a month after Easter following.

[1] A commentator on Civil Law who died 1192. Johannes Andreae died in 1348, Hostiensis in 1271.

8   WITHOUT THE PARENTS' CONSENT

Calendar of Inquisitions Post Mortem, vol. II. p. 306. A similar incident, far more interesting but much longer, is in *Paston Letters*, 1900, vol. II. pp. 364 ff.

Chester. 12 Edw. I. Cradoc de Greves, sworn and examined, says that William de Stanleghe contracted marriage with the abovesaid Joan, saying " Joan, I give thee my troth to have and hold thee for my lawful wife to my life's end," and the said Joan gave him her troth by like words ; it was before the death of the said Philip, on Sunday after St Matthew two years ago, before Adam de Hoton and Dawe de Coupeland, at the church of Asteburi ; for the said Philip, his wife and family, were at a banquet of Master John de Stanlegh ; and Joan, doubting that her father would marry her to a son of her stepmother, on that occasion accepted the said William as her husband. Robert de Bebinton and many others agree ; Adam de Hoton, Dawe de Coupeland and others agree, except as to the form of words used, viz.—" I William take thee Joan as my lawful wife, and thereto give thee my troth," and the said Joan replied " I Joan take thee William as my lawful husband."

9   ERASMUS ON MARRIAGE

Erasmus knew England so well, that we may freely appeal to his *Guide to Christian Matrimony*, written at Lord Mountjoy's request for Catharine of Aragon in 1526 (*Opera*, Leyden, 1704, vol. v. col. 613 ff.). The following passage is from pp. 677 ff.

In the ceremonies that precede our weddings, the mass of Christians sin almost more grievously than any pagans ever did or do. Nor is there here one fault alone ; for we sin in ambition, luxury, intemperance and wantonness. The first barbarous custom is that the bride and bridegroom, when they enter upon this great and serious matter, should be burdened with so many ridiculous ceremonies, according to the capricious custom of the neighbourhood, as though it were a light and laughable matter for a young man to be united to a holy and modest maiden. Let us allow, for the sacrament's sake, that the bride should be brought ceremonially to church and thence, after the service, home again.   But what end is served by those public and disorderly banquets ? by wanton dances from dinner-time to supper, wherein the tender maiden may not refuse any man, but the house is free and open to the whole city ? There the wretched maiden is forced to clasp hands (and in Britain even to exchange kisses) with drunken men, with others infected with loathsome diseases, and sometimes even with ruffians who have come rather inclined to theft than to dancing.   Then comes a tumultuous supper ; then dancing again ; then the night-cup.   Even after midnight, scarce can the outworn bride and bridegroom seek their couch.

Moreover, these and worse disorders are prolonged in some countries for three days. Why, asks the moralist, should we suffer these Corybantic orgies ?

How much sweeter would it be to hold a modest and sober wedding feast among our own relations and a few of our nearest friends ! But here, as everywhere, ambition is the prime mover of evil—ambition, with luxury in her train ! A wedding seems fit only for beggars, unless a crowd of grandees, noble ladies, rich and honoured folk, are invited to this ceremony. We call a wedding *honourable*, when vast sums have been wasted on it, when many guests have surfeited even to vomiting or fallen into fevers through sheer intemperance and weariness ; a carouse in which the greatest licence of filthy speech and folly has been permitted....Who hath taught this Bacchanalian initiation to holy wedlock ?   Is this the proper fashion to enter upon a Sacrament of the Church ?...Nay, in the church itself there is no truce to these follies.   The bridegroom, at his entrance, runs the gauntlet of fisticuffs from the other young men.   During the service there are foolish gestures and nods, and immodest words are bandied about.   Who would believe that this is a serious business?   Is it not shameful that heathen idolaters should have had holier rites of matrimony than we Christians have ?

10   MAN AND WIFE

Trevisa's *Bartholomew*, Lib. VI. c. 14.

A man is callyd Vir in latyn, and hath that name of might and stregth, as sayth Isidore.   For in myghte and strength a man passeth a woman.   A man is the hede[1] of a woman, as the appostle sayth.   And therfore a man is bounde to rule his wyfe, as the heed hath cure and rule of the body....A man hath so great love to his wyfe, that for hyr sake he aventryth hym selfe to all perylles : and settyth her love afore his mothers love : For he dwellyth with his wyfe and forsakyth father and mother, for, [as] sayth god, a man shal forsake father and mother and abyde with his wyfe.

Afore weddynge the spouse thynketh to wynne love of her that he wowethe[2], with yeftes[3], and certifyeth of his wylle with letters and messangers, and with dyvers presentes and yeveth many yeftes and moche good and cattell[4], and promyseth moche more.   And to please her he putteth hym to divers playes and games amonge gatherynge of men, and useth ofte dedes of armes, of myght and of maystry[5].   And maketh hym gaye and semely in dyvers clothynge and araye.   And all that he is prayed to gyve and to do, for her love he yeveth and dothe anone with all his myghte.   And denyeth no peticion that is made in her name and for her love.   He speketh to her plesantly, and beholdeth her chere in the face with pleasynge and gladde chere, and with a sharpe eye, and at laste assenteth to her, and telleth openly his wyll in presence of her frendes and spouseth her with a ryng, and taketh her to wyfe, and yevethe her yeftes in token of contracte of weddyng and makethe her chartres and dedes of graunt and of yeftes.   He maketh revels and festes and spowsayles, and yeveth many good yeftes to frendes and guestis, and comforteth and gladdeth his guestes with songes and pypes and other mynstralsy of musike.   And afterward, whan all this is done he bringeth her to the privetes of his chambre and maketh her felow at bed and at borde. And than he maketh her lady of his money, and of his house

---

[1] head.   [2] wooeth.   [3] gifts.   [4] chattels.   [5] victory.

and meyny[1]. And than he is no lesse diligente and carefulle
for her than he is for hym selfe : and specially lovyngly he
avysethe her yf she doo amys, and taketh good hede to kepe
hir well, and taketh hede of her bearynge and goinge, of her
spekyng and lokyng[2], of her passynge and ayene-commynge[3],
oute and home. No manne hath more welthe, than he that
hathe a good woman to his wife; and no man hath more wo
than he that hath an evyl wyfe, crieng and janglyng, chidyng
and scoldyng, dronken, lecherous, and unstedfast, and con-
trarry to him, costly, stout and gay, envious, noyfull, leping
over londes[4], moch suspicious, and wrathful....In a good spouse
and wyfe behoveth these condicions, that she be busy and
devout in goddes service, meke and serviseable to her husbond,
and fair spekyng and goodly to her meyny, mercyable and
good to wretches that bene nedy, easy and pesible to her
neyghbors, redy ware and wyse in thynges that shuld be
avoyded, myghtyfulle[5] and pacient in suffrynge, busy and diligent in her doing, manerly in clothynge, sobre in movyng, ware
in speakynge, chaste in lokyng, honeste in bearynge, sadde[6] in
goinge, shamfaste amonge the people, mery and glad with her
husbonde, and chast in privite.

11   WIFE TO HUSBAND

Paston Letters, ed. 1900, vol. I. p. 48, written in 1443.

Ryth worchipful hosbon, I recomande me to yow, desyryng
hertely to her[7] of yowr wilfar[8], thanckyng God of yowr a mend-
yng of the grete dysese[9] that ye have hade ; and I thancke
yow for the letter that ye sent me, for be[10] my trowthe my
moder and I wer nowth in hertys es[11] fro the tyme that we
woste of yowr sekenesse, tyl we woste verely of your a mend-
yng. My moder behestyd a nodyr[12] ymmage of wax of the
weytte[13] of yow to oyer[14] Lady of Walsyngham, and sche sent
iiij. nobelys[15] to the iiij. Orderys of Frerys at Norweche to pray
for yow, and I have behestyd to gon on pylgreymmays to

---

[1] retinue.   [2] looking.   [3] again-coming.   [4] given to vagabondage.
[5] strong.   [6] serious.   [7] hear.   [8] welfare.   [9] discomfort.
[10] by.   [11] not in heartsease.   [12] promised another.   [13] weight.
[14] our.   [15] nobles.

Walsingham, and to Sent Levenardys[1] for yow; be my trowth
I had never so hevy a sesyn[2] as I had from the tyme that I
woste of yowr sekenesse tyl I woste of yowr amendyng, and
zyth[3] myn hert is in no grete esse, ne nowth xal[4] be, tyl I
wott that ze ben very hal[5]. Your fader and myn was dysday
sevenyth[6] at Bekelys for a matyr of the Pryor of Bromholme....

I pray yow hertely that [ye] wol wochesaf to sende me a
letter as hastely as ze may, yf wryhyn[7] be non dysesse to yow,
and that ye wollen wochesaf to sende me worde quowe your
sor dott[8]. Yf I mythe have had my wylle, I xulde a seyne
yow er dystyme[9]; I wolde ye wern at hom, yf it wer your ese,
and your sor myth ben as wyl lokyth[10] to her as it tys ther
ze ben, now lever dan[11] a gowne zow[12] it wer of scarlette. I
pray yow, yf your sor be hol, and so that ze may indur[e] to
ryde, wan my fader com to London, that ze wol askyn leve,
and com hom wan the hors xul[13] be sentte hom a zeyn[14], for I
hope ze xulde be kepte as tenderly herr as ze ben at London.
I may non leyser[15] have to do wrytyn half a quarter so meche
as I xulde sey[16] to yow yf I myth speke with yow. I xall
sende yow a nothyr letter as hastely as I may. I thanke
yow that ze wolde wochesaffe to remember my gyrdyl, and
that ze wolde wryte to me at the tyme, for I sopose that
wrytyng was non esse to yow. Allmyth[y] God have yow in
his kepyn, and sende yow helth. Wretyn at Oxenede, in ryth
grete hast, on Sent Mikyllys Evyn.

Yorys,   M. Paston.

My modyr grette yow wel, and sendyth yow Goddys blys-
syng and hers; and sche prayeth yow, and I pray yow also,
that ye be wel dyetyd of mete and drynke, for that is the
grettest helpe that ye may have now to your helthe-ward.
Your sone faryth wel, blyssyd be God.

---

[1] St Leonard's at Norwich.   [2] season.   [3] yet.   [4] shall.
[5] really well.   [6] this day se'nnight.   [7] writing.   [8] how your sore doeth.
[9] should have seen you ere this time.   [10] looked.   [11] I would rather than.
[12] though.   [13] shall.   [14] again.   [15] leisure.   [16] say.

12   THE MODEL HOUSEWIFE

Fitzherbert, *Book of Husbandry*, ed. Skeat, 1882, p. 96.

And in the begynnynge of Marche, or a lyttell afore, is tyme for a wyfe to make her garden, and to gette as many good sedes and herbes as she canne, and specially suche as be good for the potte, and to eate:....let thy dystaffe be alwaye redye for a pastyme, that thou be not ydle. And undouted[ly] a woman can-not gette her lyvynge honestely with spynnynge on the distaffe, but it stoppeth a gap, and muste nedes be had....May fortune sometime, that thou shalt have so many thinges to do, that thou shalt not well knowe where is best to begyn....

It is convenyente for a housbande to have shepe of his owne, for many causes, and than maye his wife have part of the woll, to make her husbande and her-selfe some clothes. And at the least waye, she may have the lockes of the shepe, eyther to make clothes or blankettes and coverlettes, or bothe. And if she have no woll of her owne, she maye take wol to spynne of clothe-makers, and by that meanes she maye have a convenyent lyvynge, and many tymes to do other warkes. It is a wyves occupation, to wynowe all maner of cornes, to make malte, to wasshe and wrynge, to make heye, shere[1] corne, and in tyme of nede to helpe her husbande to fyll the mucke-wayne or dounge-carte, dryve the ploughe, to loode hey, corne, and suche other.   And to go or ride to the market, to sel butter, chese, mylke, egges, chekyns, capons, hennes, pygges, gese, and all maner of cornes.   And also to bye all maner of necessarye thynges belongynge to houssholde, and to make a trewe rekenynge and a-compte to her housbande, what she hath payed.   And yf the housbande go to the market, to bye or sell, as they ofte do, he than to shewe his wife in lyke maner.   For if one of them shoulde use to deceyve the other, he deceyveth hym-selfe, and he is not lyke to thryve.   And therfore they must be trewe eyther to other. I coulde peradventure shewe the husbandes dyverse poyntes that the wyves deceyve them in : and in lyke maner, how

---

[1] reap.

husbandes deceyve theyr wyves : but if I shulde do so, I shulde shewe mo subtyll poyntes of deceypt, than eyther of them knewe of before. And therfore me semeth beste to holde my peace, lest I shoulde do as the knyght of the toure dyd[1].

13   JEALOUSY AND REVENGE

The Knight of La Tour-Landry, E.E.T.S., 1868, p. 23. Physical violence is taken for granted almost everywhere in the Middle Ages, and in all classes of society.

I wille saie an ensaumple that it is an evelle thinge
to a woman to be in jelousie.

Ther was a gentille woman that was weddid to a squier, and she loved hym so moche that she was jelous over alle women that he spake with; for the whiche he blamed ofte her, but it was never the beter. And amonge other she was gelous of a woman that hadd a gret and an highe herte; and so on a tyme she reproved that woman with her husbonde; and she saide she saide not trae; and the wiff saide she lied. And they ranne togedres and pulled of[f] alle that ever was on her hedes, and plucked eche other bi the here of the hede right evelle. And she that was accused, caught a staffe, and smote the wiff on the nose suche a stroke that she brake her nose, and that al her lyff after she hadd her nose al croked, the whiche was a foule mayme and blemesshing of her visage; for it is the fairest membre that man or woman hathe, and sittithe in the middille of the visage. And so was the wiff fouled and maymed alle her lyff, and her husbonde saide ofte to her, that it hadde be beter that she had not be jelous, thanne forto have undone her visage as she hadd. And also for that defoulyng of her visage her husbonde might never finde in his herte to love her hertly as he dede before, and he toke other women, and thus she lost his love thorugh her jelosie and foly.

---

[1] i.e. the Knight of La Tour-Landry.

14   THE PERFECT WOMAN

Manners and Meals, E.E.T.S., 1868, p. 36, from MS. Lambeth 853, about 1430 A.D., with various readings substituted from MS. Trin. Coll. Camb. R. 3. 19.

The good wijf taughte hir doughtir
Ful manye a tyme and ofte
A ful good womman to be,
And seide "doughtir to me dere,
Sum good thou must lere
If evere thou wolt thee[1].

Doughtir, if thou wolt ben a wijf, loke wijsly that thou worche,
Loke loveli and in good lijf thou love god and holi chirche.
Go to chirche whanne thou may, loke thou spare for no reyn,
For thou farist the best that ilke day whanne thou hast god y-seyn.
He muste need weel thrive
That liveth weel al his lyve,
My leef[2] child.

Gladli geve thi tithis and thin offrynges bothe ;
The poore and the bedered[3], loke thou not lothe[4] ;
Geve of thin owne good, and be not to hard,
For seelden is that hous poore there god is steward.
Welle he proveth
That the poore loveth,
Mi leve child.

Whanne thou sittist in the chirche, thi beedis thou schalt bidde ;
Make thou no jangelynge[5] to freende nor to sibbe[6] ;
Laughe thou to scorne nouther[7] oolde bodi ne yonge,
But be of fair beerynge and of good tunge ;
Thorugh thi fair beerynge
Thi worschip hath encresynge,
Mi leve child.

If ony man biddith the worschip[8], and wolde wedde thee,
Loke that thou scorne him not, what-so-evere he be,
But schewe it to thi freendis, and forhele[9] thou it nought ;
Sitte not bi him, neither stand, there synne myghte be wrought,
For a sclaundre reisid[10] ille
Is yvel[11] for to stille,
Mi leve childe.

---

[1] thrive.   [2] dear.   [3] bedridden.   [4] see that thou hate not.
[5] chattering.   [6] kinsfolk.   [7] neither.
[8] offereth thee honour.   [9] hide.   [10] raised.   [11] evil.

That man that schal the wedde bifor god with a ryng,
Love thou him and honoure moost of ertheli thing;
Meekely thou him answere, and not as an attirling[1],
And so maist thou slake his mood, and ben his dere derlynge:
    A fair worde and a meeke
     Dooth wraththe slake,
      Mi leve child.

Fair of speche schalt thou be, gladde, and of mylde mood,
Trewe in worde and in dede, and in conscience good;
Kepe thee from synne, fro vilonye, and fro blame,
And loke that thou beere[2] thee so that men seie[3] thee no schame;
    For he that in good lijf renneth[4],
     Ful ofte weel he wynneth,
      My leve child.

Be of semeli semblaunt, wijs[5], and other good maner,
Chaunge not thi contynaunce for nought that thou may heere;
Fare not as a gigge[6], for nought that may bitide,
Laughe thou not to[7] loude, ne yane[8] thou not to wide,
    Yet lawgh thow may and mery wordys say,
      Mi leve child.

And whan thou goist in the way, go thou not to faste,
Braundische not with thin heed, thi schuldris thou ne caste[9];
Have thou not to manye wordis; to swere be thou not leefe,
For alle such maners comen to an yvel preef[10]:
    For he that cacchith to him an yvel name,
     It is to him a foule fame,
      Mi leve childe.

Go thou not into the toun as it were a gase[11]
From oon hous to another for to seke the mase[12];
Ne wende thou not to the market thi borel[13] for to selle,
And thanne to the taverne thi worschip to felle[14],
    For thei that tavernes haunten,
     Her thrifte thei adaunten[15],
      Mi leve child.

And if thou be in place where good ale is on lofte,
Whether that thou serve therof, or that thou sitte softe,
Mesurabli[16] thou take ther-of that thou falle in no blame,
For if thou be ofte drunke, it falleth thee to schame;
    For tho that ben ofte drunke,
     Thrift is from hem sunke,
      Mi leve child.

[1] venomous thing.   [2] bear.   [3] say.   [4] runneth.   [5] wise.
[6] frivolous woman.   [7] too.   [8] yawn.   [9] throw about.
[10] proof.   [11] gaze.   [12] crowd.   [13] coarse cloth.
[14] destroy.   [15] bring down.   [16] moderately.

Go not to the wrastelinge, ne to schotynge[1] at cok,
As it were a strumpet or a giggelot[2]:
Syt at hom, doughtir, and love thi werk myche[3],
And so thou schalt, my leve child, wexe[4] soone riche.
 It is evermore a myrie thing,
  A man to be served of his owne thing,
   Mi leve child.

Aqweynte thee not with eche man that gooth bi the strete;
Though ony man speke to thee, swiftli thou him grete;
Lete him go bi the wey; bi him that thou ne stonde,
That he bi no vilonye thin herte myghte fonde[5],
 For alle men ben not trewe
  That kunne fair her[6] wordis schewe,
   Mi leve child.

Also, for no coveitise, giftis that thou noon[7] take;
But thou wite right weel whi ellis[8], soone thou hem forsake,
For with giftis men may wommen over-goon
Though thei were as trewe as steel either stoon.
 Bounden forsothe sche is
  That of ony man takith giftis,
   Mi leve childe.

And wijsli governe thou thin hous and thi meyne[9]:
To bittir ne to bonour[10] with hem that thou ne be,
But loke weel what is moost neede to doone,
And sette thi meyne therto bothe ratheli[11] and soone,
 For redi is at nede
  A forn doon dede[12],
   Mi leve child.

And if thin husbonde be from hoome, lete not thi meyne go ydil,
But loke weel who dooth mykylle either[13] litil,
And he that weel dooth, thou qwite him weel his whyle[14],
And he that dooth other, serve him as the vile.
 A forn doon dede
  Wole another spede,
   Mi leve child.

And if thi nede be greet and thi tyme streite[15],
Than go thi silf therto and worche and houswijfes brayde[16],
Thanne wille thei alle do the bettir that aboute thee stande[s].
The work is the sonner do[17] that hath many handis,

---

[1] shooting.   [2] romp.   [3] much.   [4] wax.   [5] tempt.   [6] their.
[7] none.   [8] unless you see clearly some reason to the contrary.
[9] retinue.   [10] too bitter nor too easy.   [11] early.   [12] a deed done before.
[13] or.   [14] pay him well for his time.   [15] strait.
[16] urge on (*lit.* stretch out).   [17] sooner done.

For manye handis and wight
Make an hevy worke light;
Aftir thi good servise
Thi name schal arise,
    Mi leve childe.

And what so thi meyne do, aboute hem thou wende,
And as myche as thou maist, be at that oon[1] eende,
And if thou fynde ony defaute, do it soone ameende
So that thei have tyme and space and may hem defende.
    To compelle a dede to be doon, and there be no space,
    It is but tyrannye with-out temperaunce and grace,
      Mi leve child.

And loke that alle thingis be weel whanne thei her werkis lete,
And take the keies[2] in-to thi warde, loke thei ben not forgete;
And be waar to whom thou trustis, and spare for no qweyntise[3],
For myche harme hath falle to them that ben not wise;
    But, doughtir, loke that thou be wise, and do as y thee teche
    And trust noon bettir than thi silf, for no fair speche,
      Mi leve childe.

And geve thi meyne ther hire at ther terme day
Whether that thei dwelle stille or thei wende awey,
Doo weel bi hem of thi good that thou hast in welde[4],
And than schal thei seie weel of thee, bothe the yonge and oolde;
    Thi good name is to thi freendis
    Greet ioie and gladnes,
      Mi leve childe.

And if thi neigbouris wijf hath on riche a-tire,
Therfore mocke thou ne scorne, brenne not as fier[5],
But thanke god of heven for that he hath the gevene,
And so thou schalt, my doughtir, a good lijf lyv[en].
    He hath eese at weelde
    That thanketh god feele and seelde[6],
      Mi leve child.

Houswijfli thou schalt goon on the worke day, [iwis,]
Pride, reste, and ydilnes, makith onthriftines;
And whanne the holi day is come, weel schalt thou be
The holi day in worschipe, and god wole love thee;
    Have in mynde to god is worschip [ay],
    For myche pride cometh of the yvel day,
      Mi leve child.

Whanne thou art a wijf, a neighbore for to be,
Love than weel thi neighboris, as god hath comaundide thee;

[1] one.   [2] keys.   [3] craft.   [4] control.   [5] burn not as fire.
      [6] for many and few.

It bihoveth thee so for to do,
And to do to them as thou woldist be doon to.
    If ony discorde happen nyght or daye,
    Make it no worse, meende it if thou may,
        Mi leve child.

And if thou schalt be a riche wijfe, be than not to hard,
But weelcome fair thi neiboris that comen to thee-warde
With mete, drinke, and honest chere, such as thou maist to hem
    bede[1],
To ech man after his degre; and help the poore at neede;
    And also, for hap that may bitide,
    Please weel thi neighboris that dwelle thee biside,
        Mi leve child.

Doughtir, loke that thou be warre[2], what-sum-evere thee bitide,
Make not thin husbonde poore with spendinge ne with pride.
A man must spende as he may that hath but easy[3] good,
For aftir the wrenne hath veynes, men must lete hir blood[4];
    His thrifte wexith thinne
    That spendith or[5] he wynne,
        Mi leve child.

Borowe not to besely[6], nor take not thin hire first
But if the more nede it make, and grettir distresse;
Ne make thee not to seme riche with other mennis thing,
Ne therfore spende nevere the more of a ferthing;
    For though thou borowe faste,
    It must hoome agen at laste,
        Mi leve child.

And if thi children been rebel, and wole not hem bowe,
If ony of hem mys-dooth, nouther banne hem ne blowe[7],
But take a smert rodde, and bete hem on a rowe
Till thei crei mercy, and be of her gilt aknowe[8].
    Leve chylde behoveth lore,
    And ever the levyr[9] the more,
        Mi leve child.

And loke to thi doughtren, that noon of hem be lorn[10]:
Fro that ilk tyme that thei be of thee born,
Bisie thee, and gadere faste towarde her mariage,
And geve hem to spowsynge as soone as thei be of age.
    Maydens ben fair and amyable,
    But of her love ful unstable,
        Mi leve child.

[1] offer.   [2] ware.   [3] moderate.
[4] you must bleed the wren in proportion to the size of her veins.
[5] ere.   [6] busily.   [7] neither curse them nor box their ears.
[8] confessed.   [9] dearer.   [10] lost.

Now have y thee taught, doughtir, As my moder dide me;
Thinke theron nyght and day, forgete[n] that it not be;
Have mesure and lownes[1], as y have thee taught,
And what man the wedde schal, him dare care nought.
    Betere were a child unbore
    Than untaught of wijs lore,
      Mi leve child.

Now thrift and theedom[2] mote thou have, my swete barn,
Of alle oure former fadris that evere were or aren,
Of alle patriarkis and prophetis that evere weren alyve,
Her blessinge mote thou have, and weel mote thou thrive!
    For weel is the child
    That with synne wole not be filid,
      Mi leve child.

The blessynge of god mote thou have, and of his modir bright,
Of alle aungils and of alle archaungils, and of alle holy wight,
And that thou mowe have grace to wende the wey ful right
To the blis of hevene, there sittith god almyght,
              AMEN."

15   A NUNNERY VISITATION

A few injunctions for nunneries had already been accessible in English (e.g. Dugdale's *Monasticon*, ed. Caley, IV. 553, and *Yorkshire Archaeological Journal*, 1902, pp. 440, 443, 452); but Mr A. Hamilton Thompson's editions of the 15th century Lincoln Visitations, with full notes and translations, are systematically placing the real details of conventual life before the general reader now for the first time (*Lincoln Record Soc.*, 1914, etc.). In this place it will be only necessary to give one typical and less accessible visitation, from the Register of Bp Stapeldon of Exeter (ed. Hingeston-Randolph, 1892, p. 316).

Polsloe Priory, 1308. Episcopal Injunctions, abridged translation from the Norman-French[3].

Seeing that, in our visitation made of late in your chapter-house, where we enquired of your estate and that of your convent, we found certain things concerning you which we cannot suffer without amendment, for the honesty of your

---

[1] moderation and humility.   [2] prosperity.
[3] By this time Bishops seldom assumed a knowledge of Latin on the nuns' part; fourteenth-century injunctions are generally in French, and those of the next century are often in English; cf. *Myrour of our Lady*, E.E.T.S., 1873, p. 2: the book has been translated into English for the nuns of Syon because "many of you, though ye can synge and rede [Latin], yet ye can not se what the meanynge thereof ys."

Order and the salvation of your souls, therefore we ordain and command as follows for the good of your souls :

To wit, that silence be kept in due places, according to the Rule and observances of St Benedict; and, if it be desirable that any word be spoken in the aforesaid places, for any reasonable occasion, then let it be gently, and so low that it be scarce heard of the other nuns, and in as few words as may be needed for the comprehension of those who hear; and better in Latin than in any other tongue; yet the Latin need not be well-ordered by way of grammar, but thus, *candela, liber, missale, est, non, sic,* and so forth. And we will likewise that all secular women abiding with you shall keep silence in the places aforesaid, so that the Ladies of Religion be not disturbed or troubled ; and that such secular women as are wont to do otherwise be removed from the house.

Item, that all Ladies of Religion in your house, except such as are hindered by sickness or other reasonable cause, shall come with one accord and without delay to Matins, Mass, Vespers, Compline and other Services, to Collation, Chapter, and Refectory[1], there abiding until the end, and departing thence devoutly, as is decent. And before meals let them say their Grace, and after meals let them go together to the chapel to say their Grace according to the Rule ; and let no nun eat outside the Refectory in a private room, except it be with the Prioress, or for sickness or other reasonable cause. Let the sick nuns be together in the Infirmary, and not apart in several chambers, so that they may be served by one or two maids, according as they be fewer or more.

Let no Lady of Religion go to visit her friends without the Priory, unless it be once a year at the most[2], and then by permission and for a reasonable cause ; moreover, let her then be accompanied by some fully-professed nun of the same house,

[1] One of the chief difficulties in the medieval convent was the tendency of the nuns to form separate groups or even individual messes, and thus destroy that common life which was of the essence of the Rule: cf. below.

[2] Even this permission was contrary to the Bull *Periculoso*, still recent (1302), but never really kept. That Bull enjoined that nuns should conform to the original intention of St Benedict, and never leave the convent precincts if it could be avoided.

not of her own choice but as the Prioress shall assign unto her; and let not her who hath once been assigned go with her again the next time, so that each Lady have her companion changed at each visit to her friends; and the nun who hath leave to go visit her friends at certain places shall go to no other place, but if she have a fresh companion.

Item, when a Lady of Religion eateth at Exeter, or elsewhere in the neighbourhood, by leave and with reasonable cause, let it be some place whence she may return that same day or on the morrow, and let her ever have a companion and a chaplain, clerk, or squire of good repute assigned by the Prioress, who shall go, tarry, and return with them. Let them go in no other fashion, nor delay to return forthwith to the house as they are bidden, nor go afresh to Exeter, wandering from house to house, as they have oftentimes done in the past, to the dishonour of their estate and of their Order.... Let no married secular woman be received henceforth, on any account, to lodge in your house, unless it be for a month at the most; nor any other secular woman but by special leave from Us or from Our successors.

Let no corrody[1] be granted, nor any pension to secular man or woman, without leave from Us or Our successors.

Let no Lady of Religion hold long communication or parlance with secular men or women, in the parlour or elsewhere, without leave from the Prioress or Subprioress, and for some reasonable occasion; and then let it be in presence of a nun professed of your own Order; or, if she be a novice, in presence of her mistress.

Let no Lady of your Religion, novice or professed, go to the outer offices without the cloister to be let blood[2] or for other feigned occasion, but with permission from the Prioress or Subprioress; and then for some reasonable occasion; and let

---

[1] pension: generally in the form of board and lodging, and given in return for a lump sum of money or some similar gift. The monasteries thus got ready money for their immediate needs, but made a bad bargain if the corrodian lived long; hence this is one of the practices most frequently forbidden by visitors.

[2] Nuns, like monks, had periodical blood-lettings, which were taken in the later Middle Ages as "recreationes," entitling them to better food for the time, excusing them from rising to matins, etc.

her have with her some other professed nun of your Order, so that each of them may see and hear that which the other saith or doeth.

Item, we ordain that among you all ye have but one Confessor, a Regular or Secular Priest, assigned by Us or Our successors, and removable at Our will; but this time, of Our special grace, we grant you to choose either Brother John de Whateley, D.D., of the Friars Minor, or Brother Hugh de la Pole of the Friars Preachers, or both one and the other.

Item, seeing that certain Ladies of your Religion have, at certain times, had their own several serving-maids to prepare their meals apart from the rest, therefore we ordain, will, and decree that all these maids be utterly expelled from the kitchen, and that a competent man-cook with a page to help him be set to serve the whole convent.

Item, that the Dormitory, Infirmary, and Choir-stalls, and other necessary buildings be made and repaired as soon as the goods of the convent will suffice thereunto.

Item, that the accounts of all your bailiffs, reeves, and receivers [be properly kept and audited].

Item, that the Prioress do yearly, before the whole Convent or 6 Ladies by the Convent thereunto assigned, betwixt Christmas and Easter show the state of the Convent and its receipts and expenses, not in detail but in gross[1], and the debts of all debtors or creditors beyond the sum of £2; and all these things must be put into writing and kept in the common treasury, so that it may be yearly seen how your goods increase or decrease.

Finally, it is commanded that these present Ordinances be read aloud to the Convent four times a year; the nuns are solemnly adjured to keep them without diminution, and severe punishment is threatened for disobedience. The very length and emphasis of these adjurations, and of similar adjurations by other bishops at other times, tell their own tale; but we have a very plain comment on it all from the distinguished canonist John of Ayton, *temp*. Ed. III. (Lyndwood's *Provinciale*, 1679, app. p. 155). He is commenting on a legatine constitution of Ottobon (afterwards Pope Adrian V.) at the Council of London in 1269, which ends "We strictly command, in virtue of holy obedience and with appeal to the Last Judg-

---

[1] This had long been a strict Papal regulation, but was always very badly kept.

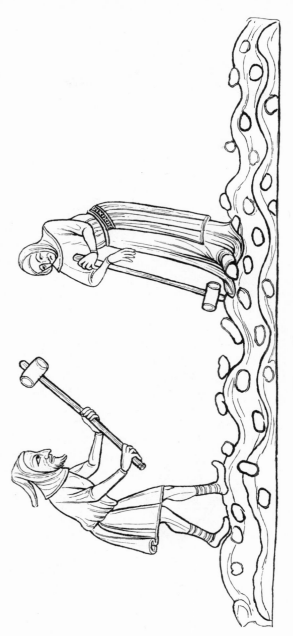

WOMAN BREAKING CLODS

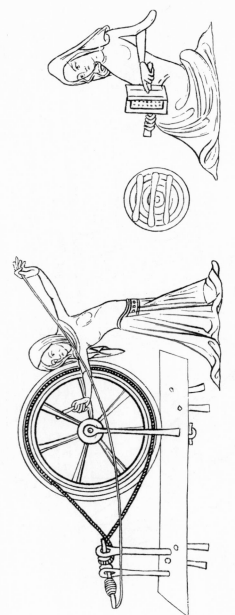

SPINSTER AND CARDER

ment, that they who find it expedient to visit the nunneries shall cause the statutes here decreed to be exactly obeyed." Upon this John of Ayton remarks (omitting his formal references to Canon Law) :

Cause to be obeyed! but certainly this almost passeth the wit of mortal man ; therefore we must here insert the proviso "so far as in them lieth."...For the nuns answer roundly to these statutes, as to others which have been decreed to check their wantonness ; "The men who made these statutes sat well at their ease when they decreed these things against us, imposing such hard and intolerable restrictions!" Therefore we see plainly that these statutes are kept either ill or not at all. Wherefore then did the Holy Fathers thus labour to beat the air? yet certainly their labour was not the less meritorious. Now the reasons why these constitutions are not kept in practice is twofold, springing from detestable faults on both sides; partly through damnable negligence on the prelates' part, and partly through hardened obstinacy and contumacious wantonness on the part of their subjects ; although, in justice, their punishment should be increased in proportion to their contumacy.

16   WOMEN'S LABOUR

Riley, *Memorials of London*, 1868, p. 277. A.D. 1355 (from the Ordinances of the Braelers, or makers of braces). Cf. Miss A. Abram's article on "Women Traders in Medieval London" (*Economic Journal*, June, 1916).

...Also, that no one of the said trade shall be so daring as to set any woman to work in his trade, other than his wedded wife or his daughter.

17   SERVANTS BY COMPULSION

The Coventry Leet Book, E.E.T.S., Part II. p. 545.

Also that no senglewoman, beyng in good hele[1] and myghty in body to labour within the age of fifty yeres, take nor kepe frohensfurth housez nor chambres be themself[2]; nor that [they] take eny Chambre within eny other persone, but that they go to service till they be maried, uppon the peyn who doth the contrarie to lese[3] at the first defalt vj s. viij d. and at the ij[de]

---

[1] health.   [2] by themselves.   [3] lose.

defalt to be comyt[ted] to prison, there to abide tyll they fynde suerte to go to service. And that every such persone [that] resceyve eny such persones, or set them eny house or Chambre, to lese at the first defalt xx s., at the ij^de defalt xl s., and at the iij^de defalt to be comyt to prison; there to remayn till he fynde suerte to conforme hym-selfe to this ordenaunce.

18　WOMEN AND GENERAL COUNCILS

William of Ockham (d. 1349) was one of the most original thinkers of the Middle Ages. In his attempt to reduce the Church from an absolute to a constitutional monarchy, he insists on the responsibility of the Pope to a General Council of Christendom. So far he is at one with his contemporary Marsiglio of Padua ; but he goes one step farther than Marsiglio in arguing that, on principle at least, no such council could be truly representative unless it contained women as well as men. The following is translated from his *Dialogus*, between a Master and his Disciple, in Goldast's *Monarchia*, vol. II. (1614) pp. 603–5. See R. L. Poole, *Illustrations of Medieval Thought*, 1884, p. 277 and note.

Lib. VI. c. 84. *We here enquire who has the right of assembling a General Council, if the Pope be an heretic, and if those who elected him still cleave to his party ; and we prove that such Council General may be assembled without the Pope.*

c. 85. *Wherein it is proved that Kings and Princes and other layfolk should come to this General Council, if they so wish.*

Master.....We should give the character of General Council to any assembly whereunto divers persons come in due form, bearing the authority and commission of every part of universal Christendom[1] to treat of the common good, with only such exceptions as those who cannot or will not come; so that, even though certain provinces were unwilling or unable to send persons bearing their commission and authority, this would be none the less a General Council....What toucheth all, should be debated and approved by all, as is noted in the Gloss on Canon Law [Gratian, *Decret.* Pars I. Dist. 96, c. 4, and *Decret. Greg.* Lib. I. tit. 33, c. 8;] where the Glossator noteth that all must be summoned who are touched by the matter in dispute. But the matters treated in a General Council touch all, since

---

[1] Goldast reads *sanitatis*, obviously misreading *Xanitatis* or some similar contraction in his MS.

in such a Council we must treat of faith and of other matters which concern all Christian folk. From which it followeth that the laity, who are concerned in the debates of a General Council, may be present if they will....Matters of faith concern not only the clergy but the laity; for God is not only the God of clerics, but of layfolk also....

Disciple. Tell me briefly wherefore it is said that women should not be excluded outright from the General Council against their will.

Master. This is by reason of the unity of men and women in the Faith which concerneth all; and wherein (as the Apostle saith in the 3rd chapter of the Epistle to the Colossians[1], speaking of the new law) there is neither male nor female. And therefore, wheresoever the wisdom or goodness or power of women be essential to the treating of faith (which is the especial matter of debate in a General Council) a woman must not be excluded from such General Council.

Disciple. I esteem this assertion concerning women (who, according to St Paul, may not teach) to be so unreasonable, that I will treat of it no more. Let us therefore dismiss this matter; and tell me what power a General Council hath over a Pope who hath been taken in heresy.

19   NEW FASHIONS

The Knight of La Tour-Landry, E.E.T.S., 1868, p. 31.

Who so takithe furst a novelte of array on hym, thei ben moche spoken of; but now a dayes, and a woman here[2] of a newe gette[3], she wille never be in pees tille she have the same. And the wives saien to her husbondes every day, "sir, suche a wyff and suche hath suche goodly arraye that besemithe her welle, and y praie you y may have of the same"; and yef[4] her husbonde saie, "wiff, yef suche have suche arraie, suche that are wiser thanne thei have it not," she wil saie, "no force it is[5]; for thei canne not were it; and yef y have it ye shull see how welle it wille become me, for y can were it." And thus with

---

[1] Rather, Gal. iii. 28. Ockham, like many medieval theologians, quoted from memory, and was thinking of the similar passage Col. iii. 11.

[2] hear.   [3] fashion.   [4] if.   [5] no matter.

her wordes her husbonde must nedis ordeine her that [which]
she desirithe, other[1] he shalle never have pees with her, for thei
wol finde so mani resones that thei wille not be werned[2]. But
the women that dothe and saithe thus, be not most wisest nor
canne[3] not best her[4] good, but thei have more her herte to
the plesaunce of the worlde thanne to her husbondes profit.
And there is a maner now amonge servyng women of lowe
astate, the whiche is comen[5], for thei furre her colers, that
hangin doune into the middil of the backe, and thei furre her
heles, the whiche is doubed[6] with filthe, and it is sengille[7] about
her brest. The whiche arraie y praise not in winter nor somer,
for hem were beter take the furre that hangithe about her
helis in the winter and sette it about her stomakes, for that
had more nede of hete thanne her helys, and in somer it were
beter awey, for flies hidethe hem therinne. And therfor y
praise not the arraye nor that novelte in a pore man, but y
saie it not be[8] women that may susteine and meintayne it atte
her lust[9]; for y caste me not to speke nor to medille me of no
thinge of her astate nor arraie that aught to displese hem,
for it longithe[10] not to me but to worshippe and to obeye hem
to my power.

20　　THE MYTH OF THE GARTER

The nucleus of this legend is in the following episode told by Froissart;
the later form of the story cannot be traced further back than Polydore
Vergil in the late 15th century, and probably rests on a confusion be-
tween this Countess of Salisbury (who was sister to John de Grandisson,
Bp of Exeter), and Joan of Kent, who afterwards married the Black Prince.
See *D.N.B.*, vol. XXXVIII. p. 213.

King David of Scotland, in 1342, sacked Durham and attacked Wark
Castle, which was presently relieved by Edward III. in person. (Berners's
Froissart, ed. 1812, vol. I. p. 97.)

The next day the kyng of scottes commaunded that every
man shulde be redy to assayle, and they within were redy to
defende; ther was a sore assaut, and a perylous: ther might a
ben sene many noble dedes on both partes. Ther was within
present, the noble countesse of Salysbury, who was as than

---

[1] or.　　[2] denied.　　[3] know.　　[4] their.　　[5] common.　　[6] daubed.
　　[7] single (unlined).　　[8] by.　　[9] pleasure.　　[10] belongeth.

reputed for the most sagest and fayrest lady of all England. The castell parteyned to her husbande, th'erle of Salisbury, who was taken prisoner, with the erle of Suffolke, before Lyle in Flanders, as ye have harde before, and was in prison as than in the Chatel[e]t of Parys; the kyng of Englande gave the same castell to the sayd erle, whan he maryed first the sayd lady, for the prowes and gode servyce that he had done before, whan he was called but sir Wyllyam Montagu. This noble lady conforted them greatly within; for by the regarde of such a lady, and by her swete conforting, a man ought to be worthe two men at nede. This assaut dured long, and the scottes lost many of their men, for they adventured themselfe hardely, and caryed wood and tymbre, to have fylled the dykes, to thyntent to bring their engyns to ye walles, but they within defended themselfe so valyantly, that the assaylantes were fayne to drawe abacke....

The same day that the scottes departyd fro the sayd castell, kyng Edward came thyder, with all his host, about noon, and came to the same place wher as the scottes had loged, and was sore displeased that he founde nat the scottes ther, for he came thyder in such hast, that his horse and men wer sore traveled. Than he commaunded to lodge ther that nyght, and sayd, howe he wolde go se the castell, and the noble lady therin, for he had nat sene her sythe she was maryed before: than every man toke his logyng as he lyst. And assone as the kyng was unarmed, he toke a x. or xii. knyghtes with hym, and went to the castell, to salute the countesse of Salisbury, and to se the maner of the assautes of the scottes, and the defence that was made agaynst them. Assone as the lady knewe of the kynges comyng, she set opyn the gates, and came out so richely besene[1], that every man ma[r]veyled of her beauty, and coude nat cease to regarde her noblenes with her great beauty, and the gracyous wordes and countenaunce that she made. Whan she came to the kyng, she knelyd downe to the yerth, thankyng hym of his socours, and so ledde hym into the castell, to make hym chere and honour, as she that coude ryght well do it. Every man regarded her marvelusly;

[1] attired.

the kyng hymselfe coude nat witholde his regardyng of her,
for he thought that he never sawe before, so noble, nor so
fayre a lady : he was stryken therewith to the hert, with a
sparcle of fyne love, that endured longe after ; he thought no
lady in the worlde so worthy to be beloved as she. Thus they
entred into the castell, hande in hande ; the lady ledde hym
first into the hall, and after into the chambre, nobly aparelled ;
the kyng regarded so the lady that [s]he was abasshed : at last
he went to a wyndo to rest hym, and so fell in a gret study.
The lady went about to make chere to the lordes and knyghtes
that were ther, and commaunded to dresse the hall for dyner :
whan she had al devysed and commaunded, thane she came
to the kyng with a mery chere, who was in a gret study, (and
she sayd) Dere syr, why do ye study so? for, your grace nat
dyspleased, it aparteyneth nat to you so to do : rather ye
shulde make good chere and be joyfull, seyng ye have chased
away your enmies, who durst nat abyde you : let other men
study for the remynant.   Than the kyng sayd, A ! dere lady,
knowe for trouthe, that syth I entred into the castell, ther is
a study come to my mynde, so that I can nat chuse but to
muse; nor I can nat tell what shall fall thereof; put it out of
my herte I can nat.   A ! sir, quoth the lady, ye ought alwayes
to make good chere, to confort therwith your peple : god hath
ayded you so in your besynes, and hath gyven you so great
graces, that ye be the moste [re]douted and honoured prince in
all christendome; and if the kyng of scottes have done you
any dyspyte or damage, ye may well amende it whan it shall
please you, as ye have done dyverse tymes or this.   Sir, leave
your musyng and come into the hall, if it please you, your dyner
is all redy.   A ! fayre lady, quoth the kyng : other thynges lyeth
at my hert that ye knowe nat of : but surely the swete behavyng,
the perfyt wysedom, the good grace, noblenes, and exellent
beauty that I se in you, hath so sore surprised my hert, that
I can nat but love you, and without your love I am but deed.
Than the lady sayde, A ! ryght noble prince, for goddessake
mocke nor tempt me nat : I can nat byleve that it is true that
ye say, nor that so noble a prince as ye be, wold thynke to
dyshonour me, and my lorde, my husbande, who is so valyant

a knight, and hath done your grace so gode seruyce, and as yet lyethe in prison for your quarell; certenly sir, ye shulde in this case have but a small prayse, and nothyng the better therby: I had never as yet such a thought in my hert, nor I trust in god never shall have, for no man lyveng. If I had any suche intencyon, your grace ought nat all onely to blame me, but also to punysshe my body, ye[1] and by true justice to be dismembred. Therwith the lady departed fro the kyng, and went into the hall to hast the dyner; than she returned agayne to the kyng, and broght some of his knyghtes with her, and sayd: Sir, yf it please you to come into the hall, your knightes abideth for you to wasshe, ye have ben to long fastyng. Than the kyng went into the hall and wassht, and sat down amonge his lordes, and the lady also. The kyng ete but lytell, he sat styll musyng; and, as he durst, he cast his eyen upon the lady: of his sadnesse his knyghtes had marvell, for he was nat acustomed so to be: some thought it was bycause the scottes were scaped fro hym. All that day the kyng taryed ther, and wyst nat what to do: somtyme he ymagined that honour and trouth defended[2] him to set his hert in such a case, to dyshonour such a lady, and so true a knyght as her husband was, who had alwayes well and truely served hym. On thother part, love so constrayned hym, that the power therof surmounted honour and trouth: thus the kyng debated in hymself all that day, and all that night; in the mornyng he arose and dysloged all his hoost, and drewe after the scottes, to chase them out of his realme. Than he toke leave of the lady, sayeng: My dere lady, to god I commende you tyll I returne agayne, requiryng you to advyse you otherwyse than ye have sayd to me. Noble prince, quoth the lady, god the father glorious be your conduct[3], and put you out of all vylayne thoughtes; sir, I am, and ever shal be redy to do your grace servyce to your honour and to myne. Therwith the kyng departed all abasshed; and soo folowed the scottes tyll he came to the cyte of Berwyke.

[1] yea. [2] forbade. [3] may God, the Father of Glory, be your guide.

21 WOMEN IN CHURCH

Bp Pecock is, so far as I know, the only medieval theologian who dares so to expound 1 Cor. xi. 3–10 as to give far greater liberty of costume than modern interpretations allow: and the fact is interesting, quite apart from the probability that Pecock mistakes his author's words (*Repressor*, R. S., I. 118).

Also noughwhere in Holi Scripture is mensioun mad or eny ensaumpling doon, that a womman schulde were upon her heer[1] and heed eny coverchief of lynnen threde or of silk. Forwhi[2] the coveryng with which a wommannys heed oughte be covered, wherof Holi Scripture spekith in the pistlis of Poul, was only the heer of wommennys heed unschorn; and of noon other coveryng to wommennys heedis spekith Holi Scripture. And, here agens[3], Holi Scripture wole[4] that men schulden lacke the coveryng which wommen schulden have; and thei schulden so lacke bi that that the heeris of her[5] heedis schulden be schorne, and schulde not growe in lengthe doun as wommanys heer schulde growe.

22 A PROTESTANT WOMAN

Margery Backster, wife of a carpenter at Martham in Norfolk, was accused of heresy before the Bishop of Norwich in 1428. Joan Cliffland deposed as follows against her (Foxe, *Acts and Monuments*, vol. III. 1844, p. 594). The episcopal register makes no further mention of Margery Backster; we do not know what became of her.

First, That the said Margery Backster did inform this deponent, that she should in no case swear; saying to her in English: "Dame, beware of the bee, for every bee will sting; and therefore take heed you swear not, neither by God, neither by our lady, neither by any other saint; and if ye do contrary, the bee will sting your tongue and venom your soul[6]."

Item, This deponent being demanded by the said Margery, what she did every day at church; she answered, that she

---

[1] hair. [2] because. [3] again. [4] wills. [5] their.

[6] Inquisitors' manuals specify, among symptoms suggestive of heresy, any strong objection to swearing. Chaucer illustrates this very plainly (*C.T.* B, 1170):
> The Persone him answerde, '*Benedicite!*
> What eyleth the man, so sinfully to swere!'
> Our Hoste answerde, 'O Jankyn, be ye there?
> I smell a Loller in the wind,' quoth he.

kneeled down and said five Pater-Nosters, in worship of the crucifix, and as many Ave Marias in worship of our lady. Whom Margery rebuked, saying, "You do evil to kneel or pray to such images in the churches, for God dwelleth not in such churches, neither shall he come down out of heaven; and he will give you no more reward for such prayer, than a candle lighted, and set under the cover of the font, will give light by night to those who are in the church": saying, moreover, in English; "Lewd wrights[1] of stocks hew and form such crosses and images, and, after that, lewd painters gleer[2] them with colours. And if you desire so much to see the true cross of Christ, I will show it you at home in your own house." Which this deponent being desirous to see, the said Margery, stretching out her arms abroad, said to this deponent: "This is the true cross of Christ, and this cross thou oughtest and mayest every day behold and worship in thine own house; and therefore it is but vain to run to the church, to worship dead crosses and images."

Item, This deponent, being demanded by the said Margery how she believed touching the sacrament of the altar, said that she believed the sacrament of the altar, after the consecration, to be the very body of Christ in form of bread. To whom Margery said; "Your belief is nought. For if every sacrament were God, and the very body of Christ, there should be an infinite number of gods, because that a thousand priests, and more, do every day make a thousand such gods, and afterwards eat them, and void them out again in places, where, if you will seek them, you may find many such gods. And, therefore, know for certainty, that by the grace of God it shall never be my god, because it is falsely and deceitfully ordained by the priests in the church, to induce the simple people to idolatry; for it is only material bread."

Moreover, The said Margery said to this deponent, that Thomas of Canterbury, whom the people called Saint Thomas, was a false traitor, and damned in hell, because he injuriously endowed the churches with possessions, and raised up many heresies in the church, which seduce the simple people; and,

---

[1] ignorant carpenters.   [2] gloss.

therefore, if God be blessed, the said Thomas is accursed; and those false priests that say that he suffered his death patiently before the altar, do lie; for, as a false cowardly traitor, he was slain in the church door, as he was flying away.

Moreover, this deponent saith, that the said Margery told her, that the cursed pope, cardinals, archbishop, and bishops, and especially the bishop of Norwich, and others that support and maintain heresies and idolatry, reigning and ruling over the people, shall shortly have the very same or worse mischief fall upon them, than that cursed man, Thomas of Canterbury, had. For they falsely and cursedly deceive the people with their false mammetries[1] and laws, to extort money from the simple folk, to sustain their pride, riot and idleness. And know assuredly that the vengeance of God will speedily come upon them, who have most cruelly slain the children of God, Father Abraham, and William White, a true preacher of the law of God, and John Wadden, with many other godly men; which vengeance had come upon the said Caiaphas, the bishop of Norwich, and his ministers, who are members of the devil, before this time, if the pope had not sent over these false pardons unto those parties, which the said Caiaphas had falsely obtained, to induce the people to make procession for the state of them and of the church; which pardons brought the simple people to cursed idolatry.

Item, The said Margery said to this deponent, that every faithful man or woman is not bound to fast in Lent, or on other days appointed for fasting by the church; and that every man may lawfully eat flesh and all other meats upon the said days and times; and that it were better to eat the fragments left upon Thursday at night on the fasting days, than to go to the market to bring themselves in debt to buy fish; and that pope Silvester made the Lent.

Item, The said Margery said to this deponent, that William White was falsely condemned for a heretic, and that he was a good and holy man; and that he willed her to follow him to the place of execution, where she saw that when he would have opened his mouth to speak unto the people to instruct

[1] idolatries.

them, a devil, (one of bishop Caiaphas's servants), struck him on the lips, and stopped his mouth, that he could in no case declare the will of God.

Item, This deponent saith, that the said Margery taught her, that she should not go on pilgrimage, neither to our lady of Walsingham, nor to any other saint or place.

Also this deponent saith, that the said Margery desired her, that she and Joan her maid would come secretly, in the night, to her chamber, and there she should hear her husband read the law of Christ unto them, which law was written in a book that her husband was wont to read to her by night: and that her husband is well learned in the christian verity....

Item, She said moreover to this deponent, that holy bread and holy water were but trifles of no effect or force; and that the bells are to be cast out of the church, and that they are excommunicated who first ordained them.

Moreover, that she should not be burned, although she were convicted of Lollardy, for that she had a charter of salvation in her body.

Also the said deponent saith, that Agnes Berthem, her servant, being sent to the house of the said Margery the Saturday after Ash-Wednesday, the said Margery not being within, found a brass pot standing over the fire, with a piece of bacon and oatmeal seething in it; as the said Agnes reported to this deponent.

SECTION XIII

ARCHITECTURE AND THE ARTS

1   THE ARTIST'S INSPIRATION

St Bruno, St Bernard, St Francis, Savonarola, and practically all the creative minds in medieval religion took a puritan view of the Fine Arts. Latitudinarian and unorthodox reformers naturally took a similar view; perhaps the fullest and most detailed architectural description in all medieval English poetry (apart from Chaucer's imaginary House of Fame[1]) is that of the great Dominican friary in *Piers Plowman's Crede*, ll. 153 ff., where the writer admires indeed, but is mainly conscious of the sinful waste.   It is astonishing how few medieval documents testify directly to the artist's love of his work: even Matthew Paris, though he tells us a little about Walter of Colchester the "pictor incomparabilis" and other artists who worked at St Albans, is disappointingly jejune on this subject.   This was mainly, however, because the medieval artist seldom (except in Italy) enjoyed literary connections; we must therefore piece out the lack of English documents by an extract from the monk Theophilus, who probably wrote in Rhineland or in N.E. France between 1150 and 1250.   It is from the Prologue to Bk III. (*Le Moine Théophile*, ed. C. de l'Escalopier, 1843).   The writer is addressing his pupil:

David, that most excellent of prophets,...uttered this saying among others: "Lord I have loved the beauty of Thine house."... It is certain that he desired the adornment of the material house of God, which is the house of prayer.   For he left to Solomon his son almost all the stores of gold, silver, brass and iron for that house, which he desired most earnestly to build, yet because he had shed men's blood (that of his enemies, indeed, yet in great abundance), therefore he de-

---

[1] For a very remarkable imaginary description of the same kind, see the Temple of the Holy Graal in *Der Jüngere Titurel*, D. 42 ff., and the illustrated monograph on this passage by Sulpiz Boisserée (1835).

served it not. For he had read in Exodus how the Lord gave Moses a command for the construction of the Tabernacle, and had chosen Masters of the Works [*operum magistros*] by name, and had filled them with the spirit of God in wisdom and in understanding and in knowledge and in all manner of workmanship in gold and silver and brass, precious stones and wood and all kinds of arts; also he had known by pious consideration that God delighteth in such adornments, which he purposed to have constructed by the teaching and authority of the Holy Ghost, believing that without His inspiration no man might bring any such thing to pass. Wherefore, most beloved son, make thou no long delay, but believe in full faith that the Spirit of God hath filled thine heart when thou hast adorned his house with so great beauty and such manifold comeliness; and, lest perchance thou distrust me, I will unfold by evident reasons that, whatsoever thou canst learn, understand, or excogitate in the arts, this is given unto thee by the grace of the Sevenfold Spirit....

Cheered by these supporting virtues, my beloved son, thou hast approached God's house in all faith, and adorned it with such abundant comeliness; and, having illuminated the vaults or the walls with divers works and divers colours, thou hast in a manner shown forth to the beholders a vision of God's paradise, bright as springtide with flowers of every hue, fresh with green grass and leaves, and refreshing the souls of the saints with crowns proportioned to their divers merits[1]; whereby thou makest them to praise God in His creatures and to preach His wonders in His works. For man's eye knoweth not whereon first to gaze; if he look up at the vaults, they are as mantles embroidered with spring flowers[2]; if he regard the walls, there is a manner of paradise; if he consider the light streaming through the windows, he marvelleth at the priceless beauty of the glass and at the variety of this most precious work. If the faithful soul chance to behold the

---

[1] These were the *aureoles*: see Coulton, *From St Francis to Dante*, 2nd ed., pp. 169, 382.

[2] *Vernant quasi pallia*; cf. the Squire in Chaucer's *Prologue*: "Embrouded was he, as it were a meede Al ful of fresshe floures whyte and reede."

effigy of our Lord's passion expressed in all its lineaments, then he is pricked to the heart; if again he see how great tortures the Saints endured in their mortal bodies, and how precious a prize of eternal life they won, then doth he receive encouragement to a better life; or, beholding how great is the joy in heaven, how awful the torments amid the flames of hell, then is he cheered with hope for his good deeds, and smitten with fear at the thought of his sins. Work therefore now, good man, happy in this life before God's face and man's, and happier still in the life to come, by whose labour and zeal so many burnt-offerings are devoted to God! Kindle thyself to a still ampler art, and set thyself with all the might of thy soul to complete that which is yet lacking in the gear of the Lord's house, without which the divine mysteries and the ministries of God's service may not stand; such as chalices, candelabra, thuribles, chrism-vases, crewets, shrines for holy relics, crosses, missals and such like, which the necessary use of the ecclesiastical order requireth. Which if thou wouldst fashion, begin after the manner thus following....

2   THE ARTIST'S ESTIMATION

Except in Italy, when the Renaissance was already dawning, it is impossible to distinguish between the medieval *artist* and *artisan*; it may truly be said that the noblest piles, like Reims, Chartres and Amiens, were built from top to bottom by artisans, who received artisans' wages, the master-mason generally getting the same as the master-carpenter or master-smith. It has sometimes been argued, however, that what these lacked in money they earned in high esteem; that they were as much respected as distinguished artists are in our own day: in support of which, we are reminded that Charles V. of France stood sponsor to the son of his master-mason Raymond du Temple, and that the boy went to the University of Orleans (Lethaby, *Medieval Art*, 1904, p. 256). This, however, is an exceptional case, just as modern royalty has sometimes condescended to stand sponsor to a gamekeeper's or gardener's child. The following extracts illustrate how the men who built our churches and castles were generally esteemed and treated as ordinary artisans. Benvenuto da Imola was a professor at Bologna who lectured on Dante's *Commedia* about a generation after the poet's death; his *Comentum super Dantis Comoediam* is a very valuable document for the student of medieval manners and thought. It must be remembered that, next to Gothic architecture, miniature was the great art of the Middle Ages, and that Benvenuto draws no distinction between Oderisi and Cimabue and Giotto.

(*a*)   Dante, tr. Cary, *Purgatorio*, XI. 79 (the Purgatory of the Proud).

          "O," I exclaim'd,
"Art thou not Oderisi? art not thou
Agobbio's glory, glory of that art
Which they of Paris call the limner's skill?"
     "Brother!" said he, "with tints that gayer smile
Bolognian Franco's pencil lines the leaves.
His all the honour now; mine borrow'd light.
In truth I had not been thus courteous to him
The whilst I liv'd, through eagerness of zeal
For that pre-eminence my heart was bent on.
Here of such pride the forfeiture is paid.
Nor were I even here if, able still
To sin, I had not turn'd me unto God.
O powers of man! how vain your glory, nipp'd
E'en in its height of verdure, if an age
Less bright succeed not! Cimabue thought
To lord it over painting's field; and now
The cry is Giotto's, and his name eclips'd."

Upon which Benvenuto comments (ed. Lacaita, Florence 1887, vol. III. p. 309):

This Oderisi was a great miniature-painter in the city of Bologna in Dante's time; and he was a very vain boaster of his art, thinking that he had no equal; wherefore Dante, who well knew how greedy his mind was of praise and glory, here purposely commendeth him over all others, that he may see whether the vain breath is now gone which once so swelled his soul....And note here that some men wonder ignorantly at this passage, saying: "Why hath Dante here named men of unknown name and low occupation [*ignoti nominis et bassae artis*], when he might more worthily have made mention of most excellent men who, in their great greed for glory, have done fair and noble deeds?" But certainly it was with great art and excellent justice that Dante did this; for thereby he giveth silently to be understood how the love of glory doth so indifferently fasten upon all men, that even petty artisans [*parvi artifices*] are anxious to earn it, as we see that painters append their names to their works,...

(*b*) F. Peck's *Antiquarian Repertory*, vol. II. p. 407 (Wardrobe accounts of Edward II.).

"Item, paid to Jak de Seint Albon, Painter Royal (whc danced on a table before the king and made him laugh beyond measure) by way of gift through the king's own hands, to help himself, his wife, and his children, 50 shillings....Item, paid at Wolmer Lodge, where the king chased the stag, to Morris Cook, of the kitchen, because he rode there before the king and fell oftentimes from his horse, whereat the king laughed heartily, in manner of gift by royal command, 20 shillings."

May not this last incident have inspired Chaucer's picture of the Cook falling from his horse at Harbledown?

(*c*) Willis and Clark, *Architectural History of the University of Cambridge*, vol. I. p. 382 (Eton College).   Foot-notes 2, 3, 4 are those of Willis and Clark.

The number of men employed varied of course according to the work, and the season of the year.   The wage-books shew that the "masons called freemasons" and the "masons called hardhewers," were retained all the year round.   They received sixpence a day; and the former were allowed their wages on Saints' days, when no work was done; the latter not, except sometimes by special command of the king.   Sixpence a day was the rate of wages for all the men, except the labourers, who received fourpence or fivepence.   Discipline was very strict, and a system of fines was enforced, by which men who misbehaved themselves lost a whole day, or half a day, for each misdemeanour.   A few of these may be cited; "for he lost a Showell[2]"; "for late cuming"; "for telling of tales"; "for chiding"; "for freghting[1]" (half-day); "for breaking of Shovoll[2]"; "for playing"; "for letting of his felowes" (whole day); "for keping of the hole owre" (half-day).   This was probably the dinner hour, and the strict observance of it by the men seems to have been a grievance with the clerk of the works, for Robert Goodgrome is fined "for he wold kepe his ouris and never go to werke till the clocke smyte."   His example apparently caused something like a mutiny, for twenty-one men are fined a whole day because

---

[1] fighting.   [2] shovel.

"they wolde not go to theire werke till ij of clocke, and al makith Goodgrome." Another lost three days "for shending[1] of a lode of strawe"; and another a whole week " for he wol not do labor but as he list himself[2]."

(p. 384.) For the next year, extending from Monday, 12 February, 1441–42, to Monday, 4 February, 1442–43, we have both a wage book and an account-book for materials supplied. The works, whether the erection of new buildings, or the repair of old ones, were evidently being carried on with increased activity, from the number of workmen of different trades employed upon them. The weekly average has now risen to 116. To give an idea of what was being done let us take the week beginning with Monday, 23 July, 1442, as a specimen. There were 53 free-masons, 9 "hardhewers," 15 "rowmasons[3]," 45 carpenters, 4 sawyers, 3 thatchers, 1 tiler, 1 plasterer, 1 smith, 5 bricklayers, and 45 labourers, making a total of 182. These workmen had to be sought out in different parts of England, and some were even pressed into service, as had been done at King's[4].

3 THE ARCHITECT'S REWARD

Léon Gautier admits that the medieval epics, while assuming palatial magnificence of architecture for the abodes of their heroes, seldom deign to name the artist who wrought all this: "Dans la *Prise d'Orange*, c'est un Sarrasin" (*La Chevalerie*, nouvelle édition, p. 468 *n.*). Ordericus Vitalis shows how the medieval architect might even have been grateful for this oblivion, and might have anticipated Figaro's epigram: "un grand nous fait assez de bien quand il ne nous fait pas de mal." (*Hist. Eccles.* lib. VIII. c. 22. Migne, *P.L.*, vol. CLXXXVIII. col. 627).

This [castle of Ivry, in Normandy] is that famous tower, vast and fortified beyond all others, which was built by

---

[1] spoiling.

[2] These instances are selected from the accounts of Roger Keys (1448–9).

[3] i.e. *rough-masons*, as distinguished from *freemasons*, the workers in fine freestone.

[4] 23 April 1442. "Robert Westurley xxv day of April in Reward for purweing[5] of Fremasons in diverse place of Engelond endentid in a bille delyvered by the handes of William lynde (clerk of the works)...xxs." 16 July 1442. "John Lynde William Lynd John Sacrys and Thomas Rigware, Row Masons of Norwyche, in reward at [t]heir going...xvj d ha."

[5] purveying.

Albereda, wife to Ralph earl of Bayeux, and which was long held against the dukes of Normandy by Hugh, bishop of Bayeux, and brother to John archbishop of Rouen. Men say that the countess aforesaid caused the castle to be built by the architect Lanfred, whom she created Master of the Works after the building of the tower of Pithiviers, a man whose skill was praised far beyond that of all other artificers of his time in France. Then, when Lanfred had completed this castle of Ivry with much labour and at great cost, she caused him to be beheaded lest he should build another equal to it elsewhere. The countess herself, in the end, was slain by her own husband on account of this same castle, because she had striven to keep him from it.

4   LINCOLN CATHEDRAL

Metrical Life of St Hugh, ed. Dimock, 1860, pp. 32 ff. abbreviated. About 1190 A.D. St Hugh set the master-mason Geoffrey de Noiers at work on the rebuilding of his cathedral of Lincoln.

With wondrous art he built the fabric of the Cathedral; whereunto he supplied not only his own wealth, and the labours of his servants, but even the sweat of his own brow; for he oftentimes bore the hod-load of hewn stone or of binding lime. In this structure, the art equals the precious materials; for the vault may be compared to a bird stretching out her broad wings to fly; planted on its firm columns, it soars to the clouds. On the other hand, the work is supported by precious columns of swarthy stone[1], not confined to one sole colour, nor loose of pore, but flecked with glittering stars and close-set in all its grain. This stone disdains to be tamed with steel until it have first been subdued by art; for its surface must first be softened by long grinding with sand, and its hardness is relaxed with strong vinegar. Moreover, it may suspend the mind in doubt whether it be jasper or marble; it is dull indeed for jasper, yet, for marble, of a most noble nature. Of this are formed those slender columns which stand round the great piers, even as a bevy of maidens stand marshalled for a dance.

[1] i.e. Purbeck marble.

5   THE PERILS OF ORIGINALITY

The medieval artist's methods were sometimes very strictly limited by his own gild; see an extremely interesting instance in Alwin Schultz's monograph on Jodocus Tauchen of Breslau (1864), p. 10. The two following documents show how much he might be trammelled also by the ecclesiastical authorities. Something, however, may be due to natural jealousy of the foreign craftsman.

(*a*) Register of Ralph Baldock, Bp of London (Canterbury and York Society, 1911), p. 19. Letter to the Prior of Holy Trinity, Aldgate.

We have heard on trustworthy authority that one Tidemann of Germany hath sold, some time since, to Geoffrey, Rector of St Mildred's in the Poultry, a certain carved Crucifix with a cross-beam which doth not represent the true form of the Cross; which crucifix the said Rector had placed in his church, and whereunto the indiscreet populace flocked in crowds as to a true image of the Cross (whereas it was no such image) whence, as We foresaw, it might chance that their souls should be imperilled—by reason of which Cross We caused the said Tidemann and Geoffrey to be summoned to Our presence, and, having made diligent inquisition from both, we have ordained as here ensueth, lest by continuance of this error yet worse things should befall : That the aforesaid Tidemann should take (and he hath indeed so taken) his oath on the Gospels that he would never henceforth make, nor suffer to be exposed for sale, within Our city or diocese of London, such Crucifix as this, or Crosses with arms contrary to the accustomed fashion, under pain of excommunication for disobedience. And because the said Tidemann claimeth to be an alien and a simple man, who might probably and innocently have ignored the accustomed mysteries of the Crucifix and the image thereunto attached, therefore We have graciously granted to him as here ensueth : That he, having first restored to Us the letter of obligation for twenty three pounds sterling which he hath from the Rector aforesaid, shall obtain restitution of this Crucifix, which hath been sequestrated and deposited in your keeping, for the avoidance of peril to men's souls, by the discreet Master Richard of Newport, who was then Our Vicar and Official. Wherefore We enjoin and command you that, having received from this Tidemann the aforesaid obligation (which you will faithfully transmit to Us), you will without delay deliver to the said Tidemann his image aforesaid; provided always that it be borne forth from your Monastery to some place without Our diocese, either at early dawn or late in the evening, when it can be done most secretly and with least scandal; and that you shall set a watch to assure the execution of this command and to intimate the same to Us. The said letter of obligation, wherein you trust, shall be sent to Us at your peril, and you shall not delay to certify Us plainly and openly by letter of all that you have done in this matter. Given at Our Palace of Fulham, Aug. 2, 1306.

(*b*)   Luke, Bp of Tuy in Spain, wrote between 1260 and 1280 a treatise against the Albigenses and other heretics of his time: one passage throws incidental light upon Bp Baldock's anxiety about Tidemann's too original crucifix and the peril to the souls of the populace. (Lucae Tudensis *De Altera Vita*, 1612, p. 93, lib. II. c. 9.)

The heretics have another method of deceiving by means of pictures; which method we have thought fit not to pass over in silence, that the faithful may know it and be the more cautious to avoid it. For they oftentimes paint or carve ill-shapen images of Saints, that by gazing on such images the devotion of simple Christian folk may be turned to loathing. In derision and scorn of Christ's Cross, they carve images of our Lord with one foot laid over the other, so that both are pierced by a single nail, thus striving either to annul or to render doubtful men's faith in the Holy Cross and the traditions of the sainted Fathers, by superinducing these diversities and novelties[1]. This we will now demonstrate more clearly by relating that which took place in the land of France, in a

---

[1] What so distressed the good bishop here was in fact the artistic evolution which was taking place in his own age. The earliest representations are not realistic at all; for some centuries after realistic representations began, the feet were still separate; and at last "in the 13th century complete realism is reached by the substitution of one nail in the feet, instead of two as in the old tradition, and the resulting crossing of the legs. All this was done from artistic motives, to bring about a more moving and devotional pose." *Catholic Encyclopaedia*, vol. IV. 1908, p. 529 (Orazio Marucchi). The note-book of Villard de Honnecourt (about 1250) shows already crucifixes of this modern type (plates 4, 14, 25).

An Ancient Crucifix

(a) A Glass-Painter
(b) Carpenter, Mason, and Clerk of the Works

town called Monculis [Montclus, Hautes-Alpes?], as hath been divulged by those who have told the facts.

In our own days, when the Manichaean heresy was spread abroad in France, and the poison of error was creeping everywhere, certain of these heretical mis-believers, instigated by the Devil, took [for their worship] a deformed and one-eyed image of the Holy Mother of God, giving this as their reason (though therein they lied wantonly, to the perdition of their own souls), that our Lord Jesus Christ so far humbled Himself as to predestine for the salvation of mankind a woman devoid of all comeliness. Thus these men thought within themselves, in their blind malice and falsehood, that they might the more easily deceive the simple, and wean their minds and thoughts from devotion to our most glorious Lady, Mary Ever-Virgin. Moreover, they suborned men who feigned themselves to be sick of divers diseases, and who seemed to be miraculously cured by this aforesaid image. These miracles were noised abroad, as though they had been true, through the towns and villages; and many even of the priests, with mistaken piety, caused like images to be made and set up in their churches. The heretics, seeing this, began now to discover what they had so long concealed, and to mock at those multitudes who flocked to pay their devotions to this image aforesaid.

About the same time, the said heretics made a cross with only three arms, whereon was carved an image with one foot laid over another, nailed by three nails only to the cross, which had no upper limb; which image the people came and adored most devoutly instead of the true Cross of Christ. Then these adversaries of the truth, disclosing the net which they had secretly spread, caught the souls of simple folk with their falsehoods, and rebuked even the Ministers of God, saying: " If those things were true which ye have hitherto believed of the Cross, then is not that true which ye now adore; and, if what ye now believe be true, ye have hitherto taught falsehood. For if Christ was nailed to the Cross with four nails, and the cross itself had four arms, as ye have taught in the past, then is this which ye now adore and preach no true similitude of the Cross of Christ. Lo now ye halt between two opinions,

and doubt, and lead ignorant folk into error by your own
devious ways! Ye have no authority; your customs con-
tradict one another!" Such blasphemies, and many more of
the same sort, these heretics uttered against the Catholics,
taking many simple souls in their snares; nay, even unto this
day they cease not to spread abroad the wicked and schismatic
doctrines which they have taken in hand.

6　AN ARTIST'S NOTEBOOK

Villard de Honnecourt, a Picard master-mason, probably built a great
church at Vaucelles about 1230, another in Hungary later, and the choir of
the Cathedral of St Quentin (destroyed only a few months ago) about 1250.
He is the only medieval architect whose sketchbook has survived; from
this we may learn much about a master-mason's mentality and methods,
which were essentially the same in all countries. His book was first published by Lassus (1858), then by Prof. Willis (1859), and lastly, in photo-
graphic facsimile (Paris 1908). The following translations are from the
edition of Lassus. Several of Villard's drawings have been reproduced
on a small scale by Prof. Lethaby in his *Medieval Art*, 1904, pp. 172, 197,
238, 249; and his celebrated description and drawing of the lion will be
found on p. 336 of my *Medieval Garner*.

Prologue (p. 61).

Here on this page you may find the figures of twelve
apostles, seated.

Villard de Honnecourt greets you, and prays all those who
work at the artifices [*engiens*] which will be found in this book
to pray for his soul, and to bear him in mind. For in this
book will be found good advice for the great power of masonry
and of engines of carpentry. You will find likewise the power
of portraiture and of design, even as the art of geometry biddeth and teacheth.

p. 73. Oftentimes have master [masons and carpenters]
disputed how to make a wheel turn of its own force. You may
see here how it may be done by an uneven number of mallets
or [bags of] quicksilver.

[*See plate* 1.]

It will be seen that, the mallets or bags being made so as to swing
freely, Villard hopes that there will always be four on the downward side
of the wheel and only three on the upward side; thus the mallet or bag
will always fall over to the left as it reaches the top, *ad infinitum.*

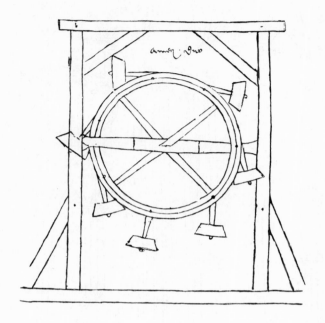

PERPETUAL MOTION

(A later hand, probably of the 15th century, has added *amen dico*—"verily I say")

Plate I to face p. 476

LAON TOWER ABOUT 1250 A.D.

NORTH-WEST TOWER OF LAON (PRESENT STATE)

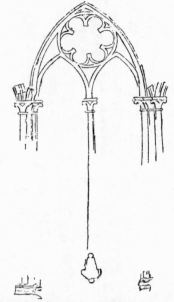

AN AISLE-WINDOW FROM REIMS

Plate IV to face p. 477

p. 93. I have been in many countries, as you may find in this book ; but in no town did I ever see such a tower as that of Laon. Here is [a plan of] its first story, with its windows. At this stage the tower is built with eight sides, flanked by four square turrets supported by columns in groups of three. Then come the little arches and the string-course; and again come turrets with eight columns, and an ox looking forth between each pair of columns. Then again come arches and a string-course, and above all a steep octagonal roof. On each side is a loophole for light. Look straight in front, and you will see well how this is ordered, and the whole elevation of the tower, and how the turrets change from story to story. And think on this ; for, if you would fain build altogether with columns and buttresses, you must choose such as have enough projection. Take good heed how you work, and then you will do as a wise and well-instructed man should.

[*See plates* 2 *and* 3.]

p. 97. Here is one of the windows of Reims Cathedral, such as they stand in each bay of the nave between each pair of pillars. I was on my way to obey a call to the land of Hungary when I drew this window, because it pleased me best of all windows.

[*See plate* 4.]

These Reims traceries, which appealed to Villard as a new and admirable design, were followed by the architect of Westminster Abbey, and thus popularized throughout England in the mid-thirteenth century. Cf. W. R. Lethaby, *Westminster Abbey*, 1906, pp. 73, 116 ff. and *Medieval Art*, p. 208.

p. 125. I was once in Hungary, where I dwelt a long time, and there I saw a church paved in this fashion [*drawings of five different patterns*].

p. 126. This is the [great wheel-]window in the Cathedral of our Lady of Chartres.

p. 127. Here is a rose-window from the Cathedral of Lausanne.

p. 150. By this means we may bridge a river, even though our beams be only twenty feet long....By this means we may measure the breadth of a river without crossing it [*i.e. by a trigonometrical measurement: cf.* p. 162]....By this means we may take the height of a tower.

p. 152. By this means we may cut the screw of a wine-press.

p. 153. By this means we may make two vessels whereof one shall contain the double of the other.

p. 162. By this means we may place an egg exactly beneath a [ripe] pear [on its tree], by [trigonometrical] measurement, so that the pear may fall plumb upon the egg.

p. 168. Take lime and pagan [*i.e. Roman*] brick powdered fine, making no more of one than of the other, except that there must be a little more brick, until its colour shall prevail over the other. Mix this cement well with linseed oil; it will be strong enough to make a vessel that will hold water.

Ibid. Take boiled quicklime and orpiment, and put them into boiling water and oil. This makes an ointment good for removing superfluous hairs.

p. 171. Thus may we make a saw that will saw by itself [*sketch of a rudimentary saw-mill*].

Ibid. Thus may we make a crossbow that cannot miss its mark [*the crossbow is fitted with a sort of pinhole-sight*].

p. 172. Thus may we make one of the strongest engines that may be to raise loads [*sketch of a screw-jack*].

p. 173. Thus may we make the eagle [on the lectern] turn his head towards the deacon when he reads the Gospel [at mass].

p. 219. Bear well in mind this that I will tell you. Take leaves of red-cabbage and of bastard-hemp. Take a herb called tansy, and hempseed. Crush these four herbs, so that there be no more of one than of the other. Then take of madder twice as much as of any of the other four herbs, stamp it in with the rest, and put these five simples into a pot, infused in the best white wine that you may procure, but so tempered that the potion be not too thick to drink. Drink not too much, for in an eggshell ye may have enough, so that the shell be full. Whatever wound or sore ye may have, this will heal you. Cleanse your wounds with a little flaxen tow, lay a leaf of red cabbage thereon, and drink of the potion morning and evening, twice a day. It is better infused in sweet must than in other wine, so that the must be good : for thus it will ferment with the simples. If you infuse it in old wine, leave it two days before you drink thereof.

7   ANGELS IN ART

Trevisa's *Bartholomew*, Lib. II. cc. 3 and 4.

Howe Angell in bodily shappe is peynted.

Also, though angels' kynde have no mater, nother lyneacions[1] and shap of body, yet angels ben paynted in bodily lyknesse, and scrypture makyth mynde that they have divers limmes and shappes.   But by denominacyons of limmes, that ben seen, unsene werkynges of hevenly inwyttes[2] bene understonde. For whan angelles bene paynted with longe lockes and cryspe heer, thereby is understonde theyr cleane affections and ordy-nate thoughtes.   For the heer of the heed tokeneth thoughtes and affections, that spryngen of the roote of thoughte and mynde.... And they bene peynted berdelesse, for to take consideration and hede that they passe never the sta[g]e of youth, neyther wexe feble in vertues, neither faile for age.... Feete they have, but as it were alwaye bare, for the mevyng[3] of theyr affeccyon to godwarde is sequestred from al deedly lykynge.... Truly they bene peynted fethered and wynged, for that they ben alyene[4] and clene from all erthly cogitacion, and they ben hoven[5] up in effecte and inwytte, and ravyshed to the innest contemplacion of the love of god.   They ben clothed in fyrye[6] redde clothes, for that they bene wrapped in the lyghte and mantell of fhe knowlege and love of god ; "they be clothed with lyght as with a garment." Psal. 103....   They ben arayed in armes and wepyn of batayle and of warre, for that by helpe of them good men ben oft socoured and def-fended in warre and in batayle of body and of soule.   And they harpe, for that they that ben worthy to be comforted, by

---

[1] no material substance, nor lineaments.   [2] minds.   [3] moving.
[4] alien.   [5] raised.   [6] fiery.

theyr helpe and prayers, falle not into sorowe of dispayre and wanhope[1]. They beare trompes in hondes[2], for that they calle and comforte and excyte us to profyte alway in goodnes. Many suche maner thinges ben writen of the araye and doynge of angelles, that betokyn theyr marvaylous werkes.

8   THE OCTAGON OF ELY

Alan de Walsingham has sometimes been called the "architect" of the great octagon at Ely; it is more probable that his strictly architectural work was limited to general suggestions. Monastic historians always exaggerate the share of the brethren; to them, the important person was not so much the artist as the employer; they constantly use *fecit* in the sense of "ordered and paid for." The following extract is from *Historia Eliensis*, in Wharton, *Anglia Sacra*, vol. I. (1691), pp. 643 ff., A.D. 1321.

[One night,] when the brethren had made their procession to the shrines in honour of St Ermengilda, and were returning to the dormitory, scarce had one or two lain down upon their beds when, behold! the central tower suddenly fell and over-whelmed the choir, with such a crash and din that men might have thought it an earthquake; yet no man was hurt or crushed by its fall....Alan [de Walsingham], our Sacrist, was sore grieved and afflicted at this most baleful and lamentable chance, not knowing whither to turn, or what possible means could be found of repairing so vast a ruin. But, plucking up courage, and putting all his trust in the help of God and of His most gracious Mother, and in the merits of the holy virgin Etheldreda, he put out his hand to strong things (Prov. xxxi. 19 *Vulg.*). First, he spent great labour and much money in removing from the Cathedral the fallen stones and beams; then he purged the holy building with all possible haste from the masses of dust which lay there. Finally he measured out in eight divisions, with the art of an architect, the place where he thought to build the new tower; and he set the workmen to dig and search for the foundations of the eight stone columns where-upon the whole building should be supported, and beneath which the choir with its stalls might afterwards be built; until at last he found solid and secure ground for all this under-

---

[1] hopelessness.   [2] trumpets in their hands.

structure. Then, when these eight places had been carefully dug out and firmly founded with stones and sand, at last he began those eight columns, with the stonework which they supported. This he completed in six years, bringing it up to the upper string-course in the year of our Lord 1328. Then, without delay, that cunningly-wrought timber structure of the new tower was begun ; a structure designed with the utmost and most marvellous subtlety of human thought, to be set upon the aforesaid stonework. This in its turn was completed, with vast and burdensome expense, especially in seeking far and wide for the great beams which were needed to support this building, which were found at last with the utmost difficulty and at great cost, and which were brought by land or sea to Ely. These beams were carved and shaped by skilful work-men, and bound together into the fabric with marvellous art ; thus at length, with God's help, the tower was brought to that honourable consummation which had long been desired. The whole cost of this new tower, during the twenty years of Alan de Walsingham's time, was £2400. 6s. 11d., whereof £206. 1s. came from gifts.

9   MASONIC LEGEND AND FACT

The word *Freemason* is probably derived from *freestone-mason* ; in early documents it always denotes the fine workman as opposed to the *rough-mason*, or *rough-hewer*, cf. no. 2 c just above. Medieval Freemasonry seems to have differed in no essential particular from other trade gilds ; only the wandering life of many masons made it advisable to bind the craft together by a few more social regulations than others, and gave it a some-what better chance of escaping from State laws regulating trade prices, etc. It is significant that the masons seem to have resisted the Statutes of Labourers more successfully than any other craft ; and that when, in the 17th century, the newborn spirit of internationalism sought some preexisting organisation to creep into, this was found among the Free-masons.

The earliest English constitutions marking this development (and probably the earliest surviving in any country) are contained in a poem which J. O. Halliwell printed from the unique MS. of the early 15th century (*Early History of Freemasonry in England*, 2nd ed. 1844). I print here continuously a very brief series of selections from the poem, with a few explanatory notes. The author, like many other medieval writers, thinks fit to commend his practical admonitions by an admixture of legend which shall give them all the sanction of hoary antiquity. With more self-restraint than later authors who have begun with the Garden of Eden, he confesses that he can trace Freemasonry no farther back than to Euclid. P. 14.

> On thys maner, throgh good wytte of gemetry,
> Bygan furst the craft of masonry :
> The clerk Euclyde on thys wise hyt fonde,
> Thys craft of gemetry yn Egypte londe.
> Fyftene artyculus[1] they ther sowghton[2]
> And fyftene poyntys they ther wroghton.

> *Hic incipit articulus primus.*

> The furste artycul of thys gemetry :—
> The mayster mason moste be ful securly[3]
> Bothe stedefast, trusty, and tr[e]we,
> Hyt shal hym never thenne arewe[4]:
> And pay thy fellows after the coste,
> As vytaylys goth thenne, wel thou woste;
> And pay them trwly, apon thy fay,
> What that they deserven may;
> And to her hure[5] take no more,
> But what that they mowe[6] serve fore.

> *Articulus secundus.*

> The secunde articul of good masonry,
> As ye mowe hyt here hyr spec[i]aly,
> That every mayster, that ys a mason,
> Most ben at the generale congregacyon,
> Or ellus[7] sekenes hath hym so stronge,
> That he may not come hem[8] amonge.

Art. 3. No apprentice to be taken for less than seven years, that he may learn his craft well.

> *Articulus quartus.*

> The fowrthe artycul thys moste be,
> That the mayster hym wel be-se[9],

---

[1] articles.   [2] sought.   [3] certainly.   [4] rue.   [5] their hire.
     [6] may   [7] unless.   [8] them.   [9] take care.

That he no bondemon[1] prentys make,
Ny[2] for no covetyse do hym take;
For the lord that he ys bonde to,
May fache[3] the prentes whersever he go.
Yef[4] yn the logge[5] he were y-take,
Muche desese[6] hyt myghth ther make,
And suche case hyt myghth befalle,
That hyt myghth greve summe or alle.
For alle the masonus that ben there
Wol stonde togedur hol y-fere[7].
By olde tyme wryten y fynde
That the sculde[8] be of gentyl kynde;
And so sumtyme grete lordys blod
Toke thys gemetry, that ys ful good.

Art. 5. The apprentice must be of legitimate birth, and not "a halt mon and a lame."

Art. 6. The master mason must not charge an employer so much for an apprentice's work as for a journeyman's.

Articulus septimus.

The seventhe artycul that ys now here,
Ful wel wol [I] telle yow, alle y-fere[9]
That no mayster, for favour ny drede,
Schal no thef nowther[10] clothe ny fede.
Theves he schal herberon[11] never won[12],
Ny hym that hath ever y-quellude[13] a mon,
Ny thylke that hath a febul[14] name,
Lest hyt wolde turne the craft to schame.

Articulus octavus.

The egthe artycul schewet yow[15] so,
That the mayster may hyt wel do,
Yef that he have any mon of crafte,
And be not also perfyt as he aughte,

---

[1] bondman.   [2] nor.   [3] fetch.   [4] if.   [5] mason's lodge.
[6] trouble.   [7] wholly combined.   [8] should.   [9] together.
[10] neither.   [11] harbour.   [12] one.   [13] killed.   [14] damaged.
[15] sheweth you.

He may hym change sone anon,
And take for hym a perfytur mon.
Suche a mon, throghe rechel-aschepe[1],
Myghth do the craft schert worschepe[2].

Art. 9.   The master must undertake no work that he is not competent
to perform, nor build on bad foundations.

Articulus decimus.

The thenthe artycul ys for to knowe,
Amonge the craft, to hye and lowe,
Ther schal no mayster supplante other,
But be togedur as systur and brother,
Ny he schal not supplante non other mon,
That hath y-take a werke hym uppon,
But yef[3] that he be gulty y-fonde,
That toke furst the werke on honde;
But yef that hyt be so y-wroghth,
That hyt turne the werke to noghth,
Thenne may a mason that werk crave,
To the lordes[4] profyt hyt for to save.

Articulus undecimus.

The eleventhe artycul y telle the,
That he ys bothe fayr and fre;
For he techyt, by hys myghth,
That no mason schulde worche be nyghth[5],
But yef hyt be yn practesynge of wytte
Yef that y cowthe[6] amende hytte.

Art. 12.   No mason must "deprave his fellow's work," but "commend
it with honest words."

Art. 13.   The master must take real pains to teach his apprentice.

Art. 14.   And therefore not take an apprentice, unless he himself have
sufficient work on hand to give him practical instruction.

---

[1] recklessness.   [2] small honour.   [3] unless.   [4] employer's.
[5] work by night.   [6] could.

Articulus quindecimus.

The fyftene artycul maketh an ende,
For to the mayster he ys a frende ;
To lere[1] hym so, that for no mon,
No fals mantenans[2] he take hym apon,
Ny maynteine hys felows yn here synne,
For no good that he myghth wynne ;
Ny no fals sware[3] sofre hem to make,
For drede of here sowles sake ;
Lest hyt wolde turne the craft to schame,
A[nd] hymself to mechul blame.

p. 22. At the same "assembly," Euclid ordained several furthe
"points" of Freemasonry :

(1) Love God and Holy Church and your fellow-masons.

(2) Labour well on work-days, to deserve your holy-day rest.

(3)

The thrydde poynt most be severele[4],
[Let] the prentes knowe hyt wele,
Hys mayster conwsel he kepe and close,
And hys felows' by hys goode purpose ;
The prevystye[5] of the chamber telle he no mon,
Ny yn the logge whatsever they done ;
Whatsever thou heryst, or systé hem do,
Telle hyt no mon, whersever thou go ;
The conwsel of halle, and yeke of bowre[6],
Kepe hyt wel to gret honowre,
Lest hyt wolde torne thyself to blame,
And brynge the craft ynto gret schame.

---

[1] teach.

[2] maintenance. *Maintenance* is generally used for supporting others in a law-suit or quarrel in which one's own interests are not involved ; in the Middle Ages, there were a good many who did this for money. See Rastell's *Les Termes de la Ley*, ed. 1642, f. 218 *b*.

[3] oath. [4] must be separate. [5] privacy. [6] eke of chamber.

(4)   Let none be disloyal to the craft.

(5)   Let the master pay wages truly, and the journeyman receive them thankfully.

(6)

Amonge the masouns, summe or alle,
Throwghe envye, or dedly hate,
Ofte aryseth ful gret debate.
Thenne owyth[1] the mason, yef that he may,
Putte hem bothe undur a day[2];
But loveday yet schul they make none,
Tyl that the werke day be clene a-gone;
Apon the holyday ye mowe wel take
Leysur[3] y-nowgh loveday to make,
Lest that hyt wolde [on] the werke day
Latte here[4] werke for suche afray.

(7)   Let the mason beware of adultery with a fellow-mason's wife.

(8)   Deal honestly with the employer who commissions the building work.

(9)   Is extremely interesting, as showing that the masons often had a common mess at their lodge.

The nynthe point we schul hym calle,
That he be st[e]warde of oure halle,
Yef that ye ben yn chambur y-fere,
Uchon serve other, with mylde chere;
Jentul[5] felows, ye most hyt knowe,
[Ought] to be stwardus alle o' rowe,
Weke after weke withoute dowte,
Stwardus to ben so alle abowte,
Lovelyche to serven uchon[6] othur,
As thawgh they were syster and brother.
Loke that thou pay wele every mon algate[7]
That thou hast y-bowght any vytayles ate,
Yet good acowntes he most make
Of such godes as he hath y-take,

---

[1] ought.   [2] appoint a "loveday" for arbitration between the two.
[3] leisure.   [4] hinder their.   [5] gentle.   [6] each one.   [7] always.

Of thy felowes goodes that thou hast spende,
Wher, and how, and to what ende,
Suche acowntes thou most come to,
When they wollen[1] that thou do.

(10) Let masons live good lives, that they shame not the craft ; black sheep are to be solemnly expelled at the yearly Assemblies.

(11)

A mason, and he thys craft wel con,
That syghth hys felow hewen on a ston,
And ys yn poynt[ts] spylle[2] that ston,
Amende hyt sone[3], yef that thou can,
And teche him then hyt to amende,
That the hole werke be not y-schende[4].
And teche hym esely hyt to amende,
With fayre wordes, that God the hath lende;
For hys sake that sytte above,
With swete wordes noresche[5] hym love.

(12)

The twelthe poynt ys of gret ryolté[6],
Ther as the semblé[7] y-holde schal be,
Ther schul be maystrys and felows also,
And other grete Lordes mony mo;
There schal be the scheref of that contré,
And also the meyr of that syté,
Knyghtes and sqwyers ther schul be,
And other aldermen, as ye schul se[8];
Suche ordynance as they maken there,
They schul maynte[ne] hyt hol y-fere[9]
Agheynus[10] that mon, whatsever he be,
That longuth to the crafte both fayr and fre.
Yef he any stryf agheynus hem make,
Ynto here warde[11] he schal be take.

(13) The mason shall swear not to steal, nor to abet a thief.

---

[1] will.   [2] spoil.   [3] soon.   [4] spoilt.   [5] nourish.   [6] royalty.   [7] assembly.
[8] It may safely be asserted, I think, that this theory is purely Utopian, and that no attempt was ever made to realize it.
[9] altogether.   [10] against.   [11] prison.

(14)   He shall swear also to keep the rules and ordinances of his craft. (This multiplicity of oaths was common, not only to the craft gilds, but to all sections of medieval society. Cf. Rashdall, *Universities of Europe*, II. 688.)

(15)   "Unbuxom" members of the craft shall be convicted before the Assembly and expelled; their goods and chattels shall be forfeited to the King. (It may safely be said that there is no trace of such forfeits among the numerous State documents in which they would have been recorded.)

(16)   The masons shall hold a yearly assembly, to enforce these statutes of King Athelstan. (This is the first we hear of Athelstan as author of the statutes, which before were ascribed to Euclid. It is probable that the Craft chose him as their eponymous hero on the strength of the *stan* (stone) in his name; just as the Paris masons of the 13th century claimed to have been freed from the burden of watch and ward by Charles Martel; a stone-hammer is one of the commonest of medieval masonic insignia. See Étienne Boileau's *Métiers de Paris*, ed. R. de l'Espinasse, 1879, Introd. p. iv and text, pp. 88 ff.)

The MS. then goes on with the story of the *Quatuor Coronati*—four masons who were fabled to have been beaten to death under Diocletian for their refusal to make "maumets" or idols; see *Golden Legend*, Nov. 8 (*Temple Classics*, vol. VI. p. 139). It passes on to a series of general religious and moral precepts, and finally to a code of good manners in "the halle, amonges the genteles," or "yn chamber, amonge the ladyes bright," resembling a brief summary of the *Stans Puer ad Mensam* (Section II., no. 27). The common assurance is given that attendance at mass will guard the mason that day from sudden death, loss of eyesight, etc., and that the Angel Gabriel measures and records "uche[1] fote that thou gost then, that holy syht for to sen[2]." At the consecration, the mason is to say that prayer which is to be found also in Myrc's *Instructions* (E.E.T.S., 1868, line 290); with this the extracts may fitly end:

> Jhesu, Lord, welcom thou be,
> Yn forme of bred, as y the se[3]!
> Now Jhesu, for thyn holy name,
> Schulde[4] me from synne and schame;
> Schryff[5] and hosel[6] thou grant me bo[7],
> Yer that y schal hennus[8] go,
> And very contrycyon of my synne,
> That y never, Lord, dye therynne;

---

[1] each.   [2] see.   [3] see.   [4] shield.   [5] shrift.   [6] eucharist.
[7] both.   [8] hence.

And, as thou were of a mayde y-bore,
Sofre[1] me never to be y-lore[2];
But when y schal hennus wende,
Grante me the blysse without ende;
Amen! Amen! so mot hyt be!
Now, swete lady, pray for me.

10   YORK CATHEDRAL MASONS

Fabric Rolls of York Minster, Surtees Soc., 1858, p. 181; regulations ordained by the Chapter. On the 31st Oct. 1370 the master-mason with his twelve fellows came before the Chapter and swore to observe these rules. The "mileway" of this document, like the "paternoster-while" of other Middle-English writers, testifies to the rarity of regular clocks: it means an average time for walking a mile: i.e. about 20 minutes.

Itte es ordayned by the Chapitre of the kirk of Saint Petyr of York that all the masonns that sall wyrke till[3] the werkes of the same kyrk of Saynte Petyr, sall fra Mighelmesse day untill the firste Sonday of Lentyn, be ilka day atte morne att thare werke, in the loge that es ordayned to the masonnes at wyrk within the close bysyde the forsayde kirk, als erly als thai may see skilfully[4] by day lyghte for till[5] wyrke; and thai sall stande thar trewly wyrkande atte thair werke all the day aftyr, als lang als thai may se skilfully for till wyrke, yf yt be alle werkday: outher elles[6], till itte be hegh none smytyn by the clocke, when halyday falles atte none....And in tyme of mete, atte none, thai sall, na tyme of the yer, dwell fra[7] the loges, ne fra thaire werke forsayde, ovyr the space of the tyme of an houre: and aftyr none thai may drynk in the loge: ande for thaire drynkyng-tyme bytwyx Mighelmes & Lentyn thai sall noghte cese no lefe[8] thare werk passand the tyme of half a mileway. Ande fra the firste Sonday of Lentyn untill Mighelmesse thai sall be in the forsayde loge atte thaire werke atte the son risyng, and stande thare trewly ande bysily wyrkande upon the forsayde werke of the kyrk all the day, untill itte be namare space than tyme of a mileway byfore the

---

[1] sufier.   [2] lost.   [3] at.   [4] reasonably.   [5] to.   [6] or else.
[7] absent themselves from.   [8] nor leave.

sone sette,...and thai sall noghte cese no[r] lefe thair werke in slepyng tyme, passande the tyme of a mileway, no[r] in drynkyng tyme aftyr none, passande the tyme of a mileway. And thai sall noghte slepe eftyre[1] none na tyme botte[2] bytwene Saynte Elenmes and Lammes; and yf any mane dwell fra the loge ande fra the werk forsayde, outher make defaute any tyme of the yer agayn this forsaide ordinance, he sall be chastyde with abaytyng of his payment, atte the loking ande devys of the maistyr masonn; and all ther tymes and houres sall by[3] reweled bi a bell ordayned tharefore. Ande, alswa[4], it es ordayned that na masonn sall be receavyde atte wyrke, to the werk of the forsayde kyrke, bot he be firste provede a weke or mare opon his well wyrkyng; and, aftyr that he es foundyn souffissant of his werke, be receavyde of the commune assente of the mayster and the kepers of the werk, ande of the maystyr masonn, and swere upon the boke that he sall trewly...hald and kepe haly all the poyntes of this forsayde ordinance,...and, wha sum evyr[5] cum agayne this ordinance and brekes itte agayn the will o the forsayde Chapitre, have he Goddy's malvson and Saynt Petirs.

11　　WYCLIF ON FREEMASONRY

Select English Works, ed. T. Arnold 1871, vol. III. p. 332 (*The Grete Sentens of Curs*, cap. XXVIII.).

Alle false conspiratours ben cursed of God and man. Conspiratours ben tho[6] that by comyn[7] assent don wrong or ony falsnesse to here neighboris. Here it semeth openly that alle freris[8], worldly clerkis, and possessioneris[9], ben openly cursed; for thei conspiren falsly aghenst the gospel and Cristis pore prestis....

Also alle newe fraternytes or gildis maad[10] of men semen openly to renne in this curs. For thei conspiren many false errours aghenst the comyn fraternyte of Crist, that alle Cristene men token in here cristendom[11], and aghenst comyn charite and

---

[1] after.　　[2] but.　　[3] be.　　[4] also.　　[5] whosoever.　　[6] those.
[7] common.　　[8] friars.　　[9] clerics (especially monks) living on endowments.
[10] made.　　[11] took at their baptism,

comyn profit of Cristene men.   And therto thei conspiren to
bere up eche other, ye[1], in wrong, and oppresse othere men in
here[2] right bi here witt and power.   And alle the goodnes that
is in thes gildes eche man owith for to do bi comyn fraternyte
of Cristendom, bi Goddis comaundement....Also men of sutel[3]
craft, as fre masons and othere, semen openly cursed bi this
sentence.   For thei conspiren togidere that no man of here
craft schal take lesse on a day than thei setten[4], though he
schulde bi good conscience take moche lesse, and that noon
of hem schal make sade trewe werk to lette othere mennus
wynnyng of the craft[5], and that non of hem schal do ought but
only hewe stone, though he myght profit his maistir twenti
pound bi o[6] daies werk bi leggyng on a wal[7], withouten harm
or penyng[8] himself.   See hou this wickid peple conspireth
aghenst treuthe and charite, and comyn profit of the lond, and
ponyschith[9] hem that helpen frely here neigheboris.

12   FREEMASONS AND TRADE-UNIONISM

Statutes of the Realm, 3rd Hen. VI. (1424), cap. I.

*Masons shall not confederate themselves in Chapiters and
Assemblies.*

First, Whereas by the yearly Congregations and Confederacies made by the Masons in their general Chapiters and
Assemblies, the good Course and Effect of the Statutes of
Labourers be openly violated and broken, in Subversion of
the Law, and to the great Damage of all the Commons ; our
said Lord the King, willing in this case to provide Remedy,
by the Advice and Assent aforesaid, and at the special Request
of the said Commons, hath ordained and established, that such
Chapiters and Congregations shall not be hereafter holden.
And if any such be made, they that cause such Chapiters and

---

[1] yea.   [2] their.   [3] subtle.   [4] have agreed among themselves.
[5] that none of them shall do steady true work, which might hinder the earnings
of other men of his craft.
[6] one.   [7] laying the stones with mortar on a wall.   [8] paining.
[9] punisheth.

Congregations to be assembled and holden, if they thereof be convict, shall be judged for Felons; and that all the other Masons that come to such Chapiters and Congregations be punished by Imprisonment of their Bodies, and make Fine and Ransom at the King's Will.

13   KING'S COLLEGE WINDOWS

From p. 40 of *King's College Chapel*, by T. J. P. Carter, 1867. Contract (A.D. 1526) of four London glaziers with the College authorities.

The said glasyiers shalle at their own propre costes and charges well, suerly, clenely, workmanly, substauncyally, curyously, and sufficiently glase and sett up, or cause to be glased and sett up eightene wyndowes of the upper story of the great churche within the kynge's college of Cambridge, whereof the wyndowe in the este ende of the seid churche to be oon, and the wyndowe in the west ende of the same churche to be another; and so seryally[1] the resydue with good, clene, sure and perfyte glasse and oryent[2] colors and imagery of the story of the olde lawe and of the newe lawe after the forme, maner, goodness, curiosytie, and clenelyness in every poynt of the glasse wyndowes of the kynge's newe chapell at Westmynster; and also accordingly and after such maner as oon Barnard Flower glasyer, late deceased, by indenture stode bounde to doo: that is to sey, six of the seid wyndowes to be clerely sette up and fynyshed after the forme aforeseid within twelve moneths next ensuyng after the date of these presentes, and that the seid Galyon, Richard, Thomas Reve and James Nycholson shall suerly bynde all the seid wyndowes with double bonds of leade for defence of great wyndes and outragious wetheringes....The aforeseid shall have for the glasse, workmanship and setting up every foot of the seid glasse by them to be provided, wrought, and sett up after the forme aboveseid eightene pence sterlinges.

[1] *seriatim.*   [2] brilliant.

14 THE BEGINNINGS OF THE SECULAR STAGE

(*a*) Mandate of Bishop John de Grandisson to the Official of the Archdeacon of Exeter and two other commissoners, 11th July, 1348. The Order here spoken of was evidently, as E. K. Chambers remarks, a *Société joyeuse.* As medieval buffoons often parodied ecclesiastical titles (e.g. Boy Bishop, Abbot of Unreason, etc.), so they sometimes gave similar satirical titles to their societies; e.g. the Abbey of Cokaygne described in MS. Harl. 913, printed partly in A. S. Cook, *Literary Middle-English Reader*, 1915, p. 369. The Order of Brothelyngham, here condemned by Grandisson, had very likely chosen its title as a parody on the only native English monastic Order, Sempringham or (as it was often written in the Middle Ages) Simplingham. *Brothel* or *brothelyng* was used of a good-for-nothing person.

Register of J. de Grandisson, ed. Hingeston-Randolph, vol. II. 1897, p. 1055.

We have heard, not without grave disquietude, that a certain abominable sect of evil-minded men, named the Order (let us rather say, the Error) of Brothelyngham, hath lately arisen by inspiration of him who soweth all evil deeds. Which men, forming no true convent but rather a plainly unlawful and sinister conventicle, have chosen for their head a certain crazy lunatic, of temper most suitable to their evil purpose. This man they call their Abbot; they dress him in monastic garb, set him up upon a stage, and adore him as their idol. Then, at the sound of a horn, which they have chosen instead of a bell, they led him not many days since through the lanes and streets of the said city of Exeter, with a great throng of horse and foot at their heels; in which procession they laid hold on clergy or laity whom they found in their way—nay, they even drew some from their own houses—and held them so long in durance, with rash, headlong, and sometimes with sacrilegious spirit, until they had extorted from them certain sums of money by way of sacrifice—nay, rather, of sacrilege. And, though they seem to do this under colour and cloke of play, or rather of buffoonery, yet this is beyond doubt no other than theft and rapine, since the money is taken from the unwilling.

The commissioners are directed to publish, next Sunday, in the Cathedral and all churches or chapels of Exeter, a strict prohibition of such proceedings, or of adhesion to such an illegal conventicle. The disobedient are to be excommunicated, and to be warned that contumacy will be met by physical force, since the Bishop will call in the royal officers.

One word which I have ventured to translate only by *stage* has received too much stress, perhaps, from those who have commented on this and the next document. The context runs "in Theatro constitutum, velud ipsorum idolum adorantes"; and, in the following piece, "in Theatro nostre Civitatis." Upon this E. K. Chambers comments (*Medieval Stage*, II. 190), "It is, however, rather surprising to find that Exeter, like Paris itself, had its regular theatre as early as 1348, more than two centuries before anything of the kind is heard of in London." The word *theatrum* can scarcely be pressed so far as this. It might, of course, mean a theatre in the modern sense; but it might also mean no more than a movable stage set up occasionally at some cross-road or other open space convenient for the games and shows of the citizens, such as the "common dancing-place" (*chorea*) of the German townships, mentioned by Jordan of Giano (see above, Section IV., no. 23, p. 240). In fact, *theatrum* might have been used of the plays of the London clerks at Clerkenwell, which Fitzstephen records as early as the 12th century. With this qualification, Grandisson's second mandate would seem to deserve all the attention it has received. It is addressed to the Archdeacon of Exeter, and dated 9th August, 1352 (*loc. cit.* p. 1120). Mr Chambers, by a slip, speaks of the *allutarii* of this document as "cloth-dressers."

(*b*) The envious enemy of mankind and instigator of all evil, who doth assiduously strive to banish from the world all delights of human tranquillity, is busy to spread the poison of his iniquity more widely in those places where he seeth most hope of mischief.

Although the mechanical arts, as experience ever shows us, should of necessity help one another, yet we have heard some time since that certain imprudent sons of our City of Exeter, given over to rioting and wantonness, and foolishly scorning that which had been profitably ordered for their own needs and those of the whole people, do purpose, and have banded themselves together, publicly to perform a certain noxious and blameworthy play, or rather buffoonery, in scorn and insult to the leather-dressers and their art, on this Sunday next to come and in the theatre of our aforesaid City of Exeter. Hence (as we are informed) there doth already breed and increase a rank growth of discord, rancour, and strife between the aforesaid artisans and the authors or abettors of this same play; so that (unless, led by a spirit of saner counsel, they shall altogether abstain and desist from their unlawful purpose), there must follow, alas! terrible assaults and aggressions, breaches of the peace of the king and his realm, blows and seditions, and even, by consequence, perils still more deplorable for men's immortal souls....

The play, therefore, is to be inhibited under pain of the greater excommunication. If, however, it shall appear that there is a just foundation for the general complaint that, "in these modern times," the aforesaid artisans are not content with a fair profit but are extorting unreasonable prices, then you must warn them, and they must be warned also from all the pulpits in the City, to refrain from these new and unauthorized exactions.

SECTION XIV

MEDICINE AND JUSTICE

1   THE PERFECT SURGEON

John Arderne was born in 1307, and was apparently attached to the households of the first Duke of Lancaster and of his son in law John of Gaunt: it is probable that Chaucer had met him.   He wrote about 1370, when, as an old and wealthy man, he could afford to let posterity into his professional confidence.   He is "the earliest example that we know at present...of a type of surgeon who has happily never been absent from England."   His fame as a pharmacist long outlived his reputation as surgeon; four of his recipes remained in use until the time of the first pharmacopœia, 1618.   The following extract is from a 15th century translation of his Treatise on Fistula, admirably edited for the E.E.T.S. (1910, pp. 1 ff.) by Mr D'Arcy Power, whose are the notes marked Ed.

I John Arderne, fro the first pestilence that was in the yere of oure lord 1349, duellid in Newerk in Notyngham-shire unto the yere of oure lord 1370, and ther I helid many men of fistula.

He here enumerates 21 cases—barons, knights, priests, merchants and friars, and proceeds:

All thise forseid cured I afore the makyng of this boke. Oure lord Jhesu y-blessid God knoweth that I lye not, and therfore no man dout[1] of this, thof-al[2] old famous men and ful clere in studie have confessed tham that thei fande nat the wey of curacion in this case.   ffor god, that is deler or rewarder of wisdom, hath hid many thingis fro wise men and slighe[3] whiche he vouchesaf aftirward for to shewe to symple men. Therfore, al men that ar to come aftirward, witte thai[4] that old maistrez war noght bisie ne pertinacez in sekyng and

---

[1] doubt.   [2] although.   [3] cunning.   [4] let them know.

serchyng of this forseid cure. But, for thai might noght take the hardnes of it[1] at the first frount, thei kest[2] it utterly byhinde thair bak. Of whiche, forsoth, som demed it holy[3] for to be incurable; other applied doutful opinions.... Therfore I pray that the grace of the holy gost be to this werke, that he vouch-saf for to spede it; that tho thingis whiche in workyng trewly I am ofte tymes experte, I may plenerly[4] explane tham in this litel boke. And this I sey that I know noght in al my tyme, ne hard[5] not in al my tyme, of any man, nouther[6] in yngland ne in partiez biyond the see, that kouthe[7] cure fistula ; outake[8] a frere minour that was with the prince of Walez in gascon and gyan[9], whiche rosed[10] and bosted hym that he had cured the forseid sekenes. And at london he deceyved many men; and when he might noght cure som man, he made suggestion to tham that no man might cure tham, and that affermed he with sweryng that yif[11] the fistule war dried, that the pacient at the next[12] shuld noght eschape dethe; whiche, forsothe, y-lefte and forsake of hym I cured perfitely. And to remove false opinions of ignorant men, for witnes I putte experience.... Netherlesse I afferme noght that I might hele al ffistulae; ffor som ben uncurable, as it shal be seid [more fully] within when I shal trete of tham. ffirst it bihoveth hym that wil profite in this crafte that he sette god afore evermore in all his werkis, and evermore calle mekely with hert and mouth his help; and som-tyme visite of his wynnyngis[13] poure men aftir his myght, that thai by thair prayers may gete hym grace of the holy goste. And that he be noght y-founden temerarie or bosteful in his seyingis[14] or in his dedes; and abstene he hym fro moche speche, and most among grete men; and answere he sleighly[15] to thingis y-asked, that he be noght y-take in his wordes.... Also, be a leche noght mich laughyng ne mich playing. And, als moche as he may withoute harme, fle he the felawshippe of knafes and of un-u[n]este[16] persones. And be he evermore occupied in thingis that

---

[1] surmount its difficulties.   [2] cast.   [3] wholly.   [4] fully.   [5] heard.
[6] neither.   [7] could.   [8] except.   [9] Guienne.   [10] vaunted.   [11] if.
[12] immediately.   [13] help from his earnings.   [14] sayings.   [15] cautiously.
[16] dishonourable.

biholdith[1] to his crafte; outhir rede he, or studie he, or write
or pray he; for the excercyse of bokes worshippeth[2] a leche.
ffor why; he shal both byholden[3] and he shal be more wise.
And aboue al thise it profiteth to hym that he be founden
evermore sobre; ffor dronkennez destroyeth al vertu and
bringith it to not, as seith a wise man, " Ebrietas frangit quic-
quid sapiencia tangit "[4]: " Dronkenes breketh what-so wisdom
toucheth." Be he content in strange places of metes and
drinkes ther y-founden, usyng mesure[5] in al thingis....Skorne
he no man....Yif ther be made speche to hym of any leche,
nouther sette he hym at nought ne preise hym to[o] mich or
commende hym, but thus may he curteysly answere; " I have
noght vrey[6] knowleche of hym, but I lerned noght ne I have
not herd of hym but gode and honeste." And of this shal
honour and thankyngis of eche party encresse and multiplie
to hym; aftur this, honour is in the honorant and noght in
the honored.   Considere[7] he noght over openly the lady or
the doughters or other fair wymmen in gret mennes [houses],
ne profre tham noght to kisse[8],...that he renne[9] noght into the
indignacion of the lord ne of noon[10] of his. In as moche as he
may, greve he no servant, but gete he thair love and thair gode
wille....When seke[11] men, forsoth, or any of tham bysyde cometh
to the leche to aske help or counsel of hym, be he noght to
tham over felle[12] ne over homely, but mene in beryng[13] aftir the
askyngis[14] of the personez; to som reverently, to som comonly.
ffor, after[15] wise men, Over moche homelynes bredeth dispisyng.
Also it spedeth that he have semyng excusacions, [*e.g.*] that he
may not incline to thair askyngis, without harmyng or without
indignacion of som gret man or frende, or for necessarie
occupacion.   Or feyne he hym hurt, or for to be seke, or som
other covenable[16] cause by whiche he may likely be excused.
Therfor, yif he will favoure to any mannes askyng, make he
covenant for his travaile, and take it byforehandez.   But
avise the leche hym-self wele that he giffe no certayn answer

---

[1] pertain.   [2] honoureth.   [3] be honoured.
[4] This saw may be found scratched on a pillar in Ashwell church, Herts.
[5] moderation.   [6] exact.   [7] look at.   [8] Cf. Section XII., no. 9.
[9] run.   [10] none.   [11] sick.   [12] stern.
[13] moderate in bearing.   [14] requirements.   [15] according to.   [16] decent.

in any cause, but he se[1] first the sikenes and the maner of it ; and whan he hath seen and assaied it, thof-al hym seme that the seke may be heled, netherlesse he shal make pronosticacion to the pacient [of] the perilez to come yif the cure be differred.   And yif he se the pacient persewe[2] bisily the cure, than, after that the state of the pacient asketh[3], aske he boldly more or lesse; but ever be he warre of scarse[4] askyngis, ffor over scarse askyngis setteth at not[5] both the markette and the thing.   Therfore for the cure of fistula...when it is curable, aske he competently of a worthi man and a gret an hundred marke or fourty pounde, with robez and feez[6] of an hundred shillyng, terme of lyfe, by yere[7].   Of lesse men fourty pounde, or fourty marke aske he without feez; and take he noght lesse than an hundred shillyngis.   ffor never in all my lyf toke I lesse than an hundred shillyng for cure of that sekenes. Netherlesse do another man as hym think better and more spedefulle.   And yif the pacientes or thair frendez or servauntz aske by how moche tyme he hopeth to hele it, evermore lat the leche byhete[8] the double that he supposeth to spede by half; that is, yif the leche hope to hele the pacient by twenty wekes—that is the comon course of curyng—adde he so many over.   ffor it is better that the terme be lengthed than the cure.   ffor prolongacion of the cure giffeth cause of dispairyng to the pacientez, when triste to the leche is moste hope of helthe.   And yif the pacient considere or wondre or aske why that he putte hym so long a tyme of curyng, sithe that he heled hym by the half, answere he that it was for that the pacient was strong-herted, and suffrid wele sharp thingis,

---

[1] see.   [2] pursue.   [3] requireth.   [4] scanty.   [5] nought.

[6] "The fees charged by Arderne are very large, if it be remembered that money had at least seventeen times and perhaps twenty times its present value. I have given some account of the fees of our ancestors in Janus (May–June 1909, pp. 287–293)."   ED.

[7] "The custom of paying for an operation by an annuity as well as by a fee lingered in England until late in the seventeenth century, for Richard Wiseman (1622?–1676), speaking of a patient, says, 'This person retired into the country afterwards and returned to London at the end of two years, and acknowledged to me his cure by settling thirty pounds a year upon me during his life and paid me sixty pounds for the two years passed.'"   ED.

[8] promise.

and that he was of gode complexion and hadde able flesshe
to hele; and feyne he othir causes pleseable to the pacient,
ffor pacientez of syche wordez are proude and delited. Also
dispose a leche hym that in clothes and othir apparalyngis be
he honeste, noght likkenyng hymself in apparalyng or berying
to mynistrallez, but in clothing and beryng shew he the
maner of clerkes. ffor why; it semeth[1] any discrete man
y-cladde with clerkis clothing for to occupie gentil mennez
bordez[2]. ¶ Have the leche also clene handes and wele
shapen nailez, and clensed fro all blaknes and filthe. And
be he curtaise at lordez bordez, and displese he noght in
wordes or dedes to the g[u]estes syttyng by; here he many
thingis but speke he but fewe....And whan he shal speke, be
the wordez short, and, als mich as he may, faire and resonable
and withoute sweryng. ¶ Be war that ther be never founden
double worde in his mouthe, ffor yif he be founden trew in his
wordes ffewe or noon shal doute in his dedez. Lere also a
yong leche gode proverbez pertenyng to his crafte in coun-
fortyng of pacientez....Also it spedeth that a leche kunne
talke of gode talez and of honest that may make the pacientes
to laugh, as wele of the biblee as of other tragediez; and
any othir thingis of which it is noght to charge[3], whilez that
they make or induce a light hert to the pacient or the sike
man. ¶ Discover never the leche unwarly the counsellez of
his pacientez, als wele of men as of wymmen, ne sette noght
oon to another at noght, thof-al he have cause, that he be
noght gilty of counsell; ffor yif a man se the hele wele[4] another
mannes counsel he wil trist[5] better in the. Many thinges,
forsothe, bene to be kepte of a leche, withoute these that ar
seid afore, that may noght be noted here for over moche
occupying....If the pacient stond[6] stedfastly that he be cured,
or aske if he may be cured, than sey the leche thus: "I dout
noght, oure lord beyng mene[7], and thi gode pacience folowyng,
yif thou wilt competently make satisfaccion to me, as sich a
cure—noght litle to be commended—asketh, that ne thingis
y-kept that ow to be kepte[8], and y-lefte that ow to be lefte, as

---

[1] is seemly for.   [2] tables.   [3] which are no trouble.   [4] thee conceal well.   [5] trust.
[6] insist.   [7] if God help us.   [8] supposing all things to be kept that ought to be kept.

AN OPERATOR IN THE FOURTEENTH CENTURY

LADY PHYSICIAN

it is seyde, I shal mow[1] bryng this cure to a loveable ende and heleful." And than acorde thay of covenant, of whiche covenaunt—al excusacione y-put abak—take he the half byfore handez; And than assigne a day to the pacient when he will bygynne[2].

2 AN ANAESTHETIC

Ibid. p. 101.

An untement slepyng[3], with which if any man be anoynted he schal mow[1] suffre kuttyng in any place of the body without felyng or akyng [*Recipe*, henbane, mandragora, hemlock, black and white poppies, opium etc.]…Also the sede alon [of henbane] giffen in wyne to drynk make[th] the drynker alsone[4] for to slepe, that he schal noght fele whatso-ever is done to hym. And this proved I myself for certayne. And witte thou that it spedeth for to draw hym that slepeth so by the nose and by the chekez and by the berde, that the spiritez be quickened, that he slepe noght over ristfully[5].

3 THE RASHNESS OF INEXPERIENCE

Ibid. p. 83. Chaucer, in his list of biting ointments, does not venture to suggest these. (C. T. *Prol.* 629 ff.)

Also witte thou that of arsenic sublimed or of realgre[6], that onez in a tyme in the bigynnyng of my practizing, when I knew noght the violence of tham, I putte of the pulver of the tuo forsayd in the leggez of tuo men; the which, forsothe, y-putte in, almost thei wer wode[7] for ake bi tuo daiez naturel and more; And thair leggez war bolned[8] out of mesure….

And witte thou that I putte noght of pulver of arsenic in the leggez of the forseid men over the quantite of a corne of senvey[9], and netherlesse the wondez that come[10] of the arsenic

---

[1] be able to.
[2] Equally interesting rules for the physician's conduct (and especially for a sharp look-out in the matter of fees, since the medieval patient was apt to be ungrateful), are quoted from contemporary French authors by Mr D'Arcy Power in his preface, pp. xx ff.
[3] soporific ointment. [4] at once. [5] deeply, restfully.
[6] disulphide of arsenic. [7] mad. [8] swollen.
[9] grain of mustard-seed. [10] wounds that came.

passed fully the lengthe and the brede of a mannez hande.
Therfor unexperte men be wele war fro the use of realgre and
arsenic sublimed, and namely[1] in the face and the leggez, and
synowy[2] placez and bony,...for, bot if thai [the patients] have
grete resistence, thai [these medicines] wirke ful cruely.

4   "FOR GOLD IN PHYSIK IS A CORDIAL"

Trevisa's *Bartholomew*, Lib. XIV. c. 4.

[Gold] hath vertue to comforte and for to clense super-
fluitees gadred[3] in bodies, and therefore it helpeth ayenst[4] lepre
and meselry[5]. The filinge of golde take in meate or in drinke,
or in medicine, preservith and letteth[6] breding of leprehede, or
namely[1] hidith it and maketh it unknowen....Also thyn plates
of gold, firy hot, quenched in wine maketh the wine proffitable
ayenst the evill of the splene, and ayenst many other evills
and passions malincolik....Also gold comforteth sore limmes,
though it be not corporate therin and though it nourisheth
them not.

5   THE MASTER-SURGEON'S OATH

H. T. Riley, *Memorials of London*, 1868, p. 337.

1369. Master John Dunheved, Master John Hyndstoke, and
Nicholas Kyldesby, surgeons, were admitted in full Husting[7],
before Simon de Mordone, [Mayor], and the Aldermen, and
sworn, as Master Surgeons of the City of London, that they
would well and faithfully serve the people, in undertaking
their cures, would take reasonably from them, etc., would faithfully follow their calling, and would present to the said Mayor
and Aldermen the defaults of others undertaking cures, so often
as should be necessary; and that they would be ready, at all
times when they should be warned, to attend the maimed or
wounded, and other persons etc.; and would give truthful
information to the officers of the city aforesaid, as to such

---

[1] especially.   [2] sinewy.   [3] gathered.   [4] against.
[5] generally used for leprosy, but also for other skin diseases.   [6] hindereth.
[7] A court composed of a committee of the general Folkmoot, which sat indoors
(therefore called *House-thing*); it met weekly, and transacted most of the city
business.

maimed, wounded, and others, whether they be in peril of death or not, etc.   And also, faithfully to do all other things touching their calling.

6   A MEDICAL INQUISITION

Ibid. p. 273.

1354.   Be it remembered, that on the Monday next after the Feast of St Matthias the Apostle [24 February], in the 28th year etc., the Prior of Hogges, Master Paschal, Master Adam de la Poletrie, and Master David de Westmerland, surgeons, were sworn before the Mayor, Aldermen, and Sheriffs, to certify them as to a certain enormous and horrible hurt, on the right side of the jaw of Thomas de Shene appearing; whether or not such injury was curable at the time when John le Spicer of Cornhulle took the same Thomas under his care, to heal the wound aforesaid.

Who say, upon their oath, that if the aforesaid John le Spicer, at the time when he took the said Thomas under his care, had been expert in his craft or art, or had called in counsel and assistance to his aid, he might have cured the injury aforesaid; and they further say that, through want of skill on part of the said John le Spicer, the said injury under his care has become apparently incurable.

7   THE QUACK'S PENANCE

Ibid. p. 464.

1382.   Roger Clerk, of Wandelesworth, on the 13th day of May in the 5th year, was attached in the Chamber of the Guildhall of London, before the Mayor and Aldermen, to make answer, as well to the Mayor and Commonalty of the City of London, as to Roger atte Hacche, in a plea of deceit and falsehood. As to which, the same Roger said, that whereas no physician or surgeon should intermeddle with any medicines or cures within the liberty of the city aforesaid, but those who are experienced in the said arts, and approved therein, the said Roger Clerk, who knew nothing of either of the arts aforesaid, being neither experienced nor approved therein, nor understood anything of letters, came to the house of him, Roger atte Hacche, in the Parish of St Martin, in Ismongereslane, in London, on Thursday, the morrow of Ash Wednesday, in the 5th year etc.; and there saw one Johanna, the wife of the aforesaid Roger atte Hacche, who was then lying ill with certain bodily infirmities, and gave the said Roger, her husband, to understand, that he was experienced and skilled in the art of medicine, and could cure the same Johanna of her maladies, if her husband desired it. Whereupon, the said Roger atte Hacche, trusting in his words, gave him 12 pence, in part payment of a larger sum which he was to pay him, in case the said Johanna should be healed. And upon this, the same Roger Clerk then and there gave to the said Roger atte Hacche an old parchment, cut or scratched across, being the leaf of a certain book, and rolled it up in a piece of cloth of gold, asserting that it would be very good for the fever and ailments of the said Johanna; and this parchment, so rolled up, he put about her neck, but in no way did it profit her; and so, falsely and maliciously, he deceived the same Roger atte Hacche. And he produced the said parchment here in Court, wrapped up in the same cloth, in proof of the matters aforesaid.

And the said Roger Clerk personally appeared, and the said parchment was shown to him by the Court, and he was asked what the virtue of such piece of parchment was; whereupon, he said that upon it was written a good charm for fevers. Upon being further asked by the Court what were the words of this charm of his, he said "*Anima Christi, sanctifica me; corpus Christi, salva me; in isanguis Christi, nebria[1] me; cum bonus Christus tu, lava me.*" And the parchment being then examined, not one of those words was found written thereon. And he was then further told by the Court, that a straw beneath his foot would be of just as much avail for fevers, as this said charm of his was; whereupon, he fully granted that it would be so. And because that the same Roger Clerk was in no way a literate man, and seeing that on the examinations aforesaid, (as well as on others afterwards made,) he was found to

---

[1] *sic*. for *sanguis Christi inebria.*

be an infidel, and altogether ignorant of the art of physic
or of surgery; and to the end that the people might not
be deceived and aggrieved by such ignorant persons, etc.; it
was adjudged that the same Roger Clerk should be led
through the middle of the City, with trumpets and pipes, he
riding on a horse without a saddle, the said parchment and
a whetstone, for his lies, being hung about his neck, an orinale
also being hung before him, and another on his back.

This was evidently a *cause célèbre*; it is told in some detail by the
chronicler Walsingham under this year 1382. Walsingham writes, "duo
ollae, quas Jordanes vulgo vocamus, ad ejus collum colligantur, cum cote
in signum quod illam mentiendo promeruit."

8 SURGEON-BARBERS

Ibid. p. 606.

1415. It was intimated in a relation, and not without
alarm, unto Thomas Fauconer, Mayor, and the Aldermen, how
that some barbers of the said city, who are inexperienced in
the art of surgery, do oftentimes take under their care many
sick and maimed persons, fraudulently obtaining possession
of very many of their goods thereby; by reason whereof, they
are oftentimes made to be worse off at their departure than
they were at their coming: and that, by reason of the inex-
perience of the same barbers, such persons are oftentimes
maimed; to the scandal of such skilful and discreet men as
practise the art of surgery, and the manifest destruction of
the people of our Lord the King.

And the said Mayor and Aldermen, wishing to obviate an
evil and a scandal such as this, as also, to provide a fitting
remedy for the same,...did ordain and enact that no barber,
practising the art of surgery within the liberty of the said
city, should presume in future to take under his care any sick
person who is in peril of death or of maiming, unless he
should shew the same person, within three days after so taking
him under his care, to the Masters inspecting for the time
being, by the barbers practising the art of surgery within the
liberty of the said city to be elected, and to the Mayor and
Aldermen presented, and by them specially to be admitted;

under a penalty of 6*s.* 8*d.*, to the Chamber of London in form underwritten to be paid, so often as, and when, against this Ordinance they should be found to act; namely, 5 shillings to the use of the Chamber of the Guildhall, and 20 pence to the use of the craft of the Barbers.

In 1417 a barber-surgeon was compelled to deposit £20 sterling, a very large sum, as security that he would keep this rule of warning the Wardens.

9　MEDICAL RECIPES

Reliquiae Antiquae, vol. I. p. 51 [from a fragment of MS. of 14th century, in possession of J. O. Halliwell, No. 335].

For hym that is in the jaunes[1]: tak warmot[2] and seth hit lange in water, and wasch the seke man with that water thrys[3] ryght wele, and gyf hym to drynk yvore[4] shavyn smal in wyne. Another: tak the rote of borage, and yf he be harde tharin stamp hit, and temper hit with a lytill ale, and do tharto saffronne, and gif hym .iij. sopes[5] thre dayes at morn and even…. Another: drynk sorell, plantayne, and chekyn-mete[6] tempered with alde[7] ale morne and even…. Another: tak yvore and saffronne, and stamp togyder, and temper hit upp with haly[8] water, and drynk hit morne and even, when thu gas[9] to bedde…. Another: tak a tenche, and clefe hit in twa al qwyk, and do away the banes, and lay hit to the herte, and to the rybbes; the seck man or woman sal drynk na strang ale, bot mengyd[10] with feble ale, no[r] ete no gees no dou[k]e[11] no roste, na na maner of beef no porke, ne noght that comes of swyne, no[r] drynk no wyne, no no new ale, ne nathyng that hate es[12], few clathes[13] bath nyght and day….

Ibid. p. 51.

For hym that haves the squynansy[14]: tak a fatte katte, and fla[15] hit wele, and clene, and draw oute the guttes, and tak the gres[16] of an urcheon[17], and the fatte of a bare[18], and resynes, and feinygreke[19], and sauge[20], and gumme of wodebynde[21], and virgyn

---

[1] jaundice.	[2] wormwood.	[3] thrice.	[4] ivory.	[5] sups.
[6] chickweed (*or* endive).		[7] old.	[8] holy.	[9] thou goest.
[10] mixed.	[11] duck.	[12] hot is.	[13] clothes.	[14] quinsy.
[15] flay.	[16] grease.	[17] hedgehog.	[18] bear.	
[19] fenugreek (*Trigonella Foenum Graecum*).			[20] sage.	[21] honeysuckle.

wax; al this mye[1] smal, and farse[2] the catte within als thu farses a gos[3], rost hit hale, and geder[4] the grees and enoynt hym therwith.

10 TOOTHACHE

(a) Trevisa's *Bartholomew*, Lib. VII. c. 25.

Wormes brede in the cheke teethe...and this is knowen by itchynge and tyckelinge and contynuall dyggynge and thyrlynge[5].... Wormes of the teethe ben slayne with myrre[6] and opium.

(b) The first of the Physicians of Myddfai lived at the end of the 12th century: he is said to have learned his art from a fairy who rose from a lake under the Black Mountains of Carmarthenshire, and who became his wife. His descendants, claiming their share of his medical skill, lived on at Myddfai until the end of the 18th century. The following recipe is from the text of *Meddygon Myddveu* by P. Diverres, 1913, printed from a MS. of the 14th century, p. 51, § 52.

Against Toothache.

Take a candle of mutton-fat, mingled with seed of sea-holly; burn this candle as close as possible to the tooth, holding a basin of cold water beneath it. The worms [which are gnawing the tooth] will fall into the water to escape the heat of the candle.

(c) Sir Thomas More, *Workes*, 1557, p. 1215a.

Besides thys, to counsayle a man never to thynke on that case, is in my mynde as much reason as the medecine that I have heard taught one for the tothe ache, to goe thryse about a church yarde, and never thynke on a fox tayle. For yf the counsayle bee not geven them, it canne not serve them. And yf it be geven them, it muste putte the poynte of the matter in theyr mynde, whiche by and by to rejecte, and thynke therein neither one thynge nor other, is a thynge that maye bee sooner bydden than obayed.

---

[1] crumble.   [2] stuff.   [3] goose.   [4] gather.   [5] boring.   [6] myrrh.

11　THE DANGERS OF WATER

Trevisa's *Bartholomew*, Lib. IX. c. 6, f. 140*a*.

Spryngynge tyme is the time of gladnesse and of love ; for in sprynging tyme all thynge semeth gladde; for the erthe wexeth grene, trees burgynne[1] and sprede, medowes bring forth flouers, heven shyneth, the see resteth and is quyete, foules synge and make theyr nestes, and al thynge that semed deed in wynter and widdered[2], ben renewed in springing time.... And water in spryngynge time is unholsome to drynke; for hit is made great and thycke with vapours that ben resolved and shed. Also it is infect with frogges and other wormes that than brede. And therefore, if it be nedefull to drynke water that tyme, Constantyne counseylleth to seeth it fyrste, that it may be clensed and pourged by boyllynge.

12　HOSPITAL FARE

Anstey, *Munimenta Academica*, R. S., I. 176, A.D. 1356 (Agreement as to rights in the suburb outside the north gate of Oxford).

Item, it is granted...that the said Chancellor of the University, or his deputies or successors, shall have in perpetuity, in the said Hundred or Suburb, jurisdiction over [the market] ...and over all flesh or fish that shall be found to be putrid, unclean, vicious, or otherwise unfit, and all manner of bad victuals, with full power of punishing delinquents in that matter, and of seizing the things thus bought or sold against the privileges of the University ; but on this condition, that the things thus forfeited be given to the Hospital of St John outside the East Gate of Oxford.

Dr Rashdall (*Univ. of Europe*, vol. II. pp. 202, 207) charitably hopes that it was the fines, and not the food, which went to the lepers. But his optimism is scarcely possible in the face of evidence from other quarters: cf. *The Athenaeum* for Aug. 27 and Sept. 3, 1898, Wheatley's *London*, p. 196, and W. Denton's *England in the Fifteenth Century*, 1888, p. 207. By an Act of the Scottish Parliament in 1386 it was provided that if any corrupt swine's flesh or salmon were offered for sale it should be confiscated by the bailie and given to the poor leper-folk ; and the borough of Berwick had a similar law, with the added proviso that "if there be no lepper-folk...the rotten pork or salmon be utterly destroyed." The most probable modern

---

[1] burgeon.　　　　[2] withered,

theory of the origin of leprosy connects it with the eating of stale fish, which was necessarily very frequent under the fasting laws of the medieval Church.   It has been suggested, with some probability, that the above-quoted regulations form the historical basis for the legend that Scottish apprentices especially stipulated not to be fed with salmon more than a certain number of days per week.   " Il y a fagots et fagots."

13   EVERY MAN HIS OWN CONSTABLE

Royal writ of 1253 for Watch and Ward: W. Stubbs, *Select Charters*, 1890, p. 375, from Rymer's *Foedera*, I. 292.   As every man in medieval Britain was required to bear arms, in case of necessity, for home defence against invasion, so also every man was bound to turn out on hearing the hue and cry against a malefactor.

(1)   That watches be held in the several townships as hath been wont, and by honest and able men.

(2)   That the hue and cry be followed according to the ancient use, so that all who neglect and refuse to follow it up shall be taken into custody as abettors of the wrongdoers, and shall be delivered up to the Sheriff.   Moreover, in every township, let four or six men be chosen according to its size, to follow the hue and cry hastily and swiftly, and to pursue the wrongdoers, if need be, with bows and arrows and other light arms, which should be provided at the common cost of the township and remain ever for the use thereof.   And to this end let two free and lawful men be chosen from the most powerful in each hundred, who shall oversee the work and see that the aforesaid watches and pursuits be rightly carried out.

(3)   That no stranger abide in the township except by day, and that he depart while it is yet daylight.

(4)   That no stranger be harboured in county townships beyond one day, or two at most, save only in time of harvest, unless his host be willing to answer for him....

(5)   That the mayor and bailiffs of all cities and boroughs be bidden that, if any merchant or stranger bearing money do show them the said money and beg for safe conduct, then they must so conduct him through the evil passes and doubtful ways ; and if he lose aught for default of such conduct or under their conduct, then let him be indemnified by the inhabitants of the said borough or city.

Compare (Stubbs, *l.c.* 145, the Assize of Clarendon 1166): no wayfarer to stay anywhere except in a borough, and even there not beyond one night, unless he or his horse be sick; after the first night "let him be taken and kept until his lord come to give pledge for him, or until he find sure pledges for himself; and let his host be arrested also...and let all sheriffs make a list of all fugitives who have fled from their counties" etc.

14   A NATION IN ARMS

In my *Chaucer and his England* and elsewhere, I have pointed out the extreme social importance of the fact that in medieval England every man was his own soldier and his own policeman; while in France national defence concerned the central government only, and the *Ordonnance* of Charles VII. riveted upon the nation the double chain of a hired army and irresponsible taxation: see e.g. R. Lodge, *Close of the Middle Ages*, 1906, p. 353. Fortescue already had an inkling of the importance of this: *Governance of England*, ed. Plummer, 1885, p. 137. But in this present passage, where Fortescue's extravagant patriotism reads *cowardice*, the modern historian must read *impotence*: the French nation then had no legal organization like our militia which could enable them to resist royal tyranny by force.

Some men have that it were good ffor the king, that the commons off Englande were made pore, as be the commons off Ffraunce. Ffor than thai wolde not rebelle, as now thai done oftentymes; wich the commons off Ffraunce do not, nor mey doo; ffor thai have no wepon, nor armour, no good to bie it with all. To theis maner off men mey be said with the phylosopher, *ad pauca respicientes de facili enunciant.* This is to say, thai that see but ffew thynges, woll sone say thair advyses[1]. Ffor soth theis ffolke consideren litill the good off the reaume off Englond, wheroff the myght stondith most uppon archers, wich be no ryche men. And yff thai were made more pouere than thai be, thai shulde not have wherwith to bie hem bowes, arroes, jakkes[2], or any other armour off defence, whereby thai myght be able to resiste owre enymes, when thai liste to come uppon us; wich thai mey do in every side (considerynge that we be an Ilelonde; and, as it is said before, we mey not sone[3] have soucour off any other reaume), wherefore we shull be a pray to all owre enymes, but yff we be myghty off owre selff; wich myght stondith most uppon owre pouere archers; and therfore thai nedun not only have

---

[1] soon give their opinion.   [2] buff-jackets.   [3] soon.

suche ablements[1] as now is spoken off, but also they nedun to be much excersised in shotynge, wich mey not be done without ryght grete expenses, as every man experte therin knowith ryght well. Wherfore the makyng pouere of the commons, wich is the makynd pouere off owre archers, shalbe the distruccion of the grettest myght off owre reaume.

Item, yff pouere men mey not lightly rise, (as is the openion of thes men, wich ffor that cause wolde have the commons pouere ;) how than, yff a myghty man made a risynge, shulde he be repressed, whan all the commons ben so pouere, that after such openyon thai mey not ffeght, and be[2] that reason not helpe the kyng with ffeghtynge? And whi makith the kynge the commons every yere to be mustered, sithen[3] (as these men ween) it were god[4] thai hade non harnes nor were able to ffight? O, howe unwyse is the oppenyon off thes men; ffor it mey not be mayntened be any reason! *Item* whan any rysinge hath be made in this londe be ffor theis dayis by commons, the pouerest men theroff have be the grettest causers and doers ther in. And thryfty men have ben loth therto, ffor drede off lesynge[5] off thai[r] gode. But yet oftentymes thai have goo[6] with thaym, through manasheynge[7] that ellis the same pouere men wolde have toke thai[r] godes, wherin it semyth that poverte hath be the holl[8] cause off all suche rysynges. The pouere man hath be sturred therto be occasion off [h]is poverte, for to gete gode; and the riche men have gone with them, because thai wolde not be pouere [by] the lesynge off ther gode. What than wolde ffall, yff all the commons were pouere? Trewly it is lyke that this lande then schulde be like unto the reaume of Boeme[9], wher the commons ffor poverte rose apon the nobles and made all thai[r] godis to be comune. *Item,* hit is the kyngis honour, and also [h]is office, to make [h]is reaume riche ; and it is dishonour whan he hath but a pouere reaume, off wich men woll say that he reigneth but uppon beggers. Yet it were moch gretter dishonour, yff he ffounde [h]is reaume riche, and then made it pouere. And it were also gretly ayenest his conciens, that awght to defende them and ther godis, yff he toke offro[10] them

---

[1] habiliments. [2] by. [3] since. [4] good. [5] losing.
[6] gone. [7] menacing. [8] whole. [9] Bohemia. [10] from.

thai[r] godis with owt lafull cause; ffrom the infame wheroff
God defende owre kyng, and gyff hym grase to augmente [h]is
reaume in riches, welth, and prosperite, to his perpetuell laude
and worshippe. *Item,*the reaume off Ffraunce givith never ffrely
off thai[r] owne gode will any subsidie to thai[r] prince, because
the commons theroff be so pouere, as thai mey not give any
thyng off thai[r] owne godis.   And the kyng ther askith never
subsidie off [h]is nobles, ffor drede that yff he charged them so,
thai wolde confedre with the commons and peraventure putt
hym doune.   But oure commons be riche, and therfore thai
give to thair kynge, at somme tymes quinsimes and dessimes[1],
and ofte tymes other grete subsidies, as he hath nede ffor the
gode and defence off his reaume.   How gret a subsidie was it,
when the reaume gaff to thair kyng a quinsime and a desime
quinqueniale, and the ix^th fflese[2] off thai[r] wolles, and also the
ix^th shefe off ther graynes, ffor the terme off v yere!   This
myght thai not have done, yff thai hade ben impovershed be
thai[r] kyng, as be the commons off Ffraunce; nor suche a
graunte hath be made by any reaume of cristendome, off wich
any cronicle makith mencion; nor non other mey or hath
cause to do so.   Ffor thai have not so much ffredome in thai[r]
owne godis, nor be entreted by so ffaverable lawes as we be,
except a ffewe regions beffor specified.   *Item,* we se dayly,
how men that have lost thair godis and be ffallen into poverte,
becomme anon robbers and theves, wich wolde not have ben
soche, yff poverte hade not brought them therto.   Howe many
a theff then were like to be in this lande, yff all the commons
were pouere?   The grettest surete trewly, and also the most
honour that may come to the kynge is, that [h]is reaume be riche
in every estate.   Ffor nothyng mey make [h]is people to arise,
but lakke off gode, or lakke off justice.   But yet sertanly when
thay lakke gode thai woll aryse, saying that thai lakke justice.
Nevertheles, yff thai be not pouere, thay will never aryse, but
yff ther prince so leve justice, that he give hym selff all to
tyranne.   Only lak off harte and cowardisse kepen the Ffrenche-
men from rysynge.

    Poverte is not the cause, whi the commons off Ffraunce

---

[1] fifteenths and tenths.   [2] fleece.

rise not ayen[1] thair soverayn lorde,...but it is cowardisse and lakke off hartes and corage, wich no Ffrenchman hath like unto a Englysh man. It hath ben offten tymes sene in Englande, that iij or iiij theves ffor poverte have sett apon vj or vij trewe men, and robbed them all. But it hath not bene sene in Ffraunce, that vj or vij theves have be hardy to robbe iij or iiij trewe men. Wherfore it is right selde that Ffrenchmen be hanged ffor robbery, ffor thai have no hartes to do so terable an acte. Ther bith ther fore mo men hanged in Englande in a yere ffor robbery and manslaughter, then ther be hanged in Ffraunce ffor such maner of crime in vij yeres. Ther is no man hanged in Scotlande in vij yere togedur[2] ffor robbery. And yet thai ben often tymes hanged ffor larceny, and stelynge off good in the absence of the owner theroff. But ther hartes serve them not to take a manys gode, while he is present, and woll defende it; wich maner of takynge is callid robbery. But the Englysh man is off another corage. Ffor yff he be pouere, and see another man havynge rychesse, wich mey be taken ffrom hym be myght, he will not spare to do so, but yff[3] that pouere man be right trewe. Wherfore it is not poverte, but it is lakke off harte and cowardisse, that kepith the Ffrenchmen ffro rysynge.

15   THE ESCAPE FROM FEUDALISM

Towns were originally under the law of their feudal lord—king, baron, or prelate—and their first step in freedom was generally the purchase of the rights of paying a fixed tax and deciding disputes by their own juries. The purchase was natural; for fines taken in the courts formed a considerable proportion of every lord's income. This step was hastened at Leicester by a picturesque incident, recorded in a document printed by C. Bémont, *Simon de Montfort*, 1884, p. 360, and by Miss Bateson, *Records of Leicester*, 1899, vol. I., p. 40. Miss Bateson's note does unintentional injustice to Prof. Bémont, who correctly identifies the Earl as Robert I. (d. 1118 A.D.). For the rules of this wager of battle see Pollock and Maitland, *Hist. of Eng. Law*, Bk II. ch. ix. § 4.

Inquest taken at Leicester in 1253.

The jury say upon their oath that, in the days of Robert de Meulan, then Earl of Leicester, it befel that two kinsmen, Nicholas son of Hacon and Geoffrey son of Nicholas of

---

[1] against.   [2] together.   [3] unless.

C.

Leicester, waged battle for a certain piece of land which
was disputed between them; and they fought from the
hour of prime till past noon.   And, as they thus strove
together, one drave the other up to a certain small ditch;
and, as he stood over it and should have fallen therein, his
kinsman cried to him, "have a care of that ditch which is
behind thee, lest thou fall therein"; whereupon there arose
such a shout and tumult from those who stood and sat
around, that the lord Earl heard their shout even in the castle
where he sat, and enquired of his men what might be the
cause thereof; and they told him how these two kinsmen
fought for the land, and how one drave the other to the ditch,
and warned him when he stood over it and should have fallen
therein.   Then the burgesses, moved with pity, made a
covenant with the said Earl, that they should give him three
pence yearly from each house which had a gable on the High
Street, on condition that he would allow them to dispute
and determine all pleas concerning the citizens by means of
24 jurats.

16   PIEPOWDER COURT

From   east the end of the 11th century onwards the royal grant
of licence to hold a fair seems to have implied licence also to hold a
court of summary jurisdiction for offences committed at the fair itself.
These obtained the name of Piepowder Courts (*piepoudreux*, *dusty-feet*,
the suitors appearing informally in their travel-stained condition).   In these,
a jury of merchants found the judgment or declared the law; thus suitors
and doomsmen were all of the same class.   England is the only country
which possesses records of the proceedings at these courts; the following
examples are from C. Gross, *Select Cases on the Law Merchant* (Selden
Soc., 1908).   All are from the records of St Ives Fair (Hunts.), which
belonged to the Abbot of Ramsey.

(p. 33.   A.D. 1288.)   William of Houghton complains of Joan
of Earith, for that whereas the said William was in front of his
gate near the waterside on Thursday last, the said Joan came
there and assaulted him with vile words, (saying that all his
life he had lived by knavery and that the measures of the
said Joan had been seized by the contrivance of the said
William,) to his dishonour to the amount of 2s. etc.

(p. 36.   A.D. 1288.)   John, son of John of Eltisely, complains of Roger Barber, for that he has unjustly broken a covenant with him, and [herein] unjustly [that,] whereas the said John was in the vill of Ramsay on Monday after Epiphany last past, a year ago, in the house of Thomas Buck, the said Roger came there and undertook to cure his, John's, head of baldness for 9*d.*, which the said John paid in advance; the next day, Tuesday, the said Roger put [a plaster on him] and did likewise on Wednesday, and afterwards withdrew from the vill, so that from that day to this he would in no way interpose, to his, John's, damage a half-mark; and he produces suit. The said Roger was present and denied [tort and force] etc., and put himself on his law, and in finding pledges of his law withdrew from the bar without leave. Therefore the said John craved judgement against him as against one who is convicted. Wherefore it is awarded that the said Roger make satisfaction to the said John for 9*d.*, the sum claimed, and for his damages, which are remitted; and that he be in mercy 6*d.* for the trespass.

(p. 42. A.D. 1291.) John, son of William, son of Agnes of Lynn, who is ten years of age, was found in the vill of St Ives near the foot of the bridge of the said vill stealing a purse during the fair; but because he is not old enough to sustain the judgement which is ordained and provided for such evil-doers, it is awarded that he abjure the vill of St Ives and the fair thereof.

(p. 75. A.D. 1300.) Ives Vickery [and five others] who were appointed to watch in Cross Lane near the canvas booth on the night of Thursday before the feast of St Dunstan, withdrew from their vigil and watched badly, so that the canvas booth was broken into by robbers, and the greater part of the canvas and other goods were carried. Therefore let them be attached to answer etc., and they are in mercy 3*s.* for the contempt.

(p. 107. Carnarvon, A.D. 1325.) Richard Brewhouse receives the merry-andrews in the midst of the fair, to the disturbance and peril of the merchants; therefore he [is in mercy] 6*d.*

17   CITY POLICE

Riley, *Memorials of London*, 1868, p. 35.

1297.   It was ordered that every bedel shall make summons by day in his own Ward, upon view of two good men, for setting watch at the Gates;—and that those so summoned shall come to the Gates in the day-time, and in the morning, at day-light, shall depart therefrom.   And such persons are to be properly armed with two pieces; namely, with haketon[1] and gambeson[2], or else with haketon and corset, or with haketon and plates.   And if they neglect to come so armed, or make default in coming, the bedel shall forthwith hire another person, at the rate of twelve pence, in the place of him who makes such default; such sum to be levied on the morrow upon the person so making default.

In like manner, if any person shall be summoned to watch within his Ward, and shall make default, the bedel shall substitute another in his place, and on the morrow shall take from him three pence, to the use of such substitute.

18   LYNCH LAW

For the process of "abjuration," or "forswearing the land," see the present writer's *Chaucer and his England*, pp. 285 ff.   The Breton was, by law, under the protection of the Church as a penitent; and his attackers theoretically incurred excommunication.   *The Brut*, E.E.T.S., 1908, p. 442.

And in the same yere, a fals Breton, betwen Ester and Witsontyde, mordrede a good wedowe in hir bedde, the which hadde found hym, for almesse[3], withoute Algate, in the suburbes of London.   And he bar a-way all that sche hadde, and after toke [f]irth of[4] holy churche at Saint Georges in Suthwerk; but at the last he toke the Crosse, and for-suore the Kyng['s] land.   And as he went his way, it happid hym to come by the same place wher he did that cursede dede.   And women of the same parish come oute to hym with stones and with canell[5] dong and there made an ende of hym in the high streit, so that he went no ferthere, not-with-stondyng the Constablis and other men also, which had hym in governaunce, to convey

---

[1] a sort of buff-coat.   [2] quilted coat.   [3] had kept him out of charity.

[4] sanctuary at.   [5] gutter.

hym forth in his way; for there was a grete companye of them; and on hym thei had neither mercie nor pite; and thus this fals thefe endede his life in this worlde, for his falsnesse.

19 BEFORE THE WARS OF THE ROSES
From Hardyng's Chronicle 1457 (*E. H. R.* Oct. 1912, p. 749).

In every shire with Jakkes[1] and Salades[2] clene
Myssereule[3] doth ryse and maketh neyghbours werre;
The wayker[4] gothe benethe, as ofte ys sene,
The myghtyest his quarell wyll preferre.

Thay kyll your men alway by one and one,
And who say ought, he shall be bette[5] doutlesse;
For in your Reme Iustyse of pese bene[6] none
That darr ought now the contekours[7] op

presse ;

The lawe is lyke unto a Walshmannes hose,
To eche mannes legge that shapen is and mete;
So mayntenours[8] subverte it and transpose,
Thurgh[9] myght it is full low layde undyr fete.

20 TORTURE BY LAW
From Fortescue's *De Laudibus*, chap. 22 (Ed. 1616, p. 46).

Of the crueltie of Rackings.

Therefore the law of France, in offences criminal, wherupon death dependeth, is not content to convict the party accused by witnesses, least, by the testimony of false persons, innocent bloud should be condemned. But that law choseth rather to torment such offenders with racking, untill they themselves confesse their own fault, rather then by the deposition of witnesses, which manye times through wicked affections, and sometimes by the subornation of evill men, are mooved to perjurie. Upon this, and such like cautels and respects, offenders and suspect persons are in that realme with so many kinds of rackings tormented, that my penne abhorreth to put

---

[1] cuirasses.   [2] open helmet.   [3] misrule.   [4] weaker.
[5] beaten.   [6] justices of the peace are.   [7] quarrellers.
[8] See note to Sect. XIII., no. 6, p. 485.   [9] through.

them in writing....My penne is both wearie and ashamed to rehearse the outragiousnes of torments devised in this behalfe: For the number of them is so great, that it can skant well be noted in a whole skinne of parchement. Moreover the Civill Lawes, for want of witnesses, doe fetch out the trueth by such rackinges: And so doe divers other Countries too. But who is so harde harted, which, being once released out of so cruell a Racke, though he bee innocent and faultlesse, would not yet rather accuse himselfe of all kindes of offences, then againe to commit himself to the intollerable crueltie of the torment once proved: and had not rather die at once (seeing death is the ende of all miseries) then so often to bee killed, and to sustaine so many hellish furies, painfuller then death it selfe: And did not you, most worthy Prince, know a certaine offender, which in such torments accused a worshippefull, yea a right good and faithfull Knyght of treason, wherein, as hee saide, they two had conspired together? which treason he himself, beeing released from the racke, afterward attempted and accomplished, thereby to acquite himselfe from comming to the torture againe. But at the last, by meane of those torments beeing so maymed in his bodie, that thereby hee was brought in despaire of his life, and thereupon receiving his howsell[1], he then swore by the same body of the Lord and by the death which he beleeved that hee should foorthwith die, that the said knight was innocent and guitlesse in all things whereof hee had accused him. Howbeit the paines, wherein hee was at the time of that his accusation, hee said were so extreme, that rather then he would feele the same againe, he would not sticke to accuse the said Knight againe, yea and his owne Father to[o]. This he said, being then at the verie point of death, which hee beleeved hee could not then escape; no, nor hee escaped not the death which hee then feared. But afterward beeing hanged, at the time of his death hee cleared the saide Knight of all crimes whereof beefore hee had defamed him. Thus (O pittifull case) doe many other wretches, not for the truthes sake, but forced thereunto by the extremitie of torments. And what certainetie then can arise of the confessions of

[1] eucharist.

miserable tormented persons? But if some innocent bodie, having his minde fixed upon eternall salvation, would in such a Babylonicall Fornace, with the three Children, blesse and magnifie the LORD, and not lye to the damnation of his owne soule, in that the Judge pronounceth him unguiltie, doth not that Judge by the selfe same judgement judge himselfe guiltie of all the cruelty and paines, wherwith hee hath tormented the innocent? O how cruell is such a Lawe, which, in that it can not condempne the syely[1] innocent, condempneth the Judge?...But the Judge peradventure will say: " I with mine owne hands did nothing in these torments." But what differeth it, whether one be a doer with his owne hands, or els bee present at the dooing, and [to exasperate] the thing that is done by his commandement. It is onely the Master of the ship that bringeth it to the haven, though by his commandement an other bee the stirresman. I beleeve that the wound where-with the minde of the Judge thus tormenting any man is plagued, will never bee healed againe, especially while hee remembreth the extremitie of the paines sustained by the poore wretch in those miserable torments.

21   THE PERILS OF THE LAW

Archbishop Courtenay of Canterbury, himself a Devonshire man, undertook in 1384 to visit the diocese of Exeter, as he was legally em-powered to do. He possibly showed want of tact; certain it is that Bishop Brantyngham of Exeter took offence, and issued a mandate on March 14 forbidding his flock to obey the Archbishop. The quarrel grew bitter; and, on the 21st, Courtenay sent an Archdeacon and two Canons to cite Brantyngham to permit a legal visitation. A letter of the Arch-deacon and Canons to the Archbishop tells the rest of the story, which is printed in vol. II. of Brantyngham's *Register*, Introd. p. xvii.

After receiving your mandate, on the said 25th day of March, we rode together to the manor-house of Clyst, where the said Bishop of Exeter was dwelling, that we might serve your citation upon him. But, as we came nigh unto the said manor, wishing to enter and to execute this mandate, we found there on the highway a great multitude assembled both of clerks and of layfolk, servants of the said Bishop, with divers

---
[1] harmless.

sorts of weapons....Wherefore, not being able safely to cite the bishop aforesaid, nor daring to approach him for fear of our lives, by reason of the power of these said servants and of this resistance which they offered unto us, we fled forthwith from that place. Yet even so we could scarce escape the temerarious hands of those same servants, who pressed after us and laid wait for us at every turn, seeking either to cast us over the bridges into the river or to slay us by some chance. At last, on that same day, when we had fled even to the town of Topsham, three esquires of the Bishop's household, viz. William Hughlot, John Ufflet, and John Moundeware, *alias* Boteller, came in arms to meet us, and compelled one of our esquires to show them our letters of citation and to tear them; after which, most inhumanly, and with fearful threats, they constrained him sorely against his will to eat the waxen seal wherewith the said letters were sealed; by reason of which impediments, and others also, we could not securely execute your mandate with any effect, nor did we dare so to do.

King and Pope were appealed to: meanwhile Archbishop and Bishop were holding rival Ordinations within the diocese: at last, on July 2, the Bishop suddenly yielded, and Courtenay was able to finish his visitation.

22   VETERINARY MEDICINE

Trevisa's *Bartholomew*, Lib. XVIII. c. 32, f. 326a.

There is soo great affinite bytwene hoves[1], clees[2], and hornes, that Aristotle commaundethe to anoynte with oyle and other medycynes bitwene the hornes a cowe that hath sore ache in the clees of the fete.

[1] hoofs.   [2] claws.

SECTION XV

SUPERSTITIONS AND MARVELS

The marvellous and the intangible so filled men's minds in every department of medieval life, that it is only necessary here to give a few illustrations complementary to the extracts in the preceding sections. Perhaps the most interesting single document relating to witchcraft is the trial of *Dame Alice Kyteler*, of Kilkenny, edited by T. Wright for the Camden Society (1843), from which the following extracts are taken, with considerable abridgment of superfluous details. Wright, in his Introduction, gives a very interesting collection of English *causes célèbres* in sorcery during the later Middle Ages.

Bishop Richard of Ossory, the Franciscan friar who is in one sense the hero of this Kyteler story, had a stormy career; see Wright's note, p. 42. About 1329, he himself was accused of heresy, and fled from Ireland for nine years; on his return, he was accused of abetting Thomas Fitzgilbert in slaying Hugh le Poer and plundering his castle. He regained the king's favour, however, and "passed the remainder of his life in great tranquillity. He obtained the king's leave for demolishing three churches without the walls, and employed the stones in building an episcopal palace near the Cathedral." He died at a great age in 1360, after an episcopate of about 42 years. At this distance of time, it will probably never be known how far the accusations against the lady on the one hand, or the Bishop on the other, were due to personal grudges or family feuds.

1   A NEST OF SORCERY

(p. 1.) [In the year 1324] these things here ensuing were done in Ireland. When the venerable father Brother Richard, Bishop of Ossory, visited his diocese, he found by solemn inquisition, whereat were five knights and a great multitude of other nobles, that there had long been in the city of Kilkenny, and still are, very many witches, practising divers sorceries which savoured of heresy. The Bishop, proceeding to investigate these, found a certain wealthy lady, Dame Alice Kyteler, mother to William Outlawe, together with her companions, entangled in various heresies.

First, he found that, in order to compass their ends by wicked sorceries, they would utterly cast off the faith of Christ and His Church for a month or a year, according as the aim of their sorcery was less or greater; so that, during this time, they believed naught that the Church believeth, nor in any way adored the Body of Christ, nor went to church, nor heard mass, nor took holy-bread or holy-water. *Secondly*, that they made to their demons sacrifices of living beasts, which they tore limb from limb and scattered about the cross-roads as an offering to a certain demon who gave himself the name of Fitz-Art, of the poorest in hell. *Thirdly*, that by their sorceries they sought counsel and answers from demons. *Fourthly*, that in their nightly conventicles they usurped the keys and jurisdiction of the Church, fulminating sentences of excommunication, with lighted candles, even against their own husbands, cursing them from the sole of the foot to the crown of the head, expressing every member singly and by name, and at the end dashing out the candles and crying *fi : fi : fi :, Amen!*[1] *Fifthly*, that having sacrificed cocks (as aforesaid) to their demons, from the intestines and inward parts of these birds, with certain loathly worms and various herbs, and dead men's nails...and garments of children that died unbaptized, and many other such detestable ingredients, boiled together over an oak-fire in the skull of a beheaded thief, they compounded divers powders, unguents and gums, and also candles of fat boiled in the same skull with sundry incantations, for the incitement of love or hatred, for the affliction or death of faithful Christian bodies, and for innumerable other purposes. *Sixthly*, that the sons and daughters of the said lady's four husbands cried urgently and publicly to the Bishop, beseeching remedy and succour against her, and openly accusing her before the people of having slain some of their fathers by her sorceries, while she had infatuated others to such a pitch of folly that they had given all their goods to

---

[1] The orthodox Roman Catholic form of excommunication ends *fiat*. *Amen!* The sorcerers may have varied this purposely, or it may be simply a scribe's abbreviation.

her and her son, to the perpetual destitution of their [or her?] children and heirs; so that even her present husband, Sir John le Poer, Knight, hath been brought to such a state with these powders and gums and sorceries, that he is horribly emaciated, and his nails and all the hairs of his body are fallen from him; but at last, warned by a certain handmaiden of the said Lady, he took the keys of her chests by violence from her hands, and, having unlocked them, the said Knight found therein a sackful of such like loathly and detestable things, which he sent to the Bishop aforesaid by the hands of two priests, men of Religion. *Seventhly,* that the said Lady hath a certain familiar spirit... named Fitz-Art or Robin Fitz-Art, who appeareth sometimes in the form of a cat, or of a black shaggy dog, or again of an Ethiopian with two companions greater and taller than himself....

Dame Alice escaped through the protection and connivance of her powerful friends, who at one time succeeded in clapping the Bishop into prison; but he finally succeeded in making an *auto da fé* of Dame Alice's unguents, etc. (p. 26), and in burning one Petronilla, her confidante and fellow-sorceress, "who, having been six times subjected to scourging by the Bishop for sorceries, was at length convicted of heresy and confessed publicly before clergy and people that, at the teaching of the said Dame Alice, she had totally cast off all faith in Christ and His Church." William Outlawe, after long resistance, was brought to his knees also, and subjected to the following "mitigated" penance (p. 28):

That he should hear for a year three masses at least every day; that he should feed a certain number of poor folk; that he should completely cover with lead, at his own cost, the choir of the cathedral church, and the whole church from the bell-steeple to the east end, and the whole of the Lady Chapel, for a perpetual memorial, that no man from henceforth should ever dare to rise up against the Church in any matter of faith, or to aid and abet heretics whether publicly or secretly. Which mitigation he gratefully admitted and accepted, in the presence of the whole people....

(p. 40.) Of the other heretics and sorcerers of the aforesaid pestilent fellowship of Robin Fitz-Art, some were publicly burned in due course of law; others, after confessing their crimes openly before the whole people, abjured their heresy and took the cross on the breast and back of their outer garments, according to custom. Others again were solemnly scourged through the city and market-place; others banished from the city and diocese; others escaped the jurisdiction of the Church and were publicly excommunicated; the rest fled in fear and lurked in secret places where they were never found. Thus then was that foul nest harried and destroyed by authority of holy Mother Church, with God's help and special grace.—Indeed we may most truly say, *of His special grace*; for throughout this arduous case—among so many difficulties, in the face of so many and so powerful adversaries and in the very teeth of so great a number of advocates most learned in the law, whom God blinded amid their own legal formalities—although the Bishop found many secret friends, and almost all men encouraged him to stand firm, yet in the whole land of Ireland not one was found who cared or dared to oppose himself publicly to these evil-doers, save this Bishop alone, who hath not yet found death in the cause of faith, although he desired and most diligently sought the same.

2   ROGER BACON'S FORECASTS

We must take the fourth chapter of Bacon's *Epistola de Secretis* (R. S., p. 532) neither too seriously nor too lightly: in many cases, Bacon grasped principles which he would have been utterly unable to realize in practice. In this connexion it is worth noting that a few of his sentences, borrowed by a 15th-century author, were among the suggestions which stimulated Columbus to his discovery of the New World.

Cap. IV. *Of marvellous artificial instruments.*

I will now proceed, therefore, to relate the works of art and miracles of nature, that I may afterwards expound the cause and the manner thereof; wherein there is nothing magical; nay rather, all magical power would seem inferior to such works, and unworthy of them. And first I will discourse through the figure and reason of art alone. For vessels might be made to move without oars or rowers, so that ships of great size might move on sea or on river, at the governance of a single man, more swiftly than if they were strongly manned. Moreover, chariots might be made to move without animal impulse at an incalculable speed; such as we suppose those scythed chariots to have been wherewith men were wont to fight in ancient days. Again, flying instruments might be made, so that a man might sit in the midst thereof, turning a certain machine whereby wings of artful composition should beat the air, after the fashion of a bird in her flight. Another instrument might be made, of small size, to raise or to lower weights of almost infinite greatness; than which nothing could be more useful in certain cases. For, by means of an instrument of the height and breadth of three fingers, and less bulk than they, a man might free himself and his companions from all peril of prison, lifting them and lowering them again. Moreover, an instrument might easily be made whereby one man could violently draw a thousand men to himself against their will, and so also of the attraction of other things. Again, instruments might be made for walking in the sea, or in rivers, even to the very bottom, without bodily danger: for Alexander the Great used these to see the secrets of the sea, as is related by Ethicus the Astronomer[1]. For these things were done of old, and have certainly also been done in our own times; except possibly the flying machine, which I have never seen, nor have I met any man who hath seen it; but I know a wise man who hath excogitated this artifice. And almost innumerable things of this kind might be made; bridges over rivers without pier or prop whatsoever, and unheard of machines and engines.

[1] An author on cosmography often quoted by Bacon. With regard to this legend Prof. D. E. Smith makes a suggestion which is far more illustrative of the attitude of the 13th century "multitude and its leaders" towards these questions, than of Bacon's own. He writes (*Roger Bacon Essays*, 1914, p. 179, note): "A propos of this quotation, there is in San Marco, Venice, a mosaic 'La Leggenda di Alessandro' of which Bacon may have heard. It follows closely the legend given by the pseudo-Callisthenes, with which Bacon was familiar, and represents Alexander as having harnessed two-winged griffins, before which two pieces of meat are held."

3　CHARMS IN MEDICINE

The charms given in Prof. A. S. Cook's *Literary Middle-English Reader* 1915, p. 379, should be compared with the following extract from so famous and advanced a doctor as John Arderne (E.E.T.S., 1910, p. 103, editor's translation, with corrections by the present compiler; the Latin text is obviously corrupt in some places).

The following charm against spasm has been found most sovran by many who have used it both at home and abroad. For at Milan in Lombardy, at the time when the Lord Lionel, son of the king of England, married the daughter of the lord of Milan, the English there were troubled with spasm due to their potations of the strong wines and the heat of the country and to too many carouses. Whereupon a certain knight, the son of Lord Reginald de Grey de Schirlond near Chesterfield, who was at Milan with the Lord Lionel and had with him the following charm, saw a certain gentleman so troubled with the spasm that his head was drawn backward nearly to his neck just like a crossbow, and he was almost dead from the pain and anguish. And when the said knight saw this he took the charm written on parchment and placed it in a purse and put it upon the neck of the patient, whilst those who stood by said the Lord's prayer and one to our lady Mary; and, as he swore faithfully to me, within four hours or five he was restored to health. And afterwards he freed many there from spasm, and the great report of that charm spread throughout that city. Again in the city of Lincoln...again in London...again in the Town of Huntingdon.

In nomine patris ✠ et filii ✠ et Spiritus sancti ✠ Amen.

⊕ Thebal ⊕ Enthe ⊕ Enthanay ⊕ In nomine Patris ⊕ et Filii ⊕ et Spiritus sancti ⊕ Amen. ⊕ Ihesu Nazarenus ⊕ Maria ⊕ Iohannes ⊕ Michael ⊕ Gabriel ⊕ Raphael ⊕ Verbum caro factum est ⊕.

Let it be closed afterwards in the manner of a letter so that it cannot be opened easily, and for this reason I used to write it in Greek letters that it might not be understood of the people. And if one carries that written charm fairly in the name of God Almighty, and believes, without doubt he will not be troubled with cramp. Let it be held in respect on account of the Lord who gave virtue to words, to stones and to herbs, and it is made secretly that every one should not know the charm, lest perchance it should lose the virtues given by God.

4 A CHARM TO FIND STOLEN GOODS

Rel. Ant. vol. I. p. 260 from Henslowe's Diary in the Library of Dulwich College, temp. Elizabeth.

To know wher a thinge is that is stolen.

Take vergine waxe and write upon yt "Jasper+Melchisor +Balthasar+," and put yt under his head to whome the good partayneth, and he shall knowe in his sleape wher the thinge is become.

5 DAMAGES FOR SORCERY

Riley, *Memorials of London*, 1868, p. 462.

A.D. 1382. On the 26th day of March, in the 5th year etc., Henry Pot, a *Duchysman* [German], was attached to make answer, as well to the Mayor and Commonalty of the City of London, as to Nicholas Freman, and Cristina, his wife, in a plea of deceit and falsehood,...that whereas one Simon Gardiner had lately lost a mazer cup, the said Henry came to him, and promised that he would let him know who had stolen the cup, and so cause him to regain it. And hereupon, the same Henry made 32 balls of white clay, and over them did sorcery, or his magic art: which done, he said that the same Cristina had stolen the cup; falsely and maliciously lying therein, and unjustly defaming the said Nicholas and Cristina, to their manifest scandal and disgrace, and to their grievance. And the same Henry, being questioned how he would acquit himself thereof, of his own accord acknowledged that he could not deny the same, but expressly admitted that he had done in manner aforesaid. And because that he thus acknowledged the same, and confessed that he had many times before practised divers like sorceries, both within the city aforesaid and without, through which various persons had undeservedly suffered injury in their character and good name; and because that sorcery, or the art magic, manifestly redounds against the doctrine of Sacred Writ; it was awarded that the same Henry should be put upon the pillory, there to remain for one hour of the day.

6   THE WITCH'S FATE

Alphabet of Tales, E.E.T.S., 1904, p. 487 (Tale DCCXXVIII.).

Cesarius tellis how som tyme ther was in Englond a womman that usid sorcerie. And on a day as sho was bown[1] to eatt, sho hard a craw cry beside hur, and sodanlie the knyfe that was in hur hande fell. And hereby sho demyd [th]at hur dead drew nere, and so sho fell seke, bown to dye. And sho sent after a monk and a non that was hur childer, and chargid thaim in hur blissyng that onone[2] as sho war dead thai sulde sew hur in a harte-skyn, and than [th]at thai sulde close hur in a tombe of stone, and [th]at thai sulde feste[3] the coveryng theron stronglie bothe with lead and strong yrn[4], and [th]at thai sulde close this stane and bynde it about with iij strang chynys[5], and than [th]at thai sulde do mes[6] and pray for hur aboute hur bodye. And if sho lay so sekurlie[7] iij dayes, than sho chargid thaim to bery hur vpp[on] the iiij day in the erth. And so all this was done, and [the] ij furste nyghtis, as clerkis was sayand ther prayers aboute hur, ffendys[8] brak the yatis[9] of the kurk, and come in unto hur and brak ij of the chynys at was at ather[10] end; and the myddyll chyne abade styll hale[11]. And vppon the iij nyght aboute cokkraw, ther come in suche a throng of fendis, [th]at thai [th]at saw it semyd [th]at the temple turnyd vpsadown. So ther come a fend [th]at was maste ugsom[12] of all, and hyer than any of the toder[13] was, and he come unto this tombe and callid hur be[14] hur name and bad hur ryse. And sho answerd agayn and sayde sho mot[15] not, for the bondis [th]at was bon[16] aboute the tombe. And he bad lowse[17] thaim, and onone at his commandement the chyne braste as it had bene hardis[18], and the coveryng of the tombe flow off. And ther he

---

[1] she was ready.   [2] anon.   [3] fasten.   [4] iron.   [5] chains.   [6] mass.
[7] safely.   [8] fiends.   [9] gates.   [10] either.   [11] whole.   [12] most ugly.
[13] others.   [14] by.   [15] could.   [16] bound.   [17] loose.   [18] tow.

tuke hur oppynlie befor all men and bare hur oute of the kurk. And ther befor the yatis ther was ordand[1] a blak hors, and that ane uglie, and here-uppon was sho sett; and than onone sho and all this felowshup vanysshid away.

7 ALCHEMIST BY ROYAL APPOINTMENT

The Coventry Leet Book, Part II., E.E.T.S., 1908.

John French, Alchemist.

Mem. that the vj[te] day of Januare the yere aforeseid, the forsaid Maire resceyved a privie signet be the handes of a servante of the kynges, the tenur wherof hereaftur ensueth :

By the kyng.

Trusty and wele-beloved, we grete you wel. And [we] late[2] you wit that it hath been shewed unto us that oure wele-beloved, Joh. ffrench, oure servaunt commonly conversyng and abydyng in oure Cite there, entendeth be[3] his labour to practise a true and a profitable conclusion in the cunnying of transmutacion of metails to oure profyte and pleasure; and, for to make a clere shewing of the same before certen oure servauntes and counsellours by us therfore appointed, it required a certain tyme to prepare his materials ; we, not willing therfore oure seid servaunt to be trobled in that he shall so werk or prepaire for oure pleasure and profite, woll[4] and charge yewe that ye ne suffre hym in eny wyse by eny persone or persones to be letted, troubled, or vexed, of his seid labour and practise; to th'entent that he, at his goode liberte, may shewe unto us and such as be by us therfore appointed, the clere effect of his said conclusion. Yeven[5] under oure signit at our palays of Westm[ynstre] the xxix[te] day of December.

For Edward IV.'s encouragement of alchemy see L. Stratford, *Edward the Fourth*, 1910, pp. 263–4. In Rymer's *Foedera*, 1711, vol. XII. p. 28 (June 18, 1476) is a similar royal letter in favour of David and John Marchaunt, who are making mercury into gold and silver, granting them protection for the next four years from "all impediment, trouble, perturbance, arrest, or grievance whatsoever from any of our Justices, Escheators, Sheriffs, Mayors, Bailiffs, constables, or other Officers of Ourselves or Our successors, or of Our liege subjects."

[1] ordained.   [2] let.   [3] by.   [4] desire.   [5] given.

8　PORTENTS

The following is a fair specimen of the mysterious significance which medieval chroniclers habitually attributed to natural phenomena, distorted or exaggerated.

The Brut, E.E.T.S., 1908, p. 313.

And this same yer [1361], in the Ascencioun, even about midday, was seyn the Eclipse of the sunne ; and ther folowed suche a newe droght that, for defaut of rayn, ther was grete bareynes of corn, froyt[1], and hey, and in the same yere, the vj kalend of Juyn, there fill a sangweyn rayne, almoost like blood, at Burgoyne ; and a sangweyn crosse, fro morwe unto pryme, was seyn and apperid at Boloigne in the eyr, the whiche meny a man sawe, and after, it mevid[2] and fill in the myd see.

And in the same tyme in Fraunce and in Engelond, and in othere meny landes, (as they had duelled in playn cuntres and desert bare wytnes), sodenly ther apperid ij castels, of the whiche wenten out ij ostes of armed men; and the to oste[3] was helid[4] and clothed in white, and the tothere yn blak ; and whan batayl bytuene them was bygunne, the white overcome the blake, and anone after, the blak token hert to them and overcome the white; and after that, they went agen into her castellis, and [after] that the castels and al the oostes vanisshed awey. And in this same yere was a grete and a houge pestilence of peple, and namely[5] of men, whos wyves, as wymmen out of governaunce, token husbondes, as wel straungers as othere lewed and symple peple; the whiche, forgetyng ther owne wurschip and berthe, coupled and maried them with them that were of lowe degre and litel reputacion.

9　OLIVER THE FLYING MAN

Trevisa's *Higden*, VII. 221.　A.D. 1066.

Seven dayes tofore May, a starre with a bright blasyng crest was i-seie[6] into al the world wyde, and was so y-seie seven dayes continuallyche. Olyver monk of Malmesbury grette[7] the sterre, and spak therto in this manere : " Thow art i-come, now thu art i-come, dwel[8] and sorwe to wel many

---

[1] fruit.　　[2] moved.　　[3] one host.　　[4] wrapped.　　[5] especially.
[6] seen.　　[7] greeted.　　[8] dule, mourning.

A Portent in the Sky

A Demon Tourney

modres ; it is yore[1] that I seie the, but now I see the more
dredeful and griseliche, that manassest[2] destroyenge of this
contray." This Olyver was thoo[3] a kunnyng man of lettrure,
and a man of grete age ; but in his yowthe by greet hardynesse
he fondede[4] forto flee as a bridde with wynges.   I not[5] by what
craft he fethered his feet and his hondes, for he wolde flee in
Dedalus his wise; and so he took a fable in stede of a sooth
sawe ; and so he stood on a hygh toure, and took the wynde,
and fligh[6] the space of a furlong and more.   But he was aferd
of the grete strengthe of the wynd and of the whirlewynde, and
[also] on caas[7] of his awne[8] folie dede, and fel doun; so that he
was lame in his thyhes[9] terme of his lyf.

10   CROCODILE TEARS

The romance of medieval natural history is best studied in the
Bestiaries; to these may be added one or two passages from Trevisa's
Bartholomew, Lib. XVIII. c. 33, f. 326*a*; a cento of detached passages.

The cocadrylle is a beaste, and dwelleth in the ryver Nilus,
and his skynne is [so] harde that [he] reccheth not though he be
strongly beten on the backe with stoones, and layeth egges in
the londe that bene greater than goos egges ; and his bityng is
venemous, his teeth ben horryble and strongly shape as a comb
or a sawe, and as a bores tuske.   And no beaste that commeth
of soo lyttelle begynnynge wexeth so great as the cocadrylle ;
and is a beaste nouryshed in greate glotenye, and eateth ryghte
moche.   And soo, whan he is ful, he lyeth by the brynke or by
the clyffe and bloweth for fulnes.   If the cocodril findeth a man
by the brim of the water or by the cliffe, he sleeth[10] hym if he
may, and then he wepeth upon hym and swoloweth hym at
the laste.

11   THE REMORA

Trevisa's *Bartholomew*, Lib. XIII. c. 19.

Enchirius is a fishe unneth[11] a fote longe, and hathe that name
of *herendo*, clevynge; for, though he be ful lytil of body, netheles
he is most of vertue.   For he clevith to the shyppe, and

---

[1] long ago.   [2] menacest.   [3] then.   [4] tried.   [5] know not.   [6] flew.
      [7] perchance.   [8] own.   [9] thighs.   [10] slayeth.   [11] scarcely.

holdeth it styll stedfastely in the see as though the shyppe
were on grounde therein, though wyndes blowe and waves
aryse strongly, and wode[1] stormes, that shyppes may not meve[2]
nother[3] passe. And that fishe holdeth not styll the shyppe by
no crafte, but only clevinge to the shippe. Latyns calle this
fyshe *Moron*. For by strenghte he maketh the shyppe to
stonde, as it is sayd.

Compare St Thomas Aquinas, *Summa Contra Gentiles*, Lib. III.
c. 102, "God alone can work miracles.... When any finite power worketh
its own proper effect, this is no miracle, though it may seem miraculous
to him who hath no comprehension of that power; as to the ignorant it
seemeth miraculous that the magnet draweth iron, or that a little fish
holdeth back a ship."

12   THE LAMPREY

Trevisa's *Bartholomew*, Lib. XIII. c. 19.

Fishars calle it [the lamprey] with hyshynge[4] and whystlyng,
and taketh her in that wise.... It is certayn that the soule
of this fishe is in the taile; for they say, unnethe[5] she is slaine,
though she be smyte on the heed.

13   THE GHOST OF THE GOG-MAGOG HILLS

Wandlebury or Wendlebury Camp is a prehistoric earthwork on the
top of the highest point of these hills, which rise close by Cambridge to
the south-east. This extract is translated from F. Liebrecht, *Gervasius
von Tilbury*, 1856, p. 26, cap. LIX. The story appears also in *Gesta
Romanorum* (ed. Swan, tale no. 155).

In England, on the confines of the diocese of Ely, is a
town named Cambridge, within whose bounds, and hard by
the town, lieth a place which men call Wandlebury, for that
the Vandals had their camp there when they invaded Britain
and cruelly slaughtered the Christians. On the spot where
they pitched their tents, at the very summit of the hill, is a
level space girt and ringed round by earthen banks, with but
one opening for ingress, after the fashion of a gate. The
aforesaid level field hath this property from time immemorial
(and common report beareth witness thereunto) that if, after
nightfall, any knight enter therein and cry aloud: "Let a

---

[1] raging.   [2] move.   [3] nor.   [4] hissing.   [5] scarcely.

knight come against this knight!" forthwith a knight will rush forward to meet him, full armed for the fray; then will the two horsemen fall upon each other; and one or other will be overthrown. Yet it must be premised, by way of warning, that the knight must enter this enclosure alone, though his companions may be suffered to wait and gaze without. In witness of this matter I add an event which is known to many, far and near, and which I have myself heard from those who were born and have dwelt near to this spot.

There was in Britain, not long since, a most doughty knight, endowed with every virtue, surpassed in power by few among the barons, and in probity by none; his name was Osbert Fitz-Hugh. One day this knight entered the town of Cambridge as a guest; and, after supper, his host's family sat by the fire to tell and listen of ancient deeds, as great men are wont to do; for his host was a man of wealth. At length one of the Cambridge men related the story of Wandlebury; whereat this doughty knight resolved to prove by experience the tale which he had heard with his ears. Choosing one of his noble squires, he went with him to the hill, and found the camp. Here, clad in full armour, he mounted his horse and drew near; and, leaving his squire without, he entered in alone and cried aloud for his adversary. Forthwith there came a knight to meet him, or the semblance of a knight, armed (as it seemed) even as he was armed. With shield displayed and levelled spears they dashed together, and the horsemen reeled with the shock of their conflicting steeds; but Osbert avoided the other's lance, which slid harmlessly from him, while he for his part unhorsed his foe. But the fallen knight started from the ground; and, seeing Osbert seize the reins of his horse, that he might take it thence for a prize, he brandished his lance, hurled it like a javelin, and pierced Osbert's thigh with a grisly wound. Our knight, for his part, whether he felt no wound for joy of his victory or that he dissembled his pain, let his adversary disappear and rode away in triumph. The horse thus won he handed over to his squire—a great charger, swift and agile and most fair to see. His household crowded to welcome his return, marvelling at this event, rejoicing in the overthrow of the fallen knight, and chanting the prowess of their renowned lord. Then Osbert disarmed ; and, taking off his steel chausses[1], he found one full of clotted blood. His household were aghast at the wound, but the lord scorned all fear. Meanwhile the townsfolk rose from their beds and were gathered together ; for the marvel grew from minute to minute, and dispelled all drowsiness even from those who had so lately been weighed down with sleep. The horse, pledge of this victory, was held with a free rein and shown to the public gaze ; men admired his flashing eyes, his proud neck, his jet-black coat and the equal blackness of his saddle and trappings. And now the first cock crowed ; whereupon the horse began to bound and prance, snorting with open nostrils and pawing the ground, until he had burst his reins and galloped off in native liberty, disappearing from the eyes of those who would have pursued him. Moreover, our noble lord kept this lifelong memorial of his wound, that yearly on this same day and this same hour the ancient scar would open and bleed afresh. Wherefore, not many years afterwards, he crossed the seas [to the Holy Land], where he fought doughtily in many battles against the pagans and ended his days in the service of God.

14   THE ENCHANTED MERE

It is difficult to choose among the many marvels related by Gervase and copied from him by later compilers such as Higden ; but the following may be taken as fairly typical.

c. LXXXVIII. p. 410. For the insulting word *Phrut*, see Section VI., no. 2. Liebrecht refers for similar legends to Grimm, *Deutsche Mythologie*, 563-5.

In the same parts [i.e. England] is *Haveringmere*. If any man sailing or rowing over this mere cry aloud :

Phrut, Haveringmere,
And alle those [that] over the fere[2] !

[1] Stockings of mail reaching almost to the waist, frequently shown on monuments of about this time, e.g. the brass of Sir Roger de Trumpington.
[2] over thee fare.

then forthwith a sudden tempest ariseth, sinking boat and man....Truly it is a great marvel that dumb waters should be capable of such indignation.

15   THE ANTIPODES

Medieval writers naturally show much difference of opinion concerning the Antipodes. St Augustine dismisses the idea with a "nulla ratione credendum est" (*De Civ. Dei* XVI. 9). In 744 we find the great missionary Saint Boniface denouncing a fellow-missionary as heretical for maintaining that there was "another world, and other men under the earth." To this denunciation Pope Zacharias replied: "Concerning this man's perverse and iniquitous teaching, which he hath uttered against God and his own soul, if indeed he be proved to have asserted that there is another world and other men under the earth, or a sun and a moon, then do thou assemble a council, deprive him of his priestly rank, and expel him from the Church" (Ep. XI., Migne, *P.L.*, vol. LXXXIX. col. 946). Dante knew the shape of the earth, but apparently held the common belief that all dry land lay in a single continuous mass, surrounded by continuous sea (except for a few outlying islands, and for his own Mountain of Purgatory). This is assumed in the medieval English term *Mydelerd*: see Section III., no. 14c. Higden's information, collected from different sources, admirably exemplifies this vagueness and confusion. (*Polychronicon*, R. S., vol. II., p. 205; version of MS. Harl.)

And...somme men say, as in fables, men callede Antipodas to be, that is to say, men to be in a contrarious parte of the worlde, and to trede with theire feete ageyne oure stappes[1]; hit is not credible by eny reason, neither the cognicion of eny story dothe not expresse hit to be soo, but that the coniecture of man movethe[2] that thynge. For thoughe the erthe be rownde and convexede withynne, neverthelesse hit is not bare of that parte, sithe that hit is circumamicte[3] with waters; and, thaughe the erthe were bare ther, hit wolde not folowe by a directe consequente that the erthe scholde conteyne men in that parte. Peraventure but if we understonde Antipodas men so namede in that maner as Marcianus dothe in his Astrology, seyenge[4] that Capricorne makethe somer to men called Antipode, and Cancer wynter; whiche thynge is supposede to be caused over the sowthe part of Ethioppe, for the stappes ther be oblike[5] and contrarious to theyme

---

[1] footsteps.   [2] suggests.   [3] clothed round.
         [4] saying.   [5] oblique.

whiche dwelle abowte the Yle callede Tyle under that pole artike[1].

Gervase of Tilbury, c. XLV. p. 24.

In Britain there is a castle among the mountains, which the people call *Peak*. Its bulwarks are almost impregnable; and in the bowels of the mountain is a cavern which, at times, belcheth forth gusts of wind as one who bloweth on a pipe. Folk wonder whence this wind cometh; and, among many marvels told of that cave, I have heard the following from that most religious man Robert, prior of [Kenilworth], who was born in those parts.

In the days when the noble William Peverel held this castle and barony—a strong and mighty man, and rich in flocks and herds—one day his swineherd, through negligence in his office, lost his noblest sow, a beast of choice ancestry, while she was big with young. Therefore, fearing the bitter words of his lord's steward at this loss, he began to think within himself whether the beast had crept into that famous Hole of the Peak, hitherto unexplored. He resolved therefore to explore that mysterious place, and crept into the cave at a time when the blast was quiet; thence, having proceeded far on his way, he at length came out of the darkness into the open air, at a place where the passage opened out into a wide plain. Here he found the land tilled far and wide, and reapers harvesting the ripe corn, and among the drooping ears his own sow, with her numerous litter of pigs. At this the swineherd marvelled, and rejoiced thus to make good his loss. Therefore he told the whole tale to the reeve of that field, who gave him his sow and sent him home rejoicing to his own herd. And, wondrous to relate! having left these subterranean folk in the harvest-field, he came back to find winter still reigning in our hemisphere.

---

[1] i.e. "For these men, as they walk, stand at an obtuse angle to those who live in the island of Thule." This still leaves room for the general belief that the southern hemisphere was almost all ocean.

16   THE GREEN CHILDREN

The similar story in the chronicler, William of Newburgh, l. 1. c. 27 (ed. Hearne, 1719, 1. 90), is worth recording in this connexion. William died about 1200 A.D.   A third, from the chronicler Walsingham, is trans-lated in *A Medieval Garner*, p. 523 ; and a fourth may be found in Giraldus Cambrensis, *Itin. Cambriae*, 1. 8, easily accessible in Bohn's translation (1863), and Dent's *Everyman's Library*.   Compare the Land of Darkness in Maundeville's *Travels*.

De Viridibus Pueris.   I must not there omit a marvel, a prodigy unheard of since the beginning of all time, which is known to have come to pass under King Stephen.   I myself long hesitated to credit it, although it was noised abroad by many folk; and I thought it ridiculous to accept a thing which had no reason to commend it, or at most some reason of great obscurity; until I was so overwhelmed with the weight of so many and such credible witnesses, that I was compelled to believe and admire that which my wit striveth vainly to reach or to fathom.

There is a village in England (it is said) some 4 or 5 miles from the noble monastery of the blessed King and Martyr Edmund; near which may be seen certain trenches of im-memorial antiquity which are called in the English tongue *Wolfpittes*, and which give their name to the adjacent village[1]. One harvest-tide, when the harvesters were gathering in the corn, there crept out from these two pits a boy and a girl, green at every point of their body, and clad in garments of strange hue and unknown texture.   These wandered dis-traught about the field, until the harvesters took them and brought them to the village, where many flocked together to see this marvel, and for some days the children took no food. At last, when they were almost dead with hunger, and yet refused every sort of food that was set before them, it chanced that some beans were brought in from the field; whereat the children caught greedily and sought in the pods, weeping bitterly to find them empty.   Then one of the bystanders offered them newly-shelled beans, which they took gladly and ate forthwith.   With this food they were nourished for some

[1] i.e. the modern Woolpit, about seven modern miles from Bury.

days, until they had learned to eat bread.　At length, under the prevailing influence of our food, they slowly changed their native hue, became as other children, and learned the English speech.　Then, at the counsel of wise folk, they received the sacrament of Holy Baptism; but the boy, who seemed the younger, lived but a brief while after this, while his sister throve and lived on, differing no whit from the girls of our land.　The story goeth that she married afterwards at Lynn, where she was said to be still living a few years since.　The children, as soon as they learned our speech, were asked who and whence they were, and are said to have answered: "We are folk of St Martin's Land; for that is the chief saint among us."　Being further asked where this land might be, and how they had come among us, they made answer: "We know not; this alone we remember, that one day we were feeding our father's flock in the field, when we heard a great noise, such as we hear now when all the bells at St Edmunds peal together.　When, therefore, we were listening with all our ears to this marvellous sound, suddenly we were rapt in the spirit and found ourselves in your harvest-field."　Being asked whether men believed in Christ there, and whether the sun rose, they said it was a Christian land, with churches of its own; "but," said they, "no sun ariseth among us; never is there open sunshine, but such a twilight as here forerunneth his rising or followeth upon his setting.　Yet a land of light is to be seen not far from ours, but severed therefrom by a stream of great breadth."　These and many other things, too long to repeat, they are said to have answered to the curious. Let all men say what they will, and reason of this as they can; I for my part am not ashamed to have related this prodigious and marvellous event.

1 7　CLOUD-SHIPS

Gervase of Tilbury, *l.c.*, cap. XIII. p. 2.　A heavy stone tomb of the kind here described, dating from the late 14th or early 15th century, may still be seen in front of the porch of St Nicholas at Lynn.　Iron door-bands in the rough form of an anchor are very common on early church doors: e.g. Sempringham (R. and J. A. Brandon, *Analysis*, vol. II. plate 6) and the modern imitation at Iffley (S. door).

There are some who say that the earth, as a centre in the midst of a circumference, is equally distant from all these extremities, and is surrounded and shut in by sea, even as it is written of the third Day of Creation, "God gathered together the waters that were under the heaven into one place, and dry land appeared."

In our own times there befel a marvellous, but well-known event to prove how the upper sea lieth above us. On a certain holyday in Great Britain, after High Mass, the folk were thronging forth from the parish church, on a morning so misty that it made a sort of twilight amid the gross and watery vapours. Here, on a stone tomb within the precincts of the churchyard[1], they found an anchor fixed, with its cable stretched tight and hanging down from the air. The people stood in amazement; and, while they were disputing among themselves of this matter, at length they saw the rope move as though men had been labouring to weigh the anchor. When therefore, for all this straining at the rope, the anchor yet clung to the tomb, they heard through the foggy air as though it had been the cries of sailors labouring with all their might to raise an anchor from the deep. Soon, when they found their labour to be in vain, they sent down one of their fellows, who, as skilfully as any shipman of our own, appeared hanging to the rope and descending with alternate interchange of hands. When, however, he had torn the anchor from the tomb, he was caught by those that stood around, in whose arms he gave up the ghost, stifled by the breath of our gross air as a shipwrecked mariner is stifled in the sea. Moreover his fellows above, judging him to be wrecked, after an hour's delay, cut the cable, left their anchor, and sailed away. In memory of which event the iron bands of the doors of that church were forged, by a cunning counsel, from that anchor; which bands are still there for all men to see.

Here again is a still more marvellous testimony. In the county of Gloucester is a town named Bristol, wealthy and full of prosperous citizens; from this port men sail for Ireland. It befel upon a time that a native of Bristol sailed to Ireland,

---

[1] Reading *septe circuitum* for Liebrecht's *septa circuitu*.

leaving his wife and children at home. Then, after a long sea-voyage, as he sailed on a far-off ocean, he chanced to sit banqueting with the mariners about the hour of tierce; and, after eating, as he washed his knife over the ship's side, it slipped suddenly from his hands. At that same hour, at Bristol, the knife fell in through the roof-window of that same citizen (which men in the English tongue call *dormer*) and stuck in the table that was set before his wife. The woman, marvelling at so strange a thing, was dumbfounded; and, laying aside this well-known knife, she learned long afterwards, on her husband's return, that his misfortune had befallen on the very day whereon she had found it. Who, then, will now doubt, after the publication of this testimony, that a sea lieth over this earth of ours, whether in the air or above the air?

INDEX

A, Richard of, 51
Abbeville, 156
"Abbot of Unreason," 493
Abel, 410
"abjuration," 516
Abraham, 108
Abraham, Father, 464
Abram, Miss A., *Women Traders in Medieval London*, 455
Acta Sanctorum Bolland., 61
Acton, 421
Adam, 11, 197, 200, 354
Adam's mother, 409
Adam (Chaucer's copyist), 105
Adam, Sir, 260
Adrian V, 454
Aelfric, Abbot of Evesham, *Dialogue*, 54
Aeneas, 99
Agnello, Bro., 249
Agnes de W., 50
Agobbio, 469
Ahasuerus, 374-5
Ailesham, Dom John, 258
Ailsi, 221-6
Ailward, 415
Aimoin, *see* Fleury
Alayn, Roger, 50
Alberede, Countess of Bayeux, 472
Albigenses, 240, 474
Albin, *see* Bolkinglas
Aldgate, Peter of, 218, 221
    De Adventu Messiae, 218
    Liber Revelationum, 218
    Pantheologus, 218
Aldham, Peter of, 26
Aldridge, Robert, 251, 255
Alexander the Great, 525
Alexander (III ?), 404
Alfred, King, 179
Alleford, John de, 322-3
Almaine, King of, 316
Alphabet of Tales, v, 196, 216, 266-8, 289, 290, 346, 404, 434
Amedeus, *see* Savoy
Anacletus, 192 n.
"Ancien Régime," 301
Andreae, Johannes, 438

Angarath, 111
Angevins, 187
Angles, 21
Anglo-Saxon Chronicle, 23, 236
Anglo-Saxon Vocabularies, 54
Angos, Robert, 258
Anjou, 296
Anjou, Duke of, 155
Anstey, *Munimenta Academica*, 64, 67-9, 508
Anthony, 190
Antichrist, 130, 189
Antioch, 23
Antipodes, the, 535
Antwerp, 252
Antwerp, Lionel of, 347
Apocalypse, 180, 187, 190, 225
"Apostate," 202 n.
Apostles, 134, 198, 419
Apulia, 23, 242
Aquitaine, Prince of, 157-8
Arabic, 256
Aragon, Catherine of, 393-4, 439
Aragon, King of, 43
Arber, vi, 83, 229, 288
Archaeologia, 377 n., 422
Archdeacon, John the, 281
Arderne, John, 496, 499 n.
    Treatise on the Fistula, 426, 496, 526
Ariège, R., 150
Aristotle, 31; "the Philosopher," 35; 47, 63, 165 n., 179, 433, 520
Arles, 385
Armagh, Abp of, 329
Armynake [Armagnac], Count of, 151, 152
Armynakes, 152
Arras, 115
Arthez, 154
Arthur, 307
Artigat, castle of, 150, 151
Artois, 360
Arundel, Constitution of Abp., 194
Arundel, Sir Thos., 279
Ascension-tide, 530
Ascham, Roger, 97

Ashburton, 261
Ashley, Sir William, *Economic History*, 342, 344 n.
Ashwell, 498 n.
Askil, William, 308
Aste, 157
Asteburi, 439
Atcham, 107
Athelstan, King, 488
Athenaeum, 508
Att Hull, Thomas, 347-8
Attilbrigge, Hankyn, 67
Augsburg, 245
Augustinian, *see* Friars
Auray, 294
"aureoles," 467 n.
Auvergne, 150; Dauphin of, 148
Avesbury, Robert of, *Historia Edwardi Tertii*, 259
Avesnes, lord of, 149
Avicenna, 63, 350
Avignon, 27, 150, 420-2
Awdelay, John, 170-1
   Poems, 170
Aylesbury, 426
Ayton, John of, 454-5

Babington, 268
Babylon, 204, 519
Bacar, Agnes de, 52
Bacar, Thos. de, 52
Bacchus, 164, 165, 378
Backster, Margery, 462-5
Bacon, Roger, 26, 129-130, 187, 192, 260 n., 525
   Opus Tertium, 62, 129
   Communia Naturalium, 129
   Communia Mathematicae, 129
   Opus Majus, 159, 350
   Opus Minus, 129
   Opera Inedita, 130, 192, 260 n.
   Compendium Studii Theologiae, 129
   Epistola de Secretis, 524
Bagdad, 123, 412
Bagnères, 153
Bailey, N., 251
"bailiff" (duties of), 303
Bailiff of Love, 87
"baker" (duties of), 305
Bakynton, 363
Baldock, Bp Ralph, 473
Baldwin, *see* Canterbury
Bâle, 204
Ball, John, 355

Baluze, *Vitae Paparum Avenionensium*, 259
Bambour, 66
Bannockburn, 409
Barbasan, 153
Barber, Roger, 515
Barbosus, 56
Barker, W., 177-8
Barre, Tiercelet de la, 149
Barri, William de, 111
Barrington, 173 n.
Bartholomaeus Anglicus, 2 n., 8, 117 n.
   De Proprietatibus Rerum, 8, 45, 47, 339, 371, 425, 433, 441, 479, 502, 507, 508, 520, 531, 532
Bartolommeo Guiscolo, Bro., 30
Bartone, Bro. William, 363
Baruch, 73 n.
Bascot, 154 n., 155
Basing, Adam de, 315
Basset, Philip, 50
Basyngwerc, 19
Bat, Thomas, 318
Bateson, Miss Mary, 315, 333, 376
   Records of Leicester, 513
Bath, archdeacon of, 281
Bath and Wells, Bps of, 346
Batman, Stephen, 9
Bavaria, Duke Albert (Aubert) of, 148, 157
Bayeux, bishops of, 472
Bayeux, Earl of, 472
"Bear-baiting," 390
Bearn, *see* Foix
Beatrice, Dante's, 28
Beauchamp, William de, 291
Beaufort, Thomas, 297 ff.
Beaumanoir, 294 ff.
Beaumont, 148
Beaumoot, 149
Beauvais, 360, 361
Bebinton, Robert de, 439
Bec, Ragenhilda of, 307
Beccles, 443
Becket, Thomas, 200, 431-2
Becket, Materials for History of Thomas, 58, 387, 431
Beck, Master J., 69
Bede, 1, 11, 63, 180, 227
Bekard [or Bocard], Peter, 309
Bémont, Charles, *Simon de Montfort*, 333, 513
Benedict (brother of Ordericus), 106
Benedictine monasteries, 39

Bergen, 125
Berkeley, 1
Berkeley Castle, 180 n.
Berkeley, Bp John de, 27 n.
Berkeley, Lord de, 1
Bernard, son of Ailsi, 223
Bernard (Fellow of Merton), 77
Berners, Lord, v, 149, 154 n., 274, 291, 294, 458
Bernewell, 309
Berthelet, 97
Berthem, Agnes, 465
Berwick, 284, 461, 508
Bestiaries, 531
Bettes, Dom William, 258
Beverley, John of, *Book of Miracles*, 407
Beverley Minster (S. John's), 407
Bible, 62, 63, 70, 102, 269, 364, 500; "God's word," 84; "the open Bible," 179; "Church = poor man's Bible," 227; *A XIV Century English Biblical Version*, 179
Bibliothèque de l'École des Chartes, 301
Bigore, 151, 153
Bishop, William, 68
Bisuthe, John, 307
Bisuthe, Gilbert, 307
Black Death, the, 199, 259, 350, 351, 496
Black Prince, 157, 158, 325, 391, 458
Blake, Thomas, 69
Bliss, W. H., *Calendar of Papal Letters*, 236, 346, 400
Blofield, 178
Blois, lords of, 148, 149, 150
Blois, Peter of, 119 n., 281
Epistolae, 281
Blomefield, *Norfolk*, 350 n.
Blond, Sir Robert, 260
Blonde of Oxford, 286
Blount, T., *Antient Tenures*, 427
Blund, John le, 318
Bockwell, Andrew, 390
Bockyngham, 79, 80
Boece, 105
Boethius, *De Disciplina Scolarium*, 63
Bohemia, 511
Bohemia, Anne of, 280
Bohemia, Wenceslas of, 154
Böhmer, 239, 245 n.
Boileau, 378

Boileau, Étienne, *Métiers de Paris*, 488
Boisserée, Sulpiz, 466
Bokkyng, 178
Bole, Richard, 329
Boleyn, Anne, 383
Bolkinglas, Albin, Abbot of, 119
Bologna, 114, 115, 468, 469
Bonatrix, Agnes, 262
Bonde, Master John, 376, 378
Bonet, Richard, 363
Boniface VIII, 190, 191
Boniface IX, 204
Bordeaux, 157
Boswell, 415
Boteller, John, 520
Botoner, *see* Worcester
Bougarber, 154
Boulogne, 360, 421, 430, 530; Our Lady of, 432
Bourbon, Étienne de, 217
Bourbon, Duke of, 148
Bourg, 154 n., 155
Bourg-S.-Andéol, 421
Bourne, Philip, Prior of, 137
Boves, Sir Geoffroy de, 297 ff.
"Boy-Bishop," 493
Boys-aliz, 424
Bozen, 244
Brabançons, 295
Brabant, 20
Brabant, Duke of, 148, 154
Brabant, Jahame, Duchess of, 148, 157
Bradele, 52
"Braelers," Ordinances of, 455
Brakelond, Jocelin of, 187, 207 n.
Brambro, 294 ff.
Brandon, R. and J. A., *Analysis of Gothic Architecture*, 538
Branscombe, 261
Brantyngham, Bp, *Register*, 519
Braundeston, Henry de, 320
Brecon, 19
Brendan, hills of, 10
Breslau, 473
Bret, Berard de la, 291
Bretons, 294, 295, 298 n., 299, 300, 516
Breton tongue, 27
Brewer, Dr, 62, 130, 130 n., 246
Brewhouse, Richard, 515
Bridges, 350
Bristol, 176, 334, 427, 539, 540
Britain, 1 ff., 10, 126, 417, 532, 536
British Sea, 108

Britons, 9
Brittany, 267, 294, 300, 349
Brixen, 244
Bromholme, Prior of, 443
Brothelyngham, Order of, 493
" Brownies," 386
Bruges, 430
Brugge, Edmund atte, 309
Brunne, Robert of, *see* Mannyng
Brunne=Bourne, 136, 137
Brunnewake, 137
Brut, The, 28, 195, 201, 275, 277, 278, 379, 409, 427, 516, 530
Brute, 17
Bryan, John, 94
Bryel, Thomas, 362
Brykelesworthe, John de, 321, 323
Buchon, 84, 148, 294
Buck, Thomas, 515
Buckingham Household Accounts, 377 n.
" bull-baiting," 390
Burgate, Peter, 258
Burgess, Peter, 308
Burgo, John de, *Pupilla Oculi*, 341
Burgundy, 530
Burton, Thomas, *Chronicon de Melsa*, 146
Bury, 537 n.
Bury, Adam de, 325
Bury, Isabel de, 320
Bury, Richard de (? Robert Holcot), *Philobiblon*, 183
Bury S. Edmunds, 394
Busch, Johann, *Liber Reformationis Monasteriorum*, 263
Buthrescas, 273
Bylney, Master, 271
Byngham, William, 53
Bynham, Dom Thomas, 257
Bysset, Ernalton, 153

Caedmon, 180
Caen, 236
Caesarius, *see* Heisterbach
Caesarius, Bro., 243
Cahors, 342
Caiaphas, Bp, 464, 465
Cain, 410
Caister, 177–8
Calabria, 23
Calais, 158, 421; S. Nicholas' shrine, 421

Calendar of Inquisitiones post mortem, 50, 52, 309, 438–9
" caligae," 78 n.
Callisthenes, pseudo-, 525 n.
Calvary, Mt., 319
Calverley, Hugh de, 297 ff.
Calvin, 47
Cam, R., 411
Camber, 17
Cambrai, 361
Cambrensis, *see* Giraldus
Cambria, 17
Cambridge, 72, 173 n., 249, 346, 532; Barnwell, 66; S. Mary's Church, 55 and note; Parliament of, 57, 330; *see also* Cooper, Peacock, Universities, Wendover
Cambridge, Earl of, 391
Cambridge History of English Literature, 83, 137
Camelton, John of, 137
Cancer, 535
Candlemas, 384, 391–3
Canon Law, 336, 339 n., 342, 406 n., 436–7, 455; Gloss on, 456
Canterbury, 111, 116, 158, 248, 258, 421, 422
  Cathedral, 222 n.
  Cathedral Priory, 247
  Priests' Spital, 247
  S. Thomas's Chapel, 115
  S. Thomas's Shrine, 422
  Abps of, 209, 211, 212, 248, 316, 336, 348
    Baldwin, 121
    Courtenay, 519
    Gervase, 222 n.
    Hubert, 357–9
    Islip, Simon, 323
    Langham, Simon, 348
    Langton, Stephen, 111, 344
    Maunsel, John, 316
    Peckham, John, 345
    Reynold, Walter, 436
    Rich, S. Edmund, 59, 436
    Richard, 118, 209–10
    S. Thomas, 39, 56, 118, 197, 463–5; Translation of, 202
    William, 350
    Winchelsea, S. Robert of, 202
Canterbury and York Society, 257, 473
" capellanus," 170
Capgrave, John, *Life of S. Richard of Chichester*, 61

Capgrave, John (*cont.*)
Life of S. Gilbert, 213, 232
"cappa,' 61
Capricorn, 535
Caraites, 414
Carcassone, 150
Carlat, 150
Carlate, 155
Carleon, 101
Carlisle, 293
Carmarthenshire (Black Mts), 507
Carmentis, 107 n.
Carnarvon, 515
Carpenter, Gilbert le, 52
Carroumois, Alain de, 296 ff.
"carters" (duties of), 305
Carter, John, 359
Carter, Robert, 308
Carter, T. J. P., *King's College Chapel*, 492
Carthusians, 39, 195
Cary, H. F., 469
Casere, 12
Casseres, 151
Castile, 43
Castyde, Henry, 161
Catechism, The Lay Folks', 206
Catholic Encyclopaedia, 474 n.
Catholics, 476
Caursins (= usurers), 342-3
Cavendish, *Life of Wolsey*, 383
Caxton, William, 205
Eneydos, 181
Dialogues in French and English, 381, 430
Cecily, 309
Cercy (?), 421
Certain, 222 n.
Chabham, Thos. de, *Penitential*, 403
Chadwick, Prof. H. M., vi
Chamberlang, Henry le, 50
Chambers, E. K., *Medieval Stage*, 403, 493-4
Champagne, 421
Champeneys, William, 50
Charles (the Bald), 179
Charles V, 148, 294, 468
Charles VII, Ordonnance of, 510
Charruel, Sir Yvain, 294 ff.
Chartes, Bibl. de l'École des, 301
Chartres, Cathedral, 468, 477
Charybdis, 4
Château-Josselin, 294 ff.
Chatillon, Sir Guy of, *see* Blois

Chaucer, Geoffrey, **v**, 78 n., 105, 127 n., 138, 149 n., 170, 239, 249, 325, 337, 347 n., 466, 470, 496
Canterbury Tales, 73 n., 117 n., 426, 462 n.
Complaint of Venus, 27
Canterbury Tales Prologue, 201 n., 216, 467 n., 501
Cook's Tales, 327
Nun's Priest's Tale, 301, 306 n.
Parson's Tale, 265 n., 379
"chausses," 534
Cheddar, 3
Chester, 4, 439
Miracle Plays, 1
Shepherd's Play, 308
S. Werburgh's, 1
Chesterfield, 526
"chests," 346
"chevisance," 337
Cheylesmore Green, 427
Chichester, Bps of, 192, 268
Children, the Three, 519
Chilterns, 389
Chimay, Chymay, 156, 162
China, 250 n.
"chorea," 494
"Christmas-box," 199 n.
Chronicles, Anglo-Saxon, 23, 236
Collection de Chroniques, 294
Eccleston's, 246, 424
French Chronicle of London, 27 n., 201, 315
Froissart's, 291, 397, 458
Hardyng's, 282, 517
Knighton's, 57, 65
London, Chronicles of Old, 315, 406
Mannyng's, 28
Newburgh's, 537
Salimbene's, 29
Chrysostom, 49 ff.
Church, Dean, *S. Anselm*, 106
"church-ales," 400
Churchegate, William atte, 309
Church Quarterly, The, 426
Cicero, 63 ; *Letters*, 183
Cimabue, 468, 469
Cirencester, 53
Cistercians, Order of, 15, 235, 346, 404 ; monasteries, 39, 102, 146
Civil Law, English, 339 n., 437-8 n. ; French, 518
Civil Law, Roman, 338 n.
Clare Castle, 102

C.

35

" claree "=claret, 117 n.
Clarence, Lionel, Duke of, 149 n., 526
Clarendon, Assize of, 510
Clarke, 207 n.
Clavyle, John, 52
Cleangre, 79
Clement IV, 129–36
Clement V, 400
Clement, Dr Vincent, 205
Clementines, the, 195
Clenchwarton, Dom John, 258
Cleomades, 86
Clere, Elizabeth, 436
Clerk, John, 362–3
Clerk, Roger, 503–5
Cleveland, Archdeacon of, 287,
Cliffland, Joan, 462–5
Clothale, Master Robert of, 319
Clynton, John of, 137
Clyst, 519
Clyst Honiton, 260
" Cock-fighting," 387
Cokaygne, Abbey of, 493
Coke, William, 307
" cokthresshyng," 332
Colchester, 359
Colchester, Walter of, 466
" Collation," 247 and note, 452
Colman, Geoffrey, 323
Colman, Thomas, 323
Colossians, Epistle to, 457
Columba's Isle, 10
Columbus, 524
Colyton, 260
Combe, Simon, 306
Commines, Philippe de, *Mémoires*, 42
Commynges, lord of, 151
" common form," 50
Commons, House of, 53, 57, 64, 397
Compare, Bourg of, 155
Compostella, *see* S. James
" compurgators," 306 n.
Condom, 201
Conquest, Norman, 20, 25, 209, 213
Constable, Messrs, vi
Constantine, 45, 46, 375, 508
Constantinople, 296; Blachernes, 413; Channel of Sophia, 414; Hippodrome, 412; Pera, 414; S. Sophia, 412; S. Stephen's Abbey, 414
Constitutions (of Abp Reynold), 436
Continent, the, 346

Cook, A. S., *Literary Middle-English Reader*, 493, 526
Cook, Morris, 470
Cooke, Roger, 324
Cooper, C. H., *Annals of Cambridge*, 66, 330, 400
Corasse, lord of, 156
Corbie, 360
" cordwainers," 362
Corinthians, Epistle to, 462
Cornewaille, Henry, 324
Cornwaile, John, 6
Cornwall, 27, 221, 222
Cornwall, Master Richard of, 26
" corona," 72 n.
" corrody," 168, 407 n., 453
Cosne, 421
Cosse, Mt. of, 150
Cosyn, Roger, 50
" cote-hardie," 149 and note
Cotton, Bartholomew de, *Historia Anglicana*, 237
Coucy, lord of, 148, 157
Coucy, Isabel of, 148
Coulton, G. G., *Chaucer and his England*, 281, 291, 400, 510, 516
From S. Francis to Dante, 467 n.
Medieval Garner, 64, 69, 81, 119 n., 130, 187, 209, 222, 260 n., 350 n., 476, 537
Medieval Studies, 257, 348
(tr.) *Pearl*, 225
Councils, Cloveshoe, 53
College, 71
General, 456
Counter-Reformation, 62
Coupeland, Dawe de, 439
Courçon, Master Robert de, 344
Courteney, Hugh de, 50
Coventry, 53, 364, 376; Earl St., 376–8; Wards of, 377
Coventry Leet Book, 310, 363, 376, 426, 455, 529
Cox, Richard, 81
Crane, T. F., 405
Cray, 219
Cray, R., 389
Creadon, Sir Richard, 161
Crécy, 291, 421
Creed, Lord's, 417
Croft, H. H. S., 97, 98, 411
Croke, Nicholas, 307
Cromwell Correspondence, 436
Croquart, Sir C., the German, 297
Cross, Hugh, 307

"cross, creeping to the," 146 n.
"crowder," 406
Crusades, the, 287; Fourth, 412
Crusaders, 414
Culmstock, William, Vicar of, 260
Cunningham, *see* Lamond
Cuthbert, Father, 246
Cutts, Dr, 336
Cymmrodorion, Transactions of the Society of, 189
Cyprus, King of, 31, 149

Dâcheux, Abbé L., *Jean Geiler*, 396
Daedalus, 531
Dagworth, 294, 295
"dairymaid" (duties of), 306
Dalderbi, John de, *see* Lincoln
[D]alyngrigge, Sir Edward, 279
Dammartin, Jehan de, 286
"Dance of Death," 410 n.
Danchyn, Peter, 151
Danett, M., 42
Danes, 5, 8
Dante, 28, 468, 535
    Purgatorio, 469
Darches, Richard, 51
Dauphiné, 267
Daventre, Richard de, 323
David, 197, 466
David, King of Scotland, 458
Dawlish, 260
de Dodebrugg, Hugh, 52
de Dodebrugg, Adam, 52
Decretals, 102
Dee, River, 4
Delisle, Léopold, 301
Demetia, 111
Dene, forest of, 53
Denmark, 418
Denton, W., *England in the Fifteenth Century*, 508
Derby, John, 309
Derbyshire, Peak of, 3
Despenser, Lord, 148
Despenser, William, 52, 53
Devon, 27
Devon, F., *Issues of the Exchequer*, 203
Devonshire, 519
Deyer, Walter le, 53
Dictionary of National Biography, 9, 176, 458
Dictionary, New English, 380 n.
Digby, Everard, *De Arte Natandi*, 411

Dimock, J. F., *ed.* Life of S. Hugh, 472
Diocletian, 488
Diodorus Siculus, 183
Dionysius [Denys], 179
"dirige," 60, 139 and note
Dissolution, the, 232
Diverres, P., *Meddygon Myddfai*, 507
Dives, 364
Dives, William of, 341
Docking, Dom Richard, 258
Dodford, 308
Dole, Robert, 52
Dole, Roger, 52
Dominicans, 129; friary of, 466
"dormer," 540
Douglas, Earl of, 149
Dover, 158, 247, 376, 421-2
Dover, Master Solomon of, 26
Doyly, 78
Drayton, 309
Drinkwater, 378
Dublin, 16 n.; [Duvelyn], 160
Dublin, Abps of, 119, 120
Dudley, Sir Edmund, *Tree of the Commonwealth*, 82, 95, 354
Dugdale-Caley, *Monasticon*, 341, 377 n., 451
Dulwich College Library, 527
Dunensis, Codex, 102
Dunes, Abbey of, 102 and note
Dunheved, Master John, 502
Dunkirk, 102
Duntone, Henry, 362-3
Duraunt, 80
Durham, 42, 291, 420, 458
Durham, Bps of, 183
Dutch language, 181

Earith, Joan of, 514
Ecclesiasticus, Book of, 185
Eccleston, Thomas of, 239
    Chronicle, 246, 424
Economic Journal, 455
Eden, Garden of, 482
Edmond, John, 323
Edmund, King, 4
Edward the Confessor, 39
Edward I, 50, 288, 317, 391, 439
Edward II, 52, 181 n., 309, 319, 347, 409; Wardrobe accounts of, 470
Edward III, 51, 52, 57, 156, 158, 159, 162, 183, 203, 291, 295,

Edward III (*cont.*)
    309, 321, 323, 324, 327, 347,
    350, 351, 352, 395, 427, 454–8
Edward IV, 30, 33, 43, 397, 529
Edward VI, 399
Edwenna, 415
Egypt, 108, 409, 482
Ekkehard IV, 111
Ekkehard V, 111
Elfeistone, Geoffrey of, 341
Elham, 79, 80, 421
Elias, Bro., 241 ff.
Elizabeth, Queen, 83, 527
Ellerby, John de, 287
Ellis, Henry, 282
Eltham, 161, 392
Eltisely, John of, 514
Ely, 532; Cathedral, 480–1; *Historia Eliensis*, 480
Elyndon, 77 ff.
Elyot, Sir Thomas, *Book of the Governour*, 97, 411
    Letters (*Cromwell Correspondence*), 436
Embleton, 422
Emeldon Church, 421
"empticii," 340
Engerant, the lord, 157
England, 1 ff., 25, 29, 42; longbow in, 397–9; "merry England," 2 n.; plague in, 344
    compared with France, 33–7
    compared with Wales, 17
Englische Studien, 420 n.
English, the, 28, 29, 30, 37, 41, 96, 294 ff.
    compared with Normans, 22, 25, 26
    compared with Welsh, 18
English costume, 379–80
English Historical Review, vi, 50, 257 n., 283, 517
English language, 6, 28, 38, 82 n., 179, 180–3, 254, 430, 451 n., 538
English verse, 423
Epistles, S. Paul's, 63
Erasmus, 97, 257, 439
    Colloquies, 251
    Guide to Christian Matrimony, 439
Eriri, 19
Esdras, Book of, 338 n.
Esmans (?), 421
Essex, 310, 323, 379 n.
Essex, John, 66

Essonne, 421
Esthamme, 323
Esther, Book of, 30, 374–5
Eston, 341
Etheldred, 4
Ethicus the Astronomer, 525
Ethiopia, 29, 535
Ethiopian, 523
Eton, 55, 69, 70, 72 n., 75 n., 81, 82 n., 251, 309, 470
Eucharist, 106
Euclid, 482–8
Eugenius III, 235
Eugenius IV, 205
Europe, 2, 20, 39, 62, 267 n., 412
Eve, 353
Evesham, 54; *see* Eynsham
Exeter, 74 n., 453, 493
Exeter, Bps of, 27, 191, 265, 451, 458, 493–4, 519
Exeter, Cathedral, 493
Exodus, 467
Extone, Nicholas, 328, 362
Eynsford, 219
Eynsham, 229, 341
Eynsham, Adam, Prior of, *Magna Vita S. Hugonis*, 195
    Revelation to the Monk of Evesham, 229
Ezekiel, 188, 200 n.

"famuli," 341
Farley, 101
Farne, isle of, 419
Fastolf, Sir John, 94, 176, 177 n., 178
Fato, 99
Fauconer, Thomas, 505
Fécamp, 247
Fécamp, William of, 236
Feckenham, John de, 52
Feltone, Thomas de, 291
Ferns, Bp of, 119
Ferrara, 149
ffelerd, John, 68, 69
Fife, Earl of, 149
Figaro, 471
Finchale, 420
Fisher, Bp, *English Works*, 49 n., 189
Fishmongers' Company, 391
Fitz-Art, Robin, 522
Fitzgilbert, Thomas, 521
Fitzherbert, Sir Anthony, *Book of Husbandry*, 310, 380, 385, 423, 444

Fitz-Hugh, Osbert, 533
Fitzosbert, William, 356–9
Fitzstephen, William, 389, 494
Materials for History of Thomas Becket, 387, 431
Fitzwalter, Lord Robert, 347
Flanders, 2, 20, 116, 149, 259, 335, 360–2, 418, 459
Flanders, Counts of, 115, 116
Flemings, 5, 7, 295
Flemish language, 38, 430
Flemming, 305 n.
Fleta, 301, 377 n.
Fleury, Aimoin of, 111 n.
Fleury, C., *Histoire Ecclésiastique*, 259
Flora, goddess, 394
Florence, 203, 334
Florentines, 28
Flowere, Bernard, 492
Fly, Eustaches de (S. German de), 344
Foix, Earl of Foix and Bearn, 150 ff.
Foizois, 152
"folkmote," 316, 502 n.
Fonblanque, E. V., *Annals of the House of Percy*, 383
"football," 332
Foreland, the, 181
Forest, the New, 274, 275
Forges [S. Forgeux?], 421
Fortescue, Sir John, 37, 41 n., 314 n., 346
De Laudibus Legum Angliae, 30, 517
On the Government of the Kingdom of England, 30 510
Fountaine sale, the, vii
Fournier, 336
Foxe, John, *Acts and Monuments*, 462
Frampton, Clifford of, vii
France, 1, 6, *passim*; usurers in, 342 ff.
Franciscan, Constitutions, 129 n., 131
convents, 8
missionary journeys, 239
Order, 8, 129, 130, 424, 521
Rule, 246
School at Oxford, 26
Franco, 469
Fraunceys, Richard, 94
Free, Hugh, 307
Freemasonry, Early History of, in England, 481

"freemasons," 471 ff., 481–9, 491, 492
Freman, Cristina, 527; Nicholas, 527
French, John (alchemist), 529
French documents, 317
French language, v, 5, 6, 136, 154, 159, 161, 179, 180–2, 196, 286, 430, 451 n.
French law, 517
French people, 29, 30, 431–2
compared with English, 21, 510–13
Frere, W. H., 146
Friars, 207 n., 208, 209, 260, 378, 442; four orders of, 442
Friars, Austin, 52, 55 n., 213
Friars, Grey, 55 n.
Friars Minor, 8, 244, 247, 248, 424, 454, 497
Friars Preachers, 248–9, 362; (church of), 363, 454
(*See also* Franciscan)
Frie, Emma de, 50
Frie, John de, 50
Friesland, 434
Frith, Hugh, 306
Froissart, v, 84–90, 149 and note, 158 n., 274, 281, 294, 298 n., 355, 360
Buisson de Jonece, 148
Chronicle, 291, 397, 458
Espinette Amoureuse, 84
Fulco, 277
Fuller, Thomas, 210
Church History, 209
Furnivall, Dr, 136, 163
Fynemer, 77 ff.

Gabriel, Angel, 488
Galatians, Epistle to, 200 n., 457 n.
Galicia, 157
Gallia, 277
Galyon, 492
Gamlingay, 347
Gardiner, Simon, 527
Garin, 109
"garlanda," 123
Garonne, R., 151, 152
Garter, Order of the, 285
Gas, Caron de Bosc de, 295, 207
Gascoigne, G., *Good-night*, 373
Gascoigne, Thomas, *Loci e Libro Veritatum*, 146, 204
Gascon language, 154

Gascons, 107
Gascony, 2, 27, 154, 201, 497
Gasquet, Cardinal, 336
  The Eve of the Reformation, 205 n.
Gaston, Earl of Foix and Bearn, 150
Gaunt, 149
Gaunt, John of, 158, 496
Gautier, Léon, 281
  La Chevalerie, 471
Geiler, Johann (of Kaysersberg), *Ship of Fools*, 396
Genesis, Book of, 340
Geney, William, 177
Geoffrey (of Leicester), 513
Gerberon, 337
German language, 38, 245, 263
German-Franciscan mission, 239 ff.
Germans, 242, 295 ff., 527
Germany, 5, 240 ff., 263, 473; *see also* Almaine
Gerounde, Maud, 309
Gesta Abbatum Monasterii S^{ti} Albani, 104
Gesta Francorum, 404
Gesta Romanorum, 217, 532
Giano, Jordan of, *Memoirs*, 239-246, 494
Gibbe, John, 328
Giffard, Abp of York, *Register*, 287
Gilbert (of Cray), 219
Gilbert, Bp of Lisieux, 109
"gilds," 315, 490-1; craft gilds, 488; trade gilds, 481
Giles, J. A., 20
Giotto, 468-9
Giraldus Cambrensis, 1, 10, 12, 16, 111-122
  De rebus a se gestis, 111
  Gemma Ecclesiastica, 111, 395
  Letters, 121
  Speculum Ecclesiae, 111
  Topographia Hibernica, 120, 121
  Itinera Cambriae, 537
Gisors [Gisorz, Gysors], 318, 320, 322
Glaber, Ralph, 111 n.
Glanvill, Ranulf de, 338, 347 n.
  De Legibus Angliae, 338
Glanville, Bartholomew de, 8
Glastonbury, 236
Gloucester, 52, 53, 203, 274, 424
Gloucester, Humphrey, Duke of, 213, 268

Gloucester, Thomas, Duke of, 158
Gloucester, Thomas, 362
Gloucestershire, 539
Godwin, Gilbert, 309
Gog-Magog Hills, 532
Goldast, *Monarchia*, 456
Golden Legend, the, 228, 488
Goliath, 66
Golofer, Sir John, 162
Gomegynes, lord of, 157
Gonfaloniero, 335
Goodgrome, Robert, 470
Gospel, Gospels, 63, 189, 198, 261, 473, 478, 490; swearing on, 69
Gospel of S. Mark, 48
  S. Luke, 375, 406 n.
  S. John, 180, 406 n.
Gotham, 77
Gothic architecture, 468; *see* Brandon
Goths, 107
Goude, la, lord of, 149
Gower, John, 170, 337, 353
  Confessio Amantis, 162
  Mirour de l'Omme, 353
Graal, Temple of the Holy, 466
Graham, Rose, 232
Grammar, Masters of, 55
Grandisson, John de, Bp, 458, 493-4
  Register, 27, 493
Granson, Sir Otho de, 27
Grantham, 93
Gratian, *Decretum*, 68 n., 192 n., 336, 339 n., 406 n., 456
Gray, Sir Thomas, *Scalacronica*, 274
Greece, 413
Greek Emperor, 415
Greek language, 179, 256
Greek letters, 526
Greek monks, 336
Greeks, 193, 413-15
Green, Godfrey, 308
Green, J. R., *Short History*, 59
Green, Mrs, *Town Life in the 15th century*, 426
Gregory IX, 246
Gregory X, 129
Gresham, John, of Walsingham, 258
Greves, Cradoc de, 439
Grey, vii
Grimm, *Deutsche Mythologie*, 534
Gross, C., *Select Cases on the Law Merchant*, 514

Grosseteste, Bp, 26, 123 and note, 189, 343, 403
Grygge, Alan, 325
Gueldres, Duchy of, 44
Guibert, *see* Nogent
Guienne, 496
Guisnes, 360
Gurnay, John le, 53
Gurnay, Sir Richard le, 53

Hacche, Johanna atte, 504
Hacche, Roger atte, 503–5
Hacon, 513
Hadle [Hadlee], John, 328, 423
Hagar, 340
Hainault, 156, 360, 361, 379
Hainault, Earl of, 160
Hainault, Philippa of, 148–162, 392
Halberstadt, 239
Hales, Master Adam of, 210
Hall, Edward, 393
Halle, 263 ff.
Halliwell, J. O., 481, 506
Hamitsri, R. Solomon, 414
" hammer of heretics," 257
Hampshire, 274
Hamund, 276
Handele, 78 ff.
Hannibal, 8
Hanover, 385
Harbledown, 470
Hardicanute, 8
Hardyng, John, 283
    Chronicle, **282**, **517**
Hardyngham, Sir Gilbert de, 318
Harinton (Bursar of Merton), 421
Harmer, Miss F. E., *Select Historical Documents*, 377 n.
Harmondsworth, Prior of, 307
Harnicourt, 222 n.
Harrow, 82 n.
Hart, G. W., 146
Hastang, *see* Longevill
Hastings, Battle of, 20
Hautes-Alpes, 475
Haveringmere, 534
" hayward," 303, 305
Hatfield, 104
Hatfield, Sir Robert of, 104
Haughmond, Abbey of, 170
Hautecombe, 201
Hayton, Adam de, 309
Hayton, William de, 309
Hearne, Thos., 259, 537
Hebrew language, 101, 256

Hebrews, the, 192
Heisterbach, Caesarius of, 111 n., 196, 217, 267, 290, 346, 434, 528
Helcoy, 299
" Helf Gott," 245 n.
Hemt, Robert le, 309
Hende, John, 278 ff.
Henley, Walter of, 301
Henry I, 221, 223, 395
Henry II, 118, 119, 232, **235**, 276, 338, 395
Henry III, 50, 122, 123, 124, 181 n., 211, 212, 315, 316, 342, 389, 390, 400
Henry IV, 57, 58, 167, 392
Henry V, 505
Henry VI, 43, 53, 200, 282, 394, 491
Henry VII, 82, 94, 103
Henry VIII, 42, 62, 82, 265, 376, 380, 383, 384, 393, 394, 398
Henry, Prince, 431
Henry III, of Spain, 43
Henryson, Robert, *Abbay Walk*, **170**
Henslowe, Philip, *Diary*, **527**
Heptarchy, 53
Hereford, Earl of, 148
" heriot," 307, 348 and note
Hertford, Earl of, 391
Hertfordshire, 389, 498
Hewith, Iseult de, 51
Hewith, John de, 51
Heygrave, Margery de, **52**
Heywood, J., 70, 72 n.
Hierman, 67
Higden, Ralph, v, 1, 72, 201
    Polychronicon, **1**, **10**, **17**, **20**, 56, **59**, **179**, **202**, 236, 274, 276, 277, **400**, 530, 534–5
Hildeyerd, Elizabeth, **52**
Hildeyerd, Emma, **52**
Hildeyerd, Thomas, **52**
Hildy, 332, 333
Hill, Walter, 307
Hob, the robber, 359
Hoccleve, Thomas, 102 n., 103, 163 ff., **167**, 171
    (trans.) *De Regimine Principum*, **164**, 167, **168**
    Dialogues, 164
    Male Regle, **164**
    Works, 102 n.
Hockday, 50
" Hock Days," **332**

Hogges, Prior of, **503**
Holcot, *see* Bury
Holland, 259
Holm, 124
Holme, Edmund de, 309
"holy bread," 261
Holy Land, 122, 287–90, 534
Homildon Hill, battle of, 282
Honnecourt, Villard de, *Album*, 474, **476–9**
Honorius III, 240
Hood, Robin, 266, 393–4
Hore, Oliver, 68
Horepoll, 308
Hospitallers, 277; Theodoric, Prior of, 122
Hostiensis, 349, 438 n.
Hoton, Adam de, 439
Houghton, William of, **514**
Hours, Book of, vii
House of Fame, 466
Hughlot, William, 520
Hull, Walter, 307
Hulle, John, 307
Hulton, *Rixae Oxonienses*, 59, **69**
Humberston, 77 ff.
Hume, 376
Hundred Years' War, 294, 400
Hungary, 240, 243, 476–7
Huntingdon, 526
Huntingdon, Henry of, *De Pre-rogativis Angliae*, 2 n.
    Historia Anglorum, **23**
Huntingdonshire, 514
"husting," 502
Hutton, Dom William, 258
Hychene, John, 362, 363
Hyndstoke, Master John, **502**

Iffley, 538
Imola, Benvenuto da, *Comentum super Dantis Comoediam*, 342, **468**
Ina, King, 195
Innocent II, 68, 400
Innocent III, 232
Innocent IV, 102, 124, 189, 343–4
Ireland, 10, 521, 524, 539
Ireland, Duchess of, 157
Ireland, Primate of, 329
Ireland, Richard of, 299
Irish clergy, 119, 120
Irish people, 9, 12, 67 n., 76 n.
Irish scholars in Oxford, 65 n.
Isaac, 379, 408

Isaiah, 197, 264, 357
Isidore, of Seville, 9, 11, 340, 441
Islip, Abbot, 426
Italian merchants, 40
Italian Relation of England, **37**, 96, **333**
Italians, 38
Italy, 99, 107 n., 240, 241, 335, 342, 466, 468
Ivry, castle of, 471–2

Jacob, 213
"Jacquerie," 360
James, Dr M. R., 165 n., *Descriptive Catalogue of MSS. in Fitz-william Museum*, vii
Jankyn, 462 n.
Janus, 499 n.
Jenette, 430
Jeremiah, Book of, 340
Jerusalem, 224, 419; church of Holy Sepulchre, 419
"Jerusalem, Laetare," 119, 300
Jessopp, Dr A., *Coming of the Friars*, 246
Jews, 48, 60, 63, 198, 344, 414
Job, 62
Jocelin, 232
John II, Abbot of S. Albans, 126
John XXII, 27, 400
John de C., 50
"John the Chaplain" (of Merton Coll., Oxford), 78
John, King, 111, 276 ff., 385
John, King of France, 157
John (of Orpington), 218
Johnson, William, 307
Jordan, 307
Jordan (Ailsi's father), 221
Jordan, Margery, 348
Jordan, William, 307
Joseph, 108
"jougleurs," 403–4
Juberothe, 156
Jubinal, 126
Judges, Book of, 29
Jusserand, J. J., 137
    Wayfaring Life, 204
Justinian, Code of, 103, 338 n.

Kalote, 146
Karyn, John, 69
Kenilworth, Robert, Prior of, 536
Kent, 5, 28, 117, 159, 389
Kent, Joan of, 458

Kestevene, 137
Kexby, John, Chancellor of Oxford Univ., 69
Keys, Roger, 471 n.
Kilkenny, 521
King's Bench, 30, 42
Kings, Book of, 32
Kingsford, Mr C. L., 9, 283
Kingstanley, 52, 53
Kitte, 138, 146
Knighton, *Chronicle*, 57, 65
Knolles, Sir Robert, 297 ff.
Kyldesby, Nicholas, 502
Kymer, Gilbert, Chancellor of Oxford Univ., 69
Kynne, Richard, 347
Kyteler, Dame Alice, 521
Kyvele, William de, 438

Lacaita, G. F., 342, 469
Lacedemonians, 335
La Cieutat, 151, 153
La Fasterne, 50
La Garde, 152
La Legh, Robert de, 51
Lamb, John, 51
Lamentations, Book of, 264
Lamond, 301
Lancashire, 83
Lancaster, Blanche, Duchess of, 148; Dukes of, 42, 158, 391, 496; Earl of, 347; Thomas, Earl of, 200–2
Lancaster, House of, 43
Lancastrian party, 30
Lane, Sir Raymond of, 152
Lanfranc, Abp, 105
Canterbury Constitutions, 101
Lanfred, 472
Langland, *see Piers Plowman*
Langton, Stephen, 111
Laon, 361; cathedral, 477
Laon, Raymond de, 131
"larvati," 407
Lassus, J. B. A., 476
Lateran, Palace of the, 190
Latimer, Hugh, 265, 271
Sermons before King Edward [VI], 310, 399
Sermon upon the Lord's Prayer, 271
Latin anecdotes, 196
Latin books, 179, 183, 213, 229
Latin documents, 317
Latin language, v, 54, 64, 71, 81,

Latin language (*cont.*)
82 n., 85, 94 n., 101, 126, 170, 179, 180, 181, 213, 245, 451 n., 452
Latins, 532
Launceston, 221 n.
Lausanne Cathedral, 477
Lawrence sale, the, vii
Layre, 151, 153
"lazars," 410
Lazarus, 364
Leach, A. F., 53, 70 n.
Educational Charters and Documents, 53, 54, 81
Leadam, I., *Star Chamber*, 341 n.
Ledeneye, 53
Ledes, castle of, 159, 160, 161
"legenda," 241 n.
Leicester, 271, 315; High St., 514; *see also* Bateson, Bémont
Leicester, Earl of, 333, 513
Leicester, Nicholas of, 513
Leland, John, 176
Léon [Lion], Sir Espaenge [Spayne] de, 150, 154, 155
"lepers," 508
l'Escalopier, C. de, 467
l'Espinasse, R. de, 488
Lesse, River, 153
Lestrange Household Book, 422
Lethaby, Prof. W. R., *Medieval Art*, 468, 476, 477
Westminster Abbey, 477
Lettenhove, Kervyn de, 102
Letters from the Northern Registers, 210
Lever, Thomas, *Sermons*, 83
Leverynton, 80
Leyecroft, 53
Liber de Antiquis Legibus, 315, 319
Libro de Dono Timoris, 267
Liebrecht, F., 389, 539 n.
Gervasius von Tilbury, 532–8
Liège, 156
Lille, 459
Lilleshall, 205
Lincoln, 20, 266, 277, 526; *see also* Thompson
Lincoln, Bishops of, 23, 51, 69, 123, 124, 233, 235; *see also* Dalderbi, Grosseteste
Lincoln Cathedral, 472
Lincoln, S. Hugh of, 229
Lincolnshire, 93, 232, 417
Lindisfarne, 419

Lion, Jean de, 102 n.
Lion, Master W. de, 102, 103
Lisieux, 107, 109
Lisle, Sir William, 159, 161
Litlington, 396
Little, Prof. A. G., 246
　Roger Bacon, 129
"livery," 407
"livre parisis," 102 n.
Llandaff, Bp of, 52
Lodge, R., *Close of the Middle Ages,*
　510
Lollards, 268 ff., 378, 462 n., 465
Lombard heretics, 242
Lombardy, 149, 240, 526
London, 20, 41, 53, 83, 118, 138, 139,
　157, 158, 178, 203, 210, 247, 248,
　259, 279, 280, 315, 317, 333–5,
　346–7, 356–8, 387, 419, 421, 422,
　443, 494, 497, 499 n., 526
　Aldgate, 317, 325, 516
　Aldgate, Holy Trinity Priory, 473
　Billingsgate, 323
　Bread St., 328
　Charing Cross, 333
　Cheapside, 328, 329, 391
　City, 315–332, 387 ff., 502, 503,
　　527
　Clerkenwell, 322, 494
　Cornhill, 138, 248, 321, 328, 389,
　　393, 394, 503
　Dovegate, 329
　Eastcheap, 165 n.
　Fleet-street, 278
　Fulham, palace of, 474
　Gracechurch, 324
　Greenwich, 393
　Guildhall, 94, 315, 323–8, 332,
　　362, 423, 503, 506; Library, vi
　Guildhall, chapel of, 329
　Inns of Court, 435
　Ironmongers Lane, 504
　Kennington, 391
　Kennington, manor of, 392
　Lambeth, 391
　Leadenhall, 389, 393
　London Bridge, 280
　London Bridge, Gate of, 317
　Ludgate, 317, 320
　Moorfields, 388
　Newgate, 165 n., 320, 323, 324,
　　329, 330, 363, 391
　Poultry, 473, 503
　R. Thames, 390
　Ropery, the, 325

London (*cont.*)
　S. Laurence Lane, 329
　Shooters Hill, 393
　Smithfield (S. Bart.'s Priory), 211
　Southwark, 391, 516
　Stepney, 394
　Strand, 334
　Tower, 43, 82, 190, 324, 427
　Wall, 318, 320
　Wandsworth, 503
　Westcheap, 331
　Westminster, 39, 122, 166, 170,
　　209, 275, 280, 320, 389–90, 477,
　　492; *see also* Lethaby
　Westminster, abbots of, 181, 396;
　　see also Litlington
　Westminster, *Consuetudinary,* 104
　Wesminster, Council of, 268
　Westminster, monks of, 124
　Westminster Muniments, 396
　Westminster, Palace of, 281, 529
London, aldermen of, 317, 323–9,
　362, 423, 502–6
　bishops of, 25, 95, 212, 319, 320,
　　343–4, 473–4
　churches, All Hallows, 320
　Our Lady at the Hill, 320
　S. Andrews (Cornhill), 394
　S. George's (Southwark), 516
　S. Laurence (Candlewick
　　Street), 318
　S. Martin, 504
　S. Mary (Bow), 358
　S. Nicholas, 329
　S. Paul's, 199 (2), 211, 259, 280,
　　319, 334, 393
　S. Paul's Cross, 83, 316
　Old S. Paul's, 410 n.
London, Council of, 454; glaziers
　in, 492; hospitals, S. Giles in
　the Field, 390; inns, etc., the
　Paul's Head, 165 n.; mayors of,
　323–9, 332, 363, 392, 502–6,
　527–9; *see also* Bockwell, Blund,
　Bury, Extone, Fauconer, Hadle,
　Hende, Gisors, Lovekyn, Mor-
　done, Riley, Robinson, Sharpe,
　Walworth, Wheatley
London, monasteries, etc., Holy
　Trinity, Aldgate, 218
　S. Mary, Clerkenwell (nunnery),
　322
　Sheriffs of, 392, 423, 503, 529,
　　see also Chronicles, Romeyn,
　　Vannere, Walworth, Wheatley

Londoners, 389
Longbeard, *see* Fitzosbert
Longevill, Beatrice de, 51
Longe Wille, 250
Lord, Richard, 309
Lord's Prayer, the, 417
Lot's wife, 174
Louis VII, 107, 115, 432
Louis, VIII, 277
Louis IX, 127
Lourde, 153
Louth, Abbey of, 15
"love-day," 486
Loveday, William, 309
Lovekyn, John, 323
Lowe, John, 323
Lowe, Dom John, 258
Lowys, 177,
Luard, H. R., 122
Lucan, 236
Lucca, 345
Luce, S., 397
Lucifer, 197, 406
Ludeworth, Walter de, 51
Luke, *see* Tudensis
Lumby, J. R., 312
Luther, Martin, 190
Luxemburg, Duke of, 154-7
Lydgate, John, 93, 171, 394
  The Babees Book, 90
  Minor Poems, 172
Lynde, John, 471 n.; William,
  471 n.
Lyndwood, Bp, 194, 204
  Provinciale, 194, 203, 348-9, 436,
  454
Lynham, Richard, 423
Lynn, 213, 232; S. Nicholas', 538
Lynn, Agnes of, 515; John of, 515;
  William of, 515
Lyons, 125, 421
Lyra, Nicholas de, 102

Macaulay, Thomas Babington, 53
Macaulay, G. C., 162
Maddeley, Walter of, 62, 424
Magdeburg, Palmerio of, 242
Mahomet, 270
Mainer, Abbot, 108-9
"maintainer," "maintenance," 75 n.,
  485, 517
Maitland, F. W., 315
  Select Pleas in Manorial Courts,
  306
  Collected Papers, 307

Maitland, Pollock and, *History of
  English Law*, 338, 339 n., 436,
  513
"male-bouche," 89
Malmesbury, Oliver of, 530
Malmesbury, William of, *De Gestis
  Regum*, 20
Malory, Sir Thomas, *Morte d'Ar-
  thur*, 274
Malvern, 144
Malvoisin, 152, 155
Malvolio, 301
Man, Alice, 51; Walter, 51
Man, Isle of, 4
"manchet," 383, 384
Manichean heresy, 475
Manly, Professor, 137
Manners and Meals, 446
Mannyng, Robert, of Brunne,
  Chronicle, 28
  Handlyng Synne, 47, 84, 136,
  137, 207, 364, 365, 401, 403
Manorbier, 111
Manuel, King, 413
MS. Harl., 17, 168, 493, 535; Lam-
  beth, 218, 221, 446; Lans-
  downe, 94; Moore, 367; Sloane,
  93; Trin. Coll., Camb., 165 n.,
  446
Map [Mapes], Walter, *De Nugis
  Curialium*, 119 n., 145 n.
  Poems, 367
Marcel, Étienne, *Letter to the Good
  Towns*, 360
Marchal, William le, 52
Marchaunt, David and John, 529
Marches, earls of the, 149
Marches, Northern, 282, 283
Marches of Wales, 119
Marcianus, 535
Marcilius Phicinus, *De triplici vita*,
  399
Mare, Gunyora de la, 341
Margaret, Queen, 30
Marisco, de, *see* Marsh
"mark," value of, 345 n.
Marsh, Adam, 62
  Letters, 26, 103 n., 189
Marsiglio, 456
Martel, Charles, 488
Martham, 462
Martres-le-Toussac, 151
Marucchi, Orazio, 474
Mascaras, 153
"masks," 392 ff.

Matrey, 245
Maubank, Alice and Philip, 438
Maulyon, 154
" maumets," 488
Maundeville, Sir John, *Travels*, 537
Maunsel, John, 315–16
Mauny, Sir Walter de, 148
May-day, 393
Meaux, 146
Meddygon Myddfai, 507
Mede, 250 ff.
Mede, John, 332–3
Medeley, 69
Medes, The, 375
Melancthon, Philip, 271
Mellont, 295
Melyador, The, 154
Ménagier de Paris, 396
Menedemus, 251
"mercator," 415
Mercia, 110
Mercians, 6
Merk, Peter, 203
Merlin, 18, 295, 297
"merry-andrews," 515
Mesendene, Nicholas de, 309
Meulan, Robt de, 515
" Middangeard," 142 n.
Middlesex, 389
Middleton, John de, 420, 422
Midleton, 79, 80
Midlond, 77
Migne, *Patrologia Latina*, 106,
117 n., 187, 281, 471, 535
Milan, 149, 205, 526
Milanese ambassador, 334
Mildenhall, William, 362
"mileway," 489
Miller, John the, 359
" Mirabilia mundi," 72 n.
Miracles, 407
Miracles of Edward, Book of the,
203
Miracle-plays, 1, 400, 402, 407
Mirror of Our Lady, 451 n.
Misrule, lord of, 392
Mittenwald, 244
Modern Language Review, 170
Mohammedans, 412
Mole, River, 108
Mollere, Nicholas, 324
Monald, James, 203
Monby, 80
Monculis, [=Montclus?], 475
Mongat, 151

Montagu, Sir William, 459
Montauban, Guillaume de, 298
Monte Gargano, 242
Monte, Pietro da, 205
" Montes Pietatis," 342, 346
Montfort, Simon de, 189, 200
Montmorency, Castellan of, 114
Montpesac, 152
Monumenta, Franciscana, 26, 103 n.,
189, 246, 424
Monumenta Germaniae, 29
Moray, earls of, 149
More, Sir Thomas, 41 n., 346
*The Third Book of Comfort
against Tribulation*, 190
Utopia, 271, 312
Works, 507
Mordone, Simon de, 502
Moreton, Earl of, 222
Moreton-Hampstead, 262
Moriaumé, lord of, 148
Morlaas, 154
Morris, William, vii
" morse," 212
"mortuary," 348, 349, 350 n.
Moses, 467
Moundeware, John, 520
Mountclare, 151
Mountgalliard, 153
Mountjoy, lord, 439
Mountmirall, 151
Mulcaster, Robert, 30
" mummers," 391
Munde the miller, 199
" murdrum," 25–6
Myddfai, 507
Mydelerd, 535
Myrc, John [Mirk], 205, 216
Book of Instructions, 205
Instructions for Parish Priests,
216, 488
Liber Festialis, 205, 227, 238
Mystic Treasury, The, 203

Namelesse, John, 359
Neilson, G., *Caudatus Anglicus*, 28
Nesta, 111
Nevers, 421
Newark, 93, 496
Newburgh, William of, *Chronicle*,
537
Newcastle, 293
Newmere, Richard of, 306
Newport, Master Richard of, 473
Newton, 421

Newton, Friar, 435
Newton, Roger de, 287
Newton S. Cyres, 261
Nicholas (son of Ailsi), 223
Nicholas (son of Hacon), 513
Nicholas III, 210, 345
Nichols, J., *Illustrations of Manners*, 377 n.
Nicholson, James, 492
Nicke, Bp, *Visitations of Dioc. Norwich*, 257
Nicostrata, *see* Carmentis
Nile, River, 531
Noah, 12, 16
Noah, William, 307
"noble," 250 and note
Nogent, Guibert of, 111 n.
Noiers, Geoffrey de, 472
Norfolk, 251, 365, 415, 462
Normandy, 2, 23, 30, 106, 108, 213, 237, 267, 471
Normandy, Dukes of, 472
Normandy, Robert of, 102–3
Norman-French language, 451
Norman language, 6
Norman, Roger the, 114
Normans, 23, 25, 104, 108, 110, 111, 236
   cp. with English, 22, 26
Norse (Mythology) 142 n.
Northampton (Borough Records of), 315
Northumberland, 292, 376, 422
Northumberland, Earl of, 383
Northumberland Household Book, 75 n., 98, 376, **383**, **386**, **422**
Northumbria, 6
Norton, 261
Norway, 125
Norway, King of, 125
Norwich, 237, 257, 442, 471; S. Leonard's, 443
Norwich, Bishops of, 123, 257, 462–5
Norwich Cathedral, 237, 261 n.
Norwich, Dom David, 258
Nottinghamshire, 93, 496

Oceanus, 252
Ockham, William of, 456–**7**
   Dialogues, **456**
Odeler, 106–8
Oderisi, 468–9
Ogbourne, Great, 308
Ogbourne, Little, **307**
Ogygius, 251

Oise, R., 360–1
Oliver, 530
Olivia, 301
Ordericus Vitalis, *Historia Ecclesiastica*, 106, **471**
Ordric, 107
Orleans, 102–3; University, 468
Orpington, 218
Orthez, 150, 154–6
Orthone, 156
Ospringe, 159
Ossory, Bp Richard of, 521
Ostrevaunt, Earl of, 157
Otto IV, 385
Ottobon, 454
Ouche, Abbey of, 106–9
Ouche, Richard, Abbot of, 109
Ouche, Roger, Abbot of, 109
Outlawe, William, 522
Ovid, 63, 182
Owen, 15
Owen, H., *Gerald the Welshman*. 111
Oweyn, 69
Oxenede, 443
Oxford, 23, 26, 52, 69, 102, 120, 129, 138, 229, 305 n., 347, 421–2, 424, 508
   East Gate, 508
   Hospital of S. John, 508
   S. Giles', 69 and note
   See also Universities
Oxford, Earl of, 286
Oxford, Synod of, 436
Oxwyke, John, 325
Oxwyke, Margaret, **325**

Padua, 456
Paganus, 224 ff.
Palaminiche, 151
Palestine, Early Travels in, 412
Palma, Helewysa, 288
Palma, Isabella, 288
Palmer, Robert, 348
Palmere, Henry, 309
Palmerio, *see* Magdeburg
Pamyers, 150
"pantler," 127 and note
Papal Bulls, 452 n. (Periculoso)
Papal legate, 277
Papal Letters, *see* Bliss
Paradise, 225–6
Paris, 113, 126, 127, 131, 360, **421**, 469; masons of, 488
   Chatel[e]t, 459

Paris (*cont.*)
Notre Dame, 114
S. Germain l'Auxerrois, 115
See also Universities
Paris, Bishop of, 129
Paris, Matthew, v, 125, 126, 187, 274, 344 n., 466
Chronica Majora, 122-6, 342-4
Historia Major, 211-12
Historia Minor, 211
Parisians, 360
Parisis ["livre parisis"], 102 n., 132
Parker, Dom Robert, 258
Parliament, 32, 36, 320, 321, 352, 398
Cambridge, Parliament of, 330
Great Parliament, 124
Scottish, 508
See also Commons
Parma, *see* Bartolommeo
Parma, John of, 240
Parsons, John, 308
Pasch [Easter], 178
Paschal, Master, 503
Paston, John, 435
Paston, Sir John, 176-9
Paston, Letters, vi, 81, 94, 176-9, 435, 439, 442
Paston, Margaret, 396, 443
"Paternoster," 38, 139, 140, 153, 198, 463; "paternoster-while," 489
Paues, Miss A. C., 179
Paul, Abbot (S. Albans), 104
Paul the Hermit, 117
Paynel, Philip, 50
Peacock, Dean, *Observations on the Statutes of the University of Cambridge*, 55
Peak, the, 536
Pearl, 225
Peasants' Revolt, 66, 337
"peciae," 102 n.
Peck, F., *Antiquarian Repertory*, 470
Peckham, Abp, 264
Registrum Epistolarum, 345, 373
Pecock, Bp Reginald, 76, 268
Repressor, 192, 268, 378, 462
Treatise on Faith, 268
Pekin, 307
Pembroke, 19, 111
Pembroke, Earl of, 148
Pencrich, 6
Pencriche, Richard, 6
Penrose, John, 321

Percy, Bp, 98 n., 265, 383
Percy family, the, 158, 159, 161, 282, 376-86
Percy Society, the, 170
Perrens, F. T., *Étienne Marcel*, 360
Peter's Pence, 195
Peter, The Venerable, *Statuta*, 117 n.
Petronilla, 523
Peverel, William, 536
Philip, King of France, 404
Philippa, *see* Hainault
Philippe-Auguste, 400
Philo, 115
"phrut," *see* "tprhurt"
Picardy, 149, 476
Picts, 5
Piepowder Court, 514
Piers Plowman, 137; "Perkyn," 144, 170, 197, 206, 236, 239, 245 n., 250, 281, 301, 308, 322, 337, 346, 350, 359, 364, 405; *P. P.'s Crede*, 466
Pilate, 198
"piment," 117 and note
"pitcher," 337 n.
Pithiviers, 472
"pittance," 208 and note
Plague, the, *see* Black Death
Placentinus, 437
Pleader, Roger, 307
Plessington, Sir John, 299
Ploërmel, 294 ff.
"plough-driver" (duties of), 304
Plummer, Charles, 510
Poer, Hugh le, 521
Poer, Sir John le, 523
Poitiers, 291, 360,
Poitiers, Count of, 127 n.
Poix, 421
Pole, Bro. Hugh de la, 454
Political Songs, 317 n.
"pollard," 262 n.
Pollard, Dr A. W., *XV Century Prose and Verse*, 179 n.
Pollock, *see* Maitland
Polsloe Priory, 451
"pomel," 319 n.
Pontefract, Priory of, 201
Poole, R. L., vi
Illustrations of Medieval Thought, 456
Ponthieu, 360
Pope (of the Greeks), 412
Porter, Robert, 328

Portlaunde, Roger de, 317
Portugal, 43, 156
"Portunus" (="Brownie"?), 386
Pot, Henry, 527
"potell," 383-4 and note
Potelyn, Alice, 52
Potelyn, John, 52
Poulart, Geoffroy, 298
Power, Mr D'Arcy, 496, 501 n.
Power, Miss E. E., 397
"pound sterling," 328 and note
Primer, William of, 307
Prise d'Orange, 471
Prophets, Books of the, 187
Protestant, 462
Provence, Eleanor of, 390
Provence, Raymond of, 390
Provençals, 212
Proverbs, Book of, 184, 192 n., 235, 480
Provins, 330
Prudhomme, Geoffrey, 324
Psalms, 100, 199, 479
Psalter, vii, 59, 139, 180, 434
Purbeck, 472 n.
Purgatory, Mountain of, 535
Purscadel, *see* Alayn
Puy, Ernalton du, 155
Pygmalion, 174
Pyne, Ernalton de, 154
Pynnock, Richard, 53
Pynson, 149,
Pyriton, 50
Pyriton, John de, 50

Quaracchi, 337
Quatuor Coronati, 488
Quiller-Couch, Sir A. T., vi
"quintain [quinten]," 115-6, 389
Quivil, Bp, 191, 192 n., 265
    Exeter Constitutions, 215

Rabanus, 340
Rabbanites, 414
Radyngton, Sir Baldwin, 279
Rainald, 108
Rait, Prof. R. S., *Life in the Me-
    dieval University,* 59, 107 n.
"Ramis-Palmarum," 145
Ramsey, 515
Ramsey, Abbot of, 514
Randolph, 261
Randolph, Hingeston-, 27, 451, 493
Ranulf, 109
Rase, Dom William, 258

Rashdall, Dr H., 58, 78 n.
    Universities of Europe, 59, 61, 62,
    64, 65 n., 70 and note, 247 n.,
    346, 488, 508
Rastell, J., *Les Termes de la Ley,*
    485 n.
Rawlings, G. B., 433
Reading, 58
Reaper, Walter, 308
Rebecca, 213
"recreationes," 453 n.
Redbourne, 104
"reeve," 536 ; (duties of), 303
Reformation, the, 62, 83, 187, 189,
    336, 436
Regham, 78
Reginald (of Durham), *Life of S.
    Godric,* 415-20
"regratress," 331 and note; re
    grating, 436
Reigner, Alice, 94, 95
Reigner, John, 94
Reims, 468, 477
Reims, Abp of, 115
Reliquiae Antiquae, 93, 94, 103,
    245 n., 367, 379 n., 409, 506,
    527
Remora, the, 531
Renascence, 42, 122, 468
Rennes, Dardaine of, 298
Reston, 52
Reve, Thomas, 492
Revue Historique, 336
Rhineland, 466
Rhys, 111
Richard, 492
Richard, Bp of London, *Dialogue
    of the Exchequer,* 25
Richard, Gilbert, 307
Richard I, 277, 355, 395
Richard II, 6, 157-163, 181 n., 203,
    278-81, 329, 330-1, 362-3, 391-
    2, 520
Ridele, 299
Rigware, Thomas, 471 n.
Riley, H. T., 319 n.
    (tr.) *Memorials of London,* vi,
    94-5, 105, 248 n., 262 n., 267 n.,
    291, 317, 319, 321, 322, 331,
    333, 362, 422, 423, 455, 502-6,
    516, 527
    Chronicles of Old London, 201,
    237, 315, 319, 322
    French Chronicles of Old London,
    320

Ripefort, 299
Ripon, 53
Ringer, 307
Ritson, Joseph, *Ancient Popular Poetry*, 367
Robinson, Dr J. Armitage, *The Abbot's House at Westminster*, 396
Robinson, Ralph, 271, 312
Roche, Geoffroy de la, 296
Rochester, 28, 29 n., 161
Rock, D., *Church of our Fathers*, 146 n.
Roger, Chancellor, 23
Roger de W., 50
Roger the Palmer, 341
Rogers, J. E. T., 146, 240
  Hist. Ag. and Prices, 77, 78 n., **101**, 215, 262 n., **346**, 377 n., 420-2
  Loci e Libro Veritatum, 146, **204**
  Oxford City Documents, 65
Rokaylle, Margaret de la, 52
Roman brick, 478
Roman law, 40, 55
Roman monks, 336
Roman Catholic schools, **59**
Romans, 8, 334
Romayn, 278
Rome, 205, 334, 417, 419
Rome, ancient, 32, 188
Rome, Church of, 195, 204
  Court of, 343, 345, 363
  Pontiff of, 190
Rome, The Stacions of, **427**
Romeyn, Thomas, 317
Romsey (nunnery of), 397
Rotuli Parliamentorum, 57, **397**
Rouen, Abps of, 109, 472
Rouen, Cathedral of, 114
Rous, Master Roger le, 262
Rousselot, Sir Jean de, 294-300
Rowland, Richard, 341
"rowmasons," 471 and note
Royal Historical Society, Transactions of the, 31
Russell, John, 323
Rutebeuf, *The Complaint of Rutebeuf*, **127**
  Lay of Charlot the Jew, 126
  The Marriage of Rutebeuf, 127
  Lay of the Poverty of Rutebeuf, **127**
  Lay of Winter Misery, **127**
Rygge, John, 325
Ryghtwys, John, 321
Rymer, *Foedera*, 509, 529

Sacrys, John, 471 **n.**
Saffron Walden, 81
S. Albans (abbey of), 104, **122-6**, 466; S. Oswin's chapel, 124; Jack of, 470
S. Ambrose, 197 n.
S. Andrew, 418
S. Anselm, *De Conceptu Virginali*, **337**
S. Anthony, 117
S. Antoine, hospital of, 267 and note
S. Asaph, Bp of, 268
S. Augustine, 5, 28, 47, 195, 197
  Confessions, 86 n., 197 and note
  De Civ. Dei, 535
S. Bartholomew's Day, 306, 319
S. Basil, 153
S. Benedict, 117, 174, 222 n.
  Rule, **100**, 101, 106, 174, 452
S. Benet (of Holm), 124
S. Bernard, 199, 466
S. Bonaventura, 129 n., 260 **n.**
  In Sententias, 337-8 n.
S. Boniface, 535
S. Botolph, 319
S. Bruno, 466
S. Catherine, 67
S. Cuthbert, 4, **419**
S. Davids, 111-12
S. Dominic, 238
S. Dunstan, Feast of, 515
S. Edmund's monastery (Woolpit), 537
S. Elphege, 4
S. Ermengilda, 480
S. Etheldreda, 480
S. Evroul, Abbey of, 106, 109
S. Francis, 239, 241, 251, 466
S. Francis's Day, 319
S. Gabriel, 300, 526
S. Gilbert, 213-14, **232**
S. Gilles, 419
S. Godric, 415-20
S. Gregory the Great, 195, 197 n., 218, 236, 336
  Decretals, 195, 456
  Dialogues, 180
  Hom. in Ezech. 187
S. Helen('s Mass), 490
S. Hugh, 195 ; *Metrical Life of*, 472
S. Ives, fair of, 514-5 ; Cross Lane, 515
S. James, 49
S. James' Day, 66, 317, **322**

S. James of Compostella, 252, 288, 419, 427, 430
S. Jerome, 115, 197 n.
Lives of the Fathers, 117
Super Matthiam, 170
S. John, vii, 49, 406, 414, 526
S. John the Baptist, 197
S. Louis, 127 n.
S. Magnus, 391
S. Martin, 408
S. Martin of Tours, 39
S. Martin's Land, 538
Sta Maria della Porziuncola, 240-1
S. Mary, 296
S. Mary Church, 261
S. Mary Magdalene, 197
S. Mary Overey (monastery of), 170
S. Matthew, 170, 206 n. ; Feast of, 439
S. Matthias, Feast of, 503
S. Maurice, 108
S. Michael, 267, 300; Eve of, 443
S. Michael's Day, 319, 331
S. Michael's Mount, 27, 267
S. Nicholas, 67, 231
S. Oswin, 124
S. Patrick, 11, 14, 16
S. Patrick II, 14
S. Patrick's Purgatory, 14, 15, 159, 160
S. Paul, 189, 197, 343, 403, 457, 462
S. Peter, 216, 254, 417, 490
S. Peter's Day, 436
S. Peter's Pence, 195
S. Philip, 86 n.
S. Quentin, Cathedral of, 476
S. Raphael, 526
S. Richard of Chichester, 61
S. Stephen, 221-6
S. Swithun, 118
S. Thomas, 294
S. Thomas Aquinas, 31, 129, 204, 260 n., 336
Summa Theol. 336
Summa contra Gentiles, 532
S. Thomas of Canterbury, *see* Canterbury
S. Tybaude, 228
S. Valentine's Day, 316
S. Winifred, 20
S. Yves, 296
See also Canterbury (Abps of)
Salcombe Regis, vicar of, 262
Salimbene, 26

Salisbury, 3
Salisbury, Bps of, 23, 278, 279, 346, 403
Salisbury, Countess of, 458
Salisbury, Earl of, 459
Salisbury, Alice de, 325
Salisbury, John of, *Policraticus*, 281
Salter, H. E., *Cartulary of the Abbey of Eynsham*, 229
Salzburg, 245
" sandall," 391
Sandars, S., vii
Sandwich, 427
Sandwich, Ralph de, 317
Saracens, 193, 270, 360, 471
Sarah, 340
Sarum, 247
Satan, 189, 406
Savonarola, 466
Savoy, 201
Savoy, Amedeus, Count of, 148
Saxon language, 5-6, 180
Saxons, 18, 232, 236
Saxony, 8, 246
" say," 391
Schep, John, 359
Schirlond, Lord Reginald de Grey de, 526
" schoolmen," 337
Schools, 53-6, 434, 436
Schools, grammar, 6
Schoonhove, 149
Schultz, Alwin, 473
Scilly Isles, 27
Scot, John the, 179
Scotland, 8-10, 513; apprentices in, 509
Scotland, King of, 43
Scots, 5, 37, 291-3, 379, 391
" scriptor," 104
Scripture, 378, 434, 462, 479
" scrivener," 105
Scrope, Stephen, 94, 435-6
" scrutinies," 77
Scylla, 4
Seaman, 307
Séez, Bp of, 109
Segrave, Gilbert of, 319
Selden, John, 301, 377 n.
Sellers, Miss Maud, *York Memorandum Book*, 315
Sempringham, 213, 232-6, 493, 538
Sempringham, Order of, 136-7, 364, 400
Sempringham, Roger of, 232

C.

" sendal," 319
Seneca, 63
"seneschal," duties of, 301
Senlis, 127
Sepulchre, the Holy, 319
Serlo, Abbot of Ouche, 109
Serlo, Bp of Séez, 109
" sester," 377 n.
Severn, R., 107
" sextary," 377 n.
Shakespeare, 9
Sharpe, Dr R. R., *Calendars of London Letter-books*, etc., 315
Sheffield, 182
Shem, 343
Shene, Thomas de, 503
Shepherd, Martin, 307
Shepherds' Play, 308
Sherde, 348
Shillingford, *Letters*, 74 n.
Shirburn, John de, 438
Shouldham, 400
Shrewsbury, 20, 106–7
Shrewsbury, Battle of, 282
Shrewsbury, Earl of, 106, 108
Shropshire, 170, 205
Sicily, 23
Sidbury, 262
"sidesmen," 260, 261 n.
Sigward, 107
Silvester, Pope, 464
Sion, 226
Skeat, W. W., 138, 140 n., 145 n., 308, 310, 380, 385, 423, 444
Skeel, Dr C. J. A., 31
Skelton, John, 182
Slipper, William, 307
Smith, Mr A. L., *Church and State in Middle Ages*, 436
Smith, Prof. D. E., *Roger Bacon Essays*, 525 n.
Smyth, John, 257–8
Snowdon, 19
"Société joyeuse," 492
Solinus, 1, 11, 12, 28
Solomon, King, 184, 466
Solomon, Books of, 63
Solomon, Brother, 248–9
Solomon of Dover, 26
Somerlesve, 427
Somerset, 423
Somme, R., 360
Song of the Schoolboy at Christmas, 93
Sorech, 109

" Soul-mass," 206 n.
" Soul-mass Day," 227–8
Southampton, 53
Southey, *British Poets*, 305 n., 373
Southwark, 118, 162
Spain, 43, 157, 240–1, 474
Spalding, 416
Spalding, William de, 400
Sperling, John, 306
Speyer, 243
Spicer, John le, 503
Spon, 427
Spyrlyng, Geoffrey, 178
" Stafford Law," 33 and note
Staneweye, Master William de. 261
Stanleghe, Joan de, 439
Stanleghe, William de, 439
Stans Puer ad Mensam, 488
Stapeldon, Bp, 27
    Register, 260, 451
Statutes, Abp Langham's, 348
    Eton College, 72
    Eton and King's College, 69, 70
    King's College, 67, 70
    Labourers, 57, 350–1, 481, 491
    at Large, 395
    of Maintenance, 75 n.
    Merton College, 69, 77
    New College, 70
    Oxford (1432), 64, 68 n.
Statutes of the Realm, 57, 62, 350, 398, 491
Staverton, 52, 262
Steele, R., *Medieval Lore*, 2 n., 9
Steeple Bumstead, 379 n.
Stephen, King, 15, 23–4, 107, 537
Sterzing, 244
Stevenson, R. L., *Essay on François Villon*, 126
Stewart, Dr H. F., vi
Stirling-Maxwell, 274
Stockton, 348
Stoke-Canon, 263
Stokes, Matthew, 55
Stonehenge, 3
Stow, John, *Survey of London*, 333, 387
Strange, Lord, 171
Stratford, 328
Stratford, L., *Edward IV*, 529
Stratton, 79
Stroud, 29 n.
Strutt, J., *Sports and Pastimes of the English People*, 332, 387

Stuarts, 83
Stubbs, W., *Select Charters*, 25, 338, 509–10
"studium," 71 n.
Stury, Sir Richard, 158–62
Sudbury, 207
Suffolk, 207
Suffolk, Duke of, 42
Suffolk, Earl of, 391, 459
Surrey, 322
Sutherland, Earl of, 149
Sutton, 77
Suttone, Robert de, 317
Swann, Charles, 532
Swavesey, 347
Swineshead, Abbey of, 277
Syon, nunnery of, 451 n.

Tabernacle, the, 467
"tables," 286 n.
Tait, Professor, 176
"tallage," 31–6
Tarbe, 153
Tarse, 250
Tarsus, Theodore of, *Poenitentiale*, 336
Tartars, 193
Tauchen, Jodocus, 473
"Taverne, la male," 421
Taverner, John le, 53
Templars, 277
Temple, Abp, 59
Temple, Raymond du, 468
Testament (Old and New), 63, 192, 218, 344
Thame, 421
Thames, R., 163, 181, 334
Thanet, 5
"theatrum," 494
Theodoric, Prior of Hospitallers, 122
Théophile, le Moine, 466
Theophrastus, 185
"thewe," 325
Thirty, Fight of the, 294–300
Thogarmim, 413
Thoissey, 421
Thomas, Mr C. C., 183
Thompson, A. Hamilton, *Lincoln Visitations*, 257, 451
Thompson, Maunde, 65, 274
Thorverton, 263
Thule, Island of, 536 n.
Thurcaston, 271
Thurstan, Abbot of Glastonbury, 236

Thursteyn, Richard, 52
Tidemann, 473
Tilburv, Gervase of, *Otia Imperialia*, 385 ; *see also* Liebrecht
Tillart, 421
Tintern Abbey, 53
Tintiniac, 299
Titurel, der Jüngere, 466
Tobit, 198
"tonsura," 72 n.
Topham, *Liber Quotidianus Ed. I.*, 377 n.
Toppesfeld, John, 324–5
Topsham, 520
Toulouse, 150
Tour-Landry, Book of the Knight of La, 433, 434, 445, 457
Tourney, 152
Tours, S. Martin of, 39
"tourte," 247 and note
Tory, Michael, 315
"tprhurt," 317–18 and note, 534
Traill, H. D., *Social England*, 315
Trecarl, Jordan of, 223
Tree, Hugh, 307
"trencher," 383–4 and note
Treng, Robert, 80 n.
Trent, Bp of, 244
Trent, R., 65
Treveris, Peter, 179
Trevisa, John of, v, 1, 9
    Description of England, 1
    Dialogue between a Lord and a Clerk, 179
    (*See also* Bartholomaeus and Higden)
Trewman, 359–60
"triennales," 206 and note
Trinity, 197, 199
Tristan, 295, 297
Trivium, the, 112
Troilus, 105
Trondhjem, 124
Troy, 18
Trumpington, Sir Roger de, 534 n.
Trygalet, castle of, 155
Tudela, Benjamin of, *Travels*, 412
Tudensis, Luca, *De Altera Vita*, 474
Turk, the great, 190
Turks, 413
Tusser, Thomas, *Five Hundred Points of Good Husbandry*, 305 n.
Tuy, Bp of, 474

Tyderynton, William de, 52
Tyler, Wat, 56; Revolt of, 350-3
Tyne, R., 292
Tyrel, Walter, 276
Tyrington, 232

Uberti, Fazio degli, **28**
   Dittamondo, **29**
Ufflet, John, 520
Umfraville, Sir Robert, 282-3
University, -ies, 53-62, 64-80, 82-4, 95, 136; "chests," 346; curriculum, 141 n.
University of Bologna, 114, 115, 468, 469
University of Cambridge, 38, 251, 271, 411; Chancellor of, 330, 341; Caius College, 367; Fitzwilliam Museum, vii; King's College, 55, 66, 69-72, 268, 471, 492; (Provost of), 218; Pembroke College, 77; Peterhouse, 70; S. John's College (Master of), 83; Trinity College, vii, 165 n.; (MS. of), 446; Vice-Chancellor, 55-6. (*See also* Carter, Peacock, Statutes, Stokes, Willis, Wood)
University of Orleans, 468
University of Oxford, 38, 55 n., 95, 101, 124, 129, 179, 183, 189, 309, 508; Chancellor of, 146, 508; Exeter College, 1; Magdalen College, 38; Merton College, 69, 77, 223, 420-2; (scrutinies of), 422; New College, 70-7, 397; Oriel College, 268; Queen's College, 1; University College, 59; S. Edmund's Hall, 59; S. John's Hall, 68. (*See also* John, Kexby, Kymer, Wood)
University of Paris, 8, 61, 112, 114, 124, 129, 135
University of Reading, 58
Unwin, Prof. G., *London Gilds and Companies*, 315
Upottery, 263
Urban VI, 203, 363, 520
Uriah, 197
Usk, 101; Adam of, 65 n., 274
Utrecht, 290
Uxbridge, 421

"vair," 331 n.
Valerius, 185

Vandals, 360, 532
Vannere, Henry, 278
Vaucelles, 476
Venetians, 415
Venice, 334-5, 349; San Marco, 525 n.
Venus, 86, 165
Vergil, Polydore, 458
Vermandois, 360
Vickery, Ives, 515
Vienne, 421
Villehardouin, Geoffroy de, 412
   Chronicle, 414
Villon, François, 126
Vincent, 190
Virgil, 28, 181, 182
Visitations, archiepiscopal, 211, 519; monastic, 77-78 n.
Vitae Patrum, 102, 218
Vitalis, *see* Ordericus
Vitry, Jacques de, 217, 266, 289, 344, 404
   Exempla, 405 n.
Voulte-s-Rhône, 421
Vulgate, 480
Vygerous, John, 323

Wace, Robert, 28
Wadden, John, 464
Wadding, L., *Annales Minorum*, 201
Wade, Roger, 406
Wadington, William of, *Manuel des Pechiez*, 136
Wailly, N. de, 414
Wales, 17, 406 n.
Wales, Prince of, 157-8, 497
Wales, S., Prince of, 111
Waleys, Henry le, 317
Waller, Mr A. R., vi
Wallingford, Sir William de, 347
Walo, 277
Walpole, 415
Walsingham, 258, 350 n.; Alan de, 480-1; Dom John, 257; Prior of, 350 n.; Priory of, 257; S. Mary of, 251, 396, 442, 465
Walsingham, Thomas de, 262, 504, 537
   Historia Brevis, 56, **359**
   Gesta Abbatum, 126
Waltam, Bp John, 279
Walworth, John, 278
Walworthe, William, 94
Wandlebury Camp, 532

Wantyng, 77–80
Warde, John, 423–4
Warham, Dom Edmund, 257
Wark Castle, 458
Warkworth Castle, 282
War, Hundred Years', 400
Wars, Barons', 133
Wars of the Roses, 43, 181 n., 517
Warwick, Earl of, 391
"Wasters," 390
"Watch and Ward," 509
Water, William at, 347
Wattenbach, *Schriftwesen des Mittelalters*, 103
Wealde, 341
Weler, Elizabeth le, 53
Weler, John le, 53
Wells, 75 n.
Wells, Dom Thomas, 258
Wellstream, 416
Welshmen, 5, 8, 18, 67 n., 76 n., 111, 517; Welsh clergy, 120; Welsh prophecies, 189
Wendover, Roger of, 122
Chronicle, 58
Wenge, John, 323
Wermuth, 51
Wessex, 195
Wessobrunn, Ludwig of, 103
Westcombe, 77–80
Westmerland, Master David de, 503
Westurley, Robert, 471 n.
Wetyndon, 53
Wexford, 120
Wharton, H., ed. *Anglia Sacra*, 218, 480
Whateley, Bro. John de, 454
Wheatley, H. B., *London*, 508
Wherwell (nunnery), 397
Whitby, 180
White, William, 307, 464
White, Geoffrey le, 309
Whyte, William, 69
Wife of Bath, 90, 185
Wilkins, D., tr. *Concilia*, 191, 215, 264
William, Abp of Rouen, 109
William the Chaplain (of Merton), 78
William the Conqueror, 21, 23, 213, 236, 334
William the Panther, 127
William Rufus, 275

Williams, J. F., *Harrow*, 82 n.
Willis and Clark, *Architectural History of the University of Cambridge*, 470
Willis, Prof., 476
Winchelsea, 427
Winchelsea, S. Robert of, 202
Winchester, 4, 70–5, 81, 82 n., 102 n., 275, 276; Bp of, 118; nunnery of S. Mary, 397
Winchester, John de, 323
Windsor, 162, 279
Winkleigh, 263
Wirhale, John, 324
Wiseman, Richard, 499 n.
Wissant, 422
"with," 393
Wobrideston, 347
Wolford, Little, 79
Wolmer Lodge, 470
Wolrington, Isabel de, 309
Wolsey, Cardinal, 383
Wood, *Hist. Univ. Oxon.*, 55 n.
Woolpit, 537
Worcester, Bps of, 180, 271
Worcester, William of [or Botoner], *Letters*, 176–9
Worcestershire, 61
Worde, Wynken de, printed *The Demaundes Joyous*, 245 n, 409
Worms, 245
Worth, 50
Wottone, William, 329
Wright, T., 70, 72 n., 81, 145, 168, 308, 317 n., 412, 521; *see also* Halliwell, Heywood, Wülcker
Wülcker, 54
Wych, 61
Wyclif, John, 76, 268, 337
De Civili Dominio, 337
The Grete Sentens of Curs, 490
Wycliffites, 179; anti-, 341
Wykeham, Bp William of, *Statutes*, 70, 72 n., 75 n.; *Injunctions*, 397
Wyliot, 78
Wyly, 77–80
Wyrfryth, Bp, 180

Yarmouth, 238
Ymer, Thomas, 307
York, 6, 42, 105, 209, 280, 334, 359; Abps of, 210, 279; Bp of, 407; churches of, S. John's, 407, S. Mary's, 359, S. Peter's, 379,

York (*cont.*)
489 ; Dukes of, 42, 158–161 ;
House of, 43 ; Minster, *Fabric
Rolls of*, 489 ; *Historians of
the Church of*, 407 ; *Memorandum Book*, 105, 315 ; Stangate,
379
York, Robert de, 362

Yorkshire, 146, 423
Yorkshire Archaeological Journal,
451
Yule, 402

Zacchaeus, 407
Zacharias, Pope, *Epistolae*, 535
Zealand, 181, 259